Ancient Christian Gospels

Ancient Christian Gospels

Their History and Development

Helmut Koester

First published in 1990

SCM Press Ltd
26–30 Tottenham Road
London N1 4BZ

Trinity Press International
3725 Chestnut Street
Philadelphia, Pa. 19104

British Library Cataloguing in Publication Data

Koester, Helmut
    Ancient Christian gospels.
    1. Bible. N. T. Gospels - Critical studies
    I. Title
    226.06

    ISBN 0-334-02459-5
    ISBN 0-334-02450-1 pbk

Library of Congress Cataloging-in-Publication Data

Koester, Helmut, 1926-
    Ancient Christian Gospels : their history and development / Helmut
    Koester.
        p.   cm.
    Includes bibliographical references.
    ISBN 0-334-02459-5
    1. Bible. N.T. Gospels--Criticism, interpretation, etc.   2. Q
hypothesis (Synoptics criticism)   3. Apocryphal Gospels--Criticism,
interpretation, etc.   4. Gnostic literature--Relation to the New
Testament.   5. Bible. N.T. Gospels--Harmonies--History and
criticism.   I. Title.
BS2555.2.K64 1990
226'.06--dc20   90-34716
                                                                        CIP

Composition by Chiron, Inc.
Cambridge, Massachusetts

A L'UNIVERSITÉ DE GENÈVE ET A SA FACULTÉ DE THÉOLOGIE
EN TÉMOIGNAGE DE GRATITUDE
POUR LA COLLATION DU DOCTORAT HONORIS CAUSE

Table of Contents

Acknowledgments

Quotations from the Bible are either my own translations or are adapted from the *Revised Standard Version* or the *New Revised Standard Version.*

Many quotations of sayings from the Synoptic Sayings Source are adapted from John Kloppenborg, *Q Parallels.*

English translations of apocryphal literature are taken from Hennecke-Schneemelcher-Wilson, *NT Apocrypha.* Nag Hammadi writings are quoted from Robinson, ed., *The Nag Hammadi Library in English,* or from the extant critical editions in Nag Hammadi Studies.

Quotations from ancient Greek, Roman, and Christian literature are usually adapted from the volumes of Loeb Classical Library.

The treatment of the *Secret Gospel of Mark* and the translation of the text are based upon the manuscript which I have submitted to Polebridge Press for its new edition of the New Testament Apocrypha.

Abbreviations

AAWG.PH	Abhandlungen der Akademie der Wissenschaften in Göttingen. Philologisch-historische Klasse.
AB	Anchor Bible
Acts Thom.	*Acts of Thomas*
Adv. haer.	*Adversus Haereses* (Irenaeus)
AnBol	*Analecta Bollandica*
ANRW	*Aufstieg und Niedergang der römischen Welt*
ANTT	Arbeiten zur neutestamentlichen Textforschung
ANTF	Abhandlungen zur neutestamentlichen Textforschung
Apocr. Jas.	*Apocryphon of James* (NHC I, 2)
ATR	*Anglican Theological Review*
BA	*Biblical Archaeologist*
Barn.	*Barnabas, Epistle of*
BBC	*Bulletin of the Bezan Club*
BEThL	Bibliotheca ephemeridum theologicarum Lovaniensium
BFChTh	Beiträge zur Förderung christlicher Theologie
BG 8502	Berlin Gnostic Papyrus 8502
BHTh	Beiträge zur historischen Theologie
BibOr	Biblica et Orientalia
BThSt	Biblisch-theologische Studien
BZ	Biblische Zeitschrift
BZNW	Beihefte zur Zeitschrift für die neutestamentliche Wissenschaft
CBM	Chester Beatty Monographs
CBQ	*Catholic Biblical Quarterly*
CChr.SA	Corpus Christianorum. Series Apocryphorum
chap(s).	chapter(s)
Clem. Al.	Clement of Alexandria

— *Ecl. Proph.*	— *Eclogae ex scripturis propheticis*
— *Exc. Theod.*	— *Excerpta ex Theodotou*
— *Strom.*	— *Stromateis*
1 *Clem.*	1 *Clement, Epistle of*
2 *Clem.*	2 *Clement, Epistle of*
CSCO	Corpus Scriptorum Christianorum Orientalium
CSSN	Corpus sacrae scripturae neerlandica medi aevi
Diogn.	*Diognetus, Epistle to*
Dial. Sav.	*Dialogue of the Savior* (NHC III,5)
Did.	*Didache (Teaching of the Twelve Apostles)*
Diog. L.	Diogenes Laërtius
Diss.	Dissertation (unpublished)
EHT.T	Europäische Hochschulschriften. Reihe 23: Theologie
EdF	Erträge der Forschung
ed(s).	edition, edited, editor(s)
EKK	Evangelisch-katholischer Kommentar zum Neuen Testament
Epiphanius	
— *Haer.*	*Panarion seu adversus lxxx haereses*
Epist. Apost.	*Epistula Apostolorum*
ET	English translation
et al.	et alii (and others)
EtB	Etudes Bibliques
EThL	*Ephemerides theologicae Lovaniensis*
ETR	*Etudes théologiques et religieuses*
EvTh	*Evangelische Theologie*
F&F	Foundations and Facets
FGNK	Forschungen zur Geschichte des neutestamentlichen Kanons
FKDG	Forschungen zur Kirchen- und Dogmengeschichte
FRLANT	Forschungen zur Religion and Literatur des Alten und Neuen Testaments
GBSNTS	Guides to Biblical Scholarship, New Testament Series
GCS	Die griechischen christlichen Schriftsteller
GGA	Göttingische Gelehrte Anzeigen
GLB	De Gruyter Lehrbuch
Gos. Egypt.	*Gospel of the Egyptians*
Gos. Pet.	*Gospel of Peter*

Gos. Thom.	*Gospel of Thomas* (NHC II,2)
Hist. eccl.	*Historia ecclesiae* (Eusebius's *Church History*)
HNT	Handbuch zum Neuen Testament
HNT.EB	Handbuch zum Neuen Testament, Ergänzungsband
HSem	Horae Semiticae
HTR	*Harvard Theological Review*
HTS	Harvard Theological Studies
Ibid.	Ibidem
IDBSup	*The Interpreter's Dictionary of the Bible, Supplementary Volume* (Nashville: Abingdon, 1976)
Ign. *Eph.*	Ignatius, *To the Ephesians*
— *Mg.*	— *To the Magnesians*
— *Trall.*	— *To the Trallians*
— *Rom.*	— *To the Romans*
— *Phld.*	— *To the Philadelphians*
— *Sm.*	— *To the Smyrnaeans*
— *Pol.*	— *To Polycarp*
inscr.	*inscriptio* (introductory phrase or sentence of a writing)
Irenaeus	
— *Adv. haer.*	*Adversus haereses*
JBL	*Journal of Biblical Literature*
JR	*Journal of Religion*
JTS	*Journal of Theological Studies*
Justin	
— *1 Apol.*	*First Apology*
— *Dial.*	*Dialogue with Trypho*
KAV	Kommentar zu den Apostolischen Vätern
KEK	Kritisch-exegetischer Kommentar über das Neue Testament
KlT	Kleine Texte für Vorlesungen und Übungen
LCL	Loeb Classical Library
LSJ	Liddell-Scott-Jones, *Greek-English Lexicon*
LXX	Septuaginta (= the Greek translation of the Old Testament)
MPG	*Migne, Patrologia Graeca*
MPL	*Migne, Patrologia Latina*
n(n).	note(s)
N.F.	Neue Folge (new series)

NHC	Nag Hammadi Corpus
NHS	Nag Hammadi Studies
Noct. Att.	*Noctes Atticae* (Aulus Gellius)
NovT	*Novum Testamentum*
NovTSup	Novum Testamentum Supplements
NT	New Testament
NTA	Neutestamentliche Abhandlungen
NTS	*New Testament Studies*
NumenSup	Supplements to Numen
OLZ	*Orientalische Literaturzeitung*
OrChr	*Oriens Christianus*
OrChrA	Orientalia Christiana Analecta
OT	Old Testament
𝔭	Papyrus of the New Testament
p(p).	page(s)
Pap. Eg. 2	*Papyrus Egerton 2*
Pap. Oxy.	*Papyrus Oxyrhynchus*
par(r).	(Synoptic) parallel(s)
PETSE	Papers of the Estonian Theological Society in Exile
Pol. *Phil.*	Polycarp, *To the Philippians*
Ps-Clem. Hom.	*Pseudo-Clementine Homilies*
PTS	Patristische Texte und Studien
Q	*Quelle: The Synoptic Sayings Source* (the chapter and verse numbers for Q are identical with those of the Gospel of Luke)
RAC	*Reallexikon für Antike und Christentum*
RB	*Revue Biblique*
RGG	*Die Religion in Geschichte und Gegenwart*
RThL	*Revue Théologique de Louvain*
RThPh	*Revue de Théologie et Philosophie*
SAQ	Sammlung ausgewählter kirchen- und dogmengeschichtlicher Quellenschriften
SBB	Stuttgarter Biblische Beiträge
SBLDS	Society of Biblical Literature Dissertation Series
SBLMS	Society of Biblical Literature Monograph Series
SBLTT	Society of Biblical Literature Texts and Translations
SBT	Studies in Biblical Theology
SC	Sources Chrétiennes

SHG	Subsidia hagiographica. Societé des Bollandistes
SHR	Studies in the History of Religions
SHW.PH	Sitzungsberichte der Heidelberger Akademie der Wissenschaften, Phil.-hist. Klasse
SJLA	Studies in Judaism in Late Antiquity
SNTS.MS	Society for New Testament Studies. Monograph Series
StD	Studies and Documents
StNT	Studien zum Neuen Testament
StTh	*Studia Theologica*
StUNT	Studien zur Umwelt des Neuen Testaments
sv. (svv.)	*sub verbo (verbis)* or *sub voce (vocis)*
TaS	Texts and Studies
Tatian, *Or.*	Tatian, *Oratio ad Graecos*
TDNT	*Theological Dictionary to the New Testament*
ThWAT	*Theologisches Wörterbuch zum Alten Testament*
ThLZ	*Theologische Literaturzeitung*
ThR	*Theologische Rundschau*
trans.	translated by
TRE	*Theologische Realenzyklopädie*
TU	Texte und Untersuchungen zur Geschichte der altchristlichen Literatur
VigChr	*Vigiliae Christianae*
VNAW	Verhandelingen [k.] nederlandse akademie van wetenschappen. Afdeling letterkunde
vol(s).	volume(s)
WdF	Wege der Forschung
WMANT	Wissenschaftliche Monographien zum Alten und Neuen Testament
vs., vss.	vers, verses
WuD	*Wort und Dienst*
WUNT	Wissenschaftliche Untersuchungen zum Neuen Testament
ZKG	*Zeitschrift für Kirchengeschichte*
ZNW	*Zeitschrift für die neutestamentliche Wissenschaft*

List of Short Titles

Aland, ed., *Die alten Übersetzungen*
> Kurt Aland, ed., *Die alten Übersetzungen des Neuen Testaments, die Kirchenväterzitate und Lektionare* (ANTT 5; Berlin: De Gruyter, 1972)

Aland, *Kurzgefaßte Liste*
> Kurt Aland, *Kurzgefaßte Liste der griechischen Handschriften des Neuen Testaments* (ANTF 1; Berlin: De Gruyter, 1963).

Aland, *Repetitorium*
> Kurt Aland, *Repetitorium der griechischen christlichen Papyri I: Biblische Papyri* (PTS 18; Berlin: De Gruyter, 1976).

Aland, *Synopsis*
> Kurt Aland, *Synopsis Quattuor Evangeliorum* (Stuttgart: Württembergische Bibelanstalt, 1963 and reprints).

Allison, "Pauline Epistles"
> Dale C. Allison, Jr., "The Pauline Epistles and the Synoptic Gospels: The Pattern of the Parallels" *NTS* 28 (1982) 1–32.

Attridge, "Greek Fragments"
> Harold W. Attridge, "The Greek Fragments," in Layton, ed., *Nag Hammadi Codex II,* 103–9.

Attridge, *Nag Hammadi Codex I*
> Harold W. Attridge, ed., *Nag Hammadi Codex I (The Jung Codex)* (2 vols.; NHS 22–23; Leiden: Brill, 1985).

Baarda, "2 Clement 12"
> Tjitze Baarda, "2 Clement 12 and the Sayings of Jesus," in Delobel, ed., *LOGIA,* 529–56.

Baarda, *Early Transmission*
> Tjitze Baarda, *Early Transmission of the Words of Jesus: Thomas, Tatian and the Text of the New Testament* (Amsterdam: Uitgiverij, 1983).

Baltzer, *Biographie*
> Klaus Baltzer, *Die Biographie der Propheten* (Neukirchen: Neukirchener Verlag, 1975).

Bauer, *Leben Jesu*
> Walter Bauer, *Das Leben Jesu im Zeitalter der neutestamentlichen Apo-kryphen* (Tübingen: Mohr/Siebeck, 1909).

Bell and Skeat, *Unknown Gospel*
> H. Idris Bell and T. C. Skeat, *Fragments of an Unknown Gospel and Other Early Christian Papyri* (London: British Museum, 1935).

Bellinzoni, *Sayings in Justin Martyr*
> Arthur Bellinzoni, *The Sayings of Jesus in the Writings of Justin Martyr* (NovTSup 17; Leiden: Brill, 1967).

Best, "1 Peter"
> Ernest Best, "1 Peter and the Gospel Tradition," *NTS* 16 (1969/70) 95–113.

Betz, *Essays*
> Hans Dieter Betz, *Essays on the Sermon on the Mount* (Philadelphia: Fortress, 1985).

Bornkamm-Barth-Held, *Tradition and Interpretation*
> Günther Bornkamm, Gerhard Barth, and Heinz-Joachim Held, *Tradition and Interpretation in Matthew* (Philadelphia: Westminster, 1963)

Bovon, *Evangelium nach Lukas*
> Francois Bovon, *Das Evangelium nach Lukas. 1. Teilband: Lk 1,1–9,50* (EKK 3/1; Zürich: Benziger Verlag, and Neukirchen: Neukirchener Verlag, 1989).

Bovon, "Synoptic Gospels"
> Francois Bovon, "The Synoptic Gospels and the Noncanonical Acts of the Apostles," *HTR* 81 (1988) 19–36.

Brown, *Birth of the Messiah*
> Raymond E. Brown, *The Birth of the Messiah: A Commentary on the Infancy Narratives of Matthew and Luke* (Garden City, NY: Doubleday, 1977).

Brown, *Gospel of John*
> Raymond E. Brown, *The Gospel According to John* (2 vols.; AB 29–30; Garden City, NJ: Doubleday, 1966–70).

Brown, "Thomas and John"
> Raymond E. Brown, "The Gospel of Thomas and St. John's Gospel," NTS 9 (1962/63) 155–77.

Bultmann, *Gospel of John*
> Rudolf Bultmann, *The Gospel of John: A Commentary* (Philadelphia: Westminster, 1971).

Bultmann, *Synoptic Tradition*
> Rudolf Bultmann, *The History of the Synoptic Tradition* (2d ed.; New York: Harper & Row, 1968).

Bultmann, *Theology*
> Rudolf Bultmann, *Theology of the New Testament* (2 vols.; New York: Scribner's, 1951–1955).

Cameron, *Apocryphon of James*
> Ron Cameron, *Sayings Traditions in the Apocryphon of James* (HTS 34; Philadelphia: Fortress, 1984).

Cameron, *Other Gospels*
> Ron Cameron, *The Other Gospels: Non-Canonical Gospel Texts* (Philadelphia: Westminster, 1982).

Cameron, *Parable and Interpretation*
> Ron Cameron, *Parable and Interpretation in the Gospel of Thomas* (F&F 2.2; Sonoma, CA: Polebridge Press, 1986).

von Campenhausen, *Ecclesiastical Authority*
> Hans von Campenhausen, *Ecclesiastical Authority and Spiritual Power* (Stanford, CA: Stanford University Press, 1969).

von Campenhausen, *Formation*
> Hans von Campenhausen, *The Formation of the Christian Bible* (Philadelphia: Fortress, 1972).

von Campenhausen, *Frühzeit*
> Hans von Campenhausen, *Aus der Frühzeit des Christentums: Studien zur Kirchengeschichte des ersten und zweiten Jahrhunderts* (Tübingen: Mohr/Siebeck, 1963).

Conzelmann, *1 Corinthians*
> Hans Conzelmann, *1 Corinthians: A Commentary on the First Epistle to the Corinthians* (Hermeneia; Philadelphia: Fortress, 1975).

Conzelmann, *Theology of St Luke*
> Hans Conzelmann, *The Theology of St Luke* (London: Faber, 1960).

Conzelmann and Lindemann, *Interpreting the NT*
> Hans Conzelmann and Andreas Lindemann, *Interpreting the New Testament: An Introduction to the Principles and Methods of N.T. Exegesis* (Peabody, MA: Hendrickson, 1988).

Crossan, *The Cross that Spoke*
> John Dominic Crossan, *The Cross that Spoke: The Origins of the Passion Narrative* (San Francisco: Harper & Row, 1988)

Crossan, *Four Other Gospels*
> John Dominic Crossan, *Four Other Gospels: Shadows on the Contours of Canon* (Minneapolis: Winston, 1985)

Crossan, *In Parable*
> John Dominic Crossan, *In Parable: The Challenge of the Historical Jesus* (New York: Harper & Row, 1973).

Daniels, *Egerton Gospel*
Jon B. Daniels, *The Egerton Gospel: Its Place in Early Christianity* (Dissertation Claremont Graduate School, Claremont, CA: 1990).

Davies, *Paul and Rabbinic Judaism*
W. D. Davies, *Paul and Rabbinic Judaism: Some Rabbinic Elements in Pauline Theology* (London: S.P.C.K., 1965).

Deissmann, *Light from the Ancient Near East*
Adolf Deissmann, *Light from the Ancient Near East* (New York: Doran, 1927).

Delobel, ed., *LOGIA*
Joël Delobel, *LOGIA: Les paroles de Jésus — The Sayings of Jesus: Memorial Joseph Coppens* (BEThL 59; Leuven: Peeters, 1982).

Dibelius, "Jungfrauensohn"
Martin Dibelius, "Jungfrauensohn und Krippenkind: Untersuchungen zur Geburtsgeschichte Jesu im Lukasevangelium," in idem, *Botschaft und Geschichte: Gesammelte Aufsätze,* vol. 1 (Tübingen: Mohr/Siebeck, 1953) 1–78.

Dibelius-Greeven, *James*
Martin Dibelius, *James: A Commentary on the Epistle of James,* rev. by Heinrich Greeven (Hermeneia, Philadelphia: Fortress, 1976).

Denker, *Petrusevangelium*
Jürgen Denker, *Die theologiegeschichtliche Stellung des Petrusevangeliums: Ein Beitrag zur Frühgeschichte des Doketismus* (EHS.T 36; Bern and Frankfurt: Lang, 1975).

Deppe, *Sayings of Jesus*
Dean B. Deppe, *The Sayings of Jesus in the Epistle of James* (Dissertation Amsterdam, Free University, 1989).

Dodd, *Historical Tradition*
C. H. Dodd, *Historical Tradition in the Fourth Gospel* (Cambridge: Cambridge University Press, 1963).

Dormeyer, *Evangelium als Gattung*
Detlev Dormeyer, *Evangelium als literarische und theologische Gattung* (EdF 263; Darmstadt: Wissenschaftliche Buchgesellschaft, 1989).

Dormeyer and Frankemölle, "Evangelium als Begriff"
Detlev Dormeyer and Hubert Frankemölle, "Evangelium als literarischer und als theologischer Begriff: Tendenzen und Aufgaben der Evangelienforschung im 20. Jahrhundert, mit einer Untersuchung des Markusevangeliums in seinem Verhältnis zur griechischen Biographie," *ANRW* 2.25/2. 1541–1704.

Emmel [Koester, Pagels], *Nag Hammadi Codex III,5*
Stephen Emmel, ed., with an introduction by Helmut Koester and Elaine Pagels, *Nag Hammadi Codex III,5: The Dialogue of the Savior* (NHS 26; Leiden: Brill, 1984).

Fallon and Cameron, "Forschungsbericht"
> Francis T. Fallon and Ron Cameron, "The Gospel of Thomas: A For-
> schungsbericht and Analysis," *ANRW* 2. 25/5, 4195–4251.

Foerster, *Gnosis*
> Werner Foerster, *Gnosis: A Selection of Gnostic Texts* (2 vols.; Oxford:
> Clarendon, 1972–74).

Frankemölle, *Evangelium: Forschungsbericht*
> Hubert Frankemölle, *Evangelium. Begriff und Gattung: Ein For-
> schungsbericht* (SBB 15; Stuttgart: Katholisches Bibelwerk, 1988).

Friedrich, "εὐαγγελίζομαι"
> Gerhard Friedrich, "εὐαγγελίζομαι, κτλ." *TDNT* 2 (1964) 707–37.

Furnish, *Theology and Ethics*
> Victor Paul Furnish, *Theology and Ethics in Paul* (Nashville: Abingdon,
> 1968).

Gibson, ed., *The Commentaries of Isho^cdad*
> M. D. Gibson, ed., *The Commentaries of Isho^cdad of Merv* (HSem 5–7; 3
> vols.; Cambridge 1911)

Hengel, *Evangelienüberschriften*
> Martin Hengel, *Die Evangelienüberschriften* (SHW.PH 1984.3; Heidel-
> berg: Winter, 1984).

Hennecke-Schneemelcher-Wilson, *NT Apocrypha*
> Edgar Hennecke, *New Testament Apocrypha* (2 vols.; 3d. ed. by Wilhelm
> Schneemelcher, trans. R. McL. Wilson; Philadelphia: Westminster,
> 1963).

Hennecke-Schneemelcher, *NT Apokryphen I*
> Edgar Hennecke, *Neutestamentliche Apokryphen in deutscher Über-
> setzung,* vol. I: *Evangelien* (5th ed. by Wilhelm Schneemelcher;
> Tübingen: Siebeck/Mohr, 1987).

Hoffmann, *Studien*
> Paul Hoffmann, *Studien zur Theologie der Logienquelle* (NTA, N.F. 8; 3d
> ed.; Münster: Aschendorff, 1982).

Huck-Greeven, *Synopsis*
> Albert Huck, *Synopsis of the First Three Gospels* (13th ed. fundamentally
> revised by Heinrich Greeven; Tübingen: Mohr/Siebeck, 1981).

Jeremias, *Parables*
> Joachim Jeremias, *The Parables of Jesus* (rev. ed.; London: SCM, New
> York: Scribner's, 1963).

Jeremias, *Unknown Sayings*
> Joachim Jeremias, *Unknown Sayings of Jesus* (2d. ed.; London: S.P.C.K.,
> 1964).

Kirchner, "Brief des Jakobus"
Dankwart Kirchner, "Brief des Jakobus," in Hennecke-Schneemelcher,
NT Apokryphen I, 234–244.

Kloppenborg, *Formation of Q*
John S. Kloppenborg, *The Formation of Q: Trajectories in Ancient
Wisdom Collections* (Studies in Antiquity and Christianity; Philadel-
phia: Fortress, 1987).

Kloppenborg, *Q Parallels*
John S. Kloppenborg, *Q Parallels: Synopsis, Critical Notes & Concordance* (F&F; Sonoma, CA: Polebridge Press, 1988).

Klostermann, *Apocrypha I*
Erich Klostermann, *Apocrypha I: Reste des Petrusevangeliums, der
Petrusapokalypse und des Kerygma Petri* (KlT 3; 3d ed.; Berlin: De
Gruyter, 1933).

Klostermann, *Apocrypha II*
Erich Klostermann, *Apocrypha II: Evangelien* (KlT 8; 3d ed.; Berlin: De
Gruyter, 1929).

Köhler, *Rezeption des Matthäusevangeliums*
Wolf-Dietrich Köhler, *Die Rezeption des Matthäusevangeliums in der
Zeit vor Irenäus* (WUNT 2/24; Tübingen: Mohr/Siebeck, 1986).

Koester, "Apocryphal and Canonical Gospels"
Helmut Koester, "Apocryphal and Canonical Gospels," *HTR* 73 (1980)
105–30.

Koester, "From Mark to Secret Mark"
Helmut Koester, "History and Development of Mark's Gospel: From
Mark to Secret Mark and 'Canonical' Mark," in: Bruce C. Corley, ed.,
*Colloquy on New Testament Studies: A Time for Reappraisal and Fresh
Approaches* (Macon, GA: Mercer University Press, 1983) 35–58.

Koester, "Gnostic Writings"
Helmut Koester, "Gnostic Writings as Witnesses for the Development of
the Sayings Tradition," in: Bentley Layton, ed., *The Rediscovery of Gnosticism,* vol. 1: *The School of Valentinus* (NumenSup 41; Leiden: Brill,
1980) 239–61.

Koester, "ΓΝΩΜΑΙ ΔΙΑΦΟΡΟΙ"
Helmut Koester, "ΓΝΩΜΑΙ ΔΙΑΦΟΡΟΙ: The Origin and Nature of
Diversification in the History of Early Christianity," in Robinson-
Koester, *Trajectories,* 114–57.

Koester, *Introduction*
Helmut Koester, *Introduction to the New Testament* (2 vols.; New York,
Berlin: De Gruyter, 1982).

Koester, "Kerygma to Gospel"
Helmut Koester, "From the Kerygma-Gospel to Written Gospels," *NTS*
35 (1989) 361–81.

Koester, "La tradition"
> Helmut Koester, "La tradition apostolique et les origines du Gnosticisme," *RThPh* 119 (1987) 1–16.

Koester, *Synoptische Überlieferung*
> Helmut Koester, *Synoptische Überlieferung bei den apostolischen Vätern* (TU 65; Berlin: Akademie-Verlag, 1957).

Kuhn, *Ältere Sammlungen*
> Heinz-Wolfgang Kuhn, *Ältere Sammlungen im Markusevangelium* (StUNT 8; Göttingen: Vandenhoeck & Ruprecht, 1971).

Kümmel, *Das Neue Testament*
> Werner Georg Kümmel, *Das Neue Testament: Geschichte der Erforschung seiner Probleme* (Orbis 3.1; Freiburg/München: Alber, 1958).

Layton, *Gnostic Scriptures*
> Bentley Layton, *The Gnostic Scriptures: A New Translation with Annotations and Introductions* (Garden City, NY: Doubleday, 1987).

Layton, *Nag Hammadi Codex II*
> Bentley Layton, ed., *Nag Hammadi Codex II,2–7 Together with XIII,2*, Brit. Lib. Or. 4926(1) and P. Oxy. 1, 654, 655* (NHS 20–21; Leiden: Brill, 1989).

Leloir, ed., *Saint Éphrem*
> Louis Leloir, ed., *Saint Éphrem, Commentaire de l'évangile concordant, version arménienne* (CSCO 137 [text] and 145; Louvain: Peeters, 1953 & 1954).

Lipsius-Bonnet, *Acta Apostolorum Apocrypha*
> Ricardus Albertus Lipsius and Maximilianus Bonnet, *Acta Apostolorum Apocrypha* (2 vols.; Leipzig: Mendelssohn, 1891–1898; reprint Darmstadt: Wissenschaftliche Buchgesellschaft, 1959).

Lührmann, *Redaktion*
> Dieter Lührmann, *Die Redaktion der Logienquelle* (WMANT 33; Neukirchen: Neukirchener Verlag, 1969).

Lührmann, *Markusevangelium*
> Dieter Lührmann, *Das Markusevangelium* (HNT 3; Tübingen: Mohr/Siebeck, 1987).

Lutz, *Matthew 1–7*
> Ulrich Lutz, *Matthew 1–7: A Commentary* (Minneapolis: Augsburg, 1989).

Marxsen, *Markus*
> Willi Marxsen, *Der Evangelist Markus* (FRLANT 67; Göttingen: Vandenhoeck & Ruprecht, 1956).

Massaux, *Influence de L'Évangile de Saint Matthieu*
> Édouard Massaux, *Influence de L'Évangile de Saint Matthieu sur la littérature chrétienne avant Saint Irénée* (reprint; Leuven: Leuven University Press, 1986).

Mayeda, *Leben-Jesu-Fragment*
Goro Mayeda, *Das Leben-Jesu-Fragment Papyrus Egerton 2 und seine Stellung in der urchristlichen Literaturgeschichte* (Bern: Haupt, 1946).

McDonald, *Formation*
Lee Martin McDonald, *The Formation of the Christian Biblical Canon* (Nashville: Abingdon, 1988).

Metzger, *Text*
Bruce Metzger, *The Text of the New Testament* (Oxford: Clarendon, 1964).

Metzger, *Textual Commentary*
Bruce Metzger, *A Textual Commentary on the Greek New Testament* (New York: United Bible Society, 1971).

Neirynck, *Minor Agreements*
Frans Neirynck, *The Minor Agreements of Matthew and Luke against Mark* (BEThL 37; Louvain: Leuven University Press, 1974).

Nestle-Aland, *NT Graece*
Erwin Nestle, *Novum Testamentum Graece* (26th ed. by Kurt Aland et al.; Stuttgart: Deutsche Bibelstiftung, 1979 and later reprints).

Niederwimmer, *Didache*
Kurt Niederwimmer, *Die Didache* (KEK, KAV 1; Göttingen: Vandenhoeck & Ruprecht, 1988).

Pearson, "Earliest Christianity in Egypt"
Birger A. Pearson, "Earliest Christianity in Egypt: Some Observations," in idem and James E. Goehring, eds., *The Roots of Egyptian Christianity* (Studies in Antiquity and Christianity; Philadelphia: Fortress, 1986) 132–56.

Pesch, *Markusevangelium*
Rudolf Pesch, *Das Markusevangelium* (2 vols.; Herders Kommentar; Freiburg: Herder, 1977)

Peterson, *The Diatessaron and Ephrem Syrus*
William L. Peterson, *The Diatessaron and Ephrem Syrus as Sources of Romanos the Melodist* (CSCO 475; Leuven: Peeters, 1985).

Robinson, "Kerygma and History"
James M. Robinson, "Kerygma and History in the New Testament," in Robinson-Koester, *Trajectories,* 20–70.

Robinson, "LOGOI SOPHON"
James M. Robinson, "LOGOI SOPHON: On the Gattung of Q," in Robinson-Koester, *Trajectories,* 71–113.

Robinson, ed., *Nag Hammadi Library*
James M. Robinson, ed., *The Nag Hammadi Library in English* (3d completely rev. ed.; San Francisco: Harper & Row, 1988).

Robinson-Koester, *Trajectories*
    James M. Robinson and Helmut Koester, *Trajectories through Early Christianity* (Philadelphia: Fortress, 1971).

Rudolph, *Gnosis*
    Kurt Rudolph, *Gnosis: The Nature and History of an Ancient Religion* (Edinburgh: Clark, 1983).

Schmithals, *Einleitung*
    Walter Schmithals, *Einleitung in die drei ersten Evangelien* (GLB; Berlin: De Gruyter, 1985).

Schmithals, *Markus*
    Walther Schmithals, *Das Evangelium nach Markus* (Ökumenischer Taschenbuchkommentar zum NT 2/1; Gütersloh: Gütersloher Verlagshaus, 1979).

Schniewind, *Euangelion*
    Julius Schniewind, *Euangelion: Ursprung und erste Gestalt des Begriffs Evangelium* (BFChTh 13; Gütersloh: Bertelsmann, 1927; reprint: Wissenschaftliche Buchgesellschaft: Darmstadt, 1970).

Schoedel, *Ignatius*
    William R. Schoedel, *Ignatius of Antioch: A Commentary on the Letters of Ignatius of Antioch* (Hermeneia; Philadelphia: Fortress, 1985).

Schulz, *Spruchquelle*
    Siegfried Schulz, *Q: Die Spruchquelle der Evangelisten* (Zürich: Theologischer Verlag, 1972).

Morton Smith, *Clement of Alexandria*
    Morton Smith, *Clement of Alexandria and a Secret Gospel of Mark* (Cambridge, MA: Harvard University Press, 1973 [transcription, plates, and translation: pp. 445–54]).

Stendahl, *School of St. Matthew*
    Krister Stendahl, *The School of St. Matthew and Its Use of the Old Testament* (2d ed.; Philadelphia: Fortress, 1968).

Streeter, *Four Gospels*
    B. H. Streeter, *The Four Gospels: A Study of Origins* (London: Macmillan, 1924).

Stuhlmacher, ed., *Evangelium und Evangelien*
    Peter Stuhlmacher, ed., *Das Evangelium und die Evangelien* (WUNT 28; Tübingen: Mohr/Siebeck, 1983).

Stuhlmacher, *Das paulinische Evangelium*
    Peter Stuhlmacher, *Das paulinische Evangelium: I. Vorgeschichte* (FRLANT 95; Göttingen: Vandenhoeck & Ruprecht, 1968).

Throckmorton, *Gospel Parallels*
    Burton H. Throckmorton, *Gospel Parallels: A Synopsis of the First Three Gospels* (4th ed.; Nashville and New York: Nelson, 1979).

Vielhauer, *Geschichte*
> Philipp Vielhauer, *Geschichte der frühchristlichen Literatur* (GLB; Berlin: De Gruyter, 1975).

Vogels, *Beiträge zur Geschichte des Diatessaron*
> Heinrich Joseph Vogels, *Beiträge zur Geschichte des Diatessaron im Abendland* (NTA 8/1: Münster: Aschendorff, 1919).

Völker, *Quellen*
> Walther Völker, *Quellen zur Geschichte der christlichen Gnosis* (SAQ 5; Tübingen: Mohr/Siebeck, 1932).

Wengst, *Didache*
> Klaus Wengst, *Didache (Apostellehre), Zweiter Clemensbrief, Schrift an Diognet* (Schriften des Urchristentums 2; Darmstadt: Wissenschaftliche Buchgesellschaft, 1984).

Williams, "Apocryphon of James"
> Francis E. Williams, ed., "The Apocryphon of James," in Harold W. Attridge, ed., *Nag Hammadi Codex I (The Jung Codex): Introductions, Texts, Translations, Notes* (NHS 22; Leiden: Brill, 1985) 13–53.

Wilson and MacRae, "Gospel According to Mary"
> R. McL. Wilson and George W. MacRae, "The Gospel According to Mary," in Douglas M. Parrott, ed., *Nag Hammadi Codices V,2–5 and VI with Papyrus Berolinensis 8502, 1 and 4* (NHS 11; Leiden: Brill, 1979) 470.

Zahn, *Kanon*
> Theodor Zahn, *Geschichte des neutestamentlichen Kanons* (2 vols.; Erlangen: Deichert, 1888–89).

Preface

Forty years ago, in the year 1950, when I visited my teacher Rudolf Bultmann at his house, Calvinstraße 14 in Marburg, he suggested that I write a dissertation on the "Gospels in the Second Century." At that time, rumors about the discovery of a *Gospel of Thomas* had not yet reached the peaceful University of Marburg. Some other apocryphal gospels were, of course, known, and my subsequent research involved me, among other things, in some frustrating study of the problem of the Jewish-Christian Gospels. But it was fortunate that a simple treatment of the "Synoptic Tradition in the Apostolic Fathers" was deemed satisfactory as a doctoral thesis and that I was thus freed from the much more ambitious aims of the thesis topic that my Doktorvater initially suggested.

However, I always felt that I should one day write a book on the gospels in the second century. My study of the gospel traditions in the Apostolic Fathers had brought me to the conclusion that gospel materials that were not dependent upon the canonical writings might indeed have survived well into the second century. But I was also aware of the prevailing opinion, which saw all apocryphal gospels as works that came into existence after the completion of the canonical writings. Attempts to discover in apocryphal materials pre-canonical traditions regularly met with severe criticism. That point of view still dominated the third edition of Edgar Hennecke's "Neutestamentliche Apokrypen," which was published by Wilhelm Schneemelcher in 1959, and which served as the basis for R. McL. Wilson's English translation of this work.[1]

The publication of the *Gospel of Thomas* in the year 1959 marks the beginning of a change. Equally important, however, was the redis-

---

[1] I was informed by the publisher Westminster/John Knox Press that an English translation of the new and thoroughly revised 5th German edition of this work, published in 1987, will be published presently.

covery of Walter Bauer's *Rechtgläubigkeit und Ketzerei im ältesten Christentum,* which had been published in 1934. The appearance of a second edition of this epochal work thirty years after its original publication and four years after the death of its author[1] as well as the publication of an English translation[2] signified a fundamental change in the climate of scholarship. It seemed as if almost two millennia of discrimination against those whom the Fathers of the church had labelled as "heretics" would come to an end. If these "heresies" were not simply secondary deviations from an already established orthodoxy, but resulted from developments in the Christian communities that occurred as early as the time of Paul's mission to the Gentiles, also their gospels could claim to be genuine continuations of the earliest stages of the formation of the traditions about Jesus of Nazareth.

What is put to the test is the "early-catholic" or "orthodox" tradition, which asserts the monopoly of the canonical gospel tradition. That there were Christians who disputed this assertion cannot be questioned. Later, in the second half of the second century, "catholic" and "heretical" Christians began to become more clearly distinguished from each other. However, the gospels discussed in this book belong to an earlier period in which these dividing lines had not yet been drawn. There were controversies, to be sure, and some of them are clearly visible as early as the the middle of the 1st century, that is, in the time of the apostle Paul. But the traditions about Jesus were shared to a large degree by all participants in these controversies. In his arguments against the heretics, the early 3d-century apologist Tertullian (*De proscriptione hereticorum*) insisted that the claims of the heretics were null and void and had to be ruled out of court because they could not prove that they existed in the very beginning. It is, however, not possible to substantiate this claim. The earliest gospel traditions and gospel writings contain the seeds of both, later heresy as well as later orthodoxy. For the description of the history and development of gospel literature in the earliest period of Christianity, the epithets "heretical" and "orthodox" are meaningless. Only dogmatic prejudice can assert that the canonical writings have an exclusive claim to apostolic origin and thus to historical priority. Whether my own reconstruction of the development of this literature is plausible, should be argued on historical and source-critical grounds.

The result of this new orientation was a shift in focus for the investigation of the apocryphal gospels. Those apocryphal writings, which

---

[1] Second edition by Georg Strecker (BHTh 10; Göttingen: Vandenhoeck & Ruprecht, 1964).

[2] *Orthodoxy and Heresy in Earliest Christianity* (Philadelphia: Fortress, 1971).

might yield insights into the earliest stages of the development of the gospel tradition, moved into the center of the scholarly debate, while the investigation of other extra-canonical writings, which were evidently dependent upon the gospels of the canon, however important and rewarding, had to take second place.

This book is the result of this shift. It includes extensive treatments of all those writings from which one might, in my judgment, learn more about the earliest stages of the history and development of gospel literature—a history that must have begun with smaller written collections of materials about Jesus and eventually resulted in the composition of a number of gospel writings, including so-called apocryphal gospels as well as the Gospels of the New Testament canon, John, Mark, Matthew, and Luke. This historical development culminated in the only partially successful attempt to create the one gospel for the church, that is, Tatian's *Diatessaron* (I thank Professor Peterson, one of the few experts of this ancient work, for contributing a chapter on the *Diatessaron,* which may well prove to be one of the most valuable parts of this book). As a consequence, I had to choose. The Synoptic Sayings Source (Q), the *Gospel of Thomas,* the *Dialogue of the Savior,* the *Unknown Gospel of Papyrus Egerton 2,* the *Apocryphon of James* and the *Gospel of Peter* seemed to have contributed to this first phase of the history of gospel literature and therefore had to be moved to center stage. But gospel writings that were dependent upon these earliest gospels and upon the Gospels of the New Testament canon, including such important writings as the Jewish-Christian Gospels, the *Epistula Apostolorum,* the *Gospel of Nicodemus* and many other non-canonical gospels and gospel fragments, had to take second place and are not included in this volume. Deo volente, some day I may be able to write a sequel to this book in which these later gospels will be discussed.

This book is the result of a still ongoing debate. I owe much to those who have expressed their disagreement with my view of these earliest non-canonical writings, and it is evident that the publication of this work will not end the controversy. I owe even more to the scholars, students, and friends, whose work has pointed into similar or analogous directions. It is perhaps appropriate, in this preface, to mention at least three friends who have been most helpful and influential on my way to the completion of this book. James M. Robinson of the Claremont Graduate School and Director of the Institute for Antiquity and Christianity in Claremont, California, to whom I am indebted for more than three decades of a shared path; François Bovon of the University of Geneva, Switzerland, who once dedicated a book to me as "le défenseur des Apocryphes"; Klaus Baltzer of the University of

Munich, Germany, whose wisdom and advice has accompanied my work throughout my career, beginning in 1954 when we both served as "assistants" of the Faculty of Theology at the University of Heidelberg.

But I also owe an apology to all those scholars whose work I failed to acknowledge. Whatever I have learned from others I have tried to indicate in every instance. I also noted in many cases my disagreements with the work of my colleagues. I have not listed what I thought was irrelevant, but I am sure that I have missed much that may very well be significant. But to achieve a complete coverage of all relevant literature became a task which I was unable to accomplish, especially with respect to the canonical Gospels. There are numerous questions that I consciously excluded. This book is not devoted to the age-old problem of the historical Jesus, nor can I claim to contribute to the more recent question of "the gospels as literature." My interest is the historical development of ancient traditions and writings, and I wish that those who want to discuss such important problems as the historical Jesus and the literary dimensions of gospel writing would pay more attention to the transmission of traditions about Jesus and to the process of the collection of materials in ancient books. If the social component of the development of these traditions is barely mentioned on the following pages, I would like to remind the reader that this will involve a thorough investigation of the relevant literary and archaeological data from the world of ancient Christianity—a work that we have scarcely even begun.

I am grateful that my student John Lanci read the manuscript and gave helpful advice in numerous instances. When I visited the University of Göttingen recently, Professor Gerd Lüdemann showed me some of the original photographs of the scholars of the "Religionsgeschichtliche Schule," of whom published pictures are well known. In several instances the originals pictured these scholars together with their wives—but their spouses had been cut out of the published photographs. My wife, Gisela Koester, has translated two theological books into German, and in the translator's preface she gives me credit for the typing of the manuscript. It is, therefore, fitting that I should express here my indebtedness to her for all her patient and helpful listening to the progress of my work and for her indulgence with respect to all sorts of things around the house that I should have done rather than working on this manuscript.

Lexington, Massachusetts
Friday, July 13, 1990

Helmut Koester

1
The Term "Gospel"

1.1 The Origin of the Term "Gospel" [1]

1.1.1 THE GREEK USAGE OF THE TERM

The English noun "gospel" is the translation of the Greek word εὐαγγέλιον (Latin *evangelium*). It is commonly understood to designate "good news" as the corresponding verb εὐαγγελίζεσθαι is normally translated "to proclaim good news" or "to preach (the) good news." Both the noun and the verb occur frequently in the New Testament and in other early Christian literature. However, in Greek literature outside of the Biblical and Christian writings both the noun and the verb are comparatively rare. The verb εὐαγγελίζεσθαι occurs for the first time in Greek literature in Aristophanes. It is used for bringing news about victories or other joyful events, but soon becomes synonymous with and stands for the bringing of any news, good or bad.[2] In classical Greek, the noun εὐαγγέλιον means "reward for good news" and, especially in the plural, "thankoffering for good news" (εὐαγγέλια θύειν). In the Roman imperial period, the noun was also used

---

[1] A discussion of the entire complex was presented by Peter Stuhlmacher, *Das paulinische Evangelium: I. Vorgeschichte* (FRLANT 95; Göttingen: Vandenhoeck & Ruprecht, 1968). The most recent extensive treatment was published by Detlev Dormeyer and Hubert Frankemölle, "Evangelium als literarischer und als theologischer Begriff: Tendenzen und Aufgaben der Evangelienforschung im 20. Jahrhundert, mit einer Untersuchung des Markusevangeliums in seinem Verhältnis zur griechischen Biographie," *ANRW* 2.25/2. 1541–1704.; see also Detlev Dormeyer, *Evangelium als literarische und theologische Gattung* (EdF 263; Darmstadt: Wissenschaftliche Buchgesellschaft, 1989). A critical discussion of the various positions in the scholarly debate can be found in Hubert Frankemölle, *Evangelium. Begriff und Gattung: Ein Forschungsbericht* (SBB 15; Stuttgart: Katholisches Bibelwerk 1988). See also Helmut Koester, "From the Kerygma-Gospel to Written Gospels," *NTS* 35 (1989) 361–81.
[2] Cf. Gerhard Friedrich, "εὐαγγελίζομαι, κτλ.," *TDNT* 2 (1964) 707–37; Stuhlmacher, *Das paulinische Evangelium,* 180–206.

to designate the good news itself.[1] Although the words are formed with the Greek prefix ευ- (= "good," "well") which gives terms composed in this way often a positive connotation, there is little reason to assume that the meaning "'good' news" was felt strongly in ordinary Greek usage. Rather, the noun normally means simply "news," "message" and particularly in Christian usage "preaching"; the verb should then be translated as "to bring a message," or "to preach." Other terms formed with the same prefix confirm this translation.[2]

1.1.2 THE USAGE OF THE TERM IN THE OLD TESTAMENT

The noun occurs only a few times in the Greek Old Testament (Septuagint).[3] It has no particular technical meaning and can be used for all sorts of messages.[4] More significant is the use of the verb εὐαγγελίζεσθαι which occurs several times in Deutero-Isaiah.[5] Εὐαγγελίζεσθαι occurs four times in Deutero-Isaiah, twice each in Isa 40:9 and 52:7. The context is theological: the proclamation of the message of the beginning of the rule of Yahweh and thus of the beginning of liberation and peace. It is used here to designate the message that announces the liberation of the people. This is even heightened in the use of the verb in Trito-Isaiah where the prophet describes his own mission as "to proclaim to the poor" (εὐαγγελίζεσθαι πτωχοῖς, Isa 61:1). This has certainly influenced the usage of the term in the New Testament. Isa

---

[1] This is not made clear in the article of Friedrich quoted above. For the use of the term in the Greco-Roman world see especially Julius Schniewind, *Euangelion: Ursprung und erste Gestalt des Begriffs Evangelium* (BFChTh 13; Gütersloh: Bertelsmann, 1927; reprint: Wissenschaftliche Buchgesellschaft: Darmstadt, 1970) 113–258.

[2] For the use of εὐχαριστία = "thanksgiving" in the NT, cf., e.g., 1 Cor 14:16; Eph 5:4; 1 Tm 2:1, 3, 4; Rev 4:9; 7:12. As a designation of the thanksgiving meal (= the Lord's Supper), cf. Ign. *Eph.* 13.1; *Phld.* 4; *Sm.* 7.1 (see Hans Conzelmann, "χάρις, εὐχαριστέω, κτλ." *TDNT* 9 [1974] 407–15). For the use of εὐλογία = "blessing" in the NT, cf. 1 Cor 10:16; Gal 3:14; Jas 3:10; Rev 5:12, 13; 7:12. In classical Greek, this term means "praise," "laudation" (cf. Hermann Wolfgang Beyer, "εὐλογέω, κτλ.," *TDNT* 2 [1964] 754–65). In its Christian usage, this term is entirely determined by the Hellenistic-Jewish language of worship and by the Septuagint where it occurs as a translation of ברכה.

[3] Εὐαγγέλιον occurs in the Septuagint only three times: 2 Kings 4:10; 18:22, 25, each time as the translation of בשרה. The feminine εὐαγγελία is used in 2 Kings 18:20, 27; 4 Kings 7:9 as a translation of the same Hebrew term. Except for 2 Kings 4:10, where it means "reward for good news," it must be translated in all instances as "news," "message."

[4] Since the Hebrew equivalent בשרה is used for "bad message" in at least one instance (1 Sam 4:17: the news of the defeat of Israel and of the death of the sons of Eli), one must assume that the term was neutral. See also the discussion and literature in O. Schilling, "בשר," *ThWAT* 1. 845–49.

[5] Each time as a translation for a Hebrew verb from the root בשר.

52:7 is quoted in Rom 10:15: "as it is written, 'how beautiful are the feet of those bringing good news'" (καθὼς γέγραπται· ὡς ὡραῖοι οἱ πόδες τῶν εὐαγγελιζομένων ἀγαθά). Matthew sees the proclamation of John the Baptist and of Jesus in terms of Isa 40:9 and 52:7. Luke 4:18 refers to Isa 61:1, cf. Luke 7:22 (= Matt 11:6). In both instances, however, the dependence upon the usage of the term in the Book of Isaiah is the product of secondary redaction of older materials.[1] There is no evidence that the earliest Christian use of εὐαγγέλιον and εὐαγγελίζεσθαι in its formative stage is in any way influenced by these prophetic passages from the Old Testament.[2] The assumption that the occurrence of the verb in Deutero-Isaiah is ultimately responsible for the widespread technical use of the noun in early Christianity is unwarranted. It must also be noted that in Isa 52:7 (which Paul quotes in Rom 10:15), the verb alone does not have the meaning "to bring good news"; rather, the meaning "good" is expressed in the object of the verb (ἀγαθά).

1.1.3 THE TERM IN THE IMPERIAL INSCRIPTIONS

More closely related to the early Christian usage of the term is the occurrence of εὐαγγέλιον in a number of inscriptions from the early Roman imperial period. Most of these inscriptions are related to the introduction of the Julian Calendar, that is, the calendar of Julius Caesar, which was generally introduced in the Roman world during the time of Augustus.[3] The inscription from Priene (9 BCE) is probably the most famous among these calendar inscriptions. It celebrates the benefactions which have come into the world through Augustus, whom divine providence has sent as a savior (σωτήρ) and who has brought the wars to an end and established an order of peace:

> ... and since the Caesar through his appearance (ἐπιφανεῖν) has exceeded the hopes of all former good messages (εὐαγγέλια), surpassing not only the benefactors who came before him, but also leaving no hope

[1] For a critical discussion of the assumption that already Jesus may have understood himself as the messenger of Deutero-Isaiah see Frankemölle, *Evangelium: Forschungsbericht,* 73–79; also idem, "Jesus als deutero-jesajanischer Freudenbote," Paper presented to the Forty-Third General Meeting of the SNTS in Cambridge, England, August 1988.

[2] Other allusions to Deutero- and Trito-Isaiah's use of εὐαγγελίζεσθαι are rare in the NT. Perhaps Acts 10:36; Eph 2:17 and 6:15 could be mentioned (see above on the use of these Isaiah passages in Matthew and Luke).

[3] On the use of εὐαγγέλιον for the announcement of the enthronement of the emperor see the materials in Friedrich, "εὐαγγέλιον," 721–25; Adolf Deissmann, *Light from the Ancient Near East* (New York: Doran, 1927) 366–67; Schniewind, *Euangelion,* 87–93; Stuhlmacher, *Das paulinische Evangelium,* 196–203.

that anyone in the future would surpass him, and since for the world the birthday of the god was the beginning of his good messages (Ἦρξεν δὲ τῷ κόσμῳ τὴν δι᾽ αὐτόν (sc. τὸν Σεβαστὸν) εὐαγγελίων ἡ γενέθλιος ἡμέρα τοῦ θεοῦ) [may it therefore be decided that . . .].[1]

All these inscriptions result from the religio-political propaganda of Augustus in which the rule of peace, initiated by Augustus's victories and benefactions, is celebrated and proclaimed as the beginning of a new age. This usage of the term εὐαγγέλιον is new in the Greco-Roman world. It elevates this term and equips it with a particular dignity. Since the Christian usage of the term for its saving message begins only a few decades after the time of Augustus, it is most likely that the early Christian missionaries were influenced by the imperial propaganda in their employment of the word.[2] Also the Christian usage is eschatological, as the missionaries proclaim the beginning of a new age and call this proclamation their "gospel."

1.2 The Use of the Term "Gospel" in the Pauline Tradition

1.2.1 THE LETTERS OF PAUL

In the earliest Christian documents, i.e., the letters of the apostle Paul, the terms "gospel" (εὐαγγέλιον) and "to preach (the gospel)" (εὐαγγελίζεσθαι) are already well-established technical terms for the Christian message and its proclamation.[3] With this meaning, both the noun and the verb appear frequently in the Pauline writings.[4] Whether

[1] For the entire Greek text of the inscription see Wilhelm Dittenberger, *Orientis Graeci inscriptiones selectae* (2 vols.; Hildesheim: Olms, 1960) # 458, vol. 2, pp. 48–60. The text quoted above is found in lines 40–42. The Greek text of the portion of the inscription quoted above is conveniently reprinted with a brief commentary in Gerhard Pfohl, ed., *Griechische Inschriften als Zeugnisse des privaten und öffentlichen Lebens* (Tusculum; München: Heimeran, no year) 134–35.

[2] Most scholars are very hesitant to see a connection of the early-Christian use and the employment of the term in the imperial propaganda; e.g., Rudolf Bultmann, *Theology of the New Testament* (2 vols.; New York: Scribner's, 1951–1955) 1. 87; cf. the discussion in Frankemölle, *Evangelium: Forschungsbericht*, 80–88.

[3] It is very difficult to establish evidence for a pre-Pauline Christian usage of these terms, *pace* Stuhlmacher (*Das paulinische Evangelium*, 209–44) who discusses Rev 10:7; 14:6; Matt 11:5 (= Luke 7:22); Luke 4:18; Mark 1:14; and Matt 4:23; 9:35; 24:14; 16:13 as possible evidence for the use of εὐαγγέλιον and εὐαγγελίζεσθαι by the Palestinian church, possibly by Jesus himself. It is more probable that the Pauline use of the terms derives from the early Hellenistic church from which Paul derives such kerygmatic formulations, called "gospel," as 1 Thess 1:9–10 and 1 Cor 15:3–5; cf. Bultmann, *Theology*, 87–89.

[4] The noun εὐαγγέλιον occurs forty-eight times in the genuine Pauline letters. In twenty-six of these occurrences it is used absolute, without a following genitive; four-

Paul says "the gospel of God"[1] of which he is the apostle,[2] or "the gospel of Christ,"[3] he is always referring to one and the same gospel. Most frequently he uses the term without a genitive as a technical term for both the action of the proclamation and for the content of the message.[4] He presupposes that the content is understood and requires no further definition or explication. This use of the word in the absolute sense reflects a distinctively Christian development. While in pagan and Jewish literature the term designates any kind of message and therefore demanded further explanation of its content, in the early Christian usage the word refers exclusively to the one and only saving message of Christ.[5]

The verb εὐαγγελίζεσθαι, however, does not have quite the same exclusive technical meaning. In 1 Thess 3:6, Paul speaks of the arrival of Timothy "who brought the (good) message" (εὐαγγελισαμένου) of the Thessalonians' faith and love. Here the verb refers to some information that Paul received. But in 1 Cor 1:17 ("Christ did not send me to baptize, but to preach," εὐαγγελίζεσθαι) the verb clearly designates the Christian missionary's activity of proclamation.[6] However, other verbs are frequently used with the same meaning; cf. Phil 1:14–17 where "to say the word" (λόγον λαλεῖν), "to announce" (κηρύσσειν), and "to proclaim" (καταγγέλειν) are used side by side in the same context.[7]

message / creed

---

teen times the genitive "of God" (τοῦ θεοῦ) or "of Christ" (τοῦ Χριστοῦ) follows. Τὸ εὐαγγέλιον ἡμῶν (1 Thess 1:5) means "the gospel that we preach." ἕτερον εὐαγγέλιον (2 Cor 11:4; Gal 1:6) is used in such a way that the implication is unmistakable: there is no such thing as "another gospel." The term has a somewhat different meaning in the phrase τὸ εὐαγγέλιον τῆς ἀκροβυστίας (Gal 2:7): it is the office of preaching to the uncircumcised, but not a different gospel that is preached to them. "My gospel" (τὸ εὐαγγέλιόν μου) in Rom 16:25 is certainly not Pauline; Rom 2:16, where the same phrase appears, may also be a later interpolation; cf. 2 Tim 2:8.   *sic 2:16*

[1] τὸ εὐαγγέλιον τοῦ θεοῦ, 1 Thess 2:2, 8–9; 2 Cor 11:7.   *(sic 2:16*

[2] Rom 1:1; 15:16.

[3] τὸ εὐαγγέλιον τοῦ Χριστοῦ, Rom 15:19; 1 Cor 9,12; 2 Cor 12:12; etc.

[4] Rom 1:16; 1 Cor 4:15; 9:14; etc.

[5] On this technical usage of the term see Bultmann, *Theology*, 1. 87–88.

[6] The verb appears nineteen times in the genuine Pauline letters. It can be used in a technical sense insofar as it means not only "to announce," "to proclaim" (1 Cor 9:16, 18; Gal 1:16, 23; 4,13; 1 Thess 3:6), but also in the full sense "to preach the gospel" (Rom 1:15; 15:20; 1 Cor 1:17; 2 Cor 10:16; Gal 1:8–9). For emphasis, Paul can also say εὐαγγελίζεσθαι τὸ εὐαγγέλιον (2 Cor 11:7; cf. Gal 2:11; 1 Cor 15:1).

[7] Full equivalents of εὐαγγελίζεσθαι are κηρύσσειν ("to proclaim," Rom 10:8, 14, 15; 1 Cor 1:23; 9:27; 15:11; Gal 2:2), καταγγέλλειν ("to announce," 1 Cor 2:1; 9:14; 11:26; Phil 1:17–18), λαλεῖν ("to speak", Phil 1:14; 1 Thess 2:2, 4, 16). In the Acts of the Apostles, διαμαρτύρεσθαι appears frequently as the equivalent of εὐαγγελίζεσθαι (Acts 2:40; 8:25; 10:42; 18:5; 20:21, 24; 28:23).

In the letters of Paul, there is no fixed formulation for the content of the "gospel." But there are some passages in which Paul characterizes the content of the gospel with words that may be described as short kerygmatic or credal formulae. The earliest of these formulae appears in 1 Thess 1:9–10:

How you turned from the idols to God in order to serve the true and living God, and to wait for his Son from heaven whom he raised from the dead, Jesus who delivers us from the wrath to come.

In 1 Cor 15:1–5 Paul reminds the Corinthians of the message that he had been proclaiming among them. The phrases used here seem to suggest a fixed formulation of the content of the gospel that was formally handed down like a piece of tradition:[1]

The gospel
that I preached to you (τὸ εὐαγγέλιον ὃ εὐαγγελισάμην ὑμῖν)
which you received (ὃ καὶ παρελάβετε),
in which you stand, by which you are also saved,
with which word we preached (εὐαγγελισάμην) to you,
... because I handed it over (παρέδωκα) to you in the beginning what I
also received (ὃ καὶ παρέλαβον),
    that Christ died for us according to the scriptures,
    that he was buried,
    that he was raised on the third day according to the scriptures
    and that he appeared to Cephas, then to the Twelve.

It is clear that Paul wants to emphasize that the gospel preached by him was not his own special gospel, but the common gospel of the entire enterprise of the Christian mission. Therefore, he emphasizes the "receiving" and "transmitting" of the gospel. This, however, does not imply that the "gospel" was a written document, nor can it be assumed that the formulation of the orally transmitted gospel was fixed and stable. Neither the formula quoted in 1 Corinthians 15, nor any other formulaic statement of the content of the gospel in Paul is ever repeated in the entire Pauline corpus. On the contrary, the heterogeneity of such formulae is striking. There are only a few central elements which appear repeatedly in these formulations, albeit in

---

[1] Of these verses, at least 1 Cor 15:3–5 can be considered part of a tradition that is introduced by a quotation formula containing terms that are analogous to the technical Pharisaic-Rabbinic terminology for the transmission of traditions. However, Paul apparently expanded the cited tradition, and he does not refer to any names in a chain of transmission which would guarantee its trustworthiness. On the whole question, see Klaus Wegenast, *Das Verständnis der Tradition bei Paulus und in den Deuteropaulinen* (WMANT 8; Neukirchen: Neukirchener Verlag, 1962) 57–70.

different combinations and in different assortments of terms. These elements are:

Christ's suffering and death
    his sacrifice "for us,"
    his cross,
    his being raised from the dead (or rising from the dead),
    his appearances,
    his coming again in the future.

1.2.2 THE LETTERS OF IGNATIUS

A further development in the history of these gospel formulae is visible in the letters of Ignatius of Antioch, written ca. 110 CE.[1] Here the "gospel" is still in general the preaching of Jesus Christ, and Ignatius never implies that he is speaking of a written text when he uses this term. But whenever the content of the gospel is quoted, the formulations—though still variable—become more fixed. Cross, death, and resurrection are more often mentioned together in formulaic expressions. In *Phld.* 8.1, Ignatius juxtaposes the gospel to the "archives," i.e., the Scriptures in which his opponents claim to possess the basis for Christian faith:

But for me the archives are Jesus Christ, the inviolable archives are his cross and death and his resurrection and faith through him.[2]

Furthermore, additional topics supplement these formulations in Ignatius: Christ's birth through the virgin and his baptism. This expansion of the gospel formula is most clearly evident in *Eph.* 18.2:

For our God, Jesus Christ, was carried in the womb by Mary according to God's plan—of the seed of David and of the Holy Spirit—who was born and baptized that by his suffering he might purify the water.[3]

The origin of these additions, particularly the birth from Mary, belong to the incipient anti-docetic controversy, that is, they are directed against a christology which denied the real humanity of Jesus. Igna-

---

[1] On the use of the term "gospel" in Ignatius's letters see Helmut Koester, *Synoptische Überlieferung bei den apostolischen Vätern* (TU 65; Berlin: Akademie-Verlag, 1957) 6–10; William R. Schoedel, *Ignatius of Antioch: A Commentary on the Letters of Ignatius of Antioch* (Hermeneia; Philadelphia: Fortress, 1985) on *Phld.* 8.2; 9.2.

[2] Other passages in which suffering or death and cross and resurrection appear together in formulaic language are Ign. *Eph.* 7.2; *Mg.* 11; *Trall.* 9.1; *Sm.* 5.3; 7.2; 12.2.

[3] See also *Eph.* 19.1 about the three mysteries that were hidden from the rulers of this age: the virginity of Mary, her giving birth, and the death of the Lord.

tius quotes a fully developed gospel formula in a clearly anti-docetic context in Trall. 9.1–2:

> Jesus Christ,
> of the family of David, of Mary,
> who was truly born,
> both ate and drank,
> was truly persecuted under Pontius Pilate,
> was truly crucified and died . . . ,
> who was also truly raised from the dead.[1]

But in spite of the evident tendency toward more comprehensive and possibly more stable formulation in Ignatius, the term "gospel" does not designate any fixed formula and it certainly does not refer to any written text enumerating the basic topics of Jesus' appearance.[2] It is rather the message of salvation in general of which the center is Christ's death and resurrection:

> . . . to pay attention to the prophets and in particular to the gospel, in which the passion is shown us and the resurrection accomplished. (*Sm.* 7.2)

> . . . the gospel has something distinctive: the coming of the Savior, our Lord Jesus Christ, his suffering and resurrection. (*Phld.* 9.2)

1.2.3 THE DEUTERO-PAULINE EPISTLES AND THE BOOK OF ACTS

The same use of the term "gospel" is found in the deutero-Pauline epistles of the New Testament. Eph 3:6 speaks of the fulfillment of the plan of salvation that the Gentiles should also be heirs of the promise "through the gospel"; cf. Eph 3:8: "(Paul) has been appointed to preach (εὐαγγελίζεσθαι) to the Gentiles the inexhaustible richness of Christ." In the later Pastoral Epistles, probably written in the first half of the 2d century CE, Paul's "gospel," that is, what he had once proclaimed,

---

[1] Traditional sentences and formulations are combined into a comprehensive credal statement—though in this form devised by Ignatius himself—in *Sm.* 1.1–2; see on this passage and on its traditional elements Schoedel, *Ignatius,* on *Sm.* 1.1–2.

[2] Gillis P:son Wetter (*Altchristliche Liturgien: Das christliche Mysterium* [FRLANT 30; Göttingen: Vandenhoeck & Ruprecht, 1921] 1. 121–22) understands εὐαγγέλιον in the letters of Ignatius as a central feature of the enactment of Christian cult, a text that represents the Christian myth of salvation so that its reading "creates life." Heinrich Schlier (*Religionsgeschichtliche Untersuchungen zu den Ignatiusbriefen* [BZNW 8; Gießen: Töpelmann, 1929] 165–66) has further elaborated this suggestion. However, there is no indication that Ignatius is actually quoting a text of any kind, nor is it evident that the wording of this gospel was fixed in any way; cf. Schoedel, *Ignatius,* especially on *Sm.* 1.1–2.

becomes the guarantee for the correct Christian proclamation; cf.
2 Tim 2:8:

> Remember Jesus Christ, risen from the dead, from the seed of David,
> according to my gospel (κατὰ τὸ εὐαγγέλιόν μου).

Also in the Acts of the Apostles, the term "gospel" designates Paul's
message of salvation that is preached to the Gentiles (Acts 15:1; 20:24).
In this respect, the terminology of Acts agrees with that of the Pauline
tradition.[1]

In the entire realm of the Pauline mission and in literature that is
dependent upon Paul and his letters, there is no evidence that the
term "gospel" was in any way related to gospel writings or to any other
form of written materials. At the beginning of the 2d century, the
term still always designates the Christian missionary preaching and
its message.[2]

1.3 The Term "Gospel" in the Gospels
of the New Testament

1.3.1 THE PROBLEM

It was apparently in the Pauline communities where the technical
use of the term "gospel" became established. All writings considered
in the previous section are dependent upon, or related to, the Pauline
churches and their traditions. The question arises whether the
authors of the Gospels of the New Testament understood their writings as "gospels," and whether the established technical meaning of
the term, "the proclaimed message about Christ's death and resurrection," had any effect on the conception and structure of their works.

The use of the noun "gospel" in the Gospels of the New Testament is
puzzling. In the Gospel of John as well as in the Johannine Epistles,
neither noun nor verb are ever used. The absence of those terms in the
Johannine writings is only one among other pieces of evidence which
prove that the beginnings of the Johannine community lay outside of
the scope of the Pauline mission area. But the Synoptic Gospels—

---

[1] On the Lukan usage see below # 1.3.2.

[2] Rev 14:6 (". . . an angel who had an eternal gospel to be proclaimed to those who
were living on earth") uses the term εὐαγγέλιον as a general, non-technical designation
for a "message." The author is not influenced by the Pauline usage of the term. Also in
Rev 10:7, ". . . as he has proclaimed (εὐηγγέλισεν) to his servants the prophets," demonstrates that the author of this book is not familiar with the technical usage of these
terms as designation for the message of Christ's death and resurrection.

Matthew, Mark, and Luke—belong to this realm and are dependent upon it. And even here the use of the term "gospel" is by no means easy to understand. In fact, it remains somewhat enigmatic and, moreover, is very different in each of the three Synoptic Gospels.

1.3.2 LUKE

In the Lukan writings, the verb is used in both parts of the Lukan work, but the noun "gospel" only in the Book of Acts.[1] In both the Gospel of Luke and in the Acts of the Apostles the verb εὐαγγελίζεσθαι can simply mean "to announce" and thus refer to any kind of good message.[2] But in most instances, it is used to designate the Christian missionary proclamation. In many cases[3] the verb has no direct object. It either means simply "to preach," or the direct object is implied: "to preach the gospel." Sometimes the object of the verb is made explicit: "the rule of God" (Luke 4:43; 8:1; cf. 16:16; Acts 8:12), "Christ Jesus" (Acts 5:42; 8:35; 11:20), "the word (of the Lord)" (Acts 8:4; 15:35), "peace" (Acts 10:36), "the promises to the fathers fulfilled" (Acts 13:32), "Jesus and the resurrection" (Acts 17:18).

If Luke does not use the noun "gospel" in the first part of his work, he also does not conceive of this writing as a "gospel." On the contrary, in the prologue to his work (Luke 1:1–4), he speaks of others who have tried to compose a "narrative" (διήγησις) about the "events" (πράγματα) which have occurred among us. "Narrative" could possibly have been the title which scribes would have given to this work.[4]

1.3.2 MATTHEW

The absence of the noun in the Gospel of Luke seems odd because the Gospel of Mark, employed by Luke as a source, had used the noun "gospel" repeatedly. However, even Matthew reproduces only a few of the Markan occurrences of the term "gospel." On the other hand, Matthew uses the term several times in non-Markan contexts and, in two instances, adds the phrase "and he preached the gospel of the kingdom" to a Markan summary statement about the activity of Jesus.[5] These are clearly redactional Matthean passages. This raises

---

[1] It occurs only twice here: 15:7 and 20:24.

[2] Luke 1:19: 2:10; Acts 14:15.

[3] Luke 3:18; 4:18 (= Isa 61:1); 7:22; 9:6; 20:1; Acts 8:25, 40; 14:7, 21; 16:10.

[4] This has been suggested by Bovon, "The Synoptic Gospels and the Non-canonical Acts of the Apostles," *HTR* 81 (1988) 23. Bovon remarks that Matthew might have been called "Beginnings" (Γέννησις) or "Life" (Βίος), and Mark could have borne the title "Memoirs" (Ὑπομνήματα).

[5] καὶ κηρύσσων τὸ εὐαγγέλιον τῆς βασιλείας, Matt 4:23; 9:35; cf. Mark 1:39; 6:6.

the question of why the author of the Gospel of Matthew, who is quite familiar with the term "gospel," does not reproduce the term when it occurs in a number of Markan passages, which he had copied from his source. The following table shows the use of the term in the respective Markan and Matthean passages.

	Mark[1]		Matthew
1:1	beginning of the gospel of Jesus Christ		———
1:15a	proclaiming the gospel of God	4:17a	he began to proclaim[2]
1:15b	and believe in the gospel	4:17b	———
8:35	on my behalf and of the gospel	16:25	on my behalf
10:29	on my behalf and on behalf of the gospel	19:29	on behalf of my name
13:10	the gospel must be proclaimed	24:14	this gospel will be proclaimed
14:9	wherever the gospel is proclaimed	26:13	wherever this gospel *announcement* of the kingdom is proclaimed

The use of the term in Mark 13:10 and 14:9 (also in 16:15) corresponds to the conventional missionary terminology of the Pauline churches.[3] Matthew, however, in the two instances in which he reproduces passages from Mark in which the term "gospel" appears, adds the demonstrative "this" to the word "gospel" and, in the first instance, also the qualifying genitive "of the kingdom." Thus, he understands the passages in question as references to a more specific message. What message is meant, is not immediately clear in Matt 26:13.[4] The phrase "gospel of the kingdom" appears, independently of Mark, also

---

[1] There is a further occurrence of the term in the secondary longer ending of Mark: "Go into all the world and proclaim the gospel to every creature" (Mark 16:15).

[2] The term used here, both in Matthew and in Mark, is κηρύσσειν.

[3] However, Mark 13:10 interrupts the close connection between 13:9 and 13:11. Can 13:10 be considered a secondary intrusion into the text of Mark from the parallel in Matthew? Commentaries usually ask whether vs. 10 was inserted into an older tradition, either by Mark or in a pre-Markan stage of the text; cf. Rudolf Pesch, *Das Markusevangelium* (2 vols; Herder Kommentar; Freiburg: Herder, 1977) 2. 285; see also idem, *Naherwartungen* (Düsseldorf: Patmos, 1968) 129–31. On the term in Markan usage in general, see Willi Marxsen, *Der Evangelist Markus* (FRLANT 67; Göttingen: Vandenhoeck & Ruprecht, 1956) 77–92.

[4] All modern commentaries agree that "this gospel" in Matt 26:13 cannot refer to the book of Matthew's Gospel. The phrase is variously understood as the gospel of Christ, the proclamation of the passion of Jesus, or the announcement of the coming of the *rule announcement of his kingship*

in Matt 4:23 and 9:25. In these two passages (as well as in Matt 24:14) the meaning of this phrase is evident: it is the message that Jesus is preaching, that is, the message of the coming of the kingdom of heaven. It is Jesus' message as it already was the message of John the Baptist (compare Matt 4:17 with 3:2). But it is not the gospel about Jesus' death and resurrection. Matthew never uses the term "gospel" in this latter meaning, which is so common in the tradition of the Pauline churches. It is characteristic that the term "gospel" is also missing in the commissioning of the disciples at the end of Matthew's Gospel (Matt 28:18–20). The difference between Matt 28:18–20 and Mark 16:15 is striking. While in the (albeit secondary) ending of Mark, Jesus commands the disciples to go into all the world to proclaim the gospel, Matthew reports Jesus' mission command as a charge to the Eleven to make all the nations disciples, to baptize them, and to teach them to observe everything that he had taught. The very distinctive understanding of "gospel" in Matthew may be the reason for his omission of the term in many of the Markan passages.

1.3.4 MARK

The use of the term "gospel" in Mark raises several problems: (1) Does the term belong to the original text of Mark in the passages in which it occurs in the extant manuscripts? (2) What is the content of the "gospel" in Mark?

It is by no means evident that Matthew read the term in his text of Mark where it now appears in our Markan manuscripts. One is tempted to argue that the term had been inserted into a number of Markan passages by a later redactor. In Mark 8:35 and 10:29, the phrase "and for the sake of the gospel" (καὶ ἕνεκεν τοῦ εὐαγγελίου) is redundant after "for my sake" (ἕνεκεν ἐμοῦ), and it is indeed missing in the Matthean parallels (16:25; 19:29).[1] There is also no Matthean correspondence to the use of the term "gospel" in Mark 1:15 (= Matt 4:17).[2]

---

kingdom of the heavens; see on this problem Stuhlmacher (*Das paulinische Evangelium*, 241–43) who argues that these passages are Matthean formulations which presuppose the technical usage of the Pauline mission, but do not identify Matthew's writing with the "gospel."

[1] See the chart above in # 1.3.3.

[2] Marxsen (*Markus*, 81) argues that Matthew used Mark 1:15 also in Matt 4:23 and 9:35. See further on this question Helmut Koester, "History and Development of Mark's Gospel: From Mark to Secret Mark and 'Canonical' Mark," in: Bruce C. Corley, ed., *Colloquy on New Testament Studies: A Time for Reappraisal and Fresh Approaches* (Macon, GA: Mercer University Press, 1983) 43–44.

In three of these Markan passages (1:15b: 8:35; 10:29), the term "gospel" appears without a genitive designating its content. This use corresponds to the use of "gospel" as a technical term in the Pauline letters.[1] It is the gospel about Jesus' death and resurrection. In Mark, this "gospel" can even assume the same dignity that is accorded to Christ himself: "on behalf of Christ and the gospel" (Mark 8:35; 10:29). Belief in Christ is identical with belief in the gospel (Mark 1:15b).[2] "The gospel of God" in Mark 1:15a is, therefore, no other gospel than the one mentioned in other Markan passages in which the term "gospel" occurs, namely, the gospel of Christ's death and resurrection. That conclusion holds in spite of the somewhat odd consequence that Jesus here is the one who proclaims that gospel which has as its content his own death and resurrection.

That same gospel is referred to in Mark 1:1, in the incipit of the Markan writing: "Beginning of the gospel of Jesus Christ." It is quite possible that a later scribe added this phrase in order to indicate the point in his manuscript at which the text of another writing began: "Beginning of the gospel of Jesus Christ."[3] As the text stands, Mark 1:1 must be understood together with Mark 1:14–15. The term "gospel" in these two passages forms an inclusio which indicates that the Baptist's message of repentance belongs together with Jesus' announcement of the nearness of the kingdom which resumes the call for repentance.[4] Mark himself does not thereby designate his own

---

[1] Stuhlmacher (*Das paulinische Evangelium,* 234–38) argues for a close relationship between Mark's use of the term and the Pauline understanding of the content of the gospel.

[2] The expression πιστεύειν ἐν is peculiar and without parallel in the NT. However, it is hard to interpret this phrase in any other way than as an equivalent of the common πιστεύειν εἰς = "to believe in"; see Marxsen, *Markus,* 90. Marxsen also argues convincingly that the term εὐαγγέλιον always occurs in redactional materials and never in any traditions or sources used by Mark. The peculiar phrase of Mark 1:15 cannot be explained by recourse to an older Aramaic tradition used by Mark (against Pesch, *Markusevangelium,* 105). Detlev Dormeyer ("Die Kompositionsmetapher 'Evangelium Jesu Christi, des Sohnes Gottes,' Mk 1.1. Ihre theologische und literarische Aufgabe in der Jesus-Biographie des Markus," *NTS* 33 [1987] 254–55) explains the choice of the preposition ἐν as a deliberate Markan finesse by which Mark wants to indicate that the gospel preached by Jesus in 1:14–15 is not the entire gospel but only one of its ingredients (*Teilmenge*).

[3] Cf. Walther Schmithals, *Das Evangelium nach Markus* (Ökumenischer Taschenbuchkommentar zum NT 2/1; Gütersloh: Gütersloher Verlagshaus, 1979) 73–74.

[4] Dormeyer ("Die Kompositionsmetapher," 452–68) has tried to demonstrate that the "genitive-syntagma" ἀρχὴ τοῦ εὐαγγελίου can be reversed to "gospel of the beginnings" and thus become the title of a writing. This suggestion overlooks the fact that "gospel" in both passages refers to a message.

work as a "gospel."[1] Ancient writings either begin with a formal dedication describing the purpose of the book (like Luke-Acts) or with a
sentence marking the first subject treated. The latter is the case in
Mark 1:1, especially when this passage is seen as a pointer to Mark
1:14–15. It is not a cryptic phrase which mysteriously suggests to the
modern interpreter that the author somehow wanted to imply that his
work was a "gospel." Rather, the sentence of Mark 1:1 says that the
proclamation of Christ's resurrection and death began with the
preaching of repentance by John the Baptist and with Jesus' own call
for repentance. Thus there is no indication whatsoever that either
Mark or any of the authors of the Gospels of the New Testament
thought that "gospel" would be an appropriate title for the literature
they produced.

1.4 "Gospel" in the Apostolic Fathers

1.4.1 THE APOSTOLIC FATHERS AS WITNESSES FOR
THE GOSPELS

Traditionally the writings of the so-called Apostolic Fathers have
been viewed as the earliest witnesses for the existence and use of written gospels.[2] Accordingly, their references to the "gospel" were understood as testimonies for the use of this term as a designation for gospel
writings. This view was challenged since the beginning of this century.[3] However, more recent publications have tried to reestablish the
position that at least the Gospel of Matthew has been widely used
in early Christian literature. In 1950, Édouard Massaux, in a
comprehensive investigation,[4] attempted to demonstrate once more
that Matthew was not only known but also used even in the earliest
writings among the Apostolic Fathers. More recently, Wolf-Dietrich

---

[1] Marxsen, *Markus,* 87–88.

[2] Most characteristic of this position is the very influential work of Theodor Zahn,
Geschichte des neutestamentlichen Kanons (2 vols.; Erlangen: Deichert, 1888–89)
1. 840, 916–41. Zahn even believed that Papias of Hierapolis, the second-century
bishop who argued strongly for the trustworthiness of the oral tradition, drew his "sayings of the Lord" from a written gospel.

[3] The first study to challenge this traditional view came from *The New Testament in
the Apostolic Fathers* by a Committee of the Oxford Society of Historical Theology
(Oxford, 1905). See further Koester, *Synoptische Überlieferung bei den Apostolischen
Vätern.*

[4] *Influence de l'Évangile de Saint Matthieu sur la littérature chrétienne avant Saint
Irénée* (reprint; BEThL 75; Leuven: Leuven University Press, 1986).

Köhler[1] has tried to come to a more differentiated judgment. He assesses each passage according to a graduated scale of the judgment about dependence which runs from "probable" (*wahrscheinlich*), "quite possible" (*gut möglich*), "at best theoretically possible" (*allenfalls theoretisch möglich*), to "rather improbable" (*eher unwahrscheinlich*). The result of Köhler's detailed, even if pedantic, investigation is that "in the overwhelming majority of the writings analyzed the use of the Gospel of Matthew is probable."[2] The question of the actual use of canonical Gospels in the New Testament, the Apostolic Fathers, and other early Christian writings will be discussed later and has to be judged on its own merits.[3] The concern here is with the problem of the employment of the term "gospel" as a designation of written documents. Even if it is possible that certain writers drew their gospel materials from written documents, this does not imply that they called such documents "gospels."

The occurrences of the term in the letters of Ignatius of Antioch have already been discussed above: Ignatius employs the term exclusively in the same way in which it had been used by Paul, that is, as a designation of the proclamation of Christ's death and resurrection.

1.4.2 THE FIRST EPISTLE OF CLEMENT AND THE EPISTLE OF BARNABAS

In the First Epistle of Clement, the oldest writing in this group of the Apostolic Fathers, sent to Corinth from Rome in the year 96 CE, the term "gospel" means preaching in general: "as Paul wrote to you in the beginning of his preaching" (*1 Clem.* 47.2). The author did not know or use a written gospel. The quotations of sayings of Jesus in *1 Clem.* 13.2 and 46.8 are drawn from the oral tradition. This is borne out by their form and wording, which does not reveal any redactional features of a known gospel author, and by the quotation formula which appears in the past tense: "he said" (εἶπεν), that is, the Lord said when he was preaching and teaching.[4]

---

[1] *Die Rezeption des Matthäusevangeliums in der Zeit vor Irenäus* (WUNT 2/24; Tübingen: Mohr/Siebeck, 1986).

[2] Ibid., 520 (translation mine).

[3] For a discussion of the literature on this subject since the publication of Massaux's work and my own *Synoptische Überlieferung bei den Apostolischen Vätern* see Frans Neirynck, "Introduction à la réimpression," in the reprint of Massaux, *Influence de l'Évangile de Saint Matthieu*, pp. vii-xv.

[4] Koester, *Synoptische Überlieferung,* 6; see below # 2.1.4.3.

In the Epistle of Barnabas, probably written at the same time or a few decades later, the term "gospel" also refers to the oral proclamation: Jesus chose the apostles in order that they should proclaim his "message" (*Barn.* 5.9).[1]

1.4.3 THE DIDACHE

It is more difficult to determine the use of the word "gospel" in the *Teaching of the Twelve Apostles* (the so-called *Didache*). This writing may have been composed as early as the last decades of the 1st century CE or early in the 2d century, although some scholars prefer a date later in the 2d century. The *Didache* is a compilation of several older sources; some of these older components may have preserved the terminology of an earlier period.[2] On the other hand, redactional passages reveal the vocabulary of the later editor.

In *Did.* 8.2, the Lord's Prayer is introduced with the words: pray "as the Lord has commanded in his gospel" (ὡς ἐκέλευσεν ὁ κύριος ἐν τῷ εὐαγγελίῳ αὐτοῦ). The form and wording of the Lord's Prayer, as it is quoted in the *Didache,* is on the whole the same as that of the Gospel of Matthew (6:9–13). However, there are a few details in the *Didache* version which are more original than the parallel expressions in Matthew's version.[3] It is also most unlikely that a Christian writer would have to copy from any written source in order to quote the Lord's Prayer. Moreover, the verb in the quotation formula appears in the past tense, which makes it quite unlikely that "his (i.e., the Lord's) gospel" refers to a written document. The quotation formula is, therefore, best understood as a reference to the preaching of Jesus during his earthly ministry.[4]

---

[1] Ibid., 6; cf. also *Barn.* 8.3.

[2] J. M. Creed, "The Didache," *JTS* 39 (1937) 370–78; Jean Paul Audet, *La Didachè: Instructions des Apôtres* (EtB; Paris: Gabalda, 1958) 104–20; Audét argues for a composition in two stages. More recent discussions of the issue and of relevant literature can be found in Klaus Wengst, *Didache (Apostellehre), Zweiter Clemensbrief, Schrift an Diognet* (Schriften des Urchristentums 2; Darmstadt: Wissenschaftliche Buchgesellschaft, 1984) 18–32; and especially in Kurt Niederwimmer, *Die Didache* (KEK, KAV 1; Göttingen: Vandenhoeck & Ruprecht, 1988) 64–80. The latter commentary gives the best account of the compilation of the Didache, although Niederwimmer's date for the final redaction (early in the 2d century) cannot be substantiated by external evidence. See also Frankemölle, *Evangelium: Forschungsbericht*, 33–34.

[3] Koester, *Synoptische Überlieferung*, 103–9. Köhler (*Rezeption des Matthäusevangeliums,* 31–36) has no doubts with respect to the dependence of *Did.* 8.1–2 upon Matthew. Massaux (*Influence de L'Évangile de Saint Matthieu,* 616–18) also argues for such dependence. However, he assumes a date for the Didache after the middle of the 2d century, while Köhler (p. 30) would prefer an early date in the last decade of the 1st or the first decade of the 2d century.

[4] Niederwimmer (*Didache,* 170–73) denies a dependence upon the text of Matthew

In the next part of the *Didache,* which deals with instructions for church officers, the following formula occurs twice: "(do this) as you have it in the gospel" (ὡς ἔχετε ἐν τῷ εὐαγγελίῳ, *Did.* 15.3 and 15.4; cf. also 11.3). This suggests that there was a document in which the respective instructions were written down.[1] But nothing in the context of these references indicates the presence of materials which were derived from any known gospel writing. Moreover, even if the phrase refers to a written document —which is by no means necessary—it obviously stems from the hand of the later editor of the *Didache,* while the materials quoted in this context are derived from an older tradition.[2] Therefore, these passages cannot be used as evidence for an early use of the term "gospel" as a designation of a written document.

There is only one instance in which sayings quoted in the *Didache* are certainly drawn from written gospels: *Did.* 1.3–5. This passage is a compilation of sayings from the Sermon on the Mount, but with distinct features of harmonization of the texts of Matthew and Luke. It is an interpolation that must have been made after the middle of the 2d century[3] and cannot, therefore, be used as evidence for the original compiler's familiarity with written gospels.[4]

1.4.4 THE SECOND EPISTLE OF CLEMENT

By the middle of the 2d century CE some proof for the use of the term "gospel" as a designation of written documents begins to appear. The so-called Second Epistle of Clement which was written ca. 150 CE,

---

and demonstrates that the doxology is not indebted to Matthew's doxology, but to the tradition of prayers from which also the meal prayers in chaps. 9–10 are derived.

[1] Niederwimmer (*Didache,* 245) sees in *Did.* 15.3–4 references to a written gospel but leaves open whether the redactor refers to the Gospel of Matthew or to some other gospel that is no longer extant.

[2] There is no external evidence which would force a date of the final composition of the *Didache* before the end of the 2d century (*pace* Wengst, *Didache,* 61–63). To be sure, the materials used in this final composition are much older. But the general references to the "gospel" may stem from the hand of the final editor; cf. Niederwimmer (*Didache,* 168–69) who shows that the phrase in *Did.* 8.2 has been clumsily interpolated into older material and argues (pp. 214, 244) that all other references to the "gospel" reveal the hand of the final redactor.

[3] Bentley Layton, "The Sources, Date and Transmission of *Didache* 1.3b–2.2," *HTR* 61 (1968) 343–83.

[4] In order to maintain his hypothesis of the *Didache*'s dependence upon the Gospel of Matthew, Wengst (*Didache,* 18–20) is forced to admit that these verses are a later interpolation, using a harmonized gospel text. See also Niederwimmer, *Didache,* 93–100 (uncommitted report about the various solutions concerning the problem of this interpolation) and pp. 115–16 (an older traditional piece which was revised by the compiler of the work).

probably even later,[1] may reveal such a use, although the evidence is somewhat ambiguous. *2 Clement* repeatedly quotes sayings of Jesus which have parallels in the Synoptic Gospels. The verbs in the quotation formulae vary. Twice a saying is introduced by "the Lord said (εἶπεν),"[2] but in other instances the present tense of the verb (λέγει) is used in the quotation formula.[3] The present tense is customarily employed for the introduction of quotations from Scripture or from any written document. This would suggest that *2 Clement* quotes sayings of Jesus from a written work. A confirmation could be found in *2 Clem.* 8.5 where a saying of Jesus is introduced with the words "because the Lord says in the gospel" (λέγει γὰρ ὁ κύριος ἐν τῷ εὐαγγελίῳ). Is this a reference to a book in which the Lord presently speaks to the church? Several of the sayings of Jesus quoted in *2 Clement* indeed reveal features which derive from the redactional activities of the authors of Matthew and Luke.[4] On the other hand, only sayings of Jesus are quoted in *2 Clement*. There is no indication that the author knew any narrative materials. If he drew his sayings from a written document, it was most likely a sayings collection which was in turn based upon the Gospels of Matthew and Luke but also included some non-canonical materials (cf. *2 Clem.* 12).[5] It must remain highly unlikely, though by no means impossible, that such a sayings collection was called a "gospel." *preaching*

1.4.5 THE SHEPHERD OF HERMAS

There are numerous instances in which passages of the *Shepherd of Hermas* seem to allude to phrases and stories of the Synoptic Gospels.[6] Actual quotations, however, never occur. But that is simply part of the

---

[1] For the date of *2 Clement* see Wengst (*Didache*, 222–27): 130–150 CE. However, since there is no external attestation for this writing before the end of the 2d century, any date in the 2d century would be possible. The use of harmonized sayings based on both Matthew and Luke with many similarities to the harmony used by Justin Martyr and the use of apocryphal materials (see below, # 5.1.2–3) would argue for a date around 150 or later; see Koester, *Synoptische Überlieferung*, 79–99. Martin Hengel (*Die Evangelienüberschriften* [SHW.PH 1984.3; Heidelberg: Winter, 1984] 34: "einige Jahrzehnte vor Justin") and especially Karl Paul Donfried (*The Setting of Second Clement in Early Christianity* [NovTSup 38; Leiden: Brill, 1974] 55–56) fail to give convincing arguments for an earlier date.

[2] εἶπεν ὁ κύριος, *2 Clem.* 4.5; 9.11.

[3] λέγει, *2 Clem.* 3.2; 5.2.

[4] Koester, *Synoptische Überlieferung*, 70–99; see below # 5.1.1–2.

[5] For further discussion of the quotations of sayings in *2 Clement* and their non-canonical parallels see below # 5.1.3.

[6] For a collection and comparison of these passages with their synoptic parallels, see Koester, *Synoptische Überlieferung*, 242–56.

particular way in which the author of this writing uses other sources and traditions. Though obviously dependent upon Scriptural passages and other traditional materials, the author rarely quotes a source.[1] It is therefore extremely difficult to determine whether the author is dependent on a particular writing or is drawing on oral tradition. Parallels to the Synoptic Gospels in the *Shepherd* show no peculiar features of the redactorial work of any of these gospels. Thus, dependence upon any of these gospels cannot be demonstrated, but neither can it be excluded.

The term "gospel" (εὐαγγέλιον) never occurs and the verb "to preach" (εὐαγγελίζεσθαι) is also missing. Thus we cannot know whether the author, if he indeed used written gospels, knew them under this designation. If an early date of ca. 100 CE can be assumed for the composition of this book,[2] it is unlikely anyway that the author would have known gospels under this title.

1.4.6 POLYCARP OF SMYRNA

The absence of the term "gospel" is equally noteworthy in the letter of bishop Polycarp of Smyrna to the Philippians. It is very likely that the major portion of the preserved letter is a writing that dates from the last decades of Polycarp's career,[3] which started at the time of Ignatius of Antioch at the beginning of the 2d century and ended with his martyrdom after the middle of that century, perhaps as late as the time of the emperor Marcus Aurelius, i.e., after 160 CE.[4] Polycarp's first letter, written at the time of Ignatius as a cover letter for sending copies of the letters of Ignatius, is preserved in chapters 13–14 of the extant document. But it is in the portions which belong to the later letter (chapters 1–12 and 15) that several quotations of gospel materials occur.

One of these quotations, Pol. *Phil.* 2.3a, is copied from the quotation of the sayings of Jesus in *1 Clem.* 13.1–2, including the quotation for-

---

[1] The only more explicit reference occurs in *Vis.* 2.3.4 where the author introduces a now lost apocryphal writing ("Eldad and Modad") with the formula "as it is written."

[2] It is tempting to identify the "Clement who will send the book to the foreign cities" (*Vis.* 2.4.3) with the the secretary of the Roman church to whom we owe *1 Clement*.

[3] The convincing thesis that the preserved letter is actually a composition of two different letters was proposed by P. N. Harrison, *Polycarp's Two Epistles to the Philippians* (Cambridge: Cambridge University Press, 1936). This thesis was endorsed by Hans von Campenhausen, *Polykarp von Smyrna und die Pastoralbriefe* (SBH.PH 1951.2; Heidelberg: Winter, 1951) 39–40, reprinted in idem, *Aus der Frühzeit des Christentums: Studien zur Kirchengeschichte des ersten und zweiten Jahrhunderts* (Tübingen: Mohr/Siebeck, 1963) 197–252.

[4] According to Eusebius, *Hist. eccl.* 3.14.10–15.1.

mula ("Remember what the Lord said when he was teaching"). However, while the quote in *1 Clem.* 13.2 had been drawn from the oral tradition, Polycarp, who knew the Gospels of Matthew and Luke, corrected the text in order to establish a more faithful agreement of Jesus' words with the wording of the written gospels from which he has also drawn his other gospel materials (*Phil.* 2.3b; 7.2; 12.3).[1] At the same time, it is remarkable that Polycarp never uses the term "gospel" for these documents and that the words of Jesus are still quoted as if they were sayings drawn from the oral tradition.

The term "gospel" appears several times in the report of Polycarp's martyrdom which was written shortly after the death of the famous bishop of Smyrna. A clear reference to a written gospel is the remark in the postscript which says "that his martyrdom happened according to the gospel of Christ" (κατὰ τὸ εὐαγγέλιον τοῦ Χριστοῦ γενόμενον, *Mart. Pol.* 19.2).[2] But neither this passage, nor the phrases which try to establish a correspondence between the martyrdom of Polycarp and the suffering of Jesus, as it is described in the Gospels of the New Testament, appear in the copy of the document that is preserved in Eusebius' *Church History*.[3] They belong to a later redaction of the story of Polycarp's martyrdom. The original report did not use the term "gospel" at all and does not show any signs of the use of written gospels in the description of the sufferings and death of the bishop of Smyrna.[4]

1.5 The Term "Gospel" in Gospels from the Nag Hammadi Library

1.5.1 THE GOSPEL OF THOMAS[5]

The manuscript of the *Gospel of Thomas* in Codex 2 of the Nag Hammadi Library does not use the term "gospel" in its text. The term occurs only in the colophon of a scribe or translator at the end of the writing: "The Gospel according to Thomas." The formulation "Gospel according to . . ." imitates the secondary titles of the canonical Gospels

---

[1] Cf. Koester, *Synoptische Überlieferung,* 114–20.

[2] Cf. also *Mart. Pol.* 4.2: ". . . for the gospel does not teach this" (ἐπειδὴ οὐχ οὕτως διδάσκει τὸ εὐαγγέλιον).

[3] *Hist. eccl.* 4.15.

[4] A critical analysis of the various layers of the report of Polycarp's martyrdom was presented by Hans von Campenhausen, *Bearbeitungen und Interpolationen des Polykarpmartyriums* (SBH.PH 1957; Heidelberg: Winter, 1957) 5–48; reprinted in idem, *Frühzeit,* 253–301.

[5] More information about the date, composition, and character of these gospels from the Nag Hammadi Library will be provided in later chapters.

which they received after their incorporation into the four-gospel canon of the New Testament. The writing itself, however, which may have been composed as early as the end of the 1st century, gives its title and the name of its author at the beginning:

> These are the secret sayings which the living Jesus spoke and which Didymus Judas Thomas wrote down. (NHC II 32,10–11)

This is the original incipit of the book. Thus the title of the book should be more appropriately "Thomas's Book of Secret Sayings." Whoever composed the book and wrote its incipit was certainly not aware of the possible designation of the work as a "gospel."

1.5.2 THE GOSPEL ACCORDING TO MARY

Also in this document from the Coptic Papyrus Berolinensis 8502 the title "[The] Gospel according to Mary" appears in the colophon of the scribe or translator, not in the document itself.[1] If there was a title in the incipit of the writing, it is now lost, because the first six pages of the Coptic manuscript are no longer extant, and the Greek fragment parallels only the last three pages of the Coptic version. However, the *Gospel according to Mary* uses the term "gospel" (εὐαγγέλιον) in its text:

> ... he (Jesus) greeted them all, saying: "... For the Son of man is within you. Follow after him! Those who seek him will find him. Go then and preach the gospel of the kingdom. Do not lay down any other rules beyond what I appointed for you...." (BG 8502 8,18–22)

> They wept greatly saying: "How shall we go to the Gentiles and preach the gospel of the kingdom of the Son of man?" (BG 8502 9,6–10)

> Levi answered and said to Peter: "... Rather, let us be ashamed and put on the perfect man and acquire him for ourselves as he commanded us, and preach the gospel, not laying down any other rule or other law beyond what the Savior said." (BG 8502 18,15–21)

The "gospel" is the message which the disciples have to proclaim. That it is twice designated as the "gospel of the kingdom" and that the command to preach the gospel is twice combined with the injunction not to

---

[1] The parallel, but very fragmentary, Greek version of the *Gospel According to Mary* in *P. Ryl. 463* has no title at the end of the writing; but it is possible that the missing lines at the end of the document were occupied by the title; cf. R. McL. Wilson and George W. MacRae, "The Gospel According to Mary," in Douglas M. Parrott, ed., *Nag Hammadi Codices V, 2–5 and VI with Papyrus Berolinensis 8502, 1 and 4* (NHS 11; Leiden: Brill, 1979) 470.

lay down any other rule, reveals a fixed technical terminology for the Christian proclamation.[1]

1.5.3 THE APOCRYPHON OF JAMES

Although this writing contains discussions of Jesus with his disciples and includes materials which belong to the tradition of Jesus' sayings, the term "gospel" does not appear.[2] A scribal colophon is missing. The document begins with a dual identification of its purpose. In the first, the writing is characterized as a letter from James to another person whose name is no longer legible (NHC I 1,1–7). The second speaks of "A Secret Book (= Apocryphon) that was revealed to me (i.e., James) and Peter by the Lord" (NHC I 1,10–12).[3]

1.5.4 THE DIALOGUE OF THE SAVIOR

The dialogues of Jesus (usually called "the Lord") with individually named disciples and the use of traditional sayings argue for the inclusion of this writing under the category of gospel literature. The title "Dialogue of the Savior" appears in the incipit (NHC III 120,1). A colophon is missing, and there are no other designations of the genre of the work or of its author. The term "gospel" never occurs.

1.5.5 THE GOSPEL OF TRUTH

This book may have been composed by the famous Gnostic teacher Valentinus, and must be dated in the middle of the 2d century. It is not a writing that belongs to the gospel literature; but it is a homily or meditation. It uses the term "gospel" in its incipit, from which it received its modern title, and twice more in the course of the writing:

> The gospel of truth is joy for those who have received from the Father of truth the grace of knowing him. . . . (NHC I 16,31–33)

> . . . in the name of the gospel is the proclamation of hope, being discovery for those who search for him. (NHC I 17,1–4)

> From this, the gospel of the one who is searched for, which was revealed to those who are perfect through the mercies of the Father, the hidden mystery, Jesus Christ, enlightened those who were in darkness through oblivion. (NHC I 18,11–19)

---

[1] This terminology is possibly related to or dependent upon the use of the same phrase in the Gospel of Matthew (see above # 1.3.2).

[2] The verb εὐαγγελίζεσθαι is used once with the meaning "to proclaim": "Blessed are they who have proclaimed the Son before his descent" (NHC I 14,37–39).

[3] For further discussion of the genre of this document see below # 3.1.2.

Although the author certainly knew and used written gospels, the term "gospel" in each instance designates the message of salvation. The *Gospel of Truth* is therefore an important 2d-century witness for the continuing use of the term "gospel" as a designation of the Christian proclamation.

1.5.6 OTHER INSTANCES OF THE USE OF THE TERM

In the Nag Hammadi library, "gospel" is used as a designation of a written source for the first time in the *Treatise on the Resurrection,* which must be dated at the end of the 2d century.[1] The reference is clearly to a written gospel, possibly to Mark 9:2–8:[2]

> For if you remember reading in the Gospel that Elijah appeared and Moses with him, do not think the resurrection is an illusion. (NHC I 48,7–11)

The author is also familiar with other writings of the New Testament, quotes a combination of Rom 8:17 and Eph 2:5–6 explicitly as said by "the Apostle" (NHC I 45,23–28), and alludes to other New Testament passages.[3]

The term "gospel" also appears in the scribal colophon of the *Gospel of Philip,* a Valentinian treatise from the end of the 2d century: "The Gospel according to Philip" (NHC II 86,18–19). Like the colophon of the *Gospel of Thomas,* the phrase seems to imitate the later designations of the canonical gospels. The genre and style of the work itself does not accord with any known gospel literature, although the author quotes a number of sayings of Jesus and refers to some narratives about him.

This brief survey of some books from the Nag Hammadi library demonstrates that the gospel writings preserved in this library never use the term "gospel" as designations for their own works. Various other titles ("Secret Sayings," "Secret Book") are used instead in the incipits of these gospels. On the other hand, whenever the term "gospel" appears in the earlier documents from this corpus, it either comes from the hand of a later scribe or translator or it designates the oral proclamation of the Christian message.

---

[1] See Malcolm L. Peel, "The Treatise on the Resurrection," in Harold W. Attridge, ed., *Nag Hammadi Codex I (The Jung Codex)* (2 vols.; NHS 22–23; Leiden: Brill, 1985) 1. 146.

[2] Ibid., 2. 192–94.

[3] Ibid., 1. 133; 2. 162–63.

1.6 Why Did Written Documents Come To Be
Called "Gospels"?

1.6.1 THE WRITTEN GOSPEL AS KERYGMA

In the second half of the 2d century certain documents came to be called "gospels." But it is not evident why the term "gospel"—once the technical term for the early Christian missionary preaching—became the title for a particular type of literature. Explanations for this change have been closely associated with the attempt to define the special genre of the gospel literature. Most commonly accepted, in one form or another, is the thesis developed by Karl Ludwig Schmidt and Julius Schniewind. It states that the gospels, specifically the four Gospels of the New Testament canon, are representatives of a literary genre *sui generis* which cannot be related to other developments in the history of literature in antiquity.[1]

In a famous carefully argued essay published in the year 1923, Karl Ludwig Schmidt[2] presented a fundamental and incisive criticism of various attempts to understand the genre of the gospels in analogy to Greek biography or other literary genres from antiquity (e.g., Jewish apocalyptic literature). Schmidt referred to Franz Overbeck's distinction between Christian "primitive literature" (*Urliteratur*) and Patristic literature.[3] According to Overbeck, the Letters and Gospels of the New Testament belong to the former category because they owe their existence to the special circumstances and requirements of Christian beginnings. Writings of this genre could no longer be reproduced in the later period because these special circumstances no longer obtained. Patristic literature, on the other hand, belongs to the "high literature" (*Hochliteratur*) of antiquity because it is influenced by established literary genres of the ancient world and their critical standards. In addition to utilizing Overbeck's distinction between these two types of literature, Schmidt relied on the insights of the form-

---

[1] The modern discussion of the kerygma genre of the written gospel has been summarized by Frankemölle, *Evangelium: Forschungsbericht,* 4–16.

[2] "Die Stellung der Evangelien in der allgemeinen Literaturgeschichte," in H. Schmidt, ed., ΕΥΧΑΡΙΣΤΗΡΙΟΝ : *Studien zur Religion und Literatur des Alten und Neuen Testaments, Hermann Gunkel zum 60. Geburtstag . . . dargebracht* (FRLANT N.F. 19/2; Göttingen: Vandenhoeck & Ruprecht, 1923) 50–134.

[3] "Über die Anfänge der patristischen Literatur," *Historische Zeitschrift* 14 (1882) 417–72; reprinted in book form: Darmstadt: Wissenschaftliche Buchgesellschaft, 1954 and 1966. On the influence of Overbeck's essay on the view of the gospels in New Testament scholarship, see Dormeyer, *Evangelium als Gattung,* 48–58.

creeded literary

critical studies of Rudolf Bultmann[1] and Martin Dibelius,[2] as well as
of his own work.[3] These publications had demonstrated that the
Synoptic Gospels of the New Testament were primarily collections of
materials which had been formed in the pre-literary, oral stages of
their transmission in the early Christian communities. Therefore,
Schmidt concluded, the genre of the gospels cannot be determined on
the basis of a comparison with the products of literary culture.
Rather, they must be understood as collections and publications of
traditions in the form of "casual literature" (*Kleinliteratur*) according
to the needs of a developing religious community.

A few years after the appearance of Karl Ludwig Schmidt's essay,
Julius Schniewind published a now-noted review article of works on
the Synoptic Gospels.[4] In this article, he proposed a further elaboration of Schmidt's arguments with respect to the use of the term
"gospel" as a designation of a literary genre. Observing the close relationship in form and content between the Synoptic Gospels and the
early Christian kerygma or creed, Schniewind concluded that the
gospels constituted a special literary genre that had no parallels
anywhere else:

creeded

> There can be no doubt: only because there was a kerygma, proclaiming a
> human being who lived "in the flesh" as "the Lord," is it possible to
> understand the origin of our gospels, including any forms of Christian
> literature that preceded them.[5]

Schniewind's explanation of the origins of this literature and of its
designation as "gospel" has been widely accepted, together with
Overbeck's distinction between Christian "primitive literature" (*Urliteratur*) as a representative of casual literature or popular cultic
writing, and Patristic literature, as representative of literary culture.[6]
Vielhauer's judgment characterizes this view:

---

[1] *The History of the Synoptic Tradition* (2d ed.; New York: Harper & Row, 1968). The
first German edition had been published two years before the appearance of Schmidt's
essay: *Die Geschichte der synoptischen Tradition* (FRLANT 29; Göttingen: Vandenhoeck & Ruprecht, 1921).

[2] *From Tradition to Gospel* (New York: Scribner's, 1934). First German edition: *Die
Formgeschichte des Evangeliums* (Tübingen: Mohr/Siebeck, 1919).

[3] Karl Ludwig Schmidt, *Der Rahmen der Geschichte Jesu* (Berlin: no publisher,
1919; reprint Darmstadt: Wissenschaftliche Buchgesellschaft, 1964, 1969).

[4] "Zur Synoptiker-Exegese," *ThR* N.F. 2 (1930) 129–89.

[5] Ibid., 183.

[6] Cf. Günther Bornkamm, "Evangelien, formgeschichtlich," *RGG* 2 (3d. ed.) 750.
For a critical discussion of this "old consensus" and full bibliography, see M. J. Suggs,
"Gospel, Genre," *IDBSup* 370–72.

The question of the literary character of the gospels and of their position within the context of the general history of literature must be answered, for the time being, in this way: the gospels do not reflect any of the genres of the contemporary Old Testament and Jewish or Greek literature; within the context of such literatures, the gospels are unique with respect to their literary character, and they do not have any predecessors or any successors.[1]

1.6.2 THE GENRE OF THE GOSPEL OF MARK: KERYGMA OR BIOGRAPHY?

The thesis of the kerygma structure of the written gospel has received support through the observation that the oldest of the gospels, the Gospel of Mark, is essentially a passion narrative with an extended introduction. Its primary purpose, therefore, was to present a narrative account of the individual topics of the Pauline kerygma which is quoted as "gospel" in 1 Cor 15:1–5. Whether or not this is in fact an appropriate description of the intent of Mark's writing, it remains to ask whether Mark and other writings of this character were called "gospels" for this very reason. And if the author of the Gospel of Mark was not aware of the kerygma structure of his writing, is it possible that Mark and other gospels were recognized later as deserving the designation "gospel" because of their close relationship to the Christian proclamation which the apostles had called "the gospel"?

One might even find a confirmation for this hypothesis in the observation that the written gospels grew in the same way in which the kerygmatic formulations were expanded. The kerygma, called "gospel" in the writings of Ignatius of Antioch, began with the virginity of Mary and the birth of Jesus,[2] just as the later Gospels of Matthew and Luke opened their accounts of the story of Jesus with narratives about the virginity of Mary and the birth of Christ.

However, our survey of the use of the term "gospel" has not turned up a single instance in which any such literature was designated with this title before the middle of the 2d century. Hengel[3] has recently tried to renew the thesis that the titles of the canonical Gospels, as they appear in the earliest manuscripts of ca. 200 CE, existed in the same form already at the beginning of the 2d century.[4] Hengel's claim

---

[1] *Geschichte der frühchristlichen Literatur* (GLB; Berlin: De Gruyter, 1975) 282.

[2] Ignatius *Trall.* 9:1–2; cf. *Eph.* 18.2: see above # 1.2.2.

[3] *Evangelienüberschriften,* passim.

[4] Dormeyer (*Evangelium als Gattung,* 17) discusses Hengel's thesis critically, but still gives too much credit to his arguments. Wilhelm Schneemelcher ("Einleitung," in Edgar Hennecke, *Neutestamentliche Apokryphen in deutscher Übersetzung,* vol. I: *Evangelien* [5th ed. by Wilhelm Schneemelcher; Tübingen: Mohr/Siebeck, 1987] 68)

that the canonical Gospels must have circulated from the very beginning under the name of specific authors may be correct.[1] But there is no evidence whatsoever that their original book titles were identical with the later "The Gospel according to . . ." (τὸ εὐαγγέλιον κατά . . .). On the contrary, there is evidence in the Nag Hammadi Library that these standard titles were later added by scribes to writings that had different original titles. Moreover, the term "gospel" continues to be used widely as a technical term designating the Christian proclamation.

In any case, the more recent discussion of the literary genre of the gospels has reopened the question of the relationship of the genre, especially the Gospel of Mark, to biography, however cautiously.[2] With respect to Hellenistic models for the genre of biography, Albrecht Dihle encouraged the attempts to understand the Gospels of the New Testament as biographies, but warned that the search for adequate models in Greco-Roman literature could be futile.[3] This warning should not be overlooked. Detlev Dormeyer, who has pursued this question vigorously in two publications,[4] has achieved a breakthrough insofar as he takes his starting point not from Greco-Roman models of biography but from Klaus Baltzer's work on the biography of the prophets.[5] Hellenistic biography is primarily interested in the character of the philosopher or the poet whose "life" (βίος) is described; "conversion" is understood as a conversion to a philosophical life, a life of "virtue" (ἀρετή). This interest is present even in the biographies of military and political figures.[6] The biography of the prophet, however, is concerned with office and function; "conversion" here is the call

---

emphasizes that Hengel's thesis simply cannot be substantiated. See for the following the useful summary by Schneemelcher, ibid., 67–68.

[1] It must be stated, however, that, except for the Papias fragments in Eusebius *Ecclesiastical History,* there is no single instance of the mention of any gospel by the name of its author before Theophilus of Antioch (ca. 170 CE); cf. Hans von Campenhausen, *The Formation of the Christian Bible* (Philadelphia: Fortress, 1972) 129.

[2] Most of the literature is treated in Dormeyer (and Frankemölle), "Evangelium als Begriff," 1581–1634. For a comprehensive discussion of gospel and Greek biography see Klaus Berger, "Hellenistische Gattungen im Neuen Testament," *ANRW* 2.25/2. 1231–45.

[3] Albrecht Dihle, "Die Evangelien und die griechische Biographie," in Peter Stuhlmacher, ed., *Das Evangelium und die Evangelien* (WUNT 28; Tübingen: Mohr/Siebeck, 1983) 383–411.

[4] Dormeyer (and Frankemölle), "Evangelium als Begriff," and idem, *Evangelium als Gattung.*

[5] Klaus Baltzer, *Die Biographie der Propheten* (Neukirchen: Neukirchener Verlag, 1975).

[6] See Plutarch's *Parallel Lives* and Suetonius's *Lives of the Emperors.*

to the office, and even the personal sufferings of the prophet are part of the exercise of the responsibilities of this office. Birth and death are only the external framework. Even within such a framework the emphasis is placed upon the individual stages of the official life. To these belong, e.g., the installations into various offices. "Life" and "office" are to a large extent identical in the presentation.[1]

It may be useful here to summarize some of the typical features of the office biography which Klaus Baltzer highlights in his brief discussion of the Gospel of Mark:[2] Just like the authors of Old Testament biographies, Mark is using various existing collections of older materials and traditions. In the design of the outline of his work he follows essentially the framework of the "biography of the prophets." He begins with Jesus' baptism (not with his birth), which is not described as a public presentation of Jesus but as the personal call which also pronounces the title of his office ("you are my beloved son," 1:11). The following chapters describe in various episodes the typical features of the conduct of office. In the story of his suffering and death, the primary concern is the legitimation of Jesus' office. That his official title is indeed "Son of God" is confirmed by the statement of the centurion (Mark 15:39) after this claim has been officially denied by the Jerusalem authorities (Mark 14:61). The ending of the Gospel of Mark (16:1–8) with its rejection of the veneration of the tomb of Jesus—this would have been appropriate for a famous sage but not for one who was holding a divine office—corresponds to the official character of the biography.[3]

Baltzer's proposal has the advantage of presenting a unified genre instead of searching for various and sundry biographical and other motifs which would have influenced Mark to different degrees in his attempt to design a framework for the story of Jesus. It may be possible to improve upon Baltzer's suggestion by investigating Greco-

---

[1] Baltzer, *Biographie,* 20.

[2] Ibid., 185–89.

[3] Baltzer's suggestions have been elaborated with some modifications in the interpretation of the Gospel of Mark by Dieter Lührmann, "Biographie des Gerechten als Evangelium: Vorstellungen zu einem Markus-Kommentar," *Wort und Dienst* N.F. 14 (1977) 25–50, and idem, *Das Markusevangelium* (HNT 3; Tübingen: Mohr/Siebeck, 1987) 42–44 and passim. It is difficult to understand Dormeyer's hesitation with respect to the acceptance of this model which he justifies with the remark that this genre had come to an end with the exile (see his *Evangelium als Gattung,* 168–73). The biography of Nehemiah and the biographical substratum of Deutero-Isaiah are certainly post-exilic. Moreover, the latter has strongly influenced the narrative of the suffering righteous and his vindication in Jewish literature after the exile; cf. George Nickelsburg, "The Genre and Function of the Markan Passion Narrative," *HTR* 73 (1980) 153–84.

failed

Roman instances of office biography, such as the Roman *commentarius,* the autobiography of the Roman official, to which Dihle has pointed as an important analogy.[1] *used*

That Mark should have ~~combined~~ the genre of the office biography ~~with the concept of~~ the "kerygma" as it appears under the term "gospel"—assuming that this term ~~was~~ a linguistic metaphor with a presupposed implicit meaning—would require the demonstration that Mark indeed knew that he was writing "a gospel." As has been shown above,[2] Mark 1:1 cannot bear this burden of proof. There is no justification whatsoever to speak of Mark's writing as an attempt to transform the oral "gospel" (= the Christian proclamation) into a literary document.[3] *rather, a written gospel into a biography*

There is indeed no evidence that the writers of the 2d century who first used the term "gospel" as a reference to a written source had any awareness of the kerygma-character of this literature. If the final redactor of the *Didache* is indeed referring to a written gospel, what he has in mind is not the kerygma that could be found in that gospel, but rules and regulations for the Christian community which were transmitted in such a writing under the authority of Jesus (as, e.g., Matthew 18).[4] What 2 *Clement* calls "gospel" is a collection of sayings of Jesus, not the story of Jesus' birth, life, death, and resurrection.[5] Marcion and Justin Martyr come closer to such a kerygma concept of the written gospel; this will be discussed in the following chapter (# 1.7). But for most of the first two-thirds of the 2d century the best characterization of the meaning of the term "gospel" is that given by Hans von Campenhausen: "'The Gospel' to which appeal is normally made, remains an elastic concept, designating the preaching of Jesus as a whole in the form in which it lives on in church tradition. The normative significance of the Lord's words, which is the most important point, ... is not transferred to the documents which record them."[6]

1.6.3 THE GENRE OF THE GOSPEL SOURCES

The problem of the literary genre of the Gospel of Mark could possibly be solved as suggested above. However, this would only explain

---

[1] "Die Evangelien und die griechische Biographie," 407–11.

[2] See above the discussion of Mark's use of the term "gospel" (# 1.3.4).

[3] It is all nigh impossible to translate the German monstrosity *Verschriftlichung des mündlichen Evangeliums* (Dormeyer, passim) into an adequate English expression.

[4] *Did.* 8.2; 15.3, 4: see above # 1.4.3.

[5] *2 Clem.* 8.5; see above # 1.4.4.

[6] von Campenhausen, *Formation,* 129.

the genre of the gospel as it was designed by Mark and as it was further developed by the later gospel writers who wrote their works on the basis of Mark's framework, i.e., Matthew and Luke and the various gospels and gospel harmonies dependent upon these gospels. But any attempt to define the genre of the written gospel in this way will not be useful as a comprehensive definition of all gospel literature because it does not include either the sources of the canonical gospels or the extant apocryphal gospel literature. To date the entire discussion of the genre of the gospel has been exclusively concerned with the gospel writings of the New Testament canon, often only with the three Synoptic Gospels at the expense of the Gospel of John.[1]

The sources used by the canonical as well as the apocryphal gospels are writings which incorporate and develop older traditions about the words and the life of Jesus. Even the Gospel of Mark, the oldest of the canonical gospels, is not the oldest representative of gospel literature, but used written sources, and there can be no doubt about the use of written sources in the later gospels of the canon. However, these sources—except for a written passion narrative—have little or no relationship to the Pauline kerygma of the death and resurrection of Jesus, *pace* the genre of biography.

Among these older gospel writings are collections of sayings (Synoptic Sayings Source), a collection of parables (the source of Mark 4), catenae of miracle stories (employed by Mark and recognizable in the Semeia Source of the Gospel of John), books of apocalyptic prophecies (Mark 13 and Matthew 24–25), and legends about Jesus' birth (Matthew 1–2; Luke 1–2). Günther Bornkamm has correctly remarked that such collections are formed "according to genres and conventions which can be observed also in other popular, secular, and religious literatures."[2] The kerygma of cross and resurrection has had no influence whatsoever upon the formation of these literatures. Rather, their genre has been determined by theological and sociological motifs of a very different character, such as "sapiential invitation," "aretalogy," and "dialogue." Moreover, these and other factors have also had an influence upon the further development of the gospel form created by Mark as well as upon the writings which are commonly known as the apocryphal gospels. Schniewind's definition and subsequent attempts to define the genre of the gospel are not only inadequate, if one considers the genre of the sources used by the canonical

---

[1] That is especially true of the more recent German discussion of this topic. In all the works cited in the preceding footnotes, one looks in vain for the mention of a single apocryphal gospel, and even the Gospel of John is rarely used.

[2] "Evangelien, formgeschichtlich," *RGG* 2 (3d ed.) 750.

gospels; they are also entirely useless for defining the literary genres which have determined the form and content of the apocryphal gospels.[1]

1.7 From the Oral Tradition to the Written Gospel

1.7.1 AUTHORITIES IN THE EARLIEST PERIOD

In the first one and one-half centuries, "scripture," i.e., authoritative writing, comprised exclusively what was later called the Old Testament.[2] Any additional authority referred to in order to underline the legitimacy of the Christian message and the teaching of the church was present in a variety of traditions which were still undefined.[3] Sometimes these were transmitted orally, sometimes in written form. Such authority could be called "the sayings of the Lord," usually transmitted orally.[4] But even the quotations of Jesus' sayings in *2 Clement*, although drawn from a written source, are still introduced as words of the Lord,[5] just as Justin (*1 Apology* 15–17) introduces the teachings of the gospels as "what Jesus said" and not as quotations from a book.

The pronouncements of Christian prophets constituted another important authority. They could be transmitted orally or in written form. Prophets were not only concerned with predicting the future;[6] they often functioned as instructors and church leaders together with "teachers" (διδάσκαλοι).[7] Prophetic writings, too, claim authority for the regulation and the renewal of the life of the church; such instructions appear as substantial sections of the Revelation of John and the *Shepherd of Hermas*.

In other cases, early Christian authors refer to "the pronouncements of the apostles," although there seems to be no particular tradition that is connected with the authority of the apostles. *1 Clement* 44 relates the offices of the church to the apostles, but in very general

---

[1] This question will be discussed below (# 1.8).

[2] von Campenhausen, *Formation*, 21–61; idem, "Das Alte Testament als Bibel der Kirche vom Ausgang des Urchristentums bis zur Entstehung des Neuen Testaments," in idem, *Frühzeit*, 152–96; Lee Martin McDonald, *The Formation of the Christian Biblical Canon* (Nashville: Abingdon, 1988) 48–68.

[3] For the use of authority in the Pauline letters see Hans von Campenhausen, "Die Begründung kirchlicher Entscheidungen beim Apostel Paulus," in idem, *Frühzeit*, 30–80.

[4] Acts 20:35; *1 Clem.* 2.8; 13.1; 46.8; *Did.* 8.2.

[5] *2 Clem.* 3.2; 4.5; 5.2–4; 6.1; 8.5; 9.11; 12.2; cf. also Polycarp *Phil.* 2.3.

[6] E.g., Acts 11:28; 21:10–11; Rev 22:6–7.

[7] Cf. Acts 13:1; *Did.* 10.7; 11.7–13.7.

terms. In 2 Pet 3:2 the apostles appear as guarantors of the Lord's commandment:

> That you should remember the predictions of the prophets and the commandment of the Lord and Savior through your apostles (μνησθῆναι ... τῆς τῶν ἀποστόλων ὑμῶν ἐντολῆς τοῦ κυρίου καὶ σωτῆρος).

The formulation is typical of the general way in which one refers to apostolic authority, though 2 Peter may have been written as late as the middle of the 2d century. *Did. inscr.* "Teaching of the Lord through the Twelve Apostles" (διδαχὴ κυρίου διὰ τῶν δώδεκα ἀποστόλων) is difficult to date; it is possible that the title was added later. It is an attempt to give material substance to the hitherto undefined authority of the apostles.[1] This presentation of the authority of the apostles in writings for the instruction of the church is continued in the subsequent production of such books as the *Catholic Didascalia of the Twelve Apostles of the Savior* and the *Apostolic Constitutions*.[2]

Apostolic authority was claimed early for writings in which the sayings of Jesus were collected. The recourse to Thomas as apostolic authority for the *Gospel of Thomas* is most likely very old, as is the reference to Matthew as authority for the "sayings" in Papias of Hierapolis (see below). Still in the second half of the 2d century, the Valentinian Ptolemy in his letter to Flora says:

> If God permit, you will learn in the future about their origin and generation, when you are accounted worthy of the apostolic tradition which we also have received by succession, because we can prove all our statements from the teaching of the Savior. (*Ptolemy to Flora* # 7.9)[3]

It seems that apostolic authority for the esoteric tradition of Jesus' pronouncements was especially favored by Gnostic writers.[4]

1.7.2 PAPIAS OF HIERAPOLIS

A closely related appeal to tradition is the citation of "the traditions of the elders." The oldest witness for the teaching authority of the "elders" or "presbyters" (πρεσβύτεροι) is bishop Papias of Hierapolis.[5] The

---

[1] On the entire question see Hans von Campenhausen, *Ecclesiastical Authority and Spiritual Power* (Stanford, CA: Stanford University Press, 1969).

[2] On the titles of these books see R. Hugh Conolly, *Didascalia Apostolorum* (Oxford: Clarendon, 1929) pp. xxvii-xxviii.

[3] ET by R. McL. Wilson in Werner Foerster, *Gnosis: A Selection of Gnostic Texts* (2 vols.; Oxford: Clarendon, 1972–74) 1. 161.

[4] Helmut Koester, "La tradition apostolique et les origines du Gnosticisme," *RThPh* 119 (1987) 1–16.

[5] The relevant fragments of his writings are quoted in Eusebius *Hist. eccl.* 3.39.3–4.

date for his writings is usually given as some time between 100 and 150 CE.[1] More abundant evidence for the presbyter traditions comes from Irenaeus and Clement of Alexandria at the end of the 2d century.[2]

Eusebius quotes the following from Papias's writing (Five Books of Interpretations of the Oracles of the Lord):

> And I shall not hesitate to append to the interpretations all that I ever learnt well from the presbyters and remember well (καλῶς ἐμνημόνευσα) . . . ; but if ever anyone came who had followed the presbyters, I inquired into the words of the presbyters, what Andrew or Peter or Philip or Thomas or James or John or Matthew, or any other of the Lord's disciples had said, and what Aristion and the presbyter John, the Lord's disciples, were saying.[3]

What Papias says about Mark reflects the use of categories which are drawn from the oral tradition:

> And the presbyter used to say this: "Mark became Peter's interpreter and wrote accurately all that he remembered (ὅσα ἐμνημόνευσεν), not, indeed, in order everything said or done by the Lord (τὰ ὑπὸ τοῦ κυρίου ἢ λεχθέντα ἢ πραχθέντα), . . . Mark did nothing wrong in thus writing down single points as he remembered them (ὅσα ἀπεμνημόνευσεν).[4]

Papias says about Matthew that he composed "the sayings" (τὰ λόγια).[5] In neither statement does Papias use the term "gospel." Even in their written form, these traditions about Jesus and of Jesus' words do not carry any greater authority than that which was transmitted orally. The written gospels' authority is assured by the same technical terms which had been established for the oral tradition. At the same time, Papias shows that these written documents did not come without the names of apostolic authors or of men who had followed the apostles. These names, which already guaranteed the trustworthiness of the oral tradition, are now used to assure the faithfulness of the written documents. The titles of such writings may have been something like "The sayings of the Lord written by Matthew (in Hebrew[6])."

---

[1] It is notoriously difficult to give a more precise date to Papias' writings; see Johannes Munck, "Presbyters and Disciples of the Lord in Papias," *HTR* 52 (1959) 223–43. On Papias references to Matthew and Mark see von Campenhausen, *Formation*, 129–35.

[2] See Günther Bornkamm, "πρεσβύς κτλ.," *TDNT* 6 (1959) 670–80; von Campenhausen, *Ecclesiastical Authority*, 162–77.

[3] Eusebius *Hist. eccl.* 3.39.3–4. Translation by Kirsopp Lake in LCL.

[4] Eusebius *Hist. eccl.* 3.39.15. ET by Kirsopp Lake in LCL.

[5] Quoted in Eusebius *Hist. eccl.* 3.39.16.

[6] It is noteworthy that the incipit of the *Apocryphon of James* says that the book was

The term "remember" (μνημονεύειν/ἀπομνημονεύειν) was decisive for the trustworthiness of the oral tradition. It played an important role in the earliest quotation formulae for sayings of Jesus.[1] It appears not only in Papias with reference to the written tradition, but also in a parallel in the *Apocryphon of James,* a writing that can be dated to approximately the same time as Papias's writing:[2]

> ... the twelve disciples [were] all sitting together at the same time and remembering what the Savior had said to each one of them, whether in secret or openly, and [putting it] in books. (NHC I 2,7–15)

The terminology of "remembering" is deliberate and, as Vielhauer had already remarked about Papias,[3] it is part of the controversy with the Gnostics. Gnostic writers were composing their written documents on the basis of the claim that they remembered well from the apostles and from those who had followed them.[4] It was important that such books could claim to rest on legitimate memory and that they carried apostolic authority. However, there was no concern with the title that was given to a particular book. Nowhere is the title "gospel" used for such books.[5]

---

written "in the Hebrew alphabet." Papias's reference to Matthew writing in Hebrew may rest upon such a statement in the original incipit of the book. Thus Papias would not be a witness to the existence for a Semitic original, but would simply report that such a reference occured in the title of the book.

[1] Acts 20:35; *1 Clem.* 13.1–2; 46.7–8.

[2] A date early in the 2d century was originally proposed by Willem van Unnik, *Evangelien aus dem Nilsand* (New York: Scheffer, 1959) 93–101. Van Unnik's argument was that this writing contained gospel materials which are still dependent upon oral tradition. In spite of some criticism of this early date (see F. E. Williams, "The Apocryphon of James," in Attridge, ed., *Nag Hammadi Codex I,* 1.26–27), van Unnik's arguments have now been confirmed by Ron Cameron, *Sayings Traditions in the Apocryphon of James* (HTS 34; Philadelphia: Fortress, 1984) 91–124.

[3] Vielhauer, *Geschichte,* 762.

[4] On this entire question see Cameron, "Remembering the Words of Jesus," in his *Apocryphon of James,* 91–124.

[5] Hengel (*Evangelienüberschriften,* 8–18) argues that Papias already presupposes the title "Gospel according to . . ." (Εὐαγγέλιον κατά . . .) with the implied meaning that this is the *one* gospel according to Matthew, Mark, etc. But there is no evidence for this in the surviving Papias fragments, and it would be completely anachronistic. That the *one* gospel was extant in different writings, which were all called "gospels" and transmitted under apostolic names, became a problem only after Marcion (see below). For Papias, all emphasis lies upon the apostolic names no matter what title could be derived from the incipit of a particular book.

1.7.3 MARCION

Hans von Campenhausen[1] suggested that the impulse for a radical change came from the Christian scholar, church leader, and reformer Marcion. At about the time when Justin Martyr arrived in Rome, coming from Ephesus, and about a decade before the publication of Justin's *Apologies,* Marcion (who was a wealthy shipowner) also came to Rome from Sinope in Pontus. Like other Christians of his time, Marcion knew the authoritative Christian scripture (the "Old Testament") and the still undefined and mostly oral traditions of the apostles and of the elders; under the same authority also some writings with the words and deeds of Jesus were transmitted. But Marcion had studied the letters of the apostle Paul, and he had become deeply impressed with the Pauline thesis of Christ as the end of the law. Marcion understood this to imply a rejection of the law and the prophets, the scriptures of Israel. Marcion's protest against the use of these scriptures in the churches also entailed a protest against what he called the Judaizing falsifications of the traditions of the apostles. He thus attacked a universally recognized authority, i.e., traditions guaranteed by names of various apostles and accepted by all churches and by many Gnostic teachers.

Moreover, Marcion thought that even the Pauline writings themselves had been contaminated by Judaizing interpretations. What he deemed necessary for a reform of the church was the dismissal of the Jewish scriptures and a new critical edition of the letters of Paul, that is, written documents under the authority of the only apostle who had fought against the Judaizers. This newly edited Corpus Paulinum, consisting of ten letters (the Pastoral Epistles are missing), became the basis of Marcion's ecclesiastical reform.

In these letters, Marcion found references of Paul to "my gospel."[2] Because of his fundamental doubts regarding the oral tradition, he understood these as references to a written document called "gospel." He may have known more than one writing which contained the reports of Jesus' words and deeds. But it is no longer possible to determine with certainty whether he was acquainted with the Gospels of Matthew and John as well as with the Gospel of Luke. Even if he knew Matthew, it is obvious that the pervasive references in this Gospel to the prophecies of Israel would have made this writing an

---

[1] *Formation,* 147–63.

[2] The phrase τὸ εὐαγγέλιόν μου appears in Rom 2:16 (Rom 16:25 is part of a secondary addition to Paul's letter); τὸ εὐαγγέλιον ἡμῶν is found in 2 Cor 4:3; 1 Thess 1:5; 2 Thess 1:8; 2:14, but see also Gal 1:11. Since Marcion did not know the Pastoral Epistles, 2 Tim 2:8 is not relevant.

unlikely choice for Marcion. In any case, Marcion believed that it must have been Luke's writing to which Paul had been referring as "my/our gospel."[1] When he published his revised edition of the letters of Paul, he included a purified version of Luke's Gospel in the novel authoritative book which he propagated as the new scriptures that were designed to replace the old scriptures of Israel.

As we have seen, there is no evidence that anyone before Marcion had used the term "gospel" as a designation for a written document. But all reports about Marcion agree that he called his revised edition of Luke "gospel."[2] Marcion introduced this novel usage in conscious protest against the still undefined and mostly oral traditions to which the churches of his day referred as their dominical and apostolic authority. Thus Marcion's new ecclesiastical organization was not only the first Christian church with its own "scripture"; it also possessed for the first time a written document called "the gospel." Marcion was excommunicated from the Roman church in 144 CE. According to the witness of Justin Martyr,[3] Marcion's church had already established itself throughout the whole world at the time of the writing of Justin's *First Apology,* i.e., less than a decade after Marcion's excommunication. It had obviously become a powerful and well-organized movement in a brief period of time, and it constituted a veritable threat to all those Christian churches which continued to insist that theology and ecclesiastical organization had to be based upon the writings of Israel, the law and the prophets, the "Holy Scripture" of Christendom.

1.7.4 JUSTIN MARTYR AND MARCION

Justin Martyr composed his writings in the later years of the emperor Antoninus Pius (150 to 160 CE). We know that Justin was involved in the earliest phase of the Marcionite controversy, because he reports in a later writing that he had published a book against Marcion.[4] But because his "Anti-Marcion" and his "Syntagma Against all Heresies" are not preserved, we do not know the details of his argu-

---

[1] The choice of Luke is interesting, because this Gospel was certainly written later than the other canonical Gospels, and "at first its standing was strikingly inferior to that of Mark and, above all, of Matthew" (von Campenhausen, *Formation,* 128).

[2] Adolf von Harnack, *Marcion: Das Evangelium vom fremden Gott* (2d ed.; Leipzig: Hinrichs, 1924 [reprint Darmstadt: Wissenschaftliche Buchgesellschaft, 1960]) 184*; von Campenhausen, *Formation,* 155–56.

[3] On Justin about Marcion see *1 Apol.* 26.5–8; 58.1–2. Cf. Eusebius *Hist. eccl.* 4.11.10.

[4] On Justin against Marcion see *1 Apol.* 26.8 ("Syntagma Against All Heresies"); Irenaeus *Adv. haer.* 4.6.9; Eusebius *Hist. eccl.* 4.11.8 (Syntagma against Marcion).

ments. However, those writings of Justin which are preserved, his two *Apologies* and his *Dialogue with Trypho,* clearly show the effects of Marcion's challenge. Most noticeable in these writings is the complete suppression of Paul and his letters. While earlier writers, even in Rome, never hesitated to refer to Paul as their authority,[1] there is not a single quote from the Pauline Corpus in Justin's writings, nor is the apostle ever mentioned. On the other hand, his writings abound with quotations from the "Old Testament" (the Septuagint) and from the Gospels of Matthew and Luke.

A positive effect of Marcion's challenge in the writings of Justin Martyr is the adoption of the concept of a written gospel and the departure from the oral tradition. Justin agrees with Marcion: reliable traditions of the church must be preserved in written records. However, while Marcion emphasized the irreconcilable contradictions between the written gospel and the Jewish scripture, Justin linked the writings which he called "Memoirs of the Apostles" as tightly as possible to the law and the prophets. While Marcion revised the Gospel of Luke in an effort to eliminate all quotations and references to the law and the prophets, Justin did not hesitate to revise the texts of Matthew and Luke on several occasions in order to establish an even closer verbal agreement between the prophecies of the Greek Bible and the record of their fulfillment in the text of the gospels.[2]

1.7.5 JUSTIN'S "MEMOIRS OF THE APOSTLES"

That Justin saw the written gospels as a more reliable record of the words and deeds of Jesus and that he advertised them as replacement of the established, but less trustworthy oral traditions about Jesus is evident in his designation of the gospels as the "Memoirs of the Apostles" (ἀπομνημονεύματα τῶν ἀποστόλων), a designation he used in many instances referring to the Gospels of Matthew, Luke, and possibly Mark. The designation occurs twice in his *First Apology*:

---

[1] In addition to numerous allusions to Paul's letters, *1 Clement* contains several explicit references: *1 Clem.* 32.5–6 = Rom 1:29–32; *1 Clem.* 37.5 = 1 Cor 12:21–22; *1 Clem.* 47.1–3 = Phil 4:15; cf. *1 Clem.* 49.5 = 1 Cor 13:5. With respect to the debated question of the dependence of 1 Peter (also written in Rome) upon Paul see Francis Wright Beare, *The First Epistle of Peter* (3d ed.; Oxford: Blackwell, 1970) 28–29, 212–16 (cf. also the literature cited on p. 28, n. 1).

[2] Helmut Koester, *Septuaginta und Synoptischer Erzählungsstoff im Schriftbeweis Justins des Märtyrers* (Habilitationsschrift Heidelberg, 1956); see also my essay "The Text of the Synoptic Gospels in the Second Century," in William L. Petersen, ed., *Gospel Traditions in the Second Century: Origins, Recensions, Text, and Transmission* (Christianity and Judaism in Antiquity 3; Notre Dame: University of Notre Dame Press, 1989) 19–37. See further below # 5.2.

The apostles in the memoirs which have come from them, which are also called gospels, have transmitted that the Lord had commanded them as follows, "that Jesus had taken bread, etc." (*1 Apol.* 66.3)

And on the day which is named after the sun there is an assembly of all those who live in each city or village; and the memoirs of the apostles or the writings of the prophets are being read as long as it is allowable; when the reader has stopped, the leader will speak and give an admonition and an invitation to imitate all these good things. (*1 Apol.* 67.3–4)[1]

It is clear here that these "memoirs" are indeed gospel writings and that they are used liturgically as instructions for the sacrament and as texts for homilies.

All other occurrences of the term are found in *Dialogue* 99–107 where Justin systematically employs gospel materials for his interpretation of Psalm 22. In this context he uses the designation "Memoirs of the Apostles" thirteen times.[2] In each instance the materials quoted derive from written gospels, usually from Matthew and Luke, in one instance from Mark, and each time the term serves to quote, or to refer to, gospel materials which demonstrate that the prophecy of the Psalm has been fulfilled in the story of Jesus. The "Memoirs of the Apostles" are used as reliable historical records.

The term "Memoirs of the Apostles" has often been explained as a title designed by Justin in order to raise the gospels to the status of Greek memoirs of a philosopher. This suggestion was first made in 1857.[3] It has been repeated by most authors because the name seemed to be "well-chosen and very appropriate in order to give to the educated Greeks the right ideas about the character of the gospels."[4] However, the term is problematic with respect to its usage for philosophical memorabilia.[5] It was never used for a philosopher's memorabilia before the Second Sophistic in the 2d century CE. The primary older example for such "Memoirs" commonly cited is Xenophon's

---

[1] But cf. also *1 Apol.* 33.5: "As those who remembered (οἱ ἀπομνημονεύσαντες) everything about the savior Jesus Christ have taught" (a quote of Luke 1:31 follows).

[2] *Dial.* 100.4; 101.3; 102.5; 103.6, 8; 104.1; 105.1, 5, 6; 106.1, 3, 4; 107.1.

[3] E. Köpke, *Über die Gattung* ἀπομνημονεύματα *in der griechischen Literatur* (Programm der Ritterakademie zu Brandenburg, 1857).

[4] Zahn, *Kanon,* 1. 471.

[5] Klaus Berger ("Hellenistische Gattungen im Neuen Testament," *ANRW* 2.25/2 [1984] 1245–47) has discussed the use of this term in detail, but he does not pay sufficient attention to the time of its earliest occurrence. Berger defines the term Ἀπομνημονεύματα as personal remembrances about particular persons which are written down, whereas Ὑπομνήματα can report all sort of things, persons, and events as well as other matters. Cf. also Nils Hyldahl, "Hegesipps Hypomnemata," *StTh* 14 (1960) 70–113.

Memorabilia of Socrates. But this Latin title was not used for Xenophon's work in antiquity; it appears for the first time in the year 1569 in Johann Lenklau's edition of Xenophon. In Plutarch and in Diodorus Siculus, ἀπομνημόνευμα means an anecdote that is heard or written down.[1] The Latin equivalent of the Greek plural ἀπομνημονεύματα, *commentarii*, is first used for Xenophon's writing in Aulus Gellius [2d century CE] *Noct. Att.* 14.3.5 (*quod Xenophon, in libris quos dictorum atque factorum Socrates commentarios composuit*). The Greek term does not appear in Xenophon's writings, but only as a title of his work in later manuscripts: "First Book of Xenophon's Memoirs of Socrates" (Ξενοφῶντος Σωκράτους ἀπομνημονευμάτων βιβλίον πρῶτον), and in the pseudepigraphical letter #18 of Xenophon from the time of the Second Sophistic: "But I am composing some memoirs of Socrates" (πεποίημαι δέ τινα ἀπομνημονεύματα Σωκράτους).[2] Xenophon himself uses the verb "to remember distinctly" (διαμνημονεύειν) once in this work: "I shall write that which I remember distinctly" (τούτων δὲ γράψω ὅποσα ἂν διαμνημονεύω, 1.3.1).

That Justin should have known the term ἀπομνημονεύματα from its occasional use in the Second Sophistic is possible, but not very likely. It is highly unlikely, however, that his choice of the term as a designation for the gospels was dependent upon this usage, and it is certainly not the case that Justin adopted the term in order to lend to the written gospels the rank of historical sources[3]—simply because ἀπομνημονεύματα did not have any such meaning at Justin's time.[4] On the other hand, the simple form of the verb "to remember" (μνημονεύειν) occurs frequently in the quotation formulae for orally transmitted sayings of Jesus.[5] The composite form of the verb "to remember" (ἀπομνημονεύειν) had been used by Papias of Hierapolis as a technical term for the transmission of oral materials about Jesus. If Justin's term "Memoirs of the Apostles" is derived from this usage, it designates the written gospels as the true recollections of the apostles, trustworthy

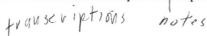

---

[1] Plutarch, *Cato maior* 9; Diodorus Siculus 1.14: "What is said in simple words briefly and clearly is for the one who speaks an ἀπόφθεγμα, for the one who has heard it an ἀπομνημόνευμα."

[2] Ed. Hercher, *Epist. Graec.*, 623); cf. also Diog. L. 4.2; 7.4, 36, 163.

[3] Dormeyer, *Evangelium als Gattung*, 15. *2 Apol.* 10 and 11 connect in no way the gospels as "memoirs" with Xenophon's *Memorabilia* of Socrates (*pace* Dormeyer, p. 15–16). Justin rather refers to a statement of Plato's *Apology* (24 b) about Socrates in *2 Apol.* 10.5, and to Xenophon's famous story about Herakles at the crossroads in *2 Apol.* 11.

[4] Trustworthy historical record would rather be designated by several other terms, such as ὑπομνήματα (= *commentarii*), συγγράμματα, see LSJ, svv.

[5] See above in the discussion of Papias of Hierapolis.

and accurate, and more reliable than any oral tradition which they are destined to replace.[1]

Moreover, when Justin composed the interpretation of Psalm 22— an earlier treatise that was later incorporated in his *Dialogue*[2]—it is evident that he knew of the presbyter tradition quoted in Papias's work. In *Dial.* 106.3 he refers to the "Memoirs of Peter" in the context of a citation from Mark 3:16–17.[3] This reveals that Justin connected the Gospel of Mark with Peter like the presbyter tradition that is quoted in Papias.[4] That Justin, relying on Papias, coined the term "Memoirs of the Apostles" with an anti-Gnostic intention, is quite possible, considering the use of the terminology of "remembering" in such writings as the *Apocryphon of James*.[5] But what is of primary importance is the fact that the use of this term advertises the written gospels as replacement for the older oral traditions under apostolic authority.

1.7.6 JUSTIN AND THE GOSPELS

Justin uses the term "gospel" only three times in his extant writings which fill almost two hundred-forty pages in a modern edition of the Greek text. Considering the large amount of quotations and references to gospel materials, this is surprising:

> The apostles in the memoirs which have come from them, which are also called gospels (ἃ εὐαγγέλια καλεῖται), have transmitted that the Lord had commanded . . . (*1 Apol.* 66.3)

[1] The first to draw attention to this close relationship of Justin's term to Papias was Richard Heard, "The ἀπομνημονεύματα in Papias, Justin, and Irenaeus," *NTS* 1 (1954–55) 122–29. Heard's thesis has been criticized by Nils Hyldahl, "Hegesipps Hypomnemata," *StTh* 14 (1960) 70–113. However, Hyldahl does not appreciate the differences between ὑπομνήματα, συγγράμματα, and ἀπομνημονεύματα, nor the fact that the latter term occurs relatively late in Greek literature.

[2] Luise Abramowski, "Die 'Erinnerungen der Apostel' bei Justin," in Stuhlmacher, ed., *Evangelium und Evangelien*, 341–53.

[3] All other references speak of memoirs of a plurality of apostles except for *Dial.* 106.3 where, after mentioning Peter, Justin speaks of "his memoirs." This is either a specific reference to the Gospel of Mark, written by the amanuensis of Peter, or—less likely—the text should be emended to "his (Jesus') apostles' memoirs." In any case, since Justin continues to refer to a Markan passage (Mark 3:16–17, there are no parallels in Matthew and Luke), the reference to the presbyter tradition that connects Peter with Mark may still be implied, even if the text must be emended.

[4] Abramowski, ibid., 353. However, this reliance on the presbyter tradition does not prove that, in general, second-century authors preferred the oral tradition to written documents; this is no longer true for Justin Martyr (*pace* E. F. Osborn, *Justin Martyr* [BHTh 47; Tübingen: Mohr/Siebeck, 1973] 125–26).

[5] Abramowski, ibid., 352.

(Trypho said:) . . . I know that your commandments which are written in the so-called gospel (ἐν τῷ λεγομένῳ εὐαγγελίῳ) are so wonderful and so great that no human being can possibly fulfill them. (Dial. 10.2)

And in the gospel it is recorded that he (Jesus) said (ἐν τῷ εὐαγγελίῳ δὲ γέγραπται εἰπών), "Everything has been handed over to me by the Father . . ." (Dial. 100.1) *all authority* *the tradition* *the father/elder*

In each of these three passages in which the term occurs, it designates a written gospel. It is evident that "gospel" refers to the same literature that Justin otherwise calls "Memoirs of the Apostles." The use of the plural in 1 Apol. 66.3 indicates that Justin knew of more than one written gospel. This is confirmed by the fact that Justin's quotations reflect the texts of the Gospels of Matthew and Luke and, at least in one instance, Mark. Moreover, he also quotes sayings which may derive from an apocryphal gospel.

These gospels, for Justin, possess the authority of written records. Although they are read in service of the church, they are not "Holy Scripture" (γραφη) like the law and the prophets. The latter are enhanced by the inspiration of the prophecies which they record,[1] but Justin never considers the "Gospels" or the "Memoirs of the Apostles" as inspired writings. While he regularly quotes the law and the prophets with the formula "it is written" (γέγραπται), he uses this term only rarely for the gospels. In the few instances where he does so, he combines this formula with other verbs. Introducing gospel quotations, the formula does not mean "it is written in Holy Scripture," but "it is recorded in a written document that Jesus said" (Dial. 100.1).[2]

The character of the gospels as historical records (rather than holy scripture) is underlined by the fact that Justin can occasionally refer to gospel materials as if they were written in secular records:

(About the dividing of Jesus garment at the crucifixion) . . . and that this happened you can learn from the acts which were recorded under Pilate (ἐκ τῶν ἐπὶ Ποντίου Πιλάτου γενομένων ἄκτων). (1 Apol. 35.9)

(About Jesus healing the sick and raising the dead) . . . that he has done these things, you can learn from the acts which were recorded under Pontius Pilate (ἐκ τῶν ἐπὶ Ποντίου Πιλάτου γενομένων ἄκτων). (1 Apol. 48.3)[3]

---

[1] 1 Apol. 32. However, Justin does not ascribe the inspiration to the text of the Greek translation (Septuagint) or to the Hebrew text, but rather to the prophets themselves whose words were recorded in Hebrew and translated into Greek.

[2] "It is written" is used in connection with the quotation of materials from the "Memoirs of the Apostles" also in Dial. 103.6, 8; 104.1; 105.6; 106.3, 4; 107.1.

[3] It is possible that the same phrase should be added to the statement in 1 Apol. 38.7: "That all these things were done to Christ by the Jews, you can learn."

(On Bethlehem as Jesus' place of birth) ... as you can learn from the census lists which were recorded under Cyrenius (ἐκ τῶν ἀπογραφῶν τῶν γενομένων ἐπὶ τοῦ Κυρηνίου), your first governor in Judea. (*1 Apol.* 34.2)

These are the earliest references to Acts of Pilate in Christian literature. The next mention of Pilate writings is found in Tertullian (*Apologeticum* 21.24):

Pilate, who was already a Christian in his conscience, reported all these things about Christ (i.e., his life activity, cross, and resurrection) to Tiberius who was Caesar at that time.

While Tertullian may have known a letter of Pilate, a Christian forgery of the late 2d century (in its preserved form mistakenly addressed to Claudius),[1] it is unlikely that Justin knew any such document.[2] But the parallel references to the "Gospels," the "Memoirs of the Apostles," and official records show why Justin values the written gospels so highly: they are records which document the historical factuality of the events of the story of Jesus. As records of this nature the gospels are, indeed, the foundations of the truth of the Christian beliefs and they substantiate the validity of the Christian kerygma. That this is the case, in Justin's understanding of their function, is not related to the "kerygmatic" character of these writings. Rather, the gospels as records document the historical fulfillment of prophecy, and thus the truth of the Christian faith. The testimony of true divinity is the fulfillment of prophecy:

It is the work of God to announce something before it happens and then to demonstrate that it happened as it was predicted. (*1 Apol.* 12.10)

In a brilliant formulation, this principle occurs in Tertullian *Apologeticum* 20.3:

---

[1] Greek Text in the *Acts of Peter and Paul,* 41–42 (Ricardus Adalbertus Lipsius and Maximilianus Bonnet, *Acta Apostolorum Apocrypha* [2 vols.; Leipzig: Mendelssohn, 1991–1898; reprint: Darmstadt: Wissenschaftliche Buchgesellschaft, 1959] 1. 196–97). There is also a Latin version, preserved as an appendix to the *Gospel of Nicodemus,* and a somewhat different Syriac translation; see F. Scheidweiler, "The Gospel of Nikodemus, Acts of Pilate and Christ's Descent into Hell," in Edgar Hennecke, *New Testament Apocrypha* (2 vols.; 3d ed. by Wilhelm Schneemelcher, trans. R. McL. Wilson; Philadelphia: Westminster, 1963) 1. 444–84 (English translation of the letter on pp. 477–78).

[2] The preserved *Acts of Pilate* are a work of the 4th century, most likely produced by a Christian as a response to a pagan writing with this title which was circulated during the Diocletian persecution as anti-Christian propaganda. On the later *Acts of Pilate,* see Stephen Gero, "Apocryphal Gospels: A Survey of Textual and Literary Problems," *ANRW* 2.25/5 (1988) 3986–88.

testimonium divinitatis veritas divinationis ("The testimony of divinity is the truth of divination").

In direct antithesis to Marcion's use of the written gospel, Justin binds these gospels to the prophetic revelation of the Old Testament scriptures.

Justin Martyr, to be sure, knows expanded kerygmatic formulations, and he closely associates their topics with narrative materials which he draws from the Gospels of Matthew and Luke. As he prepares to present his scriptural proof for the truth of the Christian faith, he quotes an expanded kerygmatic formulation:

> In the books of the prophets we find that it was proclaimed beforehand that Jesus our Christ would appear, be born by a virgin, reach manhood, heal every disease and every sickness and raise the dead, that he would be despised and denied and crucified, and that he would die and be raised up and ascend into heaven, and that he is and will be called the Son of God, and that some people would be sent by him in every nation of humanity to proclaim that . . . (*Apol.* 31.7)

He then quotes prophecies from the law and the prophets which predict each of the topics of the Christian kerygma, and quotes the corresponding sections from the gospel narratives in order to demonstrate that each of the prophecies has found its exact fulfillment in the history of Jesus. But neither does Justin ever call the kerygma or creed of the church a "gospel," nor does he show any awareness of the kerygmatic structure of the gospel writings which he is using.

1.8 Apocryphal and Canonical Gospels

1.8.1 THE PREVAILING PREJUDICE

Schniewind's definition of the genre gospel which emphasizes the kerygma structure as the constitutive element has resulted in the assumption that only the canonical gospels qualify as genuine gospel literature. We have seen, however, that the term gospel as a designation of a certain type of literature came into use without any awareness that it was their peculiar literary genre that distinguished these writings from others. Therefore a great variety of writings of very different character eventually came to be called "gospels" toward the end of the 2d century, including so-called "apocryphal" gospels.

When the kerygma structure of the canonical gospels is used as the criterion for the definition of the genre, the apocryphal gospels appear as inferior and as incompatible with this genre. Ancient and venerable prejudices—as old as the anti-heretical polemics of the Fathers of the catholic church—were reinforced. Even in recent times, scholars have characterized the apocryphal gospels as secondary, derivative, speculative, and merely concerned with the edification and entertainment of their readers, while the canonical gospels are routinely seen as original, historical, and replete with theological insight. One can still read judgments like the following in modern scholarly works:

> The Jewish-Christian Gospels are characterized by a grotesque appeal to vulgar taste and are obviously fictitious. The Gnostic Gospels are marked by an esoteric wisdom which renders Jesus' message and mission unintelligible save for the initiated few.[1]

In the third edition of *New Testament Apocrypha,* Wilhelm Schneemelcher[2] had suggested that the apocryphal gospels constitute a different genre altogether, because the exalted Lord is speaking in these writings, communicating wisdom and life—as if mediation of wisdom and life through the exalted Lord were alien to the Gospels of the New Testament! Schneemelcher distinguished two types of apocryphal gospels: (1) those connected with the Synoptic (or canonical) Gospels which are designed to edify the reader (such as the *Gospel of Peter*) and (2) those "allied with Gnosis" (to this group he assigns the *Gospel of Thomas,* the *Dialogue of the Savior,* and many others). About the latter he wrote:

> They are revelation writings the purpose of which is to convey the redeemer's words and therewith "knowledge" or "gnosis."[3]

1.8.2 CRITERIA FOR THE DEFINITION OF A "GOSPEL"

It is evident that criteria like "speculative rather than historical" and "edificational rather than theological" cannot be used in order to determine which writings should be included in a history of the

---

[1] Robert Spivey and D. Moody Smith, *Anatomy of the New Testament* (New York: Macmillan, 1969) 173.

[2] Wilhelm Schneemelcher, "Introduction," in Hennecke-Schneemelcher-Wilson, *NT Apocrypha,* 1. 80–84. In his revised "Einleitung" (pp. 71–72) in the 5th edition of *NT Apokryphen,* Schneemelcher has changed his judgment considerably and suggests that the genre "gospel," even if defined narrowly, can be applied to some of the apocryphal materials in so far as they consist of sayings and/or narrative materials related to Jesus traditions.

[3] Hennecke-Schneemelcher-Wilson, *NT Apocrypha,* 1. 83. For further discussion of such characterizations of apocryphal literature see my article, "Apocryphal and Canonical Gospels," *HTR* 73 (1980) 105–30.

development of gospel literature.

Moreover, any definition of the literary genre "gospel" on the basis of traditional classifications or theological observations is not helpful when one is faced with a rather complex and diversified corpus of literature.[1] Even for the canonical Gospels, taken by themselves, the establishment of one literary genre is not without problems. These four gospels have much in common. All four include sayings and narrative materials, and at least three of these gospels end with a passion narrative and stories about the appearances of Jesus after his resurrection.[2] But some of these common features are simply due to the fact that Matthew and Luke used the Gospel of Mark as their common source and employed a second common source for their sayings materials.

A closer scrutiny of the four canonical Gospels reveals that even here the theological definition of a gospel genre has its problems. The structure of the Gospel of Matthew is controlled by five major and a number of smaller speeches of Jesus into which the traditional sayings materials have been gathered; the passion narrative, i.e., the central piece of the "kerygma," is no longer a fundamental structural element of Matthew's Gospel. The same could be said about the Gospel of Luke, which presents the events of Jesus' life and ministry in the form of a biography of the divine man. Conversely, the Gospel of John, which is not dependent upon Mark like Matthew and Luke, is a writing of an entirely different character. It may resemble the Synoptic Gospels because of the use of a passion narrative; but its presentation of Jesus' miracles as divine epiphanies and its transformation of the sayings into revelation discourses hardly fits the definition of the genre of the gospel developed on the basis of the Gospel of Mark.

The application of such a genre definition becomes altogether impossible if one considers the sources used by the canonical gospels. The Synoptic Sayings Source, used by the Gospels of Matthew and Luke, was a collection of wisdom sayings and apocalyptic prophecies; it never contained a passion narrative. The catenae of miracle stories employed in the first part of the Mark's Gospel, the Semeia Source of the Fourth Gospel, a parable collection (Mark 4), the pamphlet of apocalyptic prophecies (Mark 13), and the legends about the birth of a divine child (Matthew 1–2; Luke 1–2)—all these are examples of

[1] Vielhauer (Geschichte, 256–57) rightly warns that any preconceived notion of the genre gospel, developed in the analysis of just one or two canonical gospels, is a dogmatic prejudice that does not do justice to the variety of writings which were indeed called "gospels" in the ancient church.

[2] Resurrection appearances are missing in the original text of the Gospel of Mark; only the secondary ending of this gospel relates such appearances.

sources and materials appearing in the gospels of the canon which
hardly fit the genre of the kerygma gospel.

On the other hand, what characterizes some of these sources reap-
pears in several of the apocryphal gospels. The *Gospel of Thomas* is a
collection of prophetic and wisdom sayings. The *Dialogue of the Savior*
preserves discourses and dialogues of Jesus with his disciples, which
are closely related to those employed by the author of the Gospel of
John. The *Infancy Gospel of Thomas* preserves legends about the
divine child—a genre that has influenced the first two chapters of the
Gospel of Luke. The *Proto-Gospel of James* tells about the virginity of
Mary and of Jesus' birth by a virgin. Only the *Gospel of Peter*—at
least in the form in which it is preserved—is constituted by a passion
narrative and stories about the appearances of the risen Christ and
thus is related to the kerygma of cross and resurrection. Whether or
not any of these apocryphal gospels are dependent upon the Gospels of
the New Testament canon, they represent, like the sources of the
canonical gospels, literary genres which have parallels in other popular and religious literatures. Genres like "wisdom book," "dialogue,"
and "aretalogy" were employed when oral traditions about Jesus were
assembled and composed in literary forms for the first time, and they
continued to be influential in the development of later gospel literature. Compared with these written compositions of Jesus traditions,
the Gospels of the New Testament appear as rather complex literary
products in which such sources are blended together in various and
distinctive ways.

On the basis of these observations one must establish a criterion by
which it can be determined whether any extant writing from the early
period of Christianity belongs to the corpus of gospel literature. This
corpus should include all those writings which are constituted by the
transmission, use, and interpretation of materials and traditions from
and about Jesus of Nazareth. Obviously, such writings belong to different literary genres. Some of these writings may have preserved the
genre which determined their character at the stage of their earliest
composition. Others may have come into being through the conflation
or combination of sources of different literary genres, or they may be
later developments or interpretations of earlier compositions.
Whether or not they are canonical, and regardless of their commitment to the kerygma of Christ's death and resurrection, all of them
must be included in a consideration of the history and development of
gospel literature.[1]

[1] For practical reasons I am excluding from this treatment some of the later gospels
which show dependence upon the canonical gospel literature, including the Jewish-

This working hypothesis provides a criterion for the exclusion of a number of writings which may appear to be gospels, or which have traditionally been known as "gospels," or received this title in the colophon of a manuscript but are not related to or constituted by the continuing development of sources containing materials from or about Jesus of Nazareth.

1.8.3 WRITINGS WHICH ARE NOT TO BE COUNTED AS GOSPELS

The following writings will, therefore, not be treated in the context of this book:

The *Gospel of Philip* (NHC II,3), a collection of aphoristic theological reflections and comments, perhaps derived from a theological treatise.

The *Gospel of Truth* (NHC I,3), a meditation about the "true gospel," i.e., about the message of gnosis brought by Jesus which creates joy among those who hear it.

The *Gospel of the Egyptians,* also called *The Holy Book of the Great Invisible Spirit* (NHC III,2 and IV,2), a mythological description of the work of salvation which was accomplished by the Great Seth, the son of Adam.[1]

The *Sophia of Jesus Christ* (NHC III,4 and BG 8502,3), a secondary elaboration in the form of a dialogue of Jesus with his disciples of the philosophical religious writing *Eugnostos the Blessed* (NHC III,3 and V,1).

The *Apocryphon of John* (NHC II,1; III,1; IV,1; BG 8502,2), a Gnostic revelation discourse containing extensive interpretations of the first chapters of the Book of Genesis. It is probably of pre-Christian origin; its only Christian element is a secondary framework which presents the entire book as a revelation discourse given by Jesus to his disciple John.

The *Pistis Sophia* (Codex Askewianus) and the *Two Books of Jeu* (Codex Brucianus), as well as other Gnostic books containing revelation discourses and dialogues of Jesus with his disciples, whenever the pattern of discourse of Jesus with his disciples is employed as a secondary stylistic devise, while the materials presented in this form have little or no relationship to the traditions from or about Jesus.

It is, of course, not always possible to draw a clear line. The *Epistula Apostolorum,* for example, is in its external form a letter of the

---

Christian Gospels, the *Epistula Apostolorum,* and the *Gospel of Nicodemus.* I have also excluded a number of fragments.

[1] This writing must be distinguished from the *Gospel According to the Egyptians* which is known through quotations from Clement of Alexandria. It belongs to the genre of gospel literature, but will not be treated in this volume.

Twelve Apostles in which they report about Jesus' discourses with them after the resurrection. Gospel materials are clearly used, especially in the introduction—a brief narrative of Jesus' ministry—and in the report of the resurrection appearance. On the other hand, large parts of the discourses are composed of church order materials and of parenetical traditions. But the writing is relevant insofar as it represents a response, based on traditional gospel materials, to the speculative gnostic discourses of Jesus with his disciples in which a relationship to traditional gospel materials is not evident.

A number of other writings called "gospel," of which often only the name or a tiny fragment or a brief quotation are known, will also not appear in the following treatment of gospel literature.[1] It is often impossible to determine the character of these writings and to be certain that their content merits inclusion.

---

[1] For a listing and brief description of these see Hennecke-Schneemelcher-Wilson, *NT Apocrypha*, vol. 1, passim.

2

The Collection of the
Sayings of Jesus

2.1 Sayings of Jesus in early Christian Writings

2.1.1 THE ATTESTATION OF THE ORAL TRADITION

During the last century scholars have critically analyzed the extant gospel writings in order to determine the sources and traditions which were used in their composition. The method employed in this endeavor, once called "literary criticism,"[1] is now commonly called "source criticism."[2] It has resulted in the hypothesis that a number of larger and smaller written documents were used by the authors of the four Gospels of the New Testament canon. These earliest written materials are in turn composed of smaller units which circulated orally during the first decades of the early Christian movement. The method by which the oral traditions about Jesus have been determined is called "form criticism" (*Formgeschichte*); it reveals the social and

---

[1] The older term "literary criticism" (*Literarkritik*) has more recently been used to designate the investigation of the literary structure of writings in their final form. Good introductions into this method are William A Beardslee, *Literary Criticism of the New Testament* (GBSNTS; Philadelphia: Fortress, 1970) and Norman R. Petersen, *Literary Criticism for New Testament Critics* (GBSNTS; Philadelphia: Fortress, 1978).

[2] There is a wealth of literature on the source criticism of the canonical gospels, mostly consisting of commentaries and monographs to individual gospels (see below on the treatment of the individual Gospels of the New Testament). The classic works on the source criticism of the Synoptic Gospels are Heinrich Julius Holtzmann, *Die synoptischen Evangelien: Ihr Ursprung und ihr geschichtlicher Charakter* (Leipzig: Engelmann, 1863); Julius Wellhausen, *Einleitung in die drei ersten Evangelien* (2d ed.; Berlin: Reimer, 1911); B. H. Streeter, *The Four Gospels: A Study of Origins* (first published London: Macmillan, 1924). Also see Martin Lehmann, *Synoptische Quellenanalyse und die Frage nach dem historischen Jesus* (BZNW 38; Berlin: De Gruyter, 1970). A comprehensive review can be found in Walter Schmithals, "Evangelien, Synoptische," *TRE* 10 (1982) 575–609.

religious function of oral traditions of and about Jesus in the early Christian community.[1]

The purpose of this chapter is to investigate the beginnings of the collection of sayings. The most natural and convenient point of departure for a discussion of the earliest formation of the gospel tradition would seem to be the life, teaching, work, and death and resurrection of Jesus of Nazareth. From here one could move on to a description of the traditions about Jesus, their growth and collection, and finally to the analysis of the extant gospel literature. To be sure, all traditions and writings which are the subject of this book are ultimately related to Jesus of Nazareth. But the collection of the oldest materials is not related directly to the life and ministry of Jesus of Nazareth.

The relationship of the earliest traditions about Jesus to the historical ministry of Jesus is complex. The earliest traditions do not give a mirror image of Jesus' ministry. The life of the community reflects the source of experience in a different way: the light that is received from its source is refracted into many colors as in a prism or in a rainbow. There are many colors close at hand instead of one unified brightness. In fact, one may see only one single color without realizing that its fount is a light of very different qualities. Our task here is not the reconstruction of the source but the description of the refracted light and of the way in which the many colors are finally composed to the various colorful (or sometimes monochrome) pictures which we call "gospels." Diversity rather than unity is the hallmark of the beginning of the traditions about Jesus.

Our story of the history and development of gospel literature, therefore, cannot start with Jesus of Nazareth but must try to determine the point at which the various and diverse traditions about Jesus begin to take form. However, the reconstruction of their formation and use is not exclusively dependent upon the internal evidence derived from the source-critical analysis of the gospels themselves, but can also rely upon some external evidence which is available in other early Christian writings, primarily the letters of Paul, which testify to

---

[1] The most important form-critical work remains Rudolf Bultmann, *The History of the Synoptic Tradition* (2d ed.; New York: Harper, 1968); cf. also idem and Karl Kundsin, *Form Criticism* (New York: Willet, Clark, 1934; reprint New York: Harper, 1962); furthermore the influential work of Martin Dibelius, *From Tradition to Gospel* (New York: Scribner's, 1934). For a brief introduction see Edgar V. McKnight, *What is Form Criticism?* (GBSNTS; Philadelphia: Fortress, 1969). An instructive collection of essays of various authors was published by Ferdinand Hahn, ed., *Zur Formgeschichte des Evangeliums* (WdF 81; Darmstadt: Wissenschaftliche Buchgesellschaft, 1985). See also the general survey with bibliography by Helmut Köster, "Formgeschichte/Formenkritik II. Neues Testament," *TRE* 11 (1983) 271–99.

the way in which Jesus' sayings and stories about Jesus were collected and used in the earliest period.

However, one immediately encounters a major difficulty. Whatever Jesus had preached did not become the content of the missionary proclamation of Paul, nor of the churches from which his proclamation took its origin, nor in other writings closely related to this missionary enterprise, i.e., most of the letters of the New Testament. The "gospel" of Paul and of the Pauline mission was the proclamation of an eschatological event: the death and resurrection of Jesus as the turning point of the ages. With this gospel, Paul proceeded to carry the missionary proclamation of the Christian community from Antioch into Asia Minor and Greece.

Antioch's church was founded within a few years after the death of Jesus by the Hellenists, Greek-speaking Jewish Christians, who had been forced to leave Jerusalem during the persecution in which Stephen was martyred. It is unlikely that any personal followers of Jesus were involved in the establishment of this church because they were still resident in Jerusalem many years thereafter (cf. Gal 1:18–19; 2:1–10). But there were contacts between the church in Antioch as well as other Gentile-Christian churches and the brothers and sisters who had remained in Jerusalem, culminating in the so-called Apostles' Council in Jerusalem (Gal 2:1–10). At this Council, the Jerusalem church was represented by Jesus' brother James and by Peter and John, all three from Galilee, while the Gentile mission from Antioch had sent its leaders Paul and Barnabas, both Greek-speaking Israelites from the diaspora, and Titus who was a converted Gentile. The credal formula quoted in 1 Cor 15:3–7 in which the "gospel" is defined as the death, burial, resurrection, and appearances of Christ makes it probable that this understanding of the gospel was shared not only by the church of Antioch from the very beginning, but also by others who are named in the citation of those to whom Jesus appeared (Peter and James). This is confirmed indirectly in Paul's report about the Apostles' Council (Gal 2:1–10). What Paul preached was never the subject of the controversy between Paul's Gentile mission and the church in Jerusalem. Jesus death and resurrection was the event upon which their common proclamation was based. Through the proclamation of this eschatological event the communities of believers became the new Israel. As new members were received into this community, they were baptized into the death of Jesus so they would share also in Jesus' resurrection (Rom 6:2–10). Looking back to the death of Jesus, they celebrated their common meals in anticipation of his return in glory (1 Cor

11:23–26).[1] What was debated was the admission of Gentiles into the community of the New Israel as well as the celebration of a common meal in which both circumcised Jews and uncircumcized Gentiles could participate together. The latter problem is evident in the conflict which arose in Antioch after Peter's move to that city, when the "people from James" came for a visit (Gal 2:11–14).

On the other hand, Paul and his fellow missionaries, like Barnabas, certainly had access to reports about Jesus' life and death and about his words and deeds. In fact, Paul reports that three years after his call he visited Peter in Jerusalem for two weeks during which stay he also saw James, though none of the other apostles (Gal 1:18). This visit can be dated as early as the year 35 CE, certainly not later than the year 38/39 CE. Moreover, Peter came to Antioch after the Council (Gal 2:11). There was no lack of opportunity for Paul and other missionaries to learn something about Jesus' words. And indeed the letters of Paul demonstrate that he was familiar with a tradition of Jesus' sayings, though they did not become part of the message that he and others proclaimed. However, we will soon discover that there were other Christians for whom the sayings of Jesus actually constituted the message of salvation upon which they based their faith.

2.1.2 JESUS' SAYINGS IN PAUL'S WRITINGS

Though explicit references to sayings of Jesus are relatively rare[2] in Paul's letters, they play a certain role in his arguments, especially

---

[1] This strictly eschatological understanding of the common meals appears everywhere in the earliest layers of the tradition, even outside of the circle of the Pauline churches; cf. Mark 14:35; Luke 22:16; *Didache* 9–10).

[2] The debate about the frequency of the use of, and allusions to, words of Jesus in Paul's letters cannot be repeated here. A critical and, for the time being, definitive review of the debate has been presented by Dale C. Allison, Jr., "The Pauline Epistles and the the Synoptic Gospels: The Pattern of the Parallels" *NTS* 28 (1982) 1–32.; see also James M. Robinson, "Early Collections of Jesus' Sayings," in Joël Delobel, ed., *LOGIA: Les Paroles de Jésus—The Sayings of Jesus: Mémorial Joseph Coppens* (BEThL 59; Leuven: Peeters, 1982) 392–93. In his zeal to discover traces of the original written gospel, Alfred Resch (*Der Paulinismus und die Logia Jesu* [TU NF 12; Leipzig: Hinrichs, 1904) found over one thousand references to the Synoptic Gospels in Paul (including the deutero-Pauline letters to the Ephesians and the Colossians and the Book of Acts). While there is general agreement that Resch vastly overstated his case, some scholars would still maintain "that it was the words of Jesus himself that formed Paul's primary source in his work as ethical διδάσκαλος" (W. D. Davies, *Paul and Rabbinic Judaism: Some Rabbinic Elements in Pauline Theology* [London: S.P.C.K., 1965] 136). For a critical assessment of this and similar positions see Allison's article quoted above; Victor Paul Furnish, *Theology and Ethics in Paul* (Nashville: Abingdon,1968) 51–64.

with respect to the order of the life of the Christian communities. There are six explicit references to sayings or traditions which derive from Jesus. All but one are references to church order materials:

1 Cor 7:10–11	Ruling against divorce	Mark 10:11–12 parr
1 Cor 7:25	No dominical command	
1 Cor 9:14	Support for apostles	Q/Luke 10:7
1 Cor 11:23–26	Institution of Lord's Supper	Mark 14:22–25 parr
1 Cor 14:37	Command concerning prophets	
1 Thess 4:15–17	Apocalyptic saying	

In addition to these, one can probably list as many as eight parallels in which Paul alludes to sayings of Jesus which are attested in the Synoptic Gospels:[1]

Rom 12:14	Blessing of the persecuted	Q/Luke 6:27
Rom 12:17; and 1 Thess 5:15	Not repaying evil with evil	Q/Luke 6:29
Rom 13:7	Paying taxes to authorities	Mark 12:13–17 par
Rom 14:13	No stumbling block	Mark 9:42 par
Rom 14:14	Nothing is unclean	Mark 7:15 par
1 Thess 5:2	Thief in the night	Q/Luke 12:39
1 Thess 5:13	Peace among yourselves	Mark 9:50

One might add to these also the following:

Rom 12:18	Have peace with everyone	Mark 9:50[2]
Rom 14:10	Do not judge	Q/Luke 6:37

Also in these allusions the predominance of church order materials is evident. 1 Thess 5:2, an apocalyptic saying, is the only exception.

With respect to these church order materials, two observations are relevant: (1) they are concentrated in certain sections of the Pauline writings (Romans 12–14; 1 Corinthians 7–14; 1 Thessalonians 5); (2) their synoptic parallels are either church-order materials of the Gospel of Mark or sayings of the Sermon on the Plain in Luke (= Q): only in one instance (1 Cor 9:14) the synoptic parallel is a Q saying

---

[1] This is the conclusion of Furnish's (*Theology and Ethics*, 55–67) discussion of W. D. Davies's (*Paul and Rabbinic Judaism*) listing of synoptic parallels in Paul. Furnish is right in arguing that all other parallels are due to common dependence upon biblical references, more general Jewish wisdom tradition, and shared proverbial materials.

[2] Charles H. Talbert ("Tradition and Redaction in Romans XII. 9–21," *NTS* 16 [1969/70] 87) mentions this verse as one of "at least four injunctions in this section (i.e., Rom 12:14–21) [which] appear to echo sayings attributed to Jesus in the existing gospel tradition." He also considers vs. 19a as an echo of Matt 5:44.

from a different context.[1] That Paul, on whatever occasion, quotes or alludes to sayings of Jesus at random is therefore very unlikely. Rather, Paul is dependent upon units of materials which have been established for the order of the communities and, moreover, have already been subject to discussion and interpretation. That Paul is familiar with such secondary interpretations which eventually found their way also into the Synoptic Gospels has been demonstrated by David Dungan in his investigation of the commands about divorce (1 Cor 7:10–11) and support for the apostles (1 Cor 9:14).[2] Paul is therefore an early witness for the development of certain units of church order materials under the authority of Jesus. These same units reappear later in the sayings collections used by Mark and by the Synoptic Sayings Source; in the latter, one of these units provided the basis for the Q collection used for the composition of Matthew's "Sermon on the Mount" (Matthew 5–7) and Luke's "Sermon on the Plain" (Luke 6:20–49).[3] Perhaps it can also be argued "that Paul knew some version of the missionary discourse."[4] However, in this respect the parallels are much less certain. That a collection of church order materials, incorporated into Mark's Gospel, was known to Paul is evident. But the extent and order of this composition of sayings is difficult to establish.[5]

Of the two apocalyptic sayings among the Synoptic Gospel materials in Paul, the first (1 Thess 4:15–17) is explicitly quoted by Paul as a saying of the Lord,[6] but there is no close synoptic parallel to this saying. With respect to its form, it is problematic as a saying of Jesus, because it speaks of Jesus in the third person (αὐτὸς ὁ κύριος ... καταβήσεται). There are, however, several elements in vs. 16 (the voice of

---

[1] The mission instructions of Mark 6:8–11 lack an explicit command about the support for the missionaries.

[2] David L. Dungan, *The Sayings of Jesus in the Churches of Paul: The Use of the Synoptic Tradition in the Regulation of Early Church Life* (Philadelphia: Fortress, 1971).

[3] See Allison, "Pauline Epistles," 11–12. Charles H. Talbert ("Tradition and Redaction in Romans XII. 9–21," *NTS* 16 [1969/70] 84–93) has tried to show that Paul used and revised an originally Semitic code; Talbert's argument is based on a critical evaluation of David Daube's thesis that Rom 12:9–19 reflects an originally Aramaic Christian ethical code; cf. David Daube, "Participle and Imperative in I Peter," Appended Note in Edward Gordon Selwyn, *The First Epistle of St. Peter* (2d ed. reprint; London: Macmillan, 1955) 467–88; idem, *The New Testament and Rabbinic Judaism* (London: Athlone, 1956) 90–97.

[4] Allison, "Pauline Epistles," 12–13.

[5] Allison (ibid., 13–15) argues for a pre-Markan collection of sayings incorporated in Mark 9:33–50. But one also has to account for the Pauline parallels to Mark 7:15; 10:11–12; 12:13–17, and possibly 14:22–25.

[6] Τοῦτο γὰρ ὑμῖν λέγομεν ἐν λόγῳ κυρίου (vs. 15).

the archangel, the trumpet of God) which have close parallels in traditional apocalyptic materials.[1] There is no question that Paul here
quotes apocalyptic tradition. But it is not clear how firmly such tradition was designated as part of the tradition of the sayings of Jesus,
because virtually the same tradition is quoted as a mystery saying
(ἰδοὺ μυστήριον ὑμῖν λέγω) in 1 Cor 15:51–52 ("We shall not all fall
asleep, but we shall all be changed . . . at the last trumpet . . ."). Such
apocalyptic sayings are designated as "mysteries" also in 1 Cor 2:7 and
Rom 11:25. As Mark 13 shows, such apocalyptic traditions were incorporated into the corpus of the sayings of Jesus. Considering the way in
which they are used by Paul, this still seems to have been an ongoing
process.

The other apocalyptic saying in Paul, "The day of the Lord is coming
like a thief in the night" (1 Thess 5:2), appears in a traditional Jewish
form. "Day of the Lord" is a standard designation of the final day of
judgment that is frequently used since the time of the prophet Amos.[2]
The same traditional statement is used in 2 Pet 3:10 and Rev 3:3
("I shall come like a thief"; cf. Rev 16:15), and it has been expanded
into the parable of the Thief transmitted by the Synoptic Sayings
Source (Q/Luke 12:39–40). The latter form is clearly secondary.
There is no indication in 1 Thess 5:2 that Paul knew this tradition as a
saying of Jesus.

2.1.3 WISDOM IN CORINTH

There is most likely another collection of sayings of Jesus of a very
different character which was known to Paul. The first chapters of
Paul's First Letter to the Corinthians reveal that there were, at a very
early date, believers who had a different perception of the central
Christian message.[3] The terminology which Paul uses in 1 Corinthians 1–4 in his debate with the wisdom theology of the Corinthians is
striking and has only few parallels elsewhere in the Pauline epistles:

"to keep secret" (ἀποκρύπτειν) 1 Cor 2:7,[4]

---

[1] See the materials cited in Beda Rigaux, *Saint Paul: Les Épitres aux Thessaloniciens* (EtB; Paris: Gabalda, 1956) 542–43.

[2] Materials in Rigaux, *Les Épitres aux Thessaloniciens,* 555–56.

[3] In the following I am repeating some of the arguments which I presented in my
article, "Gnostic Writings as Witnesses for the Development of the Sayings Tradition,"
in: Bentley Layton, ed., *The Rediscovery of Gnosticism,* vol. 1: *The School of Valentinus*
(NumenSup 41; Leiden: Brill, 1980) 239–61. See this article for further documentation.

[4] It appears only here in the genuine Pauline writings, but is used twice in deutero-
Pauline epistles (Col 1:26; Eph 3:9).

"to hide" (κρύπτειν) 1 Cor 4:5,[1]
"to uncover" (ἀποκαλύπτειν) 1 Cor 2:10; 3:13,[2]
"to reveal" (φανεροῦν) 1 Cor 4:5,[3]
"childish," "immature" (νήπιος) 1 Cor 3:1.[4]

Most striking is the frequency of the terms "wise" (σοφός) and "wisdom" (σοφία). The former occurs ten times in these four chapters of
1 Corinthians,[5] but elsewhere in Paul only four times,[6] the latter is
used sixteen times here,[7] but elsewhere only three times.[8]

This special terminology leads to a group of sayings of Jesus that
has always been noted as distinctly different from other sayings which
are preserved in the synoptic tradition:

Matt 11:25–26 = Luke 10:21
Matt 11:27 = Luke 10:22
Matt 13:16–17 = Luke 10:23–24.[9]

The first and the third in this group of sayings are alluded to in the
context of 1 Corinthians 1–4, while there seems to be no reference to
the second.[10] The most prominent of these sayings is the first (Matt
11:25–26 = Luke 10:21):[11]

---

[1] Used only here in this letter and sparingly elsewhere in Paul: Rom 1:19; 3:21; frequently in 2 Corinthians.

[2] In 1 Corinthians only here and in 14:30; elsewhere in Paul Rom 1:17, 18; 8:18; Gal
1:16; 3:23; Phil 3:15.

[3] Elsewhere in Paul Rom 1:19; 3:21 and frequently in 2 Corinthians.

[4] It is used once more in this letter (1 Cor 13:11) and in Rom 2:20; Gal 4:1, 3. The
original reading in 1 Thess 2:7 is certainly ἤπιοι ("gentle"), not νήπιοι (pace Nestle-
Aland).

[5] 1:19, 20, 25, 26, 27; 3:10, 18 (twice), 19, 20.

[6] 1 Cor 6:5; Rom 1:14, 22; 16:19 (Rom 16:27 is not Pauline).

[7] 1 Cor 1:17, 19, 20, 21 (twice), 22, 24, 30; 2:1, 4, 5, 6 (twice), 7, 13; 3:19.

[8] Rom 11:23; 1 Cor 12:8; 2 Cor 1:12. Quite striking are the frequent references to
σοφία in some deutero-Pauline letters: Eph 1:8, 17; 3:10; Col 1:9, 28; 2:3, 23; 3:16; 4:3.

[9] Bultmann (Synoptic Tradition, 166) characterizes these sayings as belonging to a
milieu that is completely different from the Aramaic environment which has produced
almost all other sayings of the synoptic tradition.

[10] I shall discuss the second saying (Matt 11:27 = Luke 10:22) in the following
chapter.

[11] The classical treatments of this passage are Adolf Harnack, The Sayings of Jesus
(New York: Putnam's, 1908) 272–310, and Eduard Norden, Agnostos Theos (Stuttgart:
Teubner, 1912; reprint Darmstadt: Wissenschaftliche Buchgesellschaft, 1956) 277–308.
Most of the following observations have been anticipated by these two treatments.
Harnack (p. 301) already pointed out the close relationship of Matt 11:25–26 and 1 Cor
1:19–21. Norden demonstrated that the formulaic (liturgical) language of this passage
belongs to a tradition which spans the entire spectrum of religious language from the
Wisdom of Solomon to the Hermetic literature. An attempt to illuminate the history-
of-religions context of this passage was made by Thomas Arvedson, Das Mysterium

I praise you, Father, Lord of heaven and earth,
that you have hidden (ἔκρυψας) these things from the wise and clever
(σοφῶν καὶ συνετῶν)
but have revealed (ἀπεκάλυψας) them to the unlearned (νηπίοις).

The hendiadys "the wise and the clever" (σοφοὶ καὶ συνετοί) appears nowhere else in the New Testament. But both terms occur in parallelism in 1 Cor 1:19 in a quote introduced by "it is written."[1] What Paul quotes here is the LXX text of Isa 29:14, "I will destroy the wisdom of the wise and the cleverness of the clever I will thwart" (ἀπολῶ τὴν σοφίαν τῶν σοφῶν καὶ τὴν σύνεσιν τῶν συνετῶν κρύψω).[2] However, also the term "unlearned" (νήπιος) of the saying Matt 11:25 par = Q/Luke 10:21), rarely used by Paul, appears in the context of Paul's discussion of wisdom in Corinth (1 Cor 3:1). In addition, there are several allusions to other sayings which speak about the contrast of hidden and revealed.

In 1 Cor 2:7 Paul speaks of "the hidden wisdom which God has predetermined before the ages." A close parallel appears in Matt 13:35:[3]

I will utter what has been hidden since the foundation of the world.

This saying is introduced by "in order to fulfill what was said by the prophet." But the most likely scriptural reference is Ps 77:2 (LXX) that is only remotely related to this Matthean saying.[4] Other sayings actually parallel this passage more closely. The small sayings collection in Mark 4 contains a similar saying, Mark 4:22:

Christi: Eine Studie zu Mt 11:25–30 (Leipzig and Uppsala: 1937). For a review of previous discussions see A. M. Hunter, "Crux Criticorum—Matt. xi.25–30—A Reappraisal," *NTS* 8 (1961–62) 241–49. The relationship of this passage to wisdom theology has been discussed in detail by J. M. Suggs, *Wisdom, Christology, and Law in Matthew's Gospel* (Cambridge, MA: Harvard University Press, 1970) 71–108.

[1] On the relationship of the passage in 1 Cor 1:19 to the text of Isaiah see Hans Conzelmann, *1 Corinthians: A Commentary on the First Epistle to the Corinthians* (Hermeneia; Philadelphia: Fortress, 1975) 42, n. 21.

[2] Paul has ἀθετήσω instead of κρύψω. Also Justin Martyr *Dial.* 78.8 quotes Isa 29:13–14 with ἀθετήσω. This suggests that the change was not made by Paul, but that both Paul and Justin were dependent on a different version of the LXX, though the two medieval manuscripts of the LXX which also have ἀθετήσω (564 and 301) as well as Eusebius may have been influenced by 1 Cor 1:19.

[3] Harnack (*The Sayings of Jesus*) noticed this parallelism. But few scholars have followed Harnack's lead.

[4] On the question of the relationship of Matt 13:35 to its assumed source, Ps 77:2 (LXX), see Krister Stendahl, *The School of St. Matthew and its Use of the Old Testament* (2d ed.; Philadelphia: Fortress, 1968) 116: the sentence is quoted in a form "differing entirely from the LXX and the later Greek versions."

> There is nothing hidden, except to be revealed;
> nor anything secret that will not come to light.

This saying appears independently also in the *Gospel of Thomas* # 5:

> Recognize what is in your sight,
> and that which is hidden from you
>   will become manifest to you.
> For there is nothing hidden
>   which will not become manifest,
> and nothing covered
>   will remain without being uncovered.

and # 6:

> . . . for all things are plain in the sight of heaven.
> For nothing hidden
>   will not become manifest,
> and nothing covered
>   will remain without being uncovered.

The same contrast between hidden and revealed is employed in 1 Cor 4:5: ". . . the Lord who will illumine the hidden things of darkness and reveal the councils of the hearts." This is best explained as a commentary on the saying Mark 4:22 and the parallel saying preserved in the *Gospel of Thomas.*

To these evident relationships of Paul's language in these chapters of 1 Corinthians to this peculiar group of sayings must be added the occurrence of the strange "quotation from scripture" in 1 Cor 2:9:[1]

> . . . what eye has not seen
> and ear has not heard,
> nor has it risen in the human heart,
> what God has prepared for those who love him.

Whereas Paul introduces the passage by "as it is written," the *Gospel of Thomas* (# 17) quotes it as a saying of Jesus:

> I shall give you what no eye has seen
> and what no ear has heard,
> and what no hand has touched,
> and what has never occurred to the human mind.[2]

---

[1] Attention to this was drawn first by James M. Robinson, "Kerygma and History in the New Testament," in idem and Helmut Koester, *Trajectories through Early Christianity* (Philadelphia: Fortress, 1971) 42–43.

[2] Unless indicated otherwise, translations from writings of the Nag Hammadi Library follow James M. Robinson, *The Nag Hammadi Library in English* (3d completely rev. ed.; San Francisco: Harper & Row, 1988).

This saying is quoted frequently in Gnostic writings in this form.[1] Its source has never been determined with certainty.[2] But it has also made its way into the Synoptic Sayings Source in a somewhat altered form in which it appears in Matt 13:16–17 = Q/Luke 10:23–24:

> Blessed are the eyes that see what you see [and the ears that hear what you hear]. ... many prophets [and righteous men] have desired to see what you see and did not see it, and to hear what you hear and did not hear it.[3]

In Luke, this saying appears in the same context as the sayings discussed above (following upon Matt 11:25–27 = Luke 10:21–22), and it is likely that this is the context in which it also appeared in Q.[4] The first part of the saying (Matt 13:16 = Luke 10:23) parallels 1 Cor 2:9 and *Gos. Thom.* #17 very closely. The second part (Matt 13:17 = Luke 10:24) appears to be a secondary elaboration which tries to set this saying into a framework of historical-biblical reference.[5]

There is another instance in which Paul reveals acquaintance with a saying that is preserved in Q. While the discussion in 1 Corinthians 1–4 is evidently concerned with wisdom theology, one wonders why Paul is introducing also the concern of "the Jews seeking signs" (1 Cor 1:22). James M. Robinson[6] has drawn attention to the fact that this

---

[1] For references to such quotes see Hans Conzelmann, *1 Corinthians*, 64. A fragment of the saying appears in *Dial. Sav.* #57 (140, 1–4: "The Lord said [. . .] ask me about a saying [. . .] which eye has not seen, [nor] have I heard it except from you"). It is also used elsewhere in the writings of the Nag Hammadi Library; cf. *Pr. Paul A* 25–29.

[2] For a full discussion and literature see Conzelmann, *1 Corinthians*, 63–64. Origen (*In Matt.* 5.29 on Matt 27:9) ascribed the saying to the *Apocryphon of Elijah*. Eckard von Nordheim ("Das Zitat des Paulus in 1 Kor 2,9," *ZNW* 65 [1974] 12–20) has argued that the quote is drawn from the Jewish *Vorlage* of the Coptic Christian *Testament of Jacob*.

[3] The two bracketed phrases occur in Matthew only. But the first of these may be original to Q, whereas the second seems to be added by Matthew.

[4] Harnack (*Sayings of Jesus,* 135) assigned the saying to this Q context. Dieter Lührmann (*Die Redaktion der Logienquelle* [WMANT 33; Neukirchen: Neukirchener Verlag, 1969] 61) is undecided. John S. Kloppenborg (*The Formation of Q: Trajectories in Ancient Wisdom Traditions* [Studies in Antiquity and Christianity; Philadelphia: Fortress, 1987] 201–2) places the saying into the context of Q = Luke 9:57–62 + 10:2–16 + 10:21–24, but remarks: "The relation of Q 10:21–22, 23–24 to the rest of the discipleship/mission sermon is more difficult to determine."

[5] It is possible that this elaboration utilizes another saying like the one which is preserved in *Gos. Thom.* #52:

> His disciples said to him, "Twenty-four prophets spoke in Israel, and all of them spoke in you." He said to them, "You have omitted the one living in your presence and have spoken (only) of the dead."

[6] "Kerygma and History," 42.

association of "signs," "kerygma," and "wisdom" occurs in only one other place in early Christianity, namely in Q (Matt 12:38–42; Luke 11:29–32). Here the demand of the Jewish leaders for a "sign" is connected with Jonah's "kerygma" and Solomon's "wisdom."

Finally, in 1 Cor 4:8 there is an ironic reference of Paul to the Corinthians as the ones who have already been satisfied, who have already become rich, and who have become kings (ἐβασιλεύσατε) without him. The verb "to be king" (βασιλεύειν) is used elsewhere in 1 Corinthians only of Christ (15:25).[1] This characterization of the Corinthians is most likely an ironic rendering of a phrase from the saying of *Gos. Thom.* # 2:[2]

> Let him who seeks continue seeking until he finds.
> When he finds, he will become astonished,
> When he becomes astonished, he will be king,
> and when he has become king, he will find rest.[3]

It must also be remembered that the democratization of the concept of kingship genuinely belongs to Jewish wisdom language.[4]

The Corinthians insisted that revelation is communicated to them through "wisdom." That most of the references to wisdom can be substantiated on the basis of wisdom literature has been demonstrated by Ulrich Wilckens.[5] But this general statement can be made more specific: wisdom sayings of Jesus must have been the vehicle on the basis of which the Corinthians claimed to have received this salvation. The various instances in which the language of these chapters reflects known wisdom sayings cannot be accidental. A collection of such sayings must have been known to both Paul and the Corinthians.

[1] Otherwise Paul uses the verb of the believers in Rom 5:17–21. There the believers rule on the basis of their having received grace, whereas in 1 Corinthians 4, those who already are kings are asked whether they can boast of anything they have not received.

[2] Robinson, ("Kerygma and History," 43) suggests that Paul's critical description of his opponents in this verse might recall the woes of the Sermon on the Plain (Luke 6:24–25). This is possible, but it would only explain the phrase, "You have already become rich," not the reference to "having become kings."

[3] This translation follows the Greek text of the *Gospel of Thomas* = *Pap. Oxy.* 654,2 (. . . θαμβηθεὶς βασιλεύσῃ, καὶ βασιλεύσας ἀναπαήσεται). This text is confirmed by the quotation in Clement of Alexandria, *Strom.* 5.14, # 96; in *Strom.* 2.9, # 43, Clement ascribes this saying to the *Gospel According to the Hebrews.*

[4] See especially Wisdom's invitation in Prov 9:6 where some important manuscripts read ἀπολείπετε ἀφροσύνην ἵνα εἰς τὸν αἰῶνα βασιλεύσητε ("leave behind foolishness so that you may become kings forever"). Editors consider this as an intrusion from Sap 6:21 and prefer the reading ζήσεσθε. But even if the latter is the original reading, the former reading may have circulated very early.

[5] *Weisheit und Torheit: Eine exegetisch-religionsgeschichtliche Untersuchung zu 1. Kor. 1 und 2* (BhTh 26; Tübingen: Mohr/Siebeck, 1959).

It is striking, however, that Paul never quotes any of these sayings directly. Rather, in one instance he quotes such a saying with the formula "as it is written" (1 Cor 2:9). In another instance he quotes a scriptural passage upon which such a wisdom saying is based (1 Cor 1:19 where Isa 29:14 is introduced by "it is written"). Paul does not use sayings as authority in a theological debate, neither here nor elsewhere.[1] Sayings of Jesus do not play a role in Paul's understanding of the event of salvation. But in this context, Paul not only alludes to the sayings which were evidently of crucial importance to his opponents, he also adopts their schema of revelation which speaks of the things that were formerly hidden, but have now been revealed.[2] This schema is characteristic of the Q sayings quoted above, though it is not really typical of the Synoptic Sayings Source as a whole.[3] In the genuine Pauline letters, it is used only in 1 Cor 2:6–16, while it occurs frequently in the deutero-Pauline letters[4] and also appears in the secondary ending of Romans (16:25–26).

For the Corinthian wisdom theology this revelation schema, of central importance for their understanding of salvation, is related to the sayings tradition by another element, namely, the recourse to the authority of certain persons: Paul, Apollos, Cephas, possibly Christ (1 Cor 1:12; 3:4–5, 22). This phenomenon is still one of the most puzzling conundrums of New Testament scholarship.[5] There are three elements which together call for an answer: (1) The Corinthians knew a number of sayings which they understood as the revelation of hidden wisdom and life-giving knowledge. (2) Paul explicitly rejects the suggestion that his calling had anything to do with baptism (1 Cor 1:15–17); the claim of belonging to a specific person may have been

---

[1] That Paul has no hesitation to use sayings from the synoptic tradition in debates concerning church order has been demonstrated in an investigation of 1 Corinthians 7 and 9 by David L. Dungan, *The Sayings of Jesus in the Churches of Paul: The Use of the Synoptic Tradition in the Regulation of Early Church Life* (Philadelphia: Fortress, 1971).

[2] See on this schema especially Dieter Lührmann, *Das Offenbarungsverständnis bei Paulus und in paulinischen Gemeinden* (WMANT 16; Neukirchen: Neukirchener Verlag, 1965) 124–33; Nils A. Dahl, "Form-critical Observations on Early Christian Preaching," in idem, *Jesus in the Memory of the Early Church* (Minneapolis: Augsburg, 1976) 31–36.

[3] Kloppenborg, *Formation of Q*, 197–99.

[4] Col 1:26–27; Eph 3:5–10; 2 Tim 1:9–10; Tit 1:2–3; cf. also 1 Pet 1:20. On the use of this revelation schema in 1 Cor 2:6–16 see Conzelmann, *1 Corinthians*, 57–60.

[5] As is well known, the literature on this problem is as immense as is the number of unsatisfactory suggestions for a solution. For a brief survey see Conzelmann, *1 Corinthians*, 33–34.

connected with the relationship of the initiate to his/her baptizer.[1]
(3) Papias, *The Gospel of Thomas, The Apocryphon of James,* and even
Ptolemy's *Letter to Flora* show that apostolic authority, appealed to
with the name of specific apostles, played a role in the transmission of
sayings of Jesus, especially in Gnostic circles.[2]

If all three observations are combined, one must conclude that Paul
faced a Corinthian faction in which believers claimed that baptism
was their initiation into the mystery of wisdom. They understood particular apostles as their mystagogues from whom they received sayings which revealed life-giving wisdom. The dual role of baptizing
mystagogue and guarantor of a tradition of wisdom sayings is quite
natural. Both the action and the sayings can be understood as μυστήριον. Paul's arguments against this understanding of salvation
become much clearer if they are understood against this background.
The well-attested reading μυστήριον, instead of μαρτύριον, in 1 Cor 2:1[3]
as well as Paul's reference to Christ's crucifixion as the "hidden mystery predetermined by God before the ages" (2:7) become understandable.[4] Nowhere else does Paul speak about the cross of Christ in such
terms.

Can the character of the collection of sayings used by the Corinthians be determined with more accuracy? It has already been said that
the Q sayings used here are not typical for this document. In fact, the
connections to Q material do not go beyond Q/Luke 10:21–24 (perhaps
also Q/Luke 11:29–32). The other sayings to which Paul alludes in
1 Corinthians 1–4 do not belong to Q: Matt 13:35; Mark 4:22; *Gos.
Thom.* ## 2, 5–6, and 17. The topic of the revelation of hidden wisdom,
at best marginal in Q, unites all the sayings to which Paul alludes in
this context. It will be seen that it is important for the sayings collections that have been used for the composition of the *Gospel of Thomas*
and which were also known in the Johannine tradition.

---

[1] Here and in the following note I must refer to my previous publications, simply
because this problem has concerned me for a long time. In a review of Ulrich Wilckens,
Weisheit und Torheit (BHTh 26; Tübingen: Mohr/Siebeck, 1959), which was published
in *Gnomon* 33 (1961) 590–95, I made the suggestion that the Corinthians understood
the apostolic authorities they referred to, possibly also Christ, as mystagogues who initiated them through baptism into the mystery of the new faith.

[2] This thesis was first put forward by von Campenhausen, *Formation.* I have
expanded this suggestion in my article "La tradition."

[3] Shunned by previous editions of Nestle's *NT Graece,* but now correctly adopted by
Aland in the 26th edition.

[4] Elsewhere in Paul the singular μυστήριον is used only of specific sayings (cf. 1 Cor
13:2; 15:51), never of the event of Christ's crucifixion or of the gospel as a whole. The
latter use appears for the first time in the Pauline corpus in Eph 3:3–4, 9; 6:19.

2.1.4 SAYINGS IN THE POST-APOSTOLIC WRITINGS

2.1.4.1 Acts and the Pastoral Epistles

There is comparatively little use of sayings of Jesus in the post-apostolic literature. Outside of the genuine Pauline letters, a saying of Jesus is quoted explicitly only once, in Acts 20:35:

> Remember the words of the Lord Jesus that he himself said, "To give is more blessed than to receive" (μακάριόν ἐστιν μᾶλλον διδόναι ἢ λαμβάνειν).

In the Book of Acts, Luke has occasionally used gospel materials,[1] but this saying is nowhere recorded in the known written gospels.[2] This "alleged word of the Lord is actually a Greek aphorism with a slight Christian touch, namely, the selection of μακάριον, "blessed," instead of ἥδιον, "more gladly."[3] 1 Clem. 2.1 (ἥδιον διδόντες ἢ λαμβάνοντες) refers to the same aphorism in the more typically Greek form without indicating any relationship to the tradition of the sayings of Jesus. Luke introduces the saying with a formula that is characteristic for the quotation of sayings from the oral tradition (μνημονεύειν τῶν λόγων τοῦ κυρίου Ἰησοῦ ὅτι αὐτὸς εἶπεν).[4] It is evidently drawn from that tradition to which Luke still had access.

Use of sayings in the deutero-Pauline epistles cannot be demonstrated with certainty. If such sayings are used in Ephesians and Colossians, they are hidden in the parenetic sections of these letters, e.g., "Let no evil talk come out of your mouths" (Eph 4:29; cf. Mark 7:15; Matt 15:11).[5] Even the Pastoral Epistles, written in Asia Minor at a time when several written gospels were known there, show no desire to refer to sayings of Jesus and never appeal to them as authorities. Most remarkable is the instance of the regulation for payment to church officials in 1 Tim 5:17–18:

---

[1] Cf. Acts 6:14: "We have heard that he (Stephen) has said that Jesus the Nazorean will destroy this place." Luke uses the accusation against Jesus from Mark 14:58 (We have heard that he said, "I shall destroy this temple . . .") which he had ommitted in his reproduction of the Markan passion narrative.

[2] There is a parallel in the *Didache* (1.5): "Blessed is he who gives according to the commandment."

[3] Hans Conzelmann, *The Acts of the Apostles: A Commentary on the Acts of the Apostles* (Hermeneia; Philadelphia: Fortress, 1987) 176; see ibid. for Greek parallels.

[4] See below on *1 Clem.* 13.

[5] Davies (*Paul and Rabbinic Judaism*, 139–40) lists eight passages in Colossians for which he assumes dependence upon sayings of Jesus. Although there are some verbal similarities, they are not sufficient to prove the actual employment of the tradition of sayings.

The presbyters who govern well as presiding officers should be deemed worthy of a double compensation, especially those who are engaged in speaking and teaching. For the scripture says, "You shall not muzzle an ox when it is treading out the grain," and "the worker is worthy of his wages."

The first of the two sayings is a scripture quotation (Deut 25:4), also used by Paul in 1 Cor 9:9; but it is debated whether the second quote is either a quote of Luke 10:7 as "scripture" or comes from a lost apocryphon that was accepted as scripture by the author of 1 Timothy.[1] In any case, it is surprizing that there is no appeal to the authority of Jesus.

2.1.4.2 The First Epistle of Peter

A more extensive use of sayings of Jesus appears in the First Epistle of Peter. However, in a critical review of assumptions about the use of sayings of Jesus in 1 Peter, Ernest Best has demonstrated that the case has been vastly overstated.[2] Only the following parallels remain as probable evidence for the use of sayings of Jesus in this New Testament letter:

1 Pet 4:14	Q/Luke 6:22
If you are reproached (ὀνειδίζεσθε) for the name of Christ, you are blessed.	Blessed are you when people hate you, and when they exclude you and and reproach (ὀνειδίσωσιν) you, and cast out your name as evil on account of the Son of man.

1 Pet 3:9	Q/Luke 6:28
Do not return evil for evil or insult for for insult, but on the contrary bless (εὐλογοῦντες) . . .	Bless (εὐλογεῖτε) those who curse you,

1 Pet 3:16	
. . . that, when you are abused, those who revile (οἱ ἐπηρεάζοντες) your good behavior in Christ may be put to shame.	pray for those who revile (τῶν ἐπηρεαζόντων) you.[3]

---

[1] See Martin Dibelius and Hans Conzelmann, *The Pastoral Epistles* (Hermeneia; Philadelphia: Fortress, 1972) 78–79.

[2] Ernest Best, "1 Peter and the Gospel Tradition," *NTS* 16 (1969/70) 95–113.

[3] These are the only two passages in which the verb ἐπηρεάζειν appears in the NT and in the Apostolic Fathers. Cf. Best, "1 Peter," 106–7. Thus this is probably a use of the saying of Q/Luke 6:28, although the two reminiscences of this saying in 1 Peter are separated by several verses.

1 Pet 2:19–20	Q/Luke 6:32–33
For this deserves credit (τοῦτο γὰρ χάρις), if . . . one endures pain while suffering unjustly. For what credit is it (ποῖον γὰρ κλέος), if when you do wrong and are beaten for it you take it patiently? But if you do good (ἀγα-θοποιοῦντες) and suffer for it and take it patiently, that is credit before God (τοῦτο χάρις παρὰ θεῷ).	If you love those who love you, what credit is that to you (ποία ὑμῖν χάρις ἐστίν)? For even sinners love those who love them. For if you also do good to those who do good to you (καὶ ἐὰν ἀγαθοποιῆτε τοὺς ἀγαθοποιοῦντας ὑμᾶς), what credit is that to you? (ποία ὑμῖν χάρις ἐστίν;).

1 Pet 3:14	Matt 5:10
But even if you suffer for righteousness sake (διὰ δικαιοσύνην), you are blessed (μακάριοι).	Blessed (μακάριοι) are those who suffer for righteousness sake (ἕνεκεν δικαιοσύνης).

1 Pet 2:12b	Matt 5:16b
Maintain good conduct among the Gentiles, so that in case they speak against you as wrongdoers, they may see your good deeds (ἐκ τῶν καλῶν ἔργων ἐποπτεύοντες) and glorify (δοξά-σωσιν) God (τὸν θεόν) on the day of visitation.	Let your light so shine before people that they may see your good works (ἴδωσιν ὑμῶν τὰ καλὰ ἔργα) and glorify (δοξάσωσιν) your Father who is in heaven (τὸν πατέρα ὑμῶν τὸν ἐν τοῖς οὐρανοῖς).

In the first three instances (1 Pet 4:14; 3:9 and 16; 2:19–20) the author of this Epistle uses material that belongs to the nucleus of the Q materials for the Sermon on the Plain/Sermon on the Mount (Q/Luke 6:22, 28, 32–33).[1] It is the same collection that also provided the sayings for Rom 12–14.

The other two uses of sayings of Jesus in 1 Peter (3:14; 2.12b) concern sayings of a typical Matthean character. Both Matt 5:10 and Matt 5:16b appear to be Matthean additions to the Q material that formed the basis for this section of the Sermon on the Mount. However, it is unlikely that these sayings are creations of the author of the Gospel of Matthew. Rather, they were already part of a Jewish-Christian document that Matthew used in chapters 5–7.[2] The makarism of those persecuted for righteousness' sake as well as the saying

---

[1] There are several other passages in 1 Peter for which dependence upon sayings of Jesus in Luke's Gospel has been assumed. For a listing and for arguments against this assumption see Best, "1 Peter," 103–8.

[2] See the several articles by Hans Dieter Betz, now collected in his *Essays on the Sermon on the Mount* (Philadelphia: Fortress, 1985).

about the visibility of the good works of the disciples[1] belong to this originally independent composition.[2] We must, therefore, conclude that 1 Peter had access to a collection of sayings that was related to or identical with Matthew's special Jewish-Christian source. Whether also the Q sayings used by 1 Peter came from this same source is difficult to determine because there is not enough extant verbal agreement with the text of either Matthew or Luke in the quotations as they appear in 1 Peter. A use of any of the Synoptic Gospels is not apparent.[3]

2.1.4.3 The First Epistle of Clement

1 Clement quotes sayings of Jesus twice, in 13.1–2 and in 46.8.[4] *1 Clem.* 13.1–2 introduces the quotation with the formula:

> Especially remember the words of the Lord Jesus which he spoke when he was teaching gentleness and longsuffering; for he spoke thus (μάλιστα μνημνημένοι τῶν λόγων τοῦ κυρίου Ἰησοῦ . . . οὕτως γὰρ εἶπεν).

A similar formula is used in *1 Clem.* 46.7–8:

> Remember the words of Jesus; for he said (μνήσθητε τῶν λόγων τοῦ κυρίου Ἰησοῦ, εἶπεν γάρ).

The use of the verb "to remember" (μνημονεύειν) as well as the aorist tense "he said" (εἶπεν) instead of the present "he/it says" (λέγει)—typical for quotations from Scripture—indicates that oral tradition is cited.[5]

The quotation in *1 Clem.* 13.2 consists of seven brief sentences of similar structure of which all but one have synoptic parallels:

[1] Betz (*Essays,* 5) calls this saying "a programmatic passage" of this document.

[2] Also Best ("1 Peter," 109) argues for this possibility. He observes that the term δικαιοσύνη and its cognates occur in contexts that "very often represent material which must have come to Matthew in the tradition peculiar to him. In fact, while the term δικαιοσύνη appears five times in the Sermon on the Mount (5:6, 10, 20; 6:1, 3), it is used only twice elsewhere in the Gospel of Matthew (3:15; 21:23)—both times in connection with John the Baptist.

[3] Best ("1 Peter," 99–102) has demonstrated that there is not a single instance in which the use of Mark or of Markan sayings materials can be assumed, nor does 1 Peter show any acquaintance with John or the Johannine tradition (Best, "1 Peter," 96–99).

[4] On these two quotations see Koester, *Synoptische Überlieferung,* 12–19; on the first of these quotations also Best, "1 Peter," 112–113.

[5] See above on the quotation formula in Acts 20:35. Closely related is the composite form of the verb "to remember" (ἀπομνημονεύειν) which is used in the Papias fragments, see above # 1.7.2. On the use of this formula in Polycarp of Smyrna's letter to the Philippians see Koester, *Synoptische Überlieferung,* 5.

1 Clem. 13.2

Be merciful that
  you may obtain mercy.

Forgive,
  that you may be forgiven.

As you do,
  so shall it be done unto you.

As you give,
  so shall it be given to you.

As you judge
  so shall you be judged.
As you are kind,
  so shall kindness be shown to you.

With what measure you measure,
  it shall be measured to you.

Matt 5:7

Blessed are the merciful,
  because they will obtain mercy

Matt 6:12

Forgive us our debts,
  as also we have forgiven our
    debtors.[1]

Q/Luke 6:31 (Matt 7:12)

As you want that people
    should do to you,
do also to them.

Q/Luke 6:38a

Give,
  and it shall be given to you.

Q/Matt 7:2a (Luke 6:37a)

By which criterion you judge,
  you shall be judged.
————
————

Q/Matt 7:2b (Luke 6:38b)

And in what measure you measure,
  it shall be measured to you.

What *1 Clement* is quoting is a fixed small catechism. The seven[2] parallel well-balanced sentences reveal that it was formulated for oral transmission. Six of the seven sentences have synoptic parallels, and all these parallels appear in the Sermon on the Mount and/or Sermon on the Plain (Matthew 5–7 and Luke 6:20–49). However, the affinity to Matthew is striking, while there is very little that parallels anything in Luke or in the version of Q used by Luke. The first sentence is paralleled by one of the beatitudes added in Matthew's version of the Sermon, though probably preserved in a more original form in *1 Clem.* 13.2. The second sentence also has only a Matthean parallel in the fifth petition of the Lord's Prayer; however, the command of Mark 11:25 to forgive each other resembles the formulation in *1 Clem.* 13.2

[1] A close parallel appears in Mark 11:25 = Matt 6:14, "Forgive, if you have anything against anyone, so that your Father also, who is in heaven, may forgive your debts."

[2] The number "seven" is not accidental; see Betz, *Essays,* 23; the numbers eight (or seven) and ten express perfection.

more closely. The third sentence, the Golden Rule, shares the positive version[1] with both Matthew and Luke, but is formulated differently; since this proverb is so widespread in antiquity,[2] a particular
source for its quotation is not required. The fourth sentence ("As you
give . . .") has no parallel in Matthew. It is a free logion that Luke has
inserted into Q/Luke 6:36–37a, 38b = Matt 5:48; 7:2. The parallel to
the following sentence in *1 Clement* appears in the same cluster of Q
sayings; however, its formulation resembles Matt 7:2a which has no
parallel in Luke. To the same context belongs the Q parallel to the last
sentence of *1 Clem.* 13.2 which shares with Matt 7:2b the simple form
of the verb "to measure" (μετρηθήσεται) instead of Luke's (6: 38b) probably secondary composite form (ἀντιμετρηθήσεται). However, the
parallels to Matt 7:2 a and b are separated by an insertion which has
no parallel anywhere in the canonical gospels. An admonition to show
kindness is incorporated in the parenetical section of Ephesians
(γίνεσθε δὲ εἰς ἀλλήλους χρηστοί, 4:32), and the verb is used once by
Paul in 1 Cor 13:4 (ἡ ἀγάπη . . . χρηστεύεται). Also the noun (χρηστότης)
appears in parenetical usage.[3] Thus, it is easily understandable that
such a parenetical sentence could be added to a catechism composed of
sayings of Jesus.[4]

It is evident that this passage of *1 Clement* cannot be explained as a
secondary composition based upon the canonical texts of Matthew and
Luke (and possibly also Mark). But neither could one argue for direct
dependence upon the Synoptic Sayings Source. These sayings belong
to the same complex of logia which we encountered already in Romans
12–14 and in 1 Peter and, once more, there may be traces of the editing
of Q materials upon which Matthew based his Sermon on the Mount.
Since both 1 Peter and *1 Clement* were written in Rome at approximately the same time, it is quite possible that they are both witnesses
to the existence in Rome of a sayings book that was identical with, or

---

[1] The negative version of the Golden Rule ("What you do not want to be done to you,
also do not do to others") appears more often, also in Christian texts; cf. *Did.* 1.2b, Acts
15:29 Western text.

[2] Albrecht Dihle (*Die Goldene Regel: Eine Einführung in die Geschichte der antiken
und frühchristlichen Vulgärethik* [Studienhefte zur Altertumswissenschaft 7; Göttingen: Vandenhoeck & Ruprecht, 1962]) presents an overview and a discussion of its
usage.

[3] Gal 5:22; Col 3:12; *Diogn.* 10.4. Elsewhere the noun usually describes the attitude
or action of God; cf. Rom 2:4; 11:22; 2 Cor 8:6; Eph 2:7; Tit 3:4; *2 Clem.* 15.5; 19.1; Ign.
Mg. 10.1; *Sm.* 7.1; *Diogn.* 8.8; 9.1–2, 6.

[4] Massaux (*Influence de L'Évangile de Saint Matthieu,* 12–13) recognizes the special
catechetical rythm of the passage, but argues for dependence upon the Sermon on the
Mount. Köhler (*Rezeption des Matthäusevangeliums,* 67–71) judges dependence upon
Matthew as "quite improbable."

related to, the Jewish-Christian writing which, as Hans Dieter Betz[1] has argued, was the source of Matthew 5–7.

But *1 Clement* also knew sayings of Jesus which did not belong to this source. This is evident in the second quote of Jesus' sayings in this letter, *1 Clem.* 46.8, to which a synoptic parallel is found in Mark (9:42) as well as in Q (Luke 17:1–2). While Luke seems to have preserved the original wording of Q, Matt 18:6–7 conflated it with the Markan version:[2]

1 Clem. 46.8	Synoptic Parallels
Woe to that man (τῷ ἀνθρώπῳ)	τῷ ἀνθρώπῳ only in Matt 18:7
	Mark 14:21
	Woe to that man through whom the Son of man is handed over;
it were good for him, if he had not been born,	it were good for him, if that man had not been born.
than that he should offend one of my select (ἐκλεκτῶν μου).	Mark 9:42: μικρῶν τούτων τῶν πιστευόντων = Matt 18:6 who adds εἰς ἐμέ.
It were better (κρεῖττον) for him	Matt: συμφέρει Mark: καλόν ἐστιν Luke 17:2: λυσιτελεῖ
that a millstone (μύλον)	Matt and Mark: μύλος ὀνικός. Luke 17:2: λίθος μυλικός.
be hung on him (περιτεθῆναι)	Matt: κρεμασθῇ. Mark and Luke: περικεῖται.
and he be drowned (καταποντισθῆναι)	Matt: καταποντισθῇ. Mark: βέβληται. Luke: ἔριπτει.
in the sea (εἰς τὴν θάλασσαν)	Matt: ἐν τῷ πελάγει τῆς θαλάσσης. Mark and Luke: εἰς τὴν θάλασσαν.
than that he should turn aside one of my select.	

Although the quote of *1 Clem.* 46.8 shares some terms with Matthew[3]

---

[1] See his *Essays*, passim.

[2] For a detailed comparison of the Greek texts see my *Synoptic Tradition*, 16–19.

[3] Köhler (*Rezeption des Matthäusevangeliums*, 62–64) finds in the appearance of the term καταποντίζομαι a strong reference for dependence upon Matthew, but assigns the quotation to the less probable category of "possible" dependence. Massaux (*Influence de L'Évangile de Saint Matthieu*, 24–27) argues for a combination of several gospel texts in this quotation.

in general and in its structure (Matthew reverses the sequence of the woe and the sentence about offences), it is more closely related to the Q version. Indeed, all terms used by the quote in *1 Clement* could have been part of the original Q version. Peculiar is the parallel with the woe in Mark 14:21. However, this Markan woe against the man who hands over the Son of man is a secondary formulation for which Mark may have used a saying like the introduction to Q/Luke 17:1-2.[1] In any case, while *1 Clem.* 13.2 reflects sayings from one of the early collections, which is also attested elsewhere, *1 Clem.* 46:8 may not have been derived from a written source *but* from the free tradition of sayings.

either *pre - Q* *or*

There may be several other passages in which *1 Clement* is dependent upon the synoptic sayings tradition. *1 Clem.* 24.4–5 recalls the parable of the Sower (Mark 4:3–9):[2]

> Let us take the crops: how and in what way does the sowing take place? "The sower went forth" and cast each of the seeds into the ground, and parched and bare they fall on to the ground and perish; then from their decay the greatness of the providence of the Lord raises them up, and from one grain many more grow and bring forth fruit.

The sentence "The sower went forth" (ἐξῆλθεν ὁ σπείρων) agrees verbatim with the first sentence of the parable of the Sower in all three synoptic versions (Mark 4:3 parr.) and in the *Gospel of Thomas* (# 9).[3] However, *1 Clement* does not give any indication that he is quoting a parable of Jesus but summarizes it, like the parable of the Vine in chapter 23.4 and the story of the Phoenix in chapter 25, without any reference to source or authority. The parable was certainly taken from the tradition in which this as well as other parables of Jesus were more generally known.

It is possible that there are other instances in which the formulation of a particular passage or sentence is influenced by a saying of Jesus. One could quote as such an instance *1 Clem.* 16.17:

> ... for if the Lord was thus humble-minded (ἐταπεινοφρόνησεν), what shall we do who have come through him under his yoke (ζυγός) of grace.

excellence

If there is indeed a recollection of Jesus' invitation to come under his yoke (ζυγός), because he is gentle and humble (ταπεινός) in his heart

---

[1] Lührmann, *Markusevangelium*, 237.

[2] Massaux (*Influence de L'Évangile de Saint Matthieu*, 32) does not argue for a dependence upon a written gospel, but assumes that *1 Clement* developed further the image of the seed which he took from the early Christian literary tradition.

[3] Mark 4:3 and *Gos. Thom.* 9 begin the sentence with ἰδού.

Come ye who are humble-minded and gentle at heart
come under my yoke of excellence
and you will find rest for your "souls" per

(Matt 11:29), it must be remembered that this was a free saying circulating in the oral tradition, attested also in the *Gospel of Thomas* (# 90).[1]

2.1.4.4 *The Epistle of James*

Were the Epistle of James indeed written by Jesus' brother James, the numerous instances in this epistle which have words and phrases in common with sayings of Jesus could be explained as personal reminiscences of these sayings.[2] But scholarship has seriously challenged this assumption of authorship. Martin Dibelius, in his influential commentary which was first published in 1920,[3] has argued that the author's affinity with Jesus' sayings is due to the following three factors: (1) formal similarity, since both consist to a large degree of parenesis; (2) similarity of style (use of short, pointed imperatives and a fixed group of metaphors); (3) both share the same convictions (ethical rigorism, warnings against worldly attitudes, piety of the poor).[4] Even closer connections exist because a large portion of Jesus' sayings in the Synoptic Gospels consists of early Christian parenesis. Therefore, any writing that is made up primarily of parenesis, like the Epistle of James, is likely to include phrases and sentences which have parallels in these gospels.[5]

There are no explicit quotations of Jesus' sayings in James, and many of the assumed parallels, as Deppe has shown in his dissertation,[6] are simply due to similarities in wording, terminology, and/or

---

[1] It is typical for the methodological weakness of Köhler's approach that he points out that the "yoke of grace" is the "yoke of Jesus" and finds "great nearness to Matthew"; therefore, this "passage can be reconciled with the assumption of the dependence (of *1 Clement*) upon Matthew," although he admits that it cannot carry the burden of proof (*Rezeption des Matthäusevangeliums,* 60). Unfortunately, Köhler never considers seriously the existence of the oral tradition or of early collections of sayings.

[2] In German scholarship, this position has been most strongly defended by Gerhard Kittel, "Der geschichtliche Ort des Jakobusbriefes," *ZNW* 41 (1942) 71–105. The extent to which this explanation is still held today has been described recently by Dean B. Deppe, *The Sayings of Jesus in the Epistle of James* (Dissertation Amsterdam, Free University, 1989). James B. Adamson, in his commentary (*The Epistle of James* [New International Commentary to the New Testament; Grand Rapids: Eerdmans, 1976]) writes about the similarities between James's Epistle and the Canonical Gospels: "We ourselves believe that this is at least mainly due not merely to James's early sharing some of the oral and written evidence to which those Gospels sooner or later were indebted, but to his own personal witness of the life and teaching of Jesus."

[3] English translation: Martin Dibelius, *James: A Commentary on the Epistle of James,* rev. by Heinrich Greeven (Hermeneia, Philadelphia: Fortress, 1976).

[4] Dibelius-Greeven, *James,* 28.

[5] Ibid., 28–29.

[6] Deppe, *Sayings of Jesus;* see especially the summary on pp. 219–21. Deppe (pp. 237–50) also presents cogent arguments against the assumption of dependency in

content. Only eight instances remain in which one can assume the use of the same tradition of a saying or a sentence of parenesis:

James	Synoptic Parallels
1:5	Q/Luke 11:9 (Matt 7:7)

But if someone among you lacks wisdom, let him ask from God—who gives to all without hesitation and without grumbling —and it will be given to him.

Ask, and it will be given to you, seek, and you will find, knock, and it will be opened to you.

4:2c–3

. . . you do not have, because you do not ask; you ask and you do not receive, because you ask with the wrong motive. . .

| 2:5 | Q/Luke 6:20b (Matt 5:3) |

Has Jesus not chosen those who are poor before the world[1] to be rich in faith and heirs of the kingdom which he has promised to those who love him?

Blessed are the poor (Matt adds: in spirit), for yours is the kingdom of God.

| 4:9 | Q/Luke 6:21b (Matt 5:4) |

Be wretched and mourn (πενθήσετε) and weep (κλαύσετε)! Let your laughter (γέλως) be turned to mourning (πένθος) and your joy to sorrow (ἡ χαρὰ εἰς κατήφειαν).

Blessed are those who weep (κλαί-οντες) now, because you will laugh (γελάσετε).

| 4:10 | Q/Luke 14:11 (Matt 23:12) |

Humble yourself before the Lord, and he will exalt you

Everyone who exalts himself will be humbled, and he who humbles himself will be exalted

(ταπεινώθητε ἐνώπιον κυρίου καὶ ὑψώσει ὑμᾶς).

(πᾶς ὁ ὑψῶν ἑαυτὸν ταπεινωθήσεται, καὶ ὁ ταπεινῶν ἑαυτὸν ὑψωθήσεται).

"The Twenty-five Most Frequently Mentioned Parallels."

[1] This translation presupposes the text πτωχοὶ τῷ κόσμῳ (p[74] ℵ A B C) rather than "the poor in the world" (πτωχοὶ ἐν τῷ κόσμῳ, some minuscules) or "the poor of the world" (πτωχοὶ τοῦ κόσμου, most manuscripts); see the discussion in Dibelius-Greeven, *James,* 137.

5:1	Luke 6:24–25
Come, you rich (οἱ πλούσιοι), weep (κλαύσετε) and wail (ὀλολύζοντες) at the miseries which are coming upon you.	(Woe to you, the rich (τοῖς πλουσίοις), for you have received your consolation. Woe to you who are full now, for you shall go hungry. Woe to you who laugh (οἱ γελῶντες) now, for you shall weep and mourn (πενθήσετε καὶ κλαύσετε).

5:2–3a	Q/Matt 6:20 (Luke 12:33b)
Your wealth has rotted (σέσηπεν) and your garments are moth-eaten (σητό-βρωτα), your gold and silver has rusted (κατίωται) and their rust will devour your flesh like fire	Lay up for yourselves treasures in heaven where neither moth nor rust corrode (οὔτε σὴς οὔτε βρῶσις ἀφανίζει) and where thieves do not dig through and steal. (Luke has only this last phrase.)

5:12	Matt 5:34–37
Above all, my brothers and sisters, do not swear (μὴ ὀμνύετε), either by heaven or by earth, *or by Jerusalem* nor with any other oath.	But I say to you not to swear at all (μὴ ὀμόσαι ὅλως), either by heaven, (because it is the throne of God,) or by earth (because it is the footstool of his feet) or by Jerusalem (because it is the city of the great king;) nor shall you swear by your head, because you cannot make a single hair white or black.
Let your yes be yes and your no be no (ἤτω δὲ ὑμῶν τὸ ναὶ ναὶ καὶ τὸ οὒ οὔ), so that you may not fall under condemnation.	Let what you say be "Yes, yes" and "No, no." Everything beyond this is from evil.

Jas 1:5 and 4:2c–3 have a parallel in a Q saying and it is certainly an expansion of the saying about prayer and faith. However, this saying of Jesus is so widespread in early Christianity[1] that a reference to a specific source is not warranted. The reference to God who gives "without grumbling" may reflect an older Jewish saying about giving rather than a saying of Jesus.[2]

The designation of the poor as the heirs of the kingdom in Jas 2:5 seems to echo the respective beatitude of the Q version of the Sermon

---

[1] See also John 16:23–24; *Gos. Thom.* 92, 94. See the discussion in Deppe, *Sayings of Jesus,* 68–70.

[2] Dibelius, *James,* 79.

on the Mount/Sermon on the Plain, without the typical Matthean interpolation "in spirit" (τῷ πνεύματι). However, nothing indicates that the author was referring to a specific beatitude of Jesus; rather, he simply states a principle of the traditional piety of the poor.[1]

Also Jas 4:9 exhibits some verbal similarities to a beatitude from the same context (Luke 6:21, following upon the blessing of the poor, Luke 6:20b). Yet, the meaning is quite different: instead of a blessing, one reads a call for repentance. In Jas 4:10 another allusion to a Q saying (Q/Luke 14:11) follows. The basic statement of Luke 14:11 is changed into an imperative and incorporated into the sequence of sayings calling for repentance; this entire sequence (vss. 7–10) may have been formulated in the parenetic tradition and was appropriated by James as a unit.[2] Thus, neither 4:9 nor 4:10 reveal a direct acquaintance of the author with Q.

Materials from the tradition of the pious poor in Jas 5:1–3 show close resemblances to several sayings from the synoptic tradition. The closest parallel to Jas 5:1 appears in special Lukan materials, the woes against the rich of Luke. In both cases, the style is prophetic, though only Luke has formulated the threats against the rich as "woes" in order to establish a formal contrast to the preceding beatitudes (Luke 6:20–23). Luke has interpolated these woes into his Q materials; they are drawn from the same tradition which has also informed James' piety of the poor. The following sentences (Jas 5:2–3a) have a parallel in the Q saying of Matt 6:20 and Luke 12:33b, but in this instance they show a closer resemblance to the Matthean version (Matt 6:20); an even closer parallel is provided by *1 Enoch* 97.8–10. Also here the terminology is not new; it had already become well established in several descriptions of the perishability of wealth in Jewish writings.[3]

In Jas 5:12 there can be no question that James is quoting the same injunction that Matthew used in the third antithesis of the Sermon on the Mount. James has preserved an earlier form.[4] The reasons given for not swearing by heaven, earth, and Jerusalem seem to be secondary explanations,[5] and the injunction against swearing by one's own head is apparently a later expansion.[6] Moreover, James's "Let your

[1] Dibelius-Greeven, *James,* Introduction, chap. 6, pp. 39–45.

[2] Ibid., 208.

[3] Ibid., 236.

[4] For the following see the detailed analysis and comparison of the two passages by Georg Strecker, "Die Antithesen des Bergpredigt," *ZNW* 69 (1978) 56–63.

[5] Strecker ("Antithesen der Bergpredigt," 60–61) points out that these expansions rest upon the LXX text of Isa 66:1 and Ps 47:3.

[6] Bultmann (*Synoptic Tradition,* 135) points out that "the first three examples, swearing by heaven, by the earth, and by Jerusalem, reject such oaths for being encroachments upon the sphere of God's majesty," whereas the last example, swearing

possible Jewish source!

IMP orig

yes be yes" recommends truthfulness in speech, whereas Matthew's "Let what you say be 'Yes, yes'" seems to be a substitute oath formula.[1] In the conclusion, the threat of judgment against untruthfulness in James's version was replaced in Matthew by a condemnation of any affirmation which goes beyond this substitute oath formula.[2] Jas 5:12 is certainly not dependent upon Matthew, but draws the saying from the parenetical tradition. It is difficult to say whether this tradition knew the injunction as a saying of Jesus. This is possible, although a quotation formula is not used.[3]

The comparison of similar sentences and materials in the Epistle of James and in the Synoptic Gospels does not reveal the use of any particular collections of sayings, but rests upon James's use of parenetic traditions which also provided materials to these gospels and/or their sources. It is quite possible that some of these sayings and injunctions were known to James as sayings of Jesus.

common source!

IMP

2.2 The Gospel of Thomas[4]

2.2.1 DISCOVERY AND ATTESTATION

A Coptic translation of the *Gospel of Thomas* was first identified in Cairo in the year 1948 in one of the codices of the Nag Hammadi Library which had been found in upper Egypt near Chenoboskion in the fall of 1945.[5] In the spring of 1948, when eleven of the original thir-

---

by one's head, "makes swearing ridiculous." Bultmann wonders whether the first three examples are later additions. That, however, is unlikely, unless one wants to argue that James is dependent upon Matthew.

[1] For the discussion of this question see Deppe, *Sayings of Jesus,* 136–40. "The teaching no longer says what one ought to *be* (i.e., truthful), but rather what one should *say* if one had to make an affirmation" (Dibelius-Greeven, *James,* 251).

[2] Strecker ("Antithesen der Bergpredigt") 57–58 shows that Matthew's last clause reveals typically Matthean language.

[3] Dibelius-Greeven (*James,* 251) considers this the only instance in which one can safely assume that the author of this epistle is indeed using a saying of Jesus. See also the discussion in Deppe, *Sayings of Jesus.*

[4] The best general presentation of the *Gospel of Thomas* with extensive bibliographies was published by Francis T. Fallon and Ron Cameron, "The Gospel of Thomas: A Forschungsbericht and Analysis," *ANRW* 2.25/5, 4195–4251.

[5] The best critical account of the story of the discovery is James M. Robinson, "The Discovery of the Nag Hammadi Codices," *BA* 42 (1979) 206–24. For a brief description see James M. Robinson, "Introduction," in idem, ed., *The Nag Hammadi Library,* 22–26; John Dominic Crossan, *Four Other Gospels: Shadows on the Contours of Canon* (Winston: Minneapolis, 1985) 15–23. The first lengthy and sometimes mystifying account was published by Jean Doresse, *Les livres secrets des Gnostiques d'Égypte*

teen codices of the Nag Hammadi Library were still in the hands of
the Cairo antiquities dealer, Phokion Tano, Jean Doresse was
retained to photograph some of the manuscripts and to prepare an
inventory of the tractates. At the end of the second tractate of Codex
II, Doresse read the words inscribed in titular fashion in the middle of
the page: πεγαγγελιον πκατα θωμας ("The Gospel According to Thomas").[1] In 1957, Pahor Labib, the director of the Coptic Museum in
Cairo, published a series of photographs of leaves from the new codices, among them the pages from Codex II containing the *Gospel of
Thomas*.[2] Within a year, Jean Doresse published a French translation,[3] and the East-German scholar Johannes Leipoldt published a
German translation of the *Gospel of Thomas*.[4] The Coptic text was
published a year later with French, German, and English translations.[5]

It soon became apparent[6] that some parts of the *Gospel of Thomas*
had indeed been known for many decades: three Greek papyri with
sayings of Jesus, all three written ca. 200 CE, had been found in Oxyrhynchus in Egypt in the years 1897, 1903, and 1904 respectively.[7]
These papyri are actually portions of the Greek original of the Coptic
Gospel of Thomas. *Pap. Oxy. 1* preserves the Greek original of *Gos.
Thom.* 28–33, *Pap. Oxy. 654* the first seven sayings, and *Pap. Oxy. 655*
sayings 37–40 of this gospel.[8] The discovery of the full Coptic text

---

(Paris: Librairie Plon, 1958; fully revised ET: *The Secret Books of the Egyptian Gnostics*
(New York: Viking, 1960) 116–36.

[1] Doresse, *Secret Books,* 120.

[2] *Coptic Gnostic Papyri in the Coptic Museum of Old Cairo.* Vol. I (Cairo: Government Press [Antiquities Department], 1956).

[3] *Secret Books,* 333–83.

[4] "Ein neues Evangelium: Das Koptische Thomasevangelium übersetzt und bespro-
chen," *ThLZ* 83 (1958) cols 481–496; reprinted in Johannes Leipoldt and Hans-Martin
Schenke, *Koptisch-gnostische Schriften aus den Papyrus-Codices von Nag Hamadi* (ThF
20; Hamburg-Bergstedt: Reich and Evangelischer Verlag, 1959).

[5] A. Guillaumont. H.-Ch. Puech, G. Quispel, W. Till and Yassah 'Abd al Masih, eds.,
The Gospel According to Thomas: Coptic Text Established and Translated (Leiden:
Brill, 1959); a reduced reprint of the editio princeps of 1959 with English translation
was published recently: San Francisco: Harper & Row, 1984.

[6] Doresse (*Secret Books,* 227) ascribes this discovery to the French scholar H.-Ph.
Puech.

[7] They were published by B. P. Grenfell and A. S. Hunt, ΛΟΓΙΑ ΙΗΣΟΥ: *Sayings of
Our Lord* (Egypt Exploration Fund; London: Frowde, 1897); idem, *New Sayings of
Jesus and Fragment of a Lost Gospel from Oxyrhynchus* (Egypt Exploration Fund; London: Frowde, 1904); idem, *The Oxyrhynchus Papyri, Part IV* (London: Egypt Exploration Fund, 1904) 1–28.

[8] For the relationship of the Greek fragments to the Coptic text see Fallon and Cameron, "Forschungsbericht," 4201–4.

made it possible to reconstruct the entire Greek text of these fragmentary papyri.[1] The definitive publication of the Coptic text and the reconstructed Greek fragments, together with translations and introductions, are now available in a volume of Nag Hammadi Studies edited by Bentley Layton.[2]

The three Oxyrhynchus Papyri had been widely discussed in the first decades of this century and valued highly by some scholars as possibly original sayings of Jesus;[3] but it was not clear whether these three papyri belonged to any particular gospel. No doubt all three Oxyrhynchus fragments are part of the Greek text of the *Gospel of Thomas*. Yet they are not portions of one single manuscript and they do not necessarily represent the Greek text from which the Coptic translation was made. Yet they do not derive from the Coptic text, but are independent developments of the Greek original underlying the Coptic translation.[4] Thus the *Gospel of Thomas* is well attested as a Greek gospel writing that circulated widely during the 2d century. The attestation is just as strong as that for the canonical gospels.[5]

That is affirmed by the early testimonies to this gospel. The earliest reference to the *Gospel of Thomas* appears in Hippolytus *Refutatio* 5.7.20 (222–235 CE in Rome):[6]

---

[1] The first reconstruction of the very fragmentary Greek texts was published by Joseph A. Fitzmyer, "The Oxyrhynchus Logoi of Jesus and the Coptic Gospel According to Thomas," now in idem, *Essays on the Semitic Background of the New Testament* (London: Chapman, 1971) 355–433; corrections were presented by Robert A. Kraft, "Oxyrhynchus Papyrus 655 Reconsidered," *HTR* 54 (1961) 253–62. A new edition of these Greek texts by Harold W. Attridge is now available in Bentley Layton, ed., *Nag Hammadi Codex II, 2–7* (see the following note).

[2] "The Gospel According to Thomas," in Bentley Layton, ed., *Nag Hammadi Codex II, 2–7 Together with XIII, 2*, Brit. Lib. Or. 4926(1) and P. Oxy. 1, 654, 655* (NHS 20–21; Leiden: Brill, 1989) 38–130: "Introduction" by Helmut Koester, "Critical Edition" by Bentley Layton, "Translation" by Thomas O. Lambdin, "Appendix: The Greek Fragments" by Harold W. Attridge. An earlier edition with French translation and commentary was published in the same series by Jacque-E. Ménard, *L'Évangile selon Thomas* (NHS 5; Leiden: Brill, 1975). Numerous translations have appeared during the last three decades. Good English translations are most conveniently available in Ron Cameron, *The Other Gospels: Non-Canonical Gospel Texts* (Philadelphia: Westminster, 1982) 23–37; Bentley Layton, *The Gnostic Scriptures: A New Translation with Annotations and Introductions* (Garden City, NY: Doubleday, 1987) 376–99. Thomas O. Lambdin's translation is also available in Robinson, ed., *Nag Hammadi Library*, 126–38. For a survey of publications of the text, translations, and basic research tools see Fallon and Cameron, "Forschungsbericht," 4197–4201.

[3] The respective literature is listed in Hennecke-Schneemelcher-Wilson, *NT Apocrypha*, 1. 99 and 105.

[4] Attridge, "The Greek Fragments," in Layton, ed., *Nag Hammadi Codex II*, 99.

[5] See my article, "Apocryphal and Canonical Gospels," 107–12.

[6] The references to the *Gospel of Thomas* are assembled by Harold W. Attridge, "The Greek Fragments," in Layton, ed., *Nag Hammadi Codex II*, 103–9. For a discussion of

2 The Collection of the Sayings of Jesus

(The Naassenes) speak ... of a nature which is both hidden and revealed at the same time, and which they call the thought-for kingdom of heaven which is in a human being. They transmit a tradition concerning this in the Gospel entitled "According to Thomas," which states expressly, "The one who seeks me will find me in children of seven years and older, for there, hidden in the fourteenth aeon, I am revealed."[1]

The second early attestation comes from the Alexandrian theologian Origen *Hom. in Luc.* 1 (233 CE):

For there circulates also the Gospel according to Thomas and the Gospel according to Matthias and many others.[2]

The *Gospel of Thomas* was also used and valued highly by Mani. This is mentioned by several Church Fathers who claim that the Manichaean gospel was actually written by one of Mani's disciples named Thomas. However, Augustine refers in this context to the phrase "he will never experience death" which echoes the first saying of the *Gospel of Thomas*.[3]

2.2.2 JUDAS THOMAS

The traditions that the apostle Thomas was the missionary to India are as old as the end of the 2d century.[4] The *Acts of Thomas,* written in eastern Syria at the beginning of the 3d century, reports the mission of the apostle Thomas to the court of King Gundaphoros (chapter 17), thus locating the activity of Thomas in North India. However, in chapters 3 and 4, the *Acts of Thomas* depict Thomas as embarking on a

---

the testimonies see also Fallon and Cameron, "Forschungsbericht," 4204.

[1] The phrase "a little child of seven" appears in saying 5 of the Coptic *Gospel of Thomas.*

[2] Later writers who also refer to these two gospels are apparently dependent upon Origen: Eusebius *Hist. eccl.* 3.25.6; Jerome *Comm. in Matt.* Prologue; Ambrose *Expositio evangelii Lucae* 1.2. See further, Attridge, "Greek Fragments," passim.

[3] *Contra epistula fundamenti* 11. See also Cyril of Jerusalem *Catechesis* 4.36; 6.31. The *Decretum Gelasianum* (5th century) lists among the heretical books "A Gospel attributed to Thomas which the Manichaean use."

[4] A survey of the relevant information can be found in A. F. J. Klijn, *The Acts of Thomas: Introduction, Text, Commentary* (NovTSup 5; Leiden: Brill, 1962) 27–29. For a discussion of the Thomas tradition and Thomas writings see Crossan, *Four Other Gospels,* 23–26. Curiously, one old piece of information about India (Eusebius *Hist. eccl.* 5.10.3) connects Indian Christianity with Bartholomew:

Pantaenus (Alexandrian teacher of Origen) ... went to the Indians, and the tradition is that he found there that among some of those there who had known Christ the Gospel according to Matthew had preceded his coming; for Bartholomew, one of the apostles, had preached to them and had left them the writing of Matthew in Hebrew letters, which was preserved until the time mentioned.

sea voyage to India; apparently the editor of this part of the book wanted to connect the mission of Thomas with South India.

All traditions agree that the authority of the apostle Thomas and the area of his mission must be located in the East, i.e., in eastern Syria, specifically in Edessa (upper Mesopotamia), and in India. In the *Acts of Thomas,* the apostle's name is "Judas who is also called Thomas" (Ἰούδας ὁ καὶ Θωμᾶς) and in chapter 1 he is introduced as "Judas Thomas who is also called Didymus" (Ἰούδας Θωμᾶς ὁ καὶ Δίδυμος).[1] This triple designation agrees with the form of the name as it appears in the original title of the *Gospel of Thomas:*

These are the secret sayings which the living Jesus spoke and which Didymus Judas Thomas wrote down.[2]

Who was Didymus Judas Thomas? Thomas appears in the lists of the "Twelve," or the "Twelve Apostles," in Matthew 10:3; Mark 3:18; Luke 6:15; and Acts 1:13. But none of these books say anything about him. However, in the Gospel of John, Thomas is mentioned several times, twice as asking a question (11:16 and 14:5) and then in the story of the "Unbelieving Thomas" (20:24–28), finally in the list of seven disciples in John 21:2. In three of these passages the phrase "who was also called Didymus" is added. In John 14:22 the Syriac translation reads "Thomas" instead of "Judas, not the Iscarioth"; obviously the translator connected the name Judas with Thomas, which corresponds to the tradition of the Syrian church. This is also reflected in the Abgar Legend about the mission in Edessa where the apostle is introduced as "Judas who is also called Thomas."[3]

"Thomas" is not a proper name but a transcription of the Aramaic word for "twin," and the Greek word "Didymus" also means "twin." The Syrian tradition as well as the *Gospel of Thomas* have preserved his given name: Judas. There are several persons with this name mentioned in the New Testament: (1) Judas Iscarioth who betrayed Jesus; (2) "Judas, the son of Jacob," listed as one of the apostles together with Thomas (Luke 6:16 = Acts 1:13; thus these were two different persons); (3) "Judas," the brother of Jesus (Mark 6:3 = Matthew 13:55). The New Testament writing known as the "Epistle of Jude" introduces as its author "Judas the brother of James" (= the brother of Jesus).

(ET Kirsopp Lake, LCL).

[1] Lipsius-Bonnet, *Acta Apostolorum Apocrypha,* 2.100, lines 4–5. The Syriac text reads instead "Judas Thomas, the Apostle."

[2] This is the reading of the Coptic text. The Greek text of *Pap. Oxy. 1* reads [. . . Ἰούδα ὁ] καὶ Θωμᾶ.

[3] Eusebius *Hist. eccl.* 1.13.11.

"Judas, the Twin, brother of Jesus" is the representative of an independent tradition of the Eastern Church.

Eventually, in the *Acts of Thomas,* he became the twin-brother of Jesus.[1] In the *Gospel of Thomas* there is a connection between James the Righteous (i.e., Jesus' brother), who is designated as the leader of the church (*Gos. Thom.* 12), and (Judas) Thomas as the apostle who knows the secret wisdom (*Gos. Thom.* 13); but no family relationship between Jesus, James, and Thomas is established. Thomas is important because he guarantees the reliability of the wisdom sayings, not because of his family ties to Jesus. Yet the significance of Thomas for the Eastern Church argues for an east-Syrian origin of the Gospel of Thomas.

2.2.3 CHARACTER AND GENRE

The designation "The Gospel of Thomas" was added later at the end of the document by the scribe who copied it. The incipit designates the writing as a "Book of Secret Sayings." Normally each saying is introduced by "Jesus said." The sayings are not embedded into a narrative framework, although occasionally the disciples are introduced as asking questions. There are no references to the story of Jesus, no mention of his birth, life, death, and resurrection; rather Jesus is simply designated as "the Living One."

The author was certainly not trying to compose a "gospel" of the type that is known from the Gospels of the New Testament. Just stringing sayings together into a written document is a mode of composition that was well known from wisdom books, like the Book of Proverbs from the Hebrew Bible, or the *Wisdom of Ben Sirah* and the *Wisdom of Solomon,* which are preserved among the so-called Old Testament Apocrypha. There are also early Christian examples for this type of literature. Most scholars believe that both Matthew and Luke used as a common source a collection of Jesus' sayings, known as the Synoptic Sayings Source (see below # 2.3). The Epistle of James in the New Testament is such a wisdom book, and also the first six chapters of the early Christian manual known as the *Didache* or *Teaching of the Twelve Apostles.*

The sayings of the *Gospel of Thomas* consist for the most part of aphorisms, proverbs, wisdom sayings, parables, prophetic sayings about the "Kingdom of the Father," and community rules.[2] "Wisdom"

---

[1] This also the case in the *Book of Thomas (the Contender)* (NHC II, 7) where Jesus address this apostle as "My brother" and as "my twin and true companion."

[2] For a listing of examples of the types of sayings in the *Gospel of Thomas* see Helmut Koester, "One Jesus and Four Primitive Gospels," in Robinson-Koester, *Trajectories,* 168–87; Fallon and Cameron, "Forschungsbericht," 4205–13.

Irenaeus creedal Faith in God Men - unique

is the theme of this writing. As in the *Wisdom of Solomon,* wisdom sayings express the truth about God and about the essence of the human self. They speak about human nature and destiny and, by extension, about the nature of the world and the proper relationship to the world in which people dwell. The wisdom sayings of the *Gospel of Thomas,* like other Jewish and Christian sayings collections of this type, contain sayings that reveal what is fundamental about people and their behavior. Still other sayings point to the tenuous nature of a human being's sojourn in the world. Such wisdom sayings, as well as many others, have parallels in the canonical gospels. Thus such sayings and the orientation they reveal are by no means unique to Thomas. They are typical of the early Christian sayings tradition to which Thomas, together with Matthew, Mark, and Luke, was heir.

What is most puzzling about the composition of sayings in this wisdom book is the arrangement and order of the sayings. There is seemingly no rhyme or reason for the odd sequence in which the sayings occur in the *Gospel of Thomas.* Moreover, in one instance, the Greek and Coptic texts differ in the order of sayings. *Pap. Oxy. 1* combines ## 30 and 77b of the Coptic text. Several attempts have been made to find the author's compositional principle,[1] none of them convincing. Some principles of order can be discovered in smaller sections. *Gos. Thom.* 62–65 brings a sequence of parables introduced by a saying that points to the mystery character of these parables. Another group of parables, each introduced by "The kingdom is like . . . ," appears in the final section of the book in ## 96, 97, 98, 107, 109. However, in this case other materials have been inserted after the first three and between the last two of these parables. Thus this is not an order established by the author of this gospel, but it reflects the use of a written source in which materials of a certain type had been grouped together. In other instances one can observe catchword associations of two or more sayings, e.g., ## 2 and 3 are obviously associated through the catchword "to be king" and "kingdom." ## 25 and 26 both speak about "your brother" and use the word "eye," though each time with a different metaphorical meaning. ## 31, 32, 33, and 35 may have been brought together through the catchwords "village," "city," "housetops," "house," though the connection to the last is obscured by the insertion of an unrelated proverb (# 34). Also in this instance, such a compositional principle is more likely a feature of the author's source.

The writer of the *Gospel of Thomas* is, in fact, not an author who deliberately composed his book according to a general master plan. He is rather a collector and compiler who used a number of smaller units

---

[1] They are surveyed by Fallon and Cameron, "Forschungsbericht," 4205–8.

of collected sayings, some perhaps available in written form, and composed them randomly. He shows no desire to express his own understanding of these sayings through the manner of composition. This can be explained by considering the hermeneutic principles employed for the interpretation of sayings: each saying has meaning in itself. In some instances, the author expresses that in the form of additional phrases. *Gos. Thom.* 16, for example, quotes three traditional sayings (= Q/Luke 12: 51, 52 and 53) and then adds "and they will stand as a single one." #78 quotes Q/Luke 7:24–25 and adds "and they are unable to discern the truth." We shall see in the further development of this tradition of sayings that the next step is the composition of dialogues which explore the deeper meaning of just one or two sayings, sometimes drawing additional sayings into the dialogue, but rarely making any attempts to bring the sayings into any rational order and sequence.[1]

The author's own understanding of traditional sayings is also expressed in the way in which he adds sayings of a different character to the collection. A number of wisdom sayings go beyond the commonplace understanding of what is wise and what is unwise in human life. They speak of divine Wisdom who invites human beings to follow her in order to find the true life here in this world and in the hereafter. Some of these Thomas sayings have parallels in the Gospels of the New Testament, for example, the famous saying in which Jesus speaks with the voice of heavenly Wisdom, inviting people to take up his yoke:

Gos. Thom. 90	Matt 11:28–30
Come unto me, for my yoke is easy and my lordship is mild, and you will find repose for yourselves.	Come to me, all who labor and are heavy laden, and I will give you rest. Take my yoke upon you and learn from me; for I am gentle and lowly in heart, and you will find rest for your souls. For my yoke is easy, and my burden is light.

It is necessary, therefore, to recognize the moment in which the words of Jesus are heard; this is expressed in a number of eschatological and prophetic sayings, for example:

His disciples said to him, "When will the repose of the dead come about, and when will the new world come?" He said to them, "What you look forward to has already come, but you do not recognize it." (*Gos. Thom.* 51)

---

[1] See below on the *Dialogue of the Savior* and on the discourses and dialogues of the Gospel of John.

His disciples said to him. "Twenty-four prophets spoke in Israel, and all
of them spoke of you." He said to them, "You have omitted the one living
in your presence, and have spoken (only) of the dead." (*Gos. Thom.* 52)

Such eschatological sayings have parallels in the canonical Gospels,
especially sayings and parables which emphasize the contrast between
the old and the new and which speak about the coming of the kingdom.

The coming of the kingdom is not dated to a future time, but is
clearly understood as an event of the present time. However, this radicalization of the eschatological expectation is not without parallel in
the canonical Gospels, as a comparison of *Gos. Thom.* 113 with its
parallel demonstrates:

Gos. Thom. 113	Lk 17:20–21
His disciples said to him, "When will the kingdom come?" Jesus said, "It will not come by looking for it. It will not be a matter of saying, 'here it is,' or 'there it is'. Rather, the kingdom of the Father is spread out upon the earth, and people do not see it."	Being asked by the Pharisees when the kingdom of God was coming, he answered them, "The kingdom of God is not coming with signs to be observed; nor will they say, 'Lo, here it is!' or 'There!' for behold, the kingdom of God is in the midst of you."

However, Thomas sees this coming of the kingdom primarily as an
event that takes place as the disciples gain a new understanding of
themselves:

Jesus said, "If those who lead you say to you, 'See, the kingdom is in the
sky,' then the birds of the sky will precede you. If they say to you, 'It is in
the sea,' then the fish will precede you. Rather the kingdom is inside of
you, and it is outside of you. When you come to know yourselves, then
you will be known, and you will realize that it is you who are the sons of
the living Father. But if you will not know yourselves, you dwell in
poverty and it is you who are that poverty." (*Gos. Thom.* 3)

To the sayings of this type, one must add those which seem to
express Gnostic themes and reveal a more radical concept of secret
knowledge. They speak of hidden truths about human existence,
heavenly origins, separation from the world, and liberation of the soul
from the body (see below). This has prompted some scholars to date
the *Gospel of Thomas* later in the 2d century CE. However, it has
become more and more evident that the rise of Gnosticism must be
dated earlier than the 2d century and that it cannot be viewed as a
relatively late Christian phenomenon. Among the tractates discovered at Nag Hammadi, one finds a number of texts which unfold a
rich legacy of Jewish Gnosticism which likely predates the beginnings

of Christianity.[1] Thus Thomas's religious perspective, even if it is "Gnostic," may have been right at home in the 1st century. In order to determine the date of the *Gospel of Thomas* relative to other early gospel traditions and writings, it is necessary to investigate the relationship of its sayings to the sayings of the canonical gospels and their sources.

2.2.4 THE GOSPEL OF THOMAS AND THE SYNOPTIC TRADITION

2.2.4.1 Thomas and the Canonical Gospels

As soon as the full text of this gospel had been recovered, it became clear that it was a book of sayings of Jesus of which many had parallels in the Gospels of Matthew, Mark, Luke, and John. Just as after the discovery of the Oxyrhynchus Papyri, scholars immediately set out to compare the sayings of the new Coptic *Gospel of Thomas* with their parallels in the canonical gospels. Scholarly opinion was divided from the very beginning. While few hailed the *Gospel of Thomas* as a collection of sayings containing the pure and unsullied words of Jesus, some interpreters believed that it represented an early tradition of sayings which was independent of the canon of the New Testament. On the other hand, many scholars saw in this gospel a heretical fabrication, a Gnostic interpretation of the teachings of Jesus, using sayings which were drawn from the the canonical gospels. The latter alternative was endorsed soon after the initial publication by a large number of authors, among them such respected scholars as Robert M. Grant of the University of Chicago,[2] and in Germany Professor Ernst Haenchen of the University of Münster.[3] The first exponents of the view that the *Gospel of Thomas* was an independent witness for the tradition of the sayings of Jesus were the Dutch scholar Gilles Quispel,[4] the Elsassian

---

[1] The most comprehensive treatment of this question can be found in Kurt Rudolph, *Gnosis: The Nature and History of an Ancient Religion* (Edinburgh: Clark, 1983); see especially pp. 275–294.

[2] "Notes on the Gospel of Thomas," *VigChr* 13 (1959) 170–180; Grant followed this article with a book coauthored with David Noel Freedman, *The Secret Sayings of Jesus* (Garden City, NY: Doubleday, 1960).

[3] In his critical survey of the first publications on the *Gospel of Thomas:* "Literatur zum Thomasevangelium," *ThR* 27 N.F. (1961/62) 147–178, 306–338; and in his translation and commentary: *Die Botschaft des Thomas-Evangeliums* (Berlin: Töpelmann, 1961).

[4] "The Gospel of Thomas and the New Testament," *VigChr* 11 (1957) 189–207. Quispel has defended and further elaborated his hypothesis in a number of subsequent articles which were published in subsequent issues of the same journal: 12 (1958) 181–96; 13 (1959) 87–117; 14 (1960) 204–15; 16 (1962) 121–53; 18 (1964) 226–35; see also idem in *NTS* 5 (1958/59) 276–90; *NTS* 12 (1965/66) 371–82.

Patristic scholar Oscar Cullmann,[1] and in England, Hugh Montefiore.[2]

Those who assume that the *Gospel of Thomas* is dependent upon the Gospels of the New Testament[3] have not been able to show that there is any concrete and consistent pattern of Thomas's dependence upon one particular gospels' version of the tradition of the sayings.[4] There is also no trace of the narrative framework into which the sayings are often embedded in the Gospels of the canon. Moreover, a number of studies have shown that in many cases a saying or parable, as it appears in the *Gospel of Thomas,* is preserved in a form that is more original than any of its canonical parallels. This means that the tradition of sayings of Jesus preserved in the *Gospel of Thomas* pre-dates the canonical Gospels[5] and rules out the possibility of a dependence

[1] "Das Thomasevangelium und die Frage nach dem Alter der in ihm enthaltenen Tradition," *ThLZ* 85 (1960) 321–334; ET in *Interpretation* 16 (1962) 418–38.

[2] "A Comparison of the Parables of the Gospel According to Thomas and the Synoptic Gospels," *NTS* 7 (1960/61) 220–248; republished in idem and H. E. W. Turner, *Thomas and the Evangelists* (SBT 35; London: SCM, 1962).

[3] In addition to the literature quoted above, see Wolfgang Schrage, *Das Verhältnis des Thomas-Evangeliums zur synoptischen Tradition und zu den koptischen Evangelienübersetzungen* (BZNW 29; Berlin: De Gruyter, 1964); with respect to Schrage's thesis of a dependence of the *Gospel of Thomas* upon the Coptic translation of the Synoptic Gospels see John Sieber, "A Redactional Analysis of the Synoptic Gospels with Regard to the Sources of the Gospel of Thomas" (Ph.D. diss., Claremont Graduate School); cf. also the important review of Schrage by R. McL. Wilson, *VigChr* 20 (1966) 118–123. Arguments for a dependence of the *Gospel of Thomas* upon the canonical Gospels have also been advanced by Jacque-E. Ménard, *L'Évangile selon Thomas* (NHS 5; Leiden Brill, 1975); idem, "La tradition synoptique et l'Évangile selon Thomas," in F. Paschke, ed., *Überlieferungsgeschichtliche Untersuchungen* (TU 125; Berlin: Akademie-Verlag, 1981) 411–26; B. Dehandshutter, "L'Évangile selon Thomas: témoin d'une tradition prélucanienne?" in: Frans Neirynck, ed., *L'Évangile de Luc* (BEThL 32; Gembloux: Duculot, 1973) 287–97; idem, "L'Évangile de Thomas comme collection des paroles de Jésus," in Delobel, ed., *LOGIA,* 507–15; J.-M. Sevrin, "L'Évangile selon Thomas: Paroles de Jésus et révélation gnostique," *RThL* 8 (1977) 265–92.

[4] Failure to demonstrate any consistency of dependence is again evident in the recent article of Klyne R. Snodgrass, "The Gospel of Thomas: A Secondary Gospel," *Second Century* 7 (1989–90) 19–38. Snodgrass completely ridicules with rhetorical questions all hypotheses about the development of the sayings tradition, and then procedes to show that the *Gospel of Thomas* has certain words and phrases in common with all four canonical Gospels. Without a theory about the pre-canonical history of the tradition, it is no wonder that dependence upon the canonical Gospels is the only possible answer. Nothing can be learned here. See the more balanced assessment and methodologically better informed essay by Charles W. Hedrick, "Thomas and the Synoptics: Aiming at a Consensus," *Second Century* 7 (1989–90) 39–56.

[5] This does not exclude intrusion of canonical sayings at a later stage of the Thomas tradition. That this tradition was not fixed, even in its written form, has correctly been emphasized by Kenneth V. Neller, "Diversity in the Gospel of Thomas," *Second Century* 7 (1989–90) 1–18. This had been stated well already by R. McL. Wilson in his review of Schrage (*Das Verhältnis des Thomas-Evangeliums zur synoptischen Tradition*) in

upon any of these Gospels.[1]

2.2.4.2 Thomas and the Synoptic Sayings Source (Q)[2]

One of the most striking features of the *Gospel of Thomas* is its silence on the matter of Jesus' death and resurrection—the keystone of Paul's missionary proclamation. But Thomas is not alone in this silence. The Synoptic Sayings Source (Q), used by Matthew and Luke, also does not consider Jesus' death a part of the Christian message. And it likewise is not interested in stories and reports about the resurrection and subsequent appearances of the risen Lord. The *Gospel of Thomas* and Q challenge the assumption that the early church was unanimous in making Jesus' death and resurrection the fulcrum of Christian faith. Both documents presuppose that Jesus' significance lay in his words, and in his words alone.

Another striking feature of the *Gospel of Thomas* is an almost total absence of christological titles, such as "Christ/Messiah," "Lord," and "Son of man." With respect to the latter title, the *Gospel of Thomas*

VigChr 20 (1966) 121: "Indeed the possibility that some logia were only added in the Coptic tradition is not to be excluded; but the direct copying of certain sayings word for word from a Coptic version of our Gospels would prove nothing for the collection as a whole—the Oxyrhynchus fragments show that some part at least was current in Greek, and moreover that this Greek version already had a manuscript tradition behind it."

[1] For a general review see Helmut Koester, "Introduction [to the Gospel of Thomas]," in Layton, ed., *Nag Hammadi Codex II,* 1. 40–43. Some of the studies which have argued for the independence of Thomas and its tradition include R. McL. Wilson, *Studies in the Gospel of Thomas* (London: Mowbray, 1960); Gilles Quispel, "Gnosis and the New Sayings of Jesus," *Eranos Jahrbuch* 38 (1969) 261–96; Robinson-Koester, *Trajectories*; J.-D. Kaestli, "L'évangile de Thomas: Son importance pour l'étude des paroles de Jésus et du gnosticisme chrétien," *Études Théologiques et Religieuses* 54 (1979) 375–96; S. L. Davis, *The Gospel of Thomas and Christian Wisdom* (New York: Seabury, 1983); John Dominic Crossan, *Four Other Gospels: Shadows on the Contours of Canon* (Winston: Minneapolis, 1985) 35–37; Layton, *Gnostic Scriptures*; now also Beate Blatz, "Das koptische Thomasevangelium," in Hennecke-Schneemelcher, *NT Apokryphen I,* 96. C. M. Tuckett (*Nag Hammadi and the Gospel Tradition* [Edinburgh: Clark, 1986]) does not deal specifically with the *Gospel of Thomas* but is open to the possibility of an independent preservation of gospel materials in this writing (see pp. 6–9). Stephen J. Patterson, has presented a detailed investigation of this question in his doctoral dissertation (Claremont Graduate School, 1988) which will be published in the near future. For this chapter of my book, I owe much to this dissertation and to the contributions of Stephen J. Patterson to our essay, "The Gospel of Thomas: Does it Contain Authentic Sayings of Jesus?" *Bible Review* 6/2 (1990) 28–39.

[2] The entire material that can be assigned to this collection of sayings is now well presented, both in the original Greek text and in an English translation, by John S. Kloppenborg, *Q Parallels: Synopsis, Critical Notes & Concordance* (F&F; Sonoma, CA: Polebridge Press, 1988).

and Q part company: In Q, the title "Son of man" plays a significant role as a designation of Jesus as the one who will appear from heaven at the end of the time: "As the lightning flashes and lights up the sky, so will the Son of man be in his day" (Luke 17:24). Similar statements about the Son of man also appear in the so-called Synoptic Apocalypse (Mark 13 and Matthew 24–25). But in recent studies, Dieter Lührmann[1] and, following him, John S. Kloppenborg,[2] have demonstrated that Q was composed in two successive stages and that the understanding of Jesus as the future Son of man was not yet present in the earlier stage of its composition. The sayings which speak about the coming of the Son of man for the final judgment and the addition of the title Son of man to older sayings[3] belong to the second stage of this document which originally presented Jesus as a teacher of wisdom and as a prophet who announced in his words the presence of the kingdom.

It is exactly with respect to the material that belongs to the earlier stage of Q, written probably within ten or twenty years of Jesus' death, that we find parallels in the *Gospel of Thomas*. Of the seventy-nine sayings of Thomas with Synoptic Gospel parallels, forty-six have parallels in Q, but the typical apocalyptic perspective of the later redaction of Q does not appear in any of these sayings. Rather, they are non-apocalyptic wisdom sayings, proverbs, prophetic sayings, parables, and community rules, as the following listing demonstrates.[4]

Q AND THOMAS

(*Q = also transmitted in Mark; Q/Matt = only in Matthew, but from Q)

Q / Luke	Thomas	Type of Saying	Title / Beginning
Q 6:20	# 54	prophetic saying	Blessed are the poor
Q 6:21	# 69b	prophetic saying	Blessed are the hungry
Q 6:22	# 68	prophetic saying	Blessed when hated
Q/Matt 5:8,10	# 69a	prophetic saying	Blessed the persecuted
Q 6:31	# 6	proverb	Golden Rule
Q 6:34a	# 95	wisdom saying	Lending at interest
Q 6:39	# 34	proverb	Blind leading the blind

[1] *Redaktion der Logienquelle.*

[2] *Formation of Q.*

[3] Cf. below the comparison of *Gos. Thom.* 68 and Luke 6:22.

[4] For the comparison of sayings in the synoptic and the apocryphal traditions, a useful synopsis of sayings in English translation has been published by John Dominic Crossan, *Sayings Parallels: A Workbook for the Jesus Tradition* (F&F; Philadelphia: Fortress, 1986).

Q 6:41–42	# 26	proverb	Speck in brother's eye
Q 6:43	# 43	proverb	Love tree, hate fruit
Q 6:44b–45	# 45	proverb	No figs from thorns
Q 7:24–25	# 78	wisdom saying	Why come into the desert
Q 7:28	# 46	prophetic saying	Superior to John
Q 9:58	# 86	wisdom saying	Foxes have holes
Q 10:2	# 73	community rule	The harvest is great
Q 10:8–9	# 14b	community rule	Eat what is before you
Q 10:22a	# 61b	wisdom saying	Given from the Father
Q 10:23–24	# 17	wisdom saying	What eye has not seen
Q 11:9–10	# 92, 94	wisdom saying	Seek and find
Q 11:27–28	# 79a	prophetic saying	Blessed the womb
*Q 11:33	# 33b	wisdom saying	Lamp under a bushel
Q 11:34–35a	# 24	wisdom saying	Eye lamp of the body
Q 11:39–40	# 89	community rule	Wash outside of the cup
Q 11:52	# 39	prophetic saying	Keys of knowledge
*Q 12:2	# 5, 6	wisdom saying	Hidden and revealed
Q 12:3	# 33a	prophetic saying	Preach from housetops
*Q 12:10	# 44	community rule	Blasphemy against Spirit
Q 12:13–14	# 73 / 72	community rule	Divide the possessions
Q 12:16–21[1]	# 63	parable	Rich fool
Q 12:22–31[2]	# 36[3]	wisdom saying	On cares
Q 12:33	# 76b	wisdom saying	Treasure in heaven
?Q 12:35	# 21c	wisdom saying	Guard against world
Q 12:39	# 21b, 103	parable	Thief in the night
Q 12:49	# 10	prophetic saying	Fire upon the earth
Q 12:51–53	# 16	prophetic saying	Peace on the earth?
Q 12:56	# 91	prophetic saying	Read face of sky & earth
*Q 13:18–19	# 20	parable	Mustard Seed
Q 13:20–21	# 96	parable	Leaven
Q 14:16–24	# 64	parable	Great banquet
Q 14:26	# 55a, 101	community rule	. . . hate his father

[1] There are no Matthean parallels to Luke 12:13–14 and 16–21. A majority of scholars hesitate to assign this and the following pericope to Q. However, there are good reasons for the inclusion: in style and wording, this section is closely related to the following Q section (12:22–46); see Kloppenborg, *Formation of Q*, 215; idem, *Q Parallels*, 128.

[2] Only parallels to vss. 22, 27a, and 31(?) are present in the Greek version of *Gos. Thom.* 36; see also the following note.

[3] The text of the Greek version in *Pap. Oxy.* 655 is much longer than the Coptic version of *Gos. Thom.* 36 ("Do not be concerned from morning until evening and from evening until morning what you will wear"); see Attridge, "Greek Fragments," 121–22 and 127.

*Q 14:27	# 55b	community rule	. . . take up his cross
Q 15:3–7	# 107	parable	Lost sheep
Q 16:13	# 47	proverb	Serving two masters
*Q 17:6	# 48	community rule	"Tree" move away
Q 17:20–21[1]	# 113	prophetic saying	Kingdom is among you
Q 17:34	# 61a	prophetic saying	Two will rest on a bed
*Q 19:26	# 41	prophetic saying	Who has will be given

Parallels in Thomas are especially frequent in sections of Q which became the basis of the Lukan Sermon on the Plain (Luke 6:20–49) and the Matthean Sermon on the Mount (Matthew 5–7). To Q/Luke 6:20–49, there are parallels to verses 20, 21, 22, 31,[2] 34, 39, 41–42, 43, 44b–45. To these sayings, which the *Gospel of Thomas* shares with Luke 6, one must add two sayings which occur in different contexts in Luke but belong to Matthew's "Sermon on the Mount" (*Gos. Thom.* 92, cf. 94, and 47a), and at least one Q saying preserved in Matthew only (Matt 5:8, 10). It is also striking that all apparent Lukan additions to Q are missing in the *Gospel of Thomas:* the curses against the rich (Luke 6:24–26)[3] and the Lukan additions to the saying about lending out money (6:34b–35).

In a number of instances Thomas has clearly preserved a more original form of the saying.

Gos. Thom. 68	Q/Luke 6:22
Blessed are you when you are hated and persecuted, and no place will be found, wherever you have been persecuted.	Blessed are you when people hate you, and when they exclude you and reproach you, and cast out your name as evil, on account of the Son of man.

The phrase "and cast out your name as evil on account of the Son of man" is certainly Lukan; it is missing in the parallel passage Matt 5:11. Moreover, the reference to persecution has disappeared in the Lukan redaction of this saying, but is preserved in Matt 5:11.

---

[1] Luke 17:20–21 is not included in Q by most scholars (see Kloppenborg, *Q Parallels,* 188). But the occurrence of the close parallel in *Gos. Thom.* 113 (see also *Gos. Thom.* 3) should prompt a reconsideration of this question.

[2] It is not certain whether this saying of the *Gospel of Thomas* is actually a parallel to the Q saying of Luke 6:31, the Golden Rule. One would have to translate *Gos. Thom.* 6 as follows: "Do not lie and do (to others) what you hate (to be done to you)."

[3] However, Lührmann (*Redaktion,* 105) assigns the curses to a later form of Q used only by Luke. Kloppenborg (*Formation of Q,* 172) states that "the close parallelism between the Lukan woes and beatitudes excludes the possibility that the woes circulated independently of 6:20–23b," but argues, at the same time, against Schürmann who defends the view that the woes are pre-Lukan; for an overview of the divided scholarly opinion see Kloppenborg, *Q Parallels,* 26.

Gos. Thom. 95	Q/Luke 6:34
If you have money, do not lend it at interest, but give [it] to one from whom you will not get back.	If you lend to those from whom you expect repayment, what credit is that to you? Even sinners lend to sinners to receive as much again.

The ending of Luke 6:34 ("Even sinners lend to sinners . . .") is a secondary addition in analogy to the ending of the preceding saying Luke 6:33 ("Even sinners do that"). Matt 5:42 reads, "Give to the one who asks you, and do not refuse one who wants to borrow from you." This may have preserved the wording of the original saying better than Luke 6:34, and Thomas's version can be best explained as a development of this form.

Gos. Thom. 47a-b	Q/Matt 6:24/Luke 16:13
It is impossible for a man to mount two horses or to stretch two bows. And it is impossible for a servant to serve two masters; otherwise he will honor the one and treat the other contemptuously.	No servant can serve two masters; for either he will hate the one and love the other or he will be loyal to the one and despise the other. You cannot serve God and mammon.

Most scholars would argue that "servant" in Luke 16:13 is a later addition, while Matthew's "no one" is an accurate reproduction of the text of Q. However, the version of Gos. Thom. 47a-b stays completely within the limits of natural expansion of a popular proverb by prefixing the analogous examples of mounting two horses or stretching two bows. Thomas's version, at the same time, shows no sign of the unnecessary duplication "hate the one and love the other" and of the secondary application of the proverb (serving God and mammon).[1] Both of these appear already in Q; thus Gos. Thom. 46b presents the form that this proverb would have had before it was incorporated into Q. Had Thomas read the final phrase in his text, he would certainly have incorporated it (cf. the rejection of worldly possessions in Gos. Thom. 110).

While the sayings in this section of Q are mostly sayings of secular wisdom, another Q section contains a larger number of prophetic sayings and community rules: Q/Luke 11:27–12:56. Here the parallels in the Gospel of Thomas are even more complete with sayings corresponding to Q = Luke 11:27–28, 33, 34–35a, 39–40, 52; 12:2, 3, 10,

---

[1] Bultmann (Synoptic Tradition, 87): "The concluding sentence in particular, with its application in the second person, gives the impression of being an edifying addition."

13–14, 16–21, 22–31, 33, 35, 39, 49, 51–53, 56. Perhaps also Luke 17:20–21, 34 belonged to the same part of Q. With these sayings of Q, the parallels in the *Gospel of Thomas* share the prophetic perspective and emphasize the eschatological presence of the salvation in Jesus and his words.

For this section of Q/Luke it is also instructive to ask which materials are not represented among the sayings of the *Gospel of Thomas*. They are mostly materials which must be assigned to the final redaction of Q.[1] The Sign of Jonah (Matt 12:38–42 = Luke 11:29–32); most of the material from the speech against the Pharisees (Luke 11:39–52);[2] only two isolated sayings appear, and only one of these is directed against the Pharisees (see below) while there is no trace in Thomas of the other materials which Matthew has assembled in his much more inclusive speech against the Pharisees (Matthew 23). There are no parallels in Thomas to the persecution sayings of Matt 10:17–20, 28–33 (= Luke 12:2–9, 11–12), nor to the allegory of the master of the house returning late from a wedding (Luke 12:36–38)—a secondary Lukan composition without a parallel in Matthew.[3] There is also no trace of the admonitions to watch for the coming of the Son of man (Matt 24:44 = Luke 12:40), of the parable of the Faithful and the Unfaithful Servant (Luke 12:41–46 = Matt 24:45–50)—both are elements of the secondary apocalyptic redaction of Q—and of the parable of the Servant's Wages (Luke 12:47–48) which was added by Luke from his special source. Finally the sayings about the coming of the Son of man in Q/Luke 17 do not appear in Thomas.

A number of observations on some of the sayings of this section confirm the thesis that the parallels of the *Gospel of Thomas* to this Q section are probably related to the very earliest stage of the composition of the Synoptic Sayings Source.

Gos. Thom. 89	Q/Luke 11:39–40
Jesus said, "Why do you wash the outside of the cup?	And the Lord said to him, "Now you Pharisees cleanse the outside of the cup and the dish, but inside you are full of extortion and wickedness? You fools!

---

[1] See Lührmann (*Redaktion,* passim) and Kloppenborg (*Formation of Q,* passim).

[2] The composition of the Q speech against the Pharisees belongs to the final stage of the development of this document; see Kloppenborg, *Formation of Q,* 139–47.

[3] Unless one wants to refer to the parable of the Ten Virgins of Matt 25:1–13.

Do you not realize that he who made the inside is the same one who made the outside?"	Did not he who made the outside make the inside also?"

(handwritten: Jewish)

This is the first of the two sayings which Thomas shares with the synoptic speech against the Pharisees. However, it can be understood as a community rule rather than a polemical saying. There is no reference to the Pharisees; the accusation that those who practice such purification "are full of extortion and wickedness" is missing, as is the slanderous "You fools!" That *Gos. Thom.* 89 reverses the order "outside/inside" in the second part of the saying is of no consequence because there is no polemical intent.

Gos. Thom. 39	Q/Luke 11:52
The Pharisees and the scribes have taken the keys of knowledge. You yourselves did not enter, and you prevented those who were trying to enter.	Woe to you lawyers (Matt: scribes and Pharisees, hypocrites)! for you have taken away the keys of knowledge and hidden them. They themselves have not entered, nor have they allowed to enter those who wish to.

In this saying, Thomas mentions explicitly the Pharisees and scribes. "Scribes and Pharisees" (Matt 23:13) is most likely the designation used in Q, rather than the typically Lukan "lawyers."[1] On the other hand, the notorious Matthean addition "hypocrites" (fourteen times in Matthew) is missing in *Gos. Thom.* 39.[2] Thomas preserves the original form of this saying.[3]

(handwritten: Every thing will be forgiven . . .)

Gos. Thom. 44	Q/Luke 12:10[4]
Whoever blasphemes against the Father, will be forgiven,	And everyone who says a word against the Son of man will be forgiven,

---

[1] Cf. Luke 7:30; 10:25; 11:45, 46, 53; 14:3.

[2] It is rare in the other Synoptic Gospels; in Mark only 7:6; in Luke only three times in 6:42; 12:56; 13:15.

[3] There is, however, another saying about the Pharisees, formulated as a curse, which has no synoptic parallel, *Gos. Thom.* 102: "Woe to the Pharisees, for they are like a dog sleeping in a manger of oxen, for neither does he eat nor does he [let] the oxen eat."

[4] A variant of this Q saying has been preserved in Mark 3:28–29. This version may have influenced the text of Matthew.

(and whoever blasphemes against the Son will be forgiven) but whoever blasphemes against the Holy Spirit will not be forgiven, either on earth or in heaven.

but the one who blasphemes against the Holy Spirit will not be forgiven. (Matt adds: either in this age or the coming one.)

The transmission of this saying in the Synoptic Gospels is complex. There are five different elements which appear in different combinations in the several variants (Luke 12:10; Mark 3:28–29; Matt 12:31–32; *Gos. Thom.* 44):

(1) Any kind of blasphemy (forgiven): Mark and Matthew.
(2) Blasphemy against the Father (forgiven): *Gospel of Thomas.*
(3) "Word" against the Son of man (forgiven): Luke and Matthew.
(4) Blasphemy against the Son (forgiven): *Gospel of Thomas.*
(5) Blasphemy against the Holy Spirit (unforgivable):
     all versions (Matthew twice).

Luke 12:10 is considered to be closest to the original Q version by most scholars; however, "Son of man" as a title of Jesus would have to be assigned to the later stage of Q. But even here it remains extremely awkward.[1] The best solution is to assume that Q, like Mark, was originally speaking about the blasphemy against the Holy Spirit,[2] uttered by "a son of man" = any human being, and that "son of man" was later misunderstood as a title of Jesus.[3] In the collection of sayings used by the *Gospel of Thomas* this saying probably was formulated like Mark 3:28–29; the elaboration in *Gos. Thom.* 44 is then best explained as an independent development. The final phrase which *Gos. Thom.* 44 and Matt 12:32 share may have been an original part of Q.

Q/Luke 12:16–21 = *Gos. Thom.* 63, the parable of the Rich Fool is presented in Thomas in a form that is clearly superior to the Lukan version (see the discussion below in the section on parables).

[1] See the detailed discussion in Kloppenborg, *Formation of Q*, 208–14.

[2] See the rule in *Did.* 11.7: "Do not test or examine any prophet who is speaking in the spirit; for every sin shall be forgiven, but this sin shall not be forgiven." This is most likely the earliest form of this community rule.

[3] "Mark has the relatively most original form: everything can be forgiven the sons of men (originally the son of man, i.e., men) save the blasphemy against the Spirit . . . (The form in Q) arose from a misunderstanding: any word spoken against the Son of man (i.e. against Jesus) can be forgiven . . ." (Bultmann, *Synoptic Tradition,* 131).

Gos. Thom. 10	Q/Luke 12:49
I have cast fire upon the world, and see, I am guarding it until it blazes.	I came to cast fire upon the earth; and would that it were already kindled.

Luke 12:50

I have a baptism to be baptized with; and how I am in anguish until it is over.

Gos. Thom. 16	Q/Luke 12:51–53
People think, perhaps, that it is peace which I have come to cast upon the world. They do not know that it is dissension which I have come to cast upon the earth: fire, sword, and war.	Do you think that I have come to give peace on earth? No, I tell you, but rather division.
For there will be five in a house: three will be against two, and two against three,	For henceforth in a house there will be five divided, three against two and two against three; they will be divided,
the father against the son, and the son against the father.	father against son, and son against father, mother against her daughter, mother-in-law against her daughter-in-law and daughter-in-law against her mother-in-law.

Thomas's version of these sayings lacks Luke 12:50, certainly an addition by the author of the Gospel.[1] Also missing in the *Gospel of Thomas* is the pedantic, and certainly secondary, enlargement of the family relationships at the end of Luke 12:53. Instead of Luke's "division" (vs. 51), *Gos. Thom.* 16 has "fire, sword, and war," probably an expansion of the original reading of Q, "sword," which is preserved in Matt 10:14.

Gos. Thom. 91	Q/Luke 12:56
You read the face of the sky and of the earth,	Hypocrites! You know how to interpret the appearance of the earth and the sky;
but you have not recognized the one who is before you, and you do not know how to read this moment?	but why do you not know how to interpret the present time?

There is no trace in Thomas of the first part of this saying (Q/Luke 12:54–55). The secondary address "hypocrites" of Luke 12:56 (no

---

[1] Cf. Bultmann (*Synoptic Tradition,* 153–54) on Luke 12:50 as a secondary development of Luke 12:49.

parallel in Matt 16:3b) is missing in Thomas as is Matthew's expansion *"the signs* of the time."

There are fewer parallels in the *Gospel of Thomas* to other sections of Q. Parallels to the Q sections about the preaching of repentance of John the Baptist, the baptism of Jesus, and the temptation story (Luke 3:22–4:13) are missing completely, though John the Baptist is mentioned (*Gos. Thom.* 46 = Q/Luke 7:28).[1] Only occasionally does Thomas bring an isolated saying paralleling any of the Q materials in Luke 8–10 and 13–16.[2] It is remarkable that there are no Thomas parallels to any of the materials which Luke draws from his special source.[3] Only once does Thomas include a saying that Luke did not draw from either Mark or Q: "No one drinks old wine and immediately desires to drink new wine" (*Gos. Thom.* 47c = Luke 5:39)—evidently a free proverb.

The materials which the *Gospel of Thomas* and Q share must belong to a very early stage of the transmission of Jesus' sayings. All of them fit well in the first composition of the Synoptic Sayings Source.[4] In a few instances, a saying reflects Matthew's rather than Luke's wording; in these instances, there are good reasons to believe that Matthew has preserved the original wording of Q. Thus, the *Gospel of Thomas* is either dependent upon the earliest version of Q or, more likely, shares with the author of Q one or several very early collections of Jesus' sayings. However, these collections are of a different character than the one used in Corinth which emphasized the mediation of secret revelation through the words of Jesus. Yet neither do they reflect a purely proverbial wisdom orientation; rather, prophetic sayings are included which incorporate the wisdom material into the perspective of a realized eschatology, centered upon the presence of revelation in the words of Jesus.

---

[1] This is the only Thomas parallel to the discussion of John the Baptist in Q/Luke 7:18–35 in which John is actually mentioned. The saying Q/Luke 7:24–25 ("What did you go out into the desert to see?") has a parallel in *Gos. Thom.* 78, but the introduction relating this saying to John is missing.

[2] The Q parables of Luke 13:18–19, 20–21; 14:16–24; 15:4–7 will be discussed in the following section.

[3] The only exceptions could be Luke 12:13–14 and 16–21, if they are assigned to Luke's special source rather than to Q.

[4] Kloppenborg (*Formation of Q,* passim) and Lührmann (*Redaktion,* passim) occasionally assign a saying of Q that has a parallel in the *Gospel of Thomas* to the later stage in the redaction of this document. However, in no instance does such a saying reflect the tendencies of the redactor.

2.2.4.3 Thomas and the Parables of Jesus

(1) *Thomas's Parables and the Synoptic Sayings Source*
There a total of twelve similitudes and parables in the Synoptic Sayings Source. The *Gospel of Thomas* includes parallels to half of these parables.

Parable		Q/Luke	Gos. Thom.
The Builders		Q 6:47–49	————
Children at Play	– 2 nd stage Q	Q 7:31–32	————
Rich Fool		Q 12:16–21[1]	# 63
‹Watchful Servants〉 2 nd Stage Q		Q 12:35–38[2]	————
Thief in the Night		Q 12:39	# 21b, 103
〈Faithful & Unfaithful Servant〉 2 nd Q		Q 12:42–46	————
Mustard Seed		Q 13:18–19[3]	# 20
Leaven		Q 13:20–21	# 96
Great Banquet		Q 14:16–24	# 64
Lost Sheep ?		Q 15:3–7	# 107
Lost Coin –		Q 15:8–10[4]	————
Talents 2 nd stage Q		Q 19:12–27	————

It cannot be determined with certainty whether the Q parables which are missing in Thomas belong to the earlier stage of Q or to its later redaction. The Builders (Q 6:47–49) is assigned to the first stage of Q.[5] Children at Play is connected with the Q pericope about John the Baptist and, in this context, would belong to the second stage of Q.[6] The section Q/Luke 7:18–25 is certainly dominated by redactional perspectives, and several layers of views of the relationship between Jesus and John are combined into a complex unit.[7] The parable itself, without the application to John the Baptist,[8] could have been part of

---

[1] It is transmitted only in Luke without a parallel in Matthew, but is most likely a Q parable; see above the discussion of Thomas and Q.

[2] A Matthean parallel is missing, unless one considers the parable of the Ten Virgins (Matt 25:1–13) to be Matthew's replacement for this Q section. For a survey of opinions see Kloppenborg, *Q Parallels*, 136.

[3] This parable is also transmitted in Mark 4:30–32. Thomas's form of the parable is more closely related to Mark than to Q and will be discussed in the next section.

[4] There is no parallel in Matthew for this Lukan parable. The close connection with the preceding parable of the Lost Sheep could indicate that the two parables were already joined in Luke's source. For a brief survey of the divided opinion of scholars, see Kloppenborg, *Q Parallels*, 176.

[5] Kloppenborg, *Formation of Q*, 185–90. It fits well into the sapiential speech character of Q 6:20–49.

[6] Kloppenborg, *Formation of Q*, 115–17.

[7] Lührmann, *Redaktion*, 24–31.

[8] For the original form of the parable see Bultmann, *Synoptic Tradition*, 172.

an earlier stage of Q, but it is difficult to assign it to a particular context.[1] The Watchful Servants (Luke 12:35–38) is not a true parable, but a secondary composition of metaphors.[2] If it was a part of Q, it certainly comes from the hand of the redactor who introduced the apocalyptic orientation. That same redactor is also responsible for the parable of the Faithful and Unfaithful Servant (Q/Luke 12:42–46), which expresses clearly the unexpected coming of the parousia.[3] Whether the Lost Coin (Luke 15:8–10) was part of Q remains uncertain at best. The last of the Q parables (19:12–27) which is missing in Thomas expresses the redactor's theme of judgment and thus belongs to the later stage of Q.[4]

All of the parables which certainly belong to the later stage of Q, and one parable which cannot be assigned to Q with certainty (Luke 15:8–10), are missing in the *Gospel of Thomas*. Of the parables included in the early composition of Q, only one does not have a parallel in Thomas (Luke 6:47–49). To be sure, it can be argued that the author of this gospel would not have chosen clearly apocalyptic materials in any case. Even so, those who argue for a dependence of the *Gospel of Thomas* upon the canonical gospels must assume that its author was quite capable of using materials whenever they suited his purposes. It it seems more likely, however, that Thomas not only had direct access to the traditions which formed the basis of Q's earliest composition, but that he also preserved forms of such materials which are more original than the forms in which they are extant in the common sayings source of Matthew and Luke. The following examples will demonstrate this.

Gos. Thom. 63	Q/Luke 12:16–21
There was a rich man who had much money. He said, "I shall put my money to use so that I may sow, reap, plant and fill my storehouse with produce, with the result that I shall lack nothing.	The land of a rich man brought forth plentifully. And he thought to himself, "What shall I do, for I have nowhere to store my crops?" And he said, "I will do this: I will pull down my granaries, and build larger ones; and there I will store all my grain and my goods. And I will say to myself,

---

[1] Luke 7:31–35 "could have been combined with the two preceding sections only after the secondary interpretation had been added to the parable, because a thematic connection (with John the Baptist) is established only through this addition" (Lührmann, *Redaktion,* 30).

[2] Bultmann, *Synoptic Tradition,* 118.

[3] "The master of the servant will come on a day when he does not expect him and at an hour he does not know" (Luke 12:46); see Kloppenborg, *Formation of Q,* 150–51.

[4] Lührmann, *Redaktion,* 70–71; Kloppenborg, *Formation of Q,* 164–65.

	'Soul, you have many goods laid up for many years; rest, eat, drink, be merry.'"
Such were his intentions, but the same night he died.	But God said to him, "Fool! this night your soul is required of you; and the things you have prepared, whose
Let him who has ears hear.	will they be?" So is whoever lays up treasure for himself, and is not rich in the sight of God.

There are two secondary features in the narrative of Luke: the conclusion[1] and the moralizing discourse. Both are missing in Thomas's version which presents this story in the more original form of a reversal parable. On the other hand, Thomas has also transferred the parable into a different milieu. The rich man is no longer a wealthy farmer but a decurion from the city who wants to invest his money successfully. The maxim at the end of *Gos. Thom.* 63 is of course secondary, but it does not reveal any knowledge of Luke's conclusion.

Gos. Thom. 21b[2]	Q/Luke 12:39–40
Therefore I say, "If the owner of a house knows that the thief is coming, he will begin his vigil before he comes and will not let him dig through into his house of his domain to carry away his goods.	But know this, if the owner of the house had known what hour the thief was coming, he would not have left his house to be dug into.
	You also must be ready; for the Son of man is coming at an hour you do not expect.

The Q version has shortened the parable, leaving out the purpose of the coming of the thief, i.e., to steal the goods of the owner of the house. That Q's parable presupposed such a continuation of the parable and was not simply an expansion of the metaphor of the "day of the Lord coming like the thief in the night" (1 Thess 5:2; Rev 3:3), is evident in the phrase "to be dug into." Thomas's version suggests that the parable was cut short Q in order to add the reference to the coming of the Son of man.

---

[1] See Bultmann, *Synoptic Tradition,* 178, who also suggests that this conclusion may not have been a part of Luke's original text because it is missing in D and in two Vetus *Latina* manuscripts.

[2] A similar version of this parable is preserved in *Gos. Thom.* 103:

Fortunate is the man who knows where the brigands will enter, so that [he] may get up, muster his domain, and arm himself before they invade.

The absence of secondary apocalyptic motifs is also evident in Thomas's version of the parable of the Great Banquet (Q/Luke 14:16–23 = *Gos. Thom.* 64).[1] Matt 25:2–10 has allegorized this parable.[2] Luke also added some allegorical features when he appended the second invitation to those "on the roads and hedges" of the countryside (Luke 14:23), apparently a reference to the Gentile mission.[3] At the end of his parable Thomas reports only the invitation to those on the streets of the city, and there are no traces of any allegorization in his version. This version is based unquestionably upon the original form of the parable and not on either Matthew or Luke. On the other hand, Thomas has changed the excuses of the first invited guests so that they reflect more closely the milieu of the city. There are four invitations, instead of three, and the excuses are "I have claims against some merchants," "I have bought a house," "My friend is to be married," and "I am on my way to collect rent from a farm." At the end Thomas adds, "Businessmen and merchants [will] not enter the places of my Father." No doubt, this is a secondary application.

Similar observations could be made with respect to the parables of the Leaven and the Lost Sheep. In the case of the latter parable, *Gos. Thom.* 107 lacks the secondary applications found in Matt 18:14 ("So it is not the will of my father who is in heaven that one of these little ones should perish") and Luke 16:7 ("There will be more joy in heaven over one sinner repenting than over ninety-nine righteous persons who need no repentance").[4] The parable of the Mustard Seed, which belongs with the parables that Thomas shares with Mark, will be discussed in the next section.

In the case of the five parables common to Q and Thomas, it is evident that they derive either from an early stage of Q or from an earlier collection which the compiler of Q also used. Such a collection was still very close to the telling of stories in the oral tradition, not a source dominated by the redactional activity of a writer who wanted to impress his theology upon the materials he used. Thus the parables of the *Gospel of Thomas* are to be read as stories in their own right, not as artificial expressions of some hidden Gnostic truth.[5]

---

[1] A detailed and helpful discussion of this Thomas parable in relation to its Synoptic parallels has been presented by Crossan, *Four Other Gospels,* 39–52.

[2] Bultmann, *Synoptic Tradition,* 175. Matthew "has allegorized the parable into an image of the history of salvation" (John Dominic Crossan, *In Parables: The Challenge of the Historical Jesus* [New York: Harper & Row, 1973] 71). See also the detailed comparison of the several versions in James Breech, *The Silence of Jesus: The Authentic Voice of the Historical Man* (Toronto: Doubleday, 1982) 114–23.

[3] Bultmann, *Synoptic Tradition,* 175; Crossan, *In Parables,* 71–72.

[4] Bultmann, *Synoptic Tradition,* 171.

[5] On this problem see my essay, "Three Thomas Parables," in A. H. B. Logan and

(2) *Thomas and Mark*

What is missing in the Synoptic Sayings Source are most of the parables which appear in the parable chapters of Mark (chapter 4) and Matthew (chapter 13).[1] In addition to the parables shared with Q, the *Gospel of Thomas* knows at least two of the parables of Mark 4: the Sower (Mark 4:3–9 = *Gos. Thom.* 9) and the Mustard Seed (Mark 4:30–32 = *Gos. Thom.* 20).[2] It is also possible that the parable of the Seed Growing Secretly (Mark 4:26–29) is reflected in *Gos. Thom.* 21 ("Let there be among you a man of understanding. When the grain ripened, he came quickly with his sickle in his hand and reaped it"). However, this latter parable may not have been part of the original Markan text (it is not reproduced by Matthew and Luke)[3] and may, therefore, not be related to the source of Mark 4.

The theory that the parables of Jesus are "secrets" (μυστήρια) is completely alien to Q. However, this theory may have served very early as a theme for the collection of some of Jesus' parables. The respective statement in Mark 4:11–12 is not attributable to Mark's redactorial work,[4] but must have been part of the source used by Mark 4. What is strange in the text of Mark is the use of the term "secret" (μυστήριον), and especially its use in the singular as a characterization of the entire parable-teaching of Jesus as a "mystery." The term does not occur anywhere else in the canonical gospels except for the two synoptic parallels of Mark 4:11 (Matt 13:11; Luke 8:10) which both read the plural "secrets" or "mysteries" (μυστήρια). In any case, it is not a typically Markan term at all. However, if Mark inherited the term together with the parables of chapter 4, the plural would have been appropriate. Matthew and Luke may have preserved the original

---

A. J. M. Wedderburn, eds., *The New Testament and Gnosis: Essays in Honor of Robert McL. Wilson* (Edinburgh: Clark, 1983) 195–203.

[1] The only overlap of Mark and Q is the parable of the Mustard Seed (Mark 4:20–32 and Q/Luke 13:18–19).

[2] Both emphasize the smallness of the mustard seed—a feature which is missing in the Q form of the parable (Luke 13:18–19).

[3] See below on the relationship of the original text of Mark to the canonical Gospel of Mark, # 4.1.2.1.

[4] Most scholars consider Mark 4:11–12 as an editorial insertion by the author of the Gospel, especially because of the introductory phrase καὶ ἔλεγεν αὐτοῖς, cf. Joachim Jeremias, *The Parables of Jesus* (rev. ed.; London: SCM, New York: Scribner's, 1963) 13–18 (however, Jeremias's view is that the saying of vss. 11–12 is an older Palestinian tradition); Heinz-Wolfgang Kuhn, *Ältere Sammlungen im Markusevangelium* (StUNT 8; Göttingen: Vandenhoeck & Ruprecht, 1971) 130–32; Dieter Lührmann, *Das Markusevangelium* (HNT 3; Tübingen: Mohr/Siebeck, 1987) 85–88.

text of Mark 4:11 and thus also of Mark's source.[1] In that case, each of the parables is designated as a "secret" which requires interpretation.[2]

That the term "secrets" belongs to an older tradition of the parables is confirmed by the *Gospel of Thomas* where the same designation appears in the plural in the introduction to a collection of three parables:

> It is to those [who are worthy of my] mysteries that I tell my mysteries.
> Do not let your left hand know what your right hand is doing. (# 62)

It is possible that the three following parables, Rich Fool (# 63), Great Banquet (# 64), and Wicked Tenants (# 65), may have formed a unit, introduced by the word about the "mysteries," before they were included into the present text of the *Gospel of Thomas*. The author of this Gospel does not make any attempt to spell out this theory of the secret with respect to the parables which follow; he also cites parables elsewhere in the gospel without ever indicating their esoteric character. All three parables of this small collection have Synoptic parallels. The Rich Fool appears in Luke only, but most likely came to Luke from the Synoptic Sayings Source (see above). The Great Banquet also belongs to Q (Matt 21:1–10 = Luke 14:16–24). However, the third parable, the Wicked Husbandmen, came to Matthew (21:33–41) and Luke (10:9–17) from the Gospel of Mark (12:1–9).

In Mark 12 as well as in *Gos. Thom.* 65, the parable of the Wicked Husbandmen is connected with the saying about the rejection of the cornerstone (Mark 12:10–11 = *Gos. Thom.* 66). This is not a Markan addition to the parable; Mark's own redactional connection, leading back into the previous context that was interrupted by the insertion of the parable, appears in 12:12–13 with an explicit reference to the parable ("they understood that he said this parable about them"). Thus the saying about the rejected cornerstone was already connected with the parable in Mark's source. However, Thomas does not reflect Mark's editorial connection of parable and saying but cites the saying as an independent unit.[3] Mark's source may have contained more

---

[1] The question of the preservation of Mark's original text in the extant manuscripts of this Gospel will be discussed below in more detail (# 4.1.2.2).

[2] Jeremias (*Parables*, 14–16) rightly argues for the traditional character of Mark 4:11–12 and also connects the meaning of "parable" with Hebrew משל = "riddle," "saying." But he fails to relate this observation to the Pauline usage where "mystery" is always a single saying or piece of tradition that requires interpretation.

[3] In Thomas the saying about the stone rejected by the builders (# 66) has its own introduction ("Jesus said"). "If one had only *Thomas,* therefore, one would not imagine any special connection between *Gos. Thom.* 65 and 66" (Crossan, *Four Other Gospels,* 54).

than one parable. The introduction (Mark 12:1) says: "And he began to speak to them in parables" but only one parable follows.[1] Whether or not this parable of Mark 12 derives from the same collection as the parables of Mark 4, it is evident that the sources of Mark and the *Gospel of Thomas* were closely related.

It has been debated, whether Thomas's version of the parable of the Wicked Tenants exhibits more original features than the allegorical version of Mark 12. *Gos. Thom.* 65 lacks the allusions to the parable of the Vineyard of Isaiah 5, and it fits very well the economic situation in Palestine of that period.[2] That this non-allegorical version still does not qualify as an original parable of Jesus[3] is no argument against the existence of such a version in a source that was used by Mark 12.[4]

That Thomas preserves a more original stage of that source of Mark is strikingly demonstrated by a comparison of the two versions of the parable of the Sower (Mark 4:3–9 = *Gos. Thom.* 9). Crossan[5] and Cameron[6] have shown that the text of the Markan parable is influenced by the allegorical interpretation which follows in Mark 4:13–20. The following synopsis will show that (secondary Markan additions in italics):

Gos. Thom. 9	Mark 4:3–9
Now the sower went out, took a handful (of seeds), and scattered them.	Behold, the sower went out to sow.
Some fell on the road; the birds came and gathered them.	And it happened in the sowing that some fell on the road; and the birds came and ate them.

---

[1] Matthew (22:33) and Luke (20:9) correct the introduction accordingly.

[2] This has been demonstrated by Martin Hengel, "Das Gleichnis von den Weingärtnern Mc 12,1–12 im Lichte der Zenopapyri und der rabbinischen Gleichnisse," *ZNW* 59 (1968) 1–39.

[3] Against Lührmann (*Markusevangelium,* 199–200) who uses this argument in order to maintain his claim that the Thomas version is "a reduction of the version of Mark."

[4] See also my essay, "Three Thomas Parables," in A. H. B. Logan and A. J. M. Wedderburn, eds., *The New Testament and Gnosis: Essays in Honor of Robert McL. Wilson* (Edinburgh: Clark, 1983) 199–200.

[5] Crossan, *In Parables,* 39–44.

[6] Ron Cameron, *Parable and Interpretation in the Gospel of Thomas* (F&F 2.2; Sonoma, CA: Polebridge Press, 1986) 20–21.

Others fell on rock, did not take root in the soil	And others fell on rock where it did not have enough soil, *and immediately it sprouted because it did not have depths of soil, and when the sun came up it was scorched* because it did not have roots, and it withered. And others fell in the thorns and it sprouted and the thorns choked it, *and it did not produce grain.*
(did not take root in the soil) and did not produce ears. And others fell on thorns, they choked the seeds and worms ate them.	
And others fell on good soil and it produced good fruit: it bore sixty per measure and a hundred and twenty per measure.	And others fell on good soil and it produced fruit, *growing up and increasing,* and it bore thirty and sixty and hundredfold.

(3) *Thomas and Matthew*

There are four parables in the *Gospel of Thomas* which have parallels only among Matthew's additions to his reproduction of the Markan parable chapter. The first of these is the parable of the Tares (*Gos. Thom.* 57 = Matt 13:24–30). Thomas tells this parable in a somewhat shorter version but, like Matthew, ends with the reference to the burning of the weeds at harvest time, possibly a reference to the last judgment. But there is no trace of the allegorical interpretation which Matthew (13:36–43) has appended. The other three parallels to Matthew 13 are found in *Gos. Thom.* 109, 76, and 8:

Gos. Thom. 109	Matt 13:44
The kingdom is like a man who had a hidden treasure in his field without knowing it. And [after] he died, he left it to his [son]. The son [did] not know (about the treasure). He inherited the field and sold [it]. And the one who bought it went plowing and [found] the treasure. He began to lend money at interest to whomever he wished.	The kingdom of heaven is like treasure hidden in a field which a man found and covered up; then in his joy he goes and sells all that he has and buys that field.

Gos. Thom. 76	Matt 13:45–46
The kingdom of the Father is like a merchant who had a consignment of merchandise and who discovered a pearl. That merchant was shrewd. He sold the merchandise and bought the pearl alone for himself.	Again the kingdom of heaven is like a merchant in search of fine pearls, who, on finding one pearl of great value, went and sold all that he had and bought that pearl.

You too seek his unfailing and   = Matt 6:19–20; Luke 12:33
enduring treasure where no moth
comes near to devour and no worm
destroys.

| | |
Gos. Thom. 8	Matt 13:47–50
The man is like a wise fisherman who cast his net into the sea and drew it up from the sea full of small fish. Among them the wise fisherman found a fine large fish. He threw all the small fish back into the sea and chose the large fish without difficulty. Whoever has ears to hear, let him hear.	The kingdom of heaven is like a net which was thrown into the sea and gathered fish of every kind; when it was full, men drew it ashore and sat down and sorted the good into a vessel, but threw away the bad. So it will be at the close of the age. The angels will come out and separate the evil from the righteous and throw them into the furnace of fire; there men will weep and gnash their teeth.

The comparison of these three parables with their Matthean counterparts is particularly instructive. In the third of these parables, the
Fisherman, Thomas has preserved the intent of the wisdom parable
better than Matthew: it is a wisdom parable, "told about the discovery
of one's own destiny," one of the stories "about a person who finds, dis-
cards, and chooses the one fine thing."[1] Matthew, changing the parable of the Fisherman into a parable of the Fishnet, has produced an
allegory for the last judgment—a secondary development.

The relationship of the other two parables in the *Gospel of Thomas*
to the original form of these parables is complex.[2] In the Pearl, the
Thomas version has been contaminated by elements from the parable
of the Treasure: the merchant is not in search of fine pearls, but finds
one by accident, like the man who "finds" a treasure in the field, and a
treasure saying is added at the end (= Matt 6:19–20; Luke 12:33).
Thus the author is quite aware of the traditional association of the two
parables.

The original parable of the Hidden Treasure, however, is not actually quoted by Thomas. If one considers *Gos. Thom.* 109 as a quotation
of that parable, one arrives at a judgment like Jeremias's, who called it
"utterly confused." But Jeremias already recognized that *Gos. Thom.*

---

[1] Cameron, *Parable and Interpretation,* 29.

[2] For a most instructive and elaborate analysis and interpretation see John Dominic
Crossan, *Finding is the First Act: Trove Folktales and Jesus' Treasure Parable* (Philadelphia: Fortress, 1979).

109 is actually a reproduction of a rabbinic parable where the story describes how angry one can get if one misses such an opportunity.[1] This story, otherwise widespread in folklore and in the complex legal Talmudic discussion about ownership of treasures found,[2] has been deliberately changed by the *Gospel of Thomas*. It says nothing about the angry reaction of the first owner of the field (who is actually dead when the treasure is discovered!), but emphasizes that the two original owners of the field "did not know about the treasure." The contrast in the parable is, therefore, between not knowing and finding, that is, "knowing."[3] Since "treasure" has at this point in the story clearly become a metaphor, the following "lending money at interest to whomever he wished" must be understood metaphorically as the communication of knowledge.[4]

In Matthew all four parables are introduced as parables of the kingdom of heaven. Thomas introduces two of these parables with "The kingdom of the Father is like. . ." (## 57 and 76) and one of them with "The kingdom is like. . ." (# 109). Moreover, many scholars have argued that in # 8 (Fishnet) the peculiar introduction "The man is like a wise fisherman" has replaced a reference to the kingdom.[5] Similar introductory phrases are used elsewhere in Thomas for parables, but they are relatively rare: "kingdom of the Father" also in ## 96, 97, and 98 (the latter two do not have synoptic parallels), "kingdom" also in # 107, and "kingdom of heaven" in # 20. *Gos. Thom.* ## 8, 9, 21a, 21b, 21d, 60, 63, 64, 65 are reproduced without a special introduction. That all four parables which Thomas shares with Matthew's special material were introduced with a reference to the kingdom could indicate that both used a common source. The parable introductions— "the kingdom is like . . ."—do not belong to the original wording of any of the parables, especially not to parables introducing the behavior or

---

[1] Jeremias, *Parables*, 32–33.

[2] See the monograph of Crossan quoted above.

[3] Crossan (ibid., 106) says: "The Gnostic story is not interested in indolence as against industry but in ignorance as against knowledge."

[4] Andreas Lindemann ("Zur Gleichnisinterpretation im Thomasevangelium," *ZNW* 71 [1980] 233–34) suggests as the (Gnostic?) interpretation that the hearer is requested to work hard with whatever he has in order to find the kingdom of God. However, in the present context the parable has a negative meaning, because what the finder does with his treasure is rejected in the following saying (# 110: "Whoever finds the world and becomes rich, let him renounce the world"). The problem with this interpretation is that the context of the sayings in the *Gospel of Thomas* is a notoriously poor guide to their interpretation, although it may well have preserved traditional associations of materials.

[5] For references to other literature see Cameron, *Parable and Interpretation*, 26–27, especially nn. 67 and 68.

action of a particular person, like the Pearl and the Treasure. In any case, Thomas draws on a tradition that contained the secondary introduction "the kingdom is like . . . ," which is also reproduced in the parables of Matthew 13.

Of the four parables of the *Gospel of Thomas* without synoptic parallels, three occur in the last part of this gospel. Two are introduced as parables of the kingdom, as are three of the parables which Thomas shares with Matthew and which are quoted in the same section of the *Gospel of Thomas*.

57	Tares	Matt 13:24–30	Kingdom of the Father
60	Samaritan with Lamb		
76	Pearl	Matt 13:45–46	Kingdom of the Father
97	Woman with Jar		Kingdom of the Father
98	Assassin		Kingdom of the Father
109	Treasure	(Matt 13:44)	Kingdom

This introduction to the parables, not often used elsewhere in Thomas, might indicate that at least some of the special parables of the *Gospel of Thomas* were drawn from the same source from which also the parables shared with Matthew were derived. They may well be older materials.[1] At least one of them expresses the same single-minded determination, e.g., *Gos. Thom.* 98:

> Jesus said, "The kingdom of the Father is like a certain man who wanted to kill a powerful man. In his own house he drew his sword and stuck it into the wall in order to find out whether his hand could carry through. Then he slew the powerful man."

The interpretation of the other special parables of Thomas is difficult and cannot be discussed here in detail. But at least one correction in the translation of the parable of the Samaritan Carrying a Lamb, suggested by Hans-Martin Schenke, needs to be emphasized: *Gos. Thom.* 60 is usually translated "*They* saw a Samaritan carrying a lamb on *his* (i.e., *the Samaritan's*) way to Judaea." But the text should certainly be restored to provide the following translation: "*He* (i.e., *Jesus*) saw a Samaritan carrying a lamb, when *he* (i.e., *Jesus*) was on his way to Judaea." The conclusion in the extant text of the *Gospel of Thomas* ("You too look for a place for yourselves, within repose, lest you become a corpse and be eaten") is probably secondary. But what the interpre-

---

[1] Klaus-Hunno Hunzinger ("Unbekannte Gleichnisse Jesu aus dem Thomas-Evangelium," in Walther Eltester, ed., *Judentum, Urchristentum, Kirche: Festschrift für Joachim Jeremias* [BZNW 26; Berlin: Töpelmann, 1960] 209–20) was the first to argue for the presence of early traditions in these parables.

leaky - hour 9/2 15

tation of this parable and of the parable of the Woman Carrying a Jar (*Gos. Thom.* 97) could have been remains an open question.

The parables which the *Gospel of Thomas* shares with the Synoptic Sayings Source have to be viewed together with other materials shared by the two documents. These common materials account for the majority of the synoptic sayings and parables in Thomas. Of the seventy-nine units in the *Gospel of Thomas* which have parallels in the Synoptic Gospels, a total of forty-six are Q materials,[1] compared to only twenty-seven sayings and parables shared with Mark (including those which Matthew and Luke drew from Mark).[2] Only twelve are shared with special materials of the Gospel of Matthew, while special Lukan material occurs only once in Thomas.

Thomas materials shared with Matthew only, apart from the parables, are relatively few and do not warrant the hypothesis of a special source shared by the two writings:

Q/Matt 5:8,10	# 69a	prophetic saying	Where there are two . . .
Matt 5:14	# 32	wisdom saying	City on a mountain
Matt 6:1–18	# 6a,14a	community rule	On Fasting and prayer
Matt 6:3	# 62b	proverb	Right and left hand
Matt 10:16	# 39b	proverb	Wise as serpents
Matt 11:28–30	# 90	wisdom saying	Invitation to heavy-laden
Matt 15:14	# 40	community rule	Plant not by the Father
Matt 18:20	# 30	community rule	Where there are two . . .

Some of these may have been Q materials, and others isolated sayings which circulated independently of any written sources. The relationship of Thomas with Mark, however, is much more striking and requires special consideration.

2.2.4.4 Thomas and the Gospel of Mark

The *Gospel of Thomas* shares a total of twenty-seven sayings and parables with the Gospel of Mark. Of these as many as seven also have parallels in Q (marked with *).

---

[1] See the listing above.

[2] *Gos. Thom.* 4b, 5, 6b, 9, 13(?), 14c, 20,, 21d, 21e, 22a, 25, 31, 33b, 35, 41, 44, 46b, 47d, 47e, 48, 55b, 62a, 65, 66, 67, 71, 99, 100, 104, 106.

Mark and Thomas

Mark	Thom.	Type	Topic
2:18–20	# 104	community rule	Fast without the bridegroom
2:21	# 47e	wisdom saying	New wine in old skins
2:22	# 47d	wisdom saying	Old patch on new garment
3:27	# 35	wisdom metaphor	House of a strong man
*3:28–29	# 44	community rule	Blasphemy against the Spirit
3:32, 34	# 99	community rule	Jesus' true relatives
4:3–8	# 9	parable	Sower
4:9	# 21e	wisdom saying	Whoever has ears to hear
4:11	# 62a	esoteric rule	Mystery of the parables
*4:21	# 33b	wisdom saying	Lamp not under a bushel
*4:22	# 5, 6	wisdom saying	Hidden and revealed
*4:25	# 41	prophetic saying	Who has will be given
4:26–29	# 21d	parable	Seed Growing Secretly
*4:30–32	# 20	parable	Mustard Seed
*6:4–5	# 31	proverb	Prophet in fatherland
7:15	# 14c	community rule	Clean and unclean
(8:27–30	# 13	(christological)	"Tell whom I am like")[1]
*8:34	# 55b	community rule	. . . take up his cross
?8:36	# 67	proverb	Gain the whole world . . .
10:13–16	# 22	community rule	Enter as children
10:31	# 4b	prophetic saying	First will be last
*11:23	# 71	community rule	Mountain move away
12:1–8	# 65	parable	Wicked Tenants
12:10	# 66	prophetic saying	Rejected cornerstone
12:14–16	# 100	community rule	Tax to Caesar
12:31	# 25	community rule	Love your brother
?13:17	# 79b	prophetic saying	Womb not conceiving[2]
14:58	# 71	prophetic saying	Destroy this temple

Only in the case of the parable of the Mustard Seed is it possible to say whether or not Thomas is closer to Mark or Q:

Gos. Thom. 20	Mark 4:30–32
The disciples said to Jesus, "Tell us what the kingdom of heaven is like." He said to them, "It is like a mustard seed. It is the smallest of all seeds.	He said, "With what shall we compare the kingdom of God, or what parable shall we use for it? It is like a mustard seed which, when it is sown

[1] This passage can hardly be counted as a true parallel. There is certainly no direct dependence upon a common tradition.

[2] Mark 13:17 is formulated as a woe over those who are pregnant or nursing. Thomas, however, is formulated as a beatitude for those who have not conceived and the breasts which have not given milk.

But when it falls on tilled soil, it produces a great plant and becomes a shelter for birds of the sky."	on the earth, is the smallest of all seeds on the earth. But when it is sown, it grows up and becomes larger than all plants and it puts forth large branches so that under its shadow the birds of the sky can dwell."

The emphasis upon the contrast of the small seed and the large plant is missing in the Q form of this parable (Luke 13:18–19), which differs from the Markan version also in other respects: it speaks of the "garden" into which the seed is thrown, and it says that it becomes a "tree" (δένδρον) and that "the birds are nesting in its branches." Mark and Thomas use the appropriate term "vegetable" (λάχανον), and they correctly describe birds as nesting under the branches. One could also argue that the contrast "small seed/large plant" is a structural element of the original parable that is lost in Q/Luke's version. In any case, Thomas's parallels with Mark do not require the assumption of a literary dependence; what both have in common are original features of the parable.[1]

It is typical in the parallels of the *Gospel of Thomas* to Markan sayings that the narrative frameworks of the Markan setting for the sayings are absent. In several cases Thomas presents a brief chria, introduced by a question of the disciples, where Mark writes an extended apophthegma.

Gos. Thom. 104	Mark 2:18–20
	And the disciples of John and the disciples of the Pharisees were fasting;
They said to Jesus, "Come, let us pray today and let us fast."	and they came and said to him, "Why do the disciples of John and the disciples of the Pharisees fast, but your disciples do not fast?"
Jesus said, "What is the sin that I have committed, or wherein have I been defeated?	And Jesus said to them, "Can the sons of the bridegroom fast as long as the bridegroom is with them? As long as they have the bridegroom with them, they cannot fast. But days are coming, when the

---

[1] One could argue that Thomas's version does not seem to reflect the technical eschatological term "dwell" (κατοκηνοῦν, cf. Jeremias, *Parables*, 147: "actually an eschatological technical term for the incorporation of the Gentiles into the people."

But when the bridegroom leaves the bridal chamber, then let them fast and pray."	bridegroom will be taken from them, and then they will fast on that day."

The first part of Jesus' answer in *Gos. Thom.* 104 is evidently a later expansion. The second part corresponds to the last sentence of this pericope in Mark, albeit without the explicit reference to "that day" with which Mark points to the day of Jesus' death.[1] There is no reference in Thomas to the disciples of John and the Pharisees. At least with respect to the latter, there would have been no reason for Thomas to delete it, had it been a part of his text or tradition.

Gos. Thom. 99	Mark 3:31–34
	And his mother and his brothers came, and standing outside they sent to him, calling him. And a crowd was seated around him,
The disciples said to him, "Your brothers and your mother	and they said to him, "Behold, your mother and your brothers and your sisters are
are standing outside." He said to them,	outside, looking for you." And Jesus answered and said to them, "Who are my mother and my brothers?" And looking around at those sitting about him, he said, "Behold, my mother and
"Those here who do the will of my Father are my brothers and my mother. It is they who will enter the kingdom of my Father."	my brothers! Whoever does the will of God is my brother and my sister and my mother."

As in the previous example, Thomas's text is a brief chria, lacking any of Mark's elaborate introductory setting of the stage and discourse. Thomas also does not share Mark's peculiarity of stating the answer first in the form of a rhetorical question. Thus Thomas's version of this pericope, except for the secondary conclusion, corresponds to its more original form.

---

[1] Lührmann (*Markusevangelium*, 63) explains the singular "on that day" after the preceding plural ("days will be coming") as a reference to the Christian practice of fasting on Fridays (the day of Jesus' death). See also Kuhn, *Ältere Sammlungen*, 69–72.

Gos. Thom. 31[1]	Mark 6:4–5
Jesus said, "A prophet is not accepted in his fatherland, nor does a physician perform healings among those who know him."	And Jesus said to them, "A prophet is not without honor except in his fatherland." And he could not do any mighty work there, except that he laid his hands on a few sick people and healed them.

This is a particularly instructive parallel. When the Greek text of *Gos. Thom.* 31 (*Pap. Oxy.* 1.6) was discovered, Emil Wendling[2] demonstrated that Mark 6:4–5 was constructed on the basis of this saying. While Mark quoted the first part of the saying at the end of his apophthegma about Jesus' rejection in Nazareth, he changed the second part into narrative. Rudolf Bultmann[3] confirmed this observation through form-critical analysis.[4] This saying, in the form in which it is preserved by Thomas, was the nucleus of the later development of the apophthegma that appears now in Mark's text.[5]

Gos. Thom. 14c	Mark 7:15
For what goes into your mouth will not defile you, but that which issues from your mouth—it is that which will defile you.	There is nothing outside a human which by going into him can defile him. But the things coming out of a human being are what defile him.

The basic difference between Thomas and Mark is that Mark states the second half in general terms ("what comes out of a human being"), while Thomas specifies "what comes out of your mouth." In this respect Thomas agrees with the form of this saying in Matt 15:11 ("but what comes out of the mouth defiles a human being"). This might argue for a dependence of Thomas upon Matthew. However, the Matthew/Thomas form of this saying is most likely original: the first half of the saying requires that the second half speak about words which the mouth utters, not excrements (see Mark 7:19). Moreover, what the *Gospel of Thomas* quotes here is the one single saying from the entire pericope that can be considered as a traditional piece and that formed the basis for the original apophthegma—consisting of

---

[1] The text offered here is a translation of the Greek text of *Pap. Oxy.* 1.6.

[2] *Die Entstehung des Marcus-Evangelium* (Tübingen: Mohr/Siebeck, 1908) 53–56.

[3] *Synoptic Tradition*, 31–32.

[4] See my discussion in "ΓΝΩΜΑΙ ΔΙΑΦΟΡΟΙ : The Origin and Nature of Diversification in the History of Early Christianity," in Robinson-Koester, *Trajectories*, 129–32.

[5] The first part of this saying, as it is quoted in Mark 6:4, is preserved independently in John 4:44.

vss. 1–2, 5, and 15—out of which the present complex text of Mark 7:1–23 has been developed.[1]

Gos. Thom. 100	Mark 12:14–16
They showed Jesus a gold coin and said to him,	And they (some of the Pharisees and the Herodians) came to Jesus and said, "Teacher, we know that you are true and do not care for anyone; for you do not regard the position of people, but truly teach the way of God.
"Caesar's men demand taxes from us."	Is it permitted to give taxes to Caesar or not? Should we pay them or should we not?" But knowing their hypocrisy, he said to them, "Why do you tempt me? Bring me a denarius that I may see it." They brought one. And he said to them, "To whom belongs the image and the inscription?" They said, "To Caesar."
He said to them, "Give Caesar what belongs to Caesar, give to God what belongs to God, (give me what is mine."	But Jesus said to them, "Give Caesar what belongs to Caesar, and (give) to God what belongs to God."
	And they were amazed at him.

In this brief chria of the *Gospel of Thomas* all of the narrative and discourse sections are missing which tie the Markan parallel to the context of Mark 12 where various people come to Jesus in order to trap him. Thomas preserves what must have been the basis of the elaborate exchange in Mark's extended apophthegma. The last phrase in Thomas ("and give me what is mine"), on the other hand, is a later expansion emphasizing the commitment to Jesus.

All these examples demonstrate that the Thomas versions of the Markan materials are closely related to the earliest stages of the transmission and development of the respective traditions. If one also considers Thomas parallels to Markan texts which have been discussed in the context of Q parallels and parables, there is no evidence that Thomas knew any of the further redactions of the Markan passages by Matthew and/or Luke.

More difficult is the question of a possible common source of the sayings materials shared by Mark and Thomas. In the case of Thomas' parallels to Q (including the shared parables), it was possible to isolate certain clusters of sayings which pointed in this direction. Except perhaps for the parables, no such clusters can be identified with respect to the numerous units shared by Mark and Thomas. There is a relatively higher number of community rules shared by both: nine out

---

[1] Cf. Lührmann, *Markusevangelium*, 125–26.

of twenty-seven units belong to this category (thirty-three percent), compared with only eight out of a total of forty-eight units in the case of Thomas and Q (sixteen percent). Was one of the common collections a small catechism? The answer to this question, as with any discussion of the sayings in Mark, is difficult as long as there is no clarity about the origin and sources of the sayings and apophthegmata in Mark's Gospel. There is general agreement that Mark did not know the Synoptic Sayings Source, but relied on various smaller collections, probably in written form, though it is difficult to define such collections with certainty.[1] If scholarship investigates further the possible contribution of the *Gospel of Thomas* to the identification of such early collections of sayings, more clarity may also be gained with respect to the sources of Mark's Gospel.

2.2.5 THE GOSPEL OF THOMAS AND THE JOHANNINE TRADITION

The first investigation of the relationship of the *Gospel of Thomas* to the Fourth Gospel of the New Testament was presented by Raymond E. Brown in 1963.[2] It was guided by the explicit question of "how much use, if any, *Gos. Thom.* makes ... of St. John's Gospel,"[3] and it ended with the conclusion that there was probably no direct use of St. John's Gospel, but that "traces of Johannine influence could be attributed to the second general source of *Gos. Thom.*," that is, a source which contained tendentious modifications of synoptic sayings and sayings "that are alien to the spirit of Jesus and without parallel in the thought of the canonical Gospels."[4] Not the author of the *Gospel of Thomas* but the compiler of that second source may have known John's Gospel.[5]

This position has prevailed among most scholars, and very little use has been made of parallels from the *Gospel of Thomas* for the interpre-

---

[1] See the helpful discussion in Lührmann, *Markusevangelium,* 12–15 (with a listing of relevant literature).

[2] "The Gospel of Thomas and St. John's Gospel," *NTS* 9 (1962/63) 155–77.

[3] Ibid., 158.

[4] Ibid., 177.

[5] Ibid. It should be noted that Brown states explicitly at the end "that this is only one possible interpretation of the evidence we have presented" (p. 177). However, in his commentary on the Gospel of John (Raymond E. Brown, *The Gospel according to John* (2 vols; AB 29–30; Garden City, NJ: Doubleday, 1966–70]), Brown essentially repeats this statement: ". . . if there is any dependence of one on the other, it is quite indirect, and the direction of the dependence would be Thomas on John" (p. liii). "Wherever these gospels (i.e., the *Gospel of Truth* and the *Gospel of Thomas*) have developed a common theme, the Gnostic documents stand at much greater distance from the primitive gospel message than does John" (p. lxxxii).

tation of the Fourth Gospel and in the investigation of its religious milieu. It is necessary to reopen the question from a different perspective: one must begin with an assessment of the life situation and purpose of the *Gospel of Thomas's* sayings, especially its "Johannine" sayings, and compare this with the role and functions of parallel materials in the Fourth Gospel and in the formation of the tradition of the Johannine community. This quest will be continued later in the treatment of the Gospel of John. It is the purpose of this chapter to investigate the tradition and collection of the sayings of Jesus insofar as this relates to these two gospels, Thomas and John.

The discourses of the Gospel of John have been developed on the basis of traditions which consisted primarily of sayings.[1] The purpose of the discourses is to explore and discuss critically the meaning and interpretation of such sayings. This is accomplished through changes of the wording of such sayings as well as by placing sayings into a particular context in the composition of a discourse so that the context becomes a critical commentary. On the other hand, the author of the *Gospel of Thomas* achieves his interpretation of traditional sayings by creating variants which thus illuminate particular aspects of understanding. In several instances, John and Thomas interpret the same traditional saying, albeit with the use of quite different hermeneutic principles. Sayings about the life-giving power of the word(s) of Jesus appear in both gospels several times:

Gos. Thom.	John
# 1: Whoever finds the interpretation of these sayings will not taste death (θανάτου οὐ μὴ γεύσηται).[2]	8:51: Whoever keeps my word will not see death (θάνατον μὴ θεωρήσῃ) in eternity.
# 111: And the one who lives from the Living One will not see death.	8:52: Whoever keeps my words will not taste death (θανάτου μὴ γεύσηται) in eternity.[3]

---

[1] We shall return to this later in the discussion of the Fourth Gospel. I have argued this case in several articles: "Dialog und Spruchüberlieferung in den gnostischen Texten von Nag Hammadi," *EvTh* 39 (1979) 532–56; "The History-of-Religions School, Gnosis, and the Gospel of John," *StTh* 40 (1986) 115–36; "Gnostic Sayings and Controversy Traditions in John 8:12–59," in Charles W. Hedrick and Robert Hodgson, Jr., eds., *Nag Hammadi, Gnosticism, and Early Christianity* (Peabody, MA: Hendrickson, 1986) 97–110.

[2] Greek version of *Pap. Oxy.* 654,1.

[3] The second quote is the repetition of the statement of Jesus by the Jews. Brown ("Thomas and John," 159) remarks that "the only difficulty is that *Gos. Thom.* has its parallel in the Jewish rephrasing of Jesus' own statement." But since this is a literary composition anyway, this does not constitute a problem.

#18b: Blessed is he who will take his place in the beginning; he will know the end and will not taste death.

6:63: It is the spirit that gives life, the flesh is of no avail. The words I have spoken to you are spirit and are life.

#19c: For there are five trees for you in paradise. . . . Whoever becomes acquainted with them will not taste death.

6:68–69: Simon Peter answered him, "Lord, to whom shall we go? You have words of eternal life, and we have come to believe and to know that you are the Holy One of God."

Thomas's hermeneutical procedure is evident. Not Jesus' words themselves, but their interpretation gives life, that is, the finding of their hidden truth. This truth is hinted at by different pointers: the finding of Jesus (the Living One), the knowledge of the trees of paradise, the knowledge of one's beginnings.

John, on the other hand, does not hesitate to quote the traditional saying about the life-giving power of Jesus' words unaltered: "The words I have spoken are spirit and are life," and "you have words of eternal life."[1] However, in the context in which these quotes appear they are immediately followed by a qualification. "But there are some of you who do not believe" (John 6:64); and (after Peter's confession) "Jesus answered them and said, 'Did I not select the twelve of you, and one of you is a traitor.'" In the other instances of the quote of this saying, John introduces a subtle change in the wording (analogous to Thomas's hermeneutic method): "Whoever keeps (τηρήσῃ) my word . . ." which is elsewhere explained as "keeping my commandments" (John 14:13, 21; 15:10). Moreover, the discussion about Jesus' claim that he is the giver of life-giving words in John 8 ends with the report that they took up stones in order to throw them at Jesus (8:59).

In a closely related saying, which connects the hearing of the words of Jesus with discipleship, John has introduced a significant change in the wording of a saying that Thomas seems to have preserved in a more original form:

Gos. Thom. #19b	John 8:31–32
If you become my disciples and listen to my words, these stones will minister to you . . .	If you abide in (μένετε ἐν) my word, you will truly be my disciples, and you will know the truth, and the truth will set you free.

For Thomas the saying implies that listening to Jesus' words will con-

---

[1] Note that the adjective "eternal" or the phrase "in eternity" occurs repeatedly in these materials common to Thomas and John. It is, however, a Johannine trait that is never repeated in any of Thomas's parallels.

vey mysterious powers to the disciples. John substitutes the term "abide in"—a typical Johannine concept which emphasizes the faithfulness of Jesus' disciples.[1] He then adds "the truth will make you free"—a Stoic maxim[2] which has no parallel in the sayings tradition. Variations of a metaphorical saying which describes the revelation as a (bubbling) spring of water occur twice in Thomas and twice in John:

Gos. Thom.	John
#13: Because you have drunk, you have become intoxicated from the bubbling spring which I have measured out.	4:14: Whoever drinks from the water that I shall give him, will not thirst in eternity, but the water that I shall give him will become in him a spring of bubbling water unto eternal life.
#108: He who will drink from my mouth will become like me. I myself shall become he, and the things that are hidden will be revealed to him.	7:37–38: If anyone thirsts, let him come [to me]; and let him drink who believes in me. As the Scripture said, "From within him shall flow streams of living water."[3]

The metaphor of drinking was widespread in various religious contexts in antiquity.[4] But there are no occurrences among the sayings of Jesus except for the four passages quoted above, which are all variations of the same saying. In John 4:14, the Johannine reformulation of the saying is visible in the phrase "unto eternal life."[5] But the interpretation is achieved by the placement of the saying in the context of a discourse. The woman's request for this water is cut short by Jesus' command to go and get her husband. The following discourse clarifies that the establishment of faith in Jesus is a more complex process, while the two passages of the *Gospel of Thomas* presuppose that drinking from this spring results immediately in inspiration (here called metaphorically "intoxication"); even more, it establishes a reciprocal identity with the revealer and the communication of secret knowledge (#108). It is especially this latter understanding that the complex reformulation of the saying in John 7:37–38 wants to avoid. Although

---

[1] "Abide in" occurs frequently in the Fourth Gospel; cf. especially John 15:4–10; also 1 John 2:6, 10, 24; 3:6, 24; 4:13, 16. On the concept see Bultmann, *Gospel of John,* on John 5:38 and 16:4.

[2] C. H. Dodd, *Historical Tradition in the Fourth Gospel* (Cambridge: Cambridge University Press, 1963) 380, cf. 330.

[3] This translation follows Brown (*Gospel of John,* 1. 319); cf. his discussion of the translation ibid., 320–22.

[4] For a survey of the evidence see Bultmann, *Gospel of John,* on John 4:11.

[5] It is used twelve times in the Gospel of John and clearly reveals the style of the author.

no particular scriptural passage can be identified as the source of the quotation,[1] the purpose of the saying's alteration is evident: Scripture confirms that Jesus remains the source of living water. The believer does not achieve mystical identity with the revealer.

Both in John and in Thomas, the synoptic sayings about the light[2] are further developed into mythological metaphors in which the revealer's and the revelation's designation as "light" describes their true nature.

Gos. Thom.	John
# 24b: There is light within a man of light and he lights up the whole world. If he does not shine, he is darkness.	11:9–10: If someone walks in the day, he does not stumble, because he sees the light of this world. But if someone walks in the night, he stumbles because the light is not in him.
	12:35–36: Walk as you have the light, that darkness may not overcome you. . . As you have the light, believe in the light so that you become sons of the light.
# 77a: It is I who am[3] the light which is above them all. It is I who am the all. ⟨them⟩	8:12: I am the light of the world. He who follows after me will not walk in the darkness, but will have the light of life.

In *Gos. Thom.* 24b, this light also describes the true identity of the believer. That the same saying is used in John 11:9–10 is evident in the final phrase ("because the light is not him"). However, John hesitates to describe the believer's metaphysical identity as "light." He prefers formulations like "having the light" (8:12) and "sons of light (12:36). On the other hand, the revealer is repeatedly identified with the light, especially in the "I am" saying (8:12; cf. 9:5; 12:46).[4] To be sure, the *Gospel of Thomas* also uses the "I am" formulation in # 77. One may doubt, however, whether John 8:12 is dependent upon such a saying. John 8:12 formulates the "I am" saying on the basis of an older saying that emphasized the contrast "light/darkness," while *Gos. Thom.* 77 is a divine self-predication contrasting divine supremacy

---

[1] See the discussion in Brown, *Gospel of John*, 321–23.

[2] Matt 6:14–16, 23; Luke 8:16; 11:33–35.

[3] This saying and # 61 are the only two passages of the *Gospel of Thomas* where the typically Johannine "I am" or "It is I" appears (ἐγώ εἰμι, Coptic: ⲁⲛⲟⲕ ⲡⲉ).

[4] See also the description of the revelation as "light" in John 1:4, 5, 7, 8–9; 3:19–21.

and the existing universe.[1] There are parallels to such statements in John:

Gos. Thom. # 77a	John 3:31
It is I who am the light which is above them all. It is I who am the all. *(them)*	He who comes from above is above all things.

However, the reformulation of the traditional saying about the light in the Gospel of John ties "belief in the light" directly with belief in Jesus who suffered and was crucified; cf. John 8:28: "When you see the Son of man being raised up (i.e., on the cross), you will recognize that I am."

Perhaps the following parallel belongs in this context:

Gos. Thom. #19a	John 8:58
Blessed is he who came into being before he came into being.	Truly, truly, I say to you, before Abraham was, I am.

For the Gnostic understanding it is crucial to know that one's own origin lies before the beginning of earthly existence. John consciously avoids this application of divine origin to all believers and restricts it to Jesus as the revealer.

This is confirmed in several sayings and statements in which John and Thomas use closely related terminology about coming from and returning to the kingdom, the light, or the Father. In each instance, John restricts these statements to Jesus whereas Thomas brings them as general statements about the believer.

Gos. Thom.	John
# 49: Blessed are the solitary and elect, for you will find the kingdom. For you are from it, and to it you will return.	16:28: I have come out from the Father and I have come into the world. I am again leaving the world and return to the Father.

---

[1] The problem of the origin of the "I am" sayings cannot be discussed in this context; see Brown, *Gospel of John,* 1. 535–38. In this as well as in other instances it seems that traditional sayings used by John are not formulated in this style; furthermore, "I am" sayings are relatively rare, or even completely absent, in such writings as the *Gospel of Thomas,* the *Dialogue of the Savior,* and the *Apocryphon of James.* This would tend to support the thesis that the Johannine "I am" sayings were created by the author of the Fourth Gospel.

50a: If they say to you, "Where did you come from?", say to them, "We came from the light, the place where the light came into being on its own accord . . ."

8:14b: . . . because I know whence I came and where I am going, but you do not know whence I came and where I am going.

1:9: The true light that enlightens every human being was coming into the world . . .

13:3: Jesus knowing that the Father had given all things into his hands and that he had come from God and was returning to God, . . .

Both John and Thomas use the same traditions, perhaps the same sayings. Is there is any dependence of one upon the other, or are both using the same older materials? If Thomas is dependent upon John, one must conclude that he deliberately generalized John's statements about the heavenly origin of Jesus and transformed them into the announcement that everyone who gains true knowledge can claim divine origin and return to it. However, there are indications that John already presupposed this generalized belief and rejected it deliberately. The believers do not arrive at salvation through knowledge about themselves, but through knowledge of Jesus. At the same time, John does not accept the alternative concept which sees Jesus as the paradigm for the Gnostic. How then do the disciples obtain salvation through Jesus in whom is present the Father and whose children they are destined to become?[1] The answer to this question is the topic of the farewell discourses in John 13–17.

In these discourses, John uses sayings which also occur in the *Gospel of Thomas*. He alludes to them repeatedly:

Gos. Thom.	John
# 38b: There will be days when you seek me and will not find me.	13:33: Only a little while I am with you. You will seek me and, as I said to the Jews so I now say to you, where I am going you cannot come.

---

[1] For the presence of the Father in Jesus see John 14:7–11; for "children of God" see John 1:12; 20:17. On this theological problem of the Fourth Gospel in its critical discussion of Gnostic alternatives see the excellent brief characterization by George W. MacRae, "Gnosticism and the Church of St. John's Gospel," in Charles W. Hedrick and Robert Hodgson, Jr., eds., *Nag Hammadi, Gnosticism, and Early Christianity* (Peabody, MA: Hendrickson, 1986), especially pp. 92–94.

7:34: I am going away and you will
seek me, and where I am going you
cannot come.

8:21: I am going away and you will
seek me, and you will die in your sins,
and where am going you cannot come.

24a: His disciples said, "Show us   14:3: I am going to prepare a place for
the place where you are, since it is   you . . . and where I am going you
necessary for us to seek it."   know the way. Thomas said, "Lord
                                              we do not know where you are going.
                                              How do we know the way?"

69a: Blessed are they who have   14:7: If you had known me, you would
been persecuted within themselves.   also know the Father; from now on
It is they who have truly come to   you have known him and have seen
know the Father.   him.

                                              8:19: You have neither known me nor
                                              the Father; if you had known me, you
                                              would also have known my Father.

37a: His disciples said, "When will   14:22: Judas[1] . . . said to him, "How is
you become revealed (ἐμφανὴς εἶναι)   it that you will reveal (ἐμφανίζειν)
to us and when shall we see you?"   yourself to us and not to the world?"

That "Jesus knew that he had come from God and was returning to
God" (John 13:3, see above) has been placed at the beginning of the
farewell discourses. The saying about "seeking me and not finding me"
(John 13:33) is then used to reject both the notion of Jesus as the paradigm for the Gnostic believer and the concept of the discovery of one's
own divine origin. The disciples are not united with Jesus by following
him, but by keeping his new commandment of loving each other as
Jesus has loved them (13:34); in this "loving each other" their belonging to Jesus will become manifest (13:35). Following Jesus to "the
place to which he goes" (14:2–3) is answered by the statement about
the presence of the Father in Jesus (14:7–11) and doing the works of
Jesus (14:12). This is the only way the Father can be known. Finally,
Jesus' revelation to the disciples (14:22) is the event of his and the
Father's return into the believer (14:23) which is, in turn, interpreted
as the coming of the Paraclete, the Spirit of Truth (14:26). This latter
statement is in sharp contrast to the saying of *Gos. Thom.* 38 where

---

[1] The Old Syriac translations read here "(Judas) Thomas."

Jesus says that he will become revealed to the disciples:

> When you disrobe without being ashamed and take up your garments and place them under your feet like little children and tread on them, then [will you see] the son of the living one, and you will not be afraid.[1]

Comments on sayings preserved in the *Gospel of Thomas* are notably present also in John 16,[2] while there are no parallels to John 17—the most "Gnostic" chapter of the farewell discourse to which Thomas might have been expected to have the greatest affinity:

Gos. Thom.	John
[# 49: Blessed are the solitary and elect, for you will find the kingdom. For you are from it, and to it you will return.]	[16:28: I have come out from the Father and I have come into the world. I am again leaving the world and return to the Father.]
# 92: Seek and you will find.	16:23b–24: Whatever you ask the Father, he shall give to you in my name . . . Ask and you will receive that your joy may be full.
Yet, what you asked me about in former times and which I did not tell you then, now I desire to tell, but you do not inquire after it.	16:4b–5: Those things I did not tell you from the beginning when I was with you. Now I am going to the one who sent me, and none of you asks me, 'Where are you going?'
	16:12: Yet many things I have to say to you, but you cannot bear them now.
	16:23a: And on that day you will not ask me anything.
	16:30: Now we know that you know all things, and you have no need that someone asks you. By that we believe that you came from God.

The last sentence in the final statement of the disciples (16:30) deliberately uses the term "to believe" (πιστεύειν) instead of "to know"

---

[1] One might also consider, whether other statements in the farewell discourses consciously refer to the question of "not being afraid," e.g., John 14:27 ("Peace I leave with you . . . let your heart not be shaken . . .").

[2] The first of these sayings has already been quoted above.

(εἰδέναι); the latter term is more often used about Jesus' own knowledge of his origin and in negative statements which characterize unbelief, cf. John 8: "for I know (οἶδα) whence I have come and where I am going, but you do not know (οὐκ οἴδατε) whence I come and where I am going."[1] For the disciples that knowledge about Jesus, and indeed also their knowledge of the Father, is faith. However, because it is faith and not knowledge, it has to face the paradox of Jesus' crucifixion and death and is therefore immediately challenged by Jesus' statement, "Do you now believe? The hour is coming, indeed it has come, when you will be scattered . . ." (John 16:31–32).

 Several discourses of the Gospel of John can be understood as interpretations of a tradition of sayings which has been preserved in the *Gospel of Thomas*. Brown[2] had observed that parallels to the *Gospel of Thomas* are concentrated in the farewell discourses and in the discourse of John 7:37–8:56. But the reason for this concentration of parallels is that John is here discussing a tradition of sayings which proclaim a salvation that is based upon the knowledge of one's origin.

Whether such sayings are also present in other instances is more difficult to decide. There are some similarities in wording and phrasing which I shall list in the following without comment.

Gos. Thom.	John
# 43: His disciples said to him, "Who are you that you should say these things to us?" [Jesus said to them,] "You do not realize who I am from what I say to you, for you have become like the Jews . . ."	8:25–26a: They said to him, "Who are you?" Jesus said to them, "First of all, what I say to you. I have many things to say and to judge about you."
# 61: I am he who exists from the undivided. I was given some of the things of my Father.	5:18: . . . but because he called God his father, making himself equal to God. 3:35: The Father loves the Son and has given everything into his hand. Cf. 13:3 (see above); 10:29.

[1] John never says that the disciples "know" whence they are coming and where they are going. But the author is familiar with the language which describes destiny by origin, cf. 8:23: "You are from below, but I am from above; you are from this world, I am not from this world." See further, Bultmann, *Gospel of John*, on John 3:1–4.

[2] "Thomas and John," 175–76.

# 11: The heavens will pass away, and the one above it will pass away. The dead are not alive, and the living will not die.	11:26: He who believes in me will live, even if he dies, and everyone who lives and believes in me will not die in eternity.

# 13: I am not your master.	15:15: No longer do I call you servants.

# 29: If the flesh came into being because of the spirit, it is a wonder. But if the spirit came into being because of the body, it is a wonder of wonders.	3:6: What is born of the flesh is flesh, and what is born of the spirit is spirit.

In the theological terminology the most striking parallel between Thomas and John is the use of the term "Father" for God. The term occurs in the *Gospel of Thomas* thirty times and is certainly part of the tradition of Thomas's sayings. It cannot be explained as the result of a casual borrowing from the Gospel of John, but characterizes the tradition of sayings that is common to both gospels. "Living Father" also appears in both documents: *Gos. Thom.* 3: ὁ πατὴρ ὁ ζῶν, John 6:57: ὁ ζῶν πατήρ.

The Gospel of John is the end product of a long development of the tradition about Jesus in the Johannine church.[1] In the beginning of this tradition the Johannine community certainly knew and interpreted sayings of Jesus which were only later expanded into lengthy speeches. One collection of such sayings also made its way into the *Gospel of Thomas* which preserved the theological perspective that must have dominated its initial stage. Like Paul's opponents in 1 Corinthians, also the Johannine Christians knew sayings of Jesus which gave life and salvation.

Connections between Thomas's sayings and those used by Paul's Corinthian opponents have already been discussed. There is no overlap between those sayings and the group of sayings which Thomas shares with John. However, there is some commonality with sayings from the Synoptic Sayings Source, notably with Q/Luke 10:22:

---

[1] A good account of some aspects of this history and development is given by Raymond E. Brown, *The Community of the Beloved Disciple: The Life, Love, and Hates of an Individual Church in New Testament Times* (New York: Paulist Press, 1979).

All things have been handed over to me by my Father, and no one knows who the Son is except the Father, or who the Father is except the Son and anyone to whom the Son wishes to reveal him.

This "Johannine" saying has always been recognized as a somewhat alien element which was probably added to Q at a later stage of its redaction,[1] though the saying is certainly older. Its presence in Q does not indicate a close relationship between the sayings common to Thomas and John on the one hand, and the Synoptic Sayings Source on the other.

2.2.6 ESOTERIC THEOLOGY [2]

"Wisdom" is the theme of this writing. As in the *Wisdom of Solomon*, wisdom sayings express the truth about God and about the essence of the human self. They speak about human nature and destiny and, by extension, about the nature of the world and of the proper relationship to the world in which people dwell. The wisdom sayings of the *Gospel of Thomas,* like other Jewish and Christian sayings collections of this type, contain sayings that reveal what is fundamental about people and their behavior. Still other sayings discuss the comportment proper to the tenuous nature of a human being's sojourn in the world. Such sayings and the orientation they reveal are by no means unique to Thomas. They are typical of the early Christian sayings tradition to which Thomas, together with Matthew, Mark, and Luke, was heir.

A number of wisdom sayings speak of divine Wisdom who invites human beings to follow her in order to find the true life here in this world and in the hereafter. It is necessary, therefore, to recognize the present moment in which the words of Jesus are heard; at this point the sayings include a prophetic element, sometimes in sayings paralleled by synoptic sayings, at other times in sayings only found in Thomas:

His disciples said to him, "When will the repose of the dead come about, and when will the new world come?" He said to them, "What you look forward to has already come, but you do not recognize it." (*Gos. Thom.* 51)

---

[1] Lührmann, *Redaktion,* 97–98; Kloppenborg, *Formation of Q,* 197–203.

[2] The following paragraphs owe much to the contributions of Steven Patterson to our jointly authored essay, "The Gospel of Thomas," in *Bible Review* 6/2 (1990) 28–39, although little of this final section of our manuscript was included in the published version.

His disciples said to him. "Twenty-four prophets spoke in Israel, and all of them spoke of you." He said to them, "You have omitted the one living in your presence, and have spoken (only) of the dead." (*Gos. Thom.* 52)

Thomas sees this coming of the kingdom primarily as an event that takes place as the disciples gain a new understanding of themselves:

Jesus said, "If those who lead you say to you, 'See, the kingdom is in the sky,' then the birds of the sky will precede you. If they say to you, 'It is in the sea,' then the fish will precede you. Rather the kingdom is inside of you, and it is outside of you. When you come to know yourselves, then you will be known, and you will realize that it is you who are the sons of the living Father. But if you will not know yourselves, you dwell in poverty and it is you who are that poverty." (*Gos. Thom.* 3)

Thomas contains a number of sayings whose meaning is not as transparent as the common wisdom forms cited thus far. But there are indications that this is by design. These sayings reveal a more radical concept of secret knowledge. They speak of hidden truths about human existence, heavenly origins, separation from the world, and liberation of the soul from the body. It is particularly this understanding of salvation that is critically interpreted in the Gospel of John. The Thomas Christians are told the truth about their divine origins, and given the secret passwords that will prove effective in the return journey to their heavenly home:

Jesus said, "Blessed are the solitary and the elect, for you will find the kingdom. For you are from it, and to it you will return" (*Gos. Thom.* 49).

Jesus said, "If they say to you, 'Where did you come from?', say to them, 'We came from the light, the place where the light came into being on its own accord and established [itself] and became manifest through their image.' If they say to you, 'Is it you?', say, 'We are its children and we are the elect of the living Father.' If they ask you, 'What is the sign of your Father in you?' say to them, 'It is movement and repose.'" (*Gos. Thom.* 50)

The religious perspective represented in such Thomas sayings as these has often been associated with Gnosticism. Gnostics believed that both their origin and their destiny lay in the supreme deity who dwells in a heavenly place removed from the evil world, the creation of a rebellious angel or demiurge. Though this demiurge seeks to hold humans in ignorance of their true identity, in sleepiness and intoxication, a divine messenger will come and awake them and relieve them from the bonds of ignorance by bringing true knowledge about themselves. In saying # 28 of the *Gospel of Thomas*, Jesus speaks with the voice of this heavenly messenger:

> Jesus said, "I took my place in the midst of the world, and I appeared to them in the flesh. I found all of them intoxicated; I found none of them thirsty. And my soul became afflicted for the human beings, because they are blind in their hearts and do not have sight; for empty they came into the world, and empty too they seek to leave the world. But for the moment they are intoxicated. When they shake off their wine, then they will repent."

However, this moment of return to which the Thomas Christians aspire requires preparation beyond the simple memorization of passwords, about which *Gos. Thom.* 50 speaks. One must also cultivate the proper understanding of the world in order to be ready to leave its confines when the time comes:

> Jesus said, "Whoever has come to understand the world, has found (only) a corpse, and whoever has found a corpse is superior to the world." (*Gos. Thom.* 56)

> Jesus said, "He who has recognized the world has found the body, but he who has found the body is superior to the world." (*Gos. Thom.* 80)

Understanding the world—a thing that is really dead—leads inevitably to a proper understanding of the body and corporeal existence. Becoming superior to the world involves deprecation of the flesh in favor of the spirit. Jesus even marvels over how it is that something so glorious as the spirit has become mired in the flesh:

> Jesus said, "If the flesh came into being because of the spirit, it is a wonder. But if spirit came into being because of the body, it is a wonder of wonders. Indeed, I am amazed at how this great wealth has made its home in this poverty." (*Gos. Thom.* 29)

Flesh and spirit, body and soul, are two different components in a human being, joined in an unholy mix which spells doom for both:

> Jesus said, "Woe to the flesh that depends upon the soul; woe to the soul that depends upon the flesh." (*Gos. Thom.* 112)

Separating the soul from corporeal existence does not mean that the soul would henceforth exist as a disembodied spirit, wandering abstractly through the cosmos without form and identity; rather, the soul freed from its prison would enter into a new kind of corporeal existence which awaits her in the heavenly realm. This new "body" is often spoken of as one's heavenly "image," which awaits the soul, but remains guarded and enclosed in the safety of the godhead until it can be properly claimed. Thus Thomas speaks of "images," for the present concealed in the Father, but waiting for the moment when their splendor will be revealed to the utter astonishment of those by whom they will be claimed:

> Jesus said, "The images are manifest to man, but the light in them remains concealed in the image of the light of the Father. He will become manifest, but his image will remain concealed by his light." (*Gos. Thom.* 83)

> Jesus said, "When you see your likeness, you rejoice. But when you see your images which came into being before you, and which neither die nor become manifest, how much will you have to bear!" (*Gos. Thom.* 84)

This understanding of human existence also involves a radical social ethos. "Knowing" is the key for the right understanding of the believers' existence in the world. But this does not mean that Thomas Christianity was a conclave of an isolated meditating elite. There are many sayings in Thomas (a number of these shared with the canonical Gospels) which specify the kind of behavior and mode of living in the world that is appropriate for those who are truly "children of the Father." At the heart of this life style is a social radicalism that rejects commonly held values. The sayings speak of rejecting the ideal of a settled life in house and home, and they require itineracy:

> Jesus said, "Become passers-by." (*Gos. Thom.* 42)

In the rejection of popular piety, Thomas's sayings are more radical than Matthew's (chapter 6) criticism of the practice of fasting, praying, and almsgiving:

> His disciples questioned him and said to him, "Do you want us to fast? How shall we pray? Shall we give alms? What diet shall we observe?" Jesus said, "Do not tell lies, and do not do what you hate, for all things are plain in the sight of heaven." (*Gos. Thom.* 6)

> Jesus said to them, "If you fast, you will give rise to sin for yourselves; and if you pray, you will be condemned; and if you give alms, you will do harm to your spirits." (*Gos. Thom.* 14a)

Shrewd business sense is rejected, in keeping with the canonical gospels (cf. Matt 5:42; Lk 6:34; 12:13–15):

> [Jesus said], "If you have money, do not lend it at interest, but give [it] to one from whom you will not get it back." (*Gos. Thom.* 95)

At the end of the parable of the Great Banquet (Matt 22:1–10; Lk 14:15–24) the *Gospel of Thomas* adds a characteristic sentence:

Businessmen and merchants [will] not enter the places of my father. (*Gos. Thom.* 64)

To be "children of the living Father" is to be free from the society and not to be bound to the world and its values. "Blessedness" does not depend upon the marks of success in this world. One's identity should not be determined by whatever is valuable for personal status in the social fabric of the world: householder, family member, religious leader, successful business person:

Jesus said: "Whoever finds the world and becomes rich, let him renounce the world." (*Gos. Thom.* 110)

But the ideal of the itinerant man, who is independent of all social and family bonds, also seems to imply that women engaged in the pursuit of common values and social conventions likewise are not fit for this role unless they accept the ideal of the ascetic man:

Simon Peter said to them, "Let Mary leave us, for women are not worthy of life." Jesus said, "I myself shall lead her in order to make her male, so that she too may become a living spirit resembling you males. For every woman who will make herself male will enter the kingdom of heaven." (*Gos. Thom.* 114)

2.3 The Synoptic Sayings Source

2.3.1 Q AND THE TWO-SOURCE HYPOTHESIS

According to the two-source hypothesis, the Gospel of Mark is the oldest of the three so-called Synoptic Gospels. It was used by the other two Synoptic Gospels, Matthew and Luke, who in addition to Mark, both used a second common source, the so-called Synoptic Sayings Source.

Markan priority was first recognized by Karl Lachmann (1835) and Gottlob Wilke (1838). Christian Hermann Weiße was the first who recognized that Matthew must have employed, in addition to Mark, a second source which consisted of a collection of sayings of Jesus (1838).[1] The architect of the two-source hypothesis and classic advocate of Markan priority is Heinrich-Julius Holtzmann.[2] The most

---

[1] On the history of the development of this hypothesis see Werner Georg Kümmel, *Das Neue Testament: Geschichte der Erforschung seiner Probleme* (Orbis 3.1; Freiburg/München: Alber, 1958) 177–91.

[2] See his *Die synoptischen Evangelien: Ihr Ursprung und ihr geschichtlicher Charac-ter* (Leipzig: Engelmann, 1863); cf. idem, *Lehrbuch der historisch-kritischen Einleitung in das Neue Testament* (Freiburg: Mohr, 1892) 342–61.

detailed elaboration of the two-source hypothesis—augmenting it by the thesis that Matthew and Luke used two other sources in addition to Mark and the Synoptic Sayings Source —was presented by B. H. Streeter.[1] In one form or another, this hypothesis has been accepted by most scholars.[2] Nevertheless, arguments against the existence of a Synoptic Sayings Source, often coupled with arguments against the priority of Mark, have been brought forward frequently.[3] The most recent challenges try to revive the so-called "Griesbach hypothesis." In 1789/90, decades before the formulation of the two-source hypothesis, Johann Jakob Griesbach had criticized the traditional view which had been generally accepted for centuries, namely, that Matthew was the oldest of the four canonical gospels, that Mark had used Matthew, and that Luke had used both Matthew and Mark. Griesbach still maintained the priority of Matthew but modified this traditional position by arguing that it was Luke who had used Matthew first, and that Mark had used both Matthew and Luke.[4] The most outspoken advocate for the more recent revival of this hypothesis, William Farmer,[5] has welcomed in particular the critique of the Markan priority by Hans-Herbert Stoldt and supported the publication of its English translation.[6]

Some of the arguments in favor of the Griesbach hypothesis rest on the observation that Matthew and Luke agree in several instances against the extant text of Mark's Gospel, the so-called minor agreements of Matthew and Luke.[7] I shall argue below in the treatment of

---

[1] *The Four Gospels: A Study of Origins* (London: Macmillan, 1924).

[2] Presentations of the arguments in favor of the two-source hypothesis and of its more recent challenges can be found in Vielhauer, *Geschichte*, 268–80, and in more detail in Schmithals, *Einleitung in die drei ersten Evangelien* (GLB; Berlin: De Gruyter, 1985) 182–233. A very helpful discussion of the Q hypothesis was published by Frans Neirynck, "Recent Developments in the Study of Q," in Delobel, ed., *LOGIA*, 29–75; see also Neirynck, "L'édition du texte du Q," in idem, *Evangelica: Gospel Studies—Études d'Évangile (Collected Essays)* (BEThL 60; Leuven: Peeters, 1982) 925–33.

[3] An excellent survey of the arguments for and against the Synoptic Sayings Source with extensive documentations of the opinions of the individual scholars in question can be found in Arthur J. Bellinzoni, Jr, *The Two-Source Hypothesis: A Critical Appraisal* (Macon, GA: Mercer University Press, 1985) 219–434.

[4] Cf. Kümmel, *Das Neue Testament*, 88–89; Schmithals, *Einleitung*, 142–45.

[5] *The Synoptic Problem* (New York: Macmillan, 1964; 2d edition Macon, GA: Mercer University Press, 1976). For Farmer's other publications see the listing in Bellinzoni, *The Two-Source Hypothesis*, 459.

[6] *History and Criticism of the Marcan Hypothesis* (Macon, GA: Mercer University Press, 1980).

[7] For a critical discussion of these arguments of Farmer (and Stoldt) in support of the Griesbach hypothesis see Frans Neirynck, *The Minor Agreements of Matthew and Luke against Mark* (BEThL 37; Louvain: Leuven University Press, 1974); furthermore several articles by the same author in his *Evangelica: Gospel Studies—Études*

the Gospel of Mark[1] that many of the minor agreements between Matthew and Luke result from the fact that both Matthew and Luke used a text of Mark that was different from the text which is preserved in the manuscript tradition of the canonical Gospel of Mark.

All attempts to disprove the two-source hypothesis favor the priority of Matthew or of some earlier form of Matthew which was possibly written in Aramaic. This is a very problematic position, burdened with great difficulties, especially with regard to the sayings materials of Matthew's Gospel. In most instances, very good arguments can be brought forward to show that the Gospel of Luke has preserved more original forms of the sayings shared by Matthew and Luke; thus Matthew cannot have been the source of these Lukan sayings. Moreover, if there was no common sayings source shared by Matthew and Luke, an explanation of the source, or sources, of Matthew's sayings must still work with the assumption of some earlier document(s) through which these sayings came to the author of the First Gospel. Scholars who deny the existence of a Synoptic Sayings Source, still have to find a theory by which the transmission of the sayings to the author of Matthew's Gospel can be explained. In other words, the rejection of the two-source hypothesis solves nothing and creates new riddles for which even more complex and more improbable hypotheses have to be proposed.

The two-source hypothesis maintains that Matthew and Luke both used Mark, or at least some form of the Gospel of Mark, as their primary source and, in addition, employed a second common source which consisted mostly of sayings of Jesus.[2] More recent research has not only made the existence of this source more probable, it has also demonstrated that one can reconstruct its formation, development, and redaction as a literary document. The observations which argue strongly for the existence of a Synoptic Sayings Source and its use by Matthew and Luke are the following:

(1) What Matthew and Luke share in addition to their common Markan pericopes consists almost exclusively of sayings. The only exceptions are: one miracle story (Matt 8:5–13 = Luke 7:1–10), materi-

---

d'Évangile (BEThL 60; Leuven: Peeters, 1982) 769–810; also C. M. Tuckett, The Revival of the Griesbach Hypothesis (NTSMS 44; Cambridge, Cambridge University Press, 1983); Schmithals, Einleitung, 150–52.

[1] See below # 4.1.

[2] For this source, the siglum "Q"—the first letter of the German word for "Source" = Quelle—has been commonly used since the beginning of this century. This designation and siglum was chosen as a neutral term that does not imply any prejudice with respect to its literary character and historical value; cf. Martin Dibelius, Botschaft und Geschichte (2 vols.; Tübingen: Mohr/Siebeck, 1953–1956) 1. 97–98.

als about John the Baptist and Jesus' baptism (parts of Matt 3:1–17 =
Luke 3:2–9, 16–17, 21–22), and the story of Jesus' temptation (Matt
4:1–11 = Luke 4:1–13). This requires the assumption of a common
source which consisted mostly of sayings of Jesus and probably of
some other shared non-Markan materials.

(2) The numerous verbal agreements of these parallel passages
cannot be explained as dependence of either Matthew upon Luke or
dependence of Luke upon Matthew because, in numerous, instances
Luke's version is evidently the more original one. But there are also
passages in which Matthew rather than Luke has preserved words
and phrases which cannot be explained as the product of Matthew's
editorial work. Indeed, in some instances what is certainly original in
a particular saying may occur partially in Luke and partially in
Matthew. A striking example is the following passage (words from
the original version of the saying are underlined):[1]

Matt 7:23	Luke 13:27	Psalm 6:9
καὶ τότε	καὶ ἐρεῖ λέγων	
ὁμολογήσω	ὑμῖν·	
αὐτοῖς ὅτι		
οὐδέποτε ἔγνων	οὐκ οἶδα	
ὑμᾶς,	πόθεν ἐστέ·	
ἀποχωρεῖτε ἀπ’	ἀπόστητε ἀπ’	ἀπόστητε ἀπ’
ἐμοῦ	ἐμοῦ πάντες	ἐμοῦ πάντες
	ἐργάται	
οἱ ἐργαζόμενοι	ἐργάται	οἱ ἐργαζόμενοι
τὴν ἀνομίαν.	ἀδικίας.	τὴν ἀνομίαν.

The second half of this saying is a quotation of Ps 6:9. But while the
first words of the sentence derived from this psalm are accurately
preserved only in Luke, the last words of the quotation have an exact
parallel only in Matthew. One must assume that there was a common
source used by both authors and that this common source quoted the
sentence exactly as it occurred in Ps 6:9.

(3) The sequence in which certain groups of sayings occur in the
Gospel of Luke often reveals an association and composition of sayings
that is more directly related to the process of the collection of oral
materials, while Matthew interrupts or disturbs such sequences whenever his motivations as an author of literature are evident. In his ver-

---

[1] I have not given an English translation because a translation would not reflect
well enough the subtle differences between the two texts.

sion of Jesus' speech for the "sending of the disciples" (Matt 9:37–11:1), Matthew parallels Luke in the reproduction of a series of sayings which instruct missionaries with respect to their conduct. But he repeatedly interpolates materials which belong to other contexts and often do not fit the genre of an older collection of originally oral sayings:

Matthew	Material	*order*	Older Q *(Luke* collection	Other Sources
9:37–38	Saying		Q 10:2	
10:1	Introduction			Mark 6:7 / *Mark 3:*
10:2–4	List of the twelve disciples			Mark 3:16–19
10:5–6	. . . not to the Samaritans			?
10:7	Instruction to preach		Q 10:9	*Mark 3:15a / Luke 9:2*
10:8	Matthean redaction			
10:9–10	Instruction about equipment		Q 10:4	Mark 6:8–9
10:11a	. . . entering a house/city		Q 10:5a	
10:11b	Expansion of command			Mark 6:10
10:12–13	Rule about stay in a house		Q 10:5b–6	
10:14	Rule about leaving		Q 10:10–11	Mark 6:11
10:15–16	Saying : *S ~ oon*		Q 10:12, 3	
10:17–22	Persecution sayings			Mark 13:9–13
10:23	Matthean redaction		*Later Q*	
10:24	Saying: master and disciple			Q 6:40
10:25	Matthean redaction			
10:26–33	Group of sayings			Q 12:2–9
10:34–35	Sayings about divisions			Q 12:51–53
10:37–38	Sayings about discipleship			Q 14:26–27
10:39	Saying about one's life			Q 17:33
10:40	Saying about acceptance			Mark 9:37
10:41	Matthean redaction			
10:42	Saying about disciple's aid			Mark 9:41
11:1	Matthean redaction			

Q/Luke 10:2–12 exhibits all the features of an early collection of rules for the conduct of the missionary. Its composition most likely took place in the oral transmission of such regulations, and Q still reflects the loose connection of such a unit of tradition. That Matthew's text is the result of a secondary redaction, revealing the use of written sources, is evident in the manner of his composition. He employed one primary source, i.e., Q, still intact in Luke's version, in order to compose a literary speech in which he included additional materials which were mostly drawn from his other major source, i.e., Mark (6:7; 3:16–19; 6:8–9; 6:10; 6:11; 13:9–13), then adding materials drawn from other contexts of both sources (Mark 13:9–13; Q 6:40; 12:2–9; 12:51–53; 14:26–27; 17:33; Mark 9:37; 9:41). In the case of Mark, the materials which Matthew used from his collection of rules about missionaries appear in the same sequence. But in the case of Q, Matthew changed their original order.

To prove the thesis that both Matthew and Luke used, in addition to Mark, such a source of sayings is not identical with the reconstruction of this source, either with respect to the sequence of its materials or with respect to the exact wording of its sayings. Moreover, although Matthew and Luke sometimes agree in their reproduction of the wording of a Q saying, there are also considerable differences, so that one wonders whether there were not two different editions of Q, one used by Matthew, the other by Luke. This is most likely with respect to the Q materials which appear in Matthew's Sermon on the Mount. Here Matthew does not appear to have used Q directly, i.e., the inaugural sermon of Jesus of Q 6:20–49, but rather a "sermon" into which a predecessor of Matthew had already incorporated sayings from other sections of Q.[1] However, such considerations do not invalidate the fundamental hypothesis of the existence of Q as a document *sui generis,* a literary composition in its own right, which can be largely reconstructed and which can be described and analyzed with respect to the stages of its development.

2.3.2 THE COMPOSITION AND REDACTION OF Q

2.3.2.1 *Some General Considerations*

The question of the composition and redaction of Q has been discussed ever since the hypothesis of its existence was proposed. Various attempts have been made to reconstruct the document and to establish its original wording.[2] In the course of the scholarly discussion a consensus has emerged with respect to several basic assumptions about Q: (1) Although there are some instances in which individual sayings reveal an Aramaic substratum, the first composition of Q was in Greek and not in Aramaic.[3] (2) The order of the sayings in Q is, in general, more faithfully preserved in Luke than in Matthew;[4] how-

---

[1] On this question see below in the chapter on the redaction of Q (# 2.3.4).

[2] See the discussion in Schmithals, *Einleitung,* 216–223; Frans Neirynck, "Recent Developments in the Study of Q," in Delobel, ed., *LOGIA,* 35–41; Kloppenborg, *Formation of Q,* 219–26. From 1984 to 1988, a seminar of the Society of Biblical Literature under the direction of James M. Robinson, now continued in regular annual working sessions as "International Q Project," is attempting to achieve a consensus in the reconstruction of this document, considering carefully all earlier attempts.

[3] Schmithals, *Einleitung,* 222–23.

[4] The relevant literature is listed in Kloppenborg, *Formation of Q,* 64–65; Schmithals, *Einleitung,* 217–19.

ever, although Matthew often moved groups of Q sayings to a different context, he often parallels Luke in the sequence of the individual sayings within such groups. (3) Luke preserves the original wording of the sayings more faithfully than Matthew, although even Luke occasionally edited his Q materials and Matthew cannot be ruled out as the document in which the original wording of its source is still extant. (4) As a rule no narrative materials but only sayings shared by Matthew and Luke should be assigned to Q—exceptions are materials concerning John the Baptist and the story of the healing of the centurion's son. (5) Convincing arguments are necessary in order to establish that sayings derive from Q whenever they are preserved only in one of the two Gospels; but the possibility cannot be excluded *a priori*. (6) The document Q must have undergone at least one substantial redaction in its development until it circulated in the form in which Matthew and Luke used it for the composition of their Gospels. (7) Q probably underwent one additional redaction before it was used by Matthew, though this latest redaction already exhibits some features, which are generally judged to be typically Matthean.

If Luke's order of the pericopae of Q can be taken as following most closely the original order of Q itself, it appears that the author of Q grouped the sayings under certain thematic headings. This observation permits the inclusion into Q of some sayings appearing in these units although they are preserved only by Luke, as well as of sayings appearing only in Matthew if they are closely connected with topics and with parallels in Q/Luke. That a saying attested only once in the parallel tradition may have been present in Q can be confirmed in numerous instances by a parallel in the *Gospel of Thomas*.[1] According to these criteria of inclusion, it is possible to determine the content and order of Q in its major subsections with a great degree of certainty.[2]

The result of this reconstruction gives us the document Q as it was used by Luke and Matthew (or a pre-Matthean redactor of Q). But this document is apparently the result of at least one major redaction of a still older document.[3] Tensions and inconsistencies which can be observed within this common source of Matthew and Luke can hardly be explained as resulting from shifts in the history of different units of oral traditions that were used in the community of Q prior to their

---

[1] On the parallels of the *Gospel of Thomas* and Q see above # 2.2.4.2.

[2] In the following I am especially indebted to Kloppenborg, *Formation of Q*, 64–80.

[3] On the several attempts of a redactional analysis of Q and the problems of such analyses see Kloppenborg, *Formation of Q*, 95–101. In the following I shall base my arguments primarily on Kloppenborg's work and refer to earlier authors only occasionally.

collection and composition into a literary document.[1] The most obvious signs of a secondary redaction of Q can be found in the apocalyptic announcement of judgment and of the coming of the Son of man which conflicts with the emphasis upon the presence of the kingdom in wisdom sayings and prophetic announcements.[2] In the following presentation of the several sections of Q, special attention will be paid to the distinction between sayings belonging to the original document and materials added by the redactor.

2.3.2.2 John the Baptist and the Temptation of Jesus

Pericope or saying	Q / Luke	Matthew	Other
Appearance of John [a]	3:2b–4	3:1–3, 5	Mark 1:3–5
Preaching of repentance[3]	3:7–9	3:7–10	
Eschatological preaching [b]	3:16–17	3:11–12	Mark 1:7–8
Baptism of Jesus [c]	(3:21–22)	3:13–17	Mark 1:9–11
Temptation of Jesus	4:1–13	4:1–11	(Mark 1:12–13)

[a] Matthew and Luke agree in the omission of the quotation from Mal 3:1 (= Mark 1:2), and both use the phrase ἡ περίχωρος τοῦ Ἰορδάνου (Matt 3:5; Luke 3:3). This justifies the inclusion of these verses into Q. It is reasonable to assume that Q must have introduced the appearance of John in some fashion.

[b] Matthew and Luke agree with Mark only in the announcement of the coming of the "Stronger One," but do not include the phrase ἐγὼ ἐβάπτισα ὑμᾶς ὕδατι, and read αὐτὸς ὑμᾶς βαπτίσει ἐν πνεύματι ἁγίῳ καὶ πυρί instead of Mark's ἐν πνεύματι ἁγίῳ. The judgment metaphor Q 3:17 has no Markan parallel.

[c] The agreements of Matthew and Luke are very slight[4] and do not justify the inclusion of this pericope.

The announcement of judgment characterizes this opening section of Q in which John the Baptist calls for repentance and announces the

---

[1] This is essentially the solution of the problems presented by Siegfried Schulz, *Q: Die Spruchquelle der Evangelisten* (Zürich: Theologischer Verlag, 1972).

[2] That these apocalyptic materials belong to the redaction of Q was first argued convincingly by Lührmann (*Redaktion*). Kloppenborg (*Formation of Q*) has presented an analysis of Q in which he characterizes the original formation of this document as a composition of sapiential speeches and, following Lührmann, its redaction as characterized by the announcement of judgment over this generation. My own view is primarily based on the observations and arguments of these two scholars.

[3] In Luke, this saying is followed by the so-called "social preaching of John" (Luke 3:10–14) which only very few scholars derive from Q; see Kloppenborg, *Q Parallels*, 10.

[4] See Kloppenborg, *Q Parallels*, 16.

coming of God ("the stronger one who is coming after me") for judgment with fire and spirit (Q 3:7–9, 16–17). Only these sayings can be assigned to Q with some degree of certainty. The temptation story in Matt 4:1–11 and Luke 4:1–13 requires a common source for these two Gospels, but it is difficult to prove that this source was Q.[1] In any case, the entire opening section must be assigned to the redaction of this document.

2.3.2.3 Inaugural Sermon to the Disciples

Pericope or Saying	Q / Luke	Matthew	Other
Introductory phrase [a]	6:12, 20a	5:1–2	
Blessing of the poor	6:20b	5:3	Gos. Thom. 54
Blessing of the hungry	6:21a	5:6	Gos. Thom. 69b
Blessing of those who weep	6:21b	5:4	Rom 12:15
Blessing of hated, persecuted [b]	6:22–23	5:10–12	Gos. Thom. 68–69a
Love your enemies	6:27–29	5:44	Rom 12:14
Give to the one who asks	6:30	5:42a	Acts 20:35
Lending money	(6:34)	5:42b	Gos. Thom. 95
Be children of your Father	6:35b	5:48	
Golden rule	6:31	7:12	Gos. Thom. 6b[2] ?
Serving two masters [c]	16:13	6:24	Gos. Thom. 47a-b
On judging	6:37–38	7:1–2	1 Clem. 13.2[3]
Plants of the Father [d]		15:13	Gos. Thom. 40
Blind leading the blind	6:39	15:14	Gos. Thom. 34[4]
Disciple not over his master	6:40	10:24–25	John 13:16[5]
Splinter in the brother's eye	6:41–42	7:3–5	
Tree and fruit	6:43	7:16–18	Gos. Thom. 43
No figs from thistles	6:44	12:33	Gos. Thom. 45a
Good things from the heart	6:45	12:34–35	Gos. Thom. 45b
"Those who say, 'Lord, Lord'"	6:46	7:21	2 Clem. 4.2
Response of the Lord [e]	13:26–27	7:22–23	2 Clem. 4.5

[a] Luke's mention of the "mountain" in 6:12 and of the disciples in 6:20, both paralleled in Matt 5:1, indicates that the "sermon" in Q was

[1] Lührmann (Redaktion, 56) argues against inclusion of this pericope in Q. But see the detailed discussion in Kloppenborg, Formation of Q, 246–62. Kloppenborg (ibid., 262) comes to the conclusion that it was a late addition to Q which signifies the movement of Q "toward a narrative or biographical cast."

[2] It is not certain that this saying of the Gospel of Thomas is a real parallel; see above # 2.2.4.2.

[3] Further parallels appear in Rom 2:1 ("... you who are judging; for in judging another you condemn yourself") and Mark 4:24.

[4] Cf. also Rom 2:19.

[5] A further parallel appears in Dial. Sav. 53 (139,11): "The disciple resembles his teacher."

introduced by a phrase that identified setting and audience.

[b] Those who are persecuted are mentioned only in Matt 5:10–11, and most scholars exclude the entire section Matt 5:5–10 from Q. But because *Gos. Thom.* 68 and 69a also blesses the disciples when they are persecuted, the persecuted were most likely also mentioned in the blessings of Q.

[c] οἰκέτης appears only in Luke and is usually considered to be secondary. However, the *Gospel of Thomas* also presupposes this word.[1]

[d] The parallel to this saying (Matt 15:13) in *Gos. Thom.* 40, and its close connection with Matt 15:14 = Q/Luke 6:39 may justify its inclusion in Q in this context.[2]

[e] Matt 7:21 and 7:22–23 belong together and may have stood together in Q.[3] That the parallel to Matt 7:22–23 appears in Luke 13:26–27 is probably due to Lukan redaction.[4] Luke 13:22–27 is a Lukan composition for which Luke has used various materials; see below the note to Q/Luke13:24.

The large number of parallels in the *Gospel of Thomas* and in other early Christian writings is striking. This section of Q has not only preserved many sayings which circulated widely at a very early date, it was most likely a cluster of sayings that existed independently in a number of variants in oral or written form before it was used by the author of Q, and it was apparently also known to Paul (Romans 12) and to the *First Epistle of Clement* (chapter 13).[5] A mixture of wisdom sayings and prophetic sayings of Jesus (to the latter category I would especially assign the beatitudes, but also the prediction of exclusion of those who only say "Lord, Lord") characterizes this portion of Q. This

---

[1] See above # 2.2.4.2.

[2] Almost all scholars exclude this saying from Q; see Kloppenborg, *Q Parallels,* 38.

[3] This, however, does not imply that the Matthean formulation of this Q saying is to be preferred over the text preserved in Luke. On the contrary, Matt 7:21–23 exhibits features which show the redaction of the pre-Matthean author of the Sermon on the Mount; see Betz, "An Episode in the Last Judgment (Matt. 7:21–23)," in idem, *Essays,* 125–57. It is difficult to determine, whether the parallel in *2 Clem.* 4 is dependent upon Matthew and Luke or upon the pre-Matthean Sermon on the Mount or at least upon the milieu in which this sermon was written (so Betz, ibid., 143–46). There are also Lukan features in *2 Clem.* 4, and the mixture of Matthean and Lukan elements in this quotation if paralleled in Justin, *1 Apol.* 16.9–12 and *Dial.* 76.5; see Koester, *Synoptische Überlieferung,* 75–91; see also below ## 5.1.2 and 5.2.1.4.

[4] Kloppenborg (*Formation of Q,* 235–36) argues for inclusion into the context of Q 13:24–14:35 and understands the saying not as directed against disciples, but "at unresponsive recipients of Christian preaching."

[5] See above, ## 2.1.2 and 2.1.4.3,

is not simply a "sapiential speech,"[1] but a prophetic, and thus eschatological, announcement of the presence of the rule of God. However, there is no trace of an apocalyptic perspective which predicts judgment and condemnation.

2.3.2.4 John, Jesus, and This Generation [2]

Saying or Pericope	Q / Luke	Matthew	Other
The centurion's son [a]	7:1–10	8:5–13	John 4:46–54
Answer to John's inquiry [b]	7:18–23	11:2–6	
Why did you go to the desert? [c]	7:24b–26	11:7–9	Gos. Thom. 78
Reference to Mal 3:1 LXX	7:27	11:10	
The smallest in the kingdom [d]	7:28	11:11	Gos. Thom. 46
The kingdom and John [e]	16:16	11:12–14	
The publicans and John	7:29–30	21:31–32	
The children of this age	7:31–35	11:16–19	

[a] This is one of only two miracle narratives in Q. In favor of its inclusion[3] is the fact that it appears right after the inaugural sermon of Jesus in both Matthew and Luke.[4] The predominance of dialogue in this story makes it an apophthegma rather than a miracle narrative.[5] It is debated whether Luke 7:3a, 4–6a should be included in the Q version (parallels are missing in Matthew). The vocabulary of these verses is Lukan, and the duplication of the sending of emissaries is awkward.[6]

[b] Most scholars consider Luke 7:21 as a Lukan addition; some would also see 7:20 as Lukan.[7]

[c] It is remarkable that, like Q 7:24b–25, the parallel in the Gospel of Thomas also does not contain a reference to John the Baptist. The relationship to John the Baptist is established in Q through the placement of the originally independent saying into this context and in Luke by the addition of 7:24a, which is clearly redactional.

---

[1] Kloppenborg (Formation of Q) uses this designation for the units of the original composition of Q.

[2] The heading is taken from Kloppenborg (Q Parallels, p. xxxi). It is difficult to find an appropriate heading for this section of Q. The materials collected in this section, or at least their application to John the Baptist, may derive from Q's later redactor. But in the final form, Q 7:1–35 is a section that is distinct from the preceding "Speech to the Disciples" and the following "Instruction for the Mission."

[3] Most authors include this pericope (Kloppenborg, Q Parallels, 50).

[4] See Bovon, Evangelium nach Lukas, 346.

[5] Bultmann, Synoptic Tradition, 38–39.

[6] Bovon (Evangelium nach Lukas, 346) suggests that at least the second sending in vs. 6 be eliminated.

[7] See Kloppenborg, Q Parallels, 52; Bovon, Evangelium nach Lukas, 370.

d Q 7:28 is a saying that praises the greatness of John (7:28a), with a secondary Christian addition which diminishes John's status (7:28b).[1] However, the form of this saying that appears in *Gos. Thom.* 46 does not contain a polemic against John the Baptist. The saying merely emphasizes the contrast between the old (from Adam to John) and the new (the kingdom). The polemical formulation ("[even] the smallest in the kingdom is greater than he") instead of "whoever becomes a child will know the kingdom and will become greater than [even] John" is thus due to the redactor of Q who inserted the saying into this context.[2]

e The placement of this saying is problematic, though most scholars agree that it appeared in Q. Matt 11:12–14 argues for a placement in this context.

Like the initial section of Q—the preaching of John the Baptist—this section points to the redactor of Q as its author. Except for two sayings (Q 7:24b-26 and 7:28) there are no parallels in the *Gospel of Thomas*. Both of these sayings are originally free sayings which do not contain any polemic against John. In its present form, with the concluding threat against "this generation" (Q 7:31–35), the composition of this entire Q section must be assigned to the redactor. However, some of the sayings used here may have stood in the earlier version of Q, although it is no longer possible to determine the context in which they originally appeared.

2.3.2.5 The Followers of Jesus and Their Mission

Pericope or saying	Q / Luke	Matthew	Other
No home for the human being [a]	9:57–58	8:19–20	Gos. Thom. 86
Let the dead bury the dead	9:59–60	8:21–22	
Who puts his hand to the plow [b]	9:61–62		
The harvest is great	10:2	9:37	Gos. Thom. 73
Like sheep among wolves	10:3	10:16a	
Clever like serpents [c]	—	10:16b	Gos. Thom. 39b
Instructions for the road [d]	10:4–7	10:9–11	Mark 6:8–13
Instruction for entering a place	10:9–12	10:7,14f	Gos. Thom. 14b
Woe over Chorazin etc. [e]	10:13–15	11:21–23a	
Those who receive me . . . [f]	10:16	10:40	John 13:20
Hidden from the wise . . . [g]	10:21	11:25–26	1 Cor 1:20

[1] Cf. Bultmann, *Synoptic Tradition*, 164.

[2] On the relationship of this saying to the present context see Lührmann, *Redaktion*, 27–29.

| Authority given to the Son | 10:22 | 11:27 | John 3:35 |
| Blessedness of the witnesses | 10:23–24 | 13:16–17 | 1 Cor 2:9 |

a In the Q version of this saying, "Son of man" was probably under-stood as title of Jesus. But the *Gospel of Thomas* never uses this title for Jesus. Thus its form of the saying has preserved the original meaning which compares the animals with the situation of human beings.[1]

b This third saying of a group of three about following Jesus has no parallel in Matthew, but its language is not Lukan; it agrees in style and content with the two preceding units, and there are good reasons why Matthew would have omitted it.[2] Torah: phor.

c The close connection between Matt 10:16a and 10:16b and the appearance of a parallel in the *Gospel of Thomas* argues for an inclu-sion of Matt 10:16b into Q.[3]

d Some of the instructions here parallel Mark quite closely. Matthew 10 has combined Mark's mission speech with the mission instructions found in Q and with other materials from a special source and from Mark 13. But Luke 10:2–16 follows Q without Markan intru-sions, while Luke reproduces the Markan mission speech elsewhere (Luke 9:1–6).

e The woe against Chorazin and Bethsaida is evidently an intrusion into an older collection of sayings concerning the mission of the disci-ples. It is an originally independent saying, and it is difficult to judge at which stage of the development of Q it was interpolated. Matt 11:23b–24 has no Lukan parallel, but may have been a part of this pro-phetic tradition.[4]

f This saying is attested frequently elsewhere; cf. Mark 9:47; 1 Thess. 4:8; *Did.* 11.4; Ignatius *Eph.* 6.1. It concludes the mission speech quite appropriately. The following sayings in Luke (10:17–20), which have no parallel in Matthew, have been considered by some authors for inclusion in Q, but there are no convincing arguments for this assumption.[5]

g This saying and the following two sayings differ markedly from other Q materials, while their parallels in 1 Corinthians 1–4 and in the *Gospel of Thomas* and the Gospel of John are striking because of their

---

[1] "Man, homeless in this world, is contrasted with the wild beasts." (Bultmann, *Synoptic Tradition*, 28); cf. Kloppenborg, *Formation of Q*, 191–92.

[2] See Kloppenborg, *Q Parallels*, 64; idem, *Formation of Q*, 190–91.

[3] Most authors would not include Matt 10:16b in Q; see Kloppenborg, *Q Parallels*, 72.

[4] See Kloppenborg, *Q Parallels*, 74.

[5] See Kloppenborg, *Q Parallels*, 76.

emphasis upon the presence of revelation in Jesus' words.[1] They are certainly very old sayings and may have been added here by the author of Q (not by the redactor, whose theological orientation is quite different) in order to emphasize the authority of the disciples.

Almost all materials in this section of Q are widely attested, both in the *Gospel of Thomas* and elsewhere. However, while the hand of the Q redactor is not visible in the composition of these sayings, they do not reflect a unified theme. The section seems to be composed of three different older clusters: (1) sayings about discipleship which imply the rejection of all normal social conditions (Q 9:57–62), (2) a collection of sayings about the mission of the disciples (Q 10:2–12,16)[2] to which a prophetic saying pronouncing the doom of the Galilean cities has been added by Q's redactor (Q 10:13–15), and (3) sayings about the presence of the revelation in Jesus' words (Q 10:21–24) which belong to an old tradition of revelation sayings that is attested as early a 1 Corinthians 1–4 and is also preserved in the Gospel of Thomas. All three clusters must have existed independently, in oral or written form, prior to the composition of Q. With rspect to the cluster of sayings about the mission of the disciples, this is evident by its appearance in Mark 6.[3] The independent existence of the cluster of revelation sayings is evident because of the parallels in 1 Corinthians 1–4, the *Gospel of Thomas,* and the Gospel of John.[4]

2.3.2.6 The Community in Conflict

Pericope or Saying	Q / Luke	Matthew	Other
The Lord's Prayer [a]	11:2–4	6:9–13	*Did.* 8.2
Request to ask and to seek [b]	11:9–13	7:7–11	*Gos. Thom.* 92, 94
Beelzebul accusation [c]	11:14–20	12:22–28	Mark 3:22–26
The house of the strong one [d]	11:21–22	12:29	*Gos. Thom.* 35
"He who is not with me . . ."	11:23	12:30	Mark 9:40
Return of the evil spirit	11:24–26	12:43–45	
True blessedness [e]	11:27–28		*Gos. Thom.* 79
The sign of Jonah [5]	11:29–32	12:38–42	

[1] See the parallel in *Gos. Thom.* 17 and possibly *Gos. Thom.* 4; cf. the discussion above in # 2.1.3.

[2] A variant of this collection is preserved in Mark 6; see below.

[3] See Philip Sellew, *Dominical Discourses: Oral Clusters in the Jesus Sayings Tradition* (to be published by Fortress Press).

[4] See above, # 2.1.3.

[5] Luke 11:16 ("Others, in order to test him, were requesting a sign from heaven") also belongs to this pericope. Its parallel in Matthew (12:38) appears in the original context.

Light not under a bushel[f]	11:33	5:15	Gos. Thom. 33b
The light of the body[g]	11:34–36	6:22–23	Gos. Thom. 24
(Pharisees) wash outside only[h]	11:39–41	23:25–26	Gos. Thom. 89
Pharisees tithe mint and rue	11:42	23:23	
Pharisees take the first seats	11:43	23:6	Mark 12:39
They are like hidden tombs	11:44	23:27	
The Pharisees' heavy burdens	11:46	23:4	
They built tombs of prophets	11:47–48	23:29–30	
The oracle of Wisdom	11:49–51	23:34–36	
They took key of knowledge[i]	11:52	23:13	Gos. Thom. 39
Lament over Jerusalem[j]	13:34–35	23:37–39	

[a] While Matthew and Luke exhibit marked differences in their versions of the Lord's Prayer, its quotation in *Did.* 8.2 is almost identical with Matthew's version. It is debated whether the Didache version is dependent upon the text of the Gospel of Matthew or derives from the same liturgical tradition.[1] An author would be more likely to write down the wording of this prayer as it was used liturgically rather than copy it from a written source. This does not necessarily raise doubts with respect to the presence of the Lord's prayer in this context of Q.[2] But it is questionable whether either Matthew or Luke copied its text from their common source.[3]

[b] Apart from the parallels in the *Gospel of Thomas* cited above (see also *Gos. Thom.* 2), there are numerous statements in the Gospel of John which are based on this saying (14:13–14; 15:7, 16; 16:23–26). Variants of this saying also appear in Mark 11:24; *Dial. Sav.* 20 (129,14–16), *Apocr. Jas.* (NHC I, 2) 10,34–34; 10,39–11,1.[4]

[c] This is the second of two miracle stories in Q. Almost all authors believe that the close agreements of Matthew and Luke against Mark—who does not report an exorcism by Jesus at the beginning of the Beelzebul controversy—justify its inclusion in Q. Because of the influence upon Matthew and Luke of the parallel collection of sayings on exorcism in Mark 3:23–30, it is difficult to determine the exact extent of Q in this pericope. But most scholars agree that Luke 11:15, 17–20 (without vs. 18b) and 23 belong to Q.[5] On the inclusion of Luke 11:21–22, see the following note.

[d] Many scholars doubt that this metaphor was included in Q, because the parallels in Matthew are too slight; both Matthew and

[1] See above, # 1.4.3.

[2] See Kloppenborg, *Q Parallels,* 84; idem, *Formation of Q,* 203–6.

[3] Whether either wording of the Lord's Prayer is more original is a different question, which cannot be answered by any hypothesis regarding its exact wording in Q.

[4] See also my documentation in "Gnostic Writings," 238–44.

[5] See the detailed discussion in Kloppenborg, *Formation of Q,* 121–27.

Luke may be dependent upon Mark. But the presence of this meta-phor in the *Gospel of Thomas* supports the arguments in favor of its inclusion.[1]

[e] The inclusion of this saying is suggested by the parallel in the *Gospel of Thomas*; there are cogent reasons to explain its omission in Matthew: he reports the Markan apophthegma of Jesus' true relatives in 12:46–50 (= Mark 3:31–35), that is, immediately after the preceding Q pericope Matt 12:43–45 = Luke 11:24–26. Thus, the Markan peri-cope substitutes for Q/Luke 11:27–28.

[f] A variant of this saying is quoted in Mark 4:21. The text of this saying in *Gos. Thom.* 33b resembles most closely Luke 11:33: both ver-sions contain the phrases "under a basket"[2] and "in a hidden place." The latter phrase does not appear in either Matt 5:15 or Mark 4:21 (= Luke 8:16). *Gos. Thom.* 33b also confirms the concluding phrase of Luke 11:33 ("that those who enter may see the light") as the original wording of Q (Matt 5:15 concludes the saying with the phrase, "and it gives light to all in the house").

[g] A further variant of this saying appears in *Dial. Sav.* 8.

[h] The parallel in *Gos. Thom.* 89 lacks the address of the saying to the Pharisees.

[i] In *Gos. Thom.* 39 this saying is addressed to the Pharisees and scribes (= Matt 23:13; Luke 11:52 is addressed to the lawyers), but the first phrase of the saying itself agrees with Luke 11:52 (". . . have taken the keys of knowledge"). The term "lawyer" (νομικός) is specifically Lukan;[3] it never appears in Mark, and only once in Matthew (22:35).[4]

[j] Only Matthew places this pericope at the end of the speech against the Pharisees; but he may have preserved the original order of Q.[5] Both, the lament about the killing of the prophets (Matt 23:34–36 = Luke 11:49–51) and the lament about Jerusalem (Matt 23:37–39 = Luke 13:34–35) are oracles of Wisdom and may have stood together in Q at the end of the woes against the Pharisees.[6] That this section in

---

[1] See Kloppenborg, *Q Parallels*, 92; idem, *Formation of Q*, 125.

[2] The words οὐδὲ ὑπὸ τὸν μόδιον are missing in p[45.78] A L Γ Ξ 0124 etc.; but they are attested in ℵ B C D W Q F etc. Older editions of the NT usually included the phrase; Nestle-Aland, *NT Graece*, encloses the phrase in brackets.

[3] It is used in Luke 7:30; 10:25; 11:45, 46, 52, 53; 14:3.

[4] This occurrence of νομικός may be caused by Matthew's source Mark, because the Lukan parallel (10:25) also uses the term. Matt 22:35 and Luke 10:25 also agree in the use of the verb "to test" (Matt: πειράζων, Luke: ἐκπειράζων), and in the address διδάσκαλε. The extant text of Mark 12:28 does not seem to preserve the Markan text that Matthew and Luke read; see below, # 4.1.2.2.

[5] See the discussion in Kloppenborg, *Q Parallels*, 158; idem, *Formation of Q*, 227–28. Kloppenborg includes Luke 13:34–35 in the sapiential speech of Q/Luke 13–14; see below.

[6] Bultmann, *Synoptic Tradition*, 114–15; Lührmann, *Redaktion*, 48.

the present text of Luke concludes with a final "woe" (against those who have hidden the keys of knowledge, Luke 11:52) is due to Lukan redaction.

This section of Q includes diverse materials, but is dominated by the Q redactor's announcement of judgment over "this generation," which is especially evident in the "woes against the Pharisees." Unfortunately, it is very difficult to determine with any certainty the original Q sequence of these seven "woes," because both Matthew and Luke seem to have disturbed this original sequence.[1] However, not all materials included in this section are therefore introduced into Q by this redactor. Apart from the three major units of controversy—the debate about the exorcism of demons and the speech against the Pharisees and the saying about the sign of Jonah—there are a number of wisdom sayings which, in themselves, have no polemical intent (Q 11:27–28, 33, 34–36 = Gos. Thom. 79, 33b, 24). They may have been part of the original version of Q. The same can be assumed for the Lord's Prayer and for the community rule about asking and praying (Q 11:2–4, 9–13). But even the two controversy units may have incorporated older Q materials such as the metaphor about the house of the strong one (Q 11:21–22 = Gos. Thom. 35) and the sayings about washing the outside of the cup (Q 11:39–41 = Gos. Thom. 89) and about the Pharisees' taking the keys of knowledge (Q 11:52 = Gos. Thom. 39). It is worth noting that the parallels to this section in the Gospel of Thomas do not reveal any of the tendencies of controversy and of judgment over this generation.[2] The wisdom oracles concluding this section of Q are not paralleled elsewhere in Christian traditions, although Thomas presents formal parallels of such wisdom sayings.[3] But the sayings which are used in the Beelzebul controversy represent an older cluster which the redactor took over as a whole and which was used independently by the Gospel of Mark.[4]

---

[1] Kloppenborg (Formation of Q, 140) reconstructs the following sequence: Luke 11:42, 39–41, 43, 44, 46, 47–48, 52. However, he makes the unlikely suggestion that the oracle of wisdom (Luke 11: 49–51) was placed in Q before the last woe (Luke 11:52).

[2] To be sure, the Pharisees and scribes are mentioned in Gos. Thom. 39, but there is no "woe" pronounced against them.

[3] On the character and origin of these wisdom oracles and on their parallels in the Gospel of Thomas see Robinson, "LOGOI SOPHON," 103–5.

[4] See Philip Sellew, Dominical Discourses: Oral Clusters in the Jesus Sayings Tradition (to be published by Fortress Press); idem, "Beelzebul in Mark 3: Dialogue, Story, or Sayings Cluster?" F&F Forum 4 (1988) 93–108.

2.3.2.7 *The Community Between This World and the Other World*

Pericope or Saying	Q / Luke	Matthew	Other
Hidden and revealed[a]	12:2	10:26	Gos. Thom. 5, 6b
"Preach from the rooftops"	12:3	10:27	Gos. Thom. 33
Fear of those who kill the body	12:4–7	10:28–31	
Fearless confession	12:8–9	10:32–33	Mark 8:38
The blasphemy not forgiven[b]	12:10	12:32	Gos. Thom. 44
The spirit's assistance[c]	12:11–12	10:19	Mark 13:9–11
Dividing the inheritance[d]	12:13–15		Gos. Thom. 72
The parable of the Rich Fool	12:16–21		Gos. Thom. 63
On cares[e]	12:22–32	6:25–34	Gos. Thom. 36
Heavenly treasure	12:33–34	6:19–21	Gos. Thom. 76b

[a] The contrast between hidden and revealed is also expressed in the saying Mark 4:22. It is likely that Paul in 1 Cor 2:7–10 comments on this saying; see above # 2.1.3.

[b] Further parallels appear in *Did.* 11:7 and Mark 3:28–30 (= Matt 12:31); see the discussion about the relationship of the several versions of this community rule, above # 2.2.4.2.

[c] Mark 13:9–11 has been combined with Q 12:11–12 in Matt 10:17–20. The original text of the Q version is preserved by Luke.

[d] This apophthegma as well as the following parable have no parallels in Matthew. But both also occur in the *Gospel of Thomas* and otherwise fit the criteria of inclusion.[1]

[e] *Gos. Thom.* 36 parallels only Q 12:22. A longer parallel is preserved in the Greek version of the *Gospel of Thomas, Pap. Oxy. 655*, which contains parallels also to Q 12:25, 27a.

The materials of this section, of which most are paralleled in the *Gospel of Thomas,* belong to the category of "rules of the community" and they exhibit features similar to those sayings in the preceding section which do not belong to the judgment speeches of the redactor. In the original version of Q, they could have belonged to a section of rules of the community which began with the Lord's Prayer. The only exceptions are Q 12:4–7 and 12:8–9, both without parallels in the Gospel of Thomas; the latter introduces Jesus as the future Son of man—here as elsewhere a sign of the hand of the redactor of Q.[2] Q 12:10, in its

---

[1] For a discussion of the incorporation into Q of this and the following pericope see Kloppenborg, *Q Parallels,* 128, and above # 2.2.4.2.

[2] On the redactional character of the introduction of this saying see Lührmann, *Redaktion,* 51–52. Lührmann (p. 51) also argues that the correspondence of a positive and a negative formulation in this saying is more original than the purely negative form of Mark 8:38.

present form, also contains a reference to the Son of man. But "Son of man" is understood as a title of Jesus only in the context of the final form of Q. Originally the contrast in this community rule must have been between the forgivable blasphemy against human beings and the unforgivable blasphemy against the Holy Spirit.[1]

2.3.2.8 The Coming Judgment

Pericope or Saying[2]	Q / Luke	Matthew	Other
Parable of the Thief[a]	12:39–40	24:43–44	Gos. Thom. 103
Faithful and Unfaithful Servant[b]	12:42–46	24:45–51	
Fire on earth[c]	12:49		Gos. Thom. 10
Not peace, but the sword	12:51–53	10:34–35	Gos. Thom. 16
Signs of the time[d]	12:54–56	16:2–3	Gos. Thom. 91
Agreement with adversary	12:57–59	5:25–26	
Parable of the Mustard Seed[e]	13:18–19	13:31–32	Gos. Thom. 20
Parable of the Leaven	13:20–21	13:33	Gos. Thom. 96

[a] The parable of the Thief occurs twice in the *Gospel of Thomas*: # 103 formulated as a beatitude ("Blessed is the man who knows where the brigands will enter . . .") and # 21 incorporated into a composite saying, followed by an admonition ("You then, be on guard against the world . . ."). In neither case do the Thomas parallels emphasize the time (Matt: ποία φυλακῇ, Luke: ποία ὥρᾳ) of the coming of the thief, nor is there an application regarding the time of the coming of the Son of man (cf. Q: ὅτι ᾗ ὥρᾳ οὐ δοκεῖτε ὁ υἱὸς τοῦ ἀνθρώπου ἔρχεται).

[b] Luke 12:41–42a and 47–48, both without a parallel in Matthew, are not to be included in Q.[3] The parable of the Faithful and Unfaithful Servant (Q 12:42b–46) cannot be understood as an older tradition, but is an allegorizing admonition which is wholly dominated by the expectation of the coming of the Son of man. In the context of Q, it explains the preceding emphasis upon the uncertainty of the hour of his coming.[4]

[1] See above, # 2.2.4.2, the discussion of this saying in the *Gospel of Thomas*.

[2] The preceding section about the watchful servants, Luke 12:35–38, is assigned to Q by some scholars because of their assumption that the parable of the Ten Virgins (Matt 25:1–13) derives from the same Q tradition (Kloppenborg, *Q Parallels*, 136). However, the resemblances are too slight and the admonition to be watchful is so widespread (I Cor 16:13; 1 Thess 5:6; 1 Pet 5:8; Rev 3:2, 3; 16:15; *Did.* 16.1) that a special written source for Matt 25:1–13 need not be presupposed.

[3] See Kloppenborg, *Q Parallels*, 140; idem, *Formation of Q*, 151, n. 212: both insertions belong together and are Lukan.

[4] For the interpretation of this "parable" see especially Lührmann, *Redaktion*, 69–70.

c Although a Matthean parallel is missing for Luke 12:49, it does not contain Lukan features and should be assigned to Q; see also the parallel in *Gos. Thom.* 10. However, the following saying, Luke 12:50 ("I must be baptized with a baptism . . ."), is a Lukan addition.[1]

d The much shorter version of the *Gospel of Thomas* agrees with Luke 12:56 in the emphasis upon recognizing "this moment" (Luke: τὸν καιρὸν τοῦτον, Matt: τὰ σημεῖα τῶν καιρῶν).

e An independent variant appears in Mark 4:30–32. *Gos. Thom.* 20 resembles Mark insofar as his version also emphasizes the smallness of the seed.

The sayings in this section must all be understood as warnings regarding the uncertainty of the coming of the Son of man. They emphasize that this uncertainty means "soon." This allowed the redactor to include sayings which actually speak about the presence of the eschatological moment in Jesus and his words. That this was the original meaning of such sayings is not only evident in the parallels of the *Gospel of Thomas,* but also in the introduction "I have come" of Q 12:49, 51, 53, and in the formulation "this moment" (Q/Luke 12:56). It is quite likely that these latter sayings had a place in the original version of Q.

2.3.2.9 Eschatological Didache[2]

Pericope or Saying	Q / Luke	Matthew	Other
The narrow gate [a]	13:24	7:13–14	
Gentiles in the kingdom [b]	13:28–30	8:11–12	
[Ox in a well][3]	14:5	12:11	
[Whoever exalts himself][4]	14:11	23:12	
Parable of the Great Banquet	14:16–24	22:1–10	Gos. Thom. 64
Whoever does not hate father	14:26	10:37	Gos. Thom. 55,101

[1] See Kloppenborg, *Q Parallels,* 142; idem, *Formation of Q,* 151, n. 213.

[2] This section of Q contains diverse materials concerned with the status and conduct of the disciples in the eschatological division, including admonitions. Kloppenborg (*Q Parallels,* p. xxxii) calls the Q materials in Luke 13 and 14 "The Two Ways." But also most of the Q materials of Luke 15:1–17:6 are parenetic in character and may have belonged to the same Q unit.

[3] That this saying belonged to Q is extremely doubtful. Matthew attached this saying in 12:11–12 to his version of the healing of the man with the withered hand (Matt 12:9–14 = Mark 3:1–6). It is more likely that this was a favorite and well-known argument against Sabbath observation which circulated in the oral tradition.

[4] This saying that Luke attaches to one of his favored meal scenes (Luke 14:7–11) and again to the story of the Pharisee and the Publican (18:14) does not require a written source but may have come from the oral tradition.

GT 55/10 (handwritten)

Whoever carries his cross	14:27	10:38	Mark 8:34
Whoever seeks his life[1]	17:33	10:39	Mark 8:35
About salt	14:34–35	5:13	Mark 9:50
Parable of the Lost Sheep	15:4–7	18:12–14	Gos. Thom. 107
Parable of the Lost Coin[2]	15:8–10		
Serving two masters	16:13	6:24	Gos. Thom. 47a
Validity of the Law[3]	16:17	5:18	Gos. Thom. 11[4]
On divorce	16:18	5:32	Mark 10:11–12
About scandals	17:1–2	18:6–7	Mark 9:42[5]
About forgiveness	17:3–4	18:15, 21	
About faith	17:6	17:20	Mark 11:22–23

(margin, handwritten: or two Q's / Matt's sermon Q is late)

a It seems that only Luke 13:24 belongs to this section of Q. The following verse, Luke 13:25, is a Lukan redaction[6] by which the Q saying of Luke 13:24 is connected to another Q passage, Luke 13:26–27 = Matt 7:22–23, that originally may have belonged to Q's inaugural sermon.[7] *(handwritten: — redaction)*

b The conclusion of this saying ("The last will be first . . . ," Luke 13:30) appears in Matt 20:16 at the end of the parable of the Laborers in the Vineyard (Matt 20:1–15). Since it is a gnomic saying from the oral tradition that was added at random in other contexts as well (cf. Mark 10:31; Matt 19:30; Gos. Thom. 4b), it is impossible to be certain about its original place in Q. The next Q saying in this Lukan context, the lament over Jerusalem (Luke 13:34–35), is better placed after Q 11:49–51; see above. *(handwritten: — maybe; good here too)*

---

[1] Since this saying belongs together with the two preceding sayings and Matthew preserved all three sayings in the same unit (Matt 10:37–39), one can assume that they also formed a unit in Q.

[2] There is no parallel either in Matthew or in the *Gospel of Thomas*. But the close connection between the two parables in Luke 15:1–10 and their parallel structure may indicate that Luke found both together in his source; cf. Kloppenborg, *Q Parallels*, 176.

[3] Luke 16:16 has been listed above because it probably belonged to the Q section about John the Baptist.

[4] The saying in the *Gospel of Thomas* parallels the first half of the Q saying, but contains no statement about the law. It probably should not be considered as a variant of Q 16:17.

[5] A variant of this saying is quoted in *1 Clem.* 46.8; see above # 2.1.4.3.

[6] Kloppenborg, *Q Parallels*, 154.

[7] See above note on Matt 7:22–23. Kloppenborg (*Formation of Q*, 224–25) includes Luke 13:26–27 in Q 13–14, but rightly excludes Luke 13:25 (ibid., p. 224–25, n. 217).

(handwritten: No)

2.3.2.10 The Coming of the Son of Man

Pericope or Saying	Q / Luke	Matthew	Other
Desiring and not finding[1]	17:22		Gos. Thom. 38
The suddenness of the coming	17:23–24	24:26–27	Gos. Thom. 113
"Where the corpse is . . ."	17:37	24:28	
The days of Noah	17:26–30	24:37–38	
"Two will be on a couch . . ."	17:34–35	24:40–41	Gos. Thom. 61a
Parable of the Talents	19:12–25	25:14–28	
"Whoever has, shall be given"	19:26	25:29	Gos. Thom. 41[2]
Judging the tribes of Israel	22:28–30	19:28	

In its final form, this section of Q with its emphasis upon the sudden appearance of the Son of man is most characteristic of the theology of the redactor of Q. Although there are some parallels to this section in the *Gospel of Thomas,* none of them mentions the Son of man. These sayings paralleled in Thomas may indeed have been included in the original composition of Q; but it is difficult to be certain about their place and context in that first version of the Synoptic Sayings Source.

2.3.3 PURPOSE AND CONTEXT OF THE COMPOSITION OF Q

John Kloppenborg[3] has made an important contribution by defining the genre of the original composition of Q as a collection of sapiential speeches. This identifies the literary genre which served as the catalyst for the composition of this document and made it more than just a random collection of sayings. This genre-critical approach to the reconstruction of Q's history and redaction supersedes older attempts which tried to determine the stages of the development of Q on the basis of certain theological assumptions.[4] The demonstration of this

---

[1] This saying is generally considered not to have been part of Q. However, the parallel in the *Gospel of Thomas* and its usage in the Gospel of John (8:21–22; cf. 7:33–34; 13:33) demonstrate that this is indeed a variant of an older saying. The unusual and most likely secondary feature of the Q/Luke version is the introduction of the title "Son of man."

[2] A parallel is preserved in the small collection of sayings in Mark 4:21–25 (4:25 = Luke 8:18b).

[3] *The Formation of Q,* passim.

[4] For the older literature see Kloppenborg, *Formation of Q,* passim. Most evident is the failure of the "theological-history" approach in Siegfried Schulz, *Q: Die Spruchquelle der Evangelisten* (Zürich: Theologischer Verlag, 1972). Schulz assigns to the older Jewish-Christian community of Q all materials related to an assumed post-Easter enthusiasm and a prophetic radicalization of Torah. Schulz (and others) have rightly emphasized that the earliest composition of Q must have contained eschatological-prophetic elements. But the type of the eschatology which characterized this early stage of Q must be determined by form- and redaction-criticial analysis.

hypothesis necessarily implied the argument that the basic parts of this wisdom book were structured as wisdom discourses. Moreover, Dieter Lührmann[1] had already identified the apocalyptic tendency of a later redaction of Q—a radical departure from the orientation of an earlier stage of Q.[2] Kloppenborg further clarified how this apocalypticizing tendency of the redactor interfered with the original structure of the sapiential discourses, because the redactor created several sections which are characterized by the apocalyptic theme of the announcement of a future judgment over "this generation." Furthermore, the redactor revised several of the eschatological sayings of the original version of Q in such a way that they could serve as predictions of the coming judgment and of the appearance of the Son of man.

The original version of Q must have included wisdom sayings as well as eschatological sayings. It cannot be argued that Q originally presented Jesus simply as a teacher of wisdom without an eschatological message. The close relationships of the *Gospel of Thomas* to Q cannot be accidental.[3] Since the typical Son of man sayings and announcements of judgments which are characteristic of the redaction of Q are never paralleled in the *Gospel of Thomas,* it is evident that its author had no knowledge of the final version of Q, nor of the secondary apocalyptic interpretation that the redactor of Q superimposed upon earlier eschatological sayings. The *Gospel of Thomas* is either dependent upon Q's earlier version or upon clusters of sayings employed in its composition.

The eschatological orientation of the original composition of Q is distinctly different from the apocalyptic perspective of the redactor. This is striking with respect to the "announcement of judgment" section which discusses the role of John the Baptist. Two sayings of the original version of Q, paralleled in the *Gospel of Thomas,* were used in its composition:

---

[1] *Die Redaktion der Logienquelle,* passim.

[2] Paul Hoffmann (*Studien zur Theologie der Logienquelle* [NTA, NF 8; 3d ed.; Münster: Aschendorff, 1982]) has presented perhaps the most impressive theological interpretation of Q that rejects the attempt of a redaction-critical analysis. Lührmann's (*Redaktion,* 8) brief criticism of this approach is still valid.

[3] It has been argued in the preceding chapter that this has implications for the reconstruction of Q: parallels in Thomas to sayings which are attested only in either Matthew or Luke may well have been Q sayings.

Q/Luke 7:24–26	Gos. Thom. 78
When the messengers of John had departed, he began to speak to the crowds concerning John: "What did you go out to the wilderness to see? A reed shaken by the wind? But what did you go out to see? A man clothed in luxurious clothing? Behold, those who are richly clothed and live in luxury are in royal palaces. But what did you go out to see? A prophet? Yes I tell you, and more than a prophet."	Jesus said: "Why have you come out to the countryside? To see a reed shaken by the wind? And to see a person dressed in rich clothing like your rulers and your powerful ones? They are dressed in rich clothing, but they cannot understand the truth."

The Q saying is forced to refer to John through the addition of a secondary introduction (7:24a: "When the messengers of John had departed . . .") and indirectly through its conclusion (7:26: "A prophet? Yes, I tell you, and more than a prophet."); but even with this conclusion the saying would not necessarily refer to John the Baptist were it not placed into this context by the redactor of Q. It would be more natural to understand it as a saying pointing to Jesus himself and to his prophetic message to the poor in contrast to the claims of the rulers of the world. This is confirmed by the absence of any reference to John the Baptist in the Thomas version of the saying. On the other hand, the reference to the rich who cannot understand the truth is in keeping with the theology of the *Gospel of Thomas*. It appears to have replaced the more original reference to Jesus' prophetic ministry. In its original understanding and place in the first composition of Q, this saying is closely related to the "blessing of the poor" (Q/Luke 6:20), the opening phrase of Jesus' "inaugural sermon."

The second older saying used in the same context is Q 7:28:

Q 7:28	Gos. Thom. 46
I tell you, among those born of women no one is greater than John; yet the least in the kingdom of God is greater than he.	Among those born of women from Adam until John the Baptist, there is no one superior to John the Baptist that his eyes should not be lowered before him. Yet I have said, whichever one of you comes to be a child will be acquainted with the kingdom and will become superior to John.

Q 7:28 has been understood as a saying that praises the greatness of John (7:28a) with, as it seems, a secondary polemical Christian addition which in turn diminishes John's status (7:28b). However, the saying as it appears in *Gos. Thom.* 46 consists of two antithetical parts which form an original unity.[1] It does not contain a polemic against John the Baptist, nor does it assign the eschatological role of a precursor to him. The saying merely emphasizes the contrast between the old (from Adam to John) and the new (the kingdom). The polemical formulation ("[even] the smallest in the kingdom is greater than he") instead of "whoever becomes a child will know the kingdom and will become greater than [even] John" is probably due to the redactor of Q who inserted the saying into this context of the "announcement of judgment" section. The more original form of the saying would have been closer to the form preserved in the *Gospel of Thomas*. It was a saying which emphasized the eschatological moment of the kingdom's presence.

Q/Luke 10:23–24 is certainly a saying that circulated very early, since it can be presupposed for the discussion of Paul with Corinthians:[2]

> Blessed are the eyes that see what you see [and the ears that hear what you hear]. For I tell you that many prophets and kings wanted to see what you are seeing and did not see it, and to hear what you are hearing and did not hear it.

The closest parallel to this saying appears in *Gos. Thom.* 17 (cf. 1 Cor 2:9):[3]

> I shall give you what no eye has seen and what no ear has heard and what no hand has touched and what has never occurred to the human mind.

The same eschatological emphasis is found in several Q sayings which now appear in the "announcement of judgment" sections of Q/Luke 11, 12 and 17 but should be assigned to the original composition of Q. Most of these have parallels in the *Gospel of Thomas*. The eschatological presence of salvation is emphasized in Q/Luke

---

[1] See the discussion in Kloppenborg, *Formation of Q*, 109, n. 30.

[2] See above, # 2.1.3.

[3] Cf. also *Gos. Thom.* 38: "Many times have you desired to hear these words which I am saying to you, and you have no one else to hear them from. There will be days when you look for me and will not find me." This may be a variant of the same saying, but it is more closely related to sayings which are used in the Gospel of John about the coming and going of the revealer; see above, # 2.2.5.

11:27–28[1] which may have followed the preceding saying in the original version of Q:[2]

> As he was saying these things, a woman from the crowd raised her voice and said to him, "Blessed is the womb that bore you and the breasts that you sucked." And he said, "Rather, blessed are those who hear the word of God and keep it."

In Q/Luke 12 there are seven units of sayings which constitute the "announcement of judgment" section of Q 12:39–59. Of these as many as five have parallels in the *Gospel of Thomas,* and in every instance an apocalyptic orientation has not yet been introduced into the sayings of Thomas' version.

Q/Luke 12:39–40	Gos. Thom. 21b, 103[3]
But recognize this, that if the householder had known what hour (Matt: in what part of the night) the thief was coming he would not have left his house to be dug into.	Therefore I say: if the owner of a house knows that a thief is coming, he will be on guard before he comes and will not let him dig through into his house of his domain to carry away his goods. You then be on guard
You also must be ready, for the Son of Man will come at an hour you do not expect.	against the world. Arm yourself with great strength, lest the robbers find a way to come to you.

In both citations of this saying in the *Gospel of Thomas* the emphasis lies on preparedness in general, not on the uncertainty with respect to the hour or the time of night at which the thief is coming. The latter perspective is the result of a secondary interpretation by the redactor of Q who also added the reference to the coming of the Son of man.[4] That the eschatological presence of the salvation which is emphasized in the original version of Q implies danger, controversy, and division is

---

[1] There is no parallel to this saying in the Gospel of Matthew. But the saying also appears in *Gos. Thom.* 79 where it is expanded by a negative statement of a more apocalyptic flavor: "For there will be days when you will say, 'Blessed are the womb which has not conceived and the breasts which have not given milk.'"

[2] According to Kloppenborg (*Formation of Q,* 121) this saying now appears in an "announcement of judgment" section that is obviously composed by the redactor: Q 11:14–52. But Kloppenborg does not think that Luke 11:27–28 was an original part of this section.

[3] The same metaphor is quoted in *Gos. Thom.* 103: "Fortunate is the man who knows where the brigands will enter, so that he may get up, muster his domain, and arm himself before they invade."

[4] On the composite character of Q 12:39–40 see Schulz, *Spruchquelle,* 268–71; Kloppenborg, *Formation of Q,* 149.

also emphasized in the three following sayings in this section which have parallels in the *Gospel of Thomas*:

Q/Luke 12:49 (cf. *Gos. Thom.* 10):
I have come to cast fire upon the earth, and how I wish that it were already ablaze!

Q/Luke 12:51 (cf. *Gos. Thom.* 16a):
Do you think that I have come to give peace upon the earth? No, I tell you, but rather division (Matt: but the sword).

Q/Luke 12:52–53 (cf. *Gos. Thom.* 16b):
For from now on there will be five in one house divided, three against two and two against three; they will be divided father against son and son against father, mother against daughter and daughter against her mother ...

In the present context these sayings, especially Q 12:52–53, speak of the apocalyptic divisions which are expected to come in the future.[1] But Q 12:49 and 51 still reveal in their formulation that they originally announced the eschatological events directly related to Jesus' coming and his message, not to an expected apocalyptic event of the future. Since also the blessing of those who are persecuted (Q 6:22–23) belongs to the original stage of Q, the saying of Q 12:52–53 "might have been understood concretely with reference to the rejection and violence experienced by members of the community itself."[2]

The final saying in this section, Q/Luke 12:54–56 (cf. *Gos. Thom.* 91), even in the form in which it is preserved by Luke,[3] emphasizes the eschatological moment and does not reveal any redactional changes which would make this saying conform more with the future-oriented eschatology of the redactor of Q:[4]

Q/Luke 12:54–56	*Gos. Thom.* 91
When you see a cloud rising in the west, you say immediately, "Rain is coming," and so it happens. And	

---

[1] For an analysis of this latter saying and its traditional apocalyptic connotations, see Schulz, *Spruchquelle*, 258–60.

[2] Kloppenborg, *Formation of Q*, 152, with reference to Hoffmann, *Studien*, 72–73.

[3] Luke 12:56 reads τὸν καιρὸν δὲ τοῦτον πῶς οὐκ οἴδατε δοκιμάζειν; Matt 16:3 has changed this to τὰ δὲ σημεῖα τῶν καιρῶν.

[4] Even Kloppenborg (*Formation of Q*, 152) admits: "Even though it does not spell out a specific apocalyptic timetable ..." But he continues to relate the saying to an impending apocalyptic catastrophe.

when a south wind is blowing, you
say, "it will be hot," and it happens.
Hypocrites, you know how to
interpret the face of the earth and the   You read the face of the sky and the
sky; but   earth, but you have not recognized
                                                 the one who is before you, and you do
why do you not know how to interpret   not know how to interpret this
the present moment?   moment.

John Kloppenborg has called "the threat of apocalyptic judgment . . .
the formative literary and theological motif in this cluster of Q sayings."[1] As these sayings appear now in the final redaction of Q, this is
undoubtedly correct. But the older Q materials used for the composition of this section did not speak about the threat of apocalyptic judgment. Rather, this theme has found expression only by means of
editorial changes in the older sayings and through the insertion of
additional apocalyptic materials. The unit that most strongly fits this
redactional tendency is the so-called parable of the Faithful and
Unfaithful Servants (Q/Luke 12:42b–46). Parallels to this unit are
missing in the *Gospel of Thomas*—no surprise, because it cannot be
understood as an older traditional saying at all. Rather, it is an
allegorizing redactional creation which is wholly dominated by the
expectation of reward and punishment in the coming judgment.

The Q apocalypse of Luke 17:20–37, in its present form the product
of the redactor, may also contain some older eschatological sayings.
There are no parallels in the *Gospel of Thomas* to the coming of the
Son of man like lightning (Q/Luke 17:23–24), nor to the expansion of
this saying by the comparison with the days of Noah (and the Sodom-
ites, Q 17:26–32). Thomas provides a parallel only to two sayings from
this apocalypse: Q/Luke 17:20–21 = *Gos. Thom.* 113 (cf. also # 3) and
Q/Luke 17:34 = *Gos. Thom.* 61a. While the latter saying, speaking
about the divisions which occur in the eschatological moment, is a
variant of the saying Q 12:51–52 = *Gos. Thom.* 16 (see above), the first
of these sayings (which has no parallel in Matthew) emphasizes the
mysterious presence of the kingdom:

Q/Luke 17:20–21	*Gos. Thom.* 113
When he was asked by the Pharisees when the kingdom of God would be coming, he answered them, and said,	His disciples said to him, "When will the kingdom come?"

---

[1] *Formation of Q*, 148.

"The kingdom of God does not come by observation, nor will they say, 'Lo, it is here,' or 'There.' For behold, the kingdom of God is among you."

Jesus said, "It will not come by waiting for it. It will not be a matter of saying, 'Here,' or 'There it is.' Rather the kingdom of the Father is spread out upon the earth, and human beings do not see it."

The phrase of Luke 17:21, which is translated here with "the kingdom of God is among you" (ἡ βασιλεία τοῦ θεοῦ ἐντὸς ὑμῶν ἐστιν), should not be interpreted either psychologically ("the kingdom of God is in your hearts") or in terms of future eschatology ("the kingdom of God will be there suddenly"),[1] although the latter interpretation may have been intended by the redactor of Q. The parallel in the *Gospel of Thomas* demonstrates that the kingdom is understood to be mysteriously present in the understanding and in the actions of the disciples. The author of the *Gospel of Thomas* may have intended a spiritualized (possibly "Gnostic") interpretation. But in the context of the original version of Q, this saying referred to the disciples' ability to grasp the significance of the eschatological moment in which their response to Jesus' words creates new dimensions of human existence.

It is in this light that one must read the wisdom discourses of the original composition of the Synoptic Sayings Source. The inaugural sermon of Jesus, Q/Luke 6:20–49, is a wisdom discourse, and even the blessings at the beginning of the inaugural sermon have their parallels in wisdom literature. However, while Wisdom calls blessed the wise who follow her precepts and do what is demanded,[2] Jesus blesses the situation in which those to whom his message comes happen to be: the poor, the hungry, those who weep, those who are persecuted. Such beatitudes are not sapiential, but prophetic.[3] The first sentences of the original version of Q introduce Jesus as a prophet, not as a teacher of wisdom.[4] His message fulfills the expectation that is, in a different context and tradition, expressed in the eschatological psalms of

---

[1] For a discussion of the various alternatives in understanding this phrase, see the commentaries.

[2] For examples of this typical wisdom makarism, see Prov 8:32, 34; Sir 14:1, 2, 20; 50:28. There are also numerous parallels in wisdom psalms: Ps 1:1; 106:3; 112:1; 119:1–2; 128:1–2. In early-Christian literature, such makarisms appear typically in writings which are dependent upon Jewish wisdom traditions: James 1:12, 25; *Did.* 1.5. See also Koester, *Synoptische Überlieferung,* 234–35.

[3] Kloppenborg (*Formation of Q,* 188–89) realizes that these beatitudes do not fit the normal pattern of sapiential blessings, but maintains that "the contents of Q 6:20b–49 are overwhelmingly sapiential."

[4] Schulz (*Spruchquelle,* 79–81) is correct in his claim for a prophetic understanding of the beatitudes. However, they should not be called "prophetic-apocalyptic," referring to the future enthronement of God.

Luke 1.[1] These eschatological makarisms are resumed in Q in the "blessedness of the witnesses" (Q 10:23–24) and the "blessedness of those hear his word" (Q 11:28).[2]

The admonitions which follow upon the beatitudes of the inaugural sermon formally correspond to the genre of the wisdom discourse.[3] However, with respect to their content, they depart radically from admonitions normally found in this genre of literature. The traditional wisdom discourse advises the followers of wisdom either with respect to prudent and merciful behavior in the existing society,[4] or it encourages them to remain faithful to the precepts of wisdom (and of the law) even in face of the rejection by the world, promising a heavenly reward and vindication. The admonitions of Q 6:27–36 are fundamentally different. To love one's enemies, to turn the other cheek, to lend to those from whom no return can be expected—these are neither admonitions to prudent and merciful behavior nor do they encourage the faithful fulfillment of wisdom's precepts in an otherwise hostile society. On the contrary, they send the disciples into the midst of the society in which their deeds will announce the eschatological moment in which new criteria for human action and interaction will change the world. Only the following admonitions on judging, blind guides, teacher and student, hypocrisy, good fruit from good trees, and building the house on firm ground (Q 6:37–45) rehearse traditional wisdom themes, albeit sometimes radicalized.[5] The conclusion, Q 6:46–49, is a typical peroration of a wisdom discourse.[6] Thus in its structure and organization, the inaugural sermon is, no doubt, sapiential.[7] The wisdom discourse is the genre which guided its literary composition. However, it incorporates a message of

---

[1] The so-called Magnificat (Luke 1:46–55) and Benedictus (Luke 1:68–79).

[2] On the different character of the beatitudes in the Sermon on the Mount (Matt 5:3–12) see Betz, *Essays*, 22–32.

[3] This, however, cannot be decided on the basis of the introduction λεγὼ ὑμῖν (Schulz, *Spruchquelle*, 79); see Kloppenborg, *Formation of Q*, 176.

[4] The examples for such wisdom admonitions which are adduced by Kloppenborg (*Formation of Q*, 177) as parallels to the command to love one's enemy (Sir 4:10; Seneca *De beneficiis* 4.26.1) prove the point: they simply recommend that one be kind to widows and orphans and bestow benefits on the ungrateful.

[5] See the references in Kloppenborg, *Formation of Q*, 178–85.

[6] Kloppenborg, *Formation of Q*, 185–87. Hoffmann (*Studien*, 155) sees the parable of the Builders in the context of the expectation of Jesus' coming as the Son of man; this view of the parable neglects the results of the redaction-critical analysis of Q. In the context of the discourse Q 6:20–49, any reference to a future eschatological figure is uncalled for.

[7] Kloppenborg, *Formation of Q*, 189.

a realized eschatology which determined the self-understanding of the early Q community.

The discourse on discipleship and mission (Q 9:57–62; 10:2–12 [13–15],[1] 16, 21–24) is introduced by radical eschatological demands. To follow Jesus means to follow the human being ("son of man") who has no place to lay his head (Q 9:57–58) and to leave it to the "dead" to bury the dead (Q 9:59–60). The mission discourse itself may indeed contain rules which resemble those given to a Cynic teacher (Q 10:4–7), but the purpose of the mission is once again the proclamation of the eschatological moment: "Heal those who are sick and say, 'the kingdom of God has come upon you'" (Q 10:9). If Q 10:13–15 belongs to the redactor, the original discourse did not speak about a future judgment awaiting those who do not repent, but assured the disciples that the rejection they experience is, in fact, a rejection of Jesus himself (Q 10:12). The thanksgiving for revelation and the blessedness of the witnesses (Q 10:21–24) demonstrate that the urgency of the mission is not dictated by the nearness of the coming judgment but by the knowledge of the present eschatological fulfillment.

More traditional wisdom and "two ways" materials appear in the Q discourse preserved in Luke 11–12. These include instructions on prayer (Q 11:2–4, 9–13),[2] the admonition not to fear those who can kill the body (Q 12:4–7), the warning not to blaspheme the spirit, and the assurance of the support of the spirit (Q 12:10–12). Perhaps also the rule against dividing inherited worldly goods and the parable of the Rich Fool (Q 12:13–21), and finally the sayings against worldly cares (Q 12:22–34) fit well into an eschatologically-oriented collection of wisdom sayings and community rules.

The final major block of materials from the original sapiential speeches is preserved in some of the Q materials of Luke 13–14. Kloppenborg[3] assigns the following materials to this section: Luke 13:24–30, 34–35; 14:16–24, 26–27; 17:33;[4] 14:34–35. However, Q/Luke

---

[1] Whether this saying, with its "woe" against Chorazin and Bethsaida, belongs to the original discourse, seems questionable. Lührmann (*Redaktion*, 60–61) assigns it to a later stage because of its close connection to Q 10:21–22, together with Q 10:2, which in his judgment presupposes the Gentile mission. Neither argument is convincing. The Gentile mission began during the very first years of the Jesus movement, and the heightened wisdom christology expressed in 10:21–22 must already be presupposed for 1 Corinthians 1–4. On the other hand, 10:13–15 reveals an apocalyptic orientation which is more characteristic of the redaction of Q.

[2] Perhaps also the instruction about clean and unclean, Q 11:39–40, which the redactor incorporated into the discourse against the Pharisees was part of this section in the non-polemical version in which it is preserved in the *Gospel of Thomas*.

[3] *Formation of Q*, 223–37.

[4] Luke 17:33 = Matt 10:39 must have followed originally upon Luke 14:26–27 = Matt 10:37–38.

13:34–35, the lament over Jerusalem, seems to be out of place and could be assigned to the "announcement of judgment" redaction of Q.[1] On the other hand, one might add Q 15:4–7 (Lost Sheep), 16:13, 17–18 (serving two masters, on the law, and on marriage and divorce) and Q 17:1–6 (on scandals, forgiveness, and faith). They fit well into a section that has been correctly characterized as the "two ways."[2] The metaphor of the "narrow gate" (Q 13:24) explicitly designates this section as "instruction" (διδαχή). However, this is not teaching for an isolated Jewish-Christian community. The following sayings in this section, Q 13:26–27 (rejection of the false teachers) and 28–30 (Gentiles in the kingdom), imply that the Q community has gone into the Gentile mission. Since 13:26 speaks of those "who have taught," it should not be construed as a rejection of unbelieving Jews, but of those who have refused to participate in the mission to the Gentiles or have hindered it.[3] The parable of the Great Supper (Q 14:16–21a, 23) continues this emphasis upon the invitation of the Gentiles.[4] Most of the community rules that follow are not typical for a Jewish-Christian community, but could be found anywhere in community regulations which are dependent upon "two ways" materials.

For the followers of Jesus whose tradition is represented in the original composition of Q, the turning point of the ages is the proclamation of Jesus. In the sayings of Jesus, his followers find the continuation of this announcement. These sayings are not only reassurance of the eschatological moment, they are also the rule of life for the community of the new age insofar as Jesus continues to speak in sayings of wisdom and in rules for the community. Jesus may indeed have been viewed as the heavenly Wisdom. This is especially evident in Q 10:21–22 which defines the relationship of Jesus to the Father in terms of the established sapiential concept of Wisdom and God.[5] If Q 13:34–35, the lament over Jerusalem, should belong to the original composition of Q, Jesus is also the one who sends Wisdom's envoys.

---

[1] Most likely, Matt 23:37–39 has preserved its original location in Q, i.e., at the end of the speech against the Pharisees. See Lührmann, *Redaktion,* 48.

[2] Kloppenborg, *Q Parallels,* p. xxxii.

[3] Luke's text is to be preferred here. Matt 7:22–23 has changed the Q text into a condemnation of Hellenistic charismatics; see below on the Sermon on the Mount, # 2.3.4.

[4] Luke 14:21b–22 is a secondary Lukan addition which expresses a special interest in the invitation of the poor to the kingdom. It seems that Luke 14:24 also is a Lukan addition; the original Q parable did not especially emphasize the rejection of those who were invited first (= Israel).

[5] Kloppenborg, *Formation of Q,* 319–20.

Just as the departure of Wisdom or of her envoy does not constitute a change in the urgency of the message, so too Jesus' death would not be seen as a crisis of his proclamation. The disciples are already called to follow in the steps of Jesus, in their discipleship (Q 9:57–62) as well as in their task to carry on his proclamation (Q 10:2–12). Jesus' departure would make this call even more urgent. The ages have already begun to turn through Jesus' announcement. Any emphasis upon Jesus' suffering, death, and resurrection would be meaningless in this context. Thus Q can not be seen as a teaching supplement for a community whose theology is represented by the Pauline kerygma. Q's theology and soteriology are fundamentally different.

If these formative concepts for the tradition and composition of Q can be explained as a continuation of wisdom teaching, a departure from these concepts is evident in two respects: (1) the ethical demands of Q are far more radical than those of traditional wisdom teaching; (2) Q's wisdom is addressed to a community in whose life the kingdom of God is present, not to an individual who follows the advise of a father or teacher. Kloppenborg[1] has emphasized that "in contrast to the generally conservative comportment of the (traditional wisdom) instruction, Q represents an ethic of radical discipleship which reverses many of the conventions which allow a society to operate, such as principles of retaliation, the orderly borrowing and lending of capital, appropriate treatment of the dead, responsible self-provision, self-defense and honor of parents."[2] Instead, the behavior which Jesus requests is a demonstration of the kingdom's presence, i.e., of a society which is governed by new principles of ethics. This not only ascribes a kerygmatic quality to the ethical demands of Jesus, it presents Jesus as a prophet rather than a teacher of wisdom. Although formal claims of Jesus to prophetic authorization, such as a vision of a calling or the introductory formula "thus says the Lord," are missing, the prophetic role of Jesus is evident in the address of these ethical demands to a community, not just to individual followers. To be sure, there are no such terms as "New Israel" in Q; these people called by Jesus are not just a sectarian group, but represent the community of the new ages, the people of God. They are the ones who will sit at table with Abraham in the banquet of the kingdom (Q 13:28–30).

It may seem surprizing that a community which claims in such a radical form the presence of a new society does not reflect, in its tradition, more vestiges of a controversy with Judaism, i.e., the religious

---

[1] Ibid., 318–21.
[2] Ibid., 318.

and social world from which it presumably emerged and which continued to form its cultural and religious matrix. There is certainly a strongly emphasized awareness of persecution (Q 6:22–23), rejection (Q 10:16), and division (Q 12:49–53); but these experiences are not understood as a rejection by "the Jews" or by "Israel." The woes against the Pharisees (Q 11:37–52) belong—except for one or two sayings—to the secondary redaction of Q, as do other polemical texts. The question encountered here is not so much a difficulty in defining the setting of the Q community, as it is a problem of the traditional understanding of what is commonly called "Judaism" and of the relationship of "Jews" and "Christians" at the beginnings of the Jesus movement. Both terms are as inappropriate as the notion that Jesus was rejected by the "Jews" and that they killed him. The context of Jesus' proclamation and of the mission of his followers after his execution (by the Roman authorities!) was one of great diversity within Israel, characterized by the not always peaceful coexistence of various groups and sects in Palestine as well as in the diaspora. Hostility and persecution that one sectarian group experienced at the hand of others was not necessarily understood as a rejection by "Israel."

Unfortunately, the texts belonging to the original composition of Q are completely silent with respect to the question of Israel's temple and law.[1] The saying about washing the outside of the cup (Q 11:39–40), originally probably not a saying against the Pharisees, gives voice to a lack of concern with respect to the technical questions of law observance. If Q 11:52,[2] accusing the Pharisees that they have taken the keys of knowledge, belongs to Q's original composition, it does not criticize the Pharisees' praxis of observing the law, but their claim to exclusive teaching authority.[3] A special problem is presented by Q 16:16, a saying which contrasts the law and the prophets "until John" with the kingdom of God. However, the original wording and meaning of the saying is so uncertain that it would be unwise to base any hypothesis upon its interpretation.[4] Moreover, it is quite unlikely

---

[1] The case would, of course, be different if one ascribed *Toraverschärfung* and polemic against the Pharisees to the seminal texts of Q (Schulz, *Spruchquelle*, 94–141).

[2] = *Gos. Thom.* 39.

[3] This is also expressed in the second saying against the Pharisees in the *Gospel of Thomas* (# 102): "Woe to the Pharisees, for they are like a dog sleeping in a manger of oxen, for neither does he eat nor does he [let] the oxen eat."

[4] "The pericope is a notorious *crux interpretum* and virtually every detail is disputed: its position in the order of Q, the original order of its two component statements (Matt 11:12–13 || Luke 16:16a, b), the reconstruction of the original saying and its meaning" (Kloppenborg, *Formation of Q*, 113). For further discussion and literature see ibid., 112–115.

that this saying can be assigned to the original composition of Q; it fits better into the redactor's interest "in the opposition between Jesus (and John) on one side, and 'this generation' on the other."[1] Q 16:17 ("It is easier for heaven and earth to pass away than for one dot of the law to be dropped") should be assigned to the redactor of Q because of its apocalyptic perspective.[2] But it certainly indicates that the law is considered as binding for the community.

As a whole the sapiential speeches of Q are not concerned with the question of law and tradition. Their message transcends the limitations of Israel and of its religious tradition; the mission of the disciples is to everyone. Jesus' command not to go to the streets of the Gentiles and to the cities of the Samaritans (Matt 10:5–6) was added later to Q's mission speech by Matthew.[3] It has no place in the older version of that speech. That the Gentiles are invited is evident in Q 13:28–30: "They will come from the East and the West . . ." But this does not imply that the community placed itself outside of Israel. Q was composed at a time when the controversy of the law had not yet emerged, and when the question of observance of the Law had not yet been used as a criterion in order to decide whether or not the followers of Jesus were within or outside of Israel. Such a situation can be assumed to have existed during the first years after the death of Jesus anywhere in Palestine or anywhere in the diaspora where the question of the law, triggered by the Pauline mission, was not yet a concern. A Greek-speaking environment is more likely than an area of towns and villages in which the predominant language was Aramaic.

2.3.4 THE REDACTION OF Q AND ITS PLACE IN ISRAEL

The redaction of Q presents a different picture. There are three new elements: (1) the announcement of judgment over "this generation"; (2) the apocalyptic expectation of Jesus' return as the Son of man; (3) the demarcation of the line that both relates and separates Jesus and John the Baptist. The third element may constitute the last stage of the redaction of Q prior to its use by Luke.

Those who do not accept the message of Jesus and oppose the community are generally called "this generation." The term occurs for the first time at the end of the discourse about John the Baptist in the

---

[1] Kloppenborg, *Formation of Q*, 114.

[2] This saying is assigned by Schulz (*Spruchquelle*, 114–16) to the oldest stratum of Q. However, Schulz correctly describes its apocalyptic orientation.

[3] It is possible that these verses had their origin in the Jewish-Christian redaction of Q that also produced the version of the Sermon on the Mount used by Matthew. On this Jewish-Christian redaction of Q see below # 2.3.4.

introduction to the parable of the Children in the Market (Q 7:31).
The opponents are characterized as those who refused to listen; John
and Jesus belong together insofar as they are two representatives of
the divine envoys whose message was ignored. In the "announcement
of judgment" section Q 11:14–52, the polemic is more explicit. In the
Beelzebul Controversy (Q 11:14–23), the opponents[1] question the
divine authorization of the work of Jesus and thus the legitimacy of
the message of the community. Q 11:19 (". . . through whom do your
sons drive out demons?") may indicate that Israel as a whole is impli-
cated.[2] But this is not stated explicitly. Even in the pericope concerning the sign of Jonah (Q 11:16,[3] 29–32), the opponents remain
anonymous: "Others, in order to test him, were seeking from him a
sign from heaven" (Q 11:16).[4]

A more specific identification of the opponents appears in the woes
against the Pharisees (Q 11:47–52). But because of the differences in
the address in Matthew and Luke, the text of Q cannot always be
reconstructed with certainty. Luke's identification of those who are
addressed in the woes changes from "Pharisees" (Φαρισαῖοι, 11:39, 42,
43) to "lawyers" (νομικοί, 11:46, 52), while Matthew addresses the woes
which derive from Q to the "scribes and Pharisees, hypocrites" (Φραμ-
ματεῖς καὶ Φαρισαῖοι ὑποκριταί, 23:13, 23, 25, 27, 29; cf. 23:2). It is usually held that the latter address is due to Matthew's redaction.[5] But
while there can be no doubt that the addition of "hypocrites" must be
ascribed to Matthew,[6] the address to the "scribes and Pharisees"
appears in Matthew 23 consistently in the introduction to materials
which derive from Q.[7] In instances of other materials and of redactional additions, Matthew uses this phrase only once (23:15); else-

---

[1] The text of Q simply introduced them as τινές ("some"); Matt 12:24 has changed
this to "the Pharisees"; cf. Mark 3:22: "The scribes who had come down from
Jerusalem."

[2] Kloppenborg, *Formation of Q*, 127.

[3] Q 11:16 has been placed into the Beelzebul controversy by Luke; its original position in Q as the introduction to the sign of Jonah pericope is beyond doubt; cf. Matt
12:38 where this sentence properly introduces that pericope (Matt 12:39–41 = Luke
11:29–32).

[4] It is again Matthew (12:38; cf. 16:1) who introduced the scribes and Pharisees as
the opponents.

[5] See, e.g., Schulz, *Spruchquelle*, 95–96; Kloppenborg, *Formation of Q*, 142 (n. 175:
"The phrase 'scribes and Pharisees' is almost certainly Matthean").

[6] Matthew adds this word also in other contexts of controversy with the Pharisees;
compare Matt 15:7 with Mark 7:6, and Matt 24:51 (μετὰ τῶν ὑποκριτῶν) with Luke
12:46 (μετὰ τῶν ἀπίστων).

[7] The mention of the "scribes and Pharisees" in Matt 23:2 also belongs to these Q
passages because it appears in the general Matthean introduction to the speech in
which Q 11:46 = Matt 23:4 is the first of the Q sayings used by Matthew.

where he prefers different addresses.[1] On the other hand, Luke's address "lawyers" is so typically Lukan that it cannot derive from Q, and Luke's assignment of the first woes to the Pharisees and the rest of the woes to the lawyers is artificial. That the woes were addressed in Q to the "scribes and Pharisees" finds a confirmation in the parallel to Q 11:52 in *Gos. Thom.* 39 ("Pharisees and scribes").[2] This would suggest that "scribes and Pharisees" are the opponents of the Q community throughout its history, from the composition of the sapiential speeches—polemic against those who took away the key of knowledge would be quite appropriate here—even to the reformulation of the Q material in the Sermon on the Mount (see below) and ultimately to the Gospel of Matthew itself. Important for the understanding of Q's polemic against the scribes and Pharisees is Q 16:17: the law will retain its validity until this world will come to an end. The redactor of Q does not place the new community outside of Israel and of its law.

Q 10:13–15 announces the coming judgment explicitly with the view to two Galilean towns, Chorazin and Bethsaida: even Tyre and Sidon will be better off in the coming judgment. And the same saying threatens that Capernaum will be condemned to Hades. Except for the lament over Jerusalem (Q 13:34–35) and the localization of John the Baptist's activity in the area of the Jordan (Q 3:3), these are the only names of places which occur in Q. It is, therefore, tempting to assume that the redaction of Q took place somewhere in Galilee and that the document as a whole reflects the experience of a Galilean community of followers of Jesus. But some caution with respect to such conclusion seems advisable for several reasons. One single saying provides a very narrow base. Polemic against the Pharisees cannot confirm Galilean provenience—Greek-speaking Pharisees could be found elsewhere in the diaspora, viz., Paul who persecuted the church in Greek-speaking synagogues, probably in Syria or Cilicia. Even the sayings used for the original composition of Q were known and used elsewhere at an early date: they were known to Paul, were used in Corinth by his opponents, employed perhaps in eastern Syria for the composition of the *Gospel of Thomas,* and quoted by *1 Clement* in Rome at the end of the 1st century. The document itself, in its final redacted form, was used for the composition of two gospel writings, Matthew and Luke, which both originated in the Greek-speaking church outside of Palestine.

---

[1] "Blind guides" (ὁδηγοὶ τυφλοί, 23:16, 24), "blind Pharisee" (Φαρισαῖε τυφλέ, 23:26), "serpents, brood of vipers" (ὄφεις, γεννήματα ἐχιδνῶν, 23:33).

[2] For the appearance of "Pharisees" in traditional sayings, cf. *Gos. Thom.* 102; for "scribes" cf. Mark 12:38.

On the other hand, the Synoptic Sayings Source is an important piece of evidence for the continuation of a theology of followers of Jesus that had no relationship to the kerygma of the cross and resurrection. It is evident now that this was not an isolated phenomenon. The opponents of Paul in 1 Corinthians 1–4, the *Gospel of Thomas,* the *Dialogue of the Savior,* and the opponents of the Gospel of John in the Johannine community[1] all shared this understanding of the significance of Jesus' coming. This in itself does not establish a date for the redaction of Q. There is, however, one feature in the redaction of Q which ties this document to a particular geographical area, namely, the expectation of the coming Son of man and the use of this term as a christological title. The redactor of Q shares this title of Jesus with apocalyptic traditions used by the Gospels of Mark and John. It occurs nowhere else in early Christian literature, and it is most probable that there is only one common origin for its emergence.

As long as one assumes that the Gospel of Mark was composed in Rome and John's Gospel in Ephesus, the explanation of their common dependence upon traditions using this title is difficult to explain. It is much more likely that all three documents—Mark, John, and Q in its final redaction—originated in the same geographical area, namely, western Syria or Palestine.[2] More important than the precise geographical location is the question of the religious ferment that triggered this novel interpretation of the role of Jesus as a coming figure of the apocalyptic drama. The Judaic War of 66–73 CE is usually the event which one associates with such ferment. But there may have been other events during the decades before the Judaic War that could have triggered a more intense apocalyptic expectation.[3]

Mark 13:14 and 14:62 (cf. 13:26) point to the Book of Daniel[4] as the scriptural text which was seminal for the development of the apocalyptic expectation of Jesus as the coming Son of man. But it is difficult to be more precise with respect to geographical origin and exact date because a literary relationship between Mark and Q cannot be demonstrated.[5] However, an organized community in which the apocalyptic

---

[1] See below, ## 3.1.1 and 3.4.4.4.

[2] With respect to Mark and John, this will be discussed further below (## 3.4 and 4.1).

[3] Schmithals (*Einleitung,* 400) dates the Markan apocalypse in the year 40 CE, when Caligula ordered his statue to be erected in the temple of Jerusalem.

[4] Explicit quotations and deliberate allusions to Dan 7:13 and 9:27 are evident in these passages.

[5] Some scholars have claimed that the redaction of Q presupposes the Gospel of Mark (see Schmithals, *Einleitung,* 398–99) because of the reference to Jesus' miracle-working in the answer to John the Baptist's disciples (Q 7:18–23). Even the Q story of the temptation of Jesus (Q 4:1–13) has been understood as a direct development of

interpretation of scripture was an ongoing activity must be presupposed.[1] The scriptural texts used are those of the Greek translation. A Greek-speaking environment is once again more likely than an area like Galilee where Aramaic would have been the more common language. On the other hand, for the redactor of Q "this generation" is represented by the (scribes and) Pharisees, the teachers of Israel. The question of unbelief in Israel weighs more heavily than rejection by the Gentile world.

The Synoptic Sayings Source was used in this revised form by the author of the Gospel of Luke, perhaps in Antioch or in Ephesus. Was it also known to Papias of Hierapolis, and should his reference to "Matthew who composed the sayings" be understood as a testimony to Q, circulating as a document under the authority of Matthew? In spite of major and weighty objections,[2] this hypothesis has merits. While Papias talks about Mark as composing the "things said and done by the Lord,"[3] he ascribes to Matthew only the composition of "the sayings" (τὰ λόγια).[4] The *Gospel of Thomas* gives conclusive evidence that the apostle Thomas was considered in the tradition as the author of a work that contained mostly sayings of Jesus. It may be more than accidental that Matthew and Thomas are mentioned side by side in the Synoptic Gospels' lists of the apostles: Mark 3:18; Matt 10:3; Luke 6:15.[5] In the *Dialogue of the Savior*, Judas (Thomas) and Matthew, together with Mary, are the disciples who question Jesus about the interpretation of his sayings. In the *Gospel of Thomas*, Peter, Matthew, and Thomas are the three disciples who respond to Jesus' question, "compare me to someone and tell me who I am like" (#13). Matthew's answer is, "You are like a wise philosopher." Thomas's answer, which follows, is evidently a reference to this apostle as the possessor of the secret tradition and thus as the author of a writing of secret sayings: Jesus draws Thomas aside and tells him three things which he cannot divulge. Does this imply that Matthew was known as

---

Mark 1:21–22. But these Q sayings do not presuppose the Gospel of Mark itself; they are dependent upon traditions also used by Mark. It is certainly absurd to see the lament over Jerusalem (Q 13:34–35) as a proleptic reference to Mark's story of Jesus' entry to Jerusalem; cf. Q 13:35b, ". . . you will not see until it happens that you say 'Blessed it the one who comes in the name of the Lord.'" This final clause of the Q saying refers to the eschatological coming of the Son of man.

[1] This is also evident in the explicit references to Genesis 7, 18, and 19 in the Q apocalypse, Luke 17:27–32.

[2] For a summary of this discussion see Cameron, *Apocryphon of James,* 108–12.

[3] Eusebius *Hist. eccl.* 3.39.15.

[4] Eusebius, *Hist. eccl.* 3.39.16.

[5] In Acts 1:13, Thomas is listed together with Philip and separated from Matthew by Bartholomew.

the authority for a book of sayings of wisdom, sapiential discourses? This question could perhaps be answered in the affirmative.

The Gospel of Matthew may have taken over the name of its author from the source of sayings that was used in its composition. But it is not likely that Matthew used Q in the same form in which it was known to Luke. While general differences in the use of Q sayings by Matthew and Luke do not necessarily require a complex hypothesis of two different redactions of Q, the Sermon on the Mount of Matthew 5–7, in which one finds almost all the sayings from Q's inaugural discourse and many other Q materials, raises the question of a further pre-Matthean redaction of Q. The past scholarly consensus was, of course, that the author of the Gospel of Matthew composed the Sermon on the Mount. In that case, one could assume that Matthew knew Q in the same form as it was used by Luke. However, this consensus has recently been questioned by Hans Dieter Betz in several articles which are now conveniently collected in one volume in English translation.[1] Betz's observations are significant for the understanding of the further development of the community of Q. He distinguishes between the concerns of the Sermon on the Mount and those of Matthew with regard to the relationship of the followers of Jesus to Judaism. The former is committed to defining the theology of the followers of Jesus in such a way that they can justify their continued legitimate existence within Judaism. Matthew, on the other hand, presupposes the situation "of the universal church which has already incorporated Jewish-Christian traditions as well as Gentile-Christian communities."[2]

The author of the Sermon on the Mount faces and solves a problem that was not yet explicit in the original composition of Q, namely, the relationship of the followers of Jesus to the law-abiding community of Israel. The controversies with "this generation" and the polemic against the Pharisees in the redaction of Q reflects, as we saw, rejection by other groups within Israel; but they did not yet raise clearly the challenge for the followers of Jesus to define in which way they could justify their claim to be counted as truly law-abiding Israelites, in whatever form they understood and interpreted the law. The urgency of an answer to this question, Betz argues,[3] was ultimately dictated by

---

[1] *Essays on the Sermon on the Mount* (Philadelphia: Fortress, 1985). Hans Dieter Betz intends to put forward a conclusive presentation of his arguments in a forthcoming commentary on the Sermon on the Mount, to be published by Fortress Press in the Hermeneia series.

[2] Hans Dieter Betz, " The Beatitudes of the Sermon on the Mount," in idem, *Essays,* 22.

[3] Ibid., 19–22.

the Pauline Gentile Christianity which had declared and propagated its freedom from the law. The author of the Sermon on the Mount, who was at the same time the pre-Matthean redactor of Q, gives an answer that firmly places the Q community within Judaism and thus transforms this group of followers of Jesus into a Jewish-Christian sect.

The primary accomplishment of this redaction was a programmatic expansion of the inaugural sermon (Q 6:20–49) into an epitome[1] of the teachings of Jesus. Quite a few Q sayings which appeared elsewhere in the earlier document were transferred into this new work.[2] The theological theme for this epitome was developed on the basis of the older saying Q 16:17 ("It is easier for heaven and earth to pass away than for one dot of the law to be dropped"), which was transferred to a central position in the first part of the Sermon on the Mount and completely reformulated (Matt 5:17–20) in order to reject explicitly the claim or accusation that Jesus had come to abolish the law and the prophets.[3] The abstract of Jesus' teaching, well-known as the "antitheses" of the Sermon on the Mount, demonstrates that Jesus is the authoritative interpreter of the law, with the implication that those who follow this interpretation in their actions will thus have heeded the request for a righteousness, i.e., a fulfillment of the law, that is better than that of the scribes and Pharisees.

The following survey demonstrates how sayings in the Sermon on the Mount from other contexts of Q are interwoven with those which come from the inaugural sermon of Q 6:20–49:

Saying or Unit	Matt	from Q 6:20–49	other Q texts
Beatitudes	5:3–12	6:20–22	
About the salt	5:13		14:34–35
About the light	5:15		11:33
About the law	5:18		16:17
Reconciliation w. opponent	5:25–26		12:58–59
On divorce	5:32		16:18

[1] This designation of the genre of the Sermon on the Mount has been suggested by Hans Dieter Betz, "The Sermon on the Mount (Matt 5:3–7:27): Its Literary Genre and Function," in idem, *Essays*, 1–16.

[2] One or the other of the Q sayings which now appear in the Sermon on the Mount may have stood already in the original inaugural sermon of Q and were transferred to another context by Luke. But on the whole, the judgment stands that Luke preserved the original order of Q more often than Matthew; cf. Kloppenborg, *Formation of Q*, 79–80.

[3] On the analysis and interpretation of this saying in its new formulation see Hans Dieter Betz, "The Hermeneutical Principles of the Sermon on the Mount (Matt. 5:17–20)," in idem, *Essays*, 37–53.

On retaliation	5:39–42	6:29–30	
Love your enemies	5:43–48	6:27–28, 32–36	
Lord's Prayer	6:9–13		11:2–4
Treasure in heaven	6:19–21		12:33–34
Metaphor of the eye	6:22–23		11:34–35
Serving two masters	6:24		16:13
On cares	6:25–34		12:22–31
On judging	7:1–5	6:37–38, 41–42	
Answer to prayer	7:7–12		11:9–13
Golden Rule	7:12	6:31	
The narrow gate	7:13–14		13:23–24
Tree and fruit	7:16–20	6:43–45	
Saying "Lord, Lord"	7:21	6:46	
Rejection of evil workers	7:22–23		13:26–27
Parable of the Builders	7:24–27	6:47–49	

The incorporation of these sayings from other contexts of Q indicates the purpose of the composition of the Sermon on the Mount. Among these sayings are especially materials from traditional "instructions" (διδαχή) so that the continuation of the Sermon on the Mount (Matthew 6–7) appears as cultic and moral teaching along the theme of the "two ways." Hans Dieter Betz has called Matt 6:1–18 "A Jewish-Christian Cultic *Didache*."[1] It presents the rules for the cultic life, almsgiving, prayer, and fasting, and emphasizes that the fulfillment in righteousness, which can expect a reward from God, requires secrecy—otherwise the reward is already received and thus wasted. The anti-Pharisaic polemic of Q is visible also here;[2] but in spite of the fact that the temple and its cult are never mentioned, these rules for cultic piety are quite in keeping with Judaism; Christian elements are nowhere visible.[3] The last section of the Sermon on the Mount consistently follows the "two ways," cf. the transfer of the "two ways" materials from other sections of Q, especially the saying of the narrow gate (Q 13:24). In keeping with the genre of "instruction" (διδαχή), the last verses are sayings of eschatological warning. They do not primarily serve as general admonitions to all believers; rather, they have a polemical intent. Those whose appeal against the eschatological verdict will be rejected are the pseudo-prophets who are "wolves in sheep's clothing" (Matt 7:15), who have not brought good fruit (Matt 7:16–20). They have said "Lord, Lord," but did not do the will of the Father in heaven (Matt 7:21). What is meant by "the will of the Father" is made explicit in the rejection of those who have pro-

---

[1] *Essays,* 55–69.

[2] Cf. the use of "hypocrites" in Matt 6:2, 5, 16.

[3] Betz, *Essays,* 62, 65.

phesied in the name of Jesus, driven out demons in the name of Jesus, and performed miracles in the name of Jesus (Matt 7:22): they are "the workers of lawlessness" (οἱ ἐργαζόμενοι τὴν ἀνομίαν), that is, they are Christian missionaries who have not fulfilled the law.[1]

If the pre-Matthean redaction of Q which produced the Sermon on the Mount reveals the final establishment of the community of Q as a law-abiding Jewish-Christian group, conclusions can be drawn with respect to the dating of Q and its redactions. The decision to remain within the limits of law-abiding Israel must be dated quite early. The Pharisees who are the opponents of this group are not yet, as in the Gospel of Matthew, the Pharisees who represent the beginnings of rabbinic Judaism after the Judaic War. They are a rival group within a framework of the religion of Israel in which the interpretation of the law that the Sermon on the Mount presents would have been quite thinkable and in keeping with Jewish tradition. The Sermon on the Mount is anti-Pharisaic, but this is a phenomenon contained completely within the community of Judaism. The polemic against the Gentile-Christian mission belongs to the time of Paul rather than to a later period. Therefore, the entire development of Q, from the first collection of the sayings of Jesus and their assembly into sapiential discourses to the apocalyptic redaction and, finally, the pre-Matthean redaction, must be dated within the first three decades after the death of Jesus. The history reflected in the development of this source is analogous to the history of the first Greek-speaking Christian communities in the diaspora of Syria, like that of Antioch. Antioch's church was founded by Greek-speaking Jewish missionaries who proclaimed a new Israel into which Gentiles were invited. These missionaries were then attacked by Pharisees like Paul. But even after Paul had joined this new effort of Gentile mission, the conflict reemerged within the circles of the followers of Jesus. Antioch's Christians where now forced to debate the question of the fulfillment of the law with their brothers and sisters in Jerusalem (the controversy known as the "Apostles' Council"), and they finally decided that the Gentile church should not be obliged to abide by the law. The Q community reflects the same stages of development. It apparently begins with an openness to the invitation to Gentiles, experiences attacks by the Pharisees, but then makes a different decision, namely, to stay

---

[1] Ibid., 19–21. Betz (Ibid., 19–20) also asks: "Can it be a coincidence that the wise disciple, whose life is represented in the parable of Matt. 7:24–27, builds his house 'upon the rock' (τεθεμελίωτο … ἐπὶ τὴν πέτραν)? Can this 'rock' be anything other than an allusion to Peter and his church, against which Paul may be polemicizing, in concealed form, in 1 Cor 3:11 ('For no other foundation can one lay than that which is laid, which is Jesus Christ')?"

within the confines of the law. According to the Sermon on the Mount, the decision for the law did not include an explicit defense of circumcision and dietary laws. This defines a position that resembles that of Peter. He took the side of the law-abiding Jewish followers of Jesus at the Jerusalem Council, but later did not hesitate to eat with the Gentiles when he visited Antioch.[1] The author of the Gospel of Matthew demonstrates dependence upon such Jewish-Christian traditions under the authority of Peter.[2] It is not unlikely that the Jewish-Christian redaction of Q used by Matthew belonged to these Peter traditions.

One final note regarding the Epistle of James can be added. It was evident in the discussion of the gospel tradition of the Epistle of James[3] that the sayings and parenetic materials used in that writing were closely related specifically to Matthew 5, and in general to a Jewish-Christian perspective that advocated adherence to the law without demanding observance of circumcision and dietary legislation. The Epistle of James also shares with the Sermon on the Mount the rejection of the Pauline thesis which claims that Christ is the end of the law. The author of this epistle and the redactor of Q who produced the Sermon on the Mount belong to the same Jewish-Christian milieu; both share the decision that the followers of Jesus belong to law-abiding Israel and that fulfillment of the law, though without any emphasis upon circumcision and ritual law, is the appropriate interpretation of the teachings of Jesus.

---

[1] Gal 2:11–14; see Hans Dieter Betz, *Galatians: A Commentary on Paul's Letter to the Churches in Galatia* (Hermeneia; Philadelphia: Fortress, 1979) on Galatians 2, especially the excursus on "The Conflict at Antioch," pp. 103–4.

[2] Cf. Matthew 16:17–19; see below # 4.3.4.

[3] See above, # 2.1.4.4.

3

From Dialogues and Narratives to the Gospel of John

3.1 Dialogue Gospels

3.1.1 THE DIALOGUE OF THE SAVIOR

3.1.1.1 The Document and its Dialogue Source

The fifth writing in Codex III of the Nag Hammadi Library, occupying pp. 120,1–147,23, is entitled by incipit and explicit "The Dialogue of the Savior."[1] This copy of the Coptic translation of the originally Greek text of the document is the only extant text of the work. The text is fragmentary; on pp. 120–32 the first or the last two to ten letters of each line are missing; pp. 137–38 and 143–46 have substantial lacunae at the top of each page; on p. 147 only a few letters of line 9 to 23 have survived.[2]

In its preserved form, this writing is a compilation of various sources and traditions; its several sections exhibit great differences in style and content. The primary source used by the author seems to have been an older dialogue gospel which can be isolated with some degree of certainty because the dialogue form appears only here, while other materials as well as the lengthy introduction of the author are written as monologues of the Savior. The title "Savior" is used for the

[1] The writing has been published with translation and notes by Stephen Emmel, ed., with an introduction by Helmut Koester and Elaine Pagels, *Nag Hammadi Codex III,5: The Dialogue of the Savior* (NHS 26; Leiden: Brill, 1984). For English translations with brief introductions see Stephen Emmel, Helmut Koester, and Elaine Pagels, "The Dialogue of the Savior," in Robinson, ed., *Nag Hammadi Library,* 244–5; Cameron, *Other Gospels,* 38–48. For a German translation see Beate Blatz, "Der Dialog des Erlösers," in Hennecke-Schneemelcher, *NT Apokryphen I,* 245–53. There is no translation of this document in Hennecke-Schneemelcher-Wilson, *NT Apocrypha I.*

[2] See the description of the manuscript by Stephen Emmel, *Nag Hammadi Codex III,5,* pp. 19–36.

speaker primarily in the secondary monologue sections, while the older dialogue gospel usually employs the title "Lord" (only twice is he called "Savior" here[1]) for Jesus in conversation with Judas, Matthew, and Mary. The four extant sections of the dialogue gospel are combined with other materials as follows:[2]

Incipit 120,1	Title
1–3[3] (120,2–124,22)	Introduction
4–14 (124,23–127,19)	Dialogue, part 1
15–18 (127,19–128,23)	Creation myth
19–20 (128,23–129,16)	Dialogue, part 2
21–24 (129,16–131,18)	Creation myth, continued
25–34a (131,19–133,21[?])	Dialogue, part 3
34b–35 (133,21[?]–134,24)	Wisdom list
36–40 (134,24–137,3)	Apocalyptic vision
41–104a (137,3–146,20)	Dialogue, part 4
104b (146,20–147,22)	Concluding instructions
Explicit (147,23)	Title

It is very difficult to ascertain the date of the composition of the document. Since it is not mentioned by any Church Father, nor is there evident use of the work in any of the other works from the Nag Hammadi Library, the *terminus ad quem* for the composition must remain the date of the extant Coptic manuscript, that is, some time in the 4th century. A *terminus a quo* cannot be established with certainty, because there is no evidence for the use of either the canonical gospels or the Pauline epistles or of any other known writing, with the possible exception of the *Gospel of Thomas*. The terms and phrases used in the author's language resemble those of the deutero-Pauline and catholic epistles.[4] This could suggest a date for the composition of the extant

---

[1] See below; the names Jesus or Jesus Christ never occur.

[2] For a more detailed argument concerning the character of the various sections see Emmel, Koester, and Pagels, *Nag Hammadi Codex III,5*, pp. 2–15; Elaine Pagels and Helmut Koester, "Report on the *Dialogue of the Savior* (CG III,5)" in R. McL. Wilson, ed., *Nag Hammadi and Gnosis: Papers Read at the First International Congress of Coptology (Cairo, December 1976)* (NHS 14; Leiden: Brill, 1987) 66–74.

[3] The first numbers refer to the units in Stephen Emmel's translation of the text. They are also used in the translation published in Robinson, ed., *Nag Hammadi Library,* and in the German translation by Beate Blatz quoted above. In the following they will be used with a paragraph sign (#) in order to distinguish them from the references to page and line(s).

[4] See the references in Koester and Pagels, *Nag Hammadi Codex III,5*, p. 10.

document in the first half of the 2d century.[1] The repeated use of the title Savior would also point to this time.

The dates to be assigned to the sources used by the author represent a different question. The dialogue sections are elaborations of sayings of Jesus which show no sign of the use of any known gospel, though some sayings as well as the arrangement of the dialogue may point to a knowledge of the *Gospel of Thomas.* Other sources used by the author do not show any specifically Christian influence; the wisdom list used in ## 34b–35, as a whole a pre-Christian product, has been expanded by a references to baptism (134,6–8) and perhaps to the knowledge of the Father and the Son (134,14–15),[2] thus suggesting a relationship to the saying used in Q/Luke 10:21–22 and John 14:7–9.[3] The dialogical elaborations of sayings of Jesus in the dialogue sections resemble those of the Gospel of John and of the *Apocryphon of James.* Thus the date for the composition of the dialogue gospel that was used by the author depends upon a determination of its relationship to the corresponding sections in these writings, specifically in the Gospel of John.

Apart from the sections which the author took from this dialogue source, the *Dialogue of the Savior* does not share any characteristics of a gospel writing. Our investigation will therefore be limited to these particular sections of the document, which comprise about sixty-five percent of the text.

Questions and answers in the dialogue[4] are usually quite brief, some units comprising only one question by one of the three disciples (sometimes by "all" the disciples) and an answer of the Lord in form of a saying. These units resemble many "sayings" in the *Gospel of Thomas* which are often introduced by a question of the disciples. In other instances, a sequence of questions and answers discusses a particular topic. A traditional saying may constitute the final answer; but sayings are also used in the formulation of a disciple's question, while the answer given by the Lord is actually a secondary interpretation of the problem posed by the understanding of the saying that was quoted at the beginning of such a dialogue unit. Several of these units of the

---

[1] This date was suggested by Koester and Pagels (*Nag Hammadi Codex III,5,* pp. 15–16). Beate Blatz (Hennecke-Schneemelcher, *NT Apokryphen I,* 247) suggests the 2d century.

[2] But the text is uncertain at this point. See Emmel, *Nag Hammadi Codex III,5,* pp. 68–69.

[3] See Koester and Pagels, *Nag Hammadi Codex III,5,* p. 8.

[4] For the following see the description of the dialogues by Koester and Pagels, *Nag Hammadi Codex III,5,* pp. 2–8.

dialogue can be compared with respective traditional sayings or passages from other gospels.

3.1.1.2 The Use of Sayings in Dialogues

Dial. Sav. ## 4–8

The text of the initial question of Matthew (# 4) is not preserved. Only fragments remain of the answer of the "Savior" (# 5), a question of Judas (# 6), and a statement by the "Lord" (# 7). But a second statement, introduced by "The Savior[1] said," is well preserved in its first part (# 8).

Dial. Sav. # 8 (125,18–126,5)	Parallels
	Matt 6:22–23[2]
The lamp [of the body] is the mind. As long as [the things inside] you are set in order, that is, [. . .]. . ., your bodies are [luminous]. As long as your hearts are [dark], the luminosity you anticipate [? will not come]. I have . . .	The lamp of the body is the eye. If your eye is single, your whole body will be luminous. But if your eye is evil, your body will also be dark. If now the light within you is darkness, how great is the darkness!

Other variations of the same saying appear in the *Gospel of Thomas* and in the Gospel of John:

Gos. Thom. 24b: There is light within a man of light and he lights up the whole world. If he does not shine, he is darkness.

John 11:9–10: If someone walks in the day, he will not stumble, because he sees the light of the world; but if someone walks in the night, he stumbles, because the light is not in him (cf. John 12:35).

The basis of this saying is identical with that of the Q saying recorded by both Matthew and Luke. In the interpretation, the word "eye" from the metaphor has been replaced by its allegorical equivalent "mind." In the subsequent passages, the contrasting pairs of enlightened heart/luminous bodies and dark heart/lack of the coming luminosity, replace the metaphors of the original saying in order to emphasize the correlation of inner enlightenment to the expected salvation into midst of the light.

---

[1] ## 5 and 8 are the only two instances in which Jesus is called "Savior."
[2] Cf. Luke 11:34–35.

Dial. Sav. ## 9–12

Dial. Sav. ## 9–12 (126,6–17)	Matt 7:7/Luke 11:9
His [disciples said, "Lord], who is it who seeks [and finds] and[1] reveals?"	Ask, and it will be given to you; seek and you will find.

	Gos. Thom. 94 (cf. 92)
[The Lord said to them], "[It is] the one who seeks [who also] reveals . . . [. . .]."	He who seeks will find, and he who knocks will be let in.

	Gos. Thom. 33a
[Matthew said, "Lord, when] I [listen . . .] and [when] I speak, who is it who [speaks and who is it] who listens?"	Preach from your housetops that which you will hear in your ear.

	John 16:13
[The Lord] said, "It is the one who speaks who also [listens], and it is the one who can see who also reveals."	(The spirit of truth) will not speak from himself, but what he hears he will speak and announce to you what is coming.

This section is an elaboration of the traditional saying about seeking and finding which is quoted in the initial question. Already there, it has been expanded to include the notion of "revealing." Sayings like *Gos. Thom.* 33a and John 16:13 may have been used in order to establish the conclusion, formulated as a new saying of the Lord, that the authority for speaking and revealing presupposes that one has not only found but also listened and seen.

Dial. Sav. ## 13–14

Dial. Sav. ## 13–14 (126,17–127,19)	Luke 6:21b
[Mary] said. "Lord, behold! Whence [do I] bear the body [while I] weep, and whence while I [laugh]?"	Blessed are those who weep now, for you shall laugh.

	John 16:20
The Lord said, "[. . .] weep on account of its works [. . .] remain and the mind laughs [. . .] . . . [. . .] . . . spirit. If one does not [stand] in darkness, he	. . . you will weep and lament, but the world will rejoice. You will be full of sorrow, but your sorrow will be turned into joy.

[1] Instead of "[and finds] and," Emmel reconstructs "who is it who also."

will [not] be able to see [the light]. So
I tell you [...] light is the darkness.
[And if one does not] stand in [the
darkness, he will] not [be able] to see
the light.

[lines 7–13 are unintelligible]

then the powers [...]... which are
above as well as those [below] will
[...] you. In that place [there will]
be weeping and [gnashing] of teeth
over the end of [all] these things."

John 12:35

Only a short time the light is among
you. Walk as you have the light, so
that darkness will not overcome you.
And he who walks in the darkness
does not know where he goes. As you
have the light, believe in the light, so
that you become children of the
light.[1]

Matt 8:12

But the sons of the kingdom will be
thrown out into the outer darkness,
and there will be weeping and
gnashing of teeth.

The use of several traditional sayings in this section is evident. But
because of the poor preservation of the text it is not possible to be certain about the interpretation. The term "weeping" forms an inclusio:
at the beginning, weeping is connected to existence in the body; at the
conclusion, it is the powers above and below who are weeping over the
end of the world. The central part seems to interpret the "laughing of
the mind" as the seeing of the light. A comparison with John 16:20
shows that, in both texts, weeping is related to the existence in the
world; but in John 16, it is existence in the world while Jesus has
departed, and joy is to come at his return as the spirit of truth, while in
the Dialogue of the Savior the liberation of the mind who has seen the
light is the cause of joy.

Dial. Sav. #19–20

This section (128,23–129,16) is a brief dialogue that has been
inserted into the narrative of the creation myth (127:19–128,23 and
129,16–131,18). It consists of a question of Matthew and a somewhat
lengthy answer of the Lord. But the text is so poorly preserved that
neither the question nor the answer are quite intelligible. In the
answer, the Lord speaks about "the means to overcome the powers
above as well as those below." This indicates that this section originally continued the dialogue of the preceding section ## 13–14. But

---

[1] See also *Gos. Thom.* 33b "... but rather he sets (the lamp) on a lampstand, so that
everyone who enters and leaves will see its light." Cf. Matt 5:15; Luke 11:33.

the conclusion of the Lord's statement clearly reflects the use of a traditional saying:

Dial. Sav. 129,14–16	John 16:24
And [let] him who [knows] seek and find and [rejoice].	Until now you have not asked anything in my name; ask and you will receive so that your joy may be full.[1]

3.1.1.3 *Dial. Sav.* ##25–30 and John 14

Dial. Sav. ## 25–30 (131,19–132,19)	John 14:2–12
[Mary] hailed her brothers [. . .], "you ask the Son about the . . . them, where are you going to put them?"	2: In my father's house are many dwellings; if not, I would have told you,
[The Lord said] to her, "Sister, [. . .] will be able to inquire about these things [. . .] . . . he has somewhere to put them in his [heart . . .] . . . to come [forth . . .] and enter . . . so that they might not hold back . . . this impoverished cosmos."	because I go to prepare a place for you. 3: . . . And I come again and take you to myself, so that where I am you also will be. 4: And where I go, you know the way.
[Matthew] said, "Lord I want to [see] that place of life, [the place] where there is no wickedness, [but rather] there is pure [light]." The Lord [said], "Brother [Matthew], you will not be able to see it [as long as you are] carrying flesh around." [Matthew] said, "Lord, [even if I will] not [be able] see it, let me [know it]."	5: Thomas said to him, "Lord, we do not know where you are going; how can we know the way?" 6: Jesus said to him, "I am the way and the truth and the life; no one comes to the Father except through me." 8: Philip said to him, "Show us the father and it will be sufficient for us."
The Lord [said], "[Everyone] who has known himself has seen [it . . .]	9: Jesus said to him, ". . . Who has seen me has seen the Father. How do

---

[1] See also the sayings about seeking/finding in Matt 7:7; Luke 11:9; *Gos. Thom.* ## 2, 92, 94.

and he ... he has ... found / will prove the place of life

because ... permitted
everything [given] to him [alone] to do
he does [...] ... and has come to
[? do / ? resemble] it in his [goodness]."

you say, 'Show us the Father?'
10: Do you not know that I am in the Father and the Father in me? ... The Father who dwells in me does his works.
12: ... He who believes in me will also do the works that I do, and will do greater ones than these.

Mary's initial question apparently raises the question of the "place of life" to which the disciples will go. The topic is formulated on the basis of a traditional saying, cf. *Gos. Thom.* 24:

> His disciples said to him, "Show us the place where you are, since it is necessary for us to seek it." He said to them, "He who has ears, let him hear. There is light within a man of light, and he lights up the whole world. If he does not shine, he is darkness.

The same question, the place of life, also introduces the dialogue of John 14:2–12. In both instances, the request is repeated in modified forms. In the *Dialogue of the Savior* the question moves from "seeing" the place to "knowing" it. In John 14 it moves from knowing the way to showing the Father. The *Dialogue of the Savior* concludes with the typical reference to knowledge of oneself as the goal of the search, once more on the basis of a traditional saying, cf. *Gos. Thom.* 3b:

> When you come to know yourselves, then you will become known, and you will realize that it is you who are the sons of the living Father. But if you will not know yourselves, you dwell in poverty, and it is you who are that poverty.

In both *Dial. Sav.* ## 25–30 and in John 14 the final stage is doing the appropriate works. As a whole, both are variants of the same composition of a brief revelation dialogue, not independently constructed on the basis of the same traditional sayings. This makes the differences even more striking. In John 14, there is no reference to self-knowledge; rather, this familiar notion is replaced quite surprisingly by a reference to knowledge of Jesus. Accordingly, the works which the believer does are not the result of one's own goodness, but they emerge from faith in Jesus and imitate the works of Jesus. John 14:2–12 appears to be a deliberate christological reinterpretation of the more traditional Gnostic dialogue, which the *Dialogue of the Savior* has preserved in its more original form. That the discourses and dialogues of John's Gospel present such reinterpretations of Gnostic dialogues in other instances will be discussed below.[1]

Dial. Sav. ## 31–34

The parable of the stone and its interpretation (132,19–134,1) could be based on older traditions and seems to employ apocalyptic materials (cf. Isa 24:18–20). In its second half, Jesus' answer alludes to several sayings that are closely related to the preceding dialogue section:

Dial. Sav. ## 34b (133,14–24)	Gos. Thom. 50
[...]...you, all the sons of [men. For] you are from [that] place. [In] the hearts of those who speak out of [joy] and truth you exist. Even if it (or he) comes forth in the body of the Father among men and is not received, still it (or he) [does (not?)] return to its (or his) place.	We came from the light, the place where the light came into being of its own accord....

Gos. Thom. 50 / *John 1:9–11*

He was the true light that enlightens every human being coming into the world, ... and the world did not know him. He came to his own, and his own did not receive him.[2]

creation in its perfection

Whoever [does not] know [the work] of perfection [knows] nothing. If one does not stand in the darkness, he will not be able to see the light.

See above on *Dial. Sav.* # 8 (125,18–126,5)

deficient world

3.1.1.4 Sayings in Dial. Sav. ## 41–104

Most of the last and most extensive portion of the dialogue, ## 41–104a (137,3–146,20), consists of smaller units, sometimes tied together by catchword association. It is not possible to recognize major units of sustained dialogue on a particular topic. In the following I shall present those portions of the dialogue which are well preserved and have evident parallels in sayings elsewhere.

Dial. Sav. ## 49–50 (138,11–20)

Judas said, "Behold, the rulers dwell above us, so it is they who will rule

of the deficient world order

---

[1] See below # 3.4.4.3.

[2] Cf. also *Gos. Thom.* 28.

over us." The Lord said, "It is you who will rule over them. But when you rid yourselves of jealousy, then you will clothe yourselves in light and enter the bridal chamber."

Gos. Thom. 75

Jesus said, "Many are standing at the door, but it is the solitary who will enter the bridal chamber.

Dial. Sav. ## 51–52
(138,20–139,7)

Judas said, "How will [our] garments be brought to us?
The Lord said, "There are some who will provide for you, and there are others who will receive [. . .]. For [it is] they [who will give you] your garments. [For] who [will] be able to reach that place [which] is [the] reward? But the garments of life were given to man

Gos. Thom. 36–37
(P. Oxy. 655, frag. 1b)

"Who could add anything to your age? He himself will give you your garment." His disciples said, "When will you become revealed to us, and when shall we see you?" Jesus said. "When you disrobe without being ashamed and take up your garments and place them under your feet like little children and tread on them, then [you will see] the son of the living one and you will not be afraid."[1]

John 14:4–5

because he knows the path by which he will leave. And it is difficult for me even to reach it."

"And where I am going, you know the way." Thomas said to him, "Lord, we do not know where you are going. How do we know the way?"

Dial. Sav. # 53 (139,8–13)

Mary said, "Thus with respect to 'the wickedness of each day,'

Matt 6:34b

Its own wickedness is sufficient for each day.[2]

Matt 10:10

and 'the laborer is worthy of his food,'

The laborer is worthy of his food.[3]

---

[1] A parallel to this saying appears in the *Gospel of the Egyptians,* see below the discussion of *2 Clem.* 12, # 5.1.3.

[2] This is the second of two free proverbs which Matthew has added to the Q collection of sayings "On cares" (Matt 6:25–33 = Luke 12:22–31).

[3] The Matthean version is quoted here. Cf. Luke 10:7: "The laborer is worthy of his wages." It is debated which of the two versions stood in Q. However, this is a free saying that is quoted frequently in both versions; cf. 1 Tim 5:18; *Did.* 13.2.

and 'the disciple resembles his teacher.'" She uttered this as a woman who had understood completely.

Matt 10:24 = Luke 6:40

A disciple is not over (his) master.[1]

Dial. Sav. ## 56–59
(139,20–140,14)

[Matthew] said, "Tell me, Lord, how the dead die [and] how the living live." The [Lord] said, "[You have] asked me about a saying [. . .] which eye has not seen, [nor] have I heard it except from you. But I say to you that when what invigorates a man is removed, he will be called 'dead.' And when what is alive leaves what is dead, what is alive will be called *l l wʻsj* upon." Judas said, "Why else, for the sake of truth, do they kill and live?" The Lord said. "Whatever is born of truth does not die.
Whatever is born of woman dies."

Gos. Thom. 11

Jesus said, ". . . The dead are not alive, and the living will not die. In the days when you consumed what is dead, you made it what is alive. . . "

Gos. Thom. 17

Jesus said, "I shall give you what no eye has seen and what no ear has heard and what no hand has touched and what has never occurred to the human mind."[2]

John 11:25

He who believes in me will live even if he dies, and everyone who lives and believes in me will not die in eternity.

Dial. Sav. ## 65–68 (141,2–11)

Matthew said, "[Why] do we not rest [at once]?" The Lord said, "When you lay down these burdens." Matthew said, "How does the small join itself to the big?" The Lord said, "When you abandon the works which will not be able to follow you, then you will rest."

Gos. Thom. 90

Come unto to me, for my yoke is easy, . . . and you will find rest for yourselves.[3]

Gos. Thom. 37

His disciples said, "When will you become revealed to us and will we see you?" Jesus said, " When you disrobe without being ashamed and take up your garments and place them under your feet like little children and tread on them, then [will you see] the son of

---

[1] Cf. John 13:16: "A servant is not greater than his master, nor is an apostle greater than the one who sent him."

[2] Cf. 1 Cor 2:9; see the discussion of this saying above, # 2.1.3.

[3] Cf. Matt 11:28–30; Gos. Thom. (P. Oxy. 654, 2) ". . . and once he has ruled, he will attain rest."

the living one, and you will not be afraid.

Dial. Sav. ## 73–74 (142,4–9)

[Judas] said, "Tell me, Lord, what the beginning of the path is." He said, "Love and goodness. For if one of these existed among the rulers, wickedness would not have come into existence."

John 14:5–6

Thomas said to him, "Lord, we do not know where you are going; how do we know the way?" Jesus said to him, "I am the way and the truth and the life. No one comes to the father except through me."

Dial. Sav. ## 75–76 (142,9–15)

Matthew said, "Lord, you have spoken about the end of everything without concern." The Lord said, "You have understood all things I have said to you and you have accepted them on faith. If you have known them, then they are [yours]. If not, then they are not yours."

Gos. Thom. 51

His disciples said to him, "When will the repose of the dead come about, and when will the new world come?" He said to them, "What you look forward to has already come, but you do not recognize it."

Dial. Sav. ## 77–78 (142,16–19)

They said to him, "What is the place to which we are going?" The [Lord] said, "Stand in the place which you can reach."

(See above the parallels to # 25 and ## 60–63)

Dial. Sav. ## 84–85 (143,11–144,1)

Judas said to Matthew, "We [want] to understand the sort of garments we are to be [clothed] with, [when] we depart the decay of the [flesh]. The Lord said. "The rulers [and] the administrators possess garments granted [only for a time], which do not last. [But] you, as children of truth, not with these transitory garments are you to clothe yourselves. Rather, I say [to] you that you will become [blessed] when you strip [yourselves]. For it is no great thing . . . [. . .] outside."

Gos. Thom. 37

His disciples said, "When will you become revealed to us and will we see you?" Jesus said, " When you disrobe without being ashamed and take up your garments and place them under your feet like little children and tread on them, then [will you see] the son of the living one, and you will not be afraid."

Dial. Sav. ## 90–95
(144,12–145,7)[1]

Judas said, "You have told us this out of the mind of truth. When we pray, how should we pray?" The Lord said, "Pray in the place where there is no woman." Matthew said, "'Pray in the place where there is no woman,' meaning, 'Destroy the works of womanhood,' not because there is any other [manner of birth], but because they will cease [giving birth]. Mary said, "Will they never be obliterated?" The Lord said, "[Who] knows that they will [not] dissolve and . . . (the remainder and # 95 are very fragmentary)

Gos. Thom. 6

His disciples questioned him and said to him, "Do you want us to fast? How should we pray? What diet shall we observe?"

Gos. Thom. 114

Simon Peter said to them, "Let Mary leave us, for women are not worthy of life." Jesus said, "I myself shall lead her in order to make her male, so that she too may become a living spirit resembling you males. For every woman who will make herself male will enter the kingdom of heaven."

Gospel of the Egyptians [2]

Salome said, "How long will human beings die?" The Lord said, "As long as women will give birth."

Dial. Sav. # 104b (147,14–22)

For I say [you . . .] . . . you take . . . [. . .] . . . you . . . [. . .] who have sought, having [understood] . . . this, will [rest . . .] he will live [forever. And] I say to [you . . .] . . . so that you will not lead [your] spirits and your souls into error.

John 6:63

It is the spirit that gives life, the flesh is of no avail; the words that I have spoken to you are spirit and life.

John 8:51

Truly, truly, I say to you, if anyone keeps my word, he will never see death.

Gos. Thom. 1

Whoever finds the interpretation of these sayings will not experience death.

An examination of the sequence of the topics which are discussed in the dialogue sections of this document as well as a comparison of the individual statements with parallels elsewhere reveals a surprising familiarity with the sayings of the *Gospel of Thomas*. The saying about seeking and finding is discussed in the first part of the dialogue (cf. *Gos. Thom.* 2), and the dialogue seems to conclude with an elabora-

[1] See also above, *Dial. Sav.* ## 56–59.
[2] Clement of Alexandria *Strom.* 3.9, 63–64; cf. ibid., 3.9, 45.

tion of the introduction to the *Gospel of Thomas* (# 1) which speaks
about the finding of life through the interpretation of the sayings. The
saying of *Gos. Thom.* 2 may also have influenced the order in which
several topics are discussed in the dialogue portions of the *Dialogue of
the Savior.* In *Gos. Thom.* 2, seeking, finding, amazement, ruling, and
resting are described as the steps of the order of salvation. *Dial. Sav.*
8 speaks about seeking and finding; # 25 raises the question of "the
place of life"; ## 47–50 discuss "who will rule over us"; # 65 raises the
question of resting. If the apocalyptic vision (*Dial. Sav.* 36–40) was
part of the original dialogue, it could be understood as a commentary
on the topic of "amazement."

This dialogue as a whole would then be a commentary on the eschatological time table which is implied in *Gos. Thom.* 2. The disciples
have sought and have found; but their rule and their rest will only
appear in the future. At the present time, the "rulers" of the cosmos
still exercise their authority, and the time at which the disciples will
rule over them, has not yet come (*Dial. Sav.* ## 47–50). The rest can
only be obtained when they can rid themselves of the burden of their
bodies (*Dial. Sav.* # 28). Mary, who recognizes this, is praised as a disciple who has understood the all (*Dial. Sav.* # 53).

The question of the "works of womanhood" (*Dial. Sav.* ## 91–95)
occupies a prominent place in the dialogue. It is a topic that belongs to
the overarching concern of wearing the body, that is, these works are
understood as the continuation of existence in the body through child-
bearing—possibly a commentary on the final saying of the *Gospel of
Thomas* (114) about Mary, the woman who is not worthy of the kingdom unless she is made male. A saying that is elsewhere preserved in
the *Gospel of the Egyptians* provides the answer: rejection of the works
of womanhood does not imply a degradation of women as such.
"Becoming male" (*Gos. Thom.* 114) would imply, in the understanding
of the *Dialogue of the Savior,* that women will stop bearing children
and, in this respect, resemble the male. This document is thus taking
a position that is diametrically opposed to the Pastoral Epistles of the
New Testament: 1 Tim 2:13–15 asserts that women will be saved by
bearing children. Moreover, the *Dialogue of the Savior* features Mary
as the most prominent of the disciples of Jesus in the discussion with
the Lord, while 1 Tim 2:11–12 demands explicitly that women should
be silent in the assembly of the church.

The dialogue gospel that the author of the extant document used
has been incorporated into a framework that can no longer be called a
"gospel" in the proper sense of the word.[1] The extant document is a

---

[1] For a more detailed discussion of the relationship of the older dialogue gospel to
the extant document, see Koester and Pagels, *Nag Hammadi Codex III,5,* pp. 9–15.

theological treatise which is concerned with the relationship of realized and future eschatology. It is probably a baptismal instruction which interprets baptism as the moment in which the time of the abandonment of labor and the attainment of rest is celebrated in an anticipatory fashion: "Already the time has come, brothers, for us to abandon our labor and stand at rest" (120,3–6). But passing through the spheres for the final attainment of rest presupposes the "time of dissolution" (122,2–3). What has already been experienced in baptism will have its consequences only once the soul passes through the powers and rulers on its way to the heavenly abode.[1] This theology is closely related to early Christian documents which come from the time of about 100 CE. Thus the date of the document in its preserved form is most likely the beginning of the 2d century CE; the dialogue gospel used by its author may have been composed during the last decades of the 1st century CE.[2]

3.1.2 THE APOCRYPHON OF JAMES

3.1.2.1 The Document

The *Apocryphon of James* (NHC I,2), often also referred to as the *Epistula Iacobi,* occupies the first pages of Codex I (1,1–16,30) of the Nag Hammadi Library.[3] The manuscript is quite well preserved except for a few lacunae at the top of the first three pages. No title appears in the manuscript. The document begins with an epistolary prescript: "[James] writes to [. . .].[4] Peace [be with you from] peace,

---

[1] The closest parallels to this anticipatory eschatology, related to the understanding of baptism, can be found in Eph. 2:1–6; Col 3:1–4; Clement of Alexandria *Exc. Theod.,* 77.1–2; *On Baptism A* (NHC XI,2b; 41,23–38); *On Baptism B* (NHC XI,2c; 42,16–19).

[2] For a discussion of the date of composition, see Koester and Pagels, *Nag Hammadi Codex III,5,* pp. 15–16.

[3] It was first published by Michel Malinine, Henri-Charles Puech, Gilles Quispel, Rudolphe Kasser, R. McL. Wilson, and Jan Zandee, eds., *Epistula Iacobi Apocrypha* (Zürich: Rascher, 1968). A new edition has been published by Francis E. Williams, ed., "The Apocryphon of James," in Harold W. Attridge, ed., *Nag Hammadi Codex I (The Jung Codex): Introductions, Texts, Translations, Notes* (2 vols.; NHS 22–23; Leiden: Brill, 1985) 1. 13–53; 2. 7–37. For English translations see Francis E. Williams, "The Apocryphon of James," in Robinson, ed., *Nag Hammadi Library,* 29–37; Cameron, *Other Gospels,* 55–64. A new German translation by Dankwart Kirchner, "Brief des Jakobus," appears in Hennecke-Schneemelcher, *NT Apokryphen I,* 234–44. There is no English translation of this document in Hennecke-Schneemelcher-Wilson, *NT Apocrypha.*

[4] Neither the name of the sender nor the name of the addressee are preserved. While it is quite clear from the following sentences that the sender must be James (the brother of Jesus?), the addressee remains uncertain. Hans-Martin Schenke ("Der Jacobusbrief aus dem Codex Jung," *OLZ* 66 [1971] 117–130) has suggested Cerinthus

[love from] love, [grace from] grace, [faith] from faith, life from holy life" (1,1–7). But the next section shows that this is only a secondary framework for the transmission of a "secret book"[1] that was revealed to James and Peter by the Lord and written by James[2] "in the Hebrew alphabet" (1,10–17). Notwithstanding this claim, there is no question that the Coptic text is a translation from a Greek original.

The first scholarly assessment of the *Apocryphon of James* saw the document as a speculative Gnostic writing, tried to locate its thought within the known framework of types of Gnostic theology, and assigned its literary genre to that of the later Gnostic dialogues.[3] A new approach for the investigation of the document was initiated by Ron Cameron.[4] He begins with the observation that the *Apocryphon of James* "states explicitly that it is providing a written record of those sayings which Jesus revealed to James and Peter."[5] As there are frequent quotations of traditional sayings in this document,[6] Cameron proposes "to analyze the *Apocryphon of James* form-critically in order to clarify the ways in which sayings of Jesus were used and transformed . . . ," including "a formal isolation of individual sayings, an identification of their traditional and redactional elements, and a reconstruction of the compositional history of the document."[7]

---

as the person to whom the letter was addressed; see also Kirchner, "Brief des Jakobus," 236–37.

[1] The Coptic transcription of the Greek word ἀπόκρυφον appears in 1,10.

[2] Because of the association of James with Peter, common in Jewish-Christian documents, it is tempting to identify James with the brother of Jesus. However, no such identification is indicated in the document. Rather, James appears, like Peter, as one of the twelve disciples. See the discussion of the name of the author in B. Dehandschutter, "L'Epistula Jacobi apocrypha de Nag Hammadi (CG I,2) comme apocryphe néotestamentaire," *ANRW* 2.25/6 (1988) 4536–39.

[3] See for this hypothesis, with a comprehensive discussion of earlier views, Dehandschutter, ibid., 4520–50. For a brief report and literature see Ron Cameron, *Sayings Traditions in the Apocryphon of James* (HTS 34; Philadelphia: Fortress, 1984). Dehandschutter does not refer to the work of Ron Cameron, which was published in 1985.

[4] Cameron, *Apocryphon of James.*

[5] Ibid., 3.

[6] See also Kirchner, "Brief des Jakobus," 237.

[7] Cameron, *Apocryphon of James,* 3. The following analysis of the sayings and dialogues of this writing is based upon the results of Cameron's investigation. Dehandschutter ("L'Epistula Jacobi apocrypha," 4540–47) presents a thorough discussion of the problem of the literary genre of this document, albeit with quite different results.

3.1.2.2 Opening Scene and Hermeneutics of the Dialogue

The opening scene of the writing (*Apocr. Jas.* 2,8–21) is important for the understanding of the hermeneutical situation in which dialogues are developed on the basis of traditional sayings: *chapters*

> ... the twelve disciples [were] all sitting together and remembering what the Savior had said to each one of them, whether in secret or openly, and [putting it] in books—[But I] was writing that which was in [my book]—lo, the Savior appeared, [after] departing from [us while we] gazed after him. And after five hundred and fifty days since he had risen from the dead, ...

"Remembering" what Jesus had said, is a key term for the oral tradition.[1] In Papias of Hierapolis, it also marks the transition from this tradition to the collection and written exposition of the sayings. The setting described in the opening section of the *Apocryphon of James* corresponds to that of Papias.[2] Whether or not the sayings are taken from a written document, the hermeneutical situation described here implies that sayings of Jesus, or collections of sayings, are transmitted in the free tradition and that the process of their interpretation is identical with the production of written documents. According to the witness of Eusebius,[3] in the case of Papias of Hierapolis the resulting books are called "Interpretation of the Sayings of the Lord" (Λογίων κυριακῶν ἐξήγησις). In the *Apocryphon of James* the writing which results is a dialogue of Jesus with two of his disciples, James and Peter, into which a few longer discourses of Jesus have been interpolated.[4] Although the setting for the writing of the document is a dialogue with Jesus after his resurrection, the basis of the work is an interpretation of traditional sayings of Jesus.[5] That is evident at the

---

[1] For the use of this term and for the following discussion and relevant literature see above, # 2.1.4.3.

[2] This has been demonstrated convincingly by Cameron, *Apocryphon of James*, especially pp. 122–23: ". . . the term 'remembering' is understood here as an introduction to a collection of 'secret sayings' of Jesus, and is used to refer to the composition of these sayings in 'secret books.'"

[3] *Hist. eccl.* 3.39.1.

[4] Several suggestions have been made with respect to possible secondary interpolations into the original dialogue; cf. Williams, "Apocryphon of James," 17–18. Williams himself (ibid., 18–19) suggests that the two longer discourses on martyrdom (4,24–6,20) and about prophecy (6,21–7,10) were inserted into an earlier work.

[5] Cameron (*Apocryphon of James*, passim) has argued convincingly for the independence of the sayings tradition of this writing. Arguments for dependence upon the canonical Gospels, especially upon the Gospel of John, are summarized and discussed by Dehandschutter, "L'Epistula Jacobi apocrypha," 4547–50; see ibid. (p. 4585) for earlier studies of this question.

very beginning of the dialogue. The first statement of Jesus which initiates the dialogue, responding to a question of the disciples ("Have you departed and removed yourself from us?"), is based on a traditional saying:

> No, but I shall go to the place whence I came. If you wish to come with me, come! (2,23–27).

This statement is a variant of an often-repeated phrase in which the one who has his or her origin in the divine world announces the return to that world.[1] It ultimately derives from the myth of Wisdom, and it made its way into the tradition of sayings of Jesus at an early date, both as a description of the disciples' return to the place of their origin and as a statement about Jesus' coming and going.[2] The former appears in the tradition of sayings in the small catechism *Gos. Thom.* 50:

> Jesus said, "If they say to you, 'Where did you come from?' say to them, 'We came from the light, the place where the light came into being . . .' If they say to you, 'Is it you?' say, 'We are its children, and we are the elect of the living Father.' If they ask you, 'What is the sign of your Father in you?' say to them, 'It is movement and repose.'"

This basic catechism is elaborated in other Gnostic texts.[3] In all these instances, the return of the disciples to the place of their origin is not dependent upon Jesus' or the revealer's own coming and returning. The disciples themselves have come to know who they are and, therefore, possess the power to return to their origin.

The saying at the beginning of the first dialogue in the *Apocryphon of James,* however, is a statement about Jesus' coming and going. This saying establishes the point of departure for an exploration of the question of the disciples' situation in view of Jesus' return.[4] An addition to the quotation of the saying initiates the dialogue: "If you wish to come with me, come!" (2,25–26). The response of the disciples is also a compositional devise for the construction of the dialogue: "They all answered and said to him, 'If you bid us, we come'" (2,26–28). Jesus' answer is again formulated on the basis of another traditional saying:

> Truly, I say unto you, no one will ever enter the kingdom of heaven at

---

[1] See the discussion of parallels in Cameron, *Apocryphon of James,* 58–62.

[2] For the latter, parallels occur most frequently in the Gospel of John; cf., e.g., "I have gone out from the Father and have come into the world; I am leaving the world again and I am going to the Father" (John 16:28).

[3] Cf. especially *1 Apocalypse of James* (NHC V,3) 33,11–34,20.

[4] This is a major topic in the dialogues of the Gospel of John, see below # 3.4.4.3.

my bidding, but (only) because you yourselves are full. (2,29–33)

The saying which is presupposed here is attested in the synoptic tradition as well as in the Gospel of John:[1]

> Truly, I say to you, whoever does not receive the kingdom of God as a child, will never enter into it. (Mark 10:15)

> Truly, truly, I say to you, unless someone is born anew (or: from above = γεννηθῇ ἄνωθεν), he can not enter the kingdom of God. (John 3:3, 5)[2]

This portion of the dialogue of *Apocr. Jas.* 2,22–33 is analogous in its formal structure to the beginning of the dialogue of John 14:2–6 which has already been quoted as a parallel to *Dial. Sav.* 25–30:[3]

Apocr. Jas.	John 14
We said to him, "Have you departed and removed yourself from us?" But Jesus said, "No, but I shall go to the place from whence I came. I you wish to come with me, come!"	2: In my father's house are many dwellings; if not, I would have told you, because I go to prepare a place for you. 3: . . . And I come again and take you to myself, so that where I am you also you will be. 4: And where I go, you know the way.
They all answered and said, "If you bid us, we come."	5: Thomas said to him, "Lord, we do not know where you are going; how can we know the way?"
He said, "Truly, I say unto you, no one will ever enter the kingdom of heaven at my bidding, but (only) because you yourselves are full."	6: Jesus said to him, "I am the way and the truth and the life; no one comes to the Father except through me."

In the *Apocryphon of James* as well as in the *Dialogue of the Savior,* the believers have to find the qualification in themselves. This agrees with the traditional saying about entering the kingdom of God that is used here; it always emphasizes that one must be reborn or become like a little child. John 14, however, connects the believers' "way"

---

[1] On the analysis of these parallels and the underlying original saying see Cameron, *Apocryphon of James,* 66–68.

[2] The more original form of the saying's Johannine version may be preserved in Justin, *1 Apol.* 61.4: "Unless you are reborn (ἀναγεννηθῆτε) you will not enter the kingdom of heaven." On the use of this saying in other contexts see Cameron, *Apocryphon of James,* 69–70.

[3] See above, # 3.1.1.

closely with the person of Jesus.

In the immediate continuation of the dialogue James and Peter are taken aside for secret instruction (2,33–39), but the beginning of this instruction is lost because the first lines of p. 3 consist of untranslatable fragments. In the following (*Apocr. Jas.* 3,8–14), the appeal to the disciples that they should be filled, which is frequently repeated in this writing,[1] is expanded by an admonition which recalls the lament of the revealer of *Gos. Thom.* 28. Moreover this lament includes the remark that human beings came into the world "empty" and seek to leave it "empty."

Apocr. Jas. 3,8–11	*Gos. Thom.* 28
Do you not, then, desire to be filled? And your heart is drunken; do you not, then, desire to be sober? Therefore, be ashamed!	I found all of them intoxicated; I found none of them thirsty; and my soul became afflicted for the sons of men, because they are blind in their hearts and do not have sight; for empty they came into the world, and empty too they seek to leave the world. But for the moment, they are intoxicated.

Without a further question of the disciples, a transitional statement explores another dimension of the theme of "remembering":

> Henceforth, waking or sleeping, remember that you have seen the Son of man, and spoken with him in person and listened to him in person (3,11–17).

This is followed by an elaborate series of woes and blessings based on a saying that the Fourth Gospel has added to the appearance of Jesus to Thomas:

Apocr. Jas. 3,17–26	John 20:29
Woe to those who have seen the Son [of] man; blessed will they be who have not seen the man, and they who have not consorted with him, and they who have not spoken with him, and they who have not listened to anything from him; yours is life.	Because you have seen me, you believe? Blessed are those who have not seen and yet believe.

This saying is used again in the discourse of *Apocr. Jas.* 12,31–13,1, which contains several additional Johannine sayings (see below). The

---

[1] *Apocr. Jas.* 2,33–35; 3,35–36; thirteen times in the section 4,1–22.

remainder of this first section of the dialogue (3,38–4,22) is an interpretation of the concept of "being full."

3.1.2.3 The Apocryphon of James and the Synoptic Tradition

A new segment of the dialogue begins with a quite different saying of Jesus:

Apocr. Jas. 4,23–30	Mark 10:28–30
But I (James) answered and said to him, "Lord, we can obey you, if you wish, for we have forsaken our fathers and our mothers and our villages and followed you.	Peter began to say to him, "Lo, we have left everything and followed you." Jesus said, "Truly, I say to you, there is no one who has left house or brothers or sisters or mother or father or children or lands, for my sake and the gospel who will not receive . . ."
Grant us, therefore, not to be tempted by the devil, the evil one."	Matt 6:13 And lead us not into temptation, but deliver us from evil.

In Mark 10:28–30 the beginning of the saying has already been used for the formulation of the question of Peter ("Lo, we have left everything and followed you").[1] In Apocr. Jas. 4,25–28 the entire saying has been transferred into the statement of James.[2] It is further combined with a request that is formulated on the basis of the last petition of the Lord's Prayer (Matt 6:13b).[3] The Apocryphon of James uses these two sayings as an introduction to a longer statement of Jesus which interprets the sayings by emphasizing obedience in spite of persecution: ". . . but if you are oppressed by Satan and persecuted, and you do his (i.e., the Father's) will, I [say] that he will love you and make you equal with me . . ." (4,38–5,3). The discourse continues to announce that the disciples will also have to suffer the fate of Jesus:

---

[1] See the discussion of the formulation of secondary introductions from sayings in Cameron, Apocryphon of James, 75–78.

[2] The text of Apocr. Jas. 4,25–28 could derive from either Mark or Matthew (19:29) or an older version of the saying. No trace of the peculiar Lukan reformulation ("wife," "parents") appears.

[3] This petition is missing in the Lukan version of the Lord's Prayer, Luke 11:2–4. But it is found in Matt 6:13 and Did. 8.2, and it may have been an original part of that prayer. Dependence of the Apocryphon of James upon the Gospel of Matthew cannot be argued on this basis.

> Or do you not know that you have yet to be abused and to be accused
> unjustly; and have yet to be shut up in prison, and condemned unlaw-
> fully, and crucified <without> reason, and buried <shamefully>, as (was)
> I myself, by the evil one. (5,9–20)

The conclusion of the discourse gives occasion for another statement of
James and a response by Jesus:

> "Scorn death, therefore, and take thought for life! Remember my cross
> and my death, and you will live."
> But I answered and said to him, "Lord, do not mention to us the cross
> and death, for they are far from you."
> The Lord answered and said, "Truly, I say unto you, none will be saved
> unless they believe in my cross. But those who have believed in my
> cross, theirs is the kingdom of God." (5,31–6,7)

The prediction of the suffering of the disciples goes further than analogous predictions of the Synoptic Gospels[1] because it uses a credal formula about Jesus' condemnation, crucifixion, death, and burial.[2] The
use of credal formulae for the creation of sayings of Jesus is most
clearly evident in the "predictions of the passion" in Mark 8:31;
9:30–32; 10:32–34. The dialogue in the *Apocryphon of James* takes
this development one step further by applying such a formula to the
prediction not only of the suffering of Jesus, but also of the suffering of
the disciples. The concluding double saying of Jesus, introduced by
"Truly, I say unto you," imitates the form of traditional sayings, but is
in reality a new formulation which draws the conclusion from the
preceding dialogue.[3]

3.1.2.4 *The* Apocryphon of James *and Johannine Sayings*

Another dialogue section of this writing that is based on several sayings appears in *Apocr. Jas.* 12,31–13,1. In this instance, parallels to
these sayings appear in the Gospel of John.

---

[1] Cf., e.g., Mark 13:9; Matt 10:17–25.

[2] The context requires that the resurrection is not mentioned.

[3] Jesus' reference to his death, James's protest, and Jesus' rejection of this protest
and subsequent call to the disciples to believe in his cross seems analogous to the dialogue between Jesus and Peter following the first prediction of the passion in Mark
8:30–34. In both instances, a credal formula is used in the construction of the dialogue.
But there is no indication of a direct dependence. See on this passage Cameron, *Apocryphon of James*, 85–90.

Apocr. Jas. 12,31–13,1	John 12:35–36
As long as I am with you, give heed to me and obey me; but when I depart from you, remember me.	The light is with you for a little longer. Walk while you have the light. . . . While you have the light, believe in the light. . . .

	John 14:9
And remember me because when I was with you, you did not know me. Blessed will they be who have known me; woe to those who have heard and have not believed.	Have I been with you so long, and yet you do not know me?

	John 20:29
Blessed will they be who have not seen, [yet have believed]!	Because you have seen me, you believe? Blessed are those who have not seen and yet believe.

The last saying had been used already in a different context (3,17–21). The first sentences in this passage of the *Apocryphon of James* are modelled on the myth of Wisdom who appears among human beings, but remains unknown.[1] Many elements of this myth are used also in the Gospel of John, especially in the farewell discourses. It is not accidental, therefore, that more parallels to the Johannine farewell discourses can be found in the *Apocryphon of James*:

Apocr. Jas. 7,1–6	John 16:29
At first I spoke to you in parables and you did not understand; now I speak to you openly, and you (still) do not perceive.	The disciples said to him, "Behold, now you speak openly and you say no parable (παροιμία)."

Apocr. Jas. 10,32–34	John 16:23b
Invoke the Father, implore God often, and he will give to you.	Truly, truly, I say to you, whatever you ask the Father in my name, he will give to you.

Apocr. Jas. 11,4–6	John 16:26
I intercede on your behalf with the Father, and he will forgive you much.	On that day you will ask in my name, and I do not say that I will request the Father in your behalf.

There is no sign of a dependence of the *Apocryphon of James* upon the Gospel of John. On the contrary, John 14:9 is a specific application of

---

[1] Cameron (*Apocryphon of James*, 47) calls it "a fragment of a farewell speech of Wisdom." See ibid. for parallels from wisdom literature.

the more general statement that the *Apocryphon of James* has preserved. The blessedness of those have believed without seeing, coupled with other blessing and woes, does not reveal any trace of the specific context and use of the saying at the end of the appearance of Jesus before Thomas in John 20:29. When Jesus emphasizes in John 16:26 that he will not intercede with the Father on behalf of the disciples, it is evidently a polemical formulation that rejects the more common belief in Jesus as the mediator, which is expressed in the parallel of the *Apocryphon of James.*

The tradition of sayings with which the *Apocryphon of James* is familiar also includes sayings from the *Gospel of Thomas* (see above the parallel to *Apocr. Jas.* 3,9–11). Also *Apocr. Jas.* 9,18–24 may recall a saying from this gospel:

Apocr. Jas. 9,18–24	*Gos. Thom.* 69a	[Q]Matt 5:11
Hearken to the word; understand knowledge, love, life, and no one will persecute you, nor will anyone oppress you, other than you yourselves.	Blessed are they who have been persecuted within themselves. It is they who have truly come to know the Father.	Blessed are you when men revile you and persecute you . . .

In *Gos. Thom.* 69a, the concept of persecution has been spiritualized. *Apocr. Jas.* 9,18–24 presupposes this secondary spiritualizing of the blessing of those who are persecuted rather than the form of the saying preserved from Q in the Gospel of Matthew.[1]

3.1.2.5 The Parables

Of special interest are the parables of the *Apocryphon of James.* There are interpretations of two parables in *Apocr. Jas.* 7,22–8,27. A list of parables has been inserted between these two parables in 8,4–10; the list is introduced (8,1–4) by Jesus saying, ". . . you have compelled me to stay with you another eighteen days for the sake of the parables. It was enough for some <to listen> to the teaching and understand:"

The Shepherds	Luke 16:4–6
and the Seed	Mark 4:3–9 parr
and the Building	Matt 7:24–27; Luke 6:47–49

---

[1] See above, # 2.3.2.

and the Lamps of the Virgins   Matt 25:1–12
and the Wage of the Workmen   Matt 20:1–15
and the Didrachmae   Luke 16:8–9
and the Woman   Luke 18:2–8   *(d. Jan)*

The identification of the Synoptic Gospels' parallels is not always certain. Luke 16:4–6 talks only about one shepherd; the Seed could refer to either Mark 4:3–9 or Mark 4:26–29, even to the parable of the Mustard Seed (Mark 4:30–32 || Q 13:18–19); the identification of the Didrachmae with the parable of the Lost Coin, and that of the Woman with the parable of the Unjust Judge is tentative at best. In any case, reference seems to be made to parables of all three Synoptic Gospels, because the parables of the Laborers in the Vineyard and the Ten Virgins appear only in Matthew, the Seed growing Secretly only in Mark, and the the Lost Coin and the Unjust Judge only in Luke. This list of parables in the *Apocryphon of James* is the only strong indication for a use of canonical gospels in this writing. Since the list is not related to either the preceding or the following parables, it is probably an interpolation.[1]

The parables which are actually quoted and interpreted in the *Apocryphon of James* do not depend upon any canonical source. The one that comes closest possibly to being derived from a canonical gospel is the parable of the Grain of Wheat which follows upon the list of parables. It is prefaced by a special introduction ("Become earnest about the word! For as to the word, its first part is faith; its second, love; the third, works; for from these comes life," 8,10–15):

Apocr. Jas. 8,16–23	Mark 4:26–29
For the word is like a grain of wheat; when someone had sown it, he had faith in it; and when it had sprouted, he loved it because he had seen many grains in place of one. And when he had worked, he was saved because he had prepared it for food, (and) again	The kingdom of God is as if a man should scatter seed upon the ground, and should sleep and rise night and day, and the seed should sprout and grow, he knows not how. The earth produces of itself, first the blade, then the ear, then the full grain in the ear.

---

[1] This is confirmed by a reference to Jesus' stay for "eighteen days" with the disciples in the introduction to the list (8,3), while the setting given at the beginning of the writing speaks of Jesus' appearance "after five hundred and fifty days after he had risen from the dead" (2,19–21). Cf. Williams, "Apocryphon of James," 19: "The difficulty at 8.1–4, where James and Peter are reproached for delaying the Savior a mysterious "eighteen days more for the sake of parables," might be solved by assuming that this passage originated in a separate source."

he left (some) to sow.   But when the grain is ripe, at once he
                                               puts in the sickle, because the
                                               harvest has come.

To be sure, both parables talk about the same, indeed rather commonplace, agricultural phenomenon. What is emphasized in each story,
however, is very different. In one instance, it is the loving and working attention that is given to the growing fruit; in the other instance, it
is exactly the opposite. It is quite difficult to explain one of the
parables as the interpretation of the other. The introduction to the
parable in the *Apocryphon of James* makes the parable an allegory
that illustrates "believing," "loving," "working," and "being saved" as
the path of salvation. Whatever its original form may have been,[1] it
has been reformulated in order to fit the theme of its introduction. But
it is evident that the topic indicated in the introduction to the parable
differs from the secondary interpretation by the author of this writing
in 8,23–27; it was part of the traditional form of the parable. The
author's interpretation appears at the end of the parable: "So also can
you yourselves receive the kingdom of heaven; unless you receive this
through knowledge, you will not be able to find it" (8,23–27).

The parable in *Apocr. Jas.* 12,20–30 uses the same imagery:

For this cause I tell you this, that you may know yourselves.
    For the kingdom of heaven is like an ear of grain after it had sprouted
in a field. And when it had ripened, it scattered its fruit and again filled
the field with ears for another year.
    You also, hasten to reap an ear of life for yourselves that you may be
filled with the kingdom.

Again the interpretation appended by the author of the writing is obviously secondary because its most important point is the "reaping of an
ear" (= to be filled with the kingdom) which is not even mentioned in
the parable itself.[2] Thus the parable must have been an independent
piece of tradition which originally spoke about the spread of the kingdom through the fruit which it produced.

The third parable of the *Apocryphon of James* is the parable of the
Palm Shoot (7,22–35). Ron Cameron has analyzed this parable in

---

[1] "The original form of this parable may be irrecoverable" (Cameron, *Parable and
Interpretation,* 8; idem, *Apocryphon of James,* 8–11).

[2] Cameron, *Parable and Interpretation,* 7; idem, *Apocryphon of James,* 12–16.

detail and has been able to explain its strange imagery.[1] I am here quoting this parable in Cameron's translation together with his analysis:[2]

(1) Introduction (7,22–23)

"Let not the kingdom of heaven wither away."

(2) Parable (7,24–28)

"For it is like a date palm (shoot) whose fruits dropped down around it. It put forth buds and, when they blossomed, they (i.e., the fruits) caused the productivity (of the date palm, literally: "the womb") to dry up."

(3) Application (7,28–32)

"Thus is it also with the fruit which comes from the single root: when it (i.e., the fruit) was (picked) fruits were collected by many."

(4) Expansion (7,33–35)

"It was really good. Is it (not) possible now to produce the plants anew for you, (and) to find it (i.e., the kingdom of heaven)?"

To understand this parable is so difficult because of the peculiar way in which date palms produce fruit. They are dioecious plants; the female tree can produce fruit only if a male tree stands nearby or if it is artificially fertilized by male pollen. Otherwise the immature fruits will drop to the ground and perish.[3] The introduction ("Let not the kingdom of heaven wither away") was written for a parable that told of the dying of the immature fruits of the female palm tree and thus of the withering of its productivity. This original parable must have been told as a warning, like the parable of the Fig Tree (Luke 13:6–9). The problems of the extant text are due two several layers of secondary interpretations which misunderstand the nature of the fruit production of the date palm. An interpolation in the parable itself ("It put forth buds and when they blossomed") and the application ("fruits were collected by many") seem to understand the story as a parable of growth, analogous to the parable of the Ear of Grain. A later (Gnostic) interpretation which emphasized the "single root" and added the "Expansion" ("find the kingdom," 7,33–35) represents the final stage of the interpretation. In all three parables, an obviously secondary Gnos-

---

[1] Cameron, *Parable and Interpretation*, 9–13; idem, *Apocryphon of James*, 17–30.

[2] *Parable and Interpretation*, 9.

[3] This was well known in antiquity, and it is frequently described. The relevant passages are quoted by Cameron, *Parable and Interpretation*, 10–11; idem, *Apocryphon of James*, 19–21.

tic interpretation appears at the end, while earlier interpretations are preserved in the introductory phrases.

3.1.2.6 Conclusions

It is still too early to draw final conclusions concerning the character and date of the *Apocryphon of James*. Further scholarly analysis is needed. Its final form may have resulted from one or several redactions. This is already evident in the dual setting and description of the document at the beginning, first as a letter from James to an unknown addressee, then as a secret book revealed by the Lord to James and Peter. The first and external frame, written as a first-person singular report by James (1,1–35; 16,2–30), is certainly the latest frame that the document has received. But even the second, and most likely more original introduction, as well as the conclusion in which James and Peter return to the other disciples and announce that they had been witnesses of Jesus' return to heaven (15,5–16,2), must be part of a secondary framework for an older dialogue gospel. The dialogues themselves do not presuppose a setting after Jesus' resurrection and ascension (2,17–21). As in the Gospel of John, they are farewell discourses in which Jesus explains what he has said before his departure, but neither resurrection nor ascension are presupposed in these discourses. There also seems to be a difference in the use of the titles for Jesus. Only in the secondary frames is Jesus called Savior (1,23; 1,32; 2,11; 16,25). In the dialogue itself, the title appears only once at the beginning (2,40);[1] otherwise the title Lord prevails.[2] This older dialogue seems to be composed on the basis of the free tradition of sayings of Jesus. Its sayings are not drawn from several written gospels (including the *Gospel of Thomas*) but represent an earlier stage of the development of the sayings tradition in which the collection of sayings coincides with their interpretation in the form of dialogues between Jesus and his disciples, analogous to the dialogue that formed the basis for the *Dialogue of the Savior*. Both documents are thus witnesses for a development of the tradition of Jesus' sayings which must be presupposed for the composition and writing of the dialogues and discourses of the Gospel of John.

---

[1] Some editors supply the title Savior also in the lacuna of 4,2; see Williams, "Apocryphon of James," note to p. 32.

[2] 4,23; 4,31; 5,36; 6,1; 6,22; 6,28; 6,32; 6,35; 13,31; 13,36. See also Cameron, *Apocryphon of James*, 4.

3.2 The Collection of Narratives about Jesus

3.2.1 MIRACLE CATENAE

It is most probable that miracle stories of Jesus were told at the very earliest stage of the Christian mission. The telling of these stories probably went hand in hand with the performance of miracles by the apostles. Such miracles are reported in the Acts of the Apostles.[1] There remains, of course, the question of the sources used by the author and of the reliability of such reports. However, Paul himself refers to his own activity of performing miracles, cf. 1 Thess 1:5:

> For our gospel came to you not only in word, but also in mighty work (δυνάμει) and in the Holy Spirit and in full conviction.

The Book of Acts also refers regularly to Jesus' miracles as part of his ministry, sometimes in standard formulae, cf. Acts 2:22:

> Jesus of Nazareth, a man attested to you by God with mighty works and wonders and signs (δυνάμεσι καὶ τέρασι καὶ σημείοις) which God did through him in your midst.

The earliest composition of stories of miracles must be located in the Christian propaganda in the Hellenistic world as Christian missionaries were confronted with competing claims of other prophets, missionaries, and miracles workers. The presence of divine and supernatural power was not only attested by the performance of a miracle or through a story told about a great miracle worker, it was also effective when it was published as a record of the superhuman accomplishments of a god or of a divine man. Records published in stone and exhibited in Asklepios sanctuaries told of the healing powers of the god.[2] Written collections of reports about the great deeds of leaders, heroes, and lawgivers are known from the realm of philosophical and religious propaganda of the Hellenistic world.[3] These must have served as models for the composition of writings, properly called aretalogies,[4] reporting the miracle stories of the apostles and of Jesus.

---

[1] Cf., e.g., Acts 3:1–10; 5:12; 6:8; 13:6–12; 14:8–18.

[2] E. and J. Edelstein, *Asklepios: A Collection and Interpretation of the Testimonies* (2 vols.; Baltimore: Johns Hopkins University Press, 1945).

[3] Ludwig Bieler, ΘΕΙΟΣ ΑΝΗΡ : *Das Bild des "göttlichen Menschen" in Spätantike und Frühchristentum* (Darmstadt: Wissenschaftliche Buchgesellschaft, 1967); Moses Hadas and Morton Smith, *Heroes and Gods: Spiritual Biography in Antiquity* (Religious Perspectives 13; New York: Harper & Row, 1965).

[4] Morton Smith, "Prolegomena to a Discussion of Aretalogies, Divine Men, the Gospels, and Jesus," *JBL* 90 (1971) 174–99.

The first evidence of such written collections comes, as Dieter Georgi has demonstrated,[1] from Paul's Second Letter to the Corinthians. The "letters of recommendation," which Paul's opponents brought to Corinth and which they solicited from the Corinthians,[2] were documents in which the great deeds were listed which these foreign missionaries had performed. These miracle reports would have contained not only stories of healings and exorcisms, but also reports of ecstasies (cf. 2 Cor 5:13), visions (cf. 2 Cor 12:1–7), and successful prayers (cf. 2 Cor 12:7–9). In the same letter Paul explicitly rejects the image of a "Christ according to the flesh" (2 Cor 5:16). This possibly refers to reports of the miracles of Christ which the opposing apostles had told.

Direct evidence for the existence of written documents recording the miracles of Jesus comes from some of the sources that were used in the Gospels of Mark and of John. It is not unlikely that such writings were originally composed as handbooks for Christian faith healers. But soon they must have been intended to communicate the powerful message of Jesus the "divine man." Stories about Jesus' power over nature, about the heavenly voice at his baptism, and eventually, about his miraculous birth, were added to these collections of healing stories.

The Gospel of Mark used one or several such collections.[3] A source of aretalogical stories seems most clearly present in Mark 4:35–6:52. It contained the following stories:

4:35–41	Stilling of the tempest
5:1–20	Gerasene demoniac[4]
5:22–24, 35–43	Raising of the daughter of Jairus
5:25–34	Healing of the woman with an issue of blood[5]
6:30–44	Feeding of the five thousand[6]

---

[1] Dieter Georgi, *The Opponents of Paul in 2 Corinthians: A Study in Religious Propaganda in Late Antiquity* (Philadelphia: Fortress, 1985).

[2] Cf. 2 Cor 3:1: "Or do we need, as some do, letters of recommendation (συστατικαὶ ἐπιστολαί) to you or from you?"

[3] Paul J. Achtemeier, "The Origin and Function of the pre-Markan Miracle Catenae," *JBL* 90 (1971) 198–221.

[4] Its length alone distinguishes this exorcism from the other exorcisms reported in Mark. Moreover, the satirical motif of this story—the demons are driven into the pigs who then drown themselves in the sea—is quite alien to the other Markan exorcisms.

[5] These two stories seem to have been artfully connected already in Mark's source.

[6] It would seem natural to include also the following story about the Walking on the Sea (6:45–52). However, the two stories are separated by the mention of Bethsaida, which apparently introduces a new cycle; see below.

Mark 6:45 mentions that Jesus and his disciples intended to go to Bethsaida. The same town is mentioned again in Mark 8:22. These two references to Bethsaida, the only two in the entire gospel literature, enclose another cycle of stories which is to some extent parallel to the cycle of Mark 5:35–6:44:[1]

First Cycle		Second Cycle	
4:35–41	Stilling of the tempest	6:45–52	Walking on the sea
5:1–20	Gerasene demoniac		
5:22–43	Daughter of Jairus		
5:25–34	Women with issue of blood	7:24–30	Canaanite woman
		7:32–36	Healing of a deaf mute
6:30–44	Feeding the five thousand	8:1–10	Feeding the four thousand
		8:22–26	Healing of a blind man

It is doubtful whether other miracles stories of the Gospel of Mark were also drawn from one or several written sources. Some of these may have belonged to written collections of a different character. The healing of the man with the withered hand (Mark 3:1–6) was apparently part of a collection of apophthegmata, short controversy stories, which Mark used in chapters 1–3. Other miracle stories, such as the healing of the leper (1:40–45), the healing of the man sick of the palsy (2:1–12), the so-called healing of the epileptic child (9:14–29), and the healing of the blind man (Bartimaeus) on the road to Jerusalem (10:46–52), could have circulated independently.

The Gospel of John permits us to discern with more certainty the source of miracle stories used in that writing. There is no question that a written source of miracles of Jesus underlies chapters 2–11 of the Gospel of John. It was a writing containing miracle stories of Jesus which may have been used in the mission and propaganda of the Johannine community. The beginning of this source is clearly marked at the end of the story of the wine miracle at Cana (2:1–11) by the remark:

This was the first of the signs (ἀρχὴν τῶν σημείων) which Jesus did in Cana of Galilee, and he revealed his glory, and his disciples believed in him. (2:11)

After the story of the healing of the son of the royal official (4:46–54) follows a similar remark:

---

[1] The entire "Bethsaida section," Mark 6:45–8:26, is not reproduced by the Gospel of Luke. This has resulted in the hypothesis that it represents a later interpolation into the Gospel of Mark; see below, # 4.1.2.

> This is the second sign (δεύτερον σημεῖον) when he came from Judea into Galilee. (5:54)

It has also been suggested that the original ending of the Semeia Source has been preserved in John 20:30–31:[1]

> Jesus did many other signs (σημεῖα) before his disciples which are not written in this book; but these are written in order that you believe that Jesus is Christ, the Son of God, and that believing in him you may have life in his name.

The name σημεῖα = "signs," "miracles" does not fit the Gospel as whole; it would be very appropriate, however, for a collection of miracle stories. Moreover, this concluding remark of the Fourth Gospel emphasizes the belief in Jesus on the basis of his miracles; similar remarks occur in the context of some other miracle stories (cf. 2:11, quoted above; 5:44; 6:2; 11:45). Because of the use of the term "signs" (σημεῖα) as a designation for miracles in the context of these stories (John 2:11; 4:45; 6:2, 14), the name Semeia Source or Source of Signs has become established among scholars as a label for this source.[2]

The following stories derive from this Semeia Source:

2:1–11	Wine miracle at the wedding feast of Cana
4:46–54	Healing of the son of a royal official
5:2–9	Healing of a lame man at the Pool of Bethzatha
6:5–14	Feeding of the six thousand
6:16–25	Tempest and walking on the sea
9:1–7	Healing of a blind man
11:1–45	Raising of Lazarus

It is evident that the Semeia Source drew its stories from the same traditions which also provided the materials for the miracle catenae of the Gospel of Mark. The story of the Feeding of the Multitudes and a miracle story connected with the Sea of Galilee appear in all three collections. The character of the Semeia Source, however, is quite different. The stories of the Markan cycles describe Jesus as a man with extraordinary powers who is not above using magical techniques; he

---

[1] On this passage see Bultmann, *Gospel of John,* 697–99; Brown, *Gospel of John,* 2.1055–58.

[2] Bultmann, *Gospel of John,* 113 and passim. A variant of this source hypothesis was suggested by Robert Thomson Fortna, *The Gospel of Signs* (Cambridge: Cambridge University Press, 1970). Fortna assumes that miracle stories and the passion narrative were both derived from one and the same narrative source. A modification of Bultmann's source hypothesis has been presented by Ernst Haenchen, *The Gospel of John* (Hermeneia; Philadelphia: Fortress, 1984) 1. 67–90.

employs magical words,[1] uses magical manipulations,[2] and holds a long discourse with a demon.[3] All of these features are absent from the stories of the Semeia Source. Here Jesus documents his power in a different way, not as magician but as a god. He changes water into wine like the Greek god Dionysos (John 2:1–10), his powerful word heals even from a distance (4:46–54), at the Pool at Bethzatha Jesus accomplishes what an angel from heaven was expected to do (5:2–9), the multitudes' expectations are not just fed by a skilled miracle worker but by a god who can walk across the Sea of Galilee and move a ship miraculously to the other shore (6:1–21), the man who receives sight has been blind from birth (9:1–7), and the raising of Lazarus who has been in his tomb for four days, presents Jesus as a god who commands power over the realm of Hades (chapter 11). The miracles of Jesus are more than miracles, they are epiphanies.

In the form in which the author of the Fourth Gospel used the Semeia Source, it was composed in Greek, though it is not impossible that it was originally written in Aramaic. In any case, it originated most likely in Syria/Palestine, like the Gospel of John itself. The inclusion of a story that once belonged to the circle of the wine god Dionysos gives clear evidence for the Hellenistic-syncretistic milieu which determined the forms of Christian propaganda in this eastern region of the Roman empire.

3.2.2 THE UNKNOWN GOSPEL OF PAPYRUS EGERTON 2

3.2.2.1 The Papyrus and the Problem of its Interpretation

In the year 1935 fragments of a papyrus from Egypt were published as *Papyrus Egerton 2*. Two damaged pages, a fragment of a third page, and a scrap of a fourth with only one readable letter contained passages from a gospel that was otherwise unknown.[4] More recently,

---

[1] Mark 5:41: ταλιθὰ κοῦμ = Greek transcription of Aramaic for "maiden rise." Mark 7:34" ἐφφαθά = Aramaic for "be open." Also the words spoken to the sea in Mark 4:39 (σιώπα, πεφίμωσο) must be understood as magical formulae.

[2] Spittle is used for the opening of the eyes of the blind man (Mark 8:23).

[3] Mark 5:7–10.

[4] H. Idris Bell and T. C. Skeat, *Fragments of an Unknown Gospel and Other Early Christian Papyri* (London: British Museum, 1935); a corrected text was published by the same authors shortly thereafter: *The New Gospel Fragments* (London: British Museum, 1935). English translations can be found in J. Jeremias, "An Unknown Gospel with Johannine Elements (Papyrus Egerton 2)," in Hennecke-Schneemelcher-Wilson, *NT Apocrypha*, 1. 94–97; Ron Cameron, *Other Gospels*, 72–75. For a recent German translation with introduction see Joachim Jeremias and Wilhelm Schneemelcher, "Papyrus Egerton 2," in Hennecke-Schneemelcher, *NT Apokryphen I*, 82–85. The English translation in Hennecke-Schneemelcher-Wilson, *NT Apocrypha*, 1. 96–97, does not yet reflect the discovery of an additional portion of *Papyrus Egerton*

another small fragment, *Pap. Köln Nr. 255,*[1] containing 5 lines, has been identified as part of *Papyrus Egerton 2.* According to the judgment of the original editors, the hand of the papyrus resembled the hands of datable papyri from the period of the late 1st and early 2d centuries.[2] However, the editor of the new fragment, Michael Gronewald, cites convincing arguments for a date of the style of the handwriting rather closer to Papyrus Bodmer II (= NT $\mathfrak{p}^{66}$), i.e., to about the year 200 CE.[3]

The Greek text of this papyrus preserves debates of Jesus with the Pharisees, the story of the healing of a leper, and a few fragmentary lines which probably belong to another miracle story. Thus the preserved fragments show that they came from a writing which contained, like the canonical Gospels, both sayings and narratives of Jesus. At the time, the discovery of such a gospel aroused considerable interest and scholarly controversy about the question of the dependence of this gospel upon the Gospels of the New Testament canon.[4] However, this debate was cut short by of the outbreak of World War II. In 1946, Goro Mayeda published his dissertation on *Papyrus Egerton 2*[5] in which he came to the conclusion that the text of this gospel was not dependent upon any of the canonical gospels.[6] This result has been debated ever since,[7] although few major investigations of the papyrus have been published since Mayeda's dissertation appeared.[8]

---

2. I acknowledge gratefully the generosity of the author who gave me access to his still unpublished dissertation and permitted me to use his new and revised English translation: Jon B. Daniels, *The Egerton Gospel: Its Place in Early Christianity* (Dissertation Claremont Graduate School, Claremont, CA: 1989).

[1] Michael Gronewald, "Unbekanntes Evangelium oder Evangelienharmonie (Fragment aus dem Evangelium Egerton)," in *Kölner Papyri (P. Köln)* vol. 6 (Abh.RWA, Sonderreihe Papyrologica Coloniensia 7; Cologne: 1987) 136–45.

[2] Bell and Skeat, *Unknown Gospel,* 1–7.

[3] See also E. G. Turner, *Greek Manuscripts of the Ancient World* (Oxford: Clarendon Press, 1971) 13.

[4] This debate is reported in Goro Mayeda, *Das Leben-Jesu-Fragment Papyrus Egerton 2 und seine Stellung in der urchristlichen Literaturgeschichte* (Bern: Haupt, 1946) 94–95. See also the literature listed in Joahim Jeremias und Wilhelm Schneemelcher, "Papyrus Egerton 2," in Hennecke-Schneemelcher, *NT Apokryphen I,* 84; cf. Joachim Jeremias, "An Unknown Gospel with Johannine Elements," in Hennecke-Schneemelcher-Wilson, *NT Apocrypha,* 1. 96.

[5] This dissertation was inspired by Martin Dibelius at the University of Heidelberg, but accepted for a degree by Rudolf Bultmann at the University of Marburg.

[6] Mayeda, *Leben-Jesu-Fragment,* passim.

[7] See Hennecke-Schneemelcher, *NT Apokryphen I,* 83; Vielhauer, *Geschichte,* 638; Brown, *Gospel of John,* 229–30.

[8] Exceptions are F.-M. Braun, *Jean le Théologien* (3 vols.; Paris: Gabalda, 1959–1966) 1. 87–94; Jeremias, *Unknown Sayings,* 18–20.

Jeremias, in his introduction to the translation of the fragments,[1] has formulated the problem of this gospel text and, at the same time, the most commonly accepted solution as follows:

> The juxtaposition of Johannine and Synoptic material and the fact that the Johannine material is shot through with Synoptic phrases and the Synoptic with Johannine usage, permits the conjecture that the author knew all and every of the canonical gospels.

If this conclusion were true, *Papyrus Egerton 2* would appear to be, even with a date of ca. 200 CE, a spectacularly early piece of evidence for the establishment of the four-gospel canon of the New Testament. Jeremias's observation, however, is not quite accurate. To be sure, both Johannine and synoptic features occur in the gospel texts of *Papyrus Egerton 2*. The problem is that this judgment, which finds a thorough mixture of synoptic and Johannine language, relies on criteria which are derived from the observation of the often strikingly different languages of the Synoptic Gospels on the one hand, and the Gospel of John on the other hand. These features, however, characterize the end-product of a long development. The presence of "synoptic" language in any "Johannine" context, and of "Johannine" language in any "synoptic" context, may well attest an earlier stage of the development in which pre-Johannine and pre-synoptic characteristics of language still existed side by side.

Most recently, Jon B. Daniels, in his learned and very detailed Claremont Graduate School dissertation,[2] has presented strong arguments for the independence of the gospel fragment preserved in *Papyrus Egerton 2*. With respect to the synoptic parallels, Daniels says, "Egerton's account of Jesus' healing a leper plausibly represents a separate tradition which did not undergo Markan redaction." With respect to the Johannine parallels, he concludes that the author's "compositional choices suggest that he or she did not make use of the Gospel of John in canonical form."[3] The following discussion of the text will demonstrate my agreement with Jon Daniels's assessment.

---

[1] In Hennecke Schneemelcher-Wilson, *NT Apocrypha*, 1. 95.

[2] See above.

[3] Quoted from the "Abstract" of the dissertation. This chapter of my book was essentially finished before I had access to Jon Daniel's dissertation, although I had learned much from discussions with the author while he was engaged in his research for the thesis. I am delighted to find almost complete confirmation of the arguments set forth in what follows.

3.2.2.2 About Scripture and Moses

The papyrus begins with a fragmentary sentence in which Jesus seems to say to the "lawyers" (νομικοί) that they may punish everyone transgressing the law. The term "lawyer" is typical for the Gospel of Luke.[1] But here as elsewhere in the papyrus, there is very little else that would suggest dependence upon Luke.

The first preserved pericope of the fragment has a close parallel in the Gospel of John, but its language sometimes is not yet as "Johannine" as that of the author of the Gospel of John.

Pap. Eg. 2, 1 verso, 7–20[2]	John 5:39–40
To the rulers of the people he said this word, "Search (ἐραυνᾶτε)[3] the scriptures in which you think you have life (ζωήν).	You search (ἐραυνᾶτε) the scriptures, because you think that in them you have eternal life (ζωὴν αἰώνιον).
These are they which bear witness of me.	These are they which bear witness of me. Yet you refuse to come to me that you may have life.
	John 5:45
Do not think that I have come to accuse you before my Father; there is one who accuses you, Moses, in whom you have set your hope."	Do not think that I shall accuse you before the Father; there is one who accuses you: Moses, in whom you have set your hope.
	John 9:28–29
And when they said (to Jesus),	. . . and they said (to the man who was blind), "You are his disciple, but we are disciples of Moses.
"We know that God has spoken to Moses; but as for you, we do not know [whence you are]."[4]	We know that God has spoken to Moses; but this one, we do not know whence he is."

---

[1] See above in the discussion of Q (# 2.3.3) on Luke 11:52.

[2] I have compared my translations of *Papyrus Egerton 2* with Jon Daniels's new reconstruction of the Greek text and have followed his translation in many instances.

[3] The Greek ἐραυνᾶτε can be translated as either an imperative ("Search!") or as in indicative ("You search"). The former translation is preferable for *Pap. Eg. 2,* the latter for John 5:39.

[4] The bracketed words translate the Greek text πόθεν εἶ which has been restored on the basis of John 9:29. With respect to arguments for this restoration, see Daniels, *Egerton Gospel,* 24, n. 1.

Jesus answered and said to them, "Now already accusation is made against your unbelief (ἀπιστία) with respect to those to whom he bore witness.[1]	John 5:46
Because if you had believed Moses, you would believe me; because it is about me that he wrote to your fathers."	Because if you had believed Moses, you would believe me; because it is about me that he wrote.

The only "synoptic" element in this passage is the address to the "rulers of the people." This term is not used in John for the opponents of Jesus; rather, here as elsewhere, Jesus' speech is addressed to "the Jews" (cf. John 5:15–16, 19), the stereotypical opponents of the Johannine Jesus. A minor difference is that *Pap. Eg. 2* uses the simple "life," whereas John 5:39 has "eternal life," which is more typical for the language of this Gospel. The phrase "Jesus answered and said" (ἀποκριθεὶς καὶ εἶπεν) is also never used in the Gospel of John, but is frequent in the Synoptic Gospels. The term "unbelief" (ἀπιστία) never occurs in the Gospel of John, but has synoptic parallels.[2] Otherwise, the language is "Johannine" throughout. But because some typical Johannine terms are missing in the parallel of *Papyrus Egerton 2,* it is possible that its text represents a pre-Johannine version of this controversy of Jesus with his opponents.

The comparison of the vocabulary cannot be conclusive. The real problem lies elsewhere. Is it possible to understand the rationale of the composition of the papyrus on the basis of the assumption that it used the Gospel of John? In that case, the author of *Papyrus Egerton 2* had taken a passage from John 5:39–47, eliminated the section 5:41–44 and the two parallel conclusions 5:40 and 5:47, but interpolated a sentence from John 9:20 between 5:45 and 5:46. It is, therefore, easier to explain John 5:39–47 as a secondary expansion of the debate between Jesus and his opponents which *Papyrus Egerton 2* has preserved in its more original form. The relationship between the original text and the Johannine redaction is presented in the following table:

5:39	"You search the scriptures in which you think you have life."	= *Papyrus Egerton 2*

---

[1] Daniels (ibid., 24) translates, "In those who have been commended by him." See ibid., n. 2.

[2] For a detailed presentation of the evidence see Mayeda, *Leben-Jesus-Fragment,* 15–27.

5:40	"But you do not want to come to me in order to have eternal life."	Johannine conclusion
5:41–44	"I do not take honor from human beings, . . . How can you believe, who receive glory from one another, and do not seek the glory that comes from the one and only God?"	Johannine interpolation
5:45	"Do not think that I have come to accuse you before my Father; there is one who accuses you: Moses in whom you have set your hope."	= *Papyrus Egerton 2*
	And when they said (to Jesus), "We know that God has spoken to Moses; but as for you, we do not know whence you are."	= *Papyrus Egerton 2* transferred by John to 9:29, addressed to the man who was blind.
	"Now already accusation is made against your unbelief with respect to those to whom he bore witness.	Omitted by John
5:46	Because if you had believed Moses, you would believe me; because it is about me that he wrote to your fathers."	= *Papyrus Egerton 2*
5:47	"But if you do not believe his writings, how will you believe my words?"	Johannine conclusion

3.2.2.3 *The Attempt to Arrest Jesus*

The priority of *Papyrus Egerton 2* is the best explanation also in the case of the report about hostility against Jesus which appears after a lacuna of several missing lines.

Pap. Eg. 2 (1 recto, 22–31)	John 7:30	John 10:31, 39
[. . . to gather] stones together [to stone] him. And the rulers laid their hands on	So they sought to arrest him.	The Jews took up stones to stone him. Again they tried to arrest him.

him to [deliver] him to
the crowd. But they
were not able to arrest
him since the hour of
his being handed over
had not yet come. But
the Lord himself
escaped from their
hands and turned
away from them.

But no one laid hands
on him,
because his hour

had not yet come.

But he escaped from
their hands.

Similar attempts to arrest Jesus are also mentioned in John 7:44 ("Some of them tried to arrest him, but no one laid his hands on him") and 8:20 ("and no one laid hands on him, because his hour had not yet come"). The parallels are once more very close.[1] An explanation of this segment of *Papyrus Egerton 2* as a secondary patchwork of several Johannine passages does not seem very appealing. The phrase "his hour had not yet come" might be considered to have been created by the author of the Gospel of John. In that case argumants for a dependence of *Papyrus Egerton 2* upon the Fourth Gospel would be persuasive. However, though references to the "hour" occur several times in John,[2] the use of the term "hour" in reference to the suffering and death of Jesus also appears in the Gethsemane pericope of Mark 14:35: "... and he prayed that, if it were possible, the hour might pass from him."[3] Thus it would seem quite possible that the reference to the "hour" of Jesus' betrayal appeared in a source of the Fourth Gospel. It is, then, preferable to explain John's multiple reference to failed attempts to arrest Jesus as reflections and usages of only one traditional report, such as the one which is preserved by *Papyrus Egerton 2*.

3.2.2.4 The Healing of a Leper

Less problematic is the third pericope of *Papyrus Egerton 2*, the story of the healing of a leper.

---

[1] On the slight difference in vocabulary see Mayeda, *Leben-Jesu-Fragment*, 27–31.

[2] See also John 2:4 ("... my hour has not yet come"); 5:25 ("Truly, truly, the hour is coming and is now that the dead will hear the voice of the Son of God . . ."); 12:23 ("The hour has come that the Son of man be glorified").

[3] The belief in the importance of the "hour," be it for the performance of a miracle, or for the determination (sometimes astrologically) of any action determined by God or by fate, is widespread in antiquity; see Bultmann, *Gospel of John*, 117, n. 1.

Pap. Eg. 2 (1 recto 34–41)	Mark 1:40–44[1]
And behold, a leper came to him and said,	[40] And a leper came to him beseeching him and kneeling said to him,
"Master Jesus, wandering with lepers and eating with them in the inn, I myself became a leper. If therefore [you will], I shall be clean."	"(Master)[2]
	if you will, you can make me clean." [41] And[3] he stretched out his hand and touched him and
Accordingly the Lord said to him, "I will, be clean!" [And immediately] the leprosy left him.	said to him, "I will, be clean!" [42] And immediately the leprosy left him. [43] And he sternly charged him and sent him away immediately.[4]
Jesus said to him,	[44] And said to him, "See that you say nothing to anyone;
"Go and show yourself to the [priests], and offer for the purification as Moses has commanded,	but go, show yourself to the priest and offer for your purification what Moses commanded for a proof to the people."

John 5:14

"Behold you have become healthy.
Sin no more that nothing worse may
and sin no more . . ."   befall you."

This miracle story is evidently identical with the one that is told by
Mark. The only element that seems to presuppose Matthew or Luke is
the address "Master" which, however, may have been an original part
of the Markan text and of the tradition that he used. That the redactional additions Mark 1:43 and 44a are missing and that no other
redactional elements of either Mark's or Matthew's or Luke's text
appear in *Papyrus Egerton 2* argues for independence of its version of

---

[1] Synoptic parallels appear in Matt 8:1–4 and Luke 5:12–14, a variant appears in
Luke 17: 11–19 (the healing of the ten lepers). However, *Papyrus Egerton 2* does not
share any special features with that account.

[2] The address "Master" (κύριε) appears only in the text of the two synoptic parallels,
Matt 8:2 and Luke 5:12. This agreement of Matthew and Luke demonstrates that the
same address stood originally also in the text of Mark. On the problem of the "common
agreements" of Matthew and Luke which may have preserved Mark's original text see
below # 4.1.2.1–3.

[3] The following phrase "moved by pity" (σπλαγχνισθείς) and the variant ὀργισθείς (D)
do not seem to have belonged to the original text of Mark. The parallel synoptic versions do not show any trace of either reading.

[4] The verse Mark 1:43 has no parallels in either Matthew or Luke. It certainly does
not belong to the original story and is probably a later interpolation into the Markan
text.

the story. The absence of a gesture of worship and the simple healing through the word of Jesus alone, may also be signs of an earlier version of the story. The expansion at the beginning which tells how the sick man contracted his leprosy—it shows unfamiliarity with the actual practice in Israel—is certainly a secondary feature. But that is no compelling reason for the assumption that the story is dependent upon any of the Synoptic Gospels.[1] As strange as the last sentence is (resembling Jesus' admonition to the invalid from the pool of Bethzatha), it is hardly enough to argue for literary dependence. There is no question anyway that the author of this gospel knew traditions and sources which were used in the Gospel of John.

3.2.2.5 Paying Taxes to the Kings

The last of the pericopes of *Papyrus Egerton 2* (2 recto, 43–59) presents a very puzzling picture. The pericope is an apophthegma that exhibits all normal features of this form:

Introduction:	. . . and they came to him testing him with questions saying, "Teacher Jesus, . . . "
Question of the opponents:	"Is it permitted to give to the kings . . . "
Jesus reaction:	But Jesus, knowing their intention, became angry.
Jesus answer:	"Why do you call me teacher with your mouth and do not do what I say?"
Expansion with a quotation from Scripture:	"Well did Isaiah prophesy concerning you . . ."

But the comparison with analogous passages from other gospels reveals that these parallels appear in quite different contexts of three or four different writings:

Pap. Eg. 2 (2 recto, 43–59)	Mark 12:13–15	John 3:2
. . . and they came to him testing him with questions saying:	And they sent to him . . . to entrap him in his talk. And they came ~~came~~ and said to	
"Teacher Jesus, we know that you have come [from God],[2]	him, "Teacher, we know that you are true and you care for no	"Rabbi, we know that you are a teacher come from God."

---

[1] I am, therefore, not convinced by the arguments in favor of the hypothesis that the author knew all three Synoptic Gospels, which have been put forward by Frans Neirynck, "Papyrus Egerton and the Healing of the Leper," *EThL* 61 (1985) 153–60.

[2] Restoration on the basis of the parallel passage John 3:2.

para alongside
the length, width of

3 From Dialogues and Narratives to the Gospel of John

for what you do bears
witness ~~beyond~~ all the
prophets.[1]

Tell us, is it permitted
to give to the kings
what pertains to their
rule? Shall we give it
or not?"
But Jesus, knowing
their intention,
became angry[2] and
said,

"Why do you call me
teacher with your
mouth and do not do
what I say?

Well did Isaiah
prophesy concerning
you when he said,

'This people honor me
with their lips, but
their heart is far away
from me. In vain do
they worship me,
[teaching] precepts of
human beings.'"

men; for you do not
regard the position of
men, but truly teach
the way of God.
Is it permitted to pay
taxes to Caesar or not?
Should we pay them or
should we not?"
But knowing their
hypocrisy, he said to
them, "Why do you put
me to the test? Show
me a coin."

Luke 6:46

Why do you call me
"Lord, Lord," and do
not do what I say?

Mark 7:6–7
(= Matt 15:7–9)

Well did Isaiah
prophesy of you
hypocrites, as it is
written,[3]
"this people honor me
with their lips, but
their heart is far away
from me. In vain do
they worship me,
teaching as doctrines
the precepts of human
beings."

This text from *Papyrus Egerton 2* indeed looks like a quilt of pieces
from at least four different New Testament passages: Mark 12:13–15;
John 3:2; Luke 6:46; and Mark 7:6–7. The problem is that there are
two solutions which are equally improbable: it is unlikely that the per-

[1] No convincing parallel can be cited for the second half of this sentence. John 10:25
(and other Johannine passages) speak about "bearing witness," but prophets are not
mentioned in such contexts. Cf. also *Gos. Thom.* 52: "His disciples said to him,
'Twenty-four prophets spoke in Israel and all of them spoke in you.'"

[2] Mark 1:43 has been quoted as a parallel to "(he) became angry." However, Mark
1:43 may not even be a part of the original Markan text; see above.

[3] "As it is written" is missing in Matthew.

icope of *Papyrus Egerton 2* is an independent older tradition, and it is equally hard to imagine that anyone would have deliberately composed this apophthegma by selecting sentences from three different gospel writings. There are no analogies to this kind of gospel composition, because this pericope is neither a harmony of parallels from different gospels, nor is it a florilegium. If one wants to uphold the hypothesis of dependence upon written gospels, one would have to assume that the pericope was written from memory.[1] But in this case, one must also ask whether the author was informed by memory of written gospels or of oral traditions. The latter seemed to be the case with respect to the story of the healing of the leper. Also concerning the pericope about paying dues to the kings, it is possible that it rests on memory of the oral tradition of the apophthegma about paying tax to Caesar (Mark 12:13–15) and of the saying about those who say "Lord, Lord" (Luke 6:46). That the parallel to Mark 12:14 has such a "Johannine" ring (cf. John 3:2) is not as strange as it may seem; the gospel of which this papyrus has preserved a fragment apparently contained other materials which were used by the author of the Fourth Gospel. What appears here is a language that is pre-johannine and pre-synoptic at the same time. The quote from Isa 29:13 (Mark 7:6–7) is, of course, not part of the oral gospel tradition; but it was known and used elsewhere in early Christian literature.[2] What is decisive is the fact that there is nothing in this pericope that clearly reveals redactional features of any of the gospels in which parallels appear. The author of *Papyrus Egerton 2* here uses individual building blocks of sayings for the composition of this dialogue;[3] none of the individual blocks has been formed by the literary activity of a previous gospel writer.[4]

If *Papyrus Egerton 2* is indeed not dependent upon the Gospel of John, it is an important witness to an earlier stage of the development of the dialogues of the Fourth Gospel. The piece of dialogue about Moses and the Scripture that is preserved here reveals controversies with (Jewish) opponents about the interpretation of Scripture which the Fourth Gospel has used and expanded also in other instances, especially in chapters 7 and 8. There they were combined with a

---

[1] Proposed by Joachim Jeremias and repeated in Hennecke-Schneemelcher, *NT Apokryphen I*, 83.

[2] It is alluded to in Col. 2:22; *1 Clem.* 15.2

[3] See the cogent arguments of Daniels, *Egerton Gospel*, 156–73.

[4] Crossan (*Four Other Gospels*, 78–87) goes one step further, and he is possibly right. He argues (ibid., 86) that Mark's source was *Pap. Eg. 2* (". . . directly dependent on the papyrus text. It might be possible that Mark is dependent on some other version exactly similar to" it).

polemic against Gnosticizing interpretations of sayings of Jesus.[1] That *Papyrus Egerton 2* shows no traces of the latter polemic would also speak against its dependence upon John.

3.2.3 THE PASSION NARRATIVE AND THE GOSPEL OF PETER

3.2.3.1 *The Discovery and Interpretation of the Gospel of Peter*

In the year 1892, a fragment of a *Gospel of Peter* was published that had been found in Akhmim in Upper Egypt in 1886/1887.[2] The Greek text and translations have been published a number of times,[3] and several monographs have appeared,[4] especially in recent years, which deal in detail with the text and the problems of its interpretation.[5]

The Akhmim fragment of this writing, an amulet found in a tomb, has been dated to the 8th or 9th centuries. No other manuscript or fragment was known until Dieter Lührmann discovered that two small papyrus fragments from Oxyrhynchus, written ca. 200 CE, which had been published in 1972,[6] actually belonged to the Gospel of Peter.[7] This confirms a *terminus ad quem* for the composition of the *Gospel of*

---

[1] See below, # 3.4.4.3.

[2] U. Bouriant, "Fragments du texte grec du livre d'Énoch et de quelques écrits attribué à saint Pierre," in: *Mémoires publiées par les membres de la mission archéologique francaise au Caire* 9 (Paris: 1892). For a brief survey of the status of the text and its evaluation see Stephen Gero, "Apocryphal Gospels: A Survey of Textual and Literary Problems," *ANRW* 2.25/5 (1988) 3985–86.

[3] H. B. Swete, *The Apocryphal Gospel of Peter: The Greek Text of the Newly Discovered Fragment* (London:1893); Klostermann, *Apocrypha I;* most recently M. G. Mara, *Évangile de Pierre: Introduction, texte critique, traduction, commentaire et index* (SC 201; Paris: Gabalda, 1973). For English translations, see Christian Maurer, "The Gospel of Peter," in *NT Apocrypha*, 1. 180–88 (but without consideration of the new fragments); Cameron, *Other Gospels,* 76–82. A new German translation (with introduction) was published by Christian Maurer and Wilhelm Schneemelcher, "Petrusevangelium," in Hennecke-Schneemelcher, *NT Apocryphen I,* 180–88.

[4] The only somewhat older detailed study is that of Léon Vaganay, *L'Évangile de Pierre* (EtB; 2d ed.; Paris: Gabalda, 1930).

[5] See Mara, *Évangile de Pierre,* quoted in note 2 above; Jürgen Denker, *Die theologiegeschichtliche Stellung des Petrusevangeliums: Ein Beitrag zur Frühgeschichte des Doketismus* (EHS.T 36; Bern and Frankfurt: Lang, 1975); John Dominic Crossan, *The Cross that Spoke: The Origins of the Passion Narrative* (San Francisco: Harper & Row, 1988); see also idem, *Four Other Gospels,* 125–181 (all subsequent references will be to the more detailed later publication of Crossan [*The Cross that Spoke*]; cf. also Benjamin A. Johnson, "The Empty Tomb Tradition in the Gospel of Peter" (Diss. Harvard University, 1965).

[6] R. A. Coles, ed., "Pap. Oxy. 2949," in G. M. Browne et al., *The Oxyrhynchus Papyri,* Vol. 41 (Cambridge: Cambridge University Press, 1972) 15–16 and plate II.

[7] Dieter Lührmann, "POx 2949: EvPt 3–5 in einer Handschrift des 2./3. Jahrhunderts," *ZNW* 72 (1981) 216–26. On this discovery see Crossan, *The Cross that Spoke,* 6–9.

Peter of 200 CE. A date before the year 200 CE had already been assumed for this document on the basis of a description of a "Gospel put forward in the name of Peter" by Bishop Serapion of Antioch, which has been preserved by Eusebius in his *Ecclesiastical History*. Eusebius dates Bishop Serapion in the reign of Commodus (180–192 CE).[1] Eusebius's quotation from Serapion's book "Concerning what is known of the Gospel of Peter," written to the church in Rhossus,[2] is as follows:[3]

> For our part, brethren, we receive both Peter and the other apostles as Christ, but the writings which falsely bear their names we reject, as men of experience, knowing that such were not handed down to us. For I myself, when I came among you, imagined that all of you clung to the true faith; and without going through the Gospel put forward by them in the name of Peter, I said: If this is the only thing that seemingly causes captious feelings among you, let it be read. But since I have now learnt, from what has been told me, that their mind was lurking in some hole of heresy, I shall give diligence to come again to you: wherefore, brethren, expect me quickly. But we, brethren, gathering to what kind of heresy Marcianus belonged . . . , were enabled by others who saw this very Gospel, that is, by the successors of those who began it, whom we call Docetae (for most of the ideas belong to their teaching)—using [the material supplied] by them, were enabled to go through it and discover that most part indeed was in accordance with the true teaching of the Savior, but that some things were added, which also we place below for your benefit. Such are the writings of Serapion.

What is preserved of the *Gospel of Peter* in the Akhmim fragment[4] is a report of the trial of Jesus, his crucifixion, death, and burial, and three epiphany accounts: in the first, the guards at the tomb are the witnesses of the resurrection; in the second, Mary Magdalene and the women are witnesses of the empty tomb; in the third, Peter and Andrew and some other disciples are witnesses of Jesus' appearance at the lake—however, the fragment ends just after a few lines introducing the third epiphany story. Peter, in the first person singular, is the narrator.

There are numerous features in these accounts which are obviously secondary: Jesus is condemned and crucified by Herod, while Pilate is completely exonerated; the anti-Jewish polemic seems intensified; the story of Jesus' resurrection from the tomb is told elaborately, introduc-

---

[1] *Hist. eccl.* 5.22.1.

[2] Rhossus is a city in Cilicia, ca. thirty miles northwest of Antioch.

[3] *Hist. eccl.* 6.12.2–6; translation from LCL.

[4] The Oxyrhynchus Papyrus fragment parallels a few lines of the first part.

ing also the cross that follows Jesus out of the tomb and speaks; a good deal of direct discourse enhances the narrative throughout. Parallels with the passion and resurrection accounts of all four canonical gospels are numerous. Therefore, the first assessment of the newly discovered document almost unanimously favored dependence of the *Gospel of Peter* upon all four Gospels of the New Testament canon and argued for a relatively late date in order to explain the uncontrolled growth of legendary features.[1] Other scholars, however, doubted that the *Gospel of Peter* could simply be understood as a patchwork of pieces and snippets from the canonical gospels. Following suggestions by Martin Dibelius, Philipp Vielhauer notices, on the one hand, an exaggeration of the fantastic and miraculous features, but also states: "The way in which the suffering of Jesus is described by the use of passages from the Old Testament without quotation formulae is, in terms of the history of the tradition, older than the explicit scriptural proof; it represents the oldest form of the description of the passion (of Jesus)."[2] Jürgen Denker[3] has used this observation as the basis for his thesis: the *Gospel of Peter* is dependent upon the traditions of interpreting Old Testament materials for the description of Jesus' suffering and death; it shares such traditions with the canonical gospels, but is not dependent upon the canonical writings. The question remains whether the close agreements with the canonical gospels are not too numerous for the hypothesis of an independent presence of such traditions in the *Gospel of Peter*.[4]

Dominic Crossan[5] has gone further. Utilizing Denker's observations about the interpretation of Scripture as the nucleus for the formation of the passion narrative, he argues that this activity resulted in the composition of a literary document at a very early date, i.e., in the middle of the 1st century CE. On the basis of a comparison of the *Gospel of Peter* with the canonical gospels and with other extracanonical traditions about Jesus' passion, he reconstructs an entire text, the *Cross Gospel,* and tries to demonstrate that this earliest of all written passion narratives was used not only by Mark, but also by Matthew and Luke (in addition to their use of Mark) and by John (in addition to

---

[1] See, e.g., J. Armitage Robinson, "The Gospel according to Peter," in idem and M. R. James, *The Gospel According to Peter, and the Revelation of Peter: Two Lectures on the Newly-Dicovered Fragments together with the Greek Text* (London: Clay, 1892) 11–36 (published in the very year of the first publication of the Akhmim Fragment); Theodor Zahn, *Das Evangelium des Petrus* (Erlangen und Leipzig: Deichert, 1893).

[2] Vielhauer, *Geschichte,* 646 (translation mine).

[3] *Petrusevangelium,* passim.

[4] Schneemelcher in Hennecke-Schneemelcher, *NT Apokryphen I,* 183.

[5] *The Cross that Spoke,* passim.

John's usage *late* of Matthew, Mark, and Luke).[1] The *Gospel of Peter* then becomes a fifth, but very important, witness for this *Cross Gospel*. It was the basis for its earliest stratum to which texts from the intra-canonical tradition were added at a later stage of its literary development.[2]

There are three major problems regarding this hypothesis. The first relates to the reliability of the extant text. It is important to remember that almost all of the Greek text of the *Gospel of Peter* is known exclusively through a single late manuscript. During the process of its transmission, copyists of its text could have been influenced by the texts of the canonical gospels. What the Akhmim fragment presents may not be identical with the original text of that writing. The question is, therefore, whether this fragment still indicates that its original—not necessarily the entire extant text—was independent of the canonical gospels, even if the extant text occasionally includes a phrase which demonstrates influence of the canonical gospels. During the first period of their transmission, all gospel texts were very unstable.[3] The text of the canonical gospels later enjoyed a certain degree of protection, beginning with the process of canonization in the 3d and 4th centuries CE. Apocryphal gospels, however, never shared that privilege.

The second problem regarding Crossan's ingenious hypothesis is his confidence in major literary compositions of a very early date as the well spring for, and almost exclusive source of, all later gospel literature.[4] In our discussion of the process of the formation of the gospel tradition, two observations applied to all relevant materials: (1) the oral tradition continued for many decades and remained an important factor, influencing even later stages of the written records; (2) the earliest written materials were relatively small compositions of special materials which paralleled the oral use of traditional materials, such as collections of wisdom sayings or of miracles stories, which were assembled for very practical purposes.

---

[1] Crossan (*The Cross that Spoke,* 17) says: "My first major proposition is that the original Cross Gospel is the one passion and resurrection narrative from which all four of the intracanonical versions derive."

[2] "My second major proposition, then, is that an intracanonical stratum was combined with that original *Cross Gospel* in the *Gospel of Peter*" (Crossan, ibid., 20).

[3] More evidence for this instability of the text of even the canonical gospels will be discussed below in the chapters on John, Mark, Matthew, and Luke.

[4] This is also evident in Crossan's view of the Synoptic Sayings Source. In view of the numerous minor agreements of Matthew and Luke in instances in which both use Mark, Crossan prefers "the theory of Mark *and* Q as twin sources for the *narratives* of Matthew and Luke" (ibid., 19; italics mine). See also his *Four Other Gospels: Shadows on the Contours of Canon* (Minneapolis: Seabury-Winston, 1985).

A third problem regarding Crossan's hypothesis is related specifically to the formation of reports about Jesus' trial, suffering, death, burial, and resurrection. The account of the passion of Jesus must have developed quite early because it is one and the same account that was used by Mark (and subsequently by Matthew and Luke) and John, and as will be argued below, by the Gospel of Peter.[1] However, except for the story of the discovery of the empty tomb, the different stories of the appearances of Jesus after his resurrection in the various gospels cannot derive from one single source. They are independent of one another. Each of the authors of the extant gospels and of their secondary endings drew these epiphany stories from their own particular tradition, not from a common source.[2]

3.2.3.2 The Passion Narrative

It is neither possible nor necessary to present here a detailed comparison of the entire passion narrative of the *Gospel of Peter* with the corresponding texts of the canonical gospels.[3] Both Denker and Crossan have contributed substantially to a better understanding of the passion narrative by demonstrating how it was developed through scriptural interpretation. The relationship of the Gospel of Peter and of the canonical Gospels to these exegetical traditions not only determines the judgment about literary dependence; it also provides insights into the growth of the narrative traditions which ultimately formed the account of Jesus' suffering and death. A few examples must suffice here.

The passion narrative of the *Gospel of Peter* parallels the canonical accounts. The fragment begins with the remark that no one among the Jews, neither Herod nor the judges, was washing his hands. Most probably, accounts of Jesus' arrest, of his trial before Pilate, and of Pilate washing his hands preceded this remark. The handwashing scene is otherwise known only from Matt 27:24–25, and on the surface

---

[1] In this respect, Crossan's reconstruction of one single source for all passion narratives seems justified. However, it is doubtful whether this account was as comprehensive and as fixed a literary document as Crossan assumes.

[2] At this point, Crossan's thesis is seriously flawed. He assigns the story of Jesus epiphany at the lake, the last partially preserved episode of the *Gospel of Peter,* to the "intracanonical stratum" (*The Cross that Spoke,* 291–93, 413). However, its "canonical" equivalent, John 21:1–14, has made it into the canon, to be sure, but is certainly not an original part of the Gospel of John. John 21 is a later addition, made to the Fourth Gospel some time after its composition at a date that can no longer be determined with any certainty. The "intracanonical tradition" of Dominic Crossan is a fiction as far as the stories of Jesus' appearances to his disciples are concerned.

[3] I refer to the detailed and expert discussions in Denker (*Petrusevangelium*) and Crossan (*The Cross that Spoke*).

it seems evident that this was the source for *Gos. Pet.* 1.1 (and whatever preceded). But the relationship of the parallels is more complex. The episode of the handwashing is one of the many features of the passion narrative that is based on the interpretation of scriptural passages, but the references to such passages are somewhat different in both instances.

The ritual on which the handwashing scene is based is described in Deut 21:6–8 (LXX):

> If someone is slain and the murderer cannot be found, the elders and judges (κριταί) shall measure the distance to the nearest city and the elders of that city shall bring a heifer, and the priests shall brake its neck. "And all the elders of that city . . . shall wash their hands over the heifer . . . and they shall testify, 'Our hands did not shed this blood, neither did our eyes see it shed.'" *man's*

The text continues (vs. 8) with a declaration of innocence which contains the phrase, "Set not the guilt of innocent blood in the midst of your people Israel, but let the guilt of blood be forgiven them." Several passages in the psalms refer to this ritual and combine with it a declaration of innocence. The scene as described by Matthew is based on Dtn 21:6–8 as well as on the psalms:

Matt 27:24–25	Ps 26 (LXX 25): 5–6
So when Pilate saw that he was gaining nothing . . . he took water and washed his hands (λαβὼν ὕδωρ ἀπενίψατο τὰς χεῖρας) before the crowd saying, "I am innocent (ἀθῷός εἰμι) of this man's blood; see to it yourselves."	I hate the company of evildoers, and I will not sit with the wicked. I wash my hands in innocence (νίψομαι ἐν ἀθῴοις τὰς χεῖρας) and go about thy altar, O Lord.[1] *around*
	Deut 21:8
And all the people answered, "His blood be on us and on our children."	Set not the guilt of innocent blood in the midst of thy people Israel.

. . .the soldiers!

The formula used by Pilate corresponds to that used in the psalms. The final declaration of the people is formulated on the basis of Deut 21:8. The guilt of the people is expressed in this last phrase in a declaration that mocks the prayer described in the ritual.

Gos. Pet. 1.1 gives the account as far as it is based on Dtn 21:6–7, but the reference to Dtn 21:8, the mockery of the prayer, is missing. Instead the guilt of Herod and of the judges (κριταί) is established

---

[1] Cf. Ps 73:13 (LXX 72:13): "All in vain have I kept my heart clean and washed my hands in innocence (ἐνίψαμεν ἐν ἀθῴοις τὰς χεῖράς μου)." The formula appears also in 2 Sam (= 2 Reg) 3:28–29.

because they do not follow the ritual of washing their hands. A formal declaration of innocence also appears in the *Gospel of Peter,* but only later in 11:46 where Pilate says: "I am clean (ἐγὼ καθαρεύω) from the blood of the Son of God." However, this declaration is not based on the psalm passages reflected in Matthew, but on a different wording of the declaration of innocence which appears in Dan 13:46 (= Sus 46): "I am clean (καθαρός) from the blood of this woman." It is evident that the accounts in the *Gospel of Peter* and in the Gospel of Matthew both derive from the same exegetical tradition, but each gospel writer has developed the nuclear tradition which was based on Deut 21:6–8 in a different way. One cannot assume literary dependence of one gospel upon the other, nor literary dependence of both upon some more original written source; rather both accounts testify to a still fluid development of an exegetical tradition within the framework of the passion narrative.

The scene of mocking and abusing Jesus appears twice in the synoptic tradition, once before the synedrion, and a second time as the mocking by the soldiers after the trial before Pilate,[1] but there is only one scene in the *Gospel of Peter.*

Gos. Pet. 3.6–9[2]	Canonical Gospels
6 So they took the Lord and pushed him in great haste (ὤθουν αὐτὸν τρέχοντες) and said, "Let us drag (σύρωμεν) the Son of God, now that we have gotten power over him."	
7 And they put upon him a purple robe (πορφύραν)	Mark 15:17: And they dressed him with a purple robe (πορφύραν). Matt 27:28: And they stripped him and put a scarlet robe upon him (χλαμύδα κοκκίνην).[3] Luke 23:11: and they put a shining garment (ἐσθῆτα λαμπράν) on him. John 19:2: and arrayed him a purple robe (ἱμάτιον πόρφυρον), cf. John 19:5.

---

[1] Luke also reports a mocking before Herod (Luke 23:11); but he omits the mocking by the soldiers (Mark 15:16–20), i.e., he transferred the motif of this latter scene to the pericope of Jesus before Herod.

[2] Translation by Crossan (modified).

[3] Some witnesses (D it) of the text of Matt 27:28 combine the readings of Mark and Matthew: καὶ ἐνδύσαντες αὐτὸν ἱμάτιον πορφυροῦν καὶ χλαμύδα κοκκίνην περιέθηκαν αὐτῷ.

and sat him on the judgment seat (ἐκάθισον αὐτὸν ἐπὶ καθέδραν κρίσεως) and said, "Judge righteously, O King of Israel!"	John 19:13: and he sat down on the judgment seat (καὶ ἐκάθισεν ἐπὶ βήματος)[1]
8 And one of them brought a crown of thorns and put it on the Lord's head.	Mark 15:17 = Matt 27:29: and plaiting a crown of thorns, they put it on him (Matt: on his head). John 19:2: and the soldiers plaited a crown of thorns and put it on his head, cf. John 19:5.
9 And others who stood by spat on his face (ἐνέπτυον αὐτοῦ ταῖς ὄψεσι),	Mark 14:65: And they began to spit at him (ἐμπτύειν αὐτῷ) = Matt 26:67: And they spat in his face (ἐνέπτυσαν τὸ πρόσωπον αὐτῷ). Mark 15:19: and they spat at him (καὶ ἐνέπτυον αὐτῷ) = Matt 27:30 (καὶ ἐμπτύσαντες εἰς αὐτόν).
and others struck him on the cheeks (τὰς σιαγόνας αὐτοῦ ἐράπισαν),	John 18:22: one of the servants standing by struck (ἔδωκεν ῥάπισμα) Jesus with his hand. John 19:3: and struck him (ἐδίδοσαν αὐτῷ ῥαπίσματα)
others pierced him with a reed (καλάμῳ ἔνυσσον),	Mark 15:19: and they struck his head with a reed (ἔτυπτον καλάμῳ). Matt 27:29: and they put a reed (κάλαμον) into his right hand . . . 30: and they took the reed (κάλαμον) and struck (ἔτυπτον) him on his head.
and some scourged (ἐμάστιζον) him saying,	John 19:1: Then Pilate took Jesus and scourged him (ἐμαστίγωσεν). Mark 15:15 = Matt 27:26: . . . and having scourged (φραγελλώσας) Jesus, he handed him over to be crucified.
"With such honor let us honor the Son of God (τιμήσωμεν τὸν υἱὸν τοῦ θεοῦ)."	Matt 27:40: save yourself, if you are the Son of God (εἰ υἱὸς εἶ τοῦ θεοῦ), and come down from the cross.[2]

[1] The extant text probably means that Pilate sat down on the judgment seat. But it is possible that the tradition used by the Gospel of John spoke about Jesus being seated on the judgment seat.

[2] This sentence belongs to the mocking of the Crucified. In the scene of the mocking before the soldiers Jesus is addressed as "King of the Jews."

"son of god" ᴄ passion → revenge-judgement ~ Son of Man
& parousia Judge
Enoch
as son of Man
Enoch

(224) 3 From Dialogues and Narratives to the Gospel of John

One can assume that the only historical information about Jesus'
suffering, crucifixion, and death was that he was condemned to death
by Pilate and crucified. The details and individual scenes of the narrative do not rest on historical memory, but were developed on the basis
of allegorical interpretation of Scripture.[1] The earliest stage and, at
the same time, the best example of such scriptural interpretation is
preserved in the *Epistle of Barnabas*.[2]

One of the important seminal scriptural passages in this process
was Isa 50:6: "I have given my back to scourges (εἰς μάστιγας), and my
cheeks to strokes (εἰς ῥαπίσματα). I hid my face (τὸ πρόσωπόν μου) from
shame and spitting (ἐμπτυσμάτων)." Of this passage, the first half is
quoted in *Barn.* 5:14 in a context in which Barnabas develops various
elements of the suffering of Jesus without any reference to traditional
narrative materials.

Other features of the scenes of the mocking of Jesus arose from a
further expansion of the interpretation of Isa 50:6 with the help of
Zach 12:10 and of the scapegoat ritual. *Barn.* 7.7–11 demonstrates
this exegetical process. *Barnabas* is not only dependent upon the
description of the scapegoat ritual of Leviticus 16, but also uses Jewish
traditions which are later attested in Mishnah and Talmud.[3] The following elements of the ritual are important:

(1) There are two identical goats, one that is sacrificed, the other
driven into the wilderness.

(2) The scapegoat is crowned with red wool on its head (τὸ ἔριον τὸ
κόκκινον περὶ τὴν κεφαλὴν αὐτοῦ).

(3) The scapegoat is put among the thorns (εἰς μέσον τῶν ἀκανθῶν
τιθέασιν).

(4) The scapegoat is spat upon (ἐμπτύσατε); this establishes a bridge
to Isa 50:6.

(5) The scapegoat is pierced (κατακεντήσατε); this establishes a link
with Zach 12:10: "Then they shall look upon the one they have pierced"
(τότε ὄψονται εἰς ὃν ἐξεκήντησαν).[4]

(6) Possibly the scapegoat was also "nudged with a reed," though
this is not included in *Barnabas*; but a parallel passage of the *Sibyl-*

---

[1] A detailed discussion of the development of the scene of the mocking of Jesus on
the basis of scriptural interpretation can be found in Crossan, *The Cross That Spoke*,
114–59; cf. also my *Synoptische Überlieferung*, 152–54.

[2] On the date of the composition of this writing see my *Introduction*, 2. 276–77;
Crossan, *The Cross That Spoke*, 120–21.

[3] See the references in Koester, *Synoptische Überlieferung*, 152–53; Crossan, *The
Cross That Spoke*, 117–20

[4] This text, as quoted also by Justin *1 Apol.* 52.12, represents the text of Lucian and
Aquila, Symmachus, and Theodotion.

line Oracles (1.373–74) mentions the reed: "they shall pierce his sides with a reed (νύξουσιν καλάμῳ) because of their law."[1] Thus, *Barn.* 7.9 can conclude:

> They will see (ὄψονται) him then on that day (i.e., of the parousia) wearing the red robe (τὸν ποδήρη τὸν κόκκινον) and they will say, "Is not this the one whom we had once crucified, reviling and piercing (κατακεντή-σαντες) and spitting (ἐμπτύσαντες); truly this was the one who once said that he was the Son of God (ἑαυτὸν υἱὸν Θεοῦ εἶναι).

In the scene of the mocking of Jesus, the crown of thorns and the red robe are derived from this exegesis of the scapegoat ritual. Possibly also the reed (κάλαμος) that is given into Jesus' hands (in Mark, Matthew, and the *Gospel of Peter*) has its origin in this ritual. Furthermore, *Barn.* 7.9 indicates that Jesus' address as the "Son of God" was part of the traditional interpretation.

On the other hand, the reports of the mocking of Jesus cannot fully be explained on this basis. There seem to be elements which derive from a different traditional topos, the "royal mocking." As an important example of this topos, Crossan[2] has drawn attention to the story of the mocking of Carabas during the Jewish pogroms under the Egyptian governor Flaccus, which Philo reported.[3] The influence of this topos on the various accounts of the mocking of Jesus is evident: the red (κόκκινος) robe, derived from the scapegoat ritual, is replaced by the royal purple (πορφύρα), Jesus is seated on a throne, the reed becomes a scepter, the eschatological acclamation of Jesus as "Son of God" is turned into the mocking of the "King of the Jews."

All these developments must be presupposed for the scenes of the mocking of Jesus in the extant gospel literature. But both the elements of the exegetical tradition and of the topos of the royal mocking are present in these accounts in such a way that simple literary dependence alone cannot explain the development. That is even evident in the case of the Synoptic Gospels. One example must suffice: in Mark 15:17, Jesus is dressed with a royal purple (πορφύρα); Matt 27:28, reproducing this Markan passage, substitutes the garment that was developed in the exegetical/scapegoat tradition and replaces Mark's royal robe with the scarlet garment (χλαμὺς κοκκίνη).

The *Gospel of Peter* reveals a very close relationship especially to

---

[1] Crossan (*The Cross That Spoke*, 151–52) proposes "that the (scapegoat) ritual included the people's hurrying the poor animal on its departure from city to desert by prodding its sides by sharpened reeds."

[2] *The Cross That Spoke*, 139–41.

[3] *In Flaccum*, 32–39.

the exegetical/scapegoat tradition, often closer than that of the canonical parallels:

Exeg. Trad.	*Gos. Pet.*	John	Synoptic Gospels
scarlet (κόκκινος) robe	purple robe (πορφύρα)	ἱμάτιον πόρφυρον.	Mark: πορφύρα Matt: χλαμὺς κοκκίνη
crown of thorns	crown of thorns	crown of thorns	crown of thorns
spitting in the face (πρόσωπον . . . ἐμπτυσμάτων)	spat on his face (ἐνέπτυον αὐτοῦ ταῖς ὄψεσι)		And they spat in his face[1] (ἐνέπτυσαν τὸ πρόσωπον αὐτῷ)
cheeks for strikes (τὰς σιαγόνας εἰς ῥαπίσματα)	struck him on the cheeks (τὰς σιαγόνας αὐτοῦ ἐράπισαν)	struck him (ἐδίδοσαν αὐτῷ ῥαπίσματα)	
pierced with a reed (νύξουσιν καλάμῳ)	pierced with a reed (καλάμῳ ἔνυσσον),	19:34: pierced with a spear (λόγχῃ ἔνυξεν)[2]	struck with a reed (ἔτυπτον καλάμῳ)
scourges (εἰς μάστιγας)	scourged (ἐμάστιζον)	scourged him (ἐμαστίγωσεν)	scourged (φραγελλώσας)
He said he was the Son of God (λέγων ἑαυτὸν υἱὸν θεοῦ εἶναι)	let us honor the Son of God (τιμήσωμεν τὸν υἱὸν τοῦ θεοῦ)		save yourself, if you are the Son of God (εἰ υἱὸς εἶ τοῦ θεοῦ)[3]

It is evident that alone in the *Gospel of Peter* all three items from the Isaiah passage appear together, while John only includes the first and the second (scourges and strikes) and Mark and Matthew only the first and the third (scourges and spitting). Moreover, only the *Gospel of Peter* and John use the same Greek terminology for "scourging" (μαστιγοῦν), in agreement with Isaiah, while Mark and Matthew substitute the more common Roman term for this punishment (φραγελλοῦν), and only Isaiah and the *Gospel of Peter* mention the cheeks (τὰς σιαγόνας) explicitly with respect to the strikes. The piercing with a reed from the scapegoat allegory is preserved only in the *Gospel of Peter,* while John has used this item for the piercing of Jesus' side after his death; Mark and Matthew misread the tradition and changed it to *poking*

[1] The term "face" (πρόσωπον) appears in Matthew only.

[2] This episode, which happens after Jesus' crucifixion is also dependent upon this exegetical tradition, but has been secondarily moved to Jesus' death.

[3] This parallel, which does belong to the scene of the mocking before the synedrion or by the soldiers, has been transferred by Matthew to the mocking of the crucified Jesus (27:40).

pokes

"strikes with a reed"; Matt 27:29 has changed this further into a royal mockery feature: the reed is given into Jesus' hand for a scepter. The reference to Jesus as the Son of God is present only in the mocking scene of the Gospel of Peter; Matthew must have known this item from the exegetical tradition but inserted it into the mocking of the crucified, where it does not appear in the Markan parallel (Mark 15:30).

The relationship of the *Gospel of Peter* to the parallel accounts of the canonical gospels cannot be explained as a random compilation of canonical passages. It is evident that the mocking scene in this gospel is a narrative version that is directly dependent upon the exegetical tradition which is visible in *Barnabas*. The narrative version of this tradition as it is preserved in the *Gospel of Peter* has not yet split the mocking account into several scenes. This is an argument for the thesis that this account is older than its various usages in the canonical gospels.

On the other hand, only Matthew has preserved the Isaiah term for "face" (πρόσωπον), while the *Gospel of Peter* has substituted a different Greek word (ὄψεις); Matthew also preserves the reference to Jesus as the Son of God. Although he is otherwise dependent upon Mark, Matthew still had access to the exegetical tradition of Isaiah interpretation which was used by the *Gospel of Peter*. This is also evident in the Gospel of John which has preserved various elements either directly from the same exegetical tradition or from an independent narrative account based upon this same tradition.[1]

Another example of the direct dependence of the *Gospel of Peter's* passion narrative upon exegetical traditions is the reference to gall and vinegar in the drink given to Jesus. *Gos. Pet.* 5.16 reports this incident after the crucifixion of Jesus:

> And one of them said, "Give him to drink gall with vinegar (χολὴν μετὰ ὄξους)." And they mixed (it) and gave him to drink.

---

[1] Luke has rarely been mentioned or quoted in the discussion. Evidently Luke is much farther removed from the original exegetical tradition. Furthermore, he has eliminated completely the scene of mocking by the soldiers (Mark 15:16–20) and transferred some features to the appearance of Jesus before Herod (Luke 23:6–12). D. R. Catchpole (*The Trial of Jesus* [Studia Postbiblica 18; Leiden: Brill] 174–83) has argued that the respective passages in Luke are altogether dependent upon a very different early account of the passion. However that may be, there is little in Luke to indicate that he was acquainted with the particular tradition of scriptural intepretation that was used by the other canonical Gospels and by the *Gospel of Peter*. See also Crossan, *The Cross That Spoke*, 147–49.

It has, of course, long been recognized that this incident has been developed on the basis of Ps 69:21 (LXX 68:22):[1]

> And they gave me gall (χολήν) in my food, and for my thirst they gave me vinegar (ὄξος) to drink.

The exegetical tradition which applied this scriptural passage to the crucifixion of Jesus is, once more, visible in *Barnabas*. In 7.3a the author makes the statement that Jesus, when he had been crucified, received vinegar and gall for a drink (ἐποτίζετο ὄξει καὶ χολῇ), and in 7.5a he introduces a repetition of this statement in the first person singular:

> ... when I am about to sacrifice my flesh on behalf of my new people, you shall give me to drink gall with vinegar (χολὴν μετὰ ὄξους).

Surprisingly, *Barnabas* does not explicitly mention or quote the psalm passages in this context nor anywhere else in his writing, although there can be little doubt that the passage *Barn.* 7.3–5 is framed by references to it. Between the two references he presents a quote and interpretation of Lev 23:29 (*Barn.* 7.3b) and a quotation of unknown origin which is introduced by "What then does he say in the prophet?" (7.4). The content of the quote is a command that, on the Day of Atonement, the priests alone shall eat the entrails of the sacrificed goat unwashed and with vinegar (μετὰ ὄξους). This quote from "the prophet," in fact, includes the reference to the fulfillment of the psalm which was quoted above (7.5a) and continues with a reference to the people's fasting while the priests eat (7.5b). It has not been possible to identify with certainty the origin of this reference to the eating of the entrails of the sacrificed goat, though there may have been a Jewish tradition about such instruction, as is indicated by a later Talmudic passage.[2]

The procedure is analogous to the one we have observed above with respect to the mocking scene. A scriptural passage forms the basis, even if it is not quoted explicitly in this case. An explanation of a sacrificial ritual on the basis of Jewish traditions follows. The result is a new insight into a detail of the circumstances of the suffering of Jesus that would eventually be developed into a narrative account.

---

[1] On the interpretation of this passage from Barnabas see my *Synoptische Überlieferung,* 148–52; Crossan, *The Cross That Spoke,* 209–12.

[2] See Hans Windisch, *Der Barnabasbrief* (HNT.EB 3; Tübingen: Mohr/Siebeck, 1920) 344; Koester, *Synoptische Überlieferung,* 150; Crossan, *The Cross That Spoke,* 210–11.

The brief narrative that appears in *Gos. Pet.* 5.16 has several parallels in the canonical gospels:

Gos. Pet.	Mark 15:23	Matt 27:34	John
	(before the crucifixion) And they gave him wine mixed with myrrh (ἐσμυρνισμένον οἶνον)	(before the crucifixion) And they gave him to drink wine mixed with gall (οἶνον μετὰ χολῆς μεμιγμένον)	

After Jesus has been crucified:

Gos. Pet.	Mark 15:36 = Matt 27:48	Luke 23:36	John 19:29–30
And one of them said, "Give him to drink gall with vinegar (χολὴν μετὰ ὄξους)." And they mixed (it) and gave him to drink.	And one of them ran and, filling a sponge full of vinegar (ὄξους), put it on a reed and gave it to him to drink.	The soldiers also mocked him, coming up and offering him vinegar (ὄξος).	A bowl full of vinegar (ὄξους μέσον) stood there; so they put a sponge full of the vinegar on a hyssop and held it to his mouth. When Jesus had received the vinegar, he said, "It is completed (τετέλεσται)."
And they fulfilled everything and completed (ἐτελείωσαν) the measure of their sins . . .			

Among the references to something to drink that is offered to Jesus, Mark 15:23 has apparently nothing to do with Ps 69:21. To offer wine mixed with myrrh to someone who was about to be crucified seems to have been a custom which was sometimes observed. It was a sedative that would diminish the pain.[1] The second incident of giving something to drink to Jesus in Mark and Matthew, at the same time the only one in the *Gospel of Peter* and in the Gospels of Luke and of John, is entirely dependent upon the interpretation of Ps 69:21. In all five reports, this incident involves vinegar. However, all four canonical gospels report that the drink was only vinegar in this case; none of

---

[1] Erich Klostermann, *Das Markusevangelium* (HNT 3; 4th ed.; Tübingen: Mohr/Siebeck, 1950) 163.

them mentions gall. Matthew, however, occupies a special position: he mentioned gall also, but he used that reference in a modification of his source, Mark 15:23, replacing the "wine mixed with myrrh" given to Jesus before the crucifixion by "wine mixed with gall" (Matt 27:34). Thus, Matthew has been able to find a place for both, the gall and the vinegar of Ps 69:21, in his Gospel.

The tradition of scriptural interpretation of the psalm which is evident in *Barnabas* originally created one single event of giving something to drink to Jesus, a drink of (poisonous) gall mixed with vinegar. *Barn.* 7.5 already indicates that this is the fulfillment of prophecy regarding the sacrifice of Jesus. The oldest narrative account which developed on this basis reported such an incident as it is preserved in the *Gospel of Peter;* this report would have appropriately added the remark "and they fulfilled everything." In the subsequent transmission of this report, the original narrative was split up into two different incidents. Mark 15:36 preserves only the second, the drink of vinegar, and so does John 19:29. But John 19:28 retains, at the same time, the reference to the fulfillment of Scripture (Jesus . . . , that the Scripture be completed, said, "I thirst," cf.: when Jesus had received the vinegar, he said, "It is completed," John 19:30).[1] Luke is simply dependent upon this curtailed tradition of scriptural interpretation which he has drawn from the Gospel of Mark, but he omitted the Markan reference to the drinking of wine mixed with myrrh for theological reasons.[2] Matthew must have had independent access to this exegetical tradition which originally mentioned both gall and vinegar.[3] Thus he replaced the Markan description of the first incident by a formulation which more appropriately described the fulfillment of Scripture. No question, the *Gospel of Peter* has preserved the most original narrative version of the tradition of scriptural interpretation. In this instance, a dependence of the *Gospel of Peter* upon any of the canonical gospels is excluded. It is unlikely that such a dependence exists with respect to any other features of the passion narrative of this gospel.[4]

---

[1] In the extant text of John, this remark has a much more pregnant significance: Jesus has completed all the works he was sent to do (cf. Bultmann, *Gospel of John,* 675). But the tradition or source of the Gospel of John probably expressed by this phrase that the fulfillment of the scripture had been accomplished.

[2] The perfect martyr, Jesus, does not need drugs in order to suffer his fate heroically.

[3] It is not very likely that "gall" was introduced by Matthew because of some misunderstanding of the Markan text; see Koester, *Synoptische Überlieferung,* 151.

[4] For further discussion of this question see Denker, *Petrusevangelium,* and Crossan, *The Cross That Spoke,* passim.

3.2.3.3 Epiphany Stories

In the passion narrative that was used by the Gospels of Mark and John and that also formed the basis for the *Gospel of Peter*'s passion narrative, the story of the discovery of the empty tomb[1] must have followed immediately upon the story of the burial of Jesus.[2] Studies of the passion narrative have shown that all gospels were dependent upon one and the same basic account of the suffering, crucifixion, death, and burial of Jesus. But this account ended with the discovery of the empty tomb. With respect to the stories of Jesus' appearances, each of the extant gospels of the canon used different traditions of epiphany stories which they appended to the one common passion account. This also applies to the *Gospel of Peter*. There is no reason to believe that any of the epiphany stories at the end of this gospel derive from the same source on which the account of the passion is based.[3]

For the stories of Jesus' burial and the discovery of the empty tomb, the *Gospel of Peter* used the source that also underlies Mark and John, which ended with the discovery of the empty tomb. Also here, the story of Jesus' burial (*Gos. Pet.* 6.23–24) is connected with Joseph (of Arimathea)[4] and with his tomb that was located in a nearby garden (cf. John 19:41). The episode of Joseph requesting the body from Pilate was relocated in the *Gospel of Peter* to a position before the scene of the mocking of Jesus (2.3–5).[5]

---

[1] Mark 16:1–6; John 20:1–10.

[2] Mark 15:42–47; John 19:38–42. Luke (23:50–56; 24:1–11) follows Mark's order. Matthew interpolated the account of the securing of the tomb (Matt 27:62–66) between the story of the burial (Matt 27:57–61) and the empty tomb pericope (Matt 28:1–10). On this interpolated account see below.

[3] In this respect, my analysis differs fundamentally with that of Crossan whose very ingenious hypothesis assumes the existence of an older "Cross Gospel" which included the epiphany story at the tomb, and into which a later redactor inserted accounts drawn from the canonical gospels, such as the account of the burial of Jesus (6.23–24), the discovery of the empty tomb (12.50–13.57), and the appearance of Jesus at the lake (14.60). Crossan's observations regarding redactional features are very astute. But, as will be seen, these redactional elements reveal the hand of the original author of the *Gospel of Peter*, who tries to connect several originally independent resurrection accounts.

[4] He is simply called "Joseph" in *Gos. Pet.* 2.3 and 6.23.

[5] Crossan (*The Cross That Spoke*, 20–23) considers the story of the burial of Jesus as one of the later interpolations from the canonical gospels (Crossan speaks of "the intra-canonical tradition") into the original "Cross Gospel," and Joseph's request for the body in *Gos. Pet.* 2.3–5 as a preparatory redactional link for this interpolation. This complicates the matter unnecessarily. There is no evidence to support the hypothesis that the report of Jesus' burial by Joseph of Arimathea in John 19:38–42 is dependent upon Mark 15:42–47; see the discussion of this question in Bultmann, *Gospel of John*, 667–68. Thus the story of the burial belongs to the source used by Mark and John and also by the *Gospel of Peter*.

However, in the *Gospel of Peter* the story of the discovery of the empty tomb does not immediately follow upon the story of the burial. Rather an elaborate story of the resurrection of Jesus from his tomb has been interpolated after the account of the burial (*Gos. Pet.* 7.25–11:49). It is a narrative full of miraculous events, but its structure reveals the basic formal features of an epiphany story. It consists of (1) an introduction which sets the scene for the epiphany, (2) the appearance of heavenly figures, (3) a miracle, (4) the epiphany of the risen Lord, and (5) the reaction of the witnesses.

Novelistic features have expanded several sections of this story, and redactional remarks have been inserted in order to connect this story with its context. But the basic elements of the older story are still evident.

(1) Introduction

This is the most novelistic part because it reports the people's unrest in view of the signs that occurred at the death of Jesus and uses this as the reason for the request for a guard at the tomb (7.25–28).[1] The older epiphany story must have featured an introduction that began with 8.29 and concluded with 9:34.

> The elders came to Pilate and said. "Give us soldiers so that we can guard his tomb for three days, lest his disciples come and steal him and the people think that he rose from the dead, and do evil to us." And Pilate gave them the centurion Petronius with soldiers to guard the tomb.
>
> [And with them, the elders and scribes went to the tomb.]
> And with the centurion and the soldiers [all who were][2] there rolled a big stone and placed it before the door of the tomb. And after they had affixed seven seals and pitched a tent they kept guard.

(2) The appearance of two heavenly figures (9.35–36)

> Now in the night in which the Lord's day dawned, when the soldiers, two by two in every watch, were keeping guard, there rang a loud voice in heaven and they saw the heavens opened and two men came down from there in great brightness and drew near to the tomb.

---

[1] Crossan (*The Cross That Spoke*, 23) has rightly identified 7.26–27 as a secondary intrusion into the introduction for the epiphany. This section describes the disciples' fear which drives them into hiding in order to prepare for the later story of Jesus' appearance before the disciples. However, 7.26–27 does not come from the hand of a later redactor who inserted canonical materials into an older "Cross Gospel."

[2] The bracketed phrases are secondary expansions in order to increase the number of people present. The elders and scribes are forgotten later in the story.

staff - The Water of Life

(3) A miracle (9.37–38a)

That stone which had been laid against the entrance to the tomb started of itself to roll and gave way to the side, and the tomb was opened, and both the young men entered in. When now the soldiers saw this, they awakened the centurion [and the elders—for they also were there to assist at the watch].[1]

(4) The epiphany of the risen Lord (10.39b–40)

They saw again three men coming out from the tomb, and two of them sustaining the other, and a cross following them, and the heads of the two reaching to heaven, but that of him who was lead by them by the hand overpassing the heavens.[2]

(5) The reaction of the witnesses (11:45)

When the centurion and his company saw this, . . .[3] they said, "In truth, he was the Son of God."[4]

The epiphany story, as reconstructed here, does not reveal any signs of a later time or tradition. What is secondary here is due to the attempt of the author of the gospel who wanted to connect the older epiphany story to the literary context of his writing and to continue his apologetics in behalf of an exoneration of Pilate.[5] If the story itself belongs to the older oral tradition of epiphany stories related to Jesus' resurrection, are there any traces of this story elsewhere in the extant gospel literature? There are indeed several indications that parts or

[1] That the centurion is awakened is necessary, since he is the primary witness. The bracketed words are a secondary expansion that wants to involve other witnesses.

[2] Two secondary insertions follow. The first (10.41–42) has been interpolated in the interest of the doctrine of the descent into Hades and the preaching to the dead: "And they heard a voice from the heavens, 'Have you preached to those who sleep?' And from the cross was heard the answer, 'Yes!'" The second insertion—the appearance of another young man from the heavens who enters the tomb (11.44)—is redactional: this angelic person is needed in the tomb for the following story of the discovery of the empty tomb (12.50–13.57). It is not a later interpolation, but belongs to the redactor who connected the different stories of the resurrection appearances (*pace* Crossan).

[3] This section has been partially changed in order to make the confession a part of the report to Pilate, which had already been prepared in the insertion of 11:43 and is continued in 11.46–49. This report to Pilate, as it stands now, is apparently due to the author of the *Gospel of Peter*. It is clearly an apologetic motif that exonerates Pilate, and it is closely connected with the description of Pilate in the passion narrative (cf. 1.1; 2.3–4).

[4] Most likely the original story continued with a report of the events to the authorities) who had ordered the guard at the tomb and the command to the soldiers to keep silence; cf. *Gos. Pet.* 11.47–49 with Matt 28:11–15. For further discussion of the relationship of these two passages, see below.

[5] See the identification of the redactional materials in the preceding notes.

fragments of this story have been used in different contexts in Mark as well as in Matthew.

The conclusion of the story with the reaction of the witnesses ends in the statement, "In truth he was the Son of God." The same statement is also reported in the Gospel of Mark after the death of Jesus (Mark 15:39):

> And when the centurion who stood facing him saw that he (Jesus) thus expired, he said, "Truly, this man was a Son of God."

In the context of Mark, this statement seems quite unmotivated. There was no spectacular event that the centurion could have witnessed.[1] Matthew has noticed this and inserted an account of miraculous occurrences (earthquake, opening of the tombs, Matt 27:51b–53) before the centurion's confession. Moreover, in Mark's account a centurion had not been mentioned before (only "soldiers" had been named). However, in the epiphany story of the *Gospel of Peter* a centurion had been introduced at the beginning of the story (8.31), and the confession at the end comes from the centurion and his company.

Three fragments of this epiphany story appear in the Gospel of Matthew: the guard at the tomb (27:62–66); the appearance of an angel from heaven (28:2–4); and the bribing of the soldiers (28:11–15). All three have very close parallels to the epiphany story of the *Gospel of Peter*.

The Guard at the Tomb

Gos. Pet. 8.28–33	Matt 27:62–66
Scribes, Pharisees and elders . . .	High priests and Pharisees . . .
Go to Pilate (immediately).	Go to Pilate on the next morning after the day of Preparation.
Ask for a guard for three days so that his disciples would not come and steal the body and the people would say that he rose from the dead.	Tell Pilate that Jesus had said that he would rise after three days. ask for a guard so that his disciples would not come and steal the body and tell the people that he rose from the dead, so that the last fraud would be worse than the first.

---

[1] Mark 15:38 reports that the curtain of the temple was torn in two; but that would be a strange motivation for a statement of someone standing at the cross of Jesus.

Pilate gives them the centurion Petronius.	Pilate gives them a guard.
They go, roll a stone before the tomb's door and seal it with seven seals and keep guard.	They go and secure the tomb and seal the stone and keep guard.

It is evident that we are dealing here with the same story. Although some features in the *Gospel of Peter* seem more exaggerated than in Matthew, e.g., the seven seals placed on the stone, there are no elements that reflect peculiarities of Matthew's version of the story. Crossan[1] thinks that the Pharisees are a secondary intrusion into the *Gospel of Peter* because they are soon forgotten; only the elders go to Pilate. But the Pharisees are also forgotten in Matt 28:11–15 where only the high priests and the elders are mentioned. The best solution is to assume that the original story mentioned only the elders. While Matthew explicitly connects the request with Jesus' predictions that he would rise "after three days,"[2] the request for guards for a three-day period in *Gos. Pet.* 8.30 may simply mean that the tomb must be secured "until the people have seen for themselves that Jesus is simply and irrevocably buried."[3] In this case the "three days" reflect the Jewish belief that the soul of a dead person remains in the neighborhood of the tomb for three days.[4] It is unclear in Matt 27:65 whether the guard is composed of Roman soldiers or is the high priests' own Jewish guard.[5] In Matt 28:11–15 it is clearly a Jewish guard which is bribed by the elders to keep silent so that the governor (Pilate) would not hear about the miraculous opening of the tomb and would think that the disciples stole the body. The ambiguity in Matt 28:11 is apparently caused by the fact that Matthew's source, like the *Gospel of Peter*, presented the guard as a cohort of Roman soldiers.[6]

Matt 27:62–66 (and 28:11–15) is usually called an apologetic legend.[7] But what Matthew reports here is not a complete story at all. It requires a continuation for which Matt 28:11–15 is not quite sufficient. What is missing is the presence of the guards as witnesses. Matthew was quite aware of that and inserted a reference to the

[1] *The Cross That Spoke,* 270.

[2] Matt 12:38–40; 16:21; 17:22–23; 20:18–19.

[3] Crossan, *The Cross That Spoke,* 270.

[4] See the story of the raising of Lazarus, John 11:17, 39, and Bultmann, *Gospel of John,* 400, n. 8.

[5] Pilate said to them ἔχετε κουστωδίαν. It is a much discussed problem whether ἔχετε is an imperative (= "take a guard!") or an indicative (= "you have a guard [your-selves]").

[6] Crossan, *The Cross That Spoke,* 397.

[7] Bultmann, *Synoptic Tradition,* 287.

guards into the story of the discovery of the empty tomb (Matt 28:2–4). However, this insertion not only has all the signs of the clumsiness of such a secondary interpolation; it also reveals that Matthew knew more of the the older epiphany story which the *Gospel of Peter* preserves.

Gos. Pet. 9.35–10.38	Matt 28:1–4
Now in the night in which the Lord's day dawned,	Now late on the Sabbath when the first day of the week was dawning, Mary Magdalene and the other Mary went to see the tomb.[1]
when the soldiers, two by two in every watch, were keeping guard, there rang a loud voice in heaven and they saw the heavens opened and two men came down from there in great brightness and drew near to the tomb. That stone which had been laid against the entrance to the tomb started of itself to roll and gave way to the side, and the tomb was opened,	And behold, there was a great earthquake; for an angel of the Lord descended from heaven (see below)
	and came and rolled back the stone and sat upon it.
(see above)	His appearance was like lightning, and his raiment white as snow.
and both the young men entered in. When now the soldiers saw this, they awakened the centurion.	And for fear of him, the guards trembled and became like dead men.

I completely agree with Crossan's statement that "Matthew is ... conflating two sources in his account of the angel and the guards."[2] That is especially evident with respect to the statement about the time at the beginning of the account.[3] These statements are perfectly clear in Mark 16:1–2 and in *Gos. Pet.* 9.35. Mark first recounts that the women buy the ointments as soon as the Sabbath is over (διαγενομένου τοῦ σαββάτου), i.e., in the evening after sunset. They go to the tomb early the next morning (λίαν πρωὶ τῇ μιᾷ τῶν σαββάτων). Matt 28:1 has combined some of that information with the time given by the epiphany story of the *Gospel of Peter*: "In the night in which the Lord's

---

[1] This verse (Matt 28:1) is taken from the Markan version of the story of the discovery of the empty tomb (Mark 16:1), but it has suffered some major alterations; see below.

[2] *The Cross That Spoke*, 352.

[3] See the detailed documentation for the following in Crossan, *The Cross That Spoke*, 352–55.

day dawned" (τῇ δὲ νυκτὶ ᾗ ἐπέφωσκεν ἡ κυριακή). This, however, indicates something like the hour of midnight, certainly still the dark of the night before sunrise. The combination of both times in Matthew results in the strange statement that the women come to the tomb "late on the Sabbath" (ὄψε τῶν σαββάτων), "when the first of the week was dawning" (τῇ ἐπιφωσκούσῃ εἰς μίαν σαββάτων). This awkwardness alone is sufficient to prove the dependence of Matthew upon the epiphany story. The verses 28:2–4 are then explained without difficulty. Matthew replaces the two figures of the epiphany story with the one figure that is needed to greet the women, and he turns the guards at the tomb into people who were "like dead," so that the angel can talk with the women without witnesses.

This is sufficient for Matthew to enable the guards to return to the high priests and report all the things that had happened (Matt 28:11). Matthew's conclusion of the account of the guard at the tomb (28:11–15) differs from *Gos. Pet.* 11:46–49. In the latter, the soldiers report directly to Pilate;[1] then a group of persons designated as "all" (πάντες) comes to Pilate and requests him to swear the centurion and the soldiers to silence. Matthew, on the other hand, had already indicated that it was a guard that reported to the Jewish authorities. Thus he changes the conclusion to have the high priests and elders bribe the guard with money so they would say that his disciples had stolen the body while they were asleep. The elimination of Pilate and the bribery to the effect that the soldiers should tell a lie, thereby even incriminating themselves (they were not supposed to fall asleep!), are evidently secondary. What Matthew has presented here is no longer a plausible story but a piece of fiction that wants to explain why "this rumor is told among the Jews until today" (28:16). The *Gospel of Peter* wants to exonerate Pilate at the expense of the Jewish authorities; the Gospel of Matthew wants to shift the entire responsibility to "the Jews."

There is a good chance that also the epiphany section of the resurrection story of the *Gospel of Peter* has survived in the Synoptic Gospels. The story of the transfiguration of Jesus (Mark 9:2–8) has been designated as a displaced resurrection account.[2] There are several features which the account of the transfiguration shares with *Gos. Pet.* 9.36–10.40 and also with Matt 28:2–4.[3] Jesus appears "in

---

[1] The author of the gospel takes this occasion to insert another declaration of innocence by Pilate: "I am clean of the blood of the Son of God; you have made this decision." See the discussion above, # 3.2.3.2.

[2] Bultmann, *Synoptic Tradition,* 259.

[3] Matt 17:1–8 has introduced some additional features drawn from the resurrection account that he used in 28:2–4: the disciples fall on their face, terrified; Jesus turns to

garments glistening, intensely white" (Mark 9:3). Two angelic figures are standing with Jesus, who are then identified as Moses and Elijah. The epiphany story, which is generally known as the "transfiguration," may indeed be nothing else but a faint echo of the account which the *Gospel of Peter* has preserved in full.[1]

The next section of the *Gospel of Peter* is the account of the discovery of the empty tomb (12.50–13.57). If the *Gospel of Peter* used a source for his passion narrative that was related to the sources of Mark and John, the story of the discovery of the empty tomb would have concluded that source. Can it be shown that *Gos. Pet.* 12.50–13.57 is indeed not dependent upon any of the accounts of the canonical gospels?[2] It must at once be recognized that this portion of the writing has been heavily edited by the redactor. It was already prepared by the redactional insertion at the end of the epiphany story, which told of another figure descending from heaven and entering into the tomb (11:44). The story of the discovery of the tomb itself has been interrupted by repeated comments referring to the fear of the Jews which are always coupled with reflections about the question of pious duty with respect to one who has died (12.50, 52, 54).[3] But apart from these secondary comments, the basic story agrees with fundamental features of its canonical parallels.

Gos. Pet. 12.50–13.57	Mark 16:1–8
	And when the Sabbath had passed,
Mary Magdalene took with her	Mary Magdalene, and Mary the
female friends	mother of James, and Salome bought
	spices so that they might go and
early in the morning of the Lord's day	anoint him. And very early on the
and went to the tomb where he had	first day of the week they went to the
been laid.	tomb when the sun had risen.
And they said,	And they were saying to one another,
". . . Who will roll away the stone for	"Who will roll away the stone for us
us that is set on the entrance of the	from the door of the tomb?"
tomb [that we may go in	

---

them saying, "Rise up, fear not" (Matt 17:6–7). See Crossan, *The Cross That Spoke,* 358.

[1] Denker, *Theologiegeschichtliche Stellung,* 99–101. I am not convinced, however, that it is possible to explain special Lukan features in the story of the transfiguration (Luke 9:30–32) as due to literary dependence upon the same source (Crossan, *The Cross That Spoke,* 359–60).

[2] Crossan (*The Cross That Spoke,* 15–30) assigns this story to the "intracanonical stratum" of the gospel.

[3] These motifs are closely related to other redactional insertions elsewhere in the writing; see *Gos. Pet.* 7.26–27; 14.59.

and sit beside him and do what is
necessary] because the stone is large
. . ." So they went and found the tomb
open.

And looking up they saw that the
stone was rolled back; for it was very
large.

And they came near, stooped down,
and saw there a young man sitting in
the midst of the tomb, beautiful and
dressed with a bright shining robe,

And they saw a young man sitting to
the right, dressed with a white robe,

and they were amazed.
But he said to them,
"Do not be amazed!

who said to them,

"Why have you come? Whom do you
seek? Not the one who was crucified?
He rose and went away. But if you do
not believe, stoop and see the place
where he lay, for he is not there. He
rose and went to the place whence he
was sent."

You seek Jesus of Nazareth who was
crucified.
He was raised; he is not here.
See the place where they laid him.

But go and tell his disciples and Peter
that he is going before you to Galilee;
there you will see him as he told you."

Then the women fled in fear.

And they went out and fled from the
tomb, for trembling and
astonishment had come upon them.
And they said nothing to anyone, for
they were afraid.

There is nothing in this account that could not have been derived from
Mark or from the source that Mark used. Special features of the parallels in Matt 28:1–10, Luke 24:1–11, and John 20:1–10 are absent. But
what is also missing in the *Gospel of Peter* are the typical Markan
redactional elements: the command to tell the disciples to go to Galilee
(Mark 16:7) and the exaggerated emphasis upon fear and astonishment (Mark 16:5, 8), perhaps also the reference to the purchase of
spices (Mark 16:1)—there is no reference to this in the parallel story in
John 20. But in agreement with John 20, Mary Magdalene is the only
woman who is explicitly named, while not one of the other names
(Mary mother of James, Salome, the other Mary) appears.

The third resurrection story in the *Gospel of Peter* is the appearance
of Jesus at the lake (14.60), but only the beginning is preserved. What
remains is the list of the disciples who were present. But this list does
not agree with the parallel account in John 21:1–14. John 21:2 names
Simon Peter, Thomas called the Twin, Nathaniel of Cana, the sons of
Zebedee, and two other disciples. *Gos. Pet.* 14.60 names Simon Peter,

his brother Andrew, and Levi the son of Alphaeus. It is not known whether any additional disciples were introduced here, because the preserved text ends at this point. Already the discrepancies in the list of names argues against any dependence of this last epiphany story upon the supplemental chapter of the Gospel of John.

The *Gospel of Peter*, as a whole, is not dependent upon any of the canonical gospels. It is a composition which is analogous to the Gospels of Mark and John. All three writings, independently of each other, use an older passion narrative which is based upon an exegetical tradition that was still alive when these gospels were composed, and to which the Gospel of Matthew also had access. All five gospels under consideration, Mark, John, and Peter, as well as Matthew and Luke, concluded their gospels with narratives of the appearances of Jesus on the basis of different epiphany stories that were told in different contexts. However, fragments of the epiphany story of Jesus being raised from the tomb, which the *Gospel of Peter* has preserved in its entirety, were employed in different literary contexts in the Gospels of Mark and Matthew.

3.3 The Transmission of the Four Canonical Gospels

3.3.1 THE MANUSCRIPTS

Four gospels from the period of early Christianity have been admitted into the canon of the New Testament writings. They are known under the names of their assumed authors Matthew, Mark, Luke, and John.[1] Because of their canonical status, these four gospels have been preserved in a very large number of manuscripts.[2]

---

[1] Editions of the Greek text of the individual gospels: Eberhard Nestle and Erwin Nestle, *Novum Testamentum Graece* (26th ed. by Kurt Aland et al.; Stuttgart: Deutsche Bibelstiftung, 1979 and later reprints); Kurt Aland et al., *The Greek New Testament* (New York: United Bible Societies, 1966 and later reprints). Synoptic edition with the text of all four gospels: Kurt Aland, *Synopsis Quattuor Evangeliorum* (Stuttgart: Württembergische Bibelanstalt, 1963 and reprints, also with English text on facing pages). Synoptic edition of Matthew, Mark, and Luke (with passages from John wherever relevant): Albert Huck, *Synopsis of the First Three Gospels* (13th ed. fundamentally revised by Heinrich Greeven; Tübingen: Mohr/Siebeck, 1981); M.-E. Boismard & A. Lamouille, *Synopsis Graeca Quattuor Evangeliorum* (Leuven: Peeters, 1986). English translation (text of the RSV) of the earlier edition of Huck, *Synopsis*: Burton H. Throckmorton, *Gospel Parallels: A Synopsis of the First Three Gospels* (4th ed.; Nashville and New York: Nelson, 1979); Kurt Aland, *Synopsis of the Four Gospels: Greek-English Edition* (6th ed.; Stuttgart: United Bible Societies, 1983).

[2] Bruce Metzger, *The Text of the New Testament* (Oxford: Clarendon, 1964); Kurt Aland, *Kurzgefaßte Liste der griechischen Handschriften des Neuen Testaments* (ANTF 1; Berlin: De Gruyter, 1963); Nestle-Aland, *NT Graece*, 684–716.

The oldest of the manuscripts transmitting all four gospels in one single codex[1] is the New Testament Papyrus p^{45},[2] written in the beginning or the middle of the 3d century CE. However, this manuscript is very fragmentary. Only chapters 20, 21, 25–26 of the Gospel of Matthew, chapters 4–13 of the Gospel of Mark, chapters 6–13 of the Gospel of Luke, and chapter 10 of the Gospel of John have been preserved. The complete text of all four Gospels of the New Testament occurs for the first time in the two oldest manuscripts which comprise the entire text of the Greek Bible: Codex Sinaiticus (‭א‬/01)[3] and Codex Vaticanus (B/03); both are uncial codices written in the middle of the 4th century CE. From the 5th century, four such codices with the text of all four gospels are preserved: Codex Alexandrinus (A/02) Codex Claromontanus (C/04), Codex Bezae Cantabrigiensis (D/05),[4] and Codex Washingtonianus (W/032).[5] A larger number of uncial manuscripts with the text of all four gospels date from the 6th,[6] 8th,[7] 9th,[8] and 10th[9] centuries. From the 9th and the following centuries an extremely large number of minuscule manuscripts with the text of the

[1] It also included the Acts of the Apostles.

[2] The major part of this manuscript is the *Chester-Beatty Papyrus I*; a small section, containing Matt 25:41–26:39, is preserved as *Pap. Graec. 31974* of the Österreichische Nationalbibliothek in Vienna. The papyrus was first published in 1933; see Metzger, *Text*, 251–52; Kurt Aland, *Repetitorium der griechischen christlichen Papyri I: Biblische Papyri* (PTS 18; Berlin: De Gruyter, 1976) 269–72.

[3] The custom to designate the uncial manuscripts of the NT with capital letters began with Wettstein's edition of 1751–52. As more and more uncial manuscript became known, Greek capital letters were also used and, in one instance—Codex Sinaiticus—a Hebrew letter was introduced. In the year 1908, Caspar René Gregory devised a new system which is now generally recognized. In this system, uncials are designated by Arabic numbers beginning with the numeral 0 (though the older designations with a capital letter are still used together with the number for the first 45 manuscripts of the list), minuscules are designated with regular numbers (not beginning with 0), lectionaries with the letter "l" followed by a number. See Kurt Aland, *Der Text des Neuen Testaments* (Stuttgart: Deutsche Bibelstiftung, 1982) 82–84.

[4] This codex, already known at the time of the Reformation, is a bilingual, containing both the Greek text and—on facing pages—the text of the Old Latin translation.

[5] This is the only major four-gospel manuscript now kept in the United States: Washington, DC, Smithsonian Institution/Freer Gallery of Art # 06.274. It has become famous because it is the only known manuscript which presents an expansion of the secondary ending of the Gospel of Mark (16:9–20) after Mark 16:14, the so-called Freer Logion.

[6] N/022, O/023, 087. Here and in the following notes, I am listing only those manuscripts which are regularly used in Nestle-Aland, *NT Graece*.

[7] E/07, L/019, Y/044, 047, 0233, 0250.

[8] F/09, G/011, H/013, K/017, M/021, U/030, V/031, X/033, Δ/037, Θ/038, Π/041, Ω/045, 0133, 0135.

[9] S/21, Γ/036, 0141.

four Gospels of the New Testament are preserved—several thousand are recorded— as well as many gospel lectionaries, i.e., manuscripts which contain only the pericopes for the gospel readings of the ecclesiastical year.[1]

3.3.2 THE TRANSLATIONS

Additional witnesses for the text of the canonical gospels are translations into other ancient languages. The oldest of these are the Old Latin translation from the end of the 2d century,[2] the Syriac translation from the 3d century,[3] and the Coptic translations of which the oldest, the translation into the Sahidic dialect, also dates from the 3d century.[4]

3.3.3 TRANSMISSION AND ATTESTATION OF THE FOUR-GOSPEL CANON

Evidence for the transmission of the four-gospel canon in one single codex appears for the first time in the middle of the 3d century. In the earliest period of the transmission of the canonical gospels their text circulated in manuscripts which contained only the text of one gospel or, in some instances, of two gospels.[5] Some of these manuscripts of individual gospels are the oldest extant witnesses of Christian writings. The custom to copy only one individual gospel continued into the later period. However, it is often not possible to determine whether a fragment with the text of only one gospel comes from a codex containing all four gospels or even the entire New Testament.

It had long been assumed that the oldest witnesses to the four-gospel canon were the *Muratorian Canon* and the *Anti-Marcionite Gospel Prologues*. The *Muratorian Canon*,[6] a list of the canonical books translated from a Greek original into a rather clumsy Latin,[7] is

---

[1] On the text of the Synoptic Gospels in the new (26th) edition of Nestle-Aland see Neirynck, "The Synoptic Gospels according to the New Textus Receptus," in idem, *Evangelica,* 883–98.

[2] On the Old Latin translation, also called *Vetus Latina,* see Metzger, *Text,* 72–79.

[3] Although the Syrian church generally used the four-gospel harmony of Tatian (the *Diatessaron*), an old translation of the four separate gospels has been preserved in two manuscripts (sy^c and sy^s). On the old Syriac translation see Metzger, *Text,* 68–71.

[4] On the several translations into Coptic dialects see Metzger, *Text,* 79–81.

[5] These manuscripts will be discussed later in the individual treatment of the canonical gospels.

[6] Latin Text in Aland, *Synopsis,* 538; English translation in Hennecke-Schneemelcher-Wilson, *NT Apocrypha,* 1. 42–45; see also Lee Martin McDonald, *The Formation of the Christian Biblical Canon* (Nashville: Abingdon, 1988) 135–37.

[7] This has been disputed; but see von Campenhausen, *Formation,* 245.

still widely believed to have been composed in Rome or Italy before the end of the 2d century.[1] It is fragmentary at the beginning: the mention of the Gospels of Matthew and Mark is not preserved. But the Gospel of Luke is discussed as "the third Gospel book," the Gospel of John follows as the fourth. If the early date of this canon list were established, its information about the four-gospel canon and the authors of two of these gospels would indeed be very valuable. However, serious doubts with respect to a 2d-century date have been raised by Albert Sundberg.[2] It is, therefore, difficult to maintain this date; the document is more likely to have been composed in the Eastern Church after the middle of the 4th century. *as a Greek*

Also with respect to the so-called *Anti-Marcionite Gospel Prologues* [3] serious questions have been raised concerning an early date.[4] These *Prologues*, originally composed in Greek, appear in several dozen Latin Bible manuscripts. Only *Prologues* for Mark, Luke, and John are extant; the *Prologue* for Luke is also preserved in Greek. It is very doubtful whether these *Prologues* can be considered as a unit. They may have been composed separately, and it is not possible to assign the same date to all three *Prologues*. While a date in the second half of *3 40* the 4th century is likely for the *Prologues* for Mark and John and the second part of the *Prologue* for Luke, the first part of the latter may have been written much earlier.[5]

Therefore, the earliest witness for the four canonical gospels as a unit remains Irenaeus, ca. 180–200:

> Matthew brought forth a written gospel among the Hebrews in their own language, while Peter and Paul in Rome were preaching the gospel and founding the church. But after their death Mark, the disciple and inter-

---

[1] Von Campenhausen, *Formation*, 243–46.

[2] "Canon Muratori: A Fourth-Century List," *HTR* 66 (1973) 1–41; see also idem, "Canon of the NT," *IDBSup* 136–40. More recently, Sundberg's arguments have been accepted and cogently supported by McDonald, *Formation*, 135–39.

[3] Critical edition: Dom Donatien De Bruyne, "Les plus anciens prologues latins des évangiles," *Revue Bénédictine* 40 (1928) 193–214. Texts in Albert Huck, *Synopse der drei ersten Evangelien* (9th ed. by Hans Lietzmann; Tübingen: Mohr/Siebeck, 1936) p. VII; Aland, *Synopsis Quattuor Evangeliorum*, 532–33.

[4] It had been widely assumed that these Prologues to the Gospels were written between 160 and 180 CE. On the problems of their interpretation and dating see J. Regul, *Die antimarcionitischen Evangelienprologe* (Vetus Latina: Die Reste der altlateinischen Bibel; Aus der Geschichte der lateinischen Bibel 6; Freiburg: Herder, 1969). Regul argues for a 4th-century date for these *Prologues*.

[5] See R. G. Heard, "The Old Gospel Prologues," *JTS* n.s. 6 (1955) 1–16. Heard argues against De Bruyne's widely accepted view (see the literature cited ibidem, p. 1, n. 1) that the Prologues were composed as a single unit. About the Lukan Prologue, see below, # 4.4.2.

preter of Peter, also himself transmitted to us in writing the things which were preached by Peter; Luke also, the follower of Paul, set down in a book the gospel which was preached by Paul. Thereafter John, the disciple of the Lord who had even rested his head on his breast, gave forth the gospel while he was staying at Ephesus.[1]

This tradition about the origin of the four canonical gospels appears, with some variations, in other Church Fathers.[2] It was a firmly established and widely used tradition by the end of the 2d century.

3.4 The Story of the Johannine Gospel [3]

3.4.1 THE TRANSMISSION

The oldest fragment of a gospel manuscript that has come to light is a small piece of a papyrus containing a few verses of the Gospel of John (18:31–33, 37–38), the New Testament $\mathfrak{p}^{52}$.[4] It was written in the first half of the 2d century and is, with the possible exception of a fragment of an extracanonical gospel (*Papyrus Egerton* 2)[5] the oldest fragment of any Christian writing that has been found to date. But it is probably not surprising that the Gospel of John is attested in Egypt at such an early date. There are more papyrological witnesses to the use of this Gospel which have come from the Egyptian deserts. $\mathfrak{p}^{66}$, written ca. 200 CE,[6] contains almost the entire text of John's Gospel.

---

[1] *Adv. haer.* 3.1.1 in Eusebius *Hist. eccl.* 5.8.2–4. Further references of Irenaeus to the four canonical gospels have been collected by Aland, *Synopsis,* 534–38.

[2] Clement of Alexandria in Eusebius *Hist. eccl.* 6.14.5–7; Origen in Eusebius *Hist. eccl.* 6.25.3–6; 6.15.1–2. For the text of these references and quotations of the relevant passages see Aland, *Synopsis,* 539–48.

[3] For a general review of recent scholarship on John see Robert Kysar, "The Fourth Gospel: A Report on Recent Research," *ANRW* 2.25/3 (1985) 2389–2480. The question of the literary genre in the scholarly debate has been reviewed by Johannes Beutler, "Literarische Gattungen im Johannesevangelium: Ein Forschungsbericht 1919–1980," *ANRW* 2.25/3 (1985) 2506–68. A representative collection of essays was published by Karl Heinrich Rengstorf, *Johannes und sein Evangelium* (WdF 82; Darmstadt: Wissenschaftliche Buchgesellschaft, 1973). Some important monographs are C. H. Dodd, *The Interpretation of the Fourth Gospel* (Cambidge: Cambridge University Press, 1953); Robert T. Fortna, *The Fourth Gospel and its Predecessor: From Narrative to Present Gospel* (Philadelphia: Fortress, 1988). Major Commentaries: Bultmann, *Gospel of John*; C. K. Barrett, *The Gospel according to St John* (London: S.P.C.K., 1958); Richard Schnackenburg, *The Gospel according to John* ((Herder's Theological Commentary on the NT; New York: Herder, 1968 and following years); Brown, *Gospel of John.*

[4] John Rylands Library, Manchester, *Pap. Graec. 457*; cf. Aland, *Repetitorium,* 286.

[5] See above, # 3.2.2.

[6] Cologny, Bibliotheca Bodmeriana, *Pap. Bodmer II*; cf. Aland, *Repetitorium,* 296–98.

p^{75} from the 3d century[1] preserves large portion of John 1–15,[2] and five other papyri from the same century are smaller fragments from manuscripts of the same Gospel.[3] Since all papyri of the New Testament from this early period have been found in Egypt, it is impossible to draw conclusions from such finds with respect to the usage and distribution of the Gospel of John in general; but there can be little doubt that this Gospel was widely known in Egypt at a very early time.[4]

However, it is very unlikely that it was written in that country; the close relationship of John's Gospel to syncretistic Judaism and to the Gnosticizing interpretation of the sayings of Jesus (see below), the ties of the Gospel with Palestinian geography (Samaria, Jordan), and the history-of-religions milieu in general point to a Syro-Palestinian origin.[5]

3.4.2 EXTERNAL ATTESTATION

The early distribution and usage of the Gospel of John in Egypt is confirmed by external evidence. Several Gnostic writings from Egypt used it,[6] and the first commentaries ever written on any gospel are

---

[1] Cologny, Bibliotheca Bodmeriana, *Pap. Bodmer XIV and XV*; cf. Aland, *Repetitorium,* 309–11.

[2] This same Papyrus also contains portions of the Gospel of Luke; see below # 4.4.1.

[3] p^5 (vss. from chaps. 1, 16, and 20), p^{22} (John 15:25–16:2; 16:21–32), p^{28} (John 6:8–12, 17–22), p^{39} (John 8:14–21), p^{80} (John 3:34).

[4] The later attestation for the text of this Gospel from Egypt is also very rich: one papyrus from the 4th century (p^6, fragments from John 10–13 in Greek and in Coptic), nine papyri from later centuries, and a total of about 30 uncial manuscripts on parchment which contain at least portions of the Fourth Gospel; the oldest of these (0162, containing John 2:11–22) was written in the 3d or 4th century.

[5] The evidence of papyrus finds should not be overestimated in the determination of the country of origin of a particular writing, since only the climatic conditions of Egypt permitted the survival of manuscripts from this early period. Scholars are divided with respect to the origin of John's Gospel. Some argue for Syrian origin (cf. Vielhauer, *Geschichte,* 445–60), others defend the ecclesiastical tradition about the disciple John of Ephesus as the author of this gospel (cf. Brown, *John,* pp. ciii-iv). On the problem concerning this ecclesiastical tradition see below.

[6] E.g., the Valentinian texts cited in Clement of Alexandria *Excerpta ex Theodotou* (Greek text in Walther Völker, *Quellen zur Geschichte der christlichen Gnosis* [SAQ 5; Tübingen: Mohr/Siebeck, 1932] 63–86; English translation in Werner Foerster, *Gnosis,* 1.222–33) and the Naassene Fragment quoted by Hippolytus *Ref.* 5.7.2–9 (Greek Text in Völker, *Quellen,* 11–26). Cf. W. von Loewenich, *Das Johannesverständnis im zweiten Jahrhundert* (BZNW 13; Gießen: Töpelmann, 1932). Some of the earlier writings from Nag Hammadi also display usage of the Fourth Gospel, e.g., the *Gospel of Philip* (NHC II,3), cf. Jacques E. Ménard, *L'Evangile selon Philip* (Paris: Letouzey & Ané, 1967)29–32; the *Testimony of Truth* (NHC IX,3), cf. Birger Pearson, *Nag Hammadi Codices IX and X* (NHS 15; Leiden: Brill, 1981) 112 and notes to the translation. In other instances, dependence upon the Gospel of John is not clear (*Gospel of Truth*) or

commentaries on the Gospel of John which derive from Egypt.[1] On the other hand, John's Gospel is not well known elsewhere. Ignatius of Antioch, although his theological language is closely related to that of John, does not seem to know this writing.[2] Nor is the Gospel of John known in Asia Minor before the middle of the 2d century: Polycarp of Smyrna, Papias of Hierapolis, and the Pastoral Epistles (written in Ephesus after the year 100) never refer to it. In Rome, neither 1 Peter nor *1 Clement* nor Justin Martyr reveal any knowledge of the Fourth Gospel. However, later in the 2d century, this Gospel begins to be used also in Asia Minor and Rome. Justin's student Tatian includes it in his four-gospel harmony, the *Diatessaron*; Irenaeus knows a tradition about the disciple John, a tradition according to which this disciple became established in Ephesus;[3] and the Montanist movement, which arose in Phrygia of Asia Minor after the middle of the 2d century, understands its prophecy as the return of the Johannine Paraclete.[4]

3.4.3 INTEGRITY OF THE TEXT

It does not appear that the text of the Gospel of John as it is extant in the oldest manuscripts has preserved the text of the autograph without changes. John 21, though belonging to the older stages of the transmission of the text, is certainly a later appendix.[5] After the story of Jesus' appearance before the disciples and Jesus' word to Thomas

---

unlikely (*Apocryphon of James, Dialogue of the Savior, Gospel of Thomas*; see the chapters on these writings).

[1] A Valentinian Exposition to the Prologue of the Gospel of John (Irenaeus *Adv. haer.* 1.8.5–6; Greek text in Völker, *Quellen*, 93–95; English translation in Foerster, *Gnosis*, 1.144–45); the commentary of Heracleon on the Gospel of John (Origen *Comm. in Joh.*, passim; Greek Texts in Völker, *Quellen*, 63–86; English translation in Foerster, *Gnosis*, 1.162–83). See Elaine H. Pagels, *The Johannine Gospel in Gnostic Exegesis: Heracleon's Commentary on John* (SBLMS 17; Nashville: Abingdon 1973).

[2] Henning Paulsen, *Studien zur Theologie des Ignatius von Antiochien* (FKDG 29; Göttingen: Vandenhoeck & Ruprecht, 1978) 36–37; Schoedel, *Ignatius*, 9.

[3] Irenaeus, the bishop of Lyon (ca. 180 CE) who came from Asia Minor, is the first author who ascribes this Gospel to "John the disciple of the Lord . . . when he was living in Ephesus" (*Adv. haer.* 3.11 = Eusebius *Hist. eccl.* 5.8.4). Older traditions also know of a presbyter (elder) John of Ephesus who may have been the author of the Book of Revelation. The best discussion of this question can be found in Vielhauer, *Geschichte*, 456–60.

[4] Materials and discussions in Adolf Hilgenfeld, *Die Ketzergeschichte des Urchristentums* (Leipzig, 1884; reprint Darmstadt: Wissenschaftliche Buchgesellschaft, 1966) 560–601. On the question of the Montanists' reliance on the Fourth Gospel see ibid., 563–64, 599–601.

[5] See the discussion in Brown, *Gospel of John*, 2.1077–85; literature on this question ibid., pp. 1143–44.

("Blessed are those who have not seen and yet believe," 20:29), John 20:30–31 gives the proper original conclusion of the gospel:[1]

> Now Jesus did many other signs in the presence of his disciples which are not written in this book; but these are written that you may believe that Jesus is the Christ, the Son of God, and that believing you may have life in his name.

John 21 adds the story of an appearance of Jesus before his disciples at the lake (21:1–14) of which at least the beginning is independently transmitted in the *Gospel of Peter*.[2] This story serves to introduce a discussion about the relationship of the tradition of the Johannine church to the authority of Peter. The leading authority for the church of the tradition under the name of Peter is confirmed through the threefold question of Jesus, "Simon, do you love me?" and the following requests, "Feed my sheep!" (21:15–17). But what about the authority of the Johannine tradition? It is represented by the "disciple whom Jesus loved," who also follows Jesus and about whom Peter asks, "Lord, what about this man?" (21:20–21) Jesus' mysterious answer, "If it is my will that he remain until I come, what is that to you?" confirms the right of the special tradition of the Beloved Disciple. It does not mean that he will not die; this is explicitly rejected (21:22–23). It means that the Johannine tradition, and specifically this written Gospel, has lasting validity.[3] That is said explicitly when the allegorical framework is finally discarded in the statement of John 21:24:

> This is the disciple who is bearing witness to these things, and who has written these things; and we know that his testimony is true.

John 20:25, once more referring to the many other things which Jesus did but could not be written in this book, imitates the original conclusion of the Gospel.

The redactor who added chapter 21 may also have been responsible for some minor additions in the text of chapters 1–20. One of these redactional passages is apparently John 6:51b–59.[4] The original

---

[1] Because it speaks of the "signs" (σημεῖα) that Jesus did, this conclusion may already have served as the ending of the Source of Signs (Semeia Source) from which John drew his miracle stories; see below # 3.4.4.1, and above # 3.2.1.

[2] See above, # 3.2.3.3.

[3] This juxtaposition of Peter and the Beloved Disciple is comparable to the one of James and Thomas in *Gos. Thom.* 12–13.

[4] Most convincing arguments for the secondary character of this disputed passage have been brought forward by Günther Bornkamm, "Die eucharistische Rede im Johannesevangelium," *ZNW* 47 (1956) 161–69. For an assessment of the discussion about these verses and bibliography see Brown, *Gospel of John*, 1. 281–94, 303–4.

discourse on the bread that has come down from heaven ended in John 6:51a with Jesus' statement, "I am the living bread which came down from heaven; those who eat of this bread will live forever." The continuation of this claim follows in John 6:60–62: the disciples find this a "hard saying," to which Jesus responds, "Then what if you were to see the Son of man ascending where he was before?" The "hard saying," thus, is Jesus' claim that he has come down from heaven, but not the content of the interpolated verses which emphasize the physical eating of Jesus' flesh and the drinking of his blood. The interpolation was made in order to emphasize the sacramental eating and drinking of Jesus' flesh and blood.

The verses John 5:27b–29; 6:39b, 40b, 44b, which present a realistic view of the resurrection on the last day, also belong to these redactional passages.[1] John 5:24–27a has stated unequivocally that those who believe in Jesus have eternal life and will not come into the judgment, and that now is the hour "that the dead will hear the voice of the Son of God, and those who hear will live." John 5:28–29 qualifies this statement through the introduction of a more traditional view of eschatology:[2]

> Do not marvel at this. For the hour is coming when all who are in the tombs will hear his voice and come forth, those who have done good, to the resurrection of life, and those who have done evil, to the resurrection of judgment.

The brief clause, "but I shall raise him on the last day," interpolated in John 6:39, 40, and 44, reveals the same traditional eschatological orientation.

That the pericope about Jesus and the adulteress, John 7:53– 8:11, did not belong to the early text of the Gospel of John is clearly shown by the manuscript tradition: it is missing in the older papyri (p^{66} and p^{75}) and in the oldest uncial codices (א, B, A) as well as in the oldest translations (sy^{s,c}, sa),[3] and appears for the first time in the 5th-century, Greek-Latin bilingual Codex D, and subsequently in most of the later manuscripts and the younger translations.[4]

---

[1] Bultmann, *Gospel of John,* 261.

[2] 5:27b, "because he is Son of man" (ὅτι υἱὸς ἀνθρώπου ἐστίν) is odd in this context. Elsewhere John always uses articles with this title. Moreover, the authority to give life and to judge was just assigned to Jesus as the Son of God. "Son of man," however, occurs in the Synoptic Gospels as the typical title for the one who is coming on the clouds for the final judgment; cf. Mark 13:26; 14:62; Luke 17:22–24.

[3] For the discussion of the manuscript evidence for this pericope see Bruce Metzger, *A Textual Commentary on the Greek New Testament* (New York: United Bible Society, 1971) 219–22; Brown, *Gospel of John,* 1. 332–38.

[4] Several later manuscripts place this pericope into the Gospel of Luke after Luke

Another aspect of the question of the integrity of the extant text of this Gospel concerns the order of its chapters and sections. Major disorder exists in two instances. The first concerns the sequence of chapters 4–7. At the end of chapter 4, Jesus is in Galilee, at the beginning of chapter 5 he goes to Jerusalem, chapter 6:1 says, "And after this Jesus went to the other side of the Sea of Galilee," and 7:1 reports that Jesus left Jerusalem and went about in Galilee, because the Jews were seeking to kill him. Moreover, John 7 continues the discussion of the theme of judgment which had been initiated in chapter 5. If the order were chapters 4, 6, 5, 7, all these difficulties would be removed.[1]

The second major disorder is apparent in John 14:30–31. At the conclusion of this first part of the farewell discourses Jesus says:

> I will no longer talk much with you, for the ruler of this world is coming. He has no power over me, but I do as the Father has commanded me, so that the world may know that I love the Father. Rise, let us go hence.

But it is only in 18:1 that this command is followed by an appropriate action:

> When Jesus had spoken these words, he went forth with his disciples across the Kidron valley where there was a garden, . . .

In spite of the clear "Rise, let us go hence" in John 14:31, chapters 15–17 continue the farewell discourses. It has been suggested that chapters 15–17 are a later interpolation. But in language, style, and content these three chapters belong with 13–14. It is clear, therefore, that they are not in the right place. Chapters 15–16 may have followed John 13:34–35, because 15:1–17 is a commentary on the commandment to love each other, and 13:36–38 seems a good continuation of 16:31.[2] This leaves John 17, the fare-well prayer of Jesus. No satisfactory solution has been found for the placement of this chapter.[3] That John 17 was added after the displacement of chapters 15–16 had already occurred, is also possible because chapter 17 is characterized by a theological interpretation of Jesus' departure that differs markedly from the farewell discourses in chapters 13–16; its orientation is more explicitly Gnostic.

21:38; see Metzger, *Textual Commentary*, 173.

[1] See Bultmann, *Gospel of John*, 209–10, following older suggestions. More recent commentators are hesitant to engage in such reordering of the chapters.

[2] Bultmann, *Gospel of John*, 459–60.

[3] Bultmann (*Gospel of John*, 460–61) suggests to place it after 13:31a, i.e., after the designation and departure of Judas and before the statement "Now is the Son of man glorified."

Rudolf Bultmann, in his landmark commentary on the Gospel of John, suggested in numerous instances the relocation of smaller units, often consisting of just a few verses.[1] The result is convincing insofar as it establishes several discourses which make much more sense than some of these chapters of the Gospel in their extant form, especially regarding chapters 7–8, 10, and 12. However, it is extremely difficult to explain what caused the disorder of the extant text. The relocation of major sections can be justified by assuming that pages in a papyrus codex became displaced. But the reconstitution of the original by relocating both some large and many very small units requires the analogy of an ancient piece of pottery that broke into several larger and many smaller pieces—unfortunately an analogy which does not fit the material transmission of ancient literature.

3.4.4 SOURCES AND COMPOSITION

3.4.4.1 The Problem of the Sources of John

The question of the sources used by the author of the Fourth Gospel is debated, but written sources were no doubt used. Various theories have been proposed.[2] The text of the Gospel shows a number of seams at which the author inserted new materials or his own comments into an older document; in many instances, it is evident that the author is adding secondary interpretations to older written or oral materials.[3] But the style of the writing is uniform throughout (even including the secondary appendix chapter 21) so that it is very difficult to determine the exact extent of the source in each single instance. Moreover, it is not possible to understand this work as the product of a single author who artfully brought together several sources, composing them into a new literary work. Whatever older written documents served as sources for this composition had already gone through a process of interpretation and commentary in the preaching, liturgy, teaching, and internal debates of the Johannine community—a process that must have been part of the community's life over a period of several

---

[1] E.g., for a chapter which he entitles "The Light of the World" he reconstructs the following original order: John 9:1–41; 8:12; 12:44–50; 8:21–29; 12:34–36; 10:19–21.

[2] Cf. the discussion and literature in Brown, *Gospel of John*, 1. pp. xxiv-xl. The most influential source hypothesis was proposed by Bultmann, *Gospel of John*. An extensive evaluation of this hypothesis has been presented by Dwight Moody Smith, *The Composition and Order of the Fourth Gospel* (New Haven: Yale University Press 1965); cf. also idem, "The Sources of the Gospel of John: an Assessment of the Present State of the Problem," *NTS* 10 (1963/64) 336–51.

[3] James M. Robinson, "The Johannine Trajectory," in Robinson-Koester, *Trajectories*, 232–68.

decades, probably of more than half a century. Several layers of interpretation that reflect the history of this community and the development of its theology had already been added to the more original materials when the author of the Gospel began to collect them in order to compose the document that we now call the Gospel of John. Moreover, the author of the Fourth Gospel is not likely to have been a stranger to the Johannine community; he must have participated himself in the effort of interpreting and shaping older traditions, ordering the community's life, and debating opponents within and without its circles. Nowhere are we told that the author produced his work in one piece in a brief period. Several earlier drafts of parts of the work may have been written and may have been used in the ongoing life of the community before the work finally reached the form in which it is preserved by the oldest manuscripts.[1]

In spite of the problems which are encountered in the attempt to define sharply the sources used in the work and distinguish them from the author's redaction, one can still point to several types of sources or traditions that provided the materials for the composition.

3.4.4.2 The Semeia Source

The character of the miracle stories used in the Gospel of John and the very fact that the miracles were apparently numbered in a way that does not always agree with the actual sequence of their occurrence in the work leaves no doubt that they were derived from a written source. This has been discussed above.[2] What is of interest here is the use of this source by the author of the Gospel. The Semeia Source was not just a random collection of sundry miracle stories, but a composition that had a message: Jesus is the divine man who strides upon the face of the earth displaying supernatural power, beginning with the miraculous change of water into wine like the god Dionysus (John 2:1–11) and ending his mission by raising the dead (John 11). The author of the Fourth Gospel has adopted this source as the basis of the first half of his writing, John 2–11, the "Book of Signs," as it has been called.

Two contradictory elements characterize the use of the Semeia Source, as it has been incorporated into the Gospel: on the one hand, nothing is taken away from the powerful effect of the miracles. On the other hand, it is repeatedly emphasized that belief in the miracles is not only insufficient; it falsifies what true belief in Jesus ought to be.

---

[1] See the theory adopted by Brown, *Gospel of John*, 1. pp. xxxiv-xxxix.
[2] See # 3.2.1.

Repeated references to the problem of the belief propagated by the Semeia Source accompany the reproduction of its stories:

At the end of the wine miracle at Cana:
This is the first of his signs Jesus did at Cana in Galilee, and manifested his glory; and his disciples believed in him. (2:11)

When Jesus thereafter appeared in Jerusalem:
Many believed (ἐπίστευσαν) in his name when they saw the signs which he did; but Jesus did not entrust himself (οὐκ ἐπίστευεν ἑαυτόν[1]) to them. (2:23–24)

In answer to the royal official whose son was ill:
"Unless you see signs and wonders (σημεῖα καὶ τέρατα) you do not believe (οὐ μὴ πιστεύσητε)." (4:48)

After the miracle of the feeding of the multitudes:
When the people saw the sign which he had done, they said, "This is indeed the prophet who has come into the world." Perceiving then that they were about to come and take him by force to make him king, Jesus withdrew again to the hills by himself. (6:14–15)

After the trials of the man who was blind, when Jesus finds him, he said, "Do you believe in the Son of man?" He answered, "Sir, who is he that I may believe in him?" Jesus said to him, "You have seen him, and it is he who speaks to you." He said, "Lord, I believe." (9:35–38)

All of these comments are due to the redactional work of the author of the gospel. Miracles call forth belief in Jesus, among the disciples, in the man who was blind, among the people. But that Jesus does not "entrust himself" to this belief, that he escapes from those who want to make him king, is confirmed in the description of the effect of the greatest miracle, the raising of Lazarus.

After the raising of Lazarus:
Many of the Jews, therefore, who had come with Mary and had seen what he did, believed in him ... So the chief priests and the Pharisees gathered the council and said, "What are we to do, for this man performs many signs. If we let him go, every one will believe in him, ..." But Caiaphas ... said, "You know nothing at all; you do not understand that it is expedient for you that one man should die for the people...." (11:45–50)

Many of the people now believe in Jesus, but the Jerusalem authori-

---

[1] The reading ἑαυτόν is found in p[66] and in the majority of manuscripts. But the alternate reading αὐτόν (ℵ A B L) can also be read as αὑτόν = "himself."

ties decide that this is cause enough to put Jesus to death. That Jesus is a divine man who displays his miraculous powers is the cause of his condemnation.

This interpretation of the Semeia Source goes hand in hand with another use of its materials: they become the basis of, and provide the topics for, the composition of some of the discourses and dialogues of the Fourth Gospel. The materials for these discourses, however, were prepared by a different type of source materials from the Johannine tradition. This will be discussed below. There is another narrative source which has been used by the author, namely, the passion narrative.

3.4.4.3 The Passion Narrative

The similarities of the Johannine and the Markan passion narratives suggest that the author of the Fourth Gospel used a written narrative source also for the second part of his writing. This assumption is confirmed by several agreements between John and the *Gospel of Peter,* the third independent witness of this passion narrative and its development on the basis of scriptural exegesis.[1]

Pericope	John	Other gospels
Conspiracy of the hierarchs	11:45–53	Mark 14:1–2 parr.
Anointing at Bethany	12:1–8	Mark 14:3–9; Matt 26:6–13
Entry into Jerusalem	12:9–19	Mark 11: 1–10 parr.
Betrayal of Judas		Mark 14:10–11 parr.
Preparation for Passover		Mark 14:12–16 parr.
Last Supper	13:1–2	Mark 14:17 parr.
Words of Institution		Mark 14:22–25 parr.
Foot Washing	13:3–11	
Designation of the traitor	13:18–30	Mark 14:18–21 parr.
Prediction of Peter's denial	13:36–38	Mark 14:26–31 parr.
Christ in Gethsemane	(18:1)	Mark 14:32–42 parr.
Jesus' arrest	18:2–12	Mark 14:43–52 parr.
Jesus before the synedrion	18:13–24	Mark 14:53–65 parr.
Denial of Peter	18:15–27	Mark 14:66–72 parr.
Mocking before the synedrion		Mark 14:65 parr.
Jesus brought before Pilate	18:28–32	Mark 15:1 parr.
The end of Judas		Matt 27:3–10
Trial before Pilate	18:33–38	Mark 15:2–5
Jesus before Herod		Luke 23:6–16
Jesus or Barabbas	18:39–40	Mark 15:6–15a parr.
Pilate's wife & handwashing		Matt 27:19, 24–25

---

[1] See above, # 3.2.3.2.

Jesus scourged	19:1	Mark 15:15b parr.
Mocking by the soldiers	19:2–3	Mark 15:16–20; Matt 27:27–31
Trial before Pilate continued	19:4–16	
Simon of Cyrene crossbearer		Mark 15:21 parr.
Woe to women of Jerusalem		Luke 23:27–32
Crucifixion	19:17–22	Mark 15:22–24a, 25–27
Dividing of the garment	19:23–24	Mark 15:24b parr.
Mocking of the Crucified		Mark 15:29–32 parr.
Jesus and the two criminals		Luke 23:39–43
Women at the cross	19:25–27	(Mark 15:40–41 parr)
Vinegar for a drink	19:28–29	Mark 15:34–36 parr.
Jesus' death	19:30	Mark 15:37 parr.
Prodigies at the death		Mark 15:38 parr.
The tombs of Saints open		Matt 27:51–53
Soldier pierces Jesus' corpse	19:31–37	
Burial of Jesus	19:38–42	Mark 15:42–47 parr.
Discovery of the empty tomb	20:1–10	Mark 16:1–8 parr.

The passion narrative source of John began, like Mark's source, with the stories of the anointing of Jesus in Bethany, John 12:1–8, and of the entry into Jerusalem, John 12:9–19,[1] and it ended with the story of the discovery of the empty tomb, John 20:1–10. As the table shows, almost all pericopes appear in the same order in which they are preserved in Mark. But dependence of John upon Mark or any of the other Synoptic Gospels is not possible for the following reasons: (1) Nowhere does John reveal a knowledge of the vocabulary and style of Mark.[2] (2) Markan expansions of his passion narrative source have no parallels in John: the preparation for the Passover (Mark 14:13–16), clearly a secondary expansion which upsets the original passion chronology; the mocking before the synedrion (Mark 14:65), a secondary variant of the scene of the mocking by the soldiers; the novelistic expansion of the Barabbas incident (Mark 15:6–15a); the episode of Simon of Cyrene who is forced to bear the cross (Mark 15:21); the mocking of the crucified Jesus (Mark 15:29–32). There are

[1] The sequence of the two stories is reversed in the Gospel of Mark. John may have preserved the original order. It would be natural that Jesus went to Bethany before entering Jerusalem. Mark had an obvious interest in using the story of the entry into Jerusalem first, in order to introduce the Jerusalem ministry of Jesus; he also wanted to tie the story of Jesus' anointing more closely with the death and burial of Jesus (cf. Mark 14:8 which has no parallel in the Johannine account).

[2] There may be a few phrases which have been added to the text of John through marginal glosses at a later date. This is most obvious with respect to the sentence, "The poor you have always with you, but you do not have always me" (John 12:8 = Matt 26:11 [Mark 14:7]). The sentence is missing in several witnesses (D sy^s) of the text of John; cf. Bultmann, *Gospel of John*, 415–16.

no parallels to any of these secondary features of Mark in the *Gospel of Peter* either. (3) There is no trace in John of any of Matthew's and Luke's additions to the Markan passion narrative (see the table above). (4) John's chronology of the last meal and the death of Jesus agrees with the chronology of Mark's source and with that of the *Gospel of Peter*. According to John 18:28 and 19:14 Jesus was crucified on the Day of Preparation, that is, in the afternoon before the First Day of Passover, which began in the evening after sunset with the eating of the Passover lamb.[1] Mark 14:1 actually presupposes the same chronology: "It was now *two* days before the Passover and the Feast of the Unleavened Bread."[2] But the interpolated story of the preparation for the Passover Meal (Mark 14:12–16) confuses this chronology. John has preserved the more original and historically accurate date.[3]

There are, on the other hand, numerous secondary features in the Johannine passion narrative. In the last meal of Jesus with his disciples (John 13:1–30; cf. Mark 14:17–25), John does not describe this meal as the institution of the Lord's Supper. At this point, John leaves the passion narrative source and inserts the farewell discourses of Jesus (John 13–17). The narrative of the source is resumed in John 18:1 with the arrest of Jesus (cf. Mark 14:43–52) and continues in the trial of Jesus before the synedrion, the betrayal of Peter, the trial before Pilate (including the Barabbas scene), the mocking by the soldiers, crucifixion, dividing of the garment, inscription on the cross, drinking of vinegar, Jesus' death and burial, and the discovery of the empty tomb. All of these are paralleled in Mark 15–16. But rarely does John follow his source verbatim. The most remarkable expansion appears in the trial before Pilate which John has rewritten in the form of various dialogues between Jesus and Pilate, and between Pilate and the accusers and the people.

The stories of the appearances of Jesus after his resurrection (John 20:11–29) have no parallels in Mark or in the other gospels;[4] they belong to the special traditions of the Johannine community.[5]

---

[1] See Bultmann, *Gospel of John*, 651.

[2] The hierarchs conspire to have Jesus executed *before* the feast in order to avoid a a tumult among the people (Mark 14:2).

[3] John is also interested in the implied symbolism: Jesus dies at the hour at which the Passover lambs are slaughtered. See Bultmann, *Gospel of John*, 664. But that does not prove that he invented that dating.

[4] The only exception is the story of Jesus' appearance at the lake in the supplement chap. 21 which is paralleled in the *Gospel of Peter*; see above, # 3.2.3.3.

[5] The remarkable differences between the stories of Jesus' appearances after the resurrection in all four canonical gospels make it certain that the passion narrative employed by John and Mark did not include any of these stories, but ended with the account of the finding of the empty tomb. Cf. Bultmann, *Synoptic Tradition*, 288–91.

3.4.4.4 Dialogue Sources

In the employment of the Semeia Source and of the Passion Narrative Source the Gospel of John shares important traditional materials with the three other Gospels of the New Testament. But the large sections of the Fourth Gospel which consist of extensive discourses of Jesus and dialogues with his disciples have no parallels in the three other Gospels of the canon. Even the major complexes of speeches of Jesus in the Gospel of Matthew (e.g., the Sermon on the Mount, Matthew 5–7, see below) cannot be cited as parallels or analogies. They are primarily the result of a compilation of traditional sayings of Jesus, while the Johannine discourses seem to contain comparatively little traditional materials and resemble more closely the revelation discourses of Gnostic writings.

Rudolf Bultmann had, therefore, presented the hypothesis that these Johannine discourses were the result of an interpretation of a pre-Christian Gnostic source containing revelation discourses which were then edited and expanded by the author of the Fourth Gospel.[1] However, it has not been possible to provide evidence for the existence of such Gnostic revelation discourses and dialogues in pre-Christian Gnosticism. Bultmann's hypothesis has, therefore, been rejected almost unanimously by subsequent scholarship. More recent commentators are normally concerned only with the description and analysis of the style and structure of the Johannine discourses and dialogues and interpret them as if they were literary products of the author of the Gospel.[2] C. H. Dodd[3] has tried to identify traditional materials which were utilized in the composition of the Johannine discourses, but with limited results because he used the Synoptic Gospels as the primary criterion in this search.

Recent discoveries of dialogues in Gnostic gospels have been more instructive in order to illuminate the origin of the Johannine dialogues and discourses.[4] They show that dialogues were initially developed in

---

However, the appearances of the Risen Lord are still showing similar formal characteristics; see Lyder Brun, *Die Auferstehung Christi in der urchristlichen Ueberlieferung* (Oslo: Aschehoug [Nygaard], 1925).

[1] Bultmann, *Gospel of John,* passim; cf. Heinz Becker, *Die Reden des Johannesevangeliums und der Stil der gnostischen Offenbarungsrede* (FRLANT 68; Göttingen: Vandenhoeck & Ruprecht, 1956). A detailed analysis of Bultmann's method and a reconstruction of the Greek text of his Redenquelle can be found in D. M. Smith, *Composition and Order,* 15–34.

[2] See Brown, *Gospel of John,* 1. pp. cxxxii–cxxxvii (with literature).

[3] *Historical Tradition in the Fourth Gospel* (Cambridge: Cambridge University Press, 1963) 335–420.

[4] See my essays "Dialog und Spruchüberlieferung in den gnostischen Texten von

the process of the interpretation of sayings of Jesus.[1] If the Johannine discourses and dialogues belong to this trajectory of the development of Jesus' sayings, they emerge as genuine gospel materials which belong to the further development of the tradition of sayings. This has become especially evident as hitherto unknown sayings were discovered in the Nag Hammadi Library, especially in the *Gospel of Thomas*.[2] In addition to these sayings, proverbs, kerygmatic formulae, and theological traditions seem to have been used. In many instances, the author of the Fourth Gospel did not compose these discourses *de novo,* but utilized and expanded older existing discourses. To demonstrate this for the entire text of the extensive discourses and dialogues of the Gospel of John is a task that still waits to be done. A few examples must suffice here.[3]

John 3:3 and 5 begin the dialogue with Nicodemus with a saying quoted by Jesus which is also attested in Justin *1 Apol.* 61.4:

John 3:3	John 3:5	Justin *1 Apol.* 61.4
Truly, truly, I say to you, unless someone is born again (or: anew), he cannot see the kingdom of God.	Truly, truly, I say to you, unless someone is born from water and spirit, he cannot enter into the kingdom of God.	Unless you are reborn, you cannot enter into the kingdom of heaven.
ἐὰν μή τις γεννηθῇ ἄνωθεν, οὐ δύναται ἰδεῖν τὴν βασιλείαν τοῦ θεοῦ.	ἐὰν μή τις γεννηθῇ ἐξ ὕδατος καὶ πνεύματος, οὐ δύναται εἰσελθεῖν εἰς τὴν βασιλείαν τοῦ θεοῦ.	ἂν μὴ ἀναγεννηθῆτε, οὐ μὴ εἰσέλθητε εἰς τὴν βασιλείαν τῶν οὐρανῶν.

The saying used by John belongs to the baptismal tradition, as Justin

---

Nag Hammadi," *EvTh* 39 (1979), 532–56; "Gnostic Sayings and Controversy Traditions in John 8:12–59," in Charles W. Hedrick and Robert Hodgson, Jr., eds., *Nag Hammadi, Gnosticism, & Early Christianity* (Peabody, MA: Hendrickson, 1986) 97–110.

[1] See above the discussions of the development of dialogues and discourses, # 3.1.1–3.

[2] The first collection of the relevant parallels to the Gospel of John was published by R. E. Brown, "Thomas and John," but he assigned these parallels in the *Gospel of Thomas* to Johannine influence upon what he deemed to be a 2d-century Gnostic writing and unfortunately did not utilize them for his analysis of the Johannine discourses.

[3] It also not possible to list all traditional sayings used in this Gospel. Parallels to sayings of the Synoptic Gospels are well known and can be easily identified; see the commentaries and Dodd, *Historical Tradition,* passim. I will, therefore, try to include as much as possible of the parallels from apocryphal gospels. But see also the above discussion of the *Gospel of Thomas* (# 2.2.5), the *Dialogue of the Savior* (# 3.1.1), and the *Apocryphon of James* (# 3.1.2).

attests.[1] The original form of the saying is better preserved in Justin than in John. The term "to be reborn" (ἀναγεννηθῆναι) belongs to baptismal language,[2] while John changes this to γεννηθῆναι ἄνωθεν, which can be understood as either "to be born again" or "to be born from above," in order to create the misunderstanding of Nicodemus (3:4) that provides the occasion for a dialogical exploration of the saying in the following verses. The second change introduced by John appears in the second part of the saying: he says "you cannot see" instead of "you cannot enter," because "to see" must be understood as equivalent to "to experience";[3] it points to present participation rather than to a future eschatological event. That John is quite aware of the baptismal setting of the saying becomes clear in 3:5 ("from water and spirit").[4] It is baptism that is explained in the following verses as being born "by the spirit," that is, "from above" (3:6–8). A traditional theological maxim, also attested by Ignatius and perhaps deriving from a liturgical context, is used to illustrate the contrast between spirit and flesh:

John 3:6, 8	Ign. Phld. 7.1
What is born by the flesh is flesh and what is born by the spirit is spirit. . . . the wind/spirit (πνεῦμα) blows where it wills . . . but you do not know whence it comes and where it goes.	If some want me to err according to the flesh, but the spirit does not err because it is from God, because it knows whence it comes and where it goes.

Nicodemus's repetition of the question (3:9) is answered by a communal confessional statement, quite unexpectedly given in the first-person plural by Jesus (3:11):

> Truly, truly, I say to you, We speak what we know and we give witness to what we have seen.

The style is similar to the introduction of 1 John ("What we have seen

---

[1] Dependence of Justin upon the Gospel of John cannot be assumed neither here nor in any other instance. There are no quotations of narrative materials from the Fourth Gospel in Justin Martyr, and typically Johannine formulations of sayings never appear; cf. Arthur Bellinzoni, *The Sayings of Jesus in the Writings of Justin Martyr* (NovT.Sup 17; Leiden: Brill, 1967) 134–38. See also below # 5.2.

[2] Cf. such passages as 1 Pet 1:3, 23.

[3] Cf. Bultmann, *Gospel of John*, 135, n.2.

[4] ὕδατος καί should not be eliminated as a later gloss, *pace* Bultmann. The manuscript evidence for the deletion consists of only a few vulgate manuscripts; a conjecture is not justified.

and what we have heard, we also proclaim to you ..." 1:3).[1] Traditional material is also evident in the verses that follow. These include: a reference to the descent and ascent of the revealer (3:13); an interpretation of Nu 21:8–9 (Moses raising the snake in the wilderness, John 3:14a) which is interpreted as an oblique reference to the crucifixion ("so the Son of man must be raised up," that is, on the cross, 3:14b); and a theological sentence about God giving his Son which is added (3:16)[2] and interpreted.

The discourse in John 5:19–47—possibly continued in John 7—reveals not only the use of isolated sayings and maxims, but of a source which presented a small dialogue of Jesus with his opponents that the author subsequently expanded into a major discourse. If the assessment of the relationship of *Pap. Egerton 2* to the Gospel of John given above[3] is correct, the discussion about the scriptures and Moses in John 5:39–40 and 45–47 are drawn from a written source. That John interrupted this source—which spoke about the witness given by the scriptures and by Moses—with a discussion about "taking honor/glory" (δόξα, 5:41–44), can be explained on the basis of the author's understanding of the parallelism between "witness" and "honor." For the evangelist, these are parallel concepts: Jesus does not bear witness to himself (5:31), and he does not seek his own glory (7:18).[4] While the source for this dialogue, represented by *Pap. Egerton 2*, wants to affirm Jesus' claim to be the legitimate heir of Moses, John's elaboration of this source discusses the paradox that the claim of the revelation can be demonstrated neither by external testimony nor by the performance of glorious deeds by the messenger (such a messenger would be the one who comes "in his own name," 5:43).

The continuation of this discourse in John 7 employs several sayings. John 7:33–34 utilizes traditional statements about the revealer leaving the world again, which appear also in other contexts of the Gospel of John:

John 7:33–34: Still a short time I shall be with you, and I am going to the one who sent me. You will seek me and not find me, and where I am you cannot come.

John 8:21–22: I am going away and you will seek me, ... Where I go you cannot come.

---

[1] See also *Dial. Sav.* 12 (126,15–17): "It is the one who speaks who also listens, and it is the one can see who also reveals." For the first person plural, cf. John 1:14.

[2] Rom 5:8.

[3] See above # 3.2.2.

[4] Cf. Bultmann, *Gospel of John*, 262–63.

John 13:33: Only a short time I shall be with you; you will seek me, and as I said to the Jews so I am saying now to you, "where I am going you cannot come."

Gos. Thom. 38: There will be days when you look for me and not find me.

Apocr. Jas. 2,23–27: "Have you departed and removed yourself from us?" But Jesus said. "No, but I shall go to the place whence I came. If you wish to come with me, come!"

Another saying appearing in this context has already been used before in the story of the encounter of Jesus with the Samaritan woman:

John 4:14: He who drinks from the water I give him, will never thirst into eternity. But the water that I will give him will become in him a spring of bubbling water for eternal life.

John 7:37–38: If anyone thirst, let him come to me and let the one who believes in me drink. As the Scripture has said,[1] from within him shall flow streams of living water.

John 8:12–59 occupies a special position with respect to the use of sayings and the development of dialogues. Traditionally, this unit has been viewed as completely disjointed.[2] But if one considers the relationship of traditional sayings to dialogue that evolves in the process of their interpretation, John 8 may represent a stage in this development that is more original than the well-organized dialogues and discourses in other sections of the Gospel. It is instructive to consider one portion of John 8—verses 12–36—in order to observe the relationship between sayings, sources, or references to scripture on the one hand, and the development of the dialogue, on the other (the secondary dialogue portions are given in italics):

Saying or Source	John 8
"There is light within a man of light, and he lights up the whole world. If	12: "I am the light of the world. He who follows after me will not walk in

[1] For this debated reference to Scripture see Bultmann, *Gospel of John,* 303–4, n. 5.

[2] Bultmann (*Gospel of John,* passim) split this section into several smaller units and assigned them to contexts as follows: 7:19–24; *8:13–20;* 7:1–14; 7:25–29; *8:48–50; 8:54–55;* 7:37–44; 7:31–36; 7:45–52; *8:41–47; 8:51–53; 8:56–59;* 9:1–41; *8:12;* 12:44–50; *8:21–29;* 12:34–36; 10:40–12:32; *8:30–40;* 6:60–71. R. E. Brown (*Gospel of John,* 1. 342) says: "An analysis of the structure of ch. viii (12.ff) is perhaps more difficult than that of any other chapter or discourse in the first part of the Gospel."

he does not shine, he is darkness."
(*Gos. Thom.* 24).[1]

"Blessed are the solitary and elect for you will find the kingdom. For you are from it and to it you will return."
(*Gos. Thom.* 49)[2]

"Only on the evidence of two witnesses, or three witnesses, shall a charge be sustained." (Deut. 19:15b)

"No one knows the Son except the Father, and no one knows the Father except the Son and anyone to whom the Son chooses to reveal him."
(Q/Luke 10:22)[3]
And the rulers laid their hands on him that they might arrest him and deliver him to the crowds; but they were not able to arrest him, because the hour of his being handed over had not yet come. (*Pap. Eg.* 2)
"Have you departed and removed yourself from us?" But Jesus said, "No, but I shall go to the place whence I came. If you wish to come, come with me." (*Apocr. Jas.* 2,23–27)

the darkness, but will have the light of life."
13: *The Pharisees then said to him, "You are bearing witness to yourself, your testimony is not true."*
14: *Jesus answered, "Even if I bear witness to myself, my testimony is true,*
because I know whence I came and where I am going. But you do not know whence I come and whither I am going.
15: *You judge according to the flesh, I judge no one. . . .*
17: *In your law it is written* that the testimony of two men is true.
18: *I bear witness to myself, and the Father who sent me bears witness to me."*
19: *They said to him, therefore, "Where is your Father?" Jesus answered,* "You do not no me or the Father; if you knew me, you would also know the Father."[4]
20: *These words he spoke in the treasury, as he taught in the temple,* but no one arrested him, because his hour had not yet come.

21: *Again he said to them, "I am going away and you will seek me, and die in your sin; where I am going you cannot come."*[5]

---

[1] There are numerous other attestations of this saying; cf. *Dial. Sav.* 127,1–6; John 11:9–10; 12:35–36.

[2] See also *Gos. Thom.* 50: "If they say to you, "Where did you come from?" say to them, "We came from the light . . .""

[3] See also *Gos. Thom.* 69; *Dial. Sav.* 134,14–15.

[4] This saying is quoted a number of times in the Gospel of John; cf. especially John 14:7–10.

[5] The same saying is used in John 7:34, 36 and 13:33.

"There will be days when you will look for me and not find me." (*Gos. Thom.* 38).

22: *Then said the Jews, "Will he kill himself, since he says, 'Where I am going you cannot come?'"* 23: *He said to them, "You are from below, I am from above; you are of this world, I am not of this world.* 24: *I told you that you would die in your sins, for you will die in your sins unless you believe that I am he."*

His disciples said to him, "Who are you that you should say these things to us?" [Jesus said to them,] "You do not realize who I am from what I say to you, but you are like the Jews, ..." (*Gos. Thom.* 43).

25: They said to him, "Who are you?" Jesus said to them, "First of all, what I say to you.[1] 26: *I have many things to say and to judge about you. But he who sent me is true, and I declare to the world what I have heard from him." They did not understand that he spoke to them of the Father.* 28: *So Jesus said, "When you have lifted up the Son of man, then you will know that I am he...." As he spoke thus, many believed in him.*

"If you become my disciples and listen to my words, these stones will minister to you. There are five trees in paradise ... Whoever becomes acquainted with them, will not experience death." (*Gos. Thom.* 19) [A Stoic maxim][2]

31: *Jesus then said to the Jews who had believed in him, "If you remain in my words, you will truly be my disciples, and you will know the truth,*

and the truth will make you free." 33: *They answered him, "We are descendents of Abraham and have never been in bondage to anyone. How is it that you say, 'You will be made free'?"*

---

[1] This sentence, τὴν ἀρχὴν ὅ τι καὶ λαλῶ ὑμῖν, presents notorious difficulties for the translator (see R. E. Brown, *Gospel of John*, note on 8:25). It is the first part of a two-fold answer (τὴν ἀρχήν = "first of all"); the first answer is the same as in the saying *Gos. Thom.* 43: whatever Jesus says represents his identity. The second answer follows in John 8:28: "When you have lifted up the Son of man, then you will know that I am he." See also below on the christology expressed in the "I am" formula.

[2] For the argument that the sentence, "The truth will make you free," is a Stoic sentence see C. H. Dodd, *Historical Tradition*, 380, cf. 330.

"Therefore no one who sins is free."
(Epictetus, *Diss.* 4.1.3)[1]

[a traditional legal or parabolic
saying][3]

34: *Jesus answered them, "Truly
truly, I say to you,* Everyone who
commits sin is a slave.[2]
The slave does not continue in the
house forever; the son continues
forever. 36: *So if the Son makes you
free, you will be free indeed."*

Many of the sayings used in this dialogue have parallels in the *Gospel
of Thomas.* These are all sayings which speak about the presence of
light and knowledge in the human beings who are saved: they have the
light in themselves, and they know that they have come from the kingdom and will return to it. Thus these sayings reveal a typically Gnostic understanding of salvation. It is characteristic for the composition
of the Johannine discourses that such claims as "having the light" or
"having come from above" are exclusively made by Jesus.

The Gnosticizing understanding of salvation that is presented by
the pre-Johannine interpretation of the sayings is refuted by the
author of the Gospel by lodging the claim to divine descent with Jesus
alone. The "I am" formula, so typical of John's Gospel, serves primarily this purpose. At the very beginning of the dialogue (in John
8:12), a traditional saying has been reformulated in this way: "I am the
light of the world." Here as elsewhere, the "I am" formulae are anti-
Gnostic devices, and they must be seen as products of the author of the
Gospel. In fact, the special type of "I am" formulae employed here[4] are
not often found in Gnostic literature.[5] They are an important
ingredient of John's anti-Gnostic christology because they assert that
it is only through belief in Jesus who is the life that salvation can be
gained, not through the discovery of light in oneself.

---

[1] C. H. Dodd, ibid.; Bultmann, *Gospel of John,* 438.

[2] Most manuscripts (except D b sy[s]) read "to sin" (τῆς ἁμαρτίας) after "a slave." But
it is certainly a later addition; see Bultmann, *Gospel of John,* 438.

[3] C. H. Dodd, *Historical Tradition,* 379–82; Bultmann, *Gospel of John,* 440.

[4] This does not deny the fact that "I am" statements are frequent in various contexts
of Hellenistic-Roman religion. Bultmann (*Gospel of John,* 225, n. 3) has analyzed the
several forms of the "I am" formula. He distinguishes four types: (1) the presentation
formula answering to the question "who are you?" (2) the qualificatory formula answering to "what are you?" (3) the identification formula in which someone identifies
him/herself with a special god or power, e.g., in magic; (4) the recognition formula
which answers the question "who is the one whom we expect?" Most of the Johannine
formulae belong to this latter group. With "I am" Jesus answers the question "who is
the bread of life, the light of the world, etc.?"

[5] The formula is rare, e.g., in the *Gospel of Thomas,* cf. # 77: "I am the light that is
above the All." However, this represents the identification formula (see the preceding
note), not the typically Johannine recognition formula. See further on the "I am" formula, R. E. Brown, *Gospel of John,* 1. 535–38.

Another use of the "I am" formula in John is closely connected with this anti-Gnostic christology. In John 8:28 Jesus says, "When you have lifted up (ὅταν ὑψώσητε) the Son of man, then you will know that I am he (ὅτι ἐγώ εἰμι)." The "lifting up" is a reference to Jesus' crucifixion.[1] This is underlined in Jesus' threefold answer "I am he" (ἐγώ εἰμι) to the the guard who comes to arrest him, who says that they are seeking Jesus of Nazareth (John 18:5, 6, 8). As John binds salvation closely to belief in Jesus, he binds this belief to Jesus as the one who is to be glorified as he is lifted up on the cross.

The farewell discourses of the Gospel of John are also largely developed on the basis of such sayings. In particular the saying about seeking and finding, and its interpretation, has played a dominant role here. This saying is, of course, well known in the tradition of sayings, in which it occurs in numerous variations.[2] It is frequently used as a challenge to seek and find life and salvation.[3] The author of the Fourth Gospel has introduced the topic of seeking early in his writing, and it occurs again at the very end. The first encounter of Jesus with another person begins with Jesus' question to two disciples of the Baptist who are following him, "What do you *seek*?" (1:38). Then Andrew comes to his brother Simon and says, "We have *found* the Messiah" (1:41). And when Philip tells Nathaniel about Jesus, he says, "We have *found* him of whom Moses and the law and also the prophets wrote" (1:45). As the encounters with Jesus begin with this question, so at the end of the Gospel, when Judas arrives with the soldiers, Jesus asks three times, "Whom do you *seek*?" And after the discovery of the empty tomb, Mary Magdalene meets Jesus and Jesus says to her, "Woman, why are you weeping? Whom do you *seek*?" (20:15).

It is evident that, for the Gospel of John, seeking Jesus—not seeking for the meaning of his words—is the central theme. For both the crowds and for the disciples, the mystery of the seeking after Jesus is captured in the statement of John 7:34 and 36:

You will seek me and not find me, and where I am you cannot come.

In John 13:33, the disciples are confronted with the same mystery:

Yet a little while I am with you. You will seek me, and as I said to the Jews so I am saying now to you, "Where I am going, you cannot come."

---

[1] See John 3:14; 8:58.

[2] Q/Luke 11:9–10 ("Ask and it will be given to you; seek and you will find; knock and it will be opened to you") is the most familiar form, and is traditionally understood as an encouragement to prayer. Cf. *Gos. Thom.* 92 and 94.

[3] See *Gos. Thom.* 1 and 2.

As far as the hostile crowds are concerned, their inability to find Jesus could simply be explained as the result of their unbelief. However, for the disciples too, the question of being with Jesus after his departure, and reaching the place to which he is going, is central for continuing belief in him. The farewell discourses of the Gospel of John are concerned with this question, because a Gnostic answer was already at hand: those who are prepared spiritually can follow the redeemer to the heavenly realms.

The farewell discourses of the Gospel of John reject this Gnostic solution explicitly. Like the parallel dialogues in the *Apocryphon of James* (1,22–33) and the *Dialogue of the Savior* (## 25–30, p. 132,5–19),[1] John 14 begins with Jesus' statement of a place to which he is going:

> "In my father's house are many rooms. If it were not so, would I have told you that I go to prepare a place for you? ... And you know the way where I am going." Thomas said to him, "Lord, we do not know where you are going. How can we know the way?" Jesus said to him, "I am the way and the truth and the life; no one comes to the Father but by me." (John 14:2–6)

This pronouncement of Jesus sounds like a direct refutation of the statement in the *Apocryphon of James,* "No one will enter the kingdom of heaven at my bidding" (2,29–34). In John 14, the believers are fully dependent upon Jesus in their quest for the way to the kingdom. As in the *Dialogue of the Savior,* the request for a visionary experience as an alternative is rejected in John 14:

> Philip said, "Lord, show us the Father and we shall be satisfied." Jesus said to him, "Have I been with you so long, and yet you do not know me, Philip? He who has seen me has seen the Father ... I am in the Father and the Father in me." (John 14:8–9)

However, in contrast to the *Dialogue of the Savior,* John 14 does not reject the vision in order to request the finding of the true knowledge of oneself in self-recognition; rather, John points to Jesus as the presence of the Father. Thus faith in Jesus is identical with the finding of eternal life. However, the works done by those who have found life in Jesus are not the works of their own goodness, but the works of Jesus:

---

[1] See above, ## 3.1.1 and 3.1.2.

> Truly, truly, I say to you, he who believes in me will also do the works
> that I do, and greater works than these he will do, because I go to the
> Father. (John 14:12)

Once more the theme of seeking and asking is resumed in the following statement of Jesus:

> Whatever you ask in my name, I will do. (John 14:14)

The disciples are still the ones who seek and who ask. But the
emphasis is no longer on the *receiving* of what they ask for, but on
Jesus' *doing* on their behalf what they have asked for.

These sentences of the Johannine farewell discourses are formulated in a direct controversy with the alternatives set forth in the
Gnostic interpretation of the same sayings. John wants to show that
there can be no answer except one: faith in Jesus. In Gnostic
discourse, the disciples will go away to find their true home in the
divine world. In John (14:18–24), Jesus will come again to the disciples; he and the Father will make their home in those who love him.
Thus the emphasis is no longer on Jesus' coming and returning to the
Father, but on Jesus' going to the Father and once more returning to
the disciples who are not taken out of the world, but remain in the
world. The Gnostic order of the descent/ascent pattern is reversed.
Jesus will return and be with the disciples forever as the Paraclete,
the Spirit of Truth, who will remind them of everything that Jesus has
said.

The theme of seeking and finding appears once more at this point.
In the *Dialogue of the Savior* (# 20; p. 129,14–15) the following variant
of this saying occurs:

> Let him who [knows] seek and find and [rejoice].

The *Apocryphon of James* (10,22–11,1) also uses this saying in a
discourse that parallels very closely themes of the Johannine farewell
discourses:

> Behold I shall depart from you and go away and do not wish to remain
> with you any longer, just as you yourselves have not wished it. Now
> therefore follow me quickly. This is why I say unto you, "for your sakes I
> came down." ... Invoke the Father and implore God often, and he will
> give to you. Blessed is he who has seen you with him, when he was pro-
> claimed among the angels and glorified among the saints; yours is life.
> Rejoice and be glad as sons of God. Keep his will that you may be saved
> ... I intercede on your behalf with the Father.

One may be tempted to view this passage as a Gnostic commentary upon John 16. However, Ron Cameron[1] has demonstrated that it is very unlikely that the discourses of this writing were based upon John's Gospel. One must assume that both writings are dependent upon a common source in which sayings of Jesus were interpreted according to Gnostic hermeneutical principles: Jesus came down for the disciples' sake; at his return the disciples are asked to follow him; they are requested to ask the Father and have the assurance that Jesus will intercede in their behalf; a reference to the vision of God as the source of life follows, to which the disciples respond rejoicing.

The author of the Fourth Gospel has reinterpreted this source once more in a reversal of the Gnostic pattern. The disciples will rejoice at the return of Jesus; the disciples will pray to the Father, but Jesus will no longer intercede with the Father on their behalf:

> Hitherto you have asked nothing in my name; ask and you will receive, that your joy may be full ... On that day you will ask in my name, and I do not say that I shall pray to the Father for you, because the Father himself loves you, because you have loved me and have believed that I came from the Father. (16:24–27)

It is no longer the religious experience of the vision of God which gives the assurance of salvation. Rather, the love of the Father and the love of Jesus and the disciples' loving each other describe the realm in which the salvation is present.

3.4.5 THE COMPOSITION

Seen as a whole, the Gospel of John is a complex literary composition employing a variety of sources and materials which themselves are already the product of a still continuing history of interpretation. It is also possible that the Fourth Gospel was written in several stages, as its sources were continuously reinterpreted during their use in the Johannine community. While an early draft of the Gospel may have come into existence soon after the middle of the 1st century, it was probably not composed in its present form until the very end of the century, and later redactional comments were added even during the 2d century, perhaps in the context of the production of the Johannine Epistles, especially 1 John.[2]

---

[1] *Apocryphon of James,* see especially pp. 116–120. See the discussion above, # 3.1.2.

[2] Raymond E. Brown, *The Community of the Beloved Disciple* (New York: Paulist Press, 1979) 93–144.

Nevertheless, the Gospel of John is not a random composition or haphazard compilation of various materials and sources. Several of its chapters are masterfully composed literary pieces. The two most striking examples are perhaps chapters 9 and 11.

John 9:1–41 begins with the reproduction of the miracle story which the author derived from the Semeia Source (9:1–7). But the usual final feature of the miracle story, the acclamation of the bystanders, has been deleted, or better, replaced by a series of encounters. These are described in a sequence of scenes with different actors: the blind man, the crowd, the parents, the Pharisees, and finally Jesus himself. Each scene discusses two questions: how is it possible that the formerly blind man can see? and, who is the one who healed him? In these encounters, the faith of the man who was blind grows into ever more certain recognition of Jesus:

Scene 1 (9:8–12)
  The neighbors,
  the man who was blind.

Are you the man who was blind?
  "I am he."
Who healed you?
  "I do not know."

Scene 2 (9:13–18)
  The Pharisees,
  the man who was blind.

How could someone who heals on the Sabbath come from God?
What do you say about him?
  "He is a prophet."

Scene 3 (9:19–23)
  The Pharisees,
  the parents.

Is this your son who was born blind?
  "Yes."
How does he see now?
  "We do not know."

Scene 4 (9:24–34)
  The Pharisees,
  the man who was blind.

Accusation: you are his disciple.
But we know that God spoke to Moses.
The man who was blind:
  "Jesus must come from God"
Pharisees: You are a sinner,
  because you were born blind.

Scene 5 (9:35–38)
  Jesus,
  the man who was blind.

Do you believe in the Son of man?
You have seen him.
The man who was blind:
  "I believe, Lord."

Scene 6 (9:39–41)	Pharisees: Are we also blind?
Jesus,	Jesus:
the Pharisees.	Because you say that you see, your
	sin remains.

John 10:40–11:54 is also developed on the basis of a traditional miracle story from the Semeia Source. In this case, the miracle story has been utilized to provide the external frame for the entire unit, while the discourses have been set in between the various segments of the traditional story. The arrangement of the sections is symmetric so that the subsections correspond to each other:

Location: Jesus is away on the other side of the Jordan (10:40–42).
Miracle story: the encounter, through messengers (11:1–7).
Jesus loved Martha and her sister and Lazarus (11:4–7).
Miracle story: Jesus and the disciples on the way to Bethany (11:7–16).
First discussion with disciples (11:8–10):
Jesus' time is limited, because he must die.
Second discussion with disciples (11:11–16):
Disciples may have to face death also.
Miracle story: arrival in Bethany (11:17–19).
Encounter with Martha who confesses her faith (11:20–27).
(begins with, "Lord, had you been here, my brother would not have died").
Encounter with Mary who weeps (11:28–32).
(ends with, "Lord, had you been here, my brother would not have died").
Miracle story: Jesus raises Lazarus (11:33–44).
Jesus weeps: How he did love Lazarus! (11:34–35)
Miracle story: reaction of the crowd (11:45–53);
results in the decision to put Jesus to death.
Location: Jesus goes away near the desert (11:54).

The Gospel of John as a whole is composed very carefully in such a way that the several sections reveal a strict correspondence to each other. The Gospel is framed by a tripartite introduction, consisting of the prologue, the preaching of John the Baptist, and the call of the disciples (1:1–51), and a three-part conclusion presenting three appearances of the risen Lord to Mary Magdalene, the disciples, and the disciples with Thomas (20:1–31). In this framework two main sections are clearly delineated: the public activity of Jesus (2:1–11:54) and the passion narrative which, in turn, frames the farewell discourses (11:55–19:42). The link between the two sections is provided by the story of the raising of Lazarus, which triggers the decision to put Jesus to death.

It is difficult, however, to construct a rationale for the arrangement of the materials within each of these two parts of the Gospel. In the first part, the author follows the sequence of the Semieia Source; but the dialogues and discourses are connected with the stories from this source in very different ways, and sometimes (chapters 7, 8, 10) not at all, while one miracle story from the source of signs (the healing of the official's son, 4:46–54) stands without an accompanying dialogue. In the second part, the author follows the sequence of events in his source for the passion narrative; but it is extremely difficult to find a principle of organization for the farewell discourses which have been inserted into this source (chapters 13–17).

Internal links between the two main parts are provided in several ways. There are pointers to the eventual raising up, or glorification, of Jesus on the cross in the first part of the Gospel;[1] a number of traditional sayings used in the dialogues of the first part reappear in the farewell discourses;[2] and the Gospel reports in its first part several unsuccessful attempts to arrest Jesus,[3] while the hour for the glorification is determined by Jesus' own decision that it is "now" (John 12:31–32).

These links between the two parts of the Gospel of John are crucial for the successful accomplishment of the impossible task that the author has set for himself: to write a biography of "Wisdom Incarnate." Jesus is the Logos, like heavenly Wisdom the mediator of creation, divine, uncreated. In traditional wisdom theology, her presence in the world remains hidden. It is present in the life of those who follow her whose true identity the world does not know. But the Gospel of John does not depict the hidden presence of Wisdom in her followers, like the Wisdom of Solomon. The author tells the story of the life of Wisdom herself, of the Logos himself, in the form of a biography of Jesus, the Wisdom/Logos incarnate. This biography, therefore, becomes a paradox. Jesus is a human being from Nazareth, and everybody knows that he comes from Galilee (7:27, 41–42), and he says, "The bread from heaven, the light of the world—it is I." Like a divine human being, the man from Nazareth does many miracles and rejects the belief which responds to these miracles, and is condemned to death because too many people believe in his miracles. Like Wisdom herself, Jesus has come from the Father and is returning to the Father, but neither the Jews nor the disciples will follow;[4] they remain in the

---

[1] E.g., John 3:14–15; 8:28.
[2] See especially the saying about Jesus going away to a place where the Jews cannot follow him (7:33–35; 8:21–22) which is repeated in 13:33.
[3] 7:30, 32, 44–45; 8:20, 59; 10:31, 39.
[4] Whoever added chap. 17 to the Gospel of John knew that this paradox required and answer, telling the disciples that they would certainly follow later. However, this answer is Gnostic.

world in which they will experience tribulations because the heavenly messenger who called them is a human being who dies on the cross which the disciples are requested to understand as the "overcoming of the world" (16:33).

The author of the Fourth Gospel knows quite well that the myth of Wisdom is always docetic, because she is never really human. Accordingly, her followers' ultimate identity is not human but divine. John's "the Word became flesh" (1:14) is pointedly anti-docetic. Biography is the vehicle of this polemical thesis, because heavenly Wisdom cannot have a true biography, though her being on earth, hidden and rejected, can be imitated by those who recognize that they themselves are a hidden divine presence on earth. Jesus' biography, as presented in the Gospel of John, cannot be imitated in the story of the life of the disciples. But the Paraclete, the Spirit of Truth, in whom Jesus returns, will remind the disciples of the new commandment that he gave to them, namely, to love each other (13:34–35). By this love they are not imitating the life of the human being Jesus, but they are imitating God who so loved the world that he gave his Son (3:16). This anti-docetic paradox is the principle of composition for the Fourth Gospel.

unic

4
The Synoptic Gospels

4.1 The Story of the Gospel of Mark[1]

4.1.1 TRANSMISSION AND ATTESTATION

Although a rather early date must be assigned to the Gospel of Mark, its earliest attestation in extant manuscripts is markedly poorer than the attestation for Matthew and Luke—not to speak of the early appearance of the Gospel of John in papyrus finds from Egypt. Mark's Gospel appears for the first time in the oldest extant manuscript containing all four canonical gospels ($\mathfrak{p}^{45}$) which was written in the middle of the 3d century CE. No other manuscript evidence for Mark exists before the 4th century, where Mark is included in the oldest uncial manuscript of the entire Greek Bible ($\aleph$ and B), in one papyrus ($\mathfrak{p}^{88}$), and in two uncial fragments (059, 0188). About twenty-five more fragments from uncial manuscripts, written between the 5th and 10th centuries present texts from Mark's Gospel. Many of these may be fragments from manuscripts containing all four canonical gospels.[2]

There are also no certain quotations from the Gospel of Mark before Clement of Alexandria and Irenaeus (last two decades of the 2d century). The only earlier passage that possibly points to a passage from

---

[1] A general review of scholarship on Mark has been presented by Petr Pokorny, "Das Markus-Evangelium: Literarische und theologische Einleitung mit Forschungsbericht," *ANRW* 2.25/3 (1985) 1969–2035; see also Gottfried Rau, "Das Markusevangelium: Komposition und Intention der ersten Darstellung christlicher Mission," *ANRW* 2.25/3 (1985) 2036–2257. A collection of representative essays was published by Rudolf Pesch, *Das Markusevangelium* (WdF 411; Darmstadt: Wissenschaftliche Buchgesellschaft, 1979). The most controversial recent monograph on Mark is Burton L. Mack, *A Myth of Innocence: Mark and Christian Origins* (Philadelphia: Fortress, 1988).

[2] On the text of Mark in the new edition (26th) of Nestle-Aland, *NT Graece,* see Frans Neirynck, "The Nestle Aland: The Text of Mark in N²⁶," in idem, *Evangelica,* 899–924.

the Gospel of Mark is found in the writings of Justin Martyr, *Dial.*
106.2–3:

> ... and when it says that he (Christ) had given the name Peter to one of
> his apostles, and when it is also written in his Memoirs that it happened
> (καὶ γεγράφθαι ἐν τοῖς ἀπομνημονεύμασιν αὐτοῦ γεγενημένον καὶ τοῦτο) after
> he had given to two other apostles, the sons of Zebedee, the name Boan-
> erges, that is Sons of Thunder.

"His Memoirs" in this text must mean "Peter's Memoirs" (not "Christ's
Memoirs"). This can only be a reference to the Gospel of Mark which
was connected with Peter in the presbyter tradition that is also quoted
by Papias of Hierapolis and by Clement of Alexandria.[1] Moreover, the
remark that follows in *Dial.* 106.3 about the sons of Zebedee demonstrates a knowledge of the text of Mark 3:17, the only passage in the
New Testament where the designation "Boanerges" of the sons of
Zebedee appears. Otherwise, there is no instance in Justin's writings
where the use of Mark can be ascertained.

But there is a noteworthy reference to this Gospel with an explicit
mention of its author in the fragments of the writings of bishop Papias
of Hierapolis (before the middle of the 2d century) which are preserved
by Eusebius (*Hist. eccl.* 3.39.15). It is reported by Papias as a statement of one of the "presbyters" (καὶ αὐτὸ ὁ πρεσβύτερος ἔλεγεν):

> Mark became the interpreter of Peter and wrote down accurately all that
> he remembered of the things said and done by the Lord (ὅσα ἐμνημόνευ-
> σεν ... τὰ ὑπὸ τοῦ κυρίου ἢ λεχθέντα ἢ πραχθέντα), not indeed in the (right)
> order, because he had not heard the Lord nor had he followed him, but
> later on, as I said, he had followed Peter who used to give his teachings
> as demanded by necessity, not, however, in order to make a composition
> of the words of the Lord (τῶν κυριακῶν λόγων). Thus Mark did nothing
> wrong in writing down individual pieces just as he remembered them.
> For only to one thing he gave his attention, to leave out nothing of what
> he had heard and to make no false statements in them.[2]

Thus, Mark's Gospel was known by the name of its author no later
than the middle of the 2d century. This is noteworthy when one considers Justin Martyr, who makes extensive use of the Gospels of

---

[1] See below on Papias and Mark and on Clement's reference to the *Secret Gospel of
Mark*. See alo the following note.

[2] This presbyter tradition is repeated in a slightly different form by Irenaeus (*Adv.
haer.* 3.1.1 = Eusebius *Hist. eccl.* 5.8.2–4) and by Clement of Alexandria *Hypotyposeis*
(in Eusebius *Hist. eccl.* 6.14.5–7). However, the letter of Clement of Alexandria which
preserves quotations from the *Secret Gospel of Mark* (see below # 4.1.5) makes a different statement about the composition of Mark, though it also connects Mark with
Peter.

Matthew and Luke without ever mentioning their assumed authors by name. That the Gospel of Mark was not quoted, referred to, or copied more frequently may be due to the fact that it was overshadowed by the other two Synoptic Gospels, Matthew and Luke, who had incorporated most of the Markan materials into their own more comprehensive compositions.

4.1.2 THE INTEGRITY OF THE TEXT

Neither Justin's nor Papias's references to the Gospel of Mark allow a judgment about the integrity of the text of this writing. There are, however, two earlier witnesses to the text of Mark: according to the two-source hypothesis[1] both Matthew and Luke, written just before or shortly after the year 100 CE, have used Mark's Gospel and have copied large portions of its text, albeit with numerous editorial alterations. A comparison of Mark's extant manuscript text with the Markan portions of Matthew and Luke raises an intriguing and difficult problem: has the text of the Gospel of Mark which Matthew and Luke used survived intact in the tradition of the manuscripts, or was the original version actually lost just as was the other major source of these two gospels, the Synoptic Sayings Source? Most important is the observation that Matthew and Luke agree in a number of instances in their reproduction of Markan passages, while differing from the extant texts of Markan manuscripts. Only a few examples can be mentioned here.[2] It is hardly possible to argue that all these minor agreements can be explained by the assumption that Matthew and Luke used a Markan text that differed from the one preserved in the canonical manuscript tradition. A large number of the minor agreements are due to common stylistic and grammatical corrections of the sometimes awkward Markan text or are caused by accidental common omissions.[3] There is also the possibility that later scribes altered the text of Luke under the influence of the better-known text of Matthew, thus creating secondary agreements of Matthew and Luke against Mark.[4] In this context I am rather concerned with those instances of agreements in which a recognizable editorial purpose could be the reason for a later

---

[1] See the discussion above in # 2.3.2.

[2] A complete list of the relevant texts of Matthew, Mark, and Luke demonstrating these agreements of the two later Gospels against their source has been published in Neirynck, *Minor Agreements,* 55–195.

[3] Neirynck (ibid., 199–288) presents a thorough classification of these agreement of Matthew and Luke against Mark.

[4] This possibility is repeatedly discussed by Francois Bovon, *Das Evangelium nach Lukas. 1. Teilband: Lk 1,1–9,50* (EKK 3/1; Zürich: Benziger Verlag, and Neukirchen: Neukirchener Verlag, 1989).

change of the Markan original text, that is, of the text that Matthew and Luke knew.[1]

4.1.2.1 "Common Omissions" of Passages from Mark

The apophthegma about plucking grain on the Sabbath, Mark 2:23–28, concludes with two sayings of Jesus, Mark 2:27, "The Sabbath was made for people, and not the people for the Sabbath," and 2:28, "The Son of man (or: every human being = ὁ υἱὸς τοῦ ἀνθρώπου) is master over the Sabbath." Matthew and Luke reproduce only the second of these two sayings. It is usually argued that the first saying, "The Sabbath was made for people ...," was too bold for the later understanding of the church and thus deleted by Matthew and Luke, although it was the more original saying of Jesus.[2] However, criticism of the Sabbath observation was pervasive at that time, as is shown by passages like Col 2:16; Ign. *Mg.* 9.1; *Barn.* 15. Thus it is more likely that the original text of Mark was later expanded by the addition of this saying. Only the saying preserved in Matthew and Luke belonged to the original text of Mark.

The parable of the Seed Growing Secretly, Mark 4:26–29, is not reproduced by either Matthew or Luke. If Matthew found the parable in his copy of Mark, one must resort to the explanation that he replaced it with the parable of the Tares (Matt 13:24–30). However, the multiple additions to the Markan parable chapter in Matthew 13 show that Matthew was eager to expand this chapter.[3] Since Luke also does not reproduce this parable in his version of the parable chapter (Luke 8:4–18) nor anywhere else in his Gospel, it is more likely that the original text of Mark did not include it.[4]

The story of the encounter of Jesus with the rich man, Mark 10:17–31, is reproduced quite faithfully and often verbatim by Matthew (20:16–30) and Luke (18:18–30). But Mark's canonical text includes two passages which are missing in the other two Synoptic Gospels and appear to be secondary expansions of a more original Markan text that Matthew and Luke still read. Mark 10:21 introduces Jesus' final answer to the rich man with the remark, "And Jesus looked at him and loved him" (ὁ δὲ Ἰησοῦς ἐμβλέψας αὐτῷ ἠγάπησεν

---

[1] See the more detailed discussion in my essay, "From Mark to Secret Mark," 35–57.

[2] Cf. Bultmann, *Synoptic Tradition,* 16–17. Bovon (*Evangelium nach Lukas,* 267–68) recognizes that Mark 2:27 does not originally belong in this context, but wonders whether Matthew and Luke still knew this saying from the oral tradition and therefore omitted it in their reproduction of Mark.

[3] Cf. Matt 13:33, 44–46, 47–50, 51–52.

[4] Vielhauer (*Geschichte,* 273–75) considers this the only certain evidence for the thesis that the original text of Mark differed from the canonical text.

αὐτόν), and Mark, after Jesus' general statement about those who have wealth (10:23), cites a repetition of Jesus' answer which is introduced by a report about the amazement of the disciples (ἐθαμβοῦντο, 10:24).[1] In the following repetition of the statement about the difficulty of entering the rule of God, the reference to wealth as an obstacle no longer appears. Not one of these Markan features of the pericope is paralleled in either Matthew or Luke.

In Mark 12:28–31 (= Matt 22:34–40 and Luke 10:25–28) the pericope about the Great Commandment is introduced by a reference to Dtn 6:4 ("Hear, O Israel . . .") and has received an appendix about "the scribe who is not far from the rule of God" (Mark 12:32–34). Neither feature has a parallel in Matthew and Luke. In a brilliant analysis, Günther Bornkamm[2] has demonstrated that this appendix is a later addition to Mark's text, written from the perspective of Hellenistic propaganda. The scribe acknowledges that Jesus "in truth" (ἐπ' ἀλη-θείας, 12:32) put forward first of all the confession of Hellenistic Jewish and Christian propaganda that "God is one"—thus the quote of Dtn 6:4, which appears only in Mark (12:29), is a secondary expansion. He then adds, in his repetition of the commandment to love God (Dtn 6:5), the phrase "out of your whole understanding" (ἐξ ὅλης τῆς συνέσεως, 12:33), and contrasts the love of one's neighbor with "burnt offerings and sacrifices" (a typical commonplace of Jewish and Christian propaganda). Finally, Jesus answers that the scribe has spoken "with understanding" (νουνεχῶς, Mark 12:34).

When Jesus is arrested, Mark 14:51–52 reports that a young man who is following Jesus, "wearing a linen cloth over his naked body" (περιβεβλημένος σινδόνα ἐπὶ γυμνοῦ), is grabbed by the armed men but lets go of the linen cloth and flees naked. Neither Matthew nor Luke show any trace of the report of this strange incidence in the texts of their Gospels.

One other passage which is completely missing in Luke but reproduced in Matthew, must be added here, though it is not a "common omission" in the strict sense: the request of the sons of Zebedee, Mark 10:35–39:

---

[1] This term appears in several other Markan passages without parallels in Matthew and Luke. It will be discussed further below.

[2] "Das Doppelgebot der Liebe," in: Walther Eltester, ed., *Neutestamentliche Studien für Rudolf Bultmann* (BZNW 21; Berlin: Töpelmann, 1954) 85–93.

Matt 20:22–23	Mark 10:38–40a
Jesus answered them and said,	But Jesus answered them,
"You do not know what you are asking.	"You do not know what you are asking.
Can you drink the cup that I shall drink?	Can you drink the cup which I drink;
	or can you be baptized with the baptism
	with which I am baptized?"
They said to him, "We can."	And they said to him, "We can."
He said to them, "The cup	He said to them, "The cup that I drink
you will drink.	you will drink;
	and with the baptism with which I am
	baptized you will be baptized.
But to sit at my right hand . . ."	But to sit at my right hand . . . "

ἀποκριθεὶς δὲ ὁ Ἰησοῦς εἶπεν·   ὁ δὲ Ἰησοῦς εἶπεν αὐτοῖς·
οὐκ οἴδατε τί αἰτεῖσθε.   οὐκ οἴδατε τί αἰτεῖσθε.
δύνασθε πιεῖν τὸ ποτήριον ὃ ἐγὼ μέλλω   δύνασθε πιεῖν τὸ ποτήριον ὃ ἐγὼ πίνω,
πίνειν;   ἢ τὸ βάπτισμα ὃ ἐγὼ βαπτίζομαι
                                 βατισθῆναι;

λέγουσιν αὐτῷ· δυνάμεθα.   οἱ δὲ εἶπαν αὐτῷ· δυνάμεθα.
λέγει αὐτοῖς·   ὁ δὲ Ἰησοῦς εἶπεν αὐτοῖς·
τὸ μὲν ποτήριόν μου πίεσθε,   τὸ ποτήριον ὃ ἐγὼ πίνω πίεσθε, καὶ τὸ
                               βάπτισμα ὃ ἐγὼ βαπτίζομαι
                               βαπτισθήσετε.

τὸ δὲ καθίσαι . . .   τὸ δὲ καθίσαι . . .

In Mark 10:38, Jesus answers the request of the sons of Zebedee with two questions, "can you drink the cup that I drink?" and "can you be baptized with the baptism with which I will be baptized?" After their affirmative response, Jesus confirms that they will indeed drink this cup and be baptized with this baptism (Mark 10:39). In the Matthean parallel (20:22–23) only the first of these double questions and confirmations appears. The reference here is certainly to martyrdom for which the image of drinking the chalice seems appropriate.[1] However, baptism as a metaphor for death or martyrdom reflects a later usage of language in Christian literature.[2] That the metaphor was used in this way in Mark's original text, written some time in the second half of the 1st century, is highly improbable. Matthew seems to have preserved the original text of Mark, while the expansions in the present text of Mark may have resulted from a secondary redaction,

[1] That "drinking the cup" appeared as a metaphor for the death of Jesus very early is confirmed by its occurrence in both Mark 14:36 parr. and John 18:11.

[2] Cf. Hans von Campenhausen, *Die Idee des Martyriums in der alten Kirche* (2d ed.; Göttingen: Vandenhoeck & Ruprecht, 1953) 60–61. Baptism is interpreted by Paul as a symbol for dying and rising with Christ in Rom 6:3–11; but the concept of martyrdom is not implied in such an interpretation.

most likely a homiletic reference to the Christian sacraments, eucharist (drinking the cup) and baptism.[1]

4.1.2.2 Original Wording Preserved in Matthew and Luke

The parables as mystery:

Matt 13:11	Mark 4:11	Luke 8:10
To you is given to know the mysteries of the kingdom of heaven.	To you is given the mystery of the kingdom of God.	To you is given to know the mysteries of the kingdom of God.
ὑμῖν δέδοται γνῶναι τὰ μυστήρια τῆς βασιλείας τῶν οὐρανῶν	ὑμῖν τὸ μυστήριον δέδοται τῆς βασιλείας τοῦ θεοῦ	ὑμῖν δέδοται γνῶναι τὰ μυστήρια τῆς βασιλείας τοῦ θεοῦ

According to the overwhelming majority of textual witnesses, the text of Mark 4:11, "To you is given the mystery of the rule of God," differs from the parallel passages in Matthew (13:11) and Luke (8:10), which agree in reading "to know" (γνῶναι) after "is given" (δέδοται) and the plural "mysteries" (μυστήρια) instead of the singular "mystery" (μυστήριον) of Mark 4:11. Thus Matthew and Luke agree in their formulations: "To you is given to know the mysteries of the rule of God" (Matthew: "of the heavens"). As far as the context is concerned, both Matthew and Luke drew everything surrounding this discourse of Jesus with the disciples (the parable of the Sower and its allegorical interpretation) from the Gospel of Mark, not from any different common source. It is difficult to avoid the conclusion that they preserved the original Markan text in the statement of Jesus to the disciples in Mark 4:11. Moreover, the plural "mysteries" is appropriate here: each of the parables is "a mystery," i.e., a mysterious saying or a riddle that must be explained.[2] This is the more original usage of the term,[3] while

[1] Morton Smith, *Clement of Alexandria and a Secret Gospel of Mark* (Cambridge, MA: Harvard University Press, 1973) 186–87.

[2] Jeremias (Parables, 13–18) has demonstrated that Mark 4:11–12 is an older saying that was originally independent. He points to the antithetical parallelism of the phrases, "to you the mystery is given" and "to those outside it comes in parables." However, Jeremias fails to explain why Mark 4:11 reads the singular "mystery" as antithesis to the plural "parables" (cf. also the plural in Mark 4:34: "to his disciples he explained all these things"). The problem is resolved if one assumes that the plural formulation in the first half of the antithesis, as it is preserved in Matt 13:11 and Luke 8:10 ("to you it is given to know the mysteries"), was also the original reading of Mark 4:11. See also the discussion above in # 2.2.4.3.

[3] As was pointed out above (# 2.2.4.3) the *Gospel of Thomas* uses the term in the plural in a saying that introduces several parables: "It is to those who are worthy of my mysteries that I give my mysteries" (# 62). Furthermore, Paul confirms the analogous

the use of the singular "mystery" as a designation of the entire preaching of Jesus or of the entire Gospel occurs only in later Christian literature.[1]

The predictions of the passion:

Matt 16:21	Mark 8:31	Luke 9:22
. . . and to be killed, and on the third day to be raised.	. . . and to be killed and to rise after three days.	. . . and to be killed, and on the third day to be raised.
. . . καὶ ἀποκτανθῆναι καὶ τῇ τρίτῃ ἡμέρᾳ ἐγερθῆναι.	. . . καὶ ἀποκτανθῆναι καὶ μετὰ τρεῖς ἡμέρας ἀναστήσεται.	. . . καὶ ἀποκτανθῆναι καὶ τῇ τρίτῃ ἡμέρᾳ ἐγερθῆναι.

Matt 16:21 and Luke 9:22 agree in their reading "and on the third day to be raised" while their common source, Mark 8:31, says: "and to *rise after* three days."[2] In his reproduction of the second and third prediction of the passion (Mark 9:31; 10:34), Matthew (17:23; 20:19) also uses the formula "and on the third day to be raised" (καὶ τῇ τρίτῃ ἡμέρᾳ ἐγερθῆναι), instead of Mark's "he will rise" (ἀναστήσεται). In these two instances, the evidence is less conclusive with respect to the original reading of Mark because a Lukan parallel to the second prediction of the passion (Mark 9:31) is missing and in the parallel to Mark 10:34, Luke (18:33) agrees with Mark's "he will rise" (ἀναστήσεται). Luke uses the formula "and he shall rise on the third day" also in 24:7, 46, though he never uses the Markan formulation "after three days." "To be raised" (ἐγερθῆναι) is more common in the oldest Christian

---

usage; when referring to an individual saying, he uses the singular (Rom 11:25; 1 Cor 15:51), otherwise the plural; cf. 1 Cor 13:2: "and if I knew all the mysteries" (see also 1 Cor 4:1; 14:2). See Günther Bornkamm, "μυστήριον," *TDNT* 4 (1967) 822–23.

[1] Typical for this later usage is the identification of "mystery" and "gospel," or the close association of the two terms; cf. Eph 6:19: "to make known the mystery of the gospel" (γνωρίσαι τὸ μυστήριον τοῦ εὐαγγελίου, see also Eph 3:1–7).

[2] Mark's "after three days" instead of "on the third day" is peculiar. It contradicts Mark's own dating of the resurrection: the empty tomb is found in the morning of the third day. Morton Smith (*Clement of Alexandria,* 163–64) points out that "after three days" actually means "on the fourth day" and that there is an interesting parallel in John 11:17 and 39, i.e., in the Johannine parallel to the story of the raising of the young man which is reported in the *Secret Gospel of Mark*: Lazarus was raised on the fourth day after his death. This will be discussed further in the treatment of the *Secret Gospel of Mark,* see below, # 4.1.5.

usage (see also 1 Cor 15:4) and is, therefore, most likely the term that appeared in Mark's original text.[1]

The story of the healing of the epileptic child, Mark 9:14–29, is the most complex miracle narrative in Mark and presents the most difficult problems for the explanation of its relationship to the parallels in Matthew (17:14–21) and Luke (9:38–43a).[2] Mark's version of the story is more than twice as long as the parallel versions in Matthew and Luke. Mark 9:14b–16, 21, 22b–24, parts of 25–27, and 28 have no parallels in either Matthew or Luke. The comparison of the three versions of the final part of the story is especially revealing:

Matt 17:18–20a	Mark 9:25–29	Luke 9:42–43
And Jesus	And when Jesus saw that a crowd came running together	And Jesus
rebuked it,	he rebuked the unclean spirit and said, "You dumb and deaf spirit, I command you, come out of him and never enter into him again."	rebuked the unclean spirit
and the demon came out of him, and the boy was healed from that hour.	And after crying aloud and shaking him much it came out. And he (the boy) became like dead, so that many said, "He died." But Jesus grasped his hand and raised him up, and he rose.	and he healed the child and returned him to his father.
		And all were astonished at the majesty of God.

[1] See also the use of ἐγείρειν in other formulaic passages in the letters of Paul (Rom 4:24; 1 Thess 1:10).

[2] Commentaries try to explain the complexity of the Markan story as the result of an inept redaction by the author of the Gospel who may have tried to conflate two older stories. However, they do not use the much simpler forms of the story in Matthew and Luke as a guide for the reconstruction of the original story in Mark. For discussion and literature, see Schmithals, *Markus*, 407–24.

And his disciples came	And when he had
to him privately and	entered the house, his
said, "Why could we	disciples asked him
not cast it out?"	privately, "Why could
	we not cast it out?"

It seems that Matthew and Luke read a version of this story in their copy of Mark which did not contain the verses of Mark to which they have no parallel. Especially the phrases and sentences of Mark 9:25–27 which are missing in the other two Synoptic Gospels have the appearance of secondary alterations or additions. Matt 17:18 and Luke 9:42b must have read a common source which reported briefly that Jesus exorcised the unclean spirit (ἐπετίμησεν κτλ.), that the child was healed (Matt: ἐθηραπεύθη, Luke: ἰάσατο), and perhaps that the crowd reacted (preserved only in Luke 9:43). The extant text of Mark, however, quotes in full the wording of an exorcistic formula, indeed the longest such formula in the Synoptic Gospels (τὸ ἄλαλον καὶ κωφὸν πνεῦμα, ἐγὼ ἐπιτάσσω σοι, ἔξελθε ἀπ' αὐτοῦ καὶ μηκέτι εἰσέλθῃς εἰς αὐτόν).[1] Surprisingly, this is an exorcism for a deaf-mute person, not for an epileptic child.[2] The redactor shows little interest in the healing of the disease. Rather, he wants to describe the effect of a powerful exorcism in order to introduce the subsequent action of Jesus, which has no parallel in Matthew and Luke: the demon departs with appropriate demonstration (κράξας καὶ πολλὰ σπαράξας), the boy is left "as if dead" (ὡσεὶ νεκρός), and the bystanders say "he died" (ἀπέθανεν). This prepares for an action of Jesus which is described as the raising of a dead person: Jesus takes him by the hand (κρατήσας τῆς χειρός), raises him, and he rises (ἤγειρεν αὐτόν, καὶ ἀνέστη). The story, as it is preserved in the extant text of Mark, appears to be a deliberate redaction of an older exorcism story which Matthew and Luke still read in their text of Mark. The redactor revised the story in such a way that it resembled a story of the raising of someone who died as a victim of demonic action.[3]

---

[1] All other exorcistic formulae cited in the Synoptic Gospels are very brief; cf. Mark 1:41; 2:11; 3:5; 10:52; Luke 8:54; 13:12; 17:14.

[2] Mark's later redactor has changed the introduction of the story (9:17) accordingly (ἔχοντα πνεῦμα ἄλαλον); the original description of the disease, epilepsy, is still visible in Mark 9:18, 20, 22.

[3] The close resemblance of this scene and its wording with the description of the raising of the young man in the *Secret Gospel of Mark* will be discussed later (see # 4.1.5).

4.1.2.3 Peculiar Terminology in the Canonical Markan Text

That a number of special terms of the Gospel of Mark are not reproduced by either Matthew or Luke is to be expected. This does not
necessarily imply that they were introduced by a later redactor.
Nevertheless, the absence of certain terms in passages which Matthew
and Luke took from Mark's Gospel is surprising. That the word "gospel" (εὐαγγέλιον) is missing in several Matthean parallels, although
Matthew uses this term in other contexts, has already been discussed.[1]

The words "to teach" (διδάσκειν) and "teaching" (διδαχή) certainly
occurred in the oldest text of the Gospel of Mark, because Matthew or
Luke or both reproduce them in their usage of the following Markan
passages: 1:21, 22; 6:2, 6; (7:7;) 11:18; 12:14; 14:49. However, there are
a number of Markan passages in which the term occurs without parallels in the corresponding passages of Matthew and Luke. In Mark
1:27, the witnesses of Jesus' exorcism (1:23–26) remark about "a new
teaching with authority" (διδαχὴ καινὴ κατ' ἐξουσίαν). The phrase
"new teaching" appears only in one other New Testament passage,
Acts 17:19: "What is this new teaching that is proclaimed by you?" (τίς
ἡ καινὴ αὕτη ἡ ὑπὸ σοῦ λαλουμένη διδαχή;). As Acts 17:32 reveals, this
new teaching is "the resurrection from the dead" (ἀκούσαντες δὲ
ἀνάστασιν νεκρῶν ...). Another important parallel occurs in the gospel
fragment *Pap. Oxy. 1224*, 2 v. col. I: "Which new teaching do they say
you teach, and which new baptism do you proclaim?" (π[ο]ίαν σέ [φασιν
διδα]χὴν καιν[ὴν διδάσκειν ἢ τί β]ά[πτισμ]α καινὸν [κηρύσσειν;]).[2]

In Mark 6:7 the Twelve are sent out "with power over the unclean
spirits"; when they return (Mark 6:30) they announce all they have
done "and what they had taught" (καὶ ὅσα ἐδίδαξεν). No such phrase
appears in the parallels of either Matthew or Luke. In the following
introduction to the story of the feeding of the five thousand, Mark 6:34
says, "and Jesus began to teach (διδάσκειν) them many things." Matt
14:14 reports instead that Jesus healed the sick; Luke 9:11 contains a
similar remark (καὶ τοὺς χρείαν ἔχοντες ἰάσατο) after a reference to
Jesus' "speaking" (ἐλάλει) about the rule of God. Mark 8:31 and 9:31
introduce the first and second predictions of the passion with the
words "he began to teach" and "he taught" (Matthew uses the verb
δεικνύειν, Luke has εἰπών). In addition to these passages, Mark 2:13;
4:1–2; 10:1; 11:17; 12:35, 37, 38 also use the word "to teach" in the

---

[1] See above # 1.3.3–4; Luke avoids the term altogether in his Gospel and can, therefore, not serve as witness to its occurrence or absence in his copy of Mark.

[2] Erich Klostermann, *Apocrypha II: Evangelien* (KlT 8; 3d ed.; Berlin: De Gruyter,
1929) 26.

description of Jesus' activity, while Matthew and Luke use different verbs in their parallel passages.

Most striking is the use of the verbs θαμβεῖσθαι and ἐκθαμβεῖσθαι in Mark. Both verbs express the amazement that befalls people when they witness extraordinary events.[1] The Gospel of Mark is the only writing in the New Testament employing these verbs; the noun also occurs in the Lukan writings. In Mark, these verbs describe the reaction of people to the exorcism in the synagogue (Mark 1:27),[2] the amazement of the people who meet Jesus as he comes down from the mountain of the transfiguration (Mark 9:15), the reaction of the disciples to Jesus' word about the difficulty of wealthy people entering the rule of God (Mark 10:24), the mood of the disciples as they follow Jesus to Jerusalem (Mark 10:32), Jesus' own mood in Gethsemane (Mark 14:33), and finally the reaction of the women as they meet the youth, dressed in a white robe, in the empty tomb (Mark 16:5; cf. 16:6).

All these features point to a redaction of the Gospel of Mark *after* its usage by Matthew and Luke. The origin and purpose of this redaction can be assessed only after the discussion of the *Secret Gospel of Mark* with which it seems closely associated (see below # 4.1.5).

4.1.2.4 The Urmarkus Hypothesis

Quite different from the question of a later redaction of Mark's text after its circulation in the form in which Matthew and Luke knew and used it, is the attempt to reconstruct a more original draft of the Gospel of Mark, known as the *Urmarkus* hypothesis.[3] External evidence for two different versions of Mark circulating at an early date can be derived only from the observation that Luke does not reproduce the section Mark 6:45–8:26. Luke 9:19 = Mark 8:27 follows directly upon Luke 9:17 = Mark 6:44. Luke may have used a copy of Mark that had accidentally lost a few pages.[4] However, there are some special features which differentiate this particular section from the rest of

---

[1] In Hellenistic religious language, these terms are employed in the context of magic performances: cf. G. Bertram, "θάμβος, κτλ.," *TDNT* 3 (1965) 4–7. Plutarch describes θάμβος as the typical result of superstition (Bertram, ibid., 4).

[2] Luke seems to have read the verb here in his copy of Mark because Luke 4:36 uses the noun θάμβος in his concluding remark about the people's reaction. The noun is also used in Luke to describe Peter's reaction to the miraculous draught of fishes in 5:9. It also occurs once in Acts (3:10).

[3] Most characteristic is the attempt of Emil Wendling, *Die Entstehung des Marcus-Evangeliums* (Tübingen: Mohr/Siebeck, 1908). On the *Urmarkus* question in general see Schmithals, *Einleitung*, 201–8.

[4] This was argued most recently by Ernst Haenchen, *Der Weg Jesu* (Berlin: Töpelmann, 1966) 303–4.

Mark's Gospel. It begins with the report of Jesus' going to Bethsaida. (Mark 6:45) and ends with the story of the healing of a blind man from Bethsaida (Mark 8:22–26). Thereafter Jesus goes to the town of Caesarea Philippi, and the town of Bethsaida never occurs again in the Gospel.[1] This section of Mark is also characterized by the appearance of a number of doublets of other Markan pericopes: 6:45–54, the walking on the water, is a variant of the stilling of the tempest (Mark 4:35–41); 8:1–10, the feeding of the four thousand, is evidently a secondary elaboration of the story of the feeding of the five thousand (Mark 6:30–44); 8:22–26 is one of two stories reporting the healing of a blind man in this Gospel (cf. Mark 10:46–52). Two of the healing stories in this section, Mark 7:32–36 and 8:22–26 (both also missing in Matthew), are the only two narratives in the Synoptic Gospels in which the healing is accomplished through elaborate manipulations; all other healings are accomplished through Jesus' word, simple gesture, or touching with or taking by the hand. Mark 6:45–8:26 exhibits some peculiar features also in its general vocabulary. E.g., the term "to understand" (συνίημι) occurs four times (6:52; 7:14; 8:17, 21), but elsewhere in Mark only once in an illusion to Isa 6:9–10 (Mark 4:12). The synonymous verb νοεῖν is found twice here (7:18; 8:17), elsewhere in Mark only in 13:14. The adjective "without insight" (ἀσύνετος) is used in Mark only in this section (8:17).[2]

The cumulative evidence of these peculiarities may allow the conclusion that an earlier version of Mark, which was used by Luke did not yet contain the "Bethsaida section" (Mark 6:45–8:26), whereas Matthew knew the expanded version which, therefore, must have come into existence very soon after the original composition of the original gospel. An *Urmarkus* hypothesis, however, cannot be established on this basis because those searching for the *Urmarkus* wanted to discover a gospel that was "more primitive" than any text that can be reconstructed on the basis of external evidence. It seems wise to limit the reconstruction of the history of Mark's text to instances that can be controlled by external evidence: the earliest version used by Luke; a text of Mark amplified by the "Bethsaida section" (Mark 6:45–8:26) which was available to Matthew; a new edition,

---

[1] Elsewhere in the canonical gospels, Bethsaida is mentioned only in Luke 9:10, in the woe over Bethsaida and Chorazin Matt 11:21 = Luke 10:13, and in John 1:45; 12:21 as the town from which Philip came. In John 5:2, the correct reading is Βηθζαθά, not Βηθσαϊδά.

[2] On the relationship of Mark and Matthew with respect to the use of this term see Gerhard Barth, "Matthew's Understanding of the Law," in Günther Bornkamm, Gerhard Barth, and Heinz-Joachim Held, *Tradition and Interpretation in Matthew* (Phildalphia: Westminster, 1963) 105–11.

characterized by various redactional features not paralleled in either
Matthew or Luke—as will be seen later, this edition is closely related
to the *Secret Gospel of Mark* ; a new edition which was admitted to the
canon of the New Testament; and, finally, a further expansion occurring in the manuscript tradition of the four canonical gospels which is
evident in the adding of appearances of the risen Lord in Mark
16:9–20.[1]

4.1.3 SOURCES AND TRADITIONAL MATERIALS

The development of the tradition which preceded the composition of
Mark cannot be discovered in the futile pursuit of an *Urmarkus,* but
only through the identification of sources used by the original author
of this Gospel. Some of these sources can be recognized with a high
degree of certainty, because Mark was more of a collector than an
author.[2] At the same time, it is not possible to determine the exact
extent and wording of such sources and traditions with certainty,
because Mark neither copied his sources slavishly nor did he make
them always subject to extensive redaction.[3]

4.1.3.1 The Miracle Stories

Among other narrative materials used by Mark were one or two
catenae of miracle stories, probably in written form.[4] They exhibit certain similarities to the material that was collected in the Semeia
Source of the Gospel of John; compare the stilling of the tempest
(Mark 4:35–41; also Mark 6:45–52) with John 6:16–21, the feeding of
the multitudes (Mark 6:30–44; also Mark 8:1–10) with John 6:1–13,

---

[1] These verses are never attested in any early papyri and are missing in the 4th-
century uncial manuscripts ℵ and B and in some manuscripts of the Syriac, Sahidic,
and Armenian translations. A further expansion of Mark 16:14, the so-called Freer
Logion, appears in the 5th-century Codex Washingtonianus (W).

[2] "Phenomena in the text of the Gospel of Mark and the comparison with Q, with
John, and with the extra-canonical tradition can support the assumption that Mark, to
a large extent, reproduces traditions which he received and can, therefore, not be
viewed as an author who has formulated everything himself for the first time"
(Lührmann, *Markusevangelium,* 13).

[3] See on this question the perceptive review article of Frans Neirynck, "L'évangile de
Marc. A propos de R. Pesch, *Das Markusevangelium,*" in idem, *Evangelica,* 491–561.

[4] Paul J. Achtemeier, "Toward the Isolation of Pre-Markan Miracle Catenae," *JBL*
89 (1970) 265–91; idem, "The Origin and Function of Pre-Markan Miracle Catenae,"
JBL 91 (1972) 198–221.

the healing of the blind man (Mark 8:22–26; also Mark 10:46–52) with John 9:1–7.[1]

The stories of Jesus' exorcisms, however, have no parallels in the Fourth Gospel and must have been derived from a different collection which could have comprised Mark 1:21–28; 5:1–20; 7:24–30; 9:14–29.[2] That such collections existed in written form prior to the composition of Mark is fairly certain. But it is not possible to determine either the exact extent of these sources or their precise wording.[3] The author of the Gospel certainly also had access to miracle stories which were freely circulating in oral form as they were used in the propaganda and mission of the church, for example the story of the healing of leper (Mark 1:40–45).[4]

4.1.3.2 Collections of Sayings and Controversy Stories

With respect to the sources for sayings materials, two written documents used by Mark are clearly recognizable: a collection of parables (4:1–34)[5] and a composition of apocalyptic materials (13:1–37).[6] Furthermore, certain groups of apophthegmata—short stories which conclude with a saying of Jesus—can be identified which must have been collected before they were incorporated into the Gospel of Mark. The first group comprises apophthegmata which deal with controversies between the Christian community and their Jewish opponents about fasting (Mark 2:18–22), observation of the Sabbath (2:23–28; 3:1–6), the authority to exorcise demons (3:20–30), the question of clean and unclean (7:1–23), and the question of marriage and divorce (10:1–12). The last of these apophthegmata could also have come from a second collection dealing with questions of church discipline, that is, resulting from debates among Christians in which the authority of Jesus was invoked. In this second group the disciples sometimes appear as the questioners: about the validity of exorcism in the name of Jesus outside of the Christian community (9:38–41); offenses

---

[1] See above, ## 3.2.1; 3.4.4.1.

[2] The latter in its more original form, i.e., like most of the other exorcisms of Mark a comparatively brief story as it is preserved by Matthew and Luke; see above.

[3] It is, e.g., quite possible that the collection of exorcisms also contained such stories as Mark 1:29–31; 2:1–12; 3:1–6 and others.

[4] On the parallel in *Papyrus Egerton 2* see above # 3.2.2.4.

[5] Heinz-Wolfgang Kuhn, *Ältere Sammlungen*.

[6] Marxsen, *Markus*, 101–40; Lars Hartman, *Prophecy Interpreted: The Formation of some Jewish Apocalyptic Texts and of the Eschatological Discourse Mark 13 Par.* (CB.NT 1; Uppsala: Almquist & Wiksells, 1966); most important, including a detailed reconstruction of the source of Mark 13, is Egon Brandenburger, *Markus 13 und die Apokalyptik* (Göttingen: Vandenhoeck & Ruprecht, 1984).

against believers (9:42); the right to excommunicate (9:43–47);[1] acceptance of children into the Christian community (10:13–16); acceptance
of wealthy people (10:17–31); ranks of honor in the community
(10:35–45). A third group comprised four or five apophthegmata which
discuss the rights and the legitimacy of the followers of Jesus as a special group within the confines of the Jewish community. These may
have their origin in the early Jerusalem community—all of these are
deliberately placed in the Jerusalem ministry of Jesus, and in each of
them a special Jewish group or its representative appears as the inter-
rogator: the followers of Jesus as a baptizing prophetic movement compared to that of John the Baptist (11:27–33); the question whether
Jesus' followers belong to those Jewish sects which are loyal to the
Roman government (12:13–17); theological identification with either
Pharisees or Sadducees (12:18–27); adherence to the Great Commandment of Judaism (12:28–34); and the significance of Jewish messianic
expectations (12:35–37).[2]

4.1.3.3 The Passion Narrative

Most evident is the use of a written source in the last section of the
Gospel, the passion narrative. Mark's source began with Jesus' entry
into Jerusalem (11:1–10),[3] continued with the anointing in Bethany
(14:3–9), the arrest of Jesus, his trial before the synedrion and before
Pilate, the mocking by the soldiers, the Barabbas incident, crucifixion,
death, and burial, and concluded with the story of the women's
discovery of the empty tomb. This source is clearly a variant of the
written report of the passion which was used by the Gospel of John.[4]
The comparison with the passion narrative of the *Gospel of Peter* [5] has
demonstrated that also this Gospel's version must be dependent upon
the same source. But Mark's version contains a number of secondary
features, e.g., the splitting up of the scene of the mocking of Jesus into
several episodes; Jesus is mocked before the synedrion (Mark 14:65),
by the soldiers (15:16–20), and by the bystanders at the cross
(15:29–32). Also secondary is Mark's insertion of the preparation for

[1] Helmut Koester, "Mark 9:43–47 and Quintilian 8.3.75," *HTR* 71 (1978) 151–53.

[2] That the fourfold scheme of questions in Mark 12 corresponds to a Rabbinic pattern has been shown by David Daube, *The New Testament and Rabbinic Judaism* (New
York: Arno, 1956) 158–69.

[3] Or perhaps with the story of the anointing in Bethany (Mark 14:3–9). In that case,
John has preserved the more original order of the stories in this source in which the
entry into Jerusalem was the second story; see above # 3.4.4.2.

[4] See above on the Johannine passion narrative source, # 3.4.4.2.

[5] See above, # 3.2.3.2.

Passover (14:12–16), which interferes with the original date of Jesus' crucifixion before the Passover that was indicated in Mark's source.[1]

4.1.4 MARK'S WORLD AND THE COMPOSITION OF HIS GOSPEL

Mark is primarily a faithful collector. Insofar as he is also an author he has created an overriding general framework for the incorporation of traditional materials, but he has still left most of his sources and materials fairly intact. His Gospel is therefore a most important witness for an early stage of the formative development of the traditions about Jesus. The world which these traditions describe rarely goes beyond the circle of Galilee, Judea, and Jerusalem,[2] which is not the world of the author nor of the readers for whom the book was written. Mark's information about Palestine and about its people is fairly accurate wherever he leaves his sources intact. But from his redaction of the sources it is clear that the author is not a Jewish-Christian and that he does not live in Palestine. Except for the importance of Jerusalem and of Jesus' journey there, geographical data have little effect upon the organization and composition of Mark's traditions and sources.

Mark composes his materials according to a theological schema which is directly related to the religious significance of the various traditions about Jesus in his own mostly Gentile-Christian environment.[3] The Gospel is characterized by a strong emphasis upon the proclamation of Jesus' death as a saving sacrifice (Mark 10:45). In concrete terms, this event is present in Mark's church in the celebration of the eucharist which remembered Jesus death as the pouring out of the blood of the covenant and looked forward to the eschatological moment of the messianic banquet (14:22–25). But it is equally present in the telling and reading of the narrative of Jesus' suffering and death as it has been developed on the basis of exegetical traditions in which Scripture provided the answer to the why and how of Jesus suffering.

There is a strong connection between the development of the passion tradition and the apostolic authority of Peter and traditions under

---

[1] Lührmann, *Markusevangelium,* 229. I agree with Lührmann that Mark 14:1–2 belongs to Mark's source; it was not created by the author of the Gospel and it agrees with the dating of the crucifixion in John, i.e., before the first day of Passover.

[2] The area of Caesarea Philippi, the capital of the tetrarch Philip near the sources of the Jordan river, were Mark locates the confession of Peter (8:27), does not belong to Galilee and would be understood as Gentile country.

[3] It will become evident that my view of this environment of Mark differs fundamentally from that of the fascinating recent book of Burton L. Mack, *A Myth of Innocence: Mark and Christian Origins* (Philadelphia: Fortress, 1988).

his name. (Simon) Peter appears repeatedly in Mark's Gospel,[1] and
he is singled out as the one who confesses Jesus to be the Christ (8:29),
though he is never appealed to as the authority behind Mark's Gospel.[2] However, Peter is attested early in Syria as an important apostolic authority:[3] as the one who confesses Jesus as a "righteous angel"
in *Gos. Thom.* 13; in the tradition about the "rock" on which Jesus will
build his church, which Matt 16:17–19 has added to the Markan pericope of the confession of Peter; as the author of the *Gospel of Peter*; and
finally as the author of two other writings, the *Apocalypse of Peter* and
the *Kerygma of Peter.*[4] The latter is of special interest because it
describes how the disciples discovered the meaning of Jesus' fate by
studying the Scripture: the disciples opened the books of the prophets
and found there predicted, partly in parables and partly literally, "his
coming, his death, his cross, and all the other torments which the Jews
inflicted on him, his resurrection and assumption . . ." All these writings and traditions belong to Syria, not to Rome.[5]

As Mark's version of the words of institution for the eucharist indicates, his community's belief in Jesus' suffering and death as saving
sacrifice is closely connected with the apocalyptic expectation of his
return. The motif itself is not new. It characterized Paul's understanding of the eucharist: "As often as you eat this bread and drink the
cup, you proclaim the Lord's death until he comes" (1 Cor 11:26).[6] But
in Mark's community it has found a specific expression as the belief in
the coming Son of man, a concept that the redactor of the Synoptic
Sayings Source shares.[7] The urgency of this expectation may have
been reinforced by the recent destruction of Jerusalem. This would
allow a date for the composition of Mark shortly after 70 CE.

Another important component of early Christian missionary
activity in Syria must have been the proclamation of Jesus as the
"divine man," which was reinforced by the apostles' performance of

---

[1] Together with his brother Andrew, he is one of the first two disciples called (1:16);
Jesus heals his mother-in-law (1:29–31); Peter is one of three witness of the
transfiguration (9:2–9) as well as being the speaker in this pericope (9:5); he also plays
a role in the passion narrative (14:29–31; 53–72; 16:7).

[2] The later tradition which describes Mark as Peter's amanuensis (see above,
4.1.1) is not expressed in the Gospel itself.

[3] It may not be accidental that Paul (Gal 2:11) is a witness for his presence in
Antioch.

[4] Fragments are preserved in Clement of Alexandria *Strom.* 6.5.39–41, 43, 48;
6.15.128.

[5] The location of Peter, and subsequently of the Gospel of Mark, in Rome is a secondary development. See Lührmann, *Markusevangelium*, 5.

[6] See also the eschatological orientation of the eucharistic prayers in *Didache* 9–10.

[7] See above # 2.3.4.

powerful miracles. The tradition of these communities about Jesus most likely consisted of aretalogies, that is, collections of miracle stories of Jesus which eventually found their way into the Semeia Source used by John and also into the miracle catenae employed by Mark. But Mark does not use these sources as just some other pieces of information about Jesus. On the the contrary, he is very aware of the religious threat that this understanding of Jesus' ministry poses to the belief in the saving sacrifice of the crucified Christ. In his Gospel he explicitly rejects the kerygmatic claims of the aretalogical tradition and, by incorporating stories of Jesus' miracles into a writing that is dominated by the passion narrative, establishes the story of Jesus' suffering as the criterion for the determination of the religious significance of the aretalogical tradition.

All of these materials, written sources as well as collections of traditions in written or oral form, have been welded together by the author of the Gospel of Mark into a work in which all of the activities of Jesus are overshadowed by the account of his suffering and death. All arrangements of the sources and traditional materials serve the theological intention of the author to present, in the form of a written document, the "messianic secret" of Jesus that God's revelation in history is not fulfilled in the demonstration of divine greatness, but in the humiliation of the divine human being in his death on the cross.[1] Jesus' opponents, Pharisees and Herodians, decide as early as Mark 3:6 that they want to destroy him. In the first part of the Gospel, the disciples who witness all of Jesus' powerful deeds exhibit a marked lack of understanding; this is expressed several times by redactional remarks at the end of miracle stories (cf. 6:52; 8:14–21). The turning point in the understanding of the disciples comes with the confession of Peter (8:27–30), whose designation of Jesus as "the Christ"[2] sums up the insight into Jesus' dignity that corresponds to the demonstration of his power in the miracles he performed. But this confession is immediately countered by Jesus' prediction that the "Son of man" must suffer and be rejected by the elders, high priests and scribes, be killed, and rise after three days (8:31)—the first of three predictions[3] of the suffering of the Son of man which from this point on determine

[1] William Wrede, *The Messianic Secret* (Library of Theological Translation; London: Clarke, 1971): English translation of a classical monograph which was first published in German in 1901; James M. Robinson, "The Messianic Secret and the Gospels Genre," in idem, *The Problem of History in Mark and other Marcan Studies* (Philadelphia: Fortress, 1982) 11–53.

[2] This is most likely the original reading. The manuscripts which add "the Son of God," or "the Son of the Living God" are influenced by the expanded text of Matt 16:16.

[3] The other two appear in 9:31–32 and 10:32–34.

the character of the narrative: Jesus is on his way to Jerusalem. The reader learns that the powerful deeds of the Christ cannot be the key to the understanding of the mission of Jesus. On the contrary, the miracles of the Christ provoked the reactions which resulted in his condemnation. As the disciples are going with Jesus to Jerusalem (8:34–10:45), they learn discipleship under the perspective of the Son of man who has come to give his life as ransom for many (10:45). It is in this section of the Gospel that the author has placed most of his church order materials. But the Son of man is also the one who will come on the clouds of heaven. Thus Mark inserted a speech of Jesus composed of apocalyptic predictions into the instructions of Jesus given before his arrest. The final juxtaposition of the titles "Christ" and "Son of man" marks the high climax of Jesus' trial before the synedrion: the high priest's question, whether he is the Christ the Son of the Blessed One, is answered positively; but the title which conveys true insight into Jesus' dignity is added immediately: "And you will see the Son of man sitting at the right hand of the Power and coming with the clouds of heaven." The Gospel of Mark is thus written as a guide to christology in narrative form. Christology is the ordering principle according to which the materials are arranged.

By combining aretalogical materials with the passion narrative, Mark produced for the first time what can be called a "biography of Jesus." This, however, is not an accidental creation. The model was the biography of the prophet. Characteristically, Mark's Gospel begins with the appointment of Jesus through the heavenly voice, "You are my beloved Son in whom I am well pleased" (Mark 1:11), directed to Jesus (not to the crowds as in Matt 3:17). Like Elijah, Jesus spends forty days in the wilderness (Mark 1:12–13). The prophetic call for repentance opens the preaching of Jesus (Mark 1:15). The hostility that Jesus experiences is the result of his conduct of office. Jesus' interpretation of Israel's law and ritual is "prophetic Torah."[1] He suffers the fate of the prophet in his death and is vindicated. This is not all that the Gospel of Mark has to say, but it is the biographical framework which provides the literary model for the writing of this "gospel."[2]

---

[1] Mark 7:1–23; 10:1–12; 12:29–31.
[2] See above the discussion of the genre of the gospel, # 1.6.

4.1.5 THE SECRET GOSPEL OF MARK[1]

4.1.5.1 Discovery, Publication, and Evaluation

The only known fragment of the *Secret Gospel of Mark* is a quotation in a letter of Clement of Alexandria. This letter was discovered 1958 by Morton Smith in the Mar Saba Monastery, twelve miles southeast of Jerusalem.[2] A learned monk had copied the letter into the back of an edition of the letters of Ignatius of Antioch by Isaac Voss that had been published in 1646.[3] The monk's handwriting can be dated to about 1750.[4] The Greek text was published 1973 by Morton Smith with extensive notes, appendices, and indices.[5] It was reprinted in a revised edition of the index volume of the publication of the works of Clement of Alexandria in the series "Die griechischen christlichen Schriftsteller" of the Berlin Academy.[6] English translations have been published by Morton Smith and by Ron Cameron.[7]

It is known that Clement of Alexandria wrote letters. But not one of these letters had survived, although quotations from Clement's letters appear in the *Sacra Parallela* attributed to John of Damascus who stayed at the Mar Saba Monastery from the beginning of the 8th century to his death (ca. 750 CE). The first question was, therefore, whether this letter was indeed the copy of a genuine letter of the Alexandrian Father. There are a number of scholars who have expressed doubts with respect to its authenticity.[8] However, vocabulary, style,

---

[1] Some of the following paragraphs are an adaptation of my introduction to the translation of the *Secret Gospel of Mark*, which is scheduled to be published by Polebridge Press in a new edition of the New Testament Apocrypha.

[2] Morton Smith, *Clement of Alexandria and a Secret Gospel of Mark* (Cambridge, MA: Harvard University Press, 1973 [transcription, plates, and translation: pp. 445–54]); idem, *The Secret Gospel: The Discovery and Interpretation of the Secret Gospel According to Mark* (New York: Harper & Row, 1973). See also Crossan, *Four Other Gospels*, 91–98.

[3] *Epistulae genuinae S. Ignatii Martyris* (Amsterdam: J. Blaeu, 1646).

[4] For information about the hand of the writer see Morton Smith, *Clement of Alexandria*, 1–4; idem, "Ἑλληνικὰ Χειρογραφία ἐν τῇ μονῇ τοῦ Ἁγίου Σάββα," *Nea Sion* 52 (1960) 110ff, 245ff.

[5] *Clement of Alexandria*, 445–54.

[6] Otto Stählin and Ursula Treu, *Clemens Alexandrinus, vol. 4.1: Register* (2d ed.; Berlin: Akademie-Verlag, 1980) pp. XVII–XVIII.

[7] M. Smith, *Clement of Alexandria*, 446–47; idem, *The Secret Gospel: The Discovery and Interpretation of the Secret Gospel According to Mark* (New York: Harper & Row, 1973) 14–17; Ron Cameron, *Other Gospels*, 67–71. For a German translation, see H. Merkel, "Das 'geheime Evangelium' nach Markus," in Hennecke-Schneemelcher, *NT Apokryphen I*, 89–92.

[8] On the heated debate about the authenticity of the letter see Wilhelm Wuellner, ed., *Longer Mark: Forgery, Interpolation, or Old Tradition?* (Colloquy 18; Berkeley, CA: The Center for Hermeneutical Studies, 1976); Morton Smith, "Clement of Alexandria

Faux 2° MI

syntax, and manner of quotation in the letter are either identical with, or similar to, that of Clement's genuine writings.[1] Skepticism is hard to justify.[2]

It is not possible to identify the addressee, a certain Theodorus. The Karpokratians who are attacked in the letter as those who had contaminated the *Secret Gospel of Mark* with their falsifications are discussed critically by Clement and in other Church Fathers.[3] Since the letter refers to an Egyptian sect, it is not unlikely that it was written during Clement's Alexandrian period, i.e., between 175 and 200 CE. But a date between 200 and 215 is also possible.[4]

The letter responds to a request from Theodorus for information about a "secret gospel" used by the Karpokratians. Clement calls their secret gospel a falsification of the genuine *Secret Gospel of Mark* which was composed by Mark himself in Alexandria[5] and was still used in the Alexandrian church in Clement's day. Following the presbyter tradition that is also used by Papias of Hierapolis and elsewhere by Clement himself, he ascribes authorship to Mark who was the amanuensis of Peter in Rome.[6] However, the ascription of a "secret gospel" to the same Mark is not attested anywhere else.

It is evident in Clement's letter that this *Secret Gospel of Mark* was an expanded edition of what Clement considers to be the first Gospel that Mark wrote. Mark, Clement says, produced the second writing to be communicated only to those who where "initiated into the great mysteries."[7] Yet a third version of a gospel written by Mark was used

---

and Secret Mark: The Score at the End of the First Decade," *HTR* 75 (1982) 449–61. For further discussion and literature see Saul Levin, "The Early History of Christianity in the Light of the 'Secret Gospel' of Mark," *ANRW* 2.25/6 (1988) 4270–92.

[1] Comparisons with parallels in Clement's writings are presented and discussed in great detail by Morton Smith, *Clement of Alexandria*, 6–85.

[2] For a general assessment and survey see Gero, "Apocryphal Gospels," 3976–78.

[3] Irenaeus, Tertullian, Hippolytus, Epiphanius, and others. For full documentation see Morton Smith, *Clement of Alexandria*, Appendix B.

[4] After leaving Alexandria at the outbreak of the persecution, Clement probably died ca. 215 CE.

[5] For a discussion of the tradition about Mark as the founder of the church in Alexandria see Birger A. Pearson, "Earliest Christianity in Egypt: Some Observations," in idem and James E. Goehring, eds., *The Roots of Egyptian Christianity* (Studies in Antiquity and Christianity; Philadelphia: Fortress, 1986) 137–45.

[6] A full presentation of these passages can be found in Morton Smith, *Clement of Alexandria*, 19–22. Two of these come from quotes from Clement's works in Eusebius (*Hist. eccl.* 2.15 and 6.14.5–7), the third from a fragment of Clement's *Hypotyposeis* (in the Latin *Adumbrationes Clementis Alexandrini in epistolas canonicas*).

[7] This may be a somewhat fancy expression, designating those Christians who were advancing to a higher degree of knowledge (γνῶσις), or it may point to another rite,

by the sect of the Karpokratians.[1] Clement calls this a "copy" (ἀπόγραφον)[2] of the genuine secret gospel. At the time at which Karpokrates
flourished in Alexandria, in the first half of the 2d century, no firmly
organized church with bishop and presbyters existed there, and it
must be assumed that anybody could obtain copies of any writing used
by Christians in Alexandria.[3] This also establishes a terminus ad
quem for this gospel early in the 2d century.

4.1.5.2 *The Relationship of* Secret Mark *to Mark's Gospel*

Clement notes two differences between *Secret Mark* and the Gospel
of Mark that was read publicly: (1) the former contained a story of the
raising of a young man, which was added to Mark's text after Mark
10:34; (2) it reported an encounter of Jesus with this young man's sister, mother and Salome, added after Mark 10:46a. On the basis of the
information that is provided by Clement, it is not possible to say
whether there were any other differences between these two gospels as
Clement knew them. Both additions are quoted in Clement's letter.
Vocabulary and style of the additions are fully compatible with the
Gospel of Mark.[4] *Secret Mark*, therefore, must belong to the same
"school" or community which had produced the canonical Gospel. Both
gospels are related to each other as closely as the Gospel of John and
its later redaction, which interpolated John 6:52b–59 and added
chapter 21 to the book.[5] This also implies that the date of composition
of *Secret Mark* should not be too far removed from the date for the
writing of the Gospel of Mark.

The story of the raising of the young man is told as follows:[6]

---

perhaps a second baptism for more mature Christians (see Morton Smith, *Clement of
Alexandria*, 168).

[1] A full treatment of Karpokrates and his sect, including a discussion of all relevant
literature, can be found in Morton Smith, *Clement of Alexandria*, 266–78 (all ancient
sources are quoted in full in Appendix B of this book, pp. 295–350).

[2] The term ἀπόγραφον may have pejorative connotations (Morton Smith, *Clement of
Alexandria*, 49).

[3] Pearson ("Earliest Christianity in Egypt," 149–151) lists a number of writings that
must have been current in Alexandria early in the 2d century.

[4] That, however, is also the case in the longer ending of Mark (16:9–20), which is
certainly secondary. It does not prove that the additions were made by the same
author.

[5] See above # 3.4.3.

[6] All translations from the *Secret Gospel of Mark* are my own. They will also appear
in the new edition of the New Testament Apocrypha to be published by Polebridge
Press. I have, of course, consulted the translation of Morton Smith in his *Clement of
Alexandria*.

And they came to Bethany, and there was a certain woman whose brother had died. And she prostrated herself before Jesus and said to him, "Son of David, have mercy on me." But the disciples rebuked her. And Jesus, being angered, went with her into the garden where the tomb was. And immediately a great voice was heard from the tomb. And Jesus, drawing near, rolled away the stone from the entrance to the tomb. And immediately, going in where the young man was, he stretched out (his) hand and raised him, grasping his hand. And the young man, looking at Jesus, loved him and began to beseech him that he might be with him. And as they came out of the tomb, they went into the house of the young man, for he was rich.

It is immediately evident that this story shows many similarities with the story of the raising of Lazarus in John 11.[1] That it is, in fact, the same story is evident in the emphasis upon the love between Jesus and the man who was raised by him (cf. John 11:3, 5, 35–36), expressed twice in the additions of *Secret Mark*.[2] Both stories are also located in Bethany. But it is impossible that *Secret Mark* is dependent upon John 11. In its version of the story, there are no traces of the rather extensive Johannine redaction (proper names, motif of the delay of Jesus' travel, measurement of space and time, discourses of Jesus with his disciples and with Martha and Mary). As to its form, *Secret Mark* represents a stage of development of the story that corresponds to the source used by John.[3] The author evidently still had access to the free tradition of stories about Jesus, or perhaps to some older written collection of miracle stories. But the story of the raising of the young man in Secret Mark has an appendix for which parallels in the Fourth Gospel's version are missing, except for the motif of love between Jesus and the man who was raised:

And the young man (νεανίσκος), looking at Jesus, loved him (ἐμβλέψας αὐτῷ ἠγάπησεν αὐτόν) and began to beseech him that he might be with him. . . . And after six days Jesus gave him an order; and when the evening had come, the young man (νεανίσκος) went to him, dressed with a linen cloth over his naked body (περιβεβλημένος σινδόνα ἐπὶ γυμνοῦ). And he remained with him that night, because Jesus taught him the mystery of the kingdom of God (ἐδίδασκε γὰρ αὐτὸν ὁ Ἰησοῦς τὸ μυστήριον τῆς βασιλείας τοῦ θεοῦ).

[1] For an analysis of this story of *Secret Mark* in relation to John 11, see Crossan, *Four Other Gospels*, 111–18.

[2] The only other canonical parallel is Mark 10:21, which will be discussed below.

[3] Morton Smith, *Clement of Alexandria*, 148–158; Koester, "From Mark to Secret Mark," 41–42.

This is evidently an addition to an older story of the raising of the young man and it could be dismissed as completely secondary were it not for the fact that exactly in these sentences a number of remarkable parallels to the preserved text of the Gospel of Mark appear. However, all Markan parallels appear in the extant manuscript text of Mark only; they are missing in Matthew's and Luke's parallel versions and do not seem to have been parts of the text of Mark that they knew.

Secret Mark	Mark
The young man, looking at Jesus, loved him (ἐμβλέψας αὐτῷ ἠγάπησεν αὐτόν).	10:21: Jesus looked at him (i.e., the rich man) and loved him (ἐμβλέψας αὐτῷ ἠγάπησεν αὐτόν).
the young man (νεανίσκος) went to him,	14:51–52: (after the arrest of Jesus) A young man (νεανίσκος) had followed him who was
dressed with a linen cloth over his naked body (περιβεβλημένος σινδόνα ἐπὶ γυμνοῦ).	dressed with a linen cloth over his naked body (περιβεβλημένος σινδόνα ἐπὶ γυμνοῦ), and they grabbed him. But he let the cloth go and fled naked.

Secret Mark	Mark 4:11	Matt 13:11; Luke 8:10
Jesus taught him the mystery of the kingdom of God (ἐδίδασκε γὰρ αὐτὸν ὁ Ἰησοῦς τὸ μυστήριον τῆς βασιλείας τοῦ θεοῦ).	To you is given the mystery of the kingdom of God. (ὑμῖν τὸ μυστήριον δέδοται τῆς βασιλείας τοῦ θεοῦ)	To you is given to know the mysteries of the kingdom of heaven/of God. (ὑμῖν δέδοται γνῶναι τὰ μυστήρια τῆς βασιλείας τῶν οὐρανῶν / τοῦ θεοῦ)

It has already been argued above that the remark "Jesus loved him" in the story of the rich man, does not seem to have been part of the original text of Mark that Matthew and Luke read.[1] It occurs nowhere else in the canonical gospels except for the story of the raising of Lazarus in John (11:5, 36). In the preserved manuscripts of the text of Mark, however, this remark appears in the story that just precedes (10:17–31) the point in Mark's textst at which Clement found the story of the raising of the young man (10:34). Mark 14:51 is the only passage in all the canonical gospels in which a young man dressed in a linen cloth over his naked body appears.[2] The singular "mystery,"

[1] On this passage and on Mark 14:51–52 see above, # 4.1.2.1.

[2] There is, of course, also the "young man dressed in a white robe" (νεανίσκον ... περιβεβλημένον στολὴν λευκήν) whom the women see in the tomb of Jesus (Mark 16:5; Gos. Pet. 13.55); but there the brightness of the robe underlines the angelic presence

employed in *Secret Mark,* is used in the canonical gospels only in Mark
4:11, and Matthew and Luke apparently read the plural "mysteries" in
their text of Mark.[1] And the extant text of the Gospel of Mark contains
numerous instances in which the terms "to teach" and "teaching"
appear without a parallel in either Matthew or Luke.[2] It seems that
the change in the text of Mark 4:11 and the additions of Mark 10:21
and 14:51–52 are due to the same redactor who inserted the story of
the raising of the young man after Mark 10:34.

This raises some questions with respect to other passages in the
text of Mark, especially in chapters 8–10, in which Matthew and Luke
have preserved the original text, while the extant text of Mark appears
to have resulted from a secondary redaction. If one assumes that
Secret Mark included these passages in the form in which they have
been preserved in the text of canonical Mark, while Matthew and Luke
represent the original Markan text, a very interesting relationship to
the story of the raising of the young man emerges:

Matt/Luke = original Mark	Revised Mark and *Secret Mark*

First prediction of the Passion

Matt 16:21 = Luke 9:21	Mark 8:31
. . . and be raised on the third day	. . . and after three days he will rise
. . . καὶ τῇ τρίτῃ ἡμέρᾳ ἐγερθῆναι.	. . . καὶ μετὰ τρεῖς ἡμέρας ἀναστήσεται.

After the Transfiguration

Matt 17:14 = Luke 9:37–38a	Mark 9:15
And when they came to crowd,	And immediately all the crowd, when they saw him, were amazed
a man came to him and kneeling before him, he said . . .	(ἐθαμβήθησαν), and they ran up to him and greeted him.

Exorcism of the Epileptic Child	*Raising the Afflicted Child*
Matt 17:18 = Luke 9:42	Mark 9:26–27
. . . and the demon departed	. . . the demon departed and the boy is left "as if dead" (ὡσεὶ νεκρός), and the bystanders say "he died" (ἀπέθανεν).

(in *Gos. Pet.* 13.55 the robe is characterized as shining most brightly [λαμπροτάτῃ]). It
is hard to imagine that Mark wants the reader to understand that this is the same
young man who fled naked.

   1 See above, # 4.1.2.2.

   2 Mark 1:27; 2:13; 4:1–2; 6:30, 34; 8:31; 9:31; 10:1; 11:17; 12:35, 37–38; see also
above, # 4.1.2.2.

	But Jesus took him by the hand (κρατήσας τῆς χειρός),
and he was healed (Matt: ἐθηραπεύθη, Luke: ἰάσατο)	raised him, and he rose (ἤγειρεν αὐτόν, καὶ ἀνέστη).

Second Prediction of the Passion

Matt 17:23 (Luke —)	Mark 9:31
. . . and be raised on the third day.	. . . and after three days he will rise.
. . . καὶ τῇ τρίτῃ ἡμέρᾳ ἐγερθῆναι.	. . . καὶ μετὰ τρεῖς ἡμέρας ἀναστήσεται.

The Rich Man

Matt 19:21 = Luke 18:22	Mark 10:21
But Jesus	But Jesus looking at him loved him (ὁ δὲ Ἰησοῦς ἐμβλέψας αὐτῷ ἠγάπησεν αὐτόν)
said to him, . . .	and said to him, . . .

Matt 19:23–24 = Luke 18:24–25	Mark 10:23–24
". . . it will be hard for a rich man to enter the kingdom of heaven."	"How hard it is for those who have riches to enter the kingdom of God." And the disciples were amazed (ἐθαμβοῦντο) at his words, but Jesus answered and said to them again, "Children, how hard it is to enter the kingdom of God!
Again I tell you,	
"It is easier for a camel to go through the eye of a needle. . ."	It is easier for a camel to go through the eye of a needle . . ."

Third Prediction of the Passion

Matt 20:17–19 = Luke 18:31–33	Mark 10:32–34
(Matt only: And when they were about to go to Jerusalem).	And they were on the road going up to Jerusalem, and Jesus was going ahead of them, and they were amazed (ἐθαμβοῦντο) and those who followed were afraid (ἐφοβοῦντο).
And he took the Twelve (Matt: in private on the road) and said to them ". . . and on the third day he will be raised" (Luke: "rise").	And taking the Twelve again, he began to tell them . . . ". . . and after three days he will rise."
καὶ τῇ τρίτῃ ἡμέρᾳ ἐγερθήσεται (Luke: ἀναστήσεται).	καὶ μετὰ τρεῖς ἡμέρας ἀναστήσεται.

The Young Man Raised

Secret Mark after Mark 10:34

There was a certain woman whose brother had died (ἀπέθανεν) . . . (Jesus) stretched out (his) hand and raised him, (ἤγειρεν αὐτόν, κρατήσας τῆς χειρός) grasping his hand. And the young man, looking at Jesus, loved him (ὁ δὲ νεανίσκος ἐμβλέψας αὐτῷ αὐτῷ ἠγάπησεν αὐτόν). . . . they went into the house of the young man, for he was rich (ἦν γὰρ πλούσιος).

The Sons of Zebedee [1]

Matt 20:22–23	Mark 10:38–40a
Jesus answered them and said, "You do not know what you are asking. Can you drink the cup that I shall drink?"	But Jesus answered them, "You do not know what you are asking. Can you drink the cup which I drink; or can you be baptized with baptism with which I am baptized?"
They said to him, "We can." He said to them, "The cup you will drink.	And they said to him, "We can." He said to them, "The cup that I drink you will drink; and with the baptism with which I am baptized you will be baptized.
But to sit at my right hand . . . "	But to sit at my right hand . . ."

In Jericho

Mark 10:46	
And they came into Jericho.	And he[2] came into Jericho, And there were the sister of the young man whom Jesus loved (τοῦ νεανίσκου ὃν ἠγάπα αὐτὸν ὁ Ἰησοῦς) and his mother and Salome, and Jesus did not receive them.

---

[1] For the Greek texts see above # 4.1.2.1

[2] Crossan (*Four Other Gospels,* 109–10) rightly calls attention to the fact that the *Secret Gospel,* as quoted by Clement, read the singular, while the manuscripts of Mark have the plural. But this does not necessarily imply that Clement's copy of the canonical Markan text also read the singular.

And when he was leaving Jericho	And when he was leaving Jericho
with his disciples and a great crowd,	with his disciples and a great crowd,
Bartimaeus, a blind beggar, ...	Bartimaeus, a blind beggar, ...

Secret Mark has arranged the original text of Mark in such a way that chapters 8–10 would have presented two stories of the raising of a dead person by Jesus, each placed after a prediction of the passion. These predictions themselves were altered so that they would speak of the "resurrection" (ἀναστῆναι) of Jesus, instead of Jesus "being raised" (ἐγερθῆναι). If these changes came from the hand of the redactor who produced the *Secret Gospel of Mark,* one would also ascribe to him the following changes in these chapters: the emphasis upon the "amazement" in the introduction to the story of the raising of the epileptic child: "All the crowd, when they saw him were greatly amazed" (ἐξεθαμβήθησαν, Mark 9:15); the statement of the amazement (ἐθαμβοῦντο) of the disciples after Jesus' saying about riches (Mark 10:24); the description of the amazement and fear of those who followed Jesus just before the insertion of the story of the raising of the young man: "and they were amazed (ἐθαμβοῦντο) and those who followed were afraid" (ἐφοβοῦντο, Mark 10:32); the expression of Jesus' love for the rich man (Mark 10:21) which creates a connection to the following story in *Secret Mark* ;[1] the addition of the baptism with which Jesus and the disciples must be baptized (Mark 10:38–39), which changes the prediction of martyrdom into a cryptic reference to baptism and eucharist; and the encounter in Jericho, which explains why the extant text of Mark 10:46 describes Jesus' entering and leaving Jericho without telling what happened there.[2]

It is difficult to be certain whether all or some of the other features in the preserved text of Mark which are not reflected in Matthew and Luke also reveal the hand of the *Secret Mark* redactor. One should certainly ascribe to him the change of the plural "mysteries" into the singular in Mark 4:11 and the insertion of the episode of the young man fleeing naked in Mark 14:51–52,[3] and perhaps also the increased

---

[1] Riddles remain here. Only Matt (19:20, 22) calls the rich man a νεανίσκος, the same term that is used in the *Secret Gospel* for the man raised by Jesus. Mark does not use this term (10: 17, 31). Only Luke, in agreement with the *Secret Gospel's* characterization of the youth who was raised, says of the rich man ἦν γὰρ πλούσιος σφόδρα (18:23), while Mark 10:22 and Matt 19:22 describes his wealth with the words ἦν γὰρ ἔχων χρήματα πολλά.

[2] Matthew's and Luke's parallels give little evidence for Mark's original text. In Matt 20:29 Jesus meets the blind man "coming out of Jericho"; in Luke 18:35 Jesus and his disciples "are approaching Jericho."

[3] For an attempt at a Gnostic interpretation of the significance of this addition see Hans-Martin Schenke,"The Mystery of the Gospel of Mark," *Second Century* 4 (1984) 65–82.

emphasis upon the "teaching" activity of Jesus.[1] In any case, the
canonical Gospel of Mark shows evidence of the redaction which was
also responsible for the insertion of the story of the raising of the
young man in *Secret Mark*. In other words, the text of canonical
Mark—it is the same text as the one known to Clement of Alexandria
as Mark's public Gospel[2]—is not the original Mark used by Matthew
and Luke, but an abbreviated version of the *Secret Gospel of Mark*.[3] It
was only the latter that had survived, and in order to make this text
suitable for public reading, the story of the raising of the young man
and his subsequent private initiation by Jesus as well as the reference
to this young man's sister and mother and Salome after Mark 10:46b
were removed.

According to Clement of Alexandria, another version of the *Secret
Gospel of Mark* was used by the Karpokratians. He explicitly quotes
only one example for the difference between the legitimate Alexandrian and the falsified Karpokratian version: after the story of the
raising of the young man, added in *Secret Mark* following Mark 10:34,
the latter contained the words, "Naked man with naked man." This
phrase, as well as some other things about which Clement's correspon-
dent wrote, were not found in the Alexandrian church's version. A
second difference between the two gospels is indicated by Clement's
remark with respect to Secret Mark's addition at Mark 10:46 where he
says that "the Secret Gospel adds *only*, 'And there were the sister of
the young man . . .' But the many other things about which you wrote
appear to be and are falsifications." These scanty remarks do not allow
any conclusions with respect to the character of the Karpokratian
Secret Gospel of Mark. It is true that the Karpokratians have been
accused of sexual license even by Clement himself.[4] However, in this
letter Clement does not indicate that the phrase "Naked man with
naked man" has any such implications. Nakedness was widely prac-
ticed in early Christian baptism,[5] and this is most likely expressed in

---

[1] See for a full discussion Koester, "From Mark to Secret Mark," 44–47.

[2] Checking the quotations from the Gospel of Mark in Clement's writings demonstrates that there is no instance in which he quotes the more original text of Mark that
Matthew and Luke used.

[3] Crossan (*Four Other Gospels*, 107–110) assumes that the *Secret Gospel of Mark*
was the most original version of this Gospel. That, however, does not excplain the fact
that Matthew and Luke used a copy of Mark which contained none of the features that
are characteristic of the *Secret Gospel*.

[4] *Strom.* 3.2, 10.1. For other evidence see Morton Smith, *Clement of Alexandria*,
Appendix B.

[5] Hippolytus (*Apostolic Tradition* 21.11) specifies that both the catechumen and the
presbyter shall stand in the water naked.

this phrase of the Karpokratian version of this new edition of Mark's Gospel.

4.2 Stories about Jesus' Birth and Childhood

4.2.1 EARLIEST INFANCY NARRATIVES[1]

Stories about Jesus' birth must have circulated long before the writing of the Gospels of Matthew and Luke, whose infancy narratives are the earliest written records of such stories. But it is very difficult to be certain about the origin and development of these narratives. Their basic genre is that of the popular "personal legend," which was well known in the world of Israel, as well as in the world of Greece and Rome. In all these legends, some kind of divine agency at the conception or the birth of a great hero, king, or religious leader is a constitutive element.

Israel's scripture itself knew of the story of Sarah and the miraculous birth of her offspring Isaac who was born, as Paul (Gal 4:23) says, "through the promise" (in contrast to the birth of Ishmael who was born "according to the flesh"). Exod 2:1–11 tells the story of the divine protection of the infant Moses. Most of all, Hannah, the mother of Samuel, whose story is told in 1 Samuel 1, became the prototype of the barren woman who, because of her prayer and piety, conceives the child that should become the new leader of the people. Against this background, one can well understand the origin of the story that tells of the wondrously announced birth of John the Baptist (Luke 1:5–25). In fact, many details in this story recall the ancient narratives of Sarah and Hannah.[2] It is the story of the birth of the new prophet of Israel in the power of Elijah who will receive the holy spirit already in his mother's womb, will bring the nation back to its God, and reconstitute Israel as God's people (Luke 1:15–17). The entire story and the announcement of the mission of John remain entirely within the

---

[1] The most comprehensive recent investigation of the infancy narratives of the canonical gospels is Raymond E. Brown, *The Birth of the Messiah: A Commentary on the Infancy Narratives of Matthew and Luke* (New York: Doubleday, 1977). For recent scholarship see idem, "Gospel Infancy Narrative Research 1976–1986," *CBQ* 48 (1986) 468–83, 660–680. A most important and seminal essay was published by Martin Dibelius in 1932 "Jungfrauensohn und Krippenkind: Untersuchungen zur Geburtsgeschichte Jesu im Lukasevangelium," and reprinted in idem, *Botschaft und Geschichte: Gesammelte Aufsätze*, vol. 1 (Tübingen: Mohr/Siebeck, 1953) 1–78. For bibliography, see also Bovon, *Evangelium nach Lukas*, 43–45; Ulrich Lutz, *Matthew 1–7: A Commentary* (Minneapolis: Augsburg, 1989) 101–2.

[2] See Bovon, *Evangelium nach Lukas*, 52–62, 94–103.

confines of Israel's tradition and expectation. There are no Hellenistic or Christian elements in this narrative. There can be little doubt that it was formed and transmitted by the community of John the Baptist which, in this story, proclaimed the memory and heritage of their great prophetic leader.

With the stories surrounding Jesus' birth in both Matthew and Luke, the reader is introduced to a similar, yet also quite different world. There is still traditional Jewish messianic language, and the Lukan stories of the annunciation (1:26–38) and of the birth of Jesus (2:1–20) formally parallel the corresponding stories about John. Even with respect to a fundamental distinction between John and Jesus, namely the attribution of royal titles to the latter, they appear to remain within the confines of Israel's traditional terminology: the child to be born will be given the throne of David, his father (Luke 1:32), and the Magi from the East come to seek the newborn king of the Jews (Matt 2:2). But the horizon is no longer that of the prophetic tradition of Israel; nor do the stories about Jesus' birth simply tell of some divine intervention at the birth of another prophet or, for that matter, of another great man like some Hellenistic legends. Rather, they speak of the birth of the divine child that marks the beginning of the new age of the history of the world. All that is old is passing away with his birth; the new age of "peace on earth for all humankind" has come (Luke 2:14). These stories utilize the genre of "personal legend" and cast it into the language of scripture, but they transcend the traditional frame of this genre. They are, first of all, eschatological proclamation. Inasmuch as nothing less than the new age of the world begins with the birth of the child, the story of God's miraculous intervention into the natural processes of birth and death[1] requires a recourse to a mythic language that is unheard of in the traditional vocabulary of Israel and has few parallels in the language of the world of Greece and Rome.

Perhaps the only true parallel to these stories can be found in the *Fourth Eclogue* of Vergil that also speaks of the turning point of the ages in the birth of the child. The boldness of Vergil's poetic language is inspired by the same eschatological tension as the vision of the narratives about the birth of Jesus and of its announcement. In spite of a multitude of publications about the birth stories of Jesus during the last six decades no modern author has been able to grasp the dimensions and the depth of spirit of these gospel stories as well as did the great scholar of classical philology and history-of-religions Eduard

---

[1] There is a correspondence between the stories of Jesus' birth and of his resurrection.

Norden in his monograph about "The Birth of the Child."[1] He has demonstrated that the roots of the concept of the birth of the divine child, who will usher in the new age, lie in Egyptian mythology and mystery language. Not that one could trace either Vergil's eclogue or any of the gospel stories directly to one or several Egyptian legends or myths. But Egyptian lore about the birth of the god Aion (= Eternity, New Age) and about the birth of Horus/Harpokrates from Isis, as well as the statuettes of Isis with her child on her lap, had become widely known in the Greco-Roman world, beginning even before the Hellenistic period.

The identification of the form and language of the legends about Jesus' birth as "scriptural"[2] is not sufficient. Of course, they were told by people who knew Isaiah's prophecies that announced the coming of the divine child.[3] But even these ancient prophecies themselves belong to the same larger world from which Vergil learned the language and the concepts of his prophetic poems. The titles of the child of Isaiah 9:6, born to rule in the new age, "Wonderful Counselor, Mighty God, Everlasting Father, Prince of Peace," are the same as those which were given to Pharaoh at his enthronement.[4] The theme of peace among the animals, which appears in Isaiah's prophecy (Isa 11:6–8) as well as in Vergil's 4th Eclogue, has a firm place in ancient Egyptian enthronement language.[5] The message of peace on earth to all people of divine pleasure may remind us of Isaiah's "prince of peace," but it also recalls the propaganda for Rome and its ruler as the guarantor of peace for the entire inhabited world, which could claim Vergil as its prophet.

It is generally agreed that the infancy narratives belong into a rela-

---

[1] Eduard Norden, *Die Geburt des Kindes: Die Geschichte einer religiösen Idee* (Leipzig: Teubner, 1924; reprint: Darmstadt: Wissenschaftliche Buchgesellschaft, 1958).

[2] It is the primary merit of the commentary on the infancy narratives of Matthew and Luke by Brown (*Birth of the Messiah*) that it presents in detail the relevant stories and prophecies of scripture which have provided, to some degree, forms, themes, and language for these narratives. Unfortunately, Brown does not place these narratives into the wider context of the continuing influence of the Egyptian throne language and its resurgence in the language of political and religious expectation in the Hellenistic and Roman world.

[3] All of Isaiah 7–11 has been very influential, not only Isa 7:14 ("behold a virgin shall conceive and bear a son and shall call his name Immanuel") and 9:6–7 ("For to us a child is born, to us a son is given, and the government shall be on his shoulder"), but also Isa 11 (the prophecy of the coming of the shoot from the root of Jesse).

[4] See Hans Wildberger, *Jesaja 1–12* (Biblischer Kommentar, Altes Testament 10/1; Neukirchen-Vluyn: Neukirchener Verlag, 1972) 376–80.

[5] Wildberger, ibid., 456–57.

tively late phase of the development of the gospel tradition. For Paul, the sonship of Jesus dates from his resurrection from the dead (Rom 1:3–4). This is reflected in the Gospel of Mark where the confession of the centurion at the cross of Jesus constitutes the first time that a human being applies the title "Son of God" to Jesus.[1] That the two later Synoptic Gospels, Matthew and Luke, date the divine sonship of Jesus from his birth is not only related to a christological development which eventually resulted in the formulation of a christology that assumed Christ's preexistence as God's Son from before the beginning of the world. It is also related to the full realization of Christianity's entrance into the world of Hellenism and Rome. Paul's message announced the salvation for Jews and Gentiles before the coming of Christ in glory. Paul knew that his message had political implications. But it was left to the next generation to spell out the Christian antithesis to the eschatological claims of Roman imperial rule. The Book of Revelation is the best known testimony, and it is no accident that this book includes a story of the birth of the messiah that borrowed heavily from Hellenistic mythology (Revelation 12). The stories of Jesus' divine conception and miraculous birth belong into the same context.

The most striking feature revealing the non-Jewish origin of the story of the birth of Jesus is the divine conception of the child. "The idea of divine generation from a virgin is not only foreign to the Old Testament and to Judaism, but it is completely impossible."[2] This statement of Rudolf Bultmann is still valid insofar as the origin of this concept is concerned, and it cannot be moderated by theological or historical reflections.[3] This concept is Hellenistic and, ultimately, Egyptian. No other religious or political tradition of antiquity can be identified as its generator. However, though Jewish circles did not create this concept, it may well have found a cautious acceptance in certain circles of Hellenistic Judaism.

The most striking example of this Hellenistic-Jewish understanding of the stories of miraculous conception and birth is indirectly preserved by Philo of Alexandria in his *De Cherubim*.[4] In this treatise, Philo speaks of four women of Israel's history (Sarah, Leah, Rebecca, and Zipporah) as examples of virtues. In doing so, he clearly draws on

[1] Elsewhere in Mark, only the heavenly voice (Mark 1:11; 9:7) and the demons (3:11; 5:7) address Jesus with this title.

[2] Bultmann, *Synoptic Tradition*, 291.

[3] See especially the two excursus "Virginal Conception" and "The Charge of Illegitimacy" in Brown, *Birth of the Messiah*, 517–542.

[4] Dibelius ("Jungfrauensohn und Krippenkind," 30–33) has drawn attention to the importance of this treatise for the understanding of the Christian infancy narratives.

older legends about the miraculous ways in which these women conceived and gave birth. According to Gen 21:1, Sarah conceives when God visits her, while she is alone (μονοθεῖσαν),[1] although the son to whom she gives birth is born to Abraham (*De Cherub.* 45). The account about Leah (*De Cherub.* 46) is even more explicit: she conceives "when God opens her womb" (Gen 29:31). Philo remarks that normally "opening the womb of a woman" is done by the husband, that is, through intercourse. Rebecca became pregnant through the one to whom Isaac sent his prayers (*De Cherub.* 47), and Zipporah became pregnant "completely without any mortal agency" (κύουσαν ἐξ οὐδενὸς θνητοῦ τὸ παράπαν, *De Cherub.* 47). If it was possible, albeit allegorically, for the Hellenistic Jew Philo to accept the concept of divine generation,[2] it must have been even less offensive to the traditional stories used by authors of the Gospels of Matthew and Luke to tell of the divine conception of the Savior whose message would challenge the political claims of the divine Augustus and his heirs.

The Synoptic Gospels record several different older stories about the birth of Jesus. All these stories are politically motivated. They share only one of these stories, namely the announcement of the conception without human (male) agency: the dream of Joseph (Matt 1:18–25) and its variant, the story of the annunciation (Luke 1:26–38). The other Synoptic stories were developed independently of each other and they do not presuppose the narrative of the miraculous conception. Matthew's account of the visit of the magi and the murder of the babes of Bethlehem (Matt 2:1–23) possibly combines two different traditional stories, namely the story of the visit of the magi and another story of the plot of Herod.[3] The last of these older stories appears in Luke 2:1–20; it records the visit of the shepherds to the cradle of the new-born child.

The two Matthean stories were formed in a very Biblical environment. The story of the coming of the magi from the East to worship the new-born king (2:1–12) exhibits features of the story of Balaam (Numbers 22–24).[4] The story of the plot of Herod (2:13–23) certainly retains a historical memory of the murderous cruelty of Herod the

---

[1] The text of Gen 21:1 does not stress explicitly that Sarah was alone at her visitation by God. But that the tradition of the interpretation had emphasized this feature is also evident in Paul, when he connects the story of Sarah's miraculous conception with Isa 54:1 (= Gal 4:27): ". . . for the desolate has more children than she who has a husband" (ὅτι πολλὰ τὰ τέκνα τῆς ἐρήμου μᾶλλον ἢ τῆς ἐχούσης τὸν ἄνδρα).

[2] See Bultmann's (*Synoptic Tradition,* 438) comment on Dibelius' article: "the abstinence of the bridegroom until birth is specifically pagan."

[3] See Brown, *Birth of the Messiah,* 188–206, 225–29.

[4] Ibid., 193–96.

Great. At the same time, it is colored also by the Biblical accounts of the Patriarch Joseph in Egypt, the birth of Moses, and the murder of the children of the Israelites by Pharaoh.[1] The Biblical and Palestinian setting of these stories is evident. However, the intention of both stories differs sharply from the parochial interests of a Jewish environment. With the "East" as the homeland of the magi and with the flight to Egypt, the horizon of the rule of the new king has become universal. It must be added that the reconstruction of the pre-Matthean stories remains extremely difficult, because Matthew not only combined elements of two stories into a new unit, he also added his own perspective by the repeated formula quotations which point to the fulfillment of scripture—not necessarily the same scriptural passages which contributed to the formation of the original stories.

The Lukan story of Jesus' birth and the proclamation to the shepherds (Luke 2:1–20) reveals a different milieu. Although the setting at Bethlehem and the shepherds may recall the city of the shepherd boy David, there is no attempt to model the story on any Biblical precedent, nor does it show any specific Palestinian coloring. There is no reason to believe that the story originated in Palestine. The introduction (2:1–5) which relates the birth of Jesus to Augustus may have been added by Luke in order to create a parallel between Jesus, the bringer of peace for the people of the earth, and Augustus who could boast that he had established peace after decades of civil war. But even the proclamation to the shepherds about the child in the manger appeals to general beliefs of the Greco-Roman world. In the Jewish tradition at the time of Jesus, shepherds are not generally seen in a very positive light.[2] But in Greco-Roman mythology, legend, and poetry the shepherd represents the golden age at which gods and human beings live in harmony and nature is at peace.[3] Like the bucolic poems of Vergil, Luke's story appeals to this romantic element of the eschatology of the Roman world.

4.2.2 THE PROTO-GOSPEL OF JAMES

The Gospels of Matthew and Luke provide the only access to the earliest stories about Jesus' birth and infancy. There seems to be no older story in any apocryphal gospel that has survived independently, although there may have been some isolated pieces of information, such as the localization of the birth of Jesus in a cave which appears in

---

[1] Ibid., 225–29 and Table VII, p. 109.

[2] See Dibelius, "Jungfrauensohn und Krippenkind," 64–65.

[3] Ibid., 72–73. The attempt to demonstrate a special relationship to the cult of Mithras has not been successful; see Dibelius, ibid., 67–73.

Justin Martyr[1] and also in the *Proto-Gospel of James*. On the other hand, the apocryphal birth and infancy gospels contain a wealth of legendary material that continues to grow throughout the following centuries.[2] Only two of the infancy gospels can be dated with some certainty into the 2nd century, the *Proto-Gospel of James* and the *Infancy Gospel of Thomas*.

The *Proto-Gospel of James*[3] is preserved in many Greek manuscripts and numerous translations of which those into Syriac, Arabic, Armenian, Coptic, and Slavonic are the most prominent.[4] None of these translations can claim to be a direct rendering of an older Greek text of this gospel. But with the exception of a few earlier fragments, even all Greek manuscripts which were known until a few years ago were written after the 10th century and show great variations in many details. A somewhat better access to the original Greek text was opened up more recently through the discovery and publication in 1958 of the *Papyrus Bodmer 5*,[5] a manuscript of the 3rd or 4th century. A fuller study of the transmission of the text of the *Proto-Gospel of James* and a new critical edition has been possible through this discovery.[6]

The discovery of *Papyrus Bodmer 5* makes clear that several parts of the later Greek manuscripts and of the translations into other ancient languages did not belong to the original story. The description, by Joseph in the first person, of the sudden cessation of nature at the moment of Jesus' birth (chapter 18.2) and the prayer of Salome (chapter 20.2) are missing in this papyrus. But even this relatively

[1] *Dial.* 78.5; see below # 5.2.2.2.

[2] See Oscar Cullmann on the younger infancy gospels in his "Kindheitsevangelien," in Hennecke-Schneemelcher, *NT Apokryphen*, 1. 363–72. This section is essentially the same as that in the English translation of the previous German edition (Hennecke-Schneemelcher-Wilson, *NT Apocrypha*, 1. 404–17).

[3] For a general discussion of this document see Edouard Cothenet, "Le Protévangile de Jaque: origine, genre et signification d'un premier midrash chrétien sur la Nativité de Marie," *ANRW* 2.25/6 (1988) 4245–69; Gero, "Apocryphal Gospels," 3978–79.

[4] See Oscar Cullmann on the "Protevangelium des Jakobus" in his "Kindheitsevangelien," in Hennecke-Schneemelcher, *NT Apocrypha*, 1. 335–36. A Latin translation did exist in ancient times; but the book was banned in the Western church. Only one fragmentary Latin manuscript of the 9th century has been discovered.

[5] M. Testuz, *Papyrus Bodmer V: Nativité de Marie* (Cologny: Bibliotheca Bodmeriana, 1958).

[6] E. de Strycker, *La forme la plus ancienne du Protévangile de Jacques: Recherches sur le Papyrus Bodmer 5 avec une édition du texte grec et une traduction annotée* (SHG 33; Brussels: 1961). The German translation in Hennecke-Schneemelcher, *NT Apokryphen*, 1. 338–49, is based upon this new edition, as is also the English translation of the previous German edition (Hennecke-Schneemelcher-Wilson, *NT Apocrypha*, 1. 374–88) which was reprinted in Cameron, *Other Gospels,* 109–21.

early papyrus includes portions that did not belong to the original work, especially the concluding chapters (22–24) which report about the death of Zacharias, the father of John the Baptist.[1] The work is entitled "The Birth of Mary, Revelation[2] of James." This has raised the question whether the entire report about the birth of Jesus (chapters 17–21) also should be viewed as a secondary expansion of the original writing, that is, whether the original writing was confined to the account of Mary's birth and virginity. But that cannot be proven.

It is evident that the author of the *Proto-Gospel of James* used the canonical gospels of Matthew and Luke. But it was certainly known to Origen, perhaps even to Clement of Alexandria. This establishes a date for its composition some time during the 2nd century CE. The pseudepigraphical author of the work is most likely "James, the brother of Jesus." However, it is not a Jewish-Christian writing like most of the other pseudepigrapha under the name of James, the brother of the Lord. The writing reveals no sectarian bias and it cannot be assigned to a particular Christian group or sect of the 2nd century. Its character differs fundamentally from any of the literature that characterized the nascent sectarian and anti-heretical writings of this period, because it is pure hagiography, perhaps the earliest hagiographical book of Christianity.

The topic of the *Proto-Gospel of James* is not the birth of Jesus, but the birth and virginity of Mary. It was written for the glorification of Mary and is, thus, a surprisingly early witness for the rapid expansion of biographical legends, not only about Jesus—that is already evident in the infancy narratives of Matthew and Luke—but also about Jesus' mother and her parents. But while the stories about the birth of Jesus still reveal the eschatological message of the proclamation of a new age with all its political implications, the *Proto-Gospel of James* exclusively caters to the interests of personal piety and, possibly, to an incipient cult of the mother of Jesus, analogous to the cult of a hero or heroine of the Hellenistic-Roman world.

The author has no real knowledge of the Temple of Jerusalem and its cult, no matter how often reference is made to Jewish ritual and purity rules. There are numerous allusions to, and borrowings from, the Biblical stories of Sarah and Hannah as well as from the canonical Gospels' story of Mary. But rarely does the author copy slavishly. Rather, the author's piety is wholly shaped by the language of the Bible. In this respect the analogy to the canonical gospel's infancy nar-

---

[1] See Cullmann in Hennecke-Schneemelcher, *NT Apokryphen*, 1. 337.

[2] This term is used in *Papyrus Bodmer 5*. Later manuscripts use "Narrative" or similar terms.

ratives is very close. However, the heroines of the story, Anna and her daughter Mary, are not Jewish women but examples of Hellenistic piety. Female sterility, the sorrow of Anna, could be a theme in any culture, Jewish, Greek, or Roman. But pregnancy of the "widow"—as is said of Anna—and virginity, combined with divine conception, here even extended to the "virgin birth," are presented in this writing as the mystery of the female that demands worship. That Mary remains a virgin even after she has given birth introduces the ascetic ideal of a life-long commitment to virginity. One is encountering a dimension of piety, in the form of a personal legend in the Hellenistic style, that is especially concerned with the role of the female in the process of the revelation's appearance in the flesh. The miraculous signs of the Synoptic Gospels' story that signify the arrival of the divine are here replaced by the wondrous virtues of virginity and ascetic dedication.

4.2.3 THE INFANCY GOSPEL OF THOMAS

While the *Proto-Gospel of James* is primarily concerned with hagiographical material and persons of the period before the birth of Jesus, the *Infancy Gospel of Thomas* focuses upon stories dealing with the childhood of Jesus. That this writing existed in some form in the 2nd century is not certain but also not improbable, although it does not seem likely that the *Epistula Apostolorum* quoted the *Infancy Gospel of Thomas*. But a reference in Irenaeus (*Adv. haer.* 1.13.1) suggests that this writing was used by the Marcosians. The title of the writing in most Greek manuscripts, "Report of the Israelite philosopher Thomas about the Childhood of the Lord"[1] claims an apostle as the author, but there is no relationship of this writing to any of the known Gnostic literature in the tradition of "Judas Thomas the Twin."[2]

No final judgment about the original form and content is possible. The variety of the available evidence in Greek manuscripts and in numerous translations is hopelessly confusing.[3] The traditions about

---

[1] Oscar Cullmann on the "Kindheitserzählung des Thomas" in his "Kindheitsevangelien," in Hennecke-Schneemelcher, *NT Apokryphen I*, 353. Cullmann, following A. de Santos Otero (see below), suggests that the Slavonic translation may have preserved the more original title "The Childhood of our Lord Jesus Christ." Thus, the name of the apostle Thomas would not have been connected with this writing in the earliest period of its transmission.

[2] See above, # 2.2.2.

[3] Cullmann in Hennecke-Schneemelcher, *NT Apokryphen*, 1. 349–360; see also idem, "The Infancy Story of Thomas" in his "Infancy Gospels," in Hennecke-Schneemelcher-Wilson, *NT Apocrypha*, 1. 388–401 (however, much of the introduction of this earlier edition must now be considered out of date). The best discussion of the problems of the transmitted texts and translations has been presented by Stephen Gero, "The Infancy

the childhood of Jesus constantly grew, were altered, and attracted new materials during a history of many centuries of transmission; later manuscripts of the *Infancy Gospel of Thomas* also include parts of the *Proto-Gospel of James*. None of the extant Greek manuscripts can be dated before the 14th century.[1] The Latin and Syriac versions are attested by manuscripts from an earlier period, but some of them remain unpublished. Arabic, Armenian, and Georgian versions seem to be secondary translations. Most important is probably the rich attestation of the *Infancy Gospel of Thomas* in the Slavonic tradition;[2] however, a satisfactory critical evaluation of the available evidence has not yet been achieved.[3]

Even if the earliest version of this gospel remains uncertain, there can be little doubt that stories about the childhood of Jesus were circulating during the 2nd century. The *Epistula Apostolorum,* written in the second half of that century, attests to one of the stories that is also contained in the various versions of the *Infancy Gospel of Thomas,* namely, the story that Jesus was sent to school where the teacher asked him to say "Alpha," whereupon Jesus responded with the request that the teacher explain to him first the meaning of "Beta" (*Epist. Apost.* 4 [15]).[4] But similar older stories may already have circulated at the time of the writing of the Gospel of Luke. To be sure, wherever the various versions of the *Infancy Gospel of Thomas* narrate the story of Jesus at twelve years in the Temple, they are clearly dependent upon the text of Luke 2:41–52. But this Lukan text itself exhibits features which suggest that the author has used an older story that told about the presence of Jesus' divine power even before his public appearance.[5] The primary interest that prompted the production of such stories is biographical.[6] The development of such stories is a comparatively late phenomenon in the formation of the

---

Gospel of Thomas: A Study of the Textual and Literary Problems," *NovT* 13 (1971) 46–80; see also idem, "Apocryphal Gospels," 3981–84.

[1] On the dates of the Greek manuscripts and of the manuscripts of all extant versions, see Gero, "The Infancy Gospel of Thomas," 49–55.

[2] All extant manuscripts derive from one or several translations made in the 10th–11th century; see Gero, ibid., 55.

[3] See Gero, ibid., 53–54, especially p. 53, n. 6 with respect to the important work of A. de Santos Otero (*Das kirchenslavische Evangelium des Thomas* [PTS 6; Berlin: De Gruyter, 1967]).

[4] For the full text of this passage, see C. Detlef G. Müller, "Epistula Apostolorum" in Hennecke-Schneemelcher, *NT Apokryphen,* 1. 208; H. Duensing, "Epistula Apostolorum," in Hennecke-Schneemelcher-Wilson, *NT Apocrypha,* 1. 193.

[5] Brown, *Birth of the Messiah,* 480–83. Brown designates such narratives as "hidden life stories."

[6] See Bovon, *Evangelium nach Lukas,* 154.

Synoptic tradition, but Luke shows that this development had begun as early as the end of the 1st century.[1]

Some of the narratives of the *Infancy Gospel of Thomas* make it evident that the childhood stories mirror the miracles of the later ministry of Jesus.[2] In the first story (chapter 2) Jesus makes twelve sparrows from clay, and a Jew complains to his father Joseph that he had violated the Sabbath; the story is modelled on gospel stories in which Jesus, during his ministry, violates the Sabbath.[3] He heals the foot of a worker who had accidentally split it with an axe (chapter 10), and saves his brother James who had been bitten by a viper. He raises a child who had fallen from the upper story of a house (chapter 9), the little child of a neighbor who had died (chapter 17),[4] and resuscitates a man who died during the building of a house. Of the several variants of the story of Jesus in school (chapters 6–7; 14 and 15), the story in chapter 15 tells of Jesus finding a book, taking it, and, without reading, by the power of the holy spirit expounding the law for all who were present; influence of the Jesus' first preaching in Nazareth (Luke 4:16–22) is evident. The parable of the sower (Mark 4:3–9 parr.) apparently provides the motif for the story of the miraculous harvest of hundred measures of wheat from a single seed that Jesus had planted (chapter 12).

But other miracle stories do not mirror any of the narratives of Jesus' ministry. They resemble more the narratives of the apocryphal Acts of the Apostles, especially the punishment miracles that tell of the death of other children who have made the boy Jesus angry (chapters 3–4) and of the death of the teacher who struck Jesus on the head (chapter 14).[5] Some stories seem to be borrowed from general popular lore.[6] The stories about the superiority of Jesus over his teachers have a parallel in stories about Buddha as child, and the

---

[1] Brown (*Birth of the Messiah*, 487–88) suggests that also the story of the wine miracle at Cana (John 2:1–12) was originally such a "hidden life" tradition.

[2] "'Hidden life' stories show that he was God's Son even as a boy by having him work miracles just as he does in the ministry" (Brown, ibid., 481).

[3] See, e.g., Mark 3:1–6; John 5:2–16.

[4] See Mark 5:35–43; Luke 7:11–17; both stories have clearly influenced the story of the raising of the neighbor's child. See also John 11.

[5] See the punishment miracles *Acts of Peter* 32; *Acts of Thomas* 8–9.

[6] This is most likely the case with respect to the story of the carrying of water in the garment (chap. 11), the miraculous stretching of a piece of wood in order to make two beams of equal length (chap. 13), and the story of Jesus and the dyer from the Arabic version of the Infancy Gospel (see Cullmann, "Infancy Gospel of Thomas" in Hennecke-Schneemelcher-Wilson, *NT Apocrypha*, 1. 400–401).

story of the clay sparrows that receive life through Jesus clapping his hands recalls the motif of an Egyptian fairy tale.[1]

It is evident that the majority of these stories are either based on the older traditions about Jesus' public ministry, especially as they are already enshrined in the canonical gospels, or are drawn from the wider store of various narratives of the ancient world. The tendency to incorporate an increasing amount of such materials into the hagiographical exploration of Jesus' childhood is richly attested in the later infancy gospels.[2]

4.3 The Gospel of Matthew [3]

4.3.1 MANUSCRIPTS

In contrast to the Gospel of Mark, the Gospel of Matthew is quite well attested in the earliest tradition of Christian communities. There are two early papyri, written about 200 CE, containing at least the fragmentary text of the Gospel of Matthew.[4] Six more papyri were written in the 3d century.[5] Rich attestation comes from the 4th century: six papyri,[6] five uncial manuscripts,[7] and of course, the two oldest manuscripts which present the entire text of the Bible (א and B, i.e., Codices Sinaiticus and Vaticanus). About three dozen uncials and two papyri from the following centuries can be added to these

---

[1] Relevant parallels are listed and discussed in Bauer, *Leben Jesu*, 95–97.

[2] Examples from these later narratives are translated by Cullmann, "Later Infancy Gospels," in Hennecke-Schneemelcher-Wilson, *NT Apocrypha*, 1. 404–17; see also Bauer, *Leben Jesu*, 97–100.

[3] For a general review of recent scholarship on the Gospel of Matthew see Graham Stanton, "The Origin and Purpose of Matthew's Gospel: Matthean Scholarship from 1945–1980," *ANRW* 2.25/3 (1985) 1889–1951. Some of the important monographs are Bornkamm-Barth-Held, *Tradition and Interpretation*; Jack Dean Kingsbury, *Matthew: Structure, Christology, Kingdom* (Philadelphia: Fortress, 1975); idem, *Matthew as Story* (2d ed.; Philadelphia: Fortress, 1988). A representative collection of important essays has been published by Joachim Lange, *Das Matthäusevangelium* (WdF 525; Darmstadt: Wissenschaftliche Buchgesellschaft, 1980).

[4] $\mathfrak{p}^{64}$ and $\mathfrak{p}^{67}$, both fragments of the same manuscript, with a few verses from Matthew 3, 5, and 26; $\mathfrak{p}^{77}$ with the text of Matt 23:30–39.

[5] $\mathfrak{p}^1$, $\mathfrak{p}^{35}$, $\mathfrak{p}^{37}$, $\mathfrak{p}^{53}$, $\mathfrak{p}^{70}$. All of these are only small fragments, containing but a few verses. $\mathfrak{p}^{45}$, presenting the text of all four canonical gospels, also preserves only a few verses of Matthew 20 and 21, and Matt 25:41–26:39. Thus there is no early attestation of the entire text of Matthew that is comparable to that for the text of the Fourth Gospel, where $\mathfrak{p}^{66}$ and $\mathfrak{p}^{75}$ have preserved considerable portions of the text; see above # 3.4.1.

[6] $\mathfrak{p}^{19}$, $\mathfrak{p}^{21}$ (both 4th or 5th century), $\mathfrak{p}^{25}$, $\mathfrak{p}^{62}$, $\mathfrak{p}^{71}$, $\mathfrak{p}^{86}$.

[7] 058, 0160, 0171, 0231, and 0242.

witnesses.[1] There can be no doubt that this Gospel was most widely used and most frequently copied in the early Byzantine period.

4.3.2 ATTESTATION

References to texts from the Gospel of Matthew and quotations from this writing appear frequently in ancient Christian literature.[2] However, the sayings quoted in *1 Clem.* 13.2 and 46.8, and the various parallels in the *Epistles of Ignatius* and the *Epistle of Barnabas* cannot be taken as evidence for the use of the Gospel of Matthew.[3] More difficult to evaluate are the quotations of sayings in *Did.* 1.3–5,[4] but this small collection of sayings of Jesus, composed from various sources, is most likely an interpolation which was made after the middle of the 2d century.[5] No use of the First Gospel can be demonstrated in any other section of the *Didache*.[6]

In the middle of the 2d century, quotations from the text of Matthew's Gospel are clearly in evidence. The sayings collection used by the author of *2 Clement* is based on the text of Matthew (and Luke, and probably an apocryphal source);[7] the Valentinian author Ptolemy, in his *Letter to Flora*,[8] uses the Gospel of Matthew frequently, and Jus-

---

[1] Among these are 𝔭⁴⁴ (6th or 7th century), 𝔭⁸³ (6th century); uncials from the 5th century A (02), C (04), D (05), W (032), and 0170; from the 6th century N (022), P (024), Z (035), Σ (042), Φ (043), 0164, and 0237; from the 7th century 0102, 0104, 0106, 0107, 0200, and 0204; from the 8th century E (07), L (019), 047, 064, 067, 071, 073, 078, 085, 087/092b, 089, 094, 0116, 0118, 0148, 0161, 0234, and 0250; from the 9th century F (09), G (011), H (013), K (017), M (021), U (030), V (031), 0128, 0135, 0136, 0196, 0197, 0255, and 0271; from the 10th century S (028), X (033), and 0249.

[2] The most comprehensive collection of materials can be found in Massaux, *Influence de l'Évangile de Saint Matthieu*. However, Massaux ascribes to the use of the Gospel of Matthew numerous instances in which quotations from the free oral tradition are more likely. See also the more balanced judgments in Köhler, *Rezeption des Matthäusevangeliums*.

[3] Koester, *Synoptische Überlieferung*, 4–61, 124–53. For the use of Matthew in the Apostolic Fathers see also *The New Testament in the Apostolic Fathers* by a Committee of the Oxford Society of Historical Theology (Oxford: 1905); Leon E. Wright, *Alterations of the Words of Jesus as quoted in the Literature of the Second Century* (Cambridge, MA: Harvard University Press, 1952). See also above ## 2.1.4.3 and 3.2.3.2.

[4] Koester, *Synoptische Überlieferung*, 220–37.

[5] Bentley Layton, "The Sources, Date and Transmission of *Didache* 1.3b–2.1," *HTR* 61 (1968) 343–83. For the discussion see also W. Rordorf, "Le Probléme de la transmission textuelle de *Didachè* 1,3b.–2,1," in: Franz Paschke, ed., *Überlieferungsgeschichtliche Untersuchungen* (TU 125; Berlin: Akademie-Verlag, 1981) 499–513; Niederwimmer, *Didache*, on *Did.* 1.3–5.

[6] Koester, *Synoptische Überlieferung*, 160–223. See above # 1.4.3.

[7] Koester, *Synoptische Überlieferung*, 70–105.

[8] In Epiphanius, *Adv. haer.* 33.3.1–7.10. The Greek text has been edited by Gilles Qispel, *Ptolémée, Lettre à Flora: Analyse, texte critique, traduction, commentaire et*

tin Martyr quotes large sections from a gospel harmony which was composed from the Gospels of Matthew and Luke, possibly also Mark.[1]

The name of Matthew, however, never appears in the context of these quotations, which is probably due to the fact that at least *2 Clement* and Justin do not use one or several separate gospels but a harmony they know as "the gospel,"[2] and not as the work of a particular author.[3]

4.3.3 AUTHOR AND INTEGRITY

Matthew as the name of an author of a writing appears for the first time in a fragment of bishop Papias of Hierapolis who lived in the first half of the 2d century:

> Matthew composed the sayings (τὰ λόγια) in the Hebrew language, and each translated them (ἡρμήνευσεν) as best he could. (Eusebius, *Hist. eccl.* 3.39.16)

This remark has been variously interpreted, and the scholarly debate has not produced a definitive and generally accepted explanation.[4] In Eusebius's report, this quote from Papias's writings follows immediately upon his quote from the same author about the Gospel of Mark.[5] Thus the reference to Matthew as the author of "the sayings" is widely understood as a reference to the canonical Gospel of Matthew, and there can be no question that this is what Eusebius thought when he copied Papias's information. But the difficulties are evident. First of all, Papias speaks only about "the sayings" of Jesus. As a reference to the Gospel of Matthew, this must seem very strange, especially in view of the fact that Papias states, with respect to the Gospel of Mark, that Mark wrote "the things said *and done* by the Lord." Second, Papias's reference to a "Hebrew" composition by Matthew is extraordinary because it is certain that there never was a Semitic (Hebrew or

---

index grec (2d ed.; SC 24; Paris: Cerf, 1966); see also Völker, *Quellen,* 87–93; English translation in Layton, *Gnostic Scriptures,* 306–15; see also Foerster, *Gnosis,* 1. 154–61.

[1] See below, # 5.2.

[2] However, Justin uses both the plural (*1 Apol.* 66.3) and the singular (*Dial.* 10.2).

[3] The only exception may be Justin, *Dial.* 106.3, where a reference to information about Peter that can come only from the Gospel of Mark (3:16–17) is said be be written in "his," i.e., Peter's memoirs. See above, # 4.1.1.

[4] The most recent comprehensive discussion can be found in Ron Cameron, *Apocryphon of James,* 108–12.

[5] See above, # 4.1.2.

Aramaic) original of the Gospel of Matthew.[1] Third, there is no evidence for the existence of various differing translations into Greek in which the Gospel of Matthew could have been circulating in its earliest period, as is claimed in Papias's statement.[2] To be sure, that Matthew was the oldest Gospel and that it was originally written in Aramaic (or Hebrew) is the traditional view, which was held from the time of the ancient church. The oldest statement comes from Irenaeus:

> Now Matthew published among the Hebrews in their own tongue also a written Gospel, while Peter and Paul were preaching in Rome and founding the church (quoted in Eusebius *Hist. eccl.* 5.8.2).

Origen's *Commentary on Matthew* refers to something that he claims to have "learned from the traditions":

> ... that first was written (the Gospel) according to Matthew, who was once a tax collector and afterwards an apostle of Christ, who published it for those who from Judaism came to believe, composed as it was in the Hebrew language (quoted in Eusebius *Hist. eccl.* 6.25.4; LCL).

Eusebius made a similar statement—without indicating a particular source—when he described the time of Domitian:

> Matthew had first preached to the Hebrews, and when he was at the point of going to others he transmitted in writing in his native language the Gospel according to himself, and thus submitted by writing the lack of his own presence to those from whom he was sent (*Hist. eccl.* 3.24.6; LCL).

It is quite probable that all these statements are ultimately inspired by Papias's tradition about "Matthew who composed the sayings in Hebrew." Through the claims of Jerome, this assumption of the originally Hebrew Gospel of Matthew was connected with the theory of its fragmentary preservation in the so-called *Gospel according to the Hebrews*.[3] The priority of a Hebrew (or Aramaic) Matthew is still held

---

[1] The Greek literary style of the Gospel of Matthew and its use of Greek sources (Mark and Q) and materials exclude this.

[2] Unless one wants to assume that Papias's information is wrong on all counts, with respect to the character of this Gospel, with respect to its original language, and with respect to the translation into Greek, Papias' remark is better understood as a reference to an altogether different writing. The writing he describes would have been a collection of sayings, composed in Hebrew (i.e., Aramaic), and translated into Greek several times. This characterization fits the Synoptic Sayings Source quite well: it was probably composed originally in Greek, but some of its part may have been translated from Aramaic into Greek more than once, and it consisted primarily of sayings of Jesus. See above # 2.3.1.

[3] For a discussion of the Jewish-Christian Gospels and the problems caused by

by some today. But hypotheses in favor of this assumption usually propose that some earlier form or part of Matthew was composed in Hebrew, and that it was this earlier version on which some of the other gospels were dependent.[1] What is actually at stake here is the integrity of the Gospel of Matthew itself. Theories developed about a more original Matthew, whether first written in Hebrew or not, always assume that there was an earlier version of this Gospel of a character that differed clearly from the Gospel of Mark and from the Synoptic Sayings Source, i.e., from the two sources used by Matthew according to the two-source hypothesis, and from the preserved Greek text of Matthew.[2] Over against such speculations, it still seems to be the most plausible assumption that the manuscript tradition of Matthew's Gospel has preserved its text more or less in its oldest form. To be sure, there are variations in the manuscript transmission. But unlike the Gospels of John and Mark, there are no indications, internal or external, that an originally Hebrew or Greek text of the Gospel of Matthew underwent substantial alteration before the emergence of the archetype(s) of the text upon which the extant manuscript tradition depends.

We do not know the author of this Gospel. That the original composition of the Matthew's Gospel was in Greek and that it depended upon earlier Greek gospel sources, makes it highly unlikely that Jesus' disciple Levi/Matthew wrote the Gospel which bears his name. However, the name Matthew may have been connected with the tradition of sayings and their written composition which the author used, i.e., with the Synoptic Sayings Source.

Jerome's ambiguous statements about the Hebrew Matthew see Philipp Vielhauer, "Jewish-Christian Gospels," in Hennecke-Schneemelcher-Wilson, *NT Apocrypha,* 1. 117–39.

[1] This was first proposed by Ferdinand Christian Baur, *Kritische Untersuchungen über die kanonischen Evangelien, ihr Verhältniß zueinander, ihren Charakter und Ursprung* (Tübingen: Fues, 1847) 572–82. On the controversies about Baur's view in the Tübingen school see R. H. Fuller, "Baur versus Hilgenfeld: A Forgotten Chapter in the Debate on the Synoptic Problem," *NTS* 24 (1977–78) 355–70. For a more recent theory of a Hebrew Proto-Matthew see Malcom Lowe and David Flusser, "Evidence Corroborating a Modified Proto-Matthean Synoptic Theory," *NTS* 29 (1983) 25–47.

[2] The most cogent, albeit it very complex, synoptic source theory recently developed, which assumes that an earlier version of Matthew existed, which functioned as a source also for the other Synoptic Gospels, was proposed by Boismard, see P. Benoit and M.-É. Boismard, *Synopse des quatres Evangîles en français,* vol. II: *Commentaire* (Paris: Cerf, 1972). Cf. also M.-É. Boismard, "The Two-Source Theory at an Impasse," *NTS* 26 (1979–80) 1–17. For criticism see F. W. Beare, "On the Synoptic Problem: A New Documentary Theory," *ATR* SS 3 (1974) 15–28.

4.3.4 SOURCES

The two-source hypothesis remains the most probable basis for a more accurate definition of the sources used by Matthew. This hypothesis says: (1) Mark is the oldest extant gospel and was used both by Matthew and Luke. (2) In addition, Matthew and Luke used a second common source, containing mostly sayings of Jesus (thus called the Synoptic Sayings Source, or "Q"), that is no longer extant but can be reconstructed with a fair degree of certainty.[1] An additional problem arises from the observation that Matthew gives evidence for having used a different edition of the document Q, especially concerning the Q materials now incorporated in the Sermon on the Mount (Matthew 5–7). This "sermon" may be the result of a special redaction of Q, as has been discussed above.[2]

The two-source hypothesis cannot fully explain the source problem of the Gospel of Matthew. The reasons are manifold: (1) as has been pointed out in the treatment of Mark,[3] the extant copies of Mark seem to derive from a revised version of that Gospel and not from the earlier version used by Matthew (and Luke); (2) the reconstruction of the Synoptic Sayings Source must necessarily remain hypothetical; (3) there are numerous sayings materials in Matthew which are not paralleled in Q and obviously derive from a special source used only by Matthew, often called "M";[4] (4) the narratives about the birth of Jesus in Matthew (chapters 1–2) have no relationship to any of these sources, nor are they in any way connected with the traditions of Luke's birth narrative[5]—thus a fourth source or tradition must be posited for these materials.

---

[1] On the recent debate about the renewal of the so-called Griesbach hypothesis see above # 2.3.1.

[2] See # 2.3.4 on the consequences of the hypothesis developed by Hans Dieter Betz, *Essays on the Sermon on the Mount.*

[3] See above, # 4.1.

[4] The hypothesis that one must assume the existence of a special source for Matthew (M) and a special source for Luke (L), in addition to Mark and Q (four-source hypothesis), was most elaborately developed by B. H. Streeter, *The Four Gospels: A Study of Origins* (London: Macmillan, 1924). However, it is not necessary to assign all the special Matthean sayings of Jesus to "M" because they may already have been incorporated into the Jewish-Christian redaction of Q that Matthew used; see above # 2.3.4.

[5] Brown, *Birth of the Messiah*; see above # 4.2.1.

4.3.5 MATTHEW'S USE OF SOURCES

The basic framework of the narrative in Matthew's Gospel is derived from Mark. In the first part of his Gospel, Matthew has somewhat rearranged the Markan order, primarily for the composition of the chapters describing Jesus' healing ministry (Matthew 8–9). Matthew at first followed Mark's narrative (with some omissions) up to Mark 1:39 = Matt 4:23–25, then left this context for the insertion of the Sermon on the Mount (Matthew 5–7), and afterwards (Matt 8:1) returned to the Markan context for two healing miracles which he uses to introduce two chapters he composed himself about Jesus' healing ministry. Mark 1:40–45 (healing of the leper) and Mark 2:1–12 (healing of the man sick with palsy) each constitute the first story of the two parts of this composition (= Matt 8:1–4; 9:1–8). Most of the other healing narratives in these two chapters are drawn from different contexts of Mark's Gospel[1] (one comes from another source, apparently Q,[2] and one may be a Matthean composition[3]). At the same time, Matthew included materials found in the same Markan context, although they did not describe Jesus' healing ministry.[4] It is also important to observe that the stories which Matthew drew from other Markan contexts in the composition of these chapters appear exactly in the same order in which they are reported in Mark. The following chart illustrates Matthew's compositional procedure:

[1] Mark 1:21–39; 4:35–41; 5:1–20, 21–43; 8:22–26(?). The latter, a story of the healing of two blind men, also contains elements of Matt 20:29–34 = Mark 10:46–52; it was perhaps composed by Matthew, as was the following story, Matt 9:32–33; see Bultmann, *Synoptic Tradition*, 212, and the next footnotes.

[2] Matt 8:5–13 = Luke 7:1–10. On the problem of the presence of this miracle narrative in Q, a writing that contained mostly sayings see Robinson, "Kerygma and History," 56–57; Lührmann, *Redaktion*, 57–58: the story as it appeared in Q contained mostly dialogue and only very little narrative material; the narrative elements of the Matthean and Lukan versions have almost nothing in common; thus they were added by the two authors independently of each other.

[3] Matt 9:32–33 (healing of a dumb demoniac) seems to be composed by Matthew on the basis of the brief story of the exorcism of a dumb demon (Matt 12:22–23 = Luke 11:14) which Q had used as introduction for the Beelzebul controversy (Q/Luke 11:15, 17–20, 23). With regard to the possible Matthean authorship of Matt 9:32–33 see Bultmann, *Synoptic Tradition*, 212.

[4] Call of Levi (Matt 9:9–13 = Mark 2:13–17), question about fasting (Matt 9:14–17 = Mark 2:18–22).

	Matthew	Mark same context	Mark other context	Other source
Summary account	4:23–25	1:39		
Sermon on the Mount	5:1–7:29			Q and M
Leper	8:1–4	1:40–45		
Centurion's servant	8:5–13			Q/Luke 7:1–10
Peter's mother	8:14–15		1:29–31	
Healing summary	8:16–17		1:32–34	
Discipleship	8:18–22			Q/Luke 9:57–60
Stilling a tempest	8:23–27		4:35–41	
Gadarene demoniacs	8:28–34		5:1–20	
Man sick with palsy	9:1–8	2:1–12		
Call of Levi	9:9–13	2:13–17		
Question of fasting	9:14–17	2:18–22		
Jairus' daughter	9:18–26		5:21–43	
Two blind men	9:27–31		8:22–26[1]	
Dumb demoniac	9:32–33			Q/Luke 11:14

Apart from these changes in the Markan order in the first part of the Gospel, other deviations are few. The pericope of the call of the Twelve (disciples) from Mark 3:13–19 and the instruction for the sending of the Twelve from Mark 6:7–13 have been used to form the introduction, and part of, the material in Matthew's sending of the twelve disciples and mission discourse (Matt 9:35; 10:1–4, 9–11, 14). Mark 1:22 (reaction to Jesus' teaching) has been used as the conclusion of the Sermon on the Mount (Matt 7:28–29), while the healing of the demoniac in the synagogue, introduced by the remark about Jesus' teaching (Mark 1:23–28), has been omitted. Also missing is the parable of the Seed Growing Secretly (Mark 4:26–29).[2]

Pericope Title	Mark	Matthew
Reaction to Jesus' teaching	1:22	7:28
Demoniac in synagogue	1:23–27	———
Report of Jesus' exorcism	1:28	4:24
Call of the Twelve	3:13	5:1
	3:14–15	———
	3:16–19	10:2–4

[1] Unless Matthew is using Mark 10:46–52 for this story; see above.

[2] However, this pericope my not have been part of the Markan text used by Matthew; see above # 4.1.2.3.

Sending of the Twelve	6:6–7	9:35–10:1
	6:8	10:5, 8, 9
	6:9–11	10:10–11, 14
	6:12–13	

Otherwise all Markan sections are reproduced by Matthew in their exact Markan order.

The use of the Gospel of Mark is even more obvious in the second half of Matthew. From 14:1 (= Mark 6:14) to the end of the work, Matthew reproduced almost all Markan pericopes in the same order in which they appear in Mark. The only sections which are omitted are the healing stories of the deaf-mute (Mark 7:32–36) and of the blind man of Bethsaida (Mark 8:22–26),[1] and the apophthegmata about the strange exorcist (Mark 9:38–41) and of the widow's mite (Mark 12:41–44). In the Synoptic Apocalypse, Matthew passes over the Markan conclusion of the discourse (13:33–37).

It is more difficult to determine the changes made by Matthew in his use of the Synoptic Sayings Source, because this source can be reconstructed only by detailed comparison with the corresponding sections reproduced by Luke. The use of Mark reveals two literary procedures. On the one hand, Matthew tends to leave the order of materials in his sources intact. On the other hand, the desire to construct larger thematic units is evidenced in the description of Jesus' healing ministry in Matthew 8 and 9; for such purposes Matthew rearranges the order of his sources. Thus it would not be out of character for the large speeches in the Gospel of Matthew to be the result of eclectic collection and redaction of sources and materials available to the author.

However, in several of his speeches, Matthew follows a set procedure. Except for the first of the five major speeches, the Sermon on the Mount (Matthew 5–7), he begins a speech with the reproduction of some Markan materials, then adds sayings from Q, and concludes with materials drawn from his special source or other contexts and traditions.

The second major discourse, recorded at the occasion of the sending of the twelve disciples (Matt 9:37–10:42), combines three smaller discourses, beginning with one from Mark (6:6–11), then adding materials from one or two discourses from Q (= Luke 10:2–16; 12:2–9), but also supplying material from other Markan contexts:

---

[1] However, this Markan story may have influenced Matt 9:27–31; see above.

Pericope or Saying	Matthew	Mark	Other Sources
Description of situation	9:35a	6:7	
Summary account	9:35b[1]		
Sheep without a shepherd	9:36	6:34	
The harvest is great	9:37		Q 10:2
Authority for the disciples	10:1	6:7	
Names of the Twelve	10:2–4	3:16–19	
"He commanded them . . ."	10:5	6:8a	
Not to the Gentiles . . .	10:5b–6		"M" source[2]
Proclamation and healing	10:7–8		Q? (Luke 9:2)
Mission instructions	10:9–11	6:8b–10	
". . . no shoes . . ."	10:10b		Q 10:4
Worker's wages	10:10c		Q 10:7
Entering a house	10:12–13		Q 10:6–10a
Leaving a place	10:14	6:11	(Q 10:10a–11)
Punishment for rejection	10:15		Q 10:12
"Like sheep among wolves"	10:16		Q 10:3
Persecution of the disciples	10:17–23[3]	13:9–13	
Disciple not over the master	10:24–25		Q 6:40
Fearless confession	10:26–33		Q 12:2–9
Division in households	10:34–36		Q 12:51–53
Conditions of discipleship	10:37–39		Q 14:26f; 17:33
Acceptance of the disciples	10:40–42	9:37, 41	

The procedure is similar in the composition of the parable speech, Matthew 13. Here as well as in the eschatological speech (Matthew 24), the Gospel of Mark already presented to Matthew materials in the form of a speech of Jesus. Thus Matthew essentially reproduces parts of the parable chapter from the Gospel of Mark (4:1–20, 25, 30–32 = Matt 13:1–13, 18–23, 31–32) and adds materials from Q (= Luke 10:32–34; 13:20–21) as well as four parables from his special source (Matt 13:24–30 and 36–43, 44, 45–46, 47–50).[4]

Parable	Matthew	Mark	Other Sources
Introduction	13:1–2	4:1–2	
The Sower	13:3–9	4:3–9	

[1] This is a Matthean composition based on Mark 1:39; 3:7–10. Matthew uses the same materials for the summary account in 4:23–25, which introduces the Sermon on the Mount; see also Luke 8:1.

[2] These instructions have no parallel either in Q or in Mark. They may be due to the Jewish-Christian redactor of Q who also composed the Sermon on the Mount; see below.

[3] Matt 10:23 seems to be a Matthean composition.

[4] About this special Matthean source for the parables and its possible relationship to a source used by the *Gospel of Thomas* see above # 2.2.4.3.

Reason for parables	13:10–12	4:10–12	
Logion	13:13	4:25	
Scriptural formula quotation	13:14–15		Isa 6:9–10
Blessed witnesses	13:16–17		Q 10:23–24
Interpretation of the Sower	13:18–23	4:13–20	
The Tares	13:24–30		Special Source
The Mustard Seed	13:31–32	4:30–32	Q 13:18–19[1]
The Leaven	13:33		Q 13:20–21
Use of parables	13:34	4:33–34	
Scriptural formula quotation	13:35		Ps 77:2(?)[2]
Interpretation of the Tares	13:36–43		Special source
The Hidden Treasure	13:44		Special source
The Pearl	13:45–46		Special source
The Fishnet	13:47–50		Special source

Some of the church order materials in Matthew's catechism (18:1–
35) were already assembled by Mark, and the discourse begins at the
point at which Matthew, in the reproduction of his source, has reached
Mark 9:33–37, that is, the pericope which he uses as the opening for
the discourse. What has been added by Matthew has been drawn from
various contexts of Q and from Matthew's special source. Again, we
can observe the peculiar method of the redactor: Mark is used at the
beginning of the discourse, then materials from Q are added, and special source materials dominate in the final portion of the discourse:

Pericope	Matthew	Mark	Other Sources
Dispute about greatness	18:1–5[3]	9:33–37	
About offences	18:6–9	9:42–48	
Parable of the Lost Sheep	18:12–14[4]		Q 15:3–7
About forgiveness	18:15		Q 17:3
Reproving a brother	18:16–17		Special source
Power of binding & losing	18:18		Special source
Prayer and fulfillment	18:19		Special source

[1] In this parable, Matthew follows the order of Mark 4, but has also used Q in the
editing of his version of the parable: λαβὼν ἄνθρωπος in vs. 31, and the verb αὐξάνω in
vs. 32 have no parallels in Mark but only in Luke 13:18–19.

[2] This passage from the Psalms, in its Greek form, is remotely related to Matt 13:35.
About more closely related sayings see above # 2.1.3.

[3] Matthew has revised this Markan pericope radically, omitting the saying of Mark
9:35 about being first (it appears later in Matt 20:27), and inserting another saying
about entering the kingdom as children (Matt 18:3), which he drew from a different
Markan context (Mark 10:15).

[4] Matt 18:10 is a saying of unknown origin; Matt 18:11 does not belong to the original text of Matthew but is an intrusion from Luke 19:10, which is missing in the most
reliable manuscripts (א B etc.).

Presence of Jesus	18:20	Special source[1]
Forgive seven times seventy	18:21–22	Q 17:4
Parable: Unmerciful Servant	18:23–35	Special source

The eschatological discourse in Matthew 24–25 is an expanded version of Mark's apocalypse (Mark 13:1–37). All verses from Mark 13 which are used by Matthew appear in the same order in which they are found in Mark. Matthew uses the same procedure that he employed in his composition of the parable speech, Matthew 13: he begins with a large section of Mark in which he maintains the Markan order of the materials; he then inserts sections from Q,[2] and he relies on special sources in the final part of the discourse:

Pericope	Matthew	Mark	Other Sources
Destruction of Jerusalem	24:1–3	13:1–4	
Signs of the parousia	24:4–8	13:5–8	
Tribulations of the disciples	24:9a–b	13:9a, 13a[3]	
	24:10–12		Special source[4]
	24:13	13:13b	
	24:14		Source?[5]
The final tribulations	24:15–25	13:14–23	
How the Son of man comes	24:26–27		Q 17:23–24
Saying about the corpse	24:28		Q 17:37
Parousia of the Son of man	24:29–31	13:24–27	
Parable of the Fig Tree	24:32–33	13:28–29	
Time of the parousia	24:34–36	13:30–32	
About watchfulness	24:37–39		Q 17:26–27
Saying about divisions	24:40–41		Q 17:35
Admonition: watchfulness	24:42	13:35	
Parable of the Thief	24:43–44		Q 12:39–40
The two servants	24:45–51		Q 12:42–46
Parable of the Ten Virgins	25:1–12		Special source[6]
Admonition: watchfulness	25:13	13:35	

[1] A parallel to this saying appears in Gos. Thom. 30.

[2] Matthew uses the Q materials here and elsewhere more freely. However, almost all of the Q materials used here have parallels in Luke 12 and 17. The eschatological prophecies of these two Lukan chapters may have formed a single unit in Q; see above, # 2.3.3–4.

[3] Mark 13:9b–12 had already been used in Matt 10:17–21.

[4] That these verses (and possibly other materials of Matthew 25) are drawn from a particular source is evident in the close parallels in Did. 16; see Koester, Synoptische Überlieferung, 173–90; John S. Kloppenborg, "Didache 16,6–8 and Special Matthaean Tradition," ZNW 70 (1979) 54–67; Niederwimmer, Didache, 250–56.

[5] This verse is probably a formulation of Matthew for which he may have used Mark 13:9–10.

[6] Matt 25:10–12 has a parallel in a passage that appears in Luke 13:25. It is debated whether this is a Q saying or a secondary formulation by the author of Luke's Gospel; see Kloppenborg, Q Parallels, 154. In any case, it is highly unlikely that Luke

| Parable of the Talents | 25:14–30 | Q 19:11–27 |
| The Last Judgment | 25:31–46 | Special source |

Some of the smaller discourses of Matthew are also expansions of Markan discourse sections. The discourse on clean and unclean, Matt 15:1–20, reproduces Mark 7:1–23, adding special materials in Matt 15:12–14.[1] The speech against the Pharisees is based on Mark 12:38–40 (= Matt 23:1, 6). However, almost all the materials of this discourse reproduce a collection of sayings from Q (Matt 23:4, 13, 23, 25–27, 29–30, 34–36 = Luke 11:46, 52, 42, 39–40, 44, 47–48, 49–51) to which Matthew adds special materials (Matt 23:2–3, 5, 8–10, 15–22, 24, 28). As in the case of the Sermon on the Mount (see below) one may doubt that the author of the First Gospel composed this discourse himself. Rather he may have used an already expanded version of the collection of sayings against the Pharisees from Q.

That the Sermon on the Mount was not a fresh creation by the author of the First Gospel is evident from a comparison with Luke's Sermon on the Plain (Luke 6:20–49); almost all the materials appearing in that discourse have parallels in Matthew 5–7.[2] Thus Q presented a discourse which was the ultimate basis for Matthew's Sermon on the Mount. Hans Dieter Betz has persuasively argued that Matthew was not directly dependent on Q/Luke 6:20–49, but upon a further expansion of this Q section, a written Jewish-Christian teaching manual which had already assembled most of the materials now incorporated in Matthew 5–7.[3] Thus with respect to the first major discourse in Matthew, the contribution of the author of the First Gos-

---

13:25 (or an older saying used here) was the basis for the formulation of the parable Matt 25:1–13.

[1] Matt 15:13 is a saying about the "Plants not planted by the Father," which Matthew probably drew from the free tradition of sayings; however, it is also attested in *Gos. Thom.* 40. Matt 15:14, the saying about the blind leading the blind, has a parallel in Luke 6:39 and *Gos. Thom.* 34. Whether or not any of these two sayings stood in Q is difficult to determine. On Matt 15:14 = Luke 6:39 see Kloppenborg, *Q Parallels*, 38.

[2] The only exceptions are Luke 6:24–26, which has no parallel at all in Matthew, and Luke 6:39–40, which Matthew has used in 15:14; 10:24–25.

[3] Hans Dieter Betz, "Die Makarismen der Bergpredigt (Matthäus 5,3–12): Beobachtungen zur literarischen Form und theologischen Bedeutung," *ZThK* 75 (1987) 3–19. Cf. also idem, "Eine judenchristliche Kult-Didache in Matthäus 6, 1–18," in Georg Strecker, ed., *Jesus Christus in Historie und Theologie: Neutestamentliche Festschrift für Hans Conzelmann zum 60. Geburtstag* (Tübingen: Mohr-Siebeck, 1975) 446–57; idem, "The Sermon on the Mount: Its Literary Genre and Function," *JR* 59 (1979) 285–97; idem, "Kosmogonie und Ethik in der Bergpredigt," *ZThK* 81 (1984) 139–71. These essays are now collected in idem, *Studien zur Bergpredigt* (Tübingen: Mohr-Siebeck, 1986); ET idem, *Essays on the Sermon on the Mount*. See above, # 2.3.4.

pel should not be overestimated. Still, it is evident that the section of Q which appears in Luke's Sermon on the Plain provided the basic structure for this speech, while Markan parallels appear only occasionally.

Pericope or Saying	Matthew	Q	Other Sources
The situation	4:25		Mark 3:7–8
The mountain setting	5:1	6:12	Mark 3:13
Beatitudes	5:3–12	**6:20–23**	
Metaphor of the salt	5:13		Mark 9:50
Metaphor of the light	5:13–16	11:33	
Relevance of the law	5:17–20		Special source
1st antithesis: murder	5:21–24		Special source
Parable about reconciliation	5:25–26	12:57–59	
2d antithesis: adultery	5:27–28		
The offending eye	5:29–30		Mark 9:43, 47f
3d antithesis: divorce	5:31–32	16:18	Mark 10:11–12
4th antithesis: swearing	5:33–37		Special source[1]
5th antithesis: retaliation	5:38–42	**6:29–30**	
6th antithesis: love & hate	5:43–45	**6:27–28**	
Sayings on loving others	5:46–47	**6:32–33**	
Conclusion	5:48	**6:36**	
On almsgiving	6:1–4		
On prayer	6:5–8		Special source[2]
Lord's Prayer	6:9–13	11:2–4	Special source
Prayer and forgiveness	6:14–15		Mark 11:25–26
On fasting	6:16–18		Special source
On treasures	6:19–21	12:33–34	
Saying on the eye	6:22–23	11:34–36	
Serving two masters	6:24	16:13	
On cares	6:25–34	12:22–31	
On judging	7:1–5	**6:37f, 41f**	
No pearls before the swine	7:6		Special source
Answer to prayer	7:7–11	11:9–13	
Golden Rule	7:12	**6:31**	
The narrow gate	7:13–14	13:23–24	
Wolves in sheep's clothing	7:15		Special source
Tree and fruit	7:16–20	**6:43–45**	
Those who say "Lord. Lord"	7:21	**6:46**	
Judgment on the lawless	7:22–23	13:26–27	
Parable of House Building	7:24–27	**6:47–49**	
Reaction to Jesus' words	7:28b–29		Mark 1:22

[1] See above on James 5:12, # 2.1.4.

[2] For this section and the following on prayer and fasting see the sayings in the *Gospel of Thomas*, # 6a, 14a.

I have highlighted the materials of the Sermon on the Mount which have parallels in Luke 6. Most of them occur in Matthew 5–7 in the same order as in Luke's Sermon on the Plain. This Q speech was certainly the basis for the composition. Other materials which have been added at numerous points are drawn mostly from other contexts of Q, while Markan sayings appear only occasionally. Thus the manner of composition differs markedly from the other major speeches in Matthew in which a Markan context and Markan materials always provide the basis for the speech. This observation would confirm the hypothesis that Matthew was not the author of the Sermon on the Mount. Rather, it was composed by an author who did not know Mark and was primarily dependent upon the Synoptic Sayings Source.

Matthew opens his Gospel with a genealogy of Jesus and narratives about Jesus' birth (Matthew 1–2). Only in 3:1 does he begin to follow his major source, the Gospel of Mark. The infancy narratives (Matt 1:18–2:23) derive from a special source which had collected popular legends about miraculous events accompanying Jesus' birth. But these narratives are dominated by an unusual motif which is a striking feature of Matthew's redaction of this source. The principle of this redaction is evident in the transformation of the narrative to a record that confirms the fulfillment of prophecy. The prophecies are explicitly quoted, introduced by the repeated elaborate formula "(this happened) in order to fulfill what had been said (by the Lord) through the prophets" (τοῦτο δὲ γέγονεν ἵνα πληρωθῇ τὸ ῥηθὲν ὑπὸ κυρίου διὰ τοῦ προφήτου λέγοντος). This formula appears four times in Matt 1:18–2:23 (1:22; 2:15, 18, 23); a differently formulated fifth reference, "thus it is written through the prophet" (οὕτως γὰρ γέγραπται διὰ τοῦ προφήτου), forms the centerpiece of the story of the visit of the Magi (2:5). This method of using narrative for the confirmation of prophecy is a characteristic editing feature of the author of this Gospel.[1] It is, therefore, likely that these first chapters of the Gospel, as they now appear in the text, have been composed by Matthew on the basis of older legends. In the process of such composition, the traditional materials lost the beauty of their legendary narrative structure and became fragmentary records confirming the theological theory of scriptural fulfillment in historical events.[2]

The tendency to use traditional materials for the proof of fulfillment of prophecy has also determined Matthew's redaction of other narra-

---

[1] This formula also appears in Matt 4:14–16; 8:17; 12:17–21; 13:14–15, 35; 21:4–5; 27:9. Cf. Krister Stendahl, *The School of St. Matthew and Its Use of the Old Testament* (2d ed.; Philadelphia: Fortress, 1968).

[2] Compare the legends used in the infancy narrative of Luke; see below, # 4.4.3.2.

tive sources used in his Gospel. Jesus' first preaching in Capernaum "in the regions of Zebulon and Naphtali" is a fulfillment of Isa 9:1–2 (Matt 4:13–16); his healing ministry fulfills Isa 53:4 (Matt 8:16–17) and Isa 42:1–2 (Matt 5:17); his preaching in parables fulfills Ps 77:2; his riding into Jerusalem is a fulfillment of Zech 9:9. This motif is also evident in the passion narrative: Jesus' suffering is necessary in order to fulfill the "scriptures of the prophets" (Matt 26:56), and the piece of land that the high priests buy with Judas's money is named in order to fulfill Jer 39:6–15 (Matt 27:9–10). In this way, Matthew changes radically the narrative impact of the stories he uses. He is not capable of just telling a story. All traditional narratives become theological proofs and are deprived of their ability to communicate "story." This apologetic feature places Matthew in the context of early Christian apologetics. His method of the interpretation of scripture in relation to fulfillment of historical record is paralleled in the apologetic procedures of Justin Martyr.

4.3.6 THE COMPOSITION OF THE GOSPEL OF MATTHEW

Whereas for the Gospel of Mark the narrative structure essentially determined the presentation of the ministry of Jesus, Matthew, though following for the most part Mark's narrative, highlights the discourses of Jesus. They become the center of Jesus' ministry. While almost all the healing activity of Jesus is described in a curtailed form in chapters 8–9, into which Matthew has assembled the Markan healing and miracle narratives, the speeches constitute the focus of Jesus' ministry. The miracles and other narratives from Mark have been drastically shortened in Matthew's text[1] and sometimes are mere skeletons. Only the appearance of Jesus as an almost superhuman being who is worshiped by those he encounters is important for Matthew; the narrative details, on the other hand, would only distract from this focus upon Jesus' dignity.

The speeches in Matthew's Gospel, however, are always more comprehensive and contain more materials than their counterparts in Mark and Q. By composing these speeches out of all the available materials from his sources and probably also from the still-fluid oral tradition of Jesus' sayings, Matthew has created five large discourses:

---

[1] Cf., e.g., the Gerasene demoniac (Mark 5:1–20 = Matt 8:28–34) is divided into 20 verses in Mark, but only 7 verses in Matthew. The story of the death of John the Baptist has 176 words in Mark 6:17–29, only 137 words in Matt 14:3–12. On the redaction of the narrative materials in Matthew, see Heinz Joachim Held, "Matthew as Interpreter of the Miracle Stories," in Bornkamm-Barth-Held, *Tradition and Interpretation*, 165–299, especially 168–92.

the Sermon on the Mount (Matt 5:1–7:29), the missionary instruction (9:35–11:1), the parable discourse (13:1–53), the discourse on the order of the church (18:1–19:1), and the eschatological discourse (24:1–26:1). Each of the first four discourses concludes with the sentence "and it happened, when Jesus had finished these words . . ."; the last discourse ends with "and it happened, when Jesus had finished *all* these words . . ." Immediately following upon this last sentence Matthew reports the hierarchs' council of death (26:1–2).

With respect to the passion narrative, Matthew follows Mark faithfully with relatively few redactions. Narrative sections are occasionally shortened. Some new materials, however, are added. The first of these is the report of the death of Judas (Matt 27:3–10); here the last of the formula quotations occurs (27:9–10, quoting a combination of verses from Zechariah and Jeremiah). As in the stories of the infancy narrative, this legendary report is entirely dominated by the desire to demonstrate the fulfillment of scripture. In these cases, Matthew is still able to draw on the exegetical tradition that was responsible for the development of the passion narrative, and he used it for apologetic purposes. In the trial scene, Matthew adds the episode with Pilate's wife (27:19) and the handwashing scene of Pilate (27:24–25).[1] After the report of the death of Jesus, Matthew inserts a description of miraculous phenomena, prodigia occurring at the death of a great human being (27:51–53); and after the story of the burial he utilizes fragments of an older epiphany story for the construction of an apologetic legend of the guard at the tomb.[2] Finally, the story of the discovery of the empty tomb is expanded by the report of the appearance of an angel who rolls away the stone from the tomb (28:2–4)—another fragment of the epiphany story preserved in the *Gospel of Peter*.

The source for the final story of the appearance of Jesus to his disciples (Matt 28:16–20) is an independent tradition. It may rest on an older epiphany account (cf. John 20:19–22), but it has been heavily redacted by the author of the First Gospel. Jesus' command to "make disciples of all nations" testifies to Matthew's unqualified endorsement of the mission to the Gentiles, while the emphasis upon "teaching them everything that I have commanded you" is a confirmation of his belief that neither the great deeds of Jesus nor his suffering and death

---

[1] The motif for these additions is clearly apologetic, but it should not be read as a polemic against "Judaism." Rather, the polemic corresponds to the established Jewish tradition of prophetic polemic against the political establishment in Jerusalem and the people who had been mislead by their leaders. With respect to the scriptural basis of the handwashing scene see the discussion above on the parallel scene in the *Gospel of Peter,* # 2.3.2.3.

[2] See above, # 2.3.2.4.

are meant to be the guiding principle of that mission. Rather, the teachings of Jesus, primarily represented in the speeches of Jesus which Matthew composed, should serve as the foundation of the church.

Nevertheless, these speeches—instruction for the churches—are not presented in the literary form of a manual of discipline. They are set forth as part of a biographical writing. The biographical framework, to be sure, has been inherited from the Gospel of Mark. But Matthew did not simply use the Markan framework as a purely external vehicle for the presentation of a church manual. The changes that he introduced reveal also his understanding of the "life of Jesus," which differs from that of Mark in two respects. First, Jesus' life, from the very beginning, is fulfillment; already his very birth fulfills what was promised. Second, the divine dignity of the person of Jesus is more strongly emphasized, although there is no single title that would summarize the entire dignity of Jesus that is pictured in the story of his birth, life, and death. Titles of Jesus may become more elaborate. The Markan formulation of the confession of Peter, "You are the Christ" (Mark 8:29) becomes, "You are the Christ, the Son of the Living God" (Matt 16:16). People approaching Jesus or witnessing his miracles "worship" him.[1] The story of the stilling of the tempest has become an allegory for the appearance of the Lord at the height of the eschatological tribulation[2] and the same risen Lord promises his disciples that he will be with them to the end of the days (Matt 28:20). But Jesus is also Wisdom who offers her mild yoke to all who wish to come (Matt 11:28–30). As Wisdom incarnate, Jesus is also the one who suffers and dies, rejected like the suffering righteous ones. The Gospel of Matthew can be called the biography of Wisdom, but Jesus as Wisdom is, at the same time, the eschatological Lord whose dignity is already visible in his earthly life and whose cross, the symbol of his suffering and death, will appear as the sign of his eschatological return.[3]

---

[1] Compare, e.g., Matt 9:18 with Mark 5:22; Matt 14:33 with Mark 6:51.

[2] Compare Matt 8:23–27 with Mark 4:35–41. See Günther Bornkamm, "The Stilling of the Storm in Matthew," in Bornkamm-Barth-Held, *Tradition and Interpretation*, 52–57.

[3] The "sign (σημεῖον) of the Son of man" (Matt 24:30) which will precede Jesus as he comes on the clouds of heaven very probably was the sign of the cross.

4.4 The Gospel of Luke [1]

4.4.1 MANUSCRIPTS

Luke's text is not as well attested as the text of John's and Matthew's Gospels, but better attested than the text of Mark. In addition to the four-gospel papyrus from the 3d century ($\mathfrak{p}^{45}$)—the only attestation of Mark before the 4th century—there are three papyri with parts of Luke's text from the 3d century.[2] Since $\mathfrak{p}^4$ preserves considerable portions of the Third Gospel, there is at least some direct evidence for the text circulating in this early period. In addition to the uncials from the 4th and the following centuries containing the text of all four canonical Gospels,[3] one papyrus and three uncial manuscripts with the text of Luke come from the 4th century,[4] and there are three papyri[5] and about two dozen uncial manuscripts containing at least portions of Luke's text from later centuries.

No manuscript preserves the work of Luke in its original form, i.e., the Gospel of Luke and the Acts of the Apostles together. They were originally two volumes of *one* work. In even the earliest extant manuscripts from ca. 200, the work had already been split into two sections of which the former was soon assigned to a collection of gospels. Thus Luke's work has not been preserved in the form in which it was published by its author.[6] The text-critical problems of Luke's text are essentially the same as those of the other canonical gospels, with one exception: the so-called Western Text[7] presents a number of interesting and controversial alternative readings.

---

[1] For literature on the Gospel of Luke in general and for the present status of scholarship see Martin Rese, "Das Lukasevangelium: Ein Forschungsbericht," *ANRW* 2.25/3 (1985) 2260–2335.

[2] $\mathfrak{p}^4$ with portions of Luke 1–6; $\mathfrak{p}^{69}$, preserving a few verses from Luke 22, and $\mathfrak{p}^{75}$ with parts of Luke 3–9; 17; and 22 (and presenting also the text of the Gospel of John; see above # 3.4.1).

[3] See above # 3.3.

[4] $\mathfrak{p}^{82}$ (Luke 7:32–34, 37–38); 0171 (verses from Luke 22 and Matt 10); 0181 (Luke 9:59–10:14). The first of these uncials may have been written ca. 300 CE.

[5] $\mathfrak{p}^3$ (6th/7th century: Luke 7:36–45; 10:38–42); $\mathfrak{p}^7$ (4th–6th century: Luke 4:1–2); $\mathfrak{p}^{42}$ (7th/8th century: Luke 1:54–55; 2:29–32).

[6] See Bovon, *Evangelium nach Lukas*, 13–14.

[7] Represented by D, some Vetus Latina manuscripts, the old Syrian translation, and quotations in several Church Fathers as early as Justin Martyr. It is therefore not possible to assign these readings of the Western Text to the 4th century. See Bovon (*Evangelium nach Lukas*, 14): the Western Text is about as old as the Egyptian Text which originated in the 2nd century and is represented by $\mathfrak{p}^{75}$, $\aleph$, B, and C.

Western Text	*Egyptian and / or Majority Text*

Luke 3:22

You are my Son, today I have begotten you (ἐγὼ σήμερον γεγέννηκά σε) = Ps 2:7	You are my beloved Son, in you I am well pleased (ἐν σοὶ εὐδόκησα) = Isa 42:1

Luke 6:5

The same day he saw someone working on the Sabbath and and said to him, "Man, if you know what you are doing, you are blessed, but if you don't know, you are cursed and a transgressor of the law."[1]	And he said to them, "The Son of man is Lord of the Sabbath."

Luke 22:17–20

And he took the cup and when he had given thanks he said, "Take this and divide it among yourselves. For I tell you, from now on I shall not drink of the fruit of the wine until the kingdom of God comes." And he took bread, and when he had given thanks he broke it and gave it to them, saying, "This is my body."	And he took a cup and when he had given thanks he said, "Take this and divide it among yourselves. For I tell you, that from now on I shall not drink of the fruit of the wine until the kingdom of God comes." And he took bread, and when he had given thanks he broke it and gave it to them, saying, "This is my body which is given for you. Do this in my remembrance." And in the same way he took the cup after the meal, saying, "This cup is the new covenant in my blood that has been poured out for you."

Another interesting variant appears in two minuscules (162, 700) and Gregory of Nyssa in the second petition of the Lord's Prayer:

Luke 11:2

Manuscript 700	*Majority Text*
Your Holy Spirit come over us and cleanse us.	Your kingdom come.
(ἐλθέτω τὸ ἅγιον πνεῦμά σου ἐφ᾽ ἡμᾶς καὶ καθαρισάτω ἡμᾶς).	(ἐλθέτω ἡ βασιλεία σου).

Scholarly opinion in textual criticism has tended to prefer the readings of the Egyptian text (represented by 𝔭⁷⁵, ℵ, B, and C) over the Western

---

[1] This saying occurs in Codex D after Luke 6:10.

Western Text, and there are good reasons for not accepting the variants offered to Luke 6:5 and 11:5. However, there is evidence for the existence of some Western Text readings as early as the middle of the 2d century.[1] For the question of the original text of Luke, it is necessary to reconsider the weight of this text as perhaps the earliest available witness.[2]

4.4.2 ATTESTATION

Nothing is said about the Gospel of Luke in the fragments of Papias of Hierapolis which are preserved in Eusebius' *Ecclesiastical History*. But it is widely attested that just before the middle of the 2d century Marcion used this Gospel as the basis for his edition of Christian Scriptures.[3] The report about Marcion's use of Luke appears for the first time in Irenaeus (ca. 180 CE):

> He mutilates the Gospel which is according to Luke, removes all that is written respecting the generation of the Lord, and sets aside a great deal of the teaching of the Lord's discourses in which the Lord is recorded as most clearly confessing that the creator of this universe is his Father. (*Adv. haer.* 1.25.1)

Thus the Gospel of Luke, perhaps written as late as the first decades of the 2d century, became the first Gospel ever to be elevated to something that could be called "canonical status," albeit in its revised Marcionite edition.

Apart from the use of Luke by Marcion, there is no certain evidence for its usage and its text before the middle of the 2d century. While Marcion apparently also knew the Gospel of Matthew but rejected it, the first early catholic writers who use the text of written gospels, Justin Martyr and *2 Clement*, use the text of Matthew as well as the text of Luke (and, in the case of Justin, also the text of Mark). In fact, apart from Marcion, a harmony of Matthew and Luke was apparently the earliest form through which the text of the Gospel Luke came to be used. This harmony is not only in evidence in Justin and *2 Clement* but also in the *Gospel of the Ebionites*.[4] The name of the author of the

---

[1] It appears in Justin *Dial.* 88 and 103.6.

[2] There are several references and discussions of this question in the recent volume of published contributions to a University of Notre Dame conference, April 15–17, 1988 on the text of the gospels in the 2d century: William L. Petersen, ed., *Gospel Traditions in the Second Century: Origins, Recensions, Text, and Transmission* (Notre Dame, IN: University of Notre Dame Press, 1989). See also Bovon, *Lukasevangelium*, 13–14.

[3] See above, # 1.7.

[4] For the Greek texts see Klostermann, *Apocrypha II*, 13–15; ET in Hennecke-Schneemelcher-Wilson, *NT Apocrypha*, 1. 156–58.

Third Gospel of the New Testament canon never appears in such contexts. Evidence for this Gospel as a separate writing under the name of Luke appears for the first time in Irenaeus in his discussion of the origin of the four canonical Gospels:

> ... and Luke also who was a follower of Paul put down in a book the gospel that was preached by him (sc. Paul).[1]

It is interesting to note that Irenaeus agrees with Marcion in assuming that Luke's Gospel is the gospel that Paul had preached. The so-called *Anti-Marcionite Prologue* has also been referred to as a testimony from the second half of the 2d century to the Gospel of Luke and to its author:[2]

> Luke is a Syrian of Antioch, a Syrian by race, a physician by profession. He had become a disciple of the apostles and later followed Paul until his (Paul's) martyrdom, having served the Lord continuously, unmarried, without children, filled with the Holy Spirit he died at the age of eighty-four years in Boeotia.[3]
>
> [Since there were already other gospels, that According to Matthew written in Judea, that According to Mark (written in) Italy, he was urged by the Holy Spirit to write his whole gospel among those in the regions of Achaea, as he indicates this in the preface that there were already other writings before him ...][4]

While the *Canon Muratori* and the *Prologues* to the Gospels of Mark and John are most likely products of the second half of the 4th century,[5] the first part of the *Prologue* to the Gospel of Luke, the only one of these prologues that is preserved in its original Greek, may have been composed in the last decades of the 2d century.[6] The former, as well as the second part of the *Prologue to Luke,* merely reflect what came to be the accepted opinion about the origin of the gospels in the ancient church. However, the first part of the *Prologue to Luke* provides information that is not reflected elsewhere: that Luke was

---

[1] Eusebius *Hist. eccl.* 5.8.3.

[2] Greek text, English translation, and critical notes in Heard, "Old Gospel Prologues," 7–9.

[3] Manuscript A reads "in Thebes, the capital of Boeotia" (Θήβαις τῇ μητροπόλει τῆς Βοιωτίας).

[4] Since the second part of the Lukan *Prologue,* bracketed above, also makes reference to the Gospels of Matthew and Mark, later also to Acts and to Revelation, it is unlikely that it was composed as an introduction for the Gospel of Luke; cf. Heard, "Old Gospel Prologues," 4.

[5] See above # 3.3.2, on the *Anti-Marcionite Prologues* to the canonical Gospels.

[6] Heard, "Old Gospel Prologues," 7–11.

unmarried and had no children, and that he died in Boeotia.[1] The historical value of this information, including the name of the author, is of dubious value. Ever since Marcion (who never mentions the name of an author for the gospel that he included in his canon), the desire to connect the author to Paul, as well as the evident information about Paul in the second half of the work, the Acts of the Apostles, would make Luke a natural choice because he was mentioned in Phlm 24, Col 4:14, and 2 Tim 4:11.

4.4.3 SOURCES AND SPECIAL MATERIALS

4.4.3.1 Luke's Sources

According to the two-source hypothesis, Luke's primary sources are the same as those of Matthew, i.e., the Gospel of Mark and the Synoptic Sayings Source. Insofar as this is the case, Luke closely resembles Matthew in form and content. In the first and third parts of his writing, Luke uses the Gospel of Mark for the outline of the events of the ministry of Jesus and inserts at certain points materials drawn from Q. In the use of both these sources, Luke is normally more conservative than Matthew because he usually leaves the sequence and wording of his sources more or less intact, and he does not try to compose major units, such as Matthew's speeches.

4.4.3.2 Luke's Special Materials

Like Matthew, Luke employs additional materials which are not drawn from either of these two sources. However, in the case of Luke, these materials are more extensive and more diversified. Most of them are usually assigned to a third source used by Luke ("L"), which differs fundamentally from both the Synoptic Sayings Source and the special source used in the Gospel of Matthew. While the latter consisted mostly of sayings, Luke's special source, or sources, also included a number of narratives as well as some example stories and parables which are attested nowhere else in the gospel traditions. Some of these materials were inserted by Luke into the Markan narrative framework; but most appear in a separate section which Luke has created as the central piece of his composition, the Lukan travel narrative (9:51–18:14). Because of the variety of the special materials in Luke, it is difficult to argue for one single source as the wellspring of

---

[1] Joseph A. Fitzmyer, S.J., *The Gospel According to Luke: Introduction, Translation, and Notes* (2 vols.; AB 28/28A; Garden City, NY: Doubleday, 1981–85) 1. 39. Bovon (*Evangelium nach Lukas*, 23–24) is more doubtful with respect to an early date for this prologue or parts of it.

all his special materials. Luke probably used several smaller collections of sayings in this section, most prominent among these a collection of parables, and also a collection of miracle stories, which Luke used in this section and elsewhere.[1] The diversity of the special materials included in Luke's Gospel warn against the assumption of just one major special source for Luke.[2] It is more likely that an educated and widely traveled author like Luke had access to a variety of written documents as well as orally circulating materials. Luke wrote at a comparatively late date, several decades after Matthew, that is, after the turn of the 1st century, when more of the gospel materials had been collected in written form. In fact, in the proem (1:1–4) Luke refers to a variety of earlier attempts to write down the traditions about Jesus. On the other hand, Luke's church does not seem to have lost the connection to the continuing and still developing free (oral) tradition of sayings of Jesus and stories about him.[3] Luke is therefore a remarkable witness for the continuing free circulation of oral or written collections of sayings of Jesus and of narratives about him as late as three generations after his death.

The most important special materials incorporated into the Gospel of Luke are the following:

Healing Miracles:

The raising of the widow's son	7:7–17
The healing of a woman with a spirit of infirmity	13:10–17
The healing of a man with dropsy	14:1–6
The healing of the ten lepers	17:11–19

Apophthegmata:

The woman that was a sinner	7:36–50
The serving women	8:1–3
Mary and Martha	10:38–42
The blessedness of the mother of Jesus	11:24–26
Dividing the inheritance	12:13–14
Call for repentance	13:1–5

---

[1] Luke 7:11–17 ("the widow's son"), 13:10–17 ("the women with a spirit of infirmity"), 14:1–6 ("the man with the dropsy"), 17:11–19 ("the ten lepers"—a variant of Mark 1:40–45).

[2] Several other hypotheses have been advanced to explain Luke's relationship to his special materials. Prominent among these is the suggestion that Q and the special materials were first combined to a "Proto-Luke" (Vincent Taylor, *Behind the Third Gospel: A Study of the Proto-Luke Hypothesis* [Oxford: Oxford University Press, 1926]). For a critique see Conzelmann and Lindemann, *Interpreting the NT,* 231–32.

[3] Bishop Papias of Hierapolis, who may have been a younger contemporary of Luke, was still able to draw on the oral traditions for the composition of his "Interpretations of the Oracles of the Lord." Cf. Eusebius *Hist. eccl.* 3.39.

| Answer to Herod | 13:31–33 |
| Zacchaeus | 19:1–10 |

Sayings (a selection):

The social teaching of John the Baptist	3:10–14
The woes against the rich	6:24–26
"I saw Satan fall like lightning . . ."	10:18–20
Punishment according to responsibility	12:47–48
"I have come to throw a fire on earth . . ."[1]	12:49
"I have to be baptized with a baptism . . ."	12:50
Order of dignity at a meal	14:7–14
Friends with the unjust mammon	16:9
Coming of the rule of God[2]	17:20–21
The destruction of Jerusalem	19:39–44
The two swords	22:35–38

Parables and Example Stories:

The Good Samaritan	10:29–37
The Friend at Midnight	11:5–8
The Rich Fool[3]	12:16–21
The Barren Figtree	13:6–9
Building a House and Waging a War	14:28–33
The Lost Coin	15:7–10
The Father who Had Two Sons (Prodigal Son)	15:11–32
The Unjust Steward	16:1–8
Dives and Lazarus	16:19–31
The Servant's Wages	17:7–10
The Unjust Judge	18:1–8
The Pharisee and the Tax Collector	18:9–14

Insertions into the Passion Narrative:

The eating of the Passover	22:15–18
The words to Peter	22:31–32
Jesus before Herod	23:6–16
The women of Jerusalem	23:27–31
Jesus and the two crucified criminals	23:32,39–43

Legends:

| The promise of the Baptist's birth | 1:5–25 |
| The annunciation | 1:26–38 |

[1] This saying, paralleled in *Gos. Thom.* 10, may be a Q saying that Matthew omitted; see above # 2.2.4.2 and 2.3.2.

[2] The parallel in *Gos. Thom.* 113 could be an indication that this saying was derived from Q; see above # 2.2.4.2. and 2.3.2.

[3] Most likely this example story came from Q and not from L; see Kloppenborg, *Q Parallels*, 128.

The birth of John the Baptist	1:57–66, 80
Mary's visit with Elizabeth	1:39–45, 56
The nativity of Jesus	2:1–20
The circumcision of Jesus	2:21–40
Jesus at twelve years in the temple	2:41–52

Epiphany Stories:	
The miraculous draught of fishes	5:1–11
The road to Emmaeus	24:13–35
The appearances of the risen Christ	24:36–49
The ascension	24:50–53

Hymnic materials:	
The Magnificat	1:46–55
The Benedictus	1:68–79
The Song of Simon	2:29–32

4.4.4 THE COMPOSITION OF THE GOSPEL OF LUKE

It must be remembered that the so-called Gospel of Luke is only the first part of a much larger work which includes the Book of the Acts of the Apostles and, in fact, describes the entire period from the birth of John the Baptist and Jesus to the arrival of the Christian message in Rome. The work was published in two volumes as a matter of convenience: as the work was first written and published in the form of scrolls, the maximum capacity of a scroll required two "volumes."[1] Thus the placing of the first volume of this work among the four Gospels of the New Testament does not correspond to its original purpose. The intention of the author is not understood at all if the Gospel of Luke is seen as a parallel to the Gospel of Matthew, although both documents have two sources in common. The author never intended to write something that would eventually be called a "gospel," and he certainly did not understand the first sentence of the Gospel of Mark ("The beginning of the gospel of Jesus Christ," Mark 1:1) as designating a literary genre.

But since the first part of Luke's work deals with Jesus and shares sources about Jesus with Matthew, some comparisons of Matthew and what we now call the "Gospel of Luke" are helpful. Like Matthew, Luke does not begin his Gospel with the appearance of John the

---

[1] The "prologue" to the Book of Acts is not the introduction of an entirely new and different work, but a resumption of the prologue of Luke 1:1–4. Thus Acts 1:1–2 functions primarily as a dedication—a Greek custom which designates the work as a piece of monographic literature.

Baptist and the baptism of Jesus, but with birth narratives (Luke 1:5–2:52). With these he also includes the story of the birth of John the Baptist (1:5–25, 57–66). The stories themselves derive from different traditions and they belong to the latest stage of the novelistic development of Synoptic narrative materials. The character of the stories relating to John the Baptist differs markedly from those about Jesus' birth. There is good reason to believe that the former came from the tradition of the followers of John. As these traditional legends appear here in the first two chapters of the Third Gospel, they owe their form and composition to the author of the work.[1] Luke has achieved the presentation of this narrative cycle not by adding occasional redactional comments, but by skillful literary arrangement which results in an introduction to his Gospel of extraordinary beauty.

The two stories of the announcement of the births (1:5–25 and 1:26–38) open the cycle; the meeting of the two mothers (1:39–56) provides a double link, on the one hand between John and Jesus, on the other hand between the announcement stories and the birth stories. Each of the birth stories (1:57–80 and 2:1–40) includes a second part in which the newly born child is greeted in the form of a kerygmatic hymn (the Benedictus of Zachariah, 1:67–79, and the Nunc Dimittis of Simeon, 2:29–32). Both birth narratives end with statements about the growth of the child that begin with exactly the same words ("And the child grew and became strong . . . ," 1:80; 2:40). The story of Jesus at twelve in the temple (2:41–52) provides the link to the following narrative about Jesus.

Announcement of John's birth	Announcement of Jesus' birth
Visit of the two mothers	
John's birth	Jesus' birth
Jesus at twelve years in the temple	

Here, as elsewhere in this Gospel, Luke expresses theological significance by the relative position of certain traditional units in the narrative. Theological purpose does not violate the fact that John the Baptist and Jesus belong together; but they meet only once, namely, in their mothers' womb. When Jesus comes to his baptism (3:21), John is already imprisoned (3:19–20). There is no longer any parallelism between the two figures.

After the infancy narratives, Luke picks up the thread of the narrative of the Gospel of Mark which he will follow for the entire first part of his writing (Mark 1:2–9:50 = Luke 3:1–9:50) and again for the third

---

[1] Bovon (*Evangelium nach Lukas,* 46–47) has shown that the composition is analogous to that of the Cornelius story in Acts 10:1–11:18).

part of the Gospel (Mark 10:13–16:8 = Luke 18:15–24:12).[1] In this use
of Mark, Luke occasionally and quite purposefully moves a pericope to
another context, and he frequently inserts materials from Q and occasionally also from a special source. The following table, comparing
Mark and Luke up to the beginning of the passion narrative, will illustrate Luke's method of composition.[2]

Pericope	Luke	Mark	Other Sources
Synchronism	3:1–2		redactional
The Baptist	3:3–6	1:2–6	
Preaching of repentance	3:7–9		from Q
Social teaching	3:10–14		from L
Messianic preaching	3:15–16	1:7–8	
Conclusion	3:17–18		from Q
John's imprisonment	3:19–20	*6:17–18*	
Baptism of Jesus	3:21–22	1:9–11	
Genealogy of Christ	3:23–38		from L (cf. Matt)
Temptation of Jesus	4:1–2	1:12–13a	
Dialogue with Satan	4:3–12		from Q
Conclusion	4:13	1:13b	
Preaching in Galilee	4:14–15	(1:14–16)	redactional
Jesus in Nazareth	4:16	*6:1–2*	
Jesus' scripture reading	4:17–21		redactional
Peoples' reaction	4:22–24	*6:3–4*	
Jesus' preaching	4:25–27		from L
Rejection	4:28–30	*6:5–6*	
Healing in the synagogue	4:31–37	1:21–28	
Peter's mother-in-law	4:38–39	1:29–31	
Healing summary	4:40–41	1:32–34	
Departure from Capernaum	4:42–44	1:35–39	
Peter's draught of fishes	5:1–11		from L
Healing of a leper	5:12–16	1:40–45	
Healing of paralytic	5:17–26	2:1–12	
Call of Levi	5:27–32	2:13–17	
Question about fasting	5:33–38	2:18–22	
Saying about old wine	5:39		oral tradition
Plucking grain on a Sabbath	6:1–5	2:23–28	
Healing of a withered hand	6:6–11	3:1–6	

[1] For a detailed analysis of the use of Mark in the Gospel of Luke see Tim Schramm,
*Der Markus-Stoff bei Lukas: Eine literarkritische und redaktionsgeschichtliche Unter-
suchung* (SNTS.MS 14; Cambridge: Cambridge University Press, 1971).

[2] "From L" points to all special materials, without prejudice regarding the source
from which Luke derived such materials. The passages from Mark are italicized whenever Luke has inserted them into a different context. I have not noted all redactional
additions of Luke within the units referred to.

Call of twelve disciples	6:12–16	*3:13–19*	
Healing summary	6:17–19	*3:7–12* [1]	
Sermon on the Plain	6:20–49		from Q
Centurio's servant healed	7:1–10		from Q
Widow's son raised	7:11–17		from L
Sayings about the Baptist	7:18–35		from Q
The women who was a sinner	7:36–50	*14:3–9* [2]	(from L?)
The ministering women	8:1–3		from L
Parable of the Sower	8:4–15	4:1–20	
Sayings about parables	8:16–18	4:21–25 [3]	
Jesus' true relatives	8:19–21	*3:31–35*	
Stilling of the tempest	8:22–25	4:35–41	
Gerasene demoniac	8:26–39	5:1–20	
Jairus' daughter	8:40–56	5:21–43	
Sending of the Twelve	9:1–6	6:6–13	
Herod about Christ	9:7–9	6:14–16	
Feeding of five thousand	9:10–17	6:30–44 [4]	
Confession of Peter	9:18–21	8:27–30	
First passion prediction	9:22	8:31 [5]	
Sayings about discipleship	9:23–27	8:34–9:1	
Transfiguration	9:28–36	9:2–8 [6]	
Healing of epileptic child	9:37–43a	9:14–29	
Second passion prediction	9:43b–45	9:30–32	
Dispute about greatness	9:46–48	9:33–37	
The strange exorcist	9:49–50	9:38–41 [7]	
Blessing of the children	18:15–17	10:13–16 [8]	
The rich young man	18:18–30	10:17–31	

[1] Mark 3 is the only Markan chapter in which Luke has made some major changes: Mark 3:7–12 and 3:13–19 have been reversed; the apophthegma about Christ's true relatives (Mark 3:31–35) has been moved to Luke 8:19–21; the Beelzebub controversy (Mark 3:20–30) has been combined with parallel Q material and moved into the travel narrative (Luke 11:18–23).

[2] This story may be a Lukan composition on the basis of Mark 14:3–9, which Luke skips in his reproduction of Mark 14.

[3] Missing from Mark's parable chapter are the parable of the Seed Growing Secretly (Mark 4:26–29)—perhaps not a part of the original version of Mark—and the parable of the Mustard Seed (Mark 4:30–32); Luke 13:18–19 cites a variant of this parable in a context dependent upon Q.

[4] The entire so-called Bethsaida section of Mark 6:45–8:26 is missing in Luke's Gospel.

[5] The rebuke of Peter, Mark 8:32–33, is missing in Luke.

[6] Luke leaves out Mark 9:9–13, the discussion about Elijah's coming.

[7] The sayings about offenses (Mark 9:42–48) have been omitted by Luke; but a variant (from Q) appears in Luke 17:1–2. A variant of the saying about the salt (Mark 9:50) appears in Luke 14:34–35, perhaps from Q = Matt 5:13.

[8] Luke omits the instructions about divorce (Mark 10:1–12).

Third passion prediction	18:31–34	10:32–34[1]	
Healing of a blind man	18:35–43	10:46–52	
Zacchaeus	19:1–10		from L
Parable of the Talents	19:11–27		from Q
Entry into Jerusalem	19:28–38	11:1–10	
Prediction of its destruction	19:39–44		from L
Christ in the temple	19:45a	11:11a[2]	
Cleansing of the temple	19:45b–48	11:15–19	
Question about authority	20:1–8	11:27–33	
Parable: wicked husbandmen	20:9–19	12:1–12	
Question of tribute to Caesar	20:20–26	12:13–17	
Question about resurrection	20:27–40	12:18–27[3]	
Question of David's son	20:41–44	12:35–37a	
Speech against Pharisees	20:45–47	12:37b–40	
The widow's mite	21:1–4	12:41–44	
Synoptic apocalypse	21:5–36	13:1–37	
Teaching in the temple	21:37–38		redactional
The council of death	22:1–2	14:1–2	
Betrayal of Judas	22:3–6	14:10–11[4]	

In the central part of Luke, the travel narrative (9:51 to 18:14), almost everything comes from Q and L. Only a few pericopes from the Gospel of Mark are used in this section of Luke. Materials from Mark 3:20–30 (Beelzebub controversy) were combined with a variant from Q in Luke 11:14–23; a Q variant of Mark 3:28–29 (the unforgivable sin) appears in Luke 12:10. The parallel to Mark 9:42–48 (about offenses) in Luke 17:1–2 is drawn from Q, not from Mark. For the introduction to the story of the Good Samaritan (10:25–28), Luke has used Mark 12:29–31. It can be assumed that the sequence of materials in the travel narrative was primarily determined by Q, if the thesis is indeed correct that Luke reproduced the sayings of Q in about the same order in which they stood in his source. Although Luke in general follows Mark's order quite faithfully, he occasionally moves a pericope to

[1] The apophthegma of Christ and the sons of Zebedee (Mark 10:35–40) was omitted by Luke and the following sayings about serving (Mark 10:41–45) have been moved into the context of the last supper (Luke 22:24–27).

[2] Mark 11:11b, Jesus' return to Bethany, is omitted by Luke, as is the following episode of the cursing of the fig tree (Mark 11:12–14) together with the discussion of this episode (Mark 11:20–25).

[3] The following question about the Great Commandment (Mark 12:28–31) has been moved to Luke 10:25–28 as an introduction to the story of the Good Samaritan. Its Markan appendix (12:29–34) is missing in both Matthew and Luke and was probably not part of Mark's original text; see above # 4.1.2.1.

[4] The material from the story of the anointing in Bethany (Mark 14:3–9) seems to have been used by Luke for his story of Jesus and the woman who was a sinner, Luke 7:36–50; see above.

another context. Therefore, he may also have moved one or the other Q saying.

It is obvious that Luke follows the Markan outline and sequence much more faithfully than Matthew. Unlike Matthew's use of Mark, there are no major rearrangements like the collecting of almost all miracle stories from Mark into one major section describing Jesus' healing ministry in Matt 8–9. Not all Lukan changes can be discussed here.[1] However, some are significant for the understanding of Luke's view of Jesus' ministry.[2]

Luke has marked the special character of the time of Jesus' ministry by a number of significant changes at the beginning of his story. These changes strongly designate Jesus' ministry as a new beginning, and they point forward to events still to come in this ministry and even subsequently in the second part of Luke's work, the Acts of the Apostles. Most remarkable is the transposition of the story of the Baptist's death. The long narrative of Mark 6:17–29 is reduced to a short note in the context of the Baptist's ministry, just before the baptism of Jesus (Mark 3:9–11 = Luke 3:21–22). The result, in Luke's text, is that John is no longer mentioned when Jesus is baptized. John is preacher and prophet rather than baptizer.[3] Jesus' ministry is thus characterized as a period no longer intertwined with that of Israel, which is represented in John the Baptist, who is Israel's last prophet (not Elijah redivivus: Luke omits the Elijah reference of Mark 9:9–13). Jesus is not the continuation of the revelation to Israel, but its fulfillment.

The story which follows, that of Jesus' temptation (Luke 4:1–3), is derived from Q, begins in the desert, but does not end with the temptation on the mountain where Satan shows Jesus all the kingdoms of the world.[4] Rather, in the last temptation, Jesus is on the pinnacle of the temple in Jerusalem. The reader will learn that the last part of Jesus'

---

[1] For further discussion see the relevant commentaries, especially Fitzmyer, *Luke*, passim; and Bovon, *Evangelium nach Lukas*, 19–22 and passim.

[2] On these Lukan redactions of Mark see Hans Conzelmann, *The Theology of St Luke* (London: Faber, 1960) passim. Conzelmann's work, which appeared in its German original first in 1953 (*Die Mitte der Zeit: Studien zur Theologie des Lukas* [BHTh 17; 3d ed.; Tübingen: Mohr/Siebeck, 1960]), has been the seminal beginning of a fresh assessment of Luke's redactional activity in his use of sources. See also Conzelmann and Lindemann, *Interpreting the NT*, 229–36. A thorough critical evaluation of the subsequent research has been published by François Bovon, *Luke the Theologian: Thirty-three Years of Research (1950–1983)* (Princeton Theological Monograph Series; Allison Park, PA: Pickwick, 1987). An anthology of this author's articles on Luke-Acts has appeared in German translation: François Bovon, *Biblisch-theologische Studien: Gesammelte Aufsätze* (BThSt 8; Neukirchen-Vluyn, Neukirchener Verlag, 1985).

[3] Bovon, *Evangelium nach Lukas*, 179.

[4] This was probably the original order of Q which Matthew preserved.

ministry took place in the temple, and that he died in Jerusalem. The sentence with which Luke describes the departure of Satan is also characteristically formulated. Mark 1:13 ends the episode of Jesus' temptation in the wilderness with the statement, "and the angels came and served him." Matt 4:11a has probably preserved the original ending from Q's story: "Then Satan left him." Luke 4:13 says: "When he had completed all temptation, the devil left him until a certain moment." This moment is most likely Luke 22:3 where Luke begins the story of Judas's betrayal with the remark, "And Satan went into Judas." The return of Satan marks the end of the time of revelation.[1] Luke 4:13 and 22:3 form a parenthesis[2] that includes the time in which Jesus' ministry is not endangered by the interference of Satan. Corresponding to this is a geographical schema designating the special character of the places of Jesus' ministry and its three periods: (1) Jesus' activity in Galilee and Judea (Luke 4:1–9:50); (2) Jesus' travel to Jerusalem (9:51–19:27); (3) Jesus' ministry in the temple (19:28–21:38).

The activity in Galilee and Judea opens with the first preaching of Jesus in Nazareth (Luke 4:16–30). The framework is taken from Mark 6:1–6, "Jesus' rejection in Nazareth," but the story has been moved to a position at the beginning of the description of Jesus' ministry and thoroughly revised. The Lukan redaction[3] presents Jesus quoting Isa 61:1–2 and announcing the fulfillment of this prophecy "today." The time of salvation begins in Jesus' home town in Galilee. The reader will know that this marks the beginning of the space in which the salvation will be at work. This designation of the locality of the beginning looks forward not only to Galilee, Judea, and Jerusalem, but ultimately to the conclusion of the Lukan work, i.e., the arrival of the Christian proclamation in Rome.

During the entire period of the first part of Jesus' ministry, he never leaves Galilee and Judea, and these two countries are treated as if they were one, and as if Jerusalem lay outside of this area.[4] This is properly the Holy Land where everything has special significance: the mountain as the place of prayer (even at the scene of the transfiguration; cf. Luke 9:28), the sea as the place for revelations to the disciples (Luke 5:1–11; 8:22–25). Thus there is no "Sermon on the

---

[1] Conzelmann, *Theology of St Luke*, 28–29 and passim.

[2] Conzelmann and Lindemann, *Interpreting the NT*, 233–34.

[3] Apparently no other source than Mark has been used here; cf. Bovon, *Evangelium nach Lukas*, 207–8.

[4] Luke's knowledge of the geography of Palestine was probably limited and inaccurate. But the primary purpose of this geographical construction is the presentation of a theological schema.

Mount"[1] or parable instruction from a boat on the lake.[2] In this Holy Land, Jesus preaches the coming of the kingdom. Here he is the divine man who performs miraculous deeds and raises the dead (7:11–17). In this land he is victorious over those who question him, and where he is not threatened by any hostility.[3]

The character of Jesus' ministry changes during the long travel to Jerusalem (9:51–19:27). There is a different urgency in Jesus' instruction to the disciples. As the travel begins, would-be followers are warned that compromises are not possible for the disciple (9:57–62). Two eschatological speeches dominate this part of Luke's Gospel (12:2–59 and 17:20–37). The nearness of the kingdom of God becomes the repeatedly emphasized single content of the message entrusted to the disciples (9:60b; 10:11b).[4] But Luke has also placed most of the church order materials and all the major parables into this section.

To understand the third part of Jesus' ministry, it is important to observe the changes which Luke has made in his use of Mark's story of the entrance into Jerusalem (Mark 11:1–11).

Mark 11	*Luke 19*
	28: And when he had said this, he went on ahead, going up to Jerusalem.
1: And when they drew near to Jerusalem to Bethphage and the Mount of Olives, he sent two of his disciples . . .	When he drew near to Bethphage and Bethany at the mount that is called "Of Olives," he sent two of the disciples . . .
8: And many spread their garments on the road and others leafy branches which they had cut from the fields.	36: And as he rode along, they spread their garments on the road.
	37: As he was now drawing near, at the descent of the Mount of Olives, the whole multitude began to rejoice . . .
	41: And as he was drawing near, he saw the city and wept over it.
11: And he entered Jerusalem and went into the temple, and when he had looked round at everything, he went out to Bethany with the Twelve.	45: And he went into the temple.

---

[1] Luke deletes this localization of the sermon in Q which Matthew has preserved (Matt 5:1) and lets Jesus preach it "on a plain" (Luke 6:17).

[2] Compare Luke 8:4 with Mark 4:1–2.

[3] Compare, e.g., Luke 6:11 with Mark 3:6.

[4] In both instances, Luke has added these sentences to the sayings from his source.

Luke deletes the mention of "Jerusalem" in Mark 11:11a so that Jesus enters directly into the temple (Luke 19:45). At the same time, he deletes the reference to Jesus' return to Bethany at night (Mark 11:11b). In this way, the entire last portion of Jesus' ministry according to Luke (19:45–21:36) is presented as ministry in the temple,[1] while Jesus goes to the Mount of Olives during the night (Luke 21:37). The pattern is taken from Ezekiel: Jesus represents the divine "glory"; as long as he resides in the temple, the temple functions as the house of Yahweh, but as he finally leaves and moves to the Mount of Olives, the destruction of the temple is imminent.[2]

Luke's redaction of the Markan text seems slight in these instances. Nevertheless, Luke has created an entirely new view of the ministry of Jesus. It begins with the fulfillment in Nazareth of the prophecy of Isaiah and ends with the last presence and final departure of the divine glory from the temple. Conzelmann has rightly called this period of Jesus' ministry "the center of time."[3] It is preceded by the time of Israel and the prophets which comes to an end with John the Baptist, and it is followed by the time of the church which begins with the passion and death of Jesus, who thus becomes the first of the martyrs of the church.

While Matthew has left the Markan passion narrative more or less intact,[4] Luke has made several changes and also inserted special material.[5] A clearly secondary feature is the explicit emphasis upon the last meal as a Passover meal (Luke 22:15). Several sayings are added to the scene of the last meal of Jesus (Luke 22:28–38). The trial before Pilate (Luke 23:2–5) differs sharply from the Markan account (Mark 15:2–5), and Luke has added an appearance of Jesus before Herod (Luke 23:6–16). The narrative of the crucifixion is enlarged by the addition of novelistic episodes: the women of Jerusalem on the road to Calvary (Luke 23:27–32); a discourse of Jesus with the two criminals (Luke 23:39–43). On the other hand, features of Luke's

---

[1] Conzelmann (*Theology of St Luke,* 75–78) has shown that this is the result of deliberate redaction by Luke of the Markan text.

[2] Klaus Baltzer, "The Meaning of the Temple in the Lukan Writings," *HTR* 58 (1965) 263–77.

[3] This is the exact translation of the title of the German original of *The Theology of St Luke: Die Mitte der Zeit.*

[4] See above, # 4.3.5–6, on Matthew's use of sources and composition.

[5] The deviations from Mark, especially in the passion narrative but also in other parts of the Gospel, have resulted in the hypothesis of an altogether different source used by Luke, at least in the passion narrative. Cf. Friedrich Rehkopf, *Die lukanische Sonderquelle: Ihr Umfang und Sprachgebrauch* (WUNT 5; Tübingen: Mohr/Siebeck, 1959); other literature in Bovon, *Evangelium nach Lukas,* 19.

source (Mark) pointing to the agonies suffered by Jesus have been left out. Instead, Jesus dies piously like a perfect martyr (23:46).

Like Matthew, Luke retains the story of the discovery of the empty tomb from the Gospel of Mark. Matthew added only one relatively brief account of the appearance of the risen Lord at the conclusion of his Gospel (Matt 28:16–20). Luke has expanded the conclusion of his Gospel by incorporating three narratives of the appearances of Jesus: the road to Emmaeus (Luke 24:13–35), the appearance in Jerusalem (Luke 24:36–49), and the ascension (Luke 24:50–53). These stories form the link to the second part of the work which begins with the repetition of the story of the ascension (Acts 1:6–11).

The story of the church begins where the story of Jesus ended, in Jerusalem. But that second part of the narrative soon goes beyond Jerusalem. As the message of Jesus began in Nazareth and was first proclaimed publicly in Galilee and Judea, so the apostles' activity begins in Jerusalem and with the public proclamation in Samaria and Syria. As Jesus traveled during the second part of his ministry, the apostles, especially Paul, travel in the Book of Acts throughout the Greek world. The goal is no longer Jerusalem but Rome, though Paul's presence in the temple paradoxically provides the cause for the Christian message to arrive in Rome. The Gospel of Luke is not only the foundation for the Christian mission; it is also its paradigm.[1] "Gospel" as a "biography" of Jesus has been incorporated into a story of the beginnings of a religious movement.

---

[1] To do justice to the Gospel of Luke would require a full treatment of the Book of Acts. This, however, would go beyond the limits of this investigation.

5

The Harmonization of
the Canonical Gospels

5.1 Quotations in the Second Epistle of Clement

The *Second Epistle of Clement* contains a number of quotations of sayings of Jesus. In one instance, such a saying is introduced with the formula, "For the Lord says in the Gospel" (λέγει γὰρ ὁ κύριος ἐν τῷ εὐαγγελίῳ, *2 Clem.* 8.5). As has been argued above,[1] this quotation formula as well as the repeated use of the present tense "he says" (λέγει)[2] instead of the aorist "he said" (εἶπεν)[3] and the quotation of one saying with the formula "another scripture says" (ἑτέρα δὲ γραφὴ λέγει, *2 Clem.* 2.4), may prove that *2 Clement* is quoting from a written source that he calls "the gospel." The character of that source, however, can only be determined on the basis of the investigation of the materials which are quoted and the determination of their relationship to known written gospels.

5.1.1 DEPENDENCE UPON EITHER MATTHEW OR LUKE

Dependence upon the redactional work of the Gospel of Matthew is evident in the quotation of Matt 10:32 (Q/Luke 12:8) in *2 Clem.* 3.2:

2 Clem. 3.2	Matt 10:32	Q/Luke 12:8
The one who confesses me before human beings,	Everyone who confesses me before human beings,	Everyone who confesses me before human beings,

[1] On this quotation formula, see above # 1.4.4.

[2] *2 Clem.* 3.2; 4.2; 5.2; 6.1; 13.4.

[3] The quotation formula "The Lord said" (εἶπεν ὁ κύριος) is used only in *2 Clem.* 4.5 and 9.11. In 5.4 and 12.2 it appears within the context of a traditional apophthegma. In 12.6, φησίν introduces the final clause of a longer pericope.

| I shall confess him before my father. | also I shall confess him before my father who is in heaven. | the Son of man will confess him before the angels of God. |

It is most likely that the reference to the Son of man in the third person in Luke 12:8 and the mention of the heavenly court as the "angels of God" represent the original wording of Q.[1] Matthew changed this to the first person statement "I shall confess . . ."[2] Thus, "my father" is also due to Matthew's redaction. The wording of this saying as it is quoted in 2 *Clem.* 3.2 is dependent upon the Gospel of Matthew.[3]

2 *Clem.* 6.2 contains a quotation of the saying about gaining the world but losing one's soul (Mark 8:36 ‖ Matt 16:26 and Luke 9:25). The version presented in the Matthean synoptic parallel is certainly the basis of the citation. Matt 16:26 had changed Mark's infinitive construction (κερδῆσαι ... ζημιωθῆναι) into a conditional clause (ἐὰν κερδήσῃ ... ζημιωθῇ).[4] It is exactly this conditional clause that is reproduced in 2 *Clem.* 6.2.[5]

However, these are the only two quotations of 2 *Clement* that can be explained by recourse to dependence upon Matthew alone. The quotation of the saying about "serving two masters" in 2 *Clem.* 6.1 points to Luke 16:13 rather than to Matt 6:24, for 2 *Clement* says "No servant" (Οὐδεὶς οἰκέτης = Luke) instead of Matthew's simple "No one" (Οὐδείς). Yet, in this case Luke may present an older form of the saying, because the same formulation also appears in the *Gospel of Thomas* (# 47a). The citation of the command to love one's enemies in 2 *Clem.* 13.4, introduced by the unique quotation formula "because God says" (ὅτι λέγει ὁ θεός), contains two phrases which are paralleled only in Luke: Οὐ χάρις ὑμῖν ... ἀλλὰ χάρις ὑμῖν (Luke 6:32: ποία ὑμῖν χάρις) and τοὺς μισοῦντας ὑμᾶς (Luke 6:27: τοῖς μισοῦσιν ὑμᾶς), while special features of the Matthean parallels (5:46, 44) do not appear.[6]

---

[1] Cf. also the negative formulation in Luke 12:9 and the variant of this saying in Mark 8:38. Both refer to the Son of man in the third person and describe the heavenly court as "the angels of God."

[2] Bultmann, *Synoptic Tradition*, 150–52.

[3] For further discussion, see Koester, *Synoptische Überlieferung*, 71–73.

[4] Luke 9:25 has changed Mark's infinitive construction into participial clauses and expanded the second part of the saying (κερδήσας ... ἀπολέσας ἢ ζημιωθείς).

[5] Koester, *Synoptische Überlieferung*, 73–74. The introductory clause of 2 *Clem.* 6.2, τί γὰρ τὸ ὄφελος, differs from the introductory formulation of all three Synoptic parallels, but is also found in the quotation of this saying in Clement of Alexandria, *Strom.* 6.14, 112.3. It is unlikely that this reflects an independent non-canonical tradition.

[6] Cf. Koester, *Synoptische Überlieferung*, 75–76.

5.1.2 HARMONIZATIONS OF MATTHEW AND LUKE

The remaining quotations of sayings in *2 Clement* reveal that the relationship of their texts to the Synoptic Gospels is much more complex. The hypothesis of dependence upon Matthew in some instances, and upon Luke in others, cannot account for their peculiar forms.

Several of the sayings quoted in *2 Clement* are harmonized versions of the Matthean and Lukan texts. This is most clearly evident in the quotation of sayings which Matthew and Luke have derived from Mark.

2 Clem. 9.11	Matt 12:50	Mark 3:35	Luke 8:21
My brothers are those who do the will of my father.	Everyone who does the will of my father in heaven, he is my brother . . .	He who does the will of God, he is my brother . . .	My mother and my brothers are those who hear the word of God and do it.
			μήτηρ μου καὶ
Ἀδελφοί μου			ἀδελφοί μου
οὗτοί εἰσιν	ὅστις γὰρ ἂν	ὃς ἂν	οὗτοί εἰσιν
οἱ ποιοῦντες	ποιήσῃ	ποιήσῃ τὸ	οἱ
τὸ θέλημα	τὸ θέλημα	θέλημα	τὸν λόγον
τοῦ πατρός μου.	τοῦ πατρός μου	τοῦ θεοῦ,	τοῦ θεοῦ
	τοῦ ἐν οὐρανοῖς,		
	αὐτός μου ἀδελφός	οὗτος ἀδελφός μου	ἀκούοντες καὶ
	. . . ἐστίν.	. . . ἐστίν.	ποιοῦντες.

2 Clem. 9:11 combines the Lukan participial formulation of the saying (οἱ ποιοῦντες) with the Matthean change of "will of God" into "will of my father." This, however, is not simply an accidental mixture of Synoptic parallels. The same harmonization of Matthean and Lukan redactional changes of Mark's text of this saying appears in its quotation in Clement of Alexandria[1] and in the *Gospel of the Ebionites*.[2] *2 Clem.* 9.11 thus presupposes a more widely known document or a tradition in which this saying already appeared in a harmonized version.

2 Clem. 5.2–4 quotes a brief dialogue which reflects Lukan vocabulary of a saying in its first part, but again exhibits harmonizations of the Matthean and Lukan version in its second part; the dialogue that connects the two sayings has no parallel in the Synoptic Gospels:

---

[1] Ἀδελφοί μου γὰρ . . . καὶ συγκληρονόμοι οἱ ποιοῦντες τὸ θέλημα τοῦ πατρός μου (*Ecl. proph.* 20.3).
[2] οὗτοί εἰσιν οἱ ἀδελφοί μου καὶ ἡ μήτηρ καὶ ἀδελφαὶ οἱ ποιοῦντες τὰ θελήματα τοῦ πατρός μου (quoted in Epiphanius *Haer.* 30.14.5). See my *Synoptische Überlieferung*, 77–79, for more detailed documentation.

2 *Clem.* 5.2–4	Matt 10:16	Luke 10:3
The Lord says (λέγει), "You will be like lambs (ἀρνία) in the midst of wolves." Answering, Peter says to him, "What if the wolves scatter the lambs?" Jesus said to Peter, "The lambs should not fear the wolves after they have died;	Behold, I am sending you like sheep (πρόβατα) in the midst of wolves.	Behold, I am sending you like lambs (ἄρνας) in the midst of wolves.

	Matt 10:28	Luke 12:4–5
and also you do not fear those who kill you and are not able to do anything to you.	and do not fear those who kill the body but are not able to kill the soul.	Do not fear those who kill the body and afterwards have no more that they can do. I will show you whom to fear:
But fear the one who after your having died has authority over soul and body to throw into the hell of fire.	But fear more the one who is able to destroy body and soul in hell.	Fear the one who after he has killed has the authority to throw into hell.

μὴ φοβεῖσθε τοὺς ἀποκτεννόντας ὑμᾶς καὶ μηδὲν ὑμῖν δυναμένους ποιεῖν, ἀλλὰ φοβεῖσθε τὸν μετὰ τὸ ἀποθανεῖν ὑμᾶς ἔχοντα ἐξουσίαν ψυχῆς καὶ σώματος τοῦ βαλεῖν εἰς γέενναν πυρός.	μὴ φοβεῖσθε ἀπὸ τῶν ἀποκτεννόντων τὸ σῶμα, τὴν δὲ ψυχὴν μὴ δυναμένων ἀποκτεῖναι. φοβεῖσθε δὲ μᾶλλον τὸν δυνάμενον καὶ ψυχὴν καὶ σῶμα ἀπολέσαι ἐν γεέννῃ.	μὴ φοβηθῆτε ἀπὸ τῶν ἀποκτεννόντων τὸ σῶμα, καὶ μετὰ ταῦτα μὴ ἐχόντων περισσότερόν τι ποιεῖν ... φοβήθητε τὸν μετὰ τὸ ἀποκτεῖναι ἔχοντα ἐξουσίαν ἐμβαλεῖν εἰς τὴν γέενναν.

The mixture of readings drawn from Matthew and from Luke is evident.[1] Two arguments speak against a direct dependence upon

---

[1] See the analysis ibid., 94–99.

Matthew and Luke for *2 Clement's* quotation. (1) It is unlikely that the author of *2 Clement* was responsible for the composition of the entire dialogue between Jesus and Peter. The first part, Jesus' initial statement about the sending of the disciples like lambs into the midst of wolves, is entirely gratuitous in the context of *2 Clement* 5. The author's argument is not based on the experience of adversities and threats of death in this world; it rather contrasts the brevity of the earthly sojourn with the great and wonderful promise of eternal life (cf. *2 Clem.* 5.5). (2) Similar harmonizations of Matt 10:28 and Luke 12:4–5 also appear in two other quotations of the passage: Justin, *1 Apol.* 19.7; *Ps-Clem. Hom.* 17.5.2.[1]

If these harmonizations must be ascribed to the source that *2 Clement* used, it is also evident that this source cannot have been a complete gospel harmony. The source must have contained only such harmonized sayings that were connected with each other through a secondary framework of questions and answers, but without any narrative materials. *2 Clem.* 5.2–4 exhibits the typical features of a secondary development of dialogical units which were formed within the tradition of sayings. The *Gospel of Thomas* and especially the *Dialogue of the Savior* provided examples for this development of the sayings tradition.[2] What is remarkable here is the fact that the sayings appearing in *2 Clement* are drawn from gospels which also contain narrative materials such as Matthew and Luke. However, the Synoptic Gospels were not the exclusive source for the sayings collection used in *2 Clement*.

5.1.3 NON-CANONICAL SAYINGS IN 2 CLEMENT

The quotation of a saying in *2 Clem.* 8.5 appears at first glance to be taken from Luke 16:10–12. Moreover, this is the only saying in *2 Clement* that is explicitly introduced with a quotation formula that refers to "the gospel." However, non-canonical parallels call for a different explanation:

2 Clem. 8.5	Luke 16:11, 12, 10	Irenaeus *Adv. haer.* 2.34.3
For the Lord says in the gospel,		And therefore the Lord said . . .

---

[1] There are a few minor differences which can easily be explained as further developments in a harmonized tradition of sayings; cf. Koester, *Synoptische Überlieferung*, 97. For further discussion of the harmonizations of sayings in Justin Martyr, see below # 5.2.1.4.

[2] See above ## 2.2.4; 3.1.1.

"If you have not preserved the small thing, the great things, who will give them to you?" ...	11 If you have not been faithful in the unjust mammon, that which is true, who will entrust it to you? 12 And if you have not been faithful in that which is another's, that which is your own, who will give it you?	"If you have not been faithful in a small thing, that which is great, who will give it to you?"
"He who is faithful in very little, is faithful also in much."	10 He who is faithful in very little, is faithful also in much; and he who is dishonest in a very little, is dishonest also in much.	

λέγει γὰρ ὁ κύριος ἐν τῷ εὐαγγελίῳ· εἰ τὸ μικρὸν οὐκ ἐτηρήσατε, τὸ μέγα τίς ὑμῖν δώσει;	11 εἰ ἐν τῷ ἀδίκῳ μαμώνα πιστοὶ οὐκ ἐγένεσθε, τὸ ἀληθινὸν τίς ὑμῖν δώσει; 12 καὶ εἰ ἐν τῷ ἀλλοτρίῳ πιστοὶ οὐκ ἐγένεσθε, τὸ ἡμέτερον τίς δώσει ὑμῖν;	Et ideo dominus dicebat ... , "Si in modico fideles non fuistis, quod magnum est, quis dabit vobis?"[1]
ὁ πιστὸς ἐν ἐλαχίστῳ καὶ ἐν πολλῷ πιστός ἐστιν.	10 ὁ πιστὸς ἐν ἐλαχίστῳ καὶ ἐν πολλῷ πιστός ἐστιν, καὶ ὁ ἐν ἐλαχίστῳ ἄδικος καὶ ἐν πολλῷ ἄδικός ἐστιν.	

The second half of the saying quoted in *2 Clem.* 8.5 agrees verbatim with Luke 16:10a. But it is unlikely that it is excerpted from the cluster of sayings in Luke 16:9–13 which are secondary additions to the parable of the Unjust Steward (Luke 16:1–8). The first half of *2 Clem.* 8.5 may reveal an alteration by the author of *2 Clement.* "If you have not preserved ..." (εἰ οὐκ ἐτηρήσατε) reflects the interests of the author who adds to the quotation of the saying the admonition, "Preserve your flesh pure" (τηρήσατε τὴν σάρκα ἁγνήν).[2] Its original wording most likely agreed with that of the quotations in Irenaeus and Hilarius (εἰ πιστοὶ οὐκ ἐγένεσθε). But this saying cannnot be derived from Luke 16. Rather, it must be assumed that it is the original form of the saying

---

[1] The same saying is quoted in Hilarius, *Epistula seu libellus*, chap. 1 (*MPL* 10.753b): Si in modico fideles non fuistis, quod maius est, quis dabit vobis?

[2] The verb τηρεῖν is frequently used in *2 Clement*, cf. 6.9; 7.6; 8.4.

that has been modified in Luke 16:11 and 12 in order to provide a commentary for the preceding parable.[1] While the original form is not preserved in Luke, it has survived in the free tradition of sayings and was incorporated into the collection which *2 Clement* used. It is very interesting that exactly in this instance *2 Clement* refers to his source as "the gospel"—possibly the earliest evidence for the designation of a sayings collection as "gospel."

In the quotation of *2 Clem.* 4.2, 5, a saying from the free tradition is combined with sayings drawn from the Synoptic Gospels . The first saying is introduced by "for he says" (λέγει γάρ), the second (4.5) by "the Lord said" (εἶπεν ὁ κύριος):

2 Clem. 4.2, 5	Matt 7:21–23	Luke 6:46; 13:26–27
[2] Not everyone who says "Lord, Lord," will be saved (σωθήσεται),	[21] Not everyone who says "Lord, Lord," will enter the kingdom of heaven,	[6:46] Why do you call me, "Lord, Lord,"
but he who does	but he who does	but do not do what I say?
the righteousness.	the will of my father in heaven.	
	[22] Many will say to me on that	[13:26] Then you will begin to say
[5a] If you were assembed in my bosom, but would not do my commandments, I would expell you.	day, "Lord, Lord, did we not prophecy in your name, and did we not cast out demons in your name, and did we not do many powerful deeds in your name?"	to me, "We ate and drank before you, and you taught in our streets.
[5b] And I shall say to you, "Depart from me, I do not know you whence you	[23] And then I shall testify to them, "I never knew you;	[27] And he will say to you, "I do not know (you)[2] whence you are;

---

[1] Luke 16:10b–12 are secondary formulations. For further discussion see Koester, *Synoptische Überlieferung*, 101. That εἰ πιστοὶ οὐκ ἐγένεσθε belongs to the original form of the saying is still visible in Luke 16:11 and 12. But it is not possible to consider *2 Clem.* 8.5a as a further secondary development on the basis of Luke (*pace* Koester, ibid.).

[2] The word ὑμᾶς is missing in 𝔭[75] B L R 070 1241 *pc* it.

are,	go away from me,	you are;
	those	stay away from me,
workers of	who are doing	all workers of
lawlessness."	lawlessness."	injustice.

καὶ ἐρῶ ὑμῖν· Ὑπάγετε	καὶ τότε ὁμολογήσω	καὶ ἐρεῖ λέγων
ἀπ' ἐμοῦ, οὐκ οἶδα ὑμᾶς,	αὐτοῖς	ὑμῖν·
πόθεν ἐστέ,	ὅτι οὐδέποτε ἔγνων ὑμᾶς,	οὐκ οἶδα (ὑμᾶς),
		πόθεν ἐστέ,
	ἀποχωρεῖτε ἀπ' ἐμοῦ οἱ	ἀπόστητε ἀπ' ἐμοῦ
ἐργάται ἀνομίας.	ἐργαζόμενοι τὴν ἀνομίαν.	πάντες ἐργάται ἀδικίας.

The parallels in Matthew belong to the same unit. But one cannot be certain whether this reflects the order of Q and the two parts of the unit were separated by Luke, or whether Matthew combined two Q sayings which were originally unconnected. Regardless of this question, both Matthean and Lukan redactional elements are evident in the quotation of *2 Clement*. Luke 6:46 apparently preserved the more original form of the saying about those who say "Lord, Lord." The construction of the sentence (οὐ πᾶς ὁ λέγων ... ἀλλ' ὁ ποιῶν) in *2 Clement* reflects Matthew's redaction.[1] Elements of Lukan redaction, however, prevail in the last part of the quotation.[2] Most evident is the mixture of Matthean and Lukan elements in the final phrase. From the quotation of Ps 6:9 (ἀπόστητε ἀπ' ἐμοῦ, πάντες οἱ ἐργαζόμενοι τὴν ἀνομίαν) which forms the basis of this phrase,[3] the citation in *2 Clem.* 4.5 preserves the term "lawlessness" in agreement with Matthew, but renders it in the genitive, while combining it with the Lukan change of οἱ ἐργαζόμενοι into ἐργάται. This mixture of Matthean and Lukan redactional elements appears once more in the quotation of the same saying in Justin, *1 Apol.* 16:11, which agrees with *2 Clement* in the reading ἐργάται τῆς ἀνομίας.[4]

Although the influence of both the texts of Matthew and of Luke is evident, *2 Clement* has replaced the central section of the saying with an altogether different description of the claim of those who want to be accepted by the Lord, "If you were assembled in my bosom ..." A

---

[1] The changes in *2 Clement*, "to do righteousness" (δικαιοσύνην) and "to be saved" (σωθήσεται) reflect the typical vocabulary of the author of this letter; see the discussion in Koester, *Synoptische Überlieferung*, 81–82.

[2] The formulation of the sentence οὐκ οἶδα ὑμᾶς, πόθεν ἐστέ in Luke 13:27 is apparently a Lukan change under the influence of the tradition quoted in Luke 13:25.

[3] The phrase must have stood in Q as an exact quote from the Psalm; see above, # 2.3.1.

[4] This is, in part, confirmed by another quotation of this passage in *Dial.* 76.5; see the further discussion of these harmonizations below, # 5.1.2.1.

parallel is preserved in a manuscript of the so-called Gospel Edition Zion. The manuscripts belonging to this group are characterized by a number of marginal notations which offer alternative readings of certain passages of Matthew, introduced by "The Jewish gospel (Τὸ Ἰου-δαϊκόν) reads here the following . . ." Minuscle 1424, which belongs to this group of manuscripts, notes in the margin to Matt 7:5 a saying that is a close variant of the central section of the quotation in *2 Clem.* 4.2, 5:

"The Jewish Gospel"[1]	*2 Clem.* 4.5a
The Jewish gospel reads here the following:	
If you were	If you were with me assembled
in my bosom and would not do	in my bosom and would not do
the will of my father in heaven,	my commandments,
I will cast you out of my bosom.	I would expell you.
Τὸ Ἰουδαϊκὸν ἐνταῦθα οὕτως ἔχει ·	εἶπεν ὁ κύριος·
ἐὰν ἦτε	ἐὰν ἦτε μετ' ἐμοῦ συνηγμένοι
ἐν τῷ κόλπῳ μου καὶ	ἐν τῷ κόλπῳ μου καὶ μὴ ποιῆτε
τὸ θέλημα τοῦ πατρός μου τοῦ ἐν	τὰς ἐντολάς μου,
τοῖς οὐρανοῖς μὴ ποιῆτε,	
ἐκ τοῦ κόλπῳ μου ἀρρίψω ὑμᾶς.	ἀποβαλῶ ὑμᾶς.

The marginal notations of this group of manuscripts are usually assigned to the Jewish-Christian Gospels, specifically to the *Gospel of the Nazoreans*.[2] This gospel was essentially an expanded edition of the Gospel of Matthew. It is, therefore, not surprising to find in the manuscript of the Gospel Edition Zion a form of this non-canonical saying which reflects the language of Matthew; cf. the phrase "the will of my father in heaven." *2 Clem.* 4.5a, however, does not exhibit any signs of the influence of Matthean language. It is, therefore unlikely that the author drew the saying from an expanded version of the Gospel of Matthew. Rather, the source of *2 Clem.* 4.2, 5 was probably the same collection of sayings that is used elsewhere in this writing, that is, a collection based on Matthew and Luke that also incorporated sayings from the free tradition.

The inclusion of such non-canonical sayings into *2 Clement's* source is also evident in the quotation of *2 Clem.* 12.2, 6.[3] Parallels to this

---

[1] Text in Klostermann, *Apocrypha II*, 7.

[2] See Vielhauer, "Jewish-Christian Gospels," in Hennecke-Schneemelcher-Wilson, *NT Apocrypha*, 1. 136, 139–46.

[3] *2 Clem.* 12.3–5 interrupts the quotation by presenting a seriatim interpretation of the three phrases of the first part of the saying.

saying are found in the *Gospel of the Egyptians*[1] and the *Gospel of Thomas*[2]:

2 Clem. 12.2, 6	*Gos. Thom.* 22	*Gos. Egypt.*
[2] When the Lord himself was asked by someone, when the kingdom of God would come,	Jesus saw infants being suckled. He said to his disciples, "These infants being suckled are like those who enter the kingdom." They said to him, "Shall we then, as children, enter the kingdom?"	When Salome inquired, when she would know the things about which she had asked,
he said (εἶπεν),	Jesus said to them,	the Lord said, "When you tread upon the garment of shame,[3]
"When the two will be one,	"When you make the two one, and when you make the inside like the outside,	and when the two become one,
and the outside like the inside,	and the outside like the inside, and the above like the below, and when you	
and the male with the female	make the male and the female	and when the male with the female

---

[1] This fragment of the *Gospel according to the Egyptians* is preserved in a quotation in Clement of Alexandria, *Strom.* 3.13, 92.2, introduced by, "What is said here, we do not have in the four gospels transmitted to us, but in the Gospel according to the Egyptians . . ." (. . . ἐν τῷ κατ' Αἰγυπτίους εὐαγγελίῳ). On the fragments of the *Gospel of the Egyptians*, see W. Schneemelcher, "The Gospel of the Egyptians," in Hennecke-Schneemelcher-Wilson, *NT Apocrypha*, 1. 166–78.

[2] A detailed discussion of *2 Clem.* 12.2, 6 with its parallels has been presented by Tjitze Baarda, "2 Clement 12 and the Sayings of Jesus," in Delobel, ed., *LOGIA*, 529–56.

[3] A parallel to this sentence appears in *Gos. Thom.* 37: "His disciples said, 'When will you become revealed to us, and when shall we see you?' Jesus said, 'When you disrobe without being ashamed, and take up your garments and place them under your feet like little children and tread on them, then [will you see] the Son of the Living One, and you will not be afraid."

neither male nor female.	one and the same, so that the male not be male nor the female female,[1]	is neither male nor female.
When you do these things, he said (φησίν),[2] the kingdom of my father will come.	then will you enter the kingdom."	

It is impossible to argue for any kind of literary dependence of one of these reproductions of this saying upon an other. In the text of the saying that is preserved in the quotation of *2 Clem.* 12, there are no secondary elaborations, and the questioner remains unnamed. *Gos. Thom.* 22 is a more complex composition.[3] The introduction which describes the situation ("Jesus saw infants being suckled") belongs to a different traditional saying about entering the kingdom of God like children; cf. Mark 10:15. The saying itself in the *Gospel of Thomas* is characterized by the addition of a series of analogous phrases. None of these secondary features is paralleled in the quotation of *2 Clem.* 12. The version of the saying from the *Gospel of the Egyptians*[4] leaves out the second of the three phrases ("and the outside like the inside"), and it combines this saying with a second saying about "treading upon the garment of shame" that is independently preserved in *Gos. Thom.* 37.[5] This, as well as the naming of the person who asks the question (Salome), argues for the secondary character of the reproduction of this traditional saying in the *Gospel of the Egyptians*.[6] The form of this saying as it is quoted in *2 Clem.* 12 is, therefore, its oldest and most original form. It must have been circulating in the free tradition

[1] The *Gospel of Thomas* inserts here: "and when you fashion eyes in the place of an eye, and a hand in the place of a hand, and a foot in place of a foot, and a likeness in the place of a likeness . . ."

[2] The word φησίν here must be understood as an introduction of a quote; cf. Baarda, "2 Clement 12," 548–49.

[3] See the detailed comparison of *2 Clem.* 12 and *Gos. Thom.* 22 by Baarda ("2 Clement 12," 544–47).

[4] It is quoted by Clement of Alexandria in the context of a refutation of the encratite teachings of Cassian, who had based his arguments on this quote; see Baarda, "2 Clement 12," 537–39.

[5] Baarda ("2 Clement 12," 542–43) suggests that either the *Gospel according to the Egyptians* or Cassian, whom Clement of Alexandria quotes, had combined the two sayings, which the *Gospel of Thomas* still preserves as two independent units.

[6] For further discussion of the relationship of *2 Clem.* 12 to the *Gospel of the Egyptians*, see Koester, *Synoptische Überlieferung*, 102–4 (note that those pages were written before the publication of the *Gospel of Thomas*).

of sayings from which the author of the sayings collection that *2 Clement* knew and used obtained also other non-canonical materials.

Several conclusions can be drawn from the observations we have made regarding the quotations of sayings in *2 Clement*. The author of this mid-2d-century work quotes from a collection of sayings of Jesus. Insofar as these sayings have parallels in the Synoptic Gospels, their text reveals a harmonization of Matthean and Lukan elements which occasionally are paralleled elsewhere, especially in Justin Martyr. In addition to these harmonized sayings from Matthew and Luke, *2 Clement's* sayings collection included sayings from the free tradition, that is, non-canonical sayings which have also found their way into so-called apocryphal gospels. However, nowhere is a direct dependence of *2 Clement* upon such apocryphal gospels indicated. Although features of the Matthean and Lukan redaction of sayings are evident, there is no trace of any narrative materials from these canonical gospels. On the other hand, the sayings in the collection that *2 Clement* used seem to have been set into a framework of brief dialogues. The possible reference to this written collection of sayings as "the gospel" argues for a date of composition after the middle of the 2d century.

5.2 The Gospel Quotations of Justin Martyr

5.2.1 SAYINGS IN JUSTIN'S WRITINGS

Justin Martyr, who wrote his Apologies for the Christians and his Dialogue with the Jew Trypho during the last decade of the rule of Antoninus Pius (138–161), is the first of the Christian writers to cite materials from written gospels extensively. He knew and quoted especially the Gospels of Matthew and Luke; he must have known the Gospel of Mark as well, though there is only one explicit reference to this Gospel;[1] he apparently had no knowledge of the Gospel of John.[2] In addition to extensive quotations of sayings in Justin's writings, his scriptural proof for the truth of the Christian message makes ample use of narrative materials from the Synoptic Gospels.

Many of the sayings quoted by Justin are grouped together under special headings in *1 Apol.* 15–17. Smaller clusters are cited in *Dial.* 17.3–4; 35.3; 51.2–3; and 76.4–7. Individual sayings appear occasionally throughout Justin's writings, and some are quoted in the context of Justin's interpretation of Psalm 22 in *Dial.* 99–107.

---

[1] *Dial.* 106.3; see above # 4.1.1.

[2] The only possible reference to the Gospel of John is the quotation of a saying in *1 Apol.* 61.4; see the discussion below.

The relationship of Justin's quotations to the tradition of sayings and to written gospels is complex, and various solutions have been proposed in order to explain the peculiar forms of his sayings.[1] The most striking feature is that these sayings exhibit many harmonizations of the texts of Matthew and Luke.[2] However, the simple assumption of a harmonized gospel source alone cannot explain all peculiarities of the quotations. It is best to consider each feature by itself; but because of the large number of sayings quoted in Justin only some characteristic passages can be discussed.

5.2.1.1 Quotations from the Free Tradition

Justin is not always dependent upon the text of a written gospel; he had access to sayings from the free tradition. This is most obvious in *1 Apol.* 61.4. The saying "Unless you are reborn, you cannot enter into the kingdom of heaven" is quoted in the context of a description of the Christian ceremony of baptism. Justin must have obtained this saying through the tradition of the baptismal liturgy, and is not dependent upon a written gospel. It has been shown above[3] that Justin's version is more original than the forms of the saying that appear in John 3:3 ("Truly, truly, I say to you, unless someone is born again [or: anew], he cannot see the kingdom of God") and John 3:5 ("Truly, truly, I say to you, unless someone is born from water and spirit, he cannot enter into the kingdom of God").[4]

In *Dial.* 35.3 Justin quotes the saying "There will be divisions and factions" ('Έσονται σχίσματα καὶ αἱρέσεις)." It has no parallel in any known written gospel[5] but is quoted elsewhere in ancient Christian literature.[6] In 1 Cor 11:18–19, Paul says: ". . . I hear that there are

---

[1] Adolf Hilgenfeld (*Kritische Untersuchungen über die Evangelien Justins, der Clementinischen Homilien und Marcions* [Halle, 1850]) argued for the use of an apocryphal gospel. Wilhelm Bousset (*Die Evangeliencitate Justins des Märtyrers in ihrem Wert für die Evangelienkritik* [Göttingen: Vandenhoeck & Ruprecht, 1891) believed that he had found evidence for the use of the Synoptic Sayings Source. Edouard Massaux ("Le texte du Sermon sur la Montagne de Matthieu utilizé par Saint Justin," *EThL* 28 [1952] 411–48) argued for exclusive use of the Synoptic Gospels.

[2] This has been argued convincingly first by Ernestus Lippelt, *Quae fuerint Justini Martyris* ΑΠΟΜΝΗΜΟΝΕΥΜΑΤΑ (Dissertationes Philologicae Halensis 15.1: 1901); see also Arthur Bellinzoni, *Sayings in Justin Martyr*.

[3] See above # 3.4.4.3.

[4] See especially the detailed arguments in Bellinzoni, *Sayings in Justin Martyr*, 134–38. Bellinzoni also discusses related quotations of this saying in Patristic literature.

[5] The origin of this saying is debated. The only saying in the Synoptic tradition that could be compared is Luke 12:51, "Do you think that I have come to give peace on earth? no, I tell you, but rather division (διαμερισμόν)"; cf. *Gos. Thom.* 16.

[6] It is also quoted in the *Didascalia* (see below), in Didymus, *De trinitate* 3.22, and

divisions (σχίσματα) among you ... For indeed there must be factions (αἱρέσεις) among you." Justin is hardly dependent upon Paul; he never refers to any of Paul's writings. But the possibility that Paul formulated his criticism of the Corinthians on the basis of this saying should not be excluded. In *Dial.* 35.3 it appears as the second in a cluster of four sayings into which it was apparently incorporated before it was quoted by Justin; see the discussion below.

It is difficult to determine the origin of the saying in *Dial.* 47.5: "Therefore, our Lord Jesus Christ said, 'In the things in which I shall overcome you, I shall also judge you' (Ἐν οἷς ἂν ὑμᾶς καταλάβω, ἐν τούτοις καὶ κρινῶ)." There are parallels to this saying in ancient Christian writers,[1] but nowhere is it quoted as a saying of Jesus. Rather, it is either identified as a pronouncement of God or as a prophecy of Ezekiel. Justin may have misunderstood a reference to "the Lord" in the introductory formula of his source (a pseudepigraphical book attributed to Ezekiel?) and thus ascribed the saying to Jesus,[2] or he may have known this saying from an oral tradition.

5.2.1.2 *Quotations that Could be Derived from Matthew*

1 Apol. 15.1 quotes Matt 5:28 ("Whoever looks at a woman in order to desire her ..."). There are no parallels to this saying in other gospels, and it is most likely a Matthean composition. The introductory formulation in Justin (Ὃς ἂν ἐμβλέψῃ) differs from Matthew (πᾶς ὁ βλέπων), but is paralleled in numerous Patristic quotations.[3] Thus, Justin may not be quoting Matthew directly, but some catechetical collection of sayings derived from Matthew.

1 Apol. 15.4 quotes Matt 19:11–12 ("There are some made eunuch by human beings ..."). There is again no parallel to this saying in any other gospel. Modifications in Justin's quotation[4] can be ascribed to his editorial work.

---

in Lactantius, *Div. Inst.* 4.30. In the latter case, it is not identified as a saying of Jesus. Dependence upon this saying is possible also in *Ps.-Clem. Hom.* 16.21.4: "There will be," as the Lord said, "false apostles, false prophets, factions (αἱρέσεις), lust for power."

[1] The texts of the quotations in Clement of Alexandria, *Quis dives salvetur* 40.1–2; Ps.-Athanasius, *Quaest. ad Antiochum* 36; *Vita S. Iohannici;* and Johannes Climacus, *Scala Paradisi* 7, can be found in Bellinzoni, *Sayings in Justin Martyr,* 132–33.

[2] Bellinzoni, *Sayings in Justin Martyr,* 134.

[3] See ibid., 57–58.

[4] Justin abbreviates the saying and reverses the order of the first two categories of eunuches.

1 Apol. 16.5 (On Swearing) has a gospel parallel only in Matt 5:34–37, but Justin's quote also shares some features with the quotation of this saying in Jas 5:12:[1]

Just. *1 Apol.* 16.5	Jas 5:12	Matt 5:34–37
	. . . my brothers and sisters,	[34] But I say to you
Do not swear at all (μὴ ὀμόσητε ὅλως)	do not swear (μὴ ὀμνύετε), either by heaven	not to swear at all (μὴ ὀμόσαι ὅλως), either by heaven, because it is the throne of God,
	or by earth,	[35] or by earth, because it is the footstool of his feet, or by Jerusalem, . . .
	nor with any other oath.	[36] nor shall you swear by your head, . . .
Let your Yes be Yes and your No be No (ἔστω δὲ ὑμῶν τὸ ναὶ ναὶ καὶ τὸ οὖ οὖ), Everything beyond these is from evil.	Let your Yes be Yes and your No be No (ἤτω δὲ ὑμῶν τὸ ναὶ ναὶ καὶ το οὖ οὖ), so that you may not fall under condemnation.	[37] Let what you say be "Yes, yes" and "No, no." (ἔστω δὲ ὁ λόγος ὑμῶν ναὶ ναί, οὖ οὖ) Everything beyond these is from evil.

That Justin is quoting Matthew and not James is evident in the first and the last clause. The absence of Matt 5:34b–36 is probably due to omission on the part of Justin. But the phrase "Let your Yes be Yes and your No be No" is identical with the corresponding sentence in Jas 5:12. Surprisingly, this phrase from Jas 5:12 also appears in a large number of Patristic quotations of Matt 5:37,[2] and a combination of this phrase with Matt 5:37b, that is, a text that is identical with that of Justin's reference, can be found twice in the *Pseudo-Clementine Homilies,* in both instances understood as a saying of Jesus.[3] Thus, also in this instance it is not likely that Justin is quoting directly from the text of Matthew, but from a catechism, whose text was influenced by the formulation preserved in Jas 5:12 but not necessarily directly dependent upon the the Epistle of James.

---

[1] See the comparison of Matt 5:34–37 and Jas 5:12 above in # 2.1.4.4.

[2] All relevant material is presented in Bellinzoni, *Sayings in Justin Martyr,* 66.

[3] Ἔστω δὲ ὑμῶν τὸ ναὶ ναὶ καὶ τὸ οὖ οὖ, τὸ γὰρ (δὲ) περισσὸν τούτων ἐκ τοῦ πονηροῦ ἐστιν (3.55.1 and 19.2.4; ed. Rehm, GCS pp. 77 and 253).

In *1 Apol.* 15.17 Justin concludes a cluster of sayings with a citation of Matt 6:1 ("... do not do this in order to be seen by people"). Again, there is no parallel in any other gospel. The quotations of Matt 6:19–20 in *1 Apol.* 15.11 and of Matt 7:21 in *1 Apol.* 16.9 appear in a series of sayings in which harmonizations of the texts of Matthew and Luke are otherwise evident.[1] It is significant that dependence on Matthew alone is restricted to sayings of Matthew that have no Synoptic parallel, and that even in these instances it is most probable that Justin is quoting from a catechism.

5.2.1.3 Sayings that Could be Derived from Luke

There are very few instances in which exclusive dependence upon Luke's Gospel is likely.[2] The only clear instance is the quotation of Luke 17:48 ("Everyone to whom much is given, of him much is required") in *1 Apol.* 17.4. There is no parallel to this saying in either Matthew or Mark; Luke has added this originally independent saying to the parable of the Servant's Wages (Luke 17:47–48a). However, in the manuscripts of Luke, this saying appears in two different versions, one in the Majority Text of the manuscripts (𝔐), the other in the so-called Western Text (D):

Justin *1 Apol.* 17.4	Luke 17:48 𝔐	Luke 17:48 D
Whom God has given more,	From everyone to whom much has been given much will be required, and from the one to whom much has been entrusted,	From everyone to whom much has been given even much more will be required, and from the one to whom much more has been entrusted,
even more will be demanded from him.	even much more will be demanded.	even more will be demanded.

---

[1] It is, therefore, misleading to classify these and similar passages as sayings which are dependent upon Matthew only (*pace* Bellinzoni, *Sayings in Justin Martyr,* 61–62, 67–69).

[2] Bellinzoni (*Sayings in Justin Martyr,* 70–73, cf. 20–22) lists *1 Apol.* 15.3; 16.1; and 16.10. But the first of these sayings (On marrying a divorced woman) actually combines elements of Luke 16:18 and Matt 5:32b (19:9). All three appear in an otherwise harmonized cluster of sayings. It would be natural that in such compositions some phrases or sentences are reflecting exclusively the version of either Matthew or Luke.

ᾧ πλέον ἔδωκεν ὁ θεός,	παντὶ δὲ ᾧ ἐδόθη πολύ, πολὺ ζητηθήσεται παρ' αὐτοῦ, καὶ ᾧ παρέθεντο πολύ,	παντὶ δὲ ᾧ ἔδωκαν πολύ, ζητήσουσιν ἀπ' αὐτοῦ περισσότερον, καὶ ᾧ παρέθεντο πολύ,
πλέον ἀπαιτηθήσεται παρ' αὐτοῦ.	περισσότερον αἰτήσουσιν αὐτόν.	πλέον ἀπαιτήσουσιν αὐτόν.

To be sure, Justin quotes this saying in an abbreviated form. But there can be no doubt that the basis of his quotation is the Western Text, as preserved in Codex D, and not the Majority Text of the Lukan manuscripts.[1] The abbreviated form of the quotation of this saying, however, does not seem to be accidental. There are several instances in Patristic literature in which a similar abbreviated form of the saying appears and, moreover, the use of the composite verb ἀπειτεῖν (Codex D) instead of the Majority Text's αἰτεῖν is pervasive in such quotes.[2] This would argue for Justin's dependence upon a special catechetical tradition also in this instance.

5.2.1.4 Harmonizations of the texts of Matthew and Luke

The vast majority of the sayings quoted in Justin's writings are harmonizations of the texts of Matthew and Luke. These harmonizations are not casual or accidental, but systematic and consistent,[3] and they involve the composition of longer sections of parallel sayings from both gospels. The consistency of the harmonizations is evident in the quotation of Matt 7:22–23 = Luke 13:26–27 which is cited by Justin twice, in *1 Apol.* 16.11 and *Dial.* 76.5:[4]

1 Apol. 16.11	Dial. 76.5	Matt 7:22–23	Luke 13:26–27
Many will say to me,	Many will say to me on that day	Many will say to me on that day	Then you will start to say,

---

[1] Special affinities of Justin's quotations with the Western text are well known and are a very strong argument for the existence of this text type in the early 2nd century; see also below.

[2] See the examples listed in Bellinzoni, *Sayings in Justin Martyr*, 73.

[3] This certainly excludes the reference to careless quotation from memory as an explanation for Justin's harmonizations.

[4] There are a total of twelve sayings that Justin quotes more than once, and not all of these can be discussed here. Bellinzoni (*Sayings in Justin Martyr*, 8–48) has demonstrated that the harmonizations of several gospel texts are consistent in most instances.

Lord, Lord, did we not in your name eat and drink	"Lord, Lord, did we not in your name eat and drink	Lord, Lord, did we not in your name	"we ate and drank before you and you have taught in our streets."
	and prophesy and	prophesy, and in your name	
	drive out demons,	drive out demons, and in your name	
do powerful deeds?"		do many powerful deeds?"	
And then I shall say to them,	And I shall say to them,	Then I shall testify to them, "I never knew you,	And he will say to you, "I do not know you whence you are.
go away from me, workers of unrighteousness."	go away from me.	go away from me, those who are working lawlessness."	Stay away from me all workers of unrighteousness."
1 Apol. 16.11	*Dial.* 76.5	Matt 7:22–23	Luke 13:26–27
πολλοὶ δὲ ἐροῦσί μοι	πολλοὶ ἐροῦσί μοι τῇ ἡμέρᾳ ἐκείνῃ·	πολλοὶ ἐροῦσί μοι τῇ ἐκείνῃ τῇ ἡμέρᾳ·	τότε ἄρξεσθε λέγειν·
κύριε κύριε, οὐ τῷ σῷ ὀνόματι ἐφάγομεν καὶ ἐπίομεν	κύριε κύριε, οὐ τῷ σῷ ὀνόματι ἐφάγομεν καὶ ἐπίομεν	κύριε κύριε, οὐ τῷ σῷ ὀνόματι	ἐφάγομεν ἐνώπιόν σου καὶ ἐπίομεν καὶ ἐν ταῖς πλατείας ἡμῶν ἐδίδαξας·
	καὶ προεφητεύσαμεν καὶ δαιμόνια ἐξεβάλομεν;	ἐπροφητεύσαμεν καὶ τῷ σῷ ὀνόματι δαιμόνια ἐξεβάλομεν καὶ τῷ σῷ ὀνόματι	
καὶ δυνάμεις ἐποιήσαμεν;		δυνάμεις πολλὰς ἐποιήσαμεν;	
καὶ τότε ἐρῶ αὐτοῖς·	καὶ ἐρῶ αὐτοῖς·	καὶ τότε ὁμολογήσω αὐτοῖς·	καὶ ἐρεῖ λέγων ὑμῖν· οὐκ οἶδα ὑμᾶς πόθεν ἐστέ·
ἀποχωρεῖτε ἀπ' ἐμοῦ ἐργάται τῆς ἀνομίας.	ἀναχωρεῖτε ἀπ' ἐμοῦ	ἀποχωρεῖτε ἀπ' ἐμοῦ οἱ ἐργαζόμενοι τὴν ἀνομίαν.	ἀπόστητε ἀπ' ἐμοῦ πάντες ἐργάται ἀδικίας.

The basis of both quotations in Justin is obviously the same harmonized text of Matthew and Luke. To be sure, each of the two quotations does not represent the entire text. But insofar as they do quote the

same words, they agree almost completely.[1] One may even assume
that the text, from which Justin quotes each time, included at least
one additional phrase which appears in neither one of his two quotations: οὐκ οἶδα ὑμᾶς πόθεν ἐστέ = Luke 13:27 (instead of Matthew's οὐδέ-
ποτε ἔγνων ὑμᾶς), because this phrase is paralleled in the harmonized
quotation of the same saying in *2 Clem.* 4.5 where one also finds the
harmonized version of the last phrase, ἐργάται (τῆς) ἀνομίας.[2] The
method of harmonization includes two different procedures: (1) whenever the texts of Matthew and Luke are closely parallel, either the
Matthean or the Lukan phrase or a conflation of both is chosen;
(2) Whenever the texts of Matthew and Luke differ considerably, as in
Matt 7:22 and Luke 13:26, major portions of the two texts are combined; thus, one finds Luke's "we were eating and drinking" as well as
Matthew's "we prophesied etc."—albeit the former is now introduced
by the Matthean "in your name" instead of Luke's "before you."

More important even than the observation of consistent harmonizations of the Matthean and Lukan parallels of individual sayings is the
question of the system of composition of sayings in this harmonized
gospel. The context of *1 Apol.* 16:9–13, in which the above quotation of
Matt 7:22–23 = Luke 12:26–27 appears, provides some insight into the
procedure of composition.[3]

1 Apol. 16.9–13	Matthew	Luke
Not everyone who says to me, "Lord, Lord" will enter into the kingdom of heaven, but the one who does the will of my father in heaven.	[7:21] Not everyone who says to me, "Lord, Lord" will enter into the kingdom of heaven, but the one who does the will of my father in heaven.	[6:46] Why do you call me, "Lord, Lord," and do not do what I say.
He who hears me and does what I say, hears	[7:24] Everyone who hears these my words and does them . . .	[6:47] Everyone who comes to me and hears my words and does them . . .

---

[1] Minor differences like ἀποχωρεῖτε for ἀναχωρεῖτε are of no concern.

[2] See above, # 5.1.3.

[3] This passage is also discussed in Bellinzoni, *Sayings in Justin Martyr,* 98–100; see
especially his diagram, p. 99; cf. Helmut Koester, "The Text of the Synoptic Gospels in
the Second Century," in: William L. Petersen, ed., *Gospel Traditions in the Second Century: Origins, Recensions, Text, and Transmission* (Christianity and Judaism in Antiquity 3; Notre Dame: Notre Dame University Press, 1989) 30.

the one who sent me.

10:16 He who hears you, hears me; he who rejects you, rejects me; and he who rejects me, rejects the one who sent me.

Many will say to me on that day, "Lord, Lord, did we not in your name eat and drink [and prophesy and cast out demons][1] and do many powerful works?"	**7:22** Many will say to me on that day, "Lord, Lord, did we not in your name prophesy and in your name cast out demons and in your name do many powerful works?"	**13:26** Then you will begin to say, "We ate and drank before you, and you taught in our streets."
And then I shall say to them, "[I do not know you whence you are.][2] Go away from me, you workers of lawlessness." There will be wailing and gnashing of teeth,	And then I shall testify to them, "I have never known you, go away from me, those who are doing lawlessness," **13:42b-43,42a** There will be wailing and gnashing of teeth.	**13:27** But he will say to you, "I do not know you whence you are. Stay away from me all workers of unrighteousness." **13:28** There will be wailing and gnashing of teeth, when you see Abraham . . .
when the righteous will shine like the sun,	Then the righteous will shine like the sun in the kingdom of their father.	
but the unrighteous will be sent into the eternal fire. Many will come in my name	And they will throw them into the furnace of fire. **24:5a** Many will come in my name, saying "I am the Christ," and they will lead many astray.[3]	

---

[1] The bracketed words occur only in the parallel quotation of this saying in *Dial.* 76.5, see above.

[2] The bracketed words are missing in Justin's citation, but are quoted in *2 Clem.* 4.5, see above # 5.1.1.3.

[3] This saying from the Synoptic apocalypse relies on Mark 13:5 and is also reproduced by Luke (21:8). This may be an accidental parallel, but it could also indicate that Justin omitted something from his source; see below.

	7:15 Beware of the false prophets who come to you	
on the outside dressed in skins of sheep, but inwardly they are ravenous wolves. From their works you will know them. Every tree that does not produce good fruit is cut down and thrown into the fire.	in sheep's clothing, but inwardly they are ravenous wolves. **7:16a** From their fruit you will know them. **7:19** Every tree that does not produce good fruit is cut down and thrown into the fire.	**3:9** Every tree that does not produce good fruit is cut down and thrown into the fire.[1]

This section of Justin's quotation of Jesus' sayings rests on a deliberate and careful composition of the parallel texts of Matthew and Luke, but is also disrupted by interpolations from different contexts. The author begins with Matt 7:21 (= Luke 6:46); he then moves to the following verse in Luke (6:47), but combines it with part of a saying that opens with a similar phrase and appears elsewhere in Luke (10:16), instead of citing the parable of the builders which is introduced by Luke 6:47. After this disruption, the cluster continues with Matt 7:22–23 and harmonizes this passage with its Lukan parallel 13:26–27. The Lukan context of this saying determines the choice of the next saying, Luke 13:28, but its continuation is taken from Matthew's parallel (13:42–43) to that Lukan passage.[2] The following saying, however, returns to the context of Matthew 7, quoting Matt 7:15–16a,[3] 19, though the introductory phrase to Matt 7:15 is perhaps drawn from Matt 24:5. Clearly, a text that was produced as a harmony of Matthew and Luke served as the basis for the composition of this cluster of sayings. However, this assumption does not solve all problems of Justin's quotation of these sayings in *1 Apol.* 16.9–13.

The intrusion of a phrase from Luke 10:16 and the opening of Matt 7:15 with a phrase from Matt 24:5 are strange. If both Luke 10:16 and

---

[1] Luke 3:9 = Matt 3:10 is a saying that belongs to the preaching of John the Baptist. Matthew has transferred the saying into the context of the Sermon on the Mount (7:19)—clear evidence that Justin is directly or indirectly dependent upon Matthew and not on a pre-Matthean collection of sayings.

[2] This is one of the sayings that might be dependent upon the text of Matthew only (see above). However, its incorporation into the present context is due to the process of harmonization, since it is chosen because its Lukan parallel follows upon a saying from Luke that had just been quoted.

[3] Matt 7:15–16a is introduced by a phrase taken from Matt 24:5. That is not accidental: the quotation of Matt 7:15–16a in *Dial.* 35.3 is also introduced in this way; see below.

Matt 24:5 were quoted in full, the character of the collection of sayings that Justin used would be become clear—it would be evident
that all the sayings deal with the problem of legitimacy of the missionary and of false prophets and teachers. But Justin has deliberately omitted from his source not only most of Luke 10:16 and the
continuation of Matt 24:5 ("saying 'I am the Christ,' and they will lead
many astray"), but also the reference to false prophets in Matt 7:22
("and prophesy and cast out demons"),[1] and the introduction to the
quote of Matt 7:15 ("Beware of the false prophets"). The reason for
these omissions is formulated by Justin himself in his introduction to
the quotation of these sayings (1 Apol. 16.8):

> Those who are not found to live as he has taught, are recognized as not
> being Christians, even if they say with their mouth the teachings of
> Christ; because he said that not those who only say, but those who do the
> works will be saved.

Thus, Justin himself did not compose this cluster of sayings for this
particular context. He used an already existing collection. But sayings that warned against false prophets would not have served his
purpose. He wanted to quote sayings speaking about hearing and
doing. Thus, he removed the respective references to false prophets.
Moreover, the cluster he used probably followed a different order: it
must have begun with Matt 7:15. Justin instead started with Matt
7:21 and moved Matt 7:15–16, 19 to the end which allowed him to
begin and to conclude the section with an emphasis upon good works.
This also explains Justin's change of "From their *fruit* you will know
them" (Matt 7:16) into "From their works you will know them."
   Justin's use of these sayings presupposes three stages of development: (1) a systematic harmonization of the texts of Matthew and
Luke, (2) the composition of a cluster of sayings which warn against
false prophets, (3) Justin's editing of this collection in order to show
that Christ's teaching speaks about the contrast between words and
works. It is necessary to distinguish the first two stages. They were
not just two different concerns in one and the same stage of composition, namely a composition of a sayings cluster that at the same time
harmonized sayings from Matthew and Luke.[2]

---

[1] That these phrases were part of Justin's source is evident from the citation of the
same passage in *Dial.* 76.5.

[2] Bellinzoni (*Sayings in Justin Martyr,* 100) collapses stage (1) and (2) of this process. He assumes that the harmonizations were made specifically for the composition
of a catechism. This assumption, however, cannot explain why also the narrative
materials quoted by Justin were drawn from a harmonized gospel text.

The existence of similar material, or even a portion of the same cluster of sayings composed of warnings against false prophets, is evident in the quotation of four sayings appearing in *Dial.* 35.3.[1] This strongly suggests that the composition of clusters was not identical with the production of a harmonized gospel text. The quotation in *Dial.* 35.3 shows that this cluster contained further sayings which were not reproduced in *1 Apol.* 16. A parallel in the *Apostolic Constitutions* (6.13) has been used to explain the reference of *Dial.* 35.3. However, it will become evident that this parallel is misleading:

Dial. 35.3	Matthew	*Apost. Const.* 6.13[2]
Many will come (ἐλεύσονται) in my name	**24:5** Many will come (ἐλεύσονται) in my name	Many will come (ἐλεύσονται) to you
	7:15 Beware of the false prophets who come (ἔρχονται) to you	
on the outside dressed in skins of sheep (ἐνδεδυμένοι δέρματα προβάτων),[3] but inwardly they are ravenous wolves.	in the dress of sheep (ἐν ἐνδύμασι προβάτων) but inwardly they are ravenous wolves.	in the dress of sheep (ἐν ἐνδύμασι προβάτων) but inwardly they are ravenous wolves.
	7:16 From their fruits you shall recognize them.	From their fruits you shall recognize them.
And: There will be divisions and factions.		[There will be factions and divisions.][4]
And: Beware of the false prophets who will come (ἐλεύσονται) to you on the outside dressed in skins of sheep (ἔξωθεν ἐνδεδυμένοι δέρματα προβάτων) but inwardly they are ravenous wolves.	**7:15** Beware of the false prophets who come (ἔρχονται) to you in the dress of sheep (ἐν ἐνδύμασι προβάτων) but inwardly they are ravenous wolves.	Beware of them.

[1] For a detailed comparison, see Bellinzoni, *Sayings in Justin Martyr,* 102–6.

[2] This passage is a reproduction of the *Didascalia* where it is preserved both in its Syriac and Latin version (Chap. 25, Connolly, pp. 210–211): "Venient ad vos in indumentis ovium, ab intus autem sunt lupi rapaces, et fructibus eorum cognoscitis eos. Adtendite vobis: exsurgent enim pseudochristi et pseudoprofetae et seducent multos."

[3] Justin uses the same formulation in the quote of *1 Apol.* 16.13.

[4] This saying appears in a different context in the *Syriac Didascalia* (Chap. 23, Connolly, p. 198), but is missing in the corresponding text of the *Apostolic Constitutions*.

And:
Many false christs and

^{24:24} False christs and
false prophets will
arise (ἐγερθήσονται)
and give great signs
and wonders so that, if
possible, they will lead
astray even the elect.

False christs and

false
apostles will arise
(ἀναστήσονται) and will
lead astray many
of the believers.

^{24:11} Many false
prophets will arise
(ἐγερθήσονται) and will
lead astray many.

false
prophets will arise
(ἀναστήσονται) and will
lead astray many.

There are several problems in the text of these four sayings. The first saying agrees verbatim with the quotation in *1 Apol.* 16.13. In both instances the reference to Matt 7:15–16a is introduced by a phrase borrowed from Matt 24:5 ("Many will come in my name"),[1] in both cases the reference to false prophets is omitted and the phrase "on the outside dressed in skins of sheep" replaces Matthew's "in the dress of sheep." The quote of this saying in *Apost. Const.* 6.13 also begins with "Many will come" and omits the reference to false prophets, but the phrase "in my name" does not appear, and the remainder of the text is an exact quotation of Matt 7:15. Thus, this is not a true parallel. What Justin is quoting here is his own edited text of the saying from *1 Apol.* 16.13.

The second saying cited by Justin, "There will be divisions and factions" (ἔσονται σχίσματα καὶ αἱρέσεις), has no parallel in the canonical gospels, but is attested elsewhere.[2] It is tempting to assume that this saying belongs to the traditional cluster of sayings quoted in *Apost. Const.* 6.13;[3] but it appears in a different context in the *Didascalia*.

A parallel to the third saying of *Dial.* 35.3 is missing in the *Didascalia* and the *Apostolic Constitutions*. What Justin is quoting here is a form of the saying that must have been the basis for the text of *1 Apol.* 16.13 and the first saying of *Dial.* 35.3. Like that quotation, the text departs from that of Matt 7:15 in the formulation "on the outside dressed in skins of sheep."

The fourth saying is a variant of Matt 24:11, and it is closely paralleled by the quotation in the *Didascalia* and the *Apostolic Constitutions*. Justin's quotation shares with Matt 24:11 the term "many" (πολλοί) before "false christs" (Matt 24:11 has "many false prophets") and

---

[1] The only difference is that *1 Apol.* 16.13 uses ἥξουσιν, *Dial.* 35.5 has ἐλεύσονται.
[2] See above.
[3] Bellinzoni, *Sayings in Justin Martyr*, 104–5.

the final phrase "they will lead astray many." But the reference to false christs does not appear in Matt 24:11; it is drawn from Matt 24:24. "False apostles" in Justin, instead of "false prophets" in Matt 24:11 (24:24) and *Apost. Const.* 6.13, seems to be a change introduced by Justin.[1] He and the *Apostolic Constitutions* both insert "false christs" from Matt 24:24 into the text of the quotation of Matt 24:11. Since Justin quotes the same conflation of these two Matthean passages also in *Dial.* 82.2,[2] it must have been a feature of his source which could have influenced later quotations of this saying. But this common feature of the quotations of Justin and of the *Didascalia* and *Apostolic Constitutions* is too small a base for the hypothesis of a common source or tradition for the entire unit. Rather, the author of the *Didascalia*, upon which the *Apostolic Constitutions* depends, is simply using Matthew, because the citation of Matt 24:11 is continued in a straightforward fashion with Matt 24:12–13. Evidence for a direct dependence upon Matthew in the *Didascalia* is so strong that it is hard to argue for the use of another kind of source that this writing shared with Justin.[3]

While the exact wording of Matthew's text occurs almost consistently in the *Didascalia*, this is not the case in Justin's sayings of *Dial.* 35.3. Rather, the wording of the variants from a special source predominates. Moreover, not only does Justin reflect this special wording in other quotations of the some of these sayings, it is also evident that he has the entire cluster in front of him whenever he quotes one of its sayings. In *Dial.* 51.2, Justin says, "he (Jesus) indicated beforehand that in the time until his parousia there would be, as I said before, factions[4] and false prophets in his name." This reference combines elements from three different sayings of the cluster about false prophets.[5]

What is hard to explain in Justin's quotation of *Dial.* 35.3 is the repetition of the variants of Matt 7:15 in the first and the third saying of this cluster. If Justin used a collection of sayings here, one must

---

[1] See Bellinzoni, *Sayings in Justin Martyr,* 103.

[2] "He said that many false prophets and false christs would come in his name and lead many astray."

[3] I disagree with the statement, "both authors used a single source or tradition that had already combined these features" (Bellinzoni, *Sayings in Justin Martyr,* 106).

[4] The manuscript text of Justin's writings reads here ἱερεῖς. Editors of Justin's text have correctly emended this to αἱρέσεις.

[5] The quote of Matt 24:11 in *Dial.* 82.2 contains the reference to the coming of the false prophets and christs "in his name," which does not appear in the quotation of Matt 24:11 in *Dial.* 35.4, but is part of other sayings of the same cluster; cf. *1 Apol.* 16.11,13 and the first saying of *Dial.* 35.4.

assume that it began with the second saying, while the first saying was added by Justin. In *Dial.* 35.2–3 he states that there are indeed people who confess the crucified Jesus as Lord and Christ but do not teach his commandments, and that Christ had predicted beforehand that this would happen in his name. A series of sayings beginning with "There will be divisions and factions" would not have served Justin's purpose too well. Therefore he prefixed to these sayings a variant of Matt 7:15 that he had formulated himself.

5.2.1.5 The character of Justin's source

Harmonizations of Matthew and Luke are evident in most of these sayings. They occur also in other clusters of sayings quoted by Justin in *1 Apol.* 15–17.[1] Whenever Justin cites a saying more than once, the same harmonizations are repeated, and in several instances quotations in other ancient Christian writings concur with Justin's harmonizations.[2] In none of these instances are narrative materials quoted in the context of the sayings. Usually, however, Justin does not seem to quote sayings directly from a harmonized gospel text. As in *2 Clement,* he is apparently relying upon collections of sayings which were composed on the basis of harmonized gospel texts and which incorporated additional sayings from the non-canonical tradition.

Justin cites clusters under special headings. These headings are Justin's own formulations, but the sayings quoted in each instance must have been grouped together thematically before their use by Justin in his writings. This was already evident in the sayings about false teachers and prophets which Justin used and revised in order to demonstrate the contrast between words and works (*1 Apol.* 16.9–13). That the sayings were originally composed into clusters for a purpose different from Justin's interpretation is evident also in other parts of these sayings clusters. *1 Apol.* 15.10–17 is a striking example. The sayings are here introduced by the statement:

> That one should share with the needy and should do nothing in order to obtain praise, he said this (εἰς δὲ τὸ κοινωνεῖν τοῖς δεομένοις καὶ μηδὲν πρὸς δόξαν ποιεῖν ταῦτα ἔφη, *1 Apol.* 15.10).

The following sayings are quoted:

---

[1] See Bellinzoni, *Sayings in Justin Martyr,* especially 76–86. Bellinzoni also argues for harmonizations of Matthew and Mark in two instances (ibid., 87–88); however, this is less convincing.

[2] Ibid., 8–48. See also the parallel between *2 Clement* and Justin discussed in the previous chapter.

1 Apol. 15.10–17	Matthew	Luke[1]
[10] Give to everyone who asks you . . .	5:42	6:30
If you lend to those from whom you hope to receive . . .	5:47a	6:34a
Even the publicans do this.	5:46b	(6:32b)
[11] Do not collect treasures for yourselves on earth.	6:19–20a	(12:33)
[12] What will it profit a human being to gain . . .	16:26	9:25
Therefore collect treasures in heaven . . .	6:20a	(12:33)
[13] Be generous and merciful like your father . . .	5:45 (48)	6:36
[14] Do not be anxious what you will eat . . .	6:25–26	12:22–24
[15] Do not be anxious . . . your father . . . knows . . .	6:31–32	12:30
[16] Seek first the kingdom of heaven . . .	6:33	12:31
Where your treasure is, . . .	6:21	12:34
[17] Do not do this in order to be seen before people	6:1	—

Only the first and the last of these sayings (16:10 and 17) are directly related to the topic mentioned by Justin in his introduction. The other sayings deal with the question of worldly treasure and are framed by Matt 6:19–21. Several of the sayings are harmonizations of the texts of Matthew and Luke.[2] But what Justin quotes is not the text of a harmonized gospel. Rather, he cites a cluster of sayings which were brought together under a particular theme. It is possible that Justin himself edited this collection so that it would serve more adequately the purpose of his citation. The addition of Matt 6:1 as a concluding sentence in particular may be due to Justin's editing.

The catechetical character of these clusters of sayings is evident in their usage in Justin, although Justin himself has sometimes provided headings which do not agree with the topic that governed their original composition. It is difficult to determine in each instance the degree to which Justin has supplemented and rearranged these collections. But it appears that the catechetical collections already existed and that Justin himself did not compose them. This does not exclude Justin's own personal knowledge of, and access to, the underlying harmonized gospel. On the contrary, in quoting narrative materials Justin certainly deals first-hand with such a gospel, and he occasionally also quotes sayings with reference to the narratives in which they are embedded.

---

[1] Texts given in parenthesis have not influenced the wording of the saying quoted by Justin.

[2] Bellinzoni (*Sayings in Justin Martyr,* passim) has discussed these sayings in detail and demonstrated the presence of harmonizations in *1 Apol.* 15:10 and 14.

5.2.2 THE GOSPEL NARRATIVES IN JUSTIN'S WRITINGS

5.2.2.1 Scriptural Proof and Gospel Narrative

Justin Martyr is the first Christian writer who makes extensive use of narrative materials from written gospels. The context is the proof of the truth of the Christian proclamation from scripture. Christ's suffering and death, understood in terms of the description of the suffering righteous, became the primary motivation for the development of the passion narrative. Study of the scriptures answered the question of the "why" of Jesus' passion and crucifixion. Luke 24:26–27 presents this question and its answer in a classic form when Jesus, still not recognized, asks the disciples on their way to Emmaus. "Was it not necessary that the Christ should suffer these things and enter into his glory?" And then Luke reports, "And beginning with Moses and all the prophets, he interpreted to them in all the scriptures the things concerning himself." But Luke already stands at the end of this phase of the development of the narrative tradition.

For Justin, the question of the "why" is no longer determinative. Rather, he now lays claim to the developed narrative and uses its agreement with scriptural prophecy as a proof for the revelatory truth of the events. Justin agrees that the story that is told about Jesus might be nothing more than the story of an ordinary human being who accomplished miracles through magical art and was therefore believed to be a Son of God (1 Apol. 30). Therefore, he defines the principles of his demonstration in this way:

> We shall set forth our demonstration not just believing those who tell the story, but of necessity persuaded by those who prophesy before it happens because of seeing with one's own eyes that it happened and is happening as it was prophesied. (1 Apol. 30)

> Because what is considered among human beings unbelievable and impossible to happen, that God has indicated beforehand through the prophetic spirit that it would happen so that, when it happened, it would not be disbelieved but believed on the basis of it's being prophesied beforehand. (1 Apol. 33.2)

The foundation of the proof for the truth of Christian faith is, therefore, the Bible of Israel—a book of venerable ancient prophecy. But the proof for the historical fulfillment of prophecy cannot be convincing as long as the correspondence between prophecy and historical fulfillment is only approximate. Justin is concerned that the evil demons already knew about such prophecy and used it for the creation of the pagan cults and their myths, falsely claiming that these cults were the institutions in which the prophecies had been fulfilled. In this way they wanted to deceive the people, but since they misunderstood some of the prophecies, it is possible to detect the mistakes they made in their fabrications of pagan myths.[1]

The Christian proclamation about Jesus as the Son of God, however, is true, because the Christians possess trustworthy historical documents—"Remembrances of the Apostles"—from which it can be shown that everything in Christ's appearance and work happened in complete agreement with prophecy. What is demonstrated to be true is the Christian kerygma, not the story of the gospels. The reports contained in the gospels are used to show that the facts about Christ which the kerygma proclaims happened in complete agreement with the prophecy that announced them.

Before beginning his proof from scripture in his First Apology, Justin quotes an expanded version of the Christian kerygma (31.7), and the following chapters then demonstrate that in each instance prophecy and fulfillment agree:

> In the books of the prophets we find it announced beforehand that he would appear, born through a virgin, grow up, heal every disease and sickness and raise the dead, and be despised and unrecognized and crucified and die and be raised and ascend to the heavens and be and be called the Son of God, and that some would be sent by him to every nation, and that the Gentiles would believe.

In his demonstration in the following chapters, Justin does not always precisely follow this order, but he begins with arguments for the time of Christ's coming (chapter 32), the miraculous nature of Jesus' birth (chapter 33), and the place of birth in Bethlehem (chapter 34). Chapter 35 discusses his growing up unrecognized, events of Jesus' passion, and the entry into Jerusalem; chapter 45 brings a prophecy about Christ's inthronization; chapter 48.1–3 speaks about his healing and raising the dead, 48.4–5 about his suffering. Finally, chapters 50–53 discuss the crucifixion, resurrection, sending of the disciples, parousia of Christ, and the faith of the nations.

Relatively little actual narrative material is quoted in the *First Apology*. The only extensive demonstration with quotations from written gospels appears in chapters 33–34 in the discussion of the announcement of Jesus' birth and of its place, Bethlehem. More extensive quotations of narrative materials appear in the *Dialogue with Trypho*, especially in the interpretation of Psalm 22 in *Dialogue* 99–107. In all instances the quotations are abbreviated, because Jus-

---

[1] See especially *1 Apology* 54.

tin wants to quote primarily those passages and phrases which correspond to the words of the prophecy. The gospel texts quoted by Justin have parallels in all three Synoptic Gospels, and sentences from Matthew and Luke (rarely if ever from Mark) are often mixed or harmonized in these quotations. In several instances, additional phrases that have no support in extant gospel texts are inserted in order to create an even more thorough correspondence between prophecy and fulfillment. The question is whether Justin composed these harmonizations and inserted additional phrases just for the purpose of his demonstration of scriptural proof or whether he drew on a written gospel text that was already harmonized and expanded.

It seems to me that we are not witnessing the work of an apologist who randomly selects pieces from various gospels and invents additional phrases for the purpose of a tight argument of literal fulfillment of scripture; nor can one solve the complex problems of Justin's quotations of gospel narrative materials by the hypothesis of a ready-made, established text of a harmonized gospel as his source. Rather, his writings permit insights into the work of a school of scriptural exegesis in which careful comparison of written gospels with the prophecies of scripture endeavored to produce an even more comprehensive new gospel text.

The materials with which Justin worked consisted of (1) traditional collections of scriptural prophetic passages related to the story of Jesus that had already been used by earlier Christian writers such as the authors of the *Epistle of Barnabas,* the *Gospel of Peter,* and the Gospel of Matthew; (2) improved texts of the Greek translation of at least some books of the Hebrew Bible; (3) several gospel writings among which Matthew and Luke predominate; (4) a harmony of the Synoptic Gospels. In this context, it is possible to discuss only the last two sets of materials in some detail, although the question of the scriptural texts used by Justin must also be considered insofar as they belong to the context of the gospel narrative.[1]

---

[1] For the traditional collections of prophecies, see Stendahl, *School of St. Matthew*; Wilhelm Bousset, *Jüdisch-christlicher Schulbetrieb in Alexandria und Rom: Literarische Untersuchungen zu Philo und Clemens Alexandrinus, Justin und Irenäus* (FRLANT N.F. 6; Göttingen: Vandenhoeck & Ruprecht, 1915); see also above # 3.2.3. For the improved Greek translation of the Hebrew Bible, see Dominique Barthélemy, O.P., "Redécouverte d'un chainon manquant de l'histoire de la Septante," *RB* 60 (1953) 18–29; idem, *Les devanciers d'Aquila: Première publication intégrale du texte des fragments du Dodécaprophéton* (Supplements to Vetus Testamentum 10; Leiden: Brill, 1963), especially pp. 203–12.

5.2.2.2 *The Narrative of Jesus' Birth*

1 Apol. 33 gives as proof concerning Jesus' birth the prophecy of Isa 7:14. The text of this scriptural passage is presented in a form that is influenced by its quotation in Matt 1:23:

Isa 7:14	Matt 1:23	1 Apol. 33.1
Behold, the virgin will conceive in the womb and bear a son, and you shall call his name Emmanuel.	Behold, the virgin will conceive in the womb and bear a son, and they will call his name Emmanuel, which is translated, "God is with us."	Behold, the virgin will conceive in the womb and bear a son, and they will say in his name, "God is with us."
ἰδοὺ ἡ παρθένος ἐν γαστρὶ λήψεται[1] καὶ τέξεται υἱόν, καὶ καλέσεις τὸ ὄνομα αὐτοῦ Ἐμμανουήλ.	ἰδοὺ ἡ παρθένος ἐν γαστρὶ ἕξει καὶ τέξεται υἱόν, καὶ καλέσουσιν[2] τὸ ὄνομα αὐτοῦ Ἐμμανουήλ, ὅ ἐστιν μεθερμηνευόμενον μεθ' ἡμῶν ὁ θεός.	ἰδοὺ ἡ παρθένος ἐν γαστρὶ ἕξει καὶ τέξεται υἱόν, καὶ ἐροῦσιν[3] ἐπὶ τῷ ὀνόματι αὐτοῦ Μεθ' ἡμῶν ὁ θεός.

Justin shares with Matthew's quotation the plural form of the verb in the second half of the sentence, although he is using a different verb (ἐροῦσιν instead of καλέσουσιν), and he repeats Matthew's translation of Ἐμμανουήλ. The focus of Justin's attention is not, strictly speaking, the Matthean form of the Isaiah quotation, for he shows no interest in the name "God with us." His primary concern is with the first part of this prophetic text that is quoted by Matthew. But in the following proof for the fulfillment of this prophecy, he turns first to the text of Luke; only later does he add elements from Matthew.

---

[1] This is the reading of the LXX manuscript B and the minuscules belonging to the so-called Lucianic recension, while LXX A reads ἕξει (= Matt 1:23). The former is the LXX text with which Justin was familiar, because it appears in his other quotations of this passage (*Dial.* 43.5; 66.2; 67.1; 68.6; 71.3).

[2] The change to the 3rd person plural instead of the 2nd person singular is deliberately introduced by Matthew, because the child's actual name is not "Emmanuel"; Matthew wants to point to the fact that he will also be called symbolically with this messianic name. See Stendahl, *School of St. Matthew*, 98.

[3] Though Justin chooses a different word, its 3rd person plural is dependent upon Matthew's text. In other quotations of the passage (*Dial.* 43.5; 66.3) Justin follows the text of the LXX (καλέσεις), and he also cites the Greek transcription of the Hebrew name (Ἐμμανουήλ), omitting the translation of the name (μεθ' ἡμῶν ὁ θεός).

Matt 1:20–21	Luke 1:31–32	1 Apol. 33.5
		. . . and the angel of God proclaimed to her and said,
What is conceived (γεννηθέν) in her, is from the Holy Spirit. She will bear a son.	And behold, you will conceive (συλλήψη) in the womb	"Behold you will conceive (συλλήψη) in the womb from the Holy Spirit and bear a son
	and bear a son, and you shall call his name Jesus. He will be great and be called Son of the Most High.	and he will be called Son of the Most High.
And you shall call his name Jesus, because he will save his people from their sins.		And you shall call his name Jesus, because he will save his people from their sins.

The text of *1 Apol.* 33.5 is a harmonization of the two angelic announcements, the one from Matthew in which the angel calls Joseph in a dream, the other from Luke's narrative of the annunciation. While the passage begins with a sentence from Luke, "from the Holy Spirit" is interpolated from Matt 1:20.[1] The naming of Jesus and the reason for this name is given according to Matt 1:21. To be sure, Justin has a special interest in this explanation of the name "Jesus," for he comments later that this Hebrew name means "savior" in Greek, and then quotes Matt 1:21 once more (*1 Apol.* 33.7–8). But in order to argue for the fulfillment of Isa 7:14 in *1 Apol.* 33.3–6, the report of the command to name the child "Jesus" did not need to refer to the Matthean form. Moreover, the quotation of Matt 1:21, that is, the angel's command to Joseph to name the child, is introduced in *1 Apol.* 33.8 by: "Therefore the angel said to the virgin." It is evident, therefore, that Justin is quoting a harmonized gospel text in which part of the angel's command to Joseph (Matt 1:21) as well as the quotation of Isa 7:14 from Matt 1:23 had already been combined with the angel's words to Mary in Luke's story of the annunciation.[2] At the same time, although quoting the text of Isa 7:14 from Matthew, Justin is quite aware of the origin of this reference. He introduces it as prophesied

---

[1] Luke mentions the Holy Spirit only in the later response of the angel to Mary's question; see below.

[2] This does not imply that this harmonized gospel narrative deleted the angel's command to Joseph entirely. *Dial.* 78.3 reports that an angel had commanded Joseph not to expel his wife, because "what is in her womb is from the holy spirit." See further below.

through Isaiah, while Matthew 1:22 only refers to "what has been said by the Lord through the prophet."

Justin's gospel text must have continued with the remainder of the Lukan pericope of the annunciation. In the introduction to the harmonization of Luke 1:31–32 and Matt 1:20–21, Justin had already alluded to the Lukan continuation of the story: *1 Apol.* 33.4 ("The power of God, coming down upon the virgin, overshadowed her and made her pregnant, although she was a virgin") recalls Luke 1:35 ("The Holy Spirit will come upon you and the power of the Most High will overshadow you"). A fuller reproduction of this passage is given in *Dial.* 100.5 in the context of an Eve/Mary typology that is reminiscent of the Adam/Christ typology of Romans 5:[1]

> Although Eve was an uncorrupted virgin, having received (συλλαβοῦσα) the word from the serpent she gave birth to disobedience and death; but the virgin Mary received faith and joy when the angel Gabriel proclaimed to her . . .

This sentence introduces a quotation of Luke 1:35 and 38 (vss. 36–37, the reference to the pregnancy of Elizabeth, is omitted):

Luke 1:35, 38	*Dial.* 100.5
"The Holy Spirit will come upon you and the power of the Most High will overshadow you; therefore the holy one that is born (from you)[2] shall be called Son of God."	. . . that the spirit of the Lord would come upon her and the power of the Most High would overshadow her; therefore the holy one that is born from her should be called Son of God,
Mary said, "Behold, I am the servant of the Lord; let it be to me according to your word."	she answered, "let it be to me according to your word."

Justin agrees with Luke's text almost completely, but has changed "Holy Spirit" to "spirit of the Lord." This is a change that was not

---

[1] This typology appears in narrative form in the *Proto-Gospel of James* (13.1) where Joseph, having discovered the pregnancy of Mary, complains (translation from Hennecke-Schneemelcher-Wilson, *NT Apocrypha*, 1. 381):

> Has the story of Adam been repeated in me? For as Adam was absent in the hour of his prayer and the serpent found Eve alone and deceived her and defiled her, so also has it happened to me.

[2] The words ἐκ σοῦ appear only in some manuscripts (C Θ *f*[1] 33 *pc* a c e [r[1]] vg[cl] sy[p]; Ir[lat] Tert Ad Epiph). This addition, however, must be presupposed for Justin. Justin should, therefore, also be listed as a witness in the text-critical apparatus of Nestle-Aland.

made *ad hoc* by Justin for the citation in *Dialogue* 100, but must have been part of his harmonized gospel text, because in that text a reference to the holy spirit had already been made in the harmonization of Luke 1:31 with Matt 1:20 ("Behold you will conceive in the womb from the Holy Spirit").

In the discussion of the prophecy for the place of Jesus' birth (*1 Apology* 34), Justin only quotes the prophecy of Micah 5:1 and then remarks that Jesus was born in this "village in the land of Judah which is 35 stades from Jerusalem" (*1 Apol.* 34.2). No actual narrative material from a gospel is quoted. But one finds here the remark that such information can be found in the "records which have been made under Cyrenius (Quirinius), the first (Roman) governor (ἐπίτροπος) of Judea." Since Cyrenius is mentioned only in Luke 2:2, a knowledge of Luke's birth narrative of Jesus is indicated.[1] However, the quotation of the text of Micah 5:1 is not given in the text of the LXX; rather, Justin follows the form of the text quoted in Matt 2:6:

Micah 5:1(2)	Matt 2:6	*1 Apol.* 34.1
And you Bethlehem, house of Ephratha, you are the smallest among the thousands of Judah. From you shall come who is to be the leader in Israel.	And you Bethlehem, land of Judah, you are by no means the smallest among the rulers of Judah, for from you shall come a ruler who is to shepherd my people Israel.	And you Bethlehem, land of Judah, you are by no means the smallest among the rulers of Judah, for from you shall come a ruler who is to shepherd my people.
Καὶ σύ, Βηθλέεμ οἶκος τοῦ Ἔφραθα, ὀλιγοστὸς εἶ τοῦ εἶναι ἐν χιλιάσιν Ἰούδα· ἐκ σοῦ μοι ἐξελεύσεται τοῦ εἶναι εἰς ἄρχοντα ἐν τῷ Ἰσραήλ.	Καὶ σὺ Βηθλέεμ, γῆ Ἰούδα, οὐδαμῶς ἐλαχίστη εἶ ἐν τοῖς ἡμεμόσιν Ἰούδα· ἐκ σοῦ γὰρ ἐξελεύσεται ἡγούμενος, ὅστις ποιμαίνει τὸν λαόν μου Ἰσραήλ.	Καὶ σὺ Βηθλέεμ, γῆ Ἰούδα, οὐδαμῶς ἐλαχίστη εἶ ἐν τοῖς ἡγεμόσιν Ἰούδα· ἐκ σοῦ γὰρ ἐξελεύσεται ἡγούμενος, ὅστις ποιμαίνει τὸν λαόν μου.

---

[1] Justin does not seem to have any independent knowledge of Cyrenius, nor of any other data of the Roman administration in Palestine. That he calls Cyrenius the *first* Roman administrator of Judea is a result of his theory of salvation history because, according to Gen 49:10 ("Not will a ruler be missing from Judah, until he comes to whom it is assigned"), Justin assumes that Jewish rulers continued in Judea until the coming of Jesus (*1 Apol.* 32.1–3).

The form of the quotation that appears in Matt 2:6 departs considerably from both the LXX and the Hebrew text. It is, in fact, a combination of Micah 5:1 and 2 Sam 5:2; only the latter speaks of the prince's function as a shepherd of Israel.[1] This conflated quotation was wholly the work of Matthew.[2] There can be no question that Justin is quoting this Matthean text.[3] On the other hand, he explicitly identifies Micah as the author of this prophecy, while Matthew 2:5 only says, "Thus it is written through the prophet." But Justin is not aware that the citation in Matthew is actually a conflation of Micah 5:1 with 2 Sam 5:2; therefore, he quotes also the clause from 2 Sam 5:2 as part of a Micah prophecy, but omits the mention of Israel at the end which comes from the text of Micah.[4]

But in references of Justin to the appearance of the star at the birth of Jesus and to the coming of the "wise men" to worship the new-born child, the absence in *1 Apol.* 34 of explicit quotations from the Matthean story of "The Visit of the Magi" (Matt 2:1–12) is striking. All of the respective statements are scriptural quotations accompanied by more general references to the fulfillment. However, even these references reveal a knowledge of gospel texts and perhaps also deliberate changes of such texts on the basis of additional exploration of scripture. Such changes become more clearly evident in his discussion of the birth narrative in *Dialogue* 77–78 (see below).

Justin speaks about the appearance of the star at the birth of Jesus for the first time in *1 Apol.* 32.13 (ἄστρον δὲ φωτεινὸν ἀνέτειλε, καὶ ἄνθος ἀνέβη ἀπὸ τῆς ῥίζης Ἰεσσαί). This statement indicates the fulfillment of a prophecy that is a conflation of three different scriptural passages:

Nu 24:17	Isa 11:1, 10	*1 Apol.* 32.12
And a star will rise from Jacob and a man will stand up from Israel		And a star will rise from Jacob
	[1] And a branch will come forth from the root of Jesse and a flower will rise up from the root.	and a flower will rise up from the root of Jesse,

---

[1] The people say to David, "And the Lord said to you, 'You shall be shepherd of my people Israel, and you shall be prince over Israel.'"

[2] See Stendahl, *School of St. Matthew,* 99–101.

[3] See also Massaux, *Influence de L'Évangile de Saint Matthieu,* 496.

[4] "Israel" is also omitted in the quotation of this passage in *Dial.* 78.1.

	¹⁰ And on that day the root of Jesse shall	
Isa 51:5	stand to lead the nations, and upon him	
. . . and upon his arm the nations will set their hope.	the nations will set their hope.	. . . and upon his arm the nations will set their hope.

Nu 24:17	Isa 11:1, 10	1 Apol. 32.12
ἀνατελεῖ ἄστρον ἐξ Ἰακὼβ καὶ ἀναστήσεται ἄνθρωπος ἐξ Ἰσραήλ		ἀνατελεῖ ἄστρον ἐξ Ἰακώβ,
	¹ Καὶ ἐξελεύσεται ῥάβδος ἐκ τῆς ῥίζης Ἰεσσαί, καὶ ἄνθος ἐκ τῇ ῥίζης ἀναβήσεται	καὶ ἄνθος ἀναβήσεται ἐκ τῆς ῥίζης Ἰεσσαί,
	¹⁰ καὶ ἔσται ἐν τῇ ἡμέρᾳ ἐκείνῃ ἡ ῥίζα τοῦ Ἰεσσαί	
Isa 51:5	καὶ ὁ ἀνιστάμενος	
. . . καὶ εἰς τὸν βραχιόνα μου ἔθνη ἐλπιοῦσιν.	ἀρχεῖν ἐθνῶν, ἐπ᾿ αὐτῷ ἔθνη ἐλπιοῦσιν.	καὶ ἐπὶ τὸν βραχιόνα αὐτοῦ ἔθνη ἐλπιοῦσιν.

This combined quote was not created by Justin, who introduces it as a quotation from Isaiah (καὶ Ἡσαίας δέ,[1] ἄλλος προφήτης, . . . οὕτως εἶπεν). Nu 24:17 and Isa 11:1 together were already known to Matthew who refers to the latter at the end of his birth narrative (2:23): "In order to fulfill what was said through the prophets, that he should be called a Nazarene" (ὅτι Ναζωραῖος κληθήσεται). Matthew here refers to the Hebrew text of Isa 11:1 which contains the term נצר, translated in the LXX with ἄνθος. Matthew was aware of this Hebrew equivalent,[2] but Justin only knew the combined quote in its Greek text and can, therefore, only make the general remark: "And a flower arose from the root of Jesse which is Christ." He does not refer to Matt 2:23 in that context.

Dial. 106.4 also connects the mention of the rising of the star at Jesus' birth with a quotation of Nu 24:17 and adds that "this is written in the memoirs of his apostles." At the same time, Justin remarks

---

[1] In his first edition of Justin's writings, Otto had emended the text to read καί instead of δέ. Thus, the impression was created that Justin was conscious of the conflated character of this quote. But Otto corrected this in later editions and explicitly rejected this misunderstanding.

[2] See Stendahl, *School of St. Matthew*, 103–4. The combination of these scriptural passages is apparently also presupposed in the *Testaments of the Twelve Patriarchs*, *Test. Judah* 24.1, 5–6.

that, at the time of the rising (ἀνατολή) of the star, "the magi of Arabia who had learned from it (i.e., from the star about the birth) came and worshiped him." Whereas Matthew (2:1) derives from Nu 24:17 (ἀνατελεῖ ἄστρον) that the Magi came from the East (ἀπὸ ἀνατολῶν), Justin relates the term directly to Jesus by adding Zech 6:12: "Behold a man, 'Rising' is his name" ('Ιδοὺ ἀνήρ, 'Ανατολὴ ὄνομα αὐτοῦ).[1] For the designation of the place from which the Magi came, Arabia, Justin relies on another scriptural passage. That is not evident in *Dialogue* 106, because in this reference to the coming of the Magi it has already become part of a revised gospel story.

But in *Dialogue* 77–78 Justin identifies Isa 8:4 as the prophecy which indicated the place from which the Magi would come: "Before the child will learn to cry 'father' or 'mother,' he will take the power of Damascus and the spoils of Samaria before the king of Assyria" (*Dial.* 77.2–3). Damascus, Justin explains, was then a city of Arabia (*Dial.* 78.10).[2] The "king of Assyria" refers to Herod "because of his godless and lawless character" (*Dial.* 77.4). This sets the stage for the rewriting of the Synoptic birth narratives (*Dialogue* 78), for which Justin uses both Matthew 2 and Luke 2. All new elements are derived from the interpretation of scriptural prophecy. The Magi are always referred to as coming from Arabia.[3] Because of Micah 5:1, Bethlehem is referred to as a city of Judah, and Joseph goes to Bethlehem with Mary "because he is from the tribe of Judah" (78.4; cf. Luke 2:4: "because he was from the house and lineage of David"). The time of the coming of the Magi is fixed "right at the time of his birth" (ἅμα τῷ γεννηθῆναι αὐτόν, 77.4).[4]

Whether the reference to the birth of the child in a cave (ἐν σπηλαίῳ τινὶ σύνεγγυς τῆς κώμης) is also a narrative element that was added on the basis of the interpretation of scripture, is less certain. Justin relates the remark explicitly to a prophecy from Isaiah (*Dial.* 78.7–8)

[1] In *Dial.* 106.4 this passage is introduced with "and another scripture says." But in *Dial.* 126.1 Justin says that Jesus was called "Rising (ἀνατολή) by Zechariah."

[2] That is historically correct, because Damascus then belonged to the realm of the Arabian Nabateans, although Justin knows, and states explicitly, that at his time Damascus belonged to Syro-Phoenecia.

[3] *Dial.* 78.1, 2, 5, 7; 102.2; 103.3; 106.4. Only in *Dial.* 78.9 does Justin call them simply "the Magi."

[4] The reason for this timing is evident in *Dial.* 77: Justin wants to make sure that the prophecy Isa 8:4 cannot refer to the king Hezekiah, because what is said in the prophecy has happened "before the child will learn to cry 'father' or 'mother.'" But the phrase "right at the time of his birth" also introduces the reference to the coming of the Magi in *Dial.* 88.1; 102.2, although there is no argument about the interpretation of Isa 8:4 in those contexts. Cf. also *Dial.* 106.4 where the appearance of the star is said to have happened "right at the time of his birth."

and adds that he had already referred to this prophecy earlier, namely in *Dial.* 70.1–2 where he discusses the falsification of a prophecy from Isaiah among the worshipers of Mithras who call their place of initiation "a cave." He then proceeds to quote Isa 33:13–19 where the Greek text of vs. 16b says: οὗτος οἰκήσει ἐν ὑψηλῷ σπηλαίῳ πέτρας ἰσχυρᾶς ("he shall dwell in a high cave of a strong rock").[1] Following his report about the birth in a cave in *Dial.* 78.5–6, Justin once more refers to the falsification of this prophecy in the cult of Mithras and the inspiration of this cult by the devil. Did Justin invent the reference to the birth in a cave on the basis of Isa 33:16? That seems very unlikely, because there is no evidence that Isa 33:16 or any part of its context ever played a role in the scriptural interpretation of the story of Jesus.[2] Does Justin follow an established tradition which identified Jesus' birthplace as a cave near Bethlehem? The *Proto-Gospel of James* (18.1) relates that Joseph, realizing that they are in a desert when Mary's hour of giving birth arrives, "found a cave there and brought her into it."[3] It is not likely that Justin's gospel text presented such a report,[4] because he never repeats it anywhere else in his writings. It has been suggested that Justin, coming from Palestine himself, personally knew of a place of worship in a cave near Bethlehem.[5] That there was such a place is evident in a remark of Origen in his *Contra Celsum* (1.51).[6] But Origen wrote this two or three generations later, and one cannot be sure that a cave cult that remembered the birth of Jesus existed near Bethlehem at the time of Justin. Perhaps the knowledge of the story of Mithras' birth in a cave and the designation of Mithras sanctuaries as "caves" prompted Justin to discuss the question of the falsification of prophecy with respect to Jesus' birth. The reference to the scriptural prophecy mentioning the cave would then be an afterthought and not the source of a new piece of information about the story of Jesus.

In *Dial.* 78.7–8 Justin finally reports about the murder of the innocents by Herod and the flight to Egypt. In the details of his report as

---

[1] The words σπηλαίῳ πέτρας ἰσχυρᾶς translate the Hebrew text סלעים משׂגבו מצדות = סלעים משׂגבו מצדות "his defense will be the fortress of rocks." The reason the Greek translates the first of these Hebrew terms with σπηλαίον is unclear.

[2] Dibelius, "Jungfrauensohn," 76.

[3] For other early Christian reports about Jesus' birth in a cave, see Dibelius, ibid., 75–77; Bauer, *Leben Jesu,* 61–68. Neither in the *Proto-Gospel of James* nor anywhere else is the reference to Isa 33:16 repeated.

[4] That he is dependent upon the *Proto-Gospel of James* is highly unlikely.

[5] Joachim Jeremias, *Golgotha* (Leipzig: 1926) 14–16; see also Dibelius, "Jungfrauensohn," 76–77.

[6] Dibelius, "Jungfrauensohn," 75.

well as in the quotation of the respective scripture (Jer 31:15), Justin is simply dependent upon Matt 2:13–18. He quotes Jeremiah exactly like Matthew, whose citation "comes the nearest to giving an abbreviated translation of the M.T. (Massoretic Hebrew text), possibly with some influence from the LXX."[1]

Perhaps what is visible in this treatment of the Synoptic birth narratives is not the finished product of a harmony of Matthew and Luke, but the process of the production of such a harmony by an author who seeks to update the narrative information of the two gospel writings with additional exploration of scriptural prophecy. Justin introduces some new passages from scripture, from which he derives more details of the narrative; but he also uses and reapplies prophecies that are already recorded in the gospel story. The purpose of the harmonizations is not to achieve a richer unified narrative, but to produce a more complete record of the fulfillment of scripture. Matthew had begun this process in his own gospel because speaking about the birth of Jesus is for him a demonstration of its legitimacy: it fulfills scripture. Justin continues this process. If one attempted to reconstruct Justin's harmonized gospel—or the one that was in the process of being produced in his school—one would probably find that it was more a record of incidents of fulfillment of prophecy than the story of a wonderful arrival of the divine savior in this world.

5.2.2.3 John the Baptist and the Narrative of Jesus' Baptism

Gospel materials about John the Baptist in Justin's *Dialogue with Trypho*[2] are used in two different contexts. In *Dialogue* 49–51 Justin wants to show that the prophecy of the coming of Elijah before the appearance of the Messiah has been fulfilled in the coming of John the Baptist. In *Dialogue* 88 the demonstration is concerned with the question of Christ's full preexistent possession of divine power and spirit (*Dialogue* 87); the narrative of Jesus' baptism is discussed in order to reject the idea that he received the spirit only at that moment. In both instances, Justin emphasizes that the presence of the divine spirit, and thus also of prophecy, had ceased with the coming of Jesus and that all spiritual gifts are now at work among the Christians. In each instance the selections of gospel narratives that are quoted or summarized are influenced by the purpose of the discussion. But they also share some peculiar features that differ from the narrative of any particular gospel.

---

[1] Stendahl, *School of St. Matthew*, 102.
[2] Justin does not discuss the Baptist in his *First Apology*.

About the appearance of John the Baptist, Justin always says that he "was stationed at the Jordan":

Dial. 49.3 ... who sat at the Jordan crying out.
Dial. 51.2 ... when he was still sitting at the Jordan river.
Dial. 51.2 ... when John was still sitting at the Jordan.

Dial. 49.3 ὅστις ἐπὶ τὸν Ἰορδάνην καθεζόμενος ἐβόα.
Dial. 51.2 ἔτι αὐτοῦ καθεζομένου ἐπὶ τοῦ Ἰορδάνου ποταμοῦ.
Dial. 51.2 Ἰωάννου γὰρ καθεζομένου ἐπὶ τοῦ Ἰορδάνου.

The description of the locality of his activity as stationary[1] at the Jordan is peculiar. In Mark 1:4 John appears "in the desert," in Matt 3:1 "in the desert of Judea." Only Luke 3:3 deliberately restricts the area of John's activity to "all the districts of the Jordan" (ἦλθεν εἰς πᾶσαν τὴν περίχωρον τοῦ Ἰορδάνου), but Luke still allows John to walk around like an itinerant preacher, rather than making him stationary.[2] In most later traditions, the only locale with which John is connected is "the Jordan."[3] Justin here shows that his gospel text is influenced by this tendency of the tradition rather than by any specific passages from the canonical gospels.

The two terms "to cry out" (βοᾶν) and "to proclaim" (κηρύσσειν) are always used to describe the character of his message:

Dial. 49.3 ... who sat at the Jordan crying out.
Dial. 51.2 John went before him and cried out to the people to repent.
Dial. 88.2 John went before him as the herald of his coming.
Dial. 88.7a John ... proclaiming a baptism of repentance.
Dial. 88.7b ... and he cried out.

Dial. 49.3 ἐπὶ τὸν Ἰορδάνην καθεζόμενος ἐβόα.
Dial. 51.2 Ἰωάννης προελήλυθε βοῶν τοῖς ἀνθρώποις μετανοεῖν.
Dial. 88.2 προελήλυθεν Ἰωάννης κῆρυξ αὐτοῦ τῆς παρουσίας.
Dial. 88.7a Ἰωάννου ... κηρύσσοντος βάπτισμα μετανοίας.
Dial. 88.7b ... καὶ αὐτὸς ἐβόα.

The term "to proclaim" (κηρύσσειν) also occurs in Mark 1:7 and Luke 3:3; but while Justin is using exclusively these two verbs for the description of John's preaching, all canonical gospels also employ other

---

[1] καθίζομαι has the meaning of being (permanently) resident in one particular place; cf. Bauer, *Leben Jesu*, 103.

[2] The Gospel of John attempts to define more specifically various places of John's activity: "in Bethany beyond the Jordan, where John was baptizing" (John 1:28), "at Aenon near Salim, because there was much water there" (3:23).

[3] Bauer, *Leben Jesu*, 103.

terms.[1] The description of John as "herald" (κῆρυξ) is missing altogether in the canonical Gospels. The verb "to cry out" (βοᾶν) appears in the Synoptic Gospels only in the quotation of Isa 40:3 (φωνὴ βοῶντος);[2] it is not used in the description of John's preaching. Justin (*Dial.* 50.3–5) quotes the entire passage Isa 39:8–40:17, including verse 6: "A voice saying, 'Cry out!' and I said, 'What shall I cry?'" (φωνὴ λέγοντος· Βόησον. καὶ εἶπον· Τί βοήσω;). Throughout the *Dialogue with Trypho*, he prefers the verb "to cry" for the introduction of prophetic speech,[3] while it is used only rarely for a saying of Jesus.[4] The use of this verb for the proclamation of John the Baptist clearly marks his speech as prophetic announcement. He is the "prophet" (προφήτης, *Dial.* 49.3, 4; cf. 51.2) and the "proclaimer" ("herald" = κῆρυξ, *Dial.* 88.2) of the coming of Christ. Although the Synoptic Gospels also designate John as a "prophet,"[5] the term is never used in the story of his ministry.[6] Since all of Justin's alterations of the description of John are consistent and appear repeatedly, it is probable that they were already incorporated into the text of his gospel.

That this gospel text was a harmony is evident in many details of Justin's description of John's appearance and preaching:

Dial. 88.7	Matt 3:1	Mark 1:4	Luke 3:3
When John was sitting at the Jordan.	in the wilderness of Judea	in the wilderness	into all the region around the Jordan
Ἰωάννου γὰρ καθεζομένου ἐπὶ τοῦ Ἰορδάνου	ἐν τῇ ἐρήμῳ τῆς Ἰουδαίας	ἐν τῇ ἐρήμῳ	εἰς πᾶσαν τὴν περίχωρον τοῦ Ἰορδάνου

---

[1] λέγων Matt 3:1; Mark 1:7; John 1:26; λέγει John 1:21, 29; εἶπεν Matt 3:7; John 1:22; ἔλεγεν Luke 3:7; ἀπεκρίνατο λέγων Luke 3:11; ὡμολόγησεν John 1:20.

[2] Matt 3:3 and Mark 1:2 quote only this verse (Mark combines it with Mal 3:1); Luke 3:4–6 expands the citation to include also Isa 40:4–5.

[3] *Dial.* 12.1; 14.1; 17.2; 20.4; 24.3; 25.1; 27.2, 3; etc.

[4] *Dial.* 17.3, 4; 76.7. For sayings of Jesus, Justin prefers εἶπεν (*1 Apol.* 15.1, 8; 16.9; 19.6; etc.; *Dial.* 35.3; 47.5; 49.3, etc.), διδάσκειν (*1 Apol.* 15.9; 17.1) and other verbs.

[5] The term occurs occasionally, e.g., Mark 6:15 par; Matt 14:5; Q/Luke 7:26.

[6] John 1:21–25 explicitly rejects the identification of John the Baptist as a prophet. That appears even more clearly, if vss. 22–23 (the quote of Isa 40:3) have been interpolated by a later redactor; cf. Bultmann, *Gospel of John,* on 1:22–23.

Dial. 88.7	Matt 3:1	Mark 1:4	Luke 3:3
proclaiming a baptism of repentance	proclaiming	proclaiming a baptism of repentance for the forgiveness of sins	proclaiming a baptism of repentance for the forgiveness of sins
κηρύσσοντος βάπτισμα μετανοίας	κηρύσσων	κηρύσσων βάπτισμα μετανοίας εἰς ἄφεσιν ἁμαρτιῶν	κηρύσσων βάπτισμα μετανοίας εἰς ἄφεσιν ἁμαρτιῶν

As has been stated above with respect to the location of John's activity, Justin is closest to Luke's text. The description of the content of his proclamation, "baptism of repentance," could have been derived from Luke, but also from Mark, while there is no equivalent in Matthew.

Dial. 88.7: καὶ ζώνην δερματίνην καὶ ἔδυμα ἀπὸ τριχῶν καμήλου μόνον φοροῦντος καὶ μηδὲν ἐσθίοντος πλὴν ἀκρίδας καὶ μέλι ἄγριον.	Matt 3:4: εἶχον τὸ ἔνδυμα αὐτοῦ ἀπὸ τριχῶν καμήλου καὶ ζώνην δερματίνην περὶ τὴν ὀσφὺν αὐτοῦ· ἡ δὲ τροφὴ αὐτοῦ ἀκρίδες καὶ μέλι ἄγριον.
	Mark 1:6: καὶ ἦν ... ἐνδεδυμένος τρίχας καμήλου καὶ ζώνην δερματίνην περὶ τὴν ὀσφὺν αὐτοῦ, καὶ ἐσθίων ἀκρίδας καὶ μέλι ἄγριον.

For a description of John's dress and nourishment, either Matthew or Mark could have been Justin's source; in the use of the verb ἐσθίειν Justin agrees with Mark. There is no equivalent in Luke's Gospel to this description.

Dial. 88.7	Luke 3:15–16a	John 1:19–20
The people assumed	As the people were filled with expectation and all were questioning in their hearts, whether John might	When they sent . . . to ask him, "Who are you?"
that he was the Christ; to them he cried out,	be the Christ, John answered all of them by saying,	. . . and he confessed,
"I am not the Christ,	"I baptize you with water . . ."	"I am not the Christ."
but the voice of one crying . . ."		cf. vs. 23: "I am the voice of one crying out in the wilderness. . ."

Dial. 88.7	Luke 3:15–16a	John 1:19–20
οἱ ἄνθρωποι ὑπελάμβανον αὐτὸν	Προσδοκοῦντος δὲ τοῦ λαοῦ καὶ διαλογίζομενον πάντων ἐν ταῖς καρδίαις αὐτῶν περὶ τοῦ Ἰωάννου, μήποτε αὐτὸς	ὅτε ἀπέστειλαν ... ἵνα ἐρωτήσωσιν αὐτόν· σὺ τίς εἶ; ...
εἶναι τὸν Χριστόν· πρὸς οὓς καὶ αὐτὸς ἐβόα·	εἴη ὁ Χριστός, ἀπεκρίνατο λέγων πᾶσιν ὁ Ἰωάννης·	καὶ ὡμολόγησεν ὅτι
Οὐκ εἰμὶ ὁ Χριστός, ἀλλὰ φωνὴ βοῶντος.	ἐγὼ μὲν βαπτίζω ...[1]	ἐγὼ οὐκ εἰμὶ ὁ Χριστός, cf. vs. 23: ἐγὼ φωνὴ βοῶντος ἐν τῇ ἐρήμῳ ...

Only Luke formulates the thoughts of the people, concerning whether John might be the Christ, in such a way that his text could have served as the basis of Justin's formulation. However, the answer "I am not the Christ" has a parallel only in the Gospel of John; the continuation of the Baptist's answer in Justin ("but the voice of a crier") also recalls the text of the Fourth Gospel. That Justin knew the Gospel of John, or the tradition about John the Baptist that was used in this Gospel, cannot be categorically excluded. But this singular similarity with John's text is too weak to be a basis for the argument of Justin's acquaintance with the Fourth Gospel. It is possible that Justin developed the answer of the Baptist on the basis of Luke's text[2] and the Isaiah prophecy.[3]

The proclamation of John the Baptist about the one who is coming after him presupposes both Matthew's and Luke's text:[4]

Dial. 49.3 (88.7)[5]	Matt 3:11–12	Luke 3:16b–17
I baptize you with water for repentance, but the one who is stronger than I is coming;	I baptize you with water for repentance, but one who is stronger than I is coming after me;	I baptize you with water, but the one who is stronger than I is coming;

[1] John's answer in Luke 3:16b–17 is the saying about the stronger one who is coming after him; see below.

[2] See also Acts 13:25, where Luke quotes the same passage from his Gospel, but notes that John answered, "I am not he" (οὐκ εἰμὶ ἐγώ).

[3] See the discussion in Wilhelm Bousset, *Die Evangelienzitate Justins des Märtyrers in ihrem Wert für die Evangelienkritik* (Göttingen: Vandenhoeck & Ruprecht, 1891) 66–68; cf. also Massaux, *Influence de L'Évangile de Saint Matthieu*, 517–18, 547–48.

[4] No peculiar features of Mark's text are reflected in Justin's quotations.

[5] The quotation in *Dial.* 88.7 contains only the second sentence, beginning with ἥξει.

I am not worthy to
carry his sandals.
He will
baptize you with the
Holy Spirit and fire.
His winnowing fork is
in his hand and he will
clear his thrashing
floor and to gather the
wheat into the
grannary; and the
chaff he will burn with
unquenchable fire.

I am not worthy to
carry his sandals.
He will
baptize you with the
Holy Spirit and fire.
The winnowing fork is
in his hand and he will
clear his thrashing
floor and to gather his
wheat into the
grannary; and the
chaff he will burn with
unquenchable fire.

I am not worthy to
untie the thong of his
sandals. He will
baptize you with the
Holy Spirit and fire.
His winnowing fork is
in his hand in order to
clear his thrashing
floor and to gather the
wheat into his
grannary; but the chaff
he will burn with
unquenchable fire.

Dial. 49.3 (88.7)

Ἐγὼ μὲν ὑμᾶς βαπτίζω ἐν
ὕδατι εἰς μετάνοιαν· ἥξει
δὲ ὁ
ἰσχυρότερός μου
οὗ οὐκ εἰμὶ ἱκανὸς
τὰ ὑποδήματα
βαστάσαι·
αὐτὸς ὑμᾶς βαπτίσει ἐν
πνεύματι ἁγίῳ καὶ πυρί.
οὗ τὸ πτύον αὐτοῦ ἐν τῇ
χειρὶ αὐτοῦ,
καὶ διακαθαριεῖ τὴν
ἄλωνα αὐτοῦ καὶ τὸν
σῖτον συνάξει εἰς τὴν
ἀποθήκην, καὶ τὸ ἄχυρον
κατακαύσει πυρὶ
ἀσβέστῳ.

Matt 3:11–12

Ἐγὼ μὲν ὑμᾶς βαπτίζω ἐν
ὕδατι εἰς μετάνοιαν· ὁ δὲ
ὀπίσω μου ἐρχόμενος
ἰσχυρότερός μού
ἐστιν, οὗ οὐκ εἰμὶ ἱκανὸς
τὰ ὑποδήματα
βαστάσαι·
αὐτὸς ὑμᾶς βαπτίσει ἐν
πνεύματι ἁγίῳ καὶ πυρί.
οὗ τὸ πτύον αὐτοῦ ἐν τῇ
χειρὶ αὐτοῦ,
καὶ διακαθαριεῖ τὴν
ἄλωνα αὐτοῦ καὶ τὸν
σῖτον συνάξει εἰς τὴν
ἀποθήκην, καὶ τὸ ἄχυρον
κατακαύσει πυρὶ
ἀσβέστῳ.

Luke 3:16b–17

Ἐγὼ μὲν ὕδατι βαπτίζω
ὑμᾶς· ἔρχεται δὲ ὁ
ἰσχυρότερός μου, οὗ οὐκ
εἰμὶ ἱκανὸς λῦσαι τὰ
ἱμάντα τῶν ὑποδημάτων
αὐτοῦ·
αὐτὸς ὑμᾶς βαπτίσει ἐν
πνεύματι ἁγίῳ καὶ πυρί.
οὗ τὸ πτύον αὐτοῦ ἐν τῇ
χειρὶ αὐτοῦ,
διακαθαριεῖ τὴν ἄλωνα
αὐτοῦ καὶ τὸν
σῖτον συνάξει εἰς τὴν
ἀποθήκην, καὶ τὸ ἄχυρον
κατακαύσει πυρὶ
ἀσβέστῳ.

On the whole, there is considerable agreement between the versions of
Justin, Matthew and Luke.[1] As Justin reflects special formulations of
both Matthew and Luke, there can be no question that his quote harmonizes the text of these two Synoptic Gospels.

Similar harmonizations of special features of the texts of these two
Gospels are also present in Justin's report about the baptism of Jesus.
In *Dial.* 88, Justin twice reports the coming of the holy spirit upon
Jesus at his baptism. He gives this report in order to demonstrate the
fulfillment of the prophecies of Isa 11:1–3 and Joel 2:28–29 about the
coming of the spirit which he had quoted in *Dial.* 87.2 and 6.

---

[1] There are no special features of Mark 1:7–8 in Justin's quotation. Moreover the
saying of Matt 3:12 = Luke 3:17 is missing in Mark altogether.

Dial. 88.3	*Dial.* 88.8	Matt 3:13–17	Luke 3:21–22
And then, when Jesus came to the Jordan river, where John was baptizing, and when Jesus came down into the water, and a fire was kindled in the Jordan, and when Jesus emerged from the water,	And when Jesus came to the Jordan	Then Jesus came from Galilee ro the Jordan to John to be baptized by him . . .	But it happened when all the people were baptized,
		when Jesus had been baptized, just as he came up from the water, and behold, the heavens were opened and he saw	and when Jesus had been baptized and was praying, the heaven was opened
the Holy Spirit flew down upon . . .	the Holy Spirit flew down upon him in the form of a dove, and with it a voice came down from heaven, "You are my Son, today I have begotten you."	the spirit of God descending like a dove and alighting upon him. And a voice from heaven said, "This is my beloved Son with whom I am well pleased."	and the Holy Spirit descended upon him in bodily form like a dove. And a voice came from heaven, "You are my Son, today I have begotten you."

Dial. 88.3	*Dial.* 88.8	Matt 3:13–17	Luke 3:21–22
καὶ τότε ἐλθόντος τοῦ Ἰησοῦ ἐπὶ τὸν Ἰορδάνην ποταμόν, ἔνθα ὁ Ἰωάννης ἐβάπτιζε,	καὶ ἐλθόντος τοῦ Ἰησοῦ ἐπὶ τὸν Ἰορδάνην	Τότε παραγίνεται ὁ Ἰησοῦς ἀπὸ τῆς Γαλιλαίας ἐπὶ τὸν Ἰορδάνην πρὸς τὸν Ἰωάννην τοῦ βαπτισθῆναι ὑπ' αὐτοῦ . . .	Ἐγένετο ἐν τῷ βαπτισθῆναι ἅπαντα τὸν λαὸν
κατελθόντος τοῦ Ἰησοῦ ἐπὶ τὸ ὕδωρ καὶ πῦρ ἀνήφθη ἐν τῷ Ἰορδάνῃ,			
καὶ ἀναδύντος αὐτοῦ ἀπὸ τοῦ ὕδατος		βαπτισθεὶς δὲ ὁ Ἰησοῦς εὐθὺς ἀνέβη ἀπὸ τοῦ ὕδατος· καὶ ἰδοὺ ἠνεῴχθησαν οἱ οὐρανοί,	καὶ Ἰησοῦ βαπτισθέντος καὶ προσευχομένου ἀνεῳχθῆναι τὸν οὐρανόν,

ὡς περιστερὰν τὸ ἅγιον πνεῦμα	τὸ πνεῦμα τὸ ἅγιον ἐν εἴδει περιστερᾶς	καὶ εἶδεν πνεῦμα θεοῦ καταβαῖνον ὡσεὶ περιστεράν,	καὶ καταβῆναι τὸ πνεῦμα τὸ ἅγιον σωματικῷ εἴδει ὡς περιστερὰν
ἐπιπτῆναι ἐπ' αὐτόν,...	ἐπέπτη αὐτῷ, καὶ φωνὴ ἐκ τῶν οὐρανῶν ἅμα ἐληλύθει· υἱός μου εἶ σύ· ἐγὼ σήμερον γεγέννηκά σε.	ἐρχόμενον ἐπ' αὐτόν· καὶ ἰδοὺ φωνὴ ἐκ τῶν οὐρανῶν λέγουσα· οὗτός ἐστιν ὁ υἱός μου ὁ ἀγαπητός, ἐν ᾧ εὐδόκησα.	ἐπ' αὐτόν, καὶ φωνὴ ἐξ οὐρανοῦ γενέσθαι· υἱός μου εἶ σύ, ἐγὼ σήμερον γεγέννηκά σε.[1]

Justin's reports are based upon the Synoptic accounts. But they again demonstrate a harmonization of the texts of Matthew and Luke.[2] That John was baptizing at the Jordan when Jesus came is reported in Matthew (and Mark), but not in Luke, where neither John nor the Jordan are mentioned.[3] Also the report of Jesus' baptism requires Matthew's Gospel rather than Luke's terse remark "when Jesus was baptized." But the "Holy Spirit" (Matthew: "spirit of God," Mark: "spirit") is clearly Lukan. This term must have been given in Justin's text, because the quote of Isa 11:1–3 actually contains the phrase "spirit of God" (= Matthew). "In the form (ἐν εἴδει) of a dove" also presupposes Luke's "in bodily form (σωματικῷ εἴδει), as a dove." Finally, the heavenly voice is given by Justin in a citations of Ps 2:7, while Mark and Matthew present a wording of the heavenly voice which is a conflation of Isa 42:1 and 44:2. Only the Western text of Luke 3:22 presents the heavenly voice in the form that must be presupposed for Justin's source.[4] Justin cannot have been the author of this form of the heavenly voice; he had no special interest in proving

[1] This text of Luke 3:22 appears only in the so-called Western Text (D it; Meth Hil Aug). This is the accepted text in Huck-Greeven, *Synopsis,* but is rejected by Aland (*Synopsis*) and Nestle-Aland (*NT Graece*) in favor of the majority reading σὺ εἶ ὁ υἱός μου ὁ ἀγαπητός, ἐν σοὶ εὐδόκησα = Mark 1:11.

[2] Mark 1:9–11 also could have been the basis of some elements of Justin's report; but there are no peculiar Markan features in his text.

[3] Luke reports the imprisonment of John the Baptist before the baptism of Jesus (Luke 3:19–20) in order to create a clear, albeit superficial, separation of John and Jesus. "The reference to the imprisonment in iii, 19f. divides the section concerning John from the section concerning Jesus in the sense of drawing a distinction between the epochs of salvation . . ." (Conzelmann, *Theology of St Luke,* 21).

[4] The question of the original text of Luke 3:22 is not up for debate here; on this problem see Bovon, *Evangelium nach Lukas,* on Luke 3:22. That Justin quotes Luke in this form indicates that readings of the Western Text existed as early as the middle of the 2nd century.

the fulfillment of this scriptural text, although he is quite aware of its appearance in scripture as a word of David, i..e, a psalm that David wrote.[1] That Justin's source already contained this form of the heavenly voice is confirmed in *Dial.* 103.6, where he refers to it once more in passing; introducing a remark about Jesus temptation, he again quotes the exact text of Luke 2:22 D = Ps 2:7.

In order to prove the fulfillment of the prophecies of Isa 11:1–3 and Joel 2:28–29, Justin only had to report the coming of the spirit upon Jesus. But not only does he add the report about the heavenly voice, he also mentions "that a fire was lit in the Jordan." Nothing in the context of Justin's discussion requires a mention of this phenomenon. It must have been part of the text Justin is quoting. It is difficult to determine the origin of this new element in the account of Jesus' baptism.[2] The *Gospel of the Ebionites*[3] tells of an appearance of light after Jesus' baptism. However, it is doubtful whether *fire* and *light* can simply be identified.[4] A discussion of the complex history-of-religions problem of the appearance of fire at the event of an epiphany may not be necessary at this point. In the Synoptic Sayings Source, John the Baptist announces the one who comes after him who will baptize "with the Holy Spirit and with fire" (Q/Luke 3:16). Once this prophecy, originally referring to the coming of God for the final judgment, is applied to Jesus' coming, it seems natural that the report of Jesus' baptism would contain not only an account of the coming of the Holy Spirit upon Jesus, but also an account of the appearance of fire at the event of his baptism. Thus, Justin is using a report about the baptism of Jesus that reveals a further consistent development which goes beyond the account of the Synoptic Gospels but finds its natural explanation in the inherent dynamics of the evolving text itself. The baptism of Jesus is seen as the complete fulfillment of John the Baptist's prophecy.

5.2.2.4 The Passion Narrative

Materials from the passion narrative appear in Justin's writings in two different settings: (1) in the context of various traditional scrip-

---

[1] Only a portion of the manuscripts of the LXX designates this psalm as a "Psalm of David." This designation is missing in the Massoretic tradition of the Hebrew text of Psalm 2.

[2] On the apocryphal reports about the appearance of light or fire in the reports about Jesus' baptism see Bauer, *Leben Jesu,* 134–39.

[3] Epiphanius, *Haer.* 30.13; see also below on the *Diatessaron* # 5.3.5.2.

[4] For the Pseudo-Clementines (*Hom.* 11.26.4; *Rec.* 6.9; 9.7.10) fire and light are clearly two different elements: it is the water that quenches the fire.

ture quotations that have played a role in the development of the passion narrative, (2) in Justin's detailed interpretation of Psalm 21 [22]
(*Dial.* 99–106).

Clusters of traditional scriptural prophecies are quoted three times:
1 Apol. 35; 38; and *Dial.* 97. In most instances, the same scriptural
passages have been used elsewhere in the formation of the narrative of
Jesus passion and death.

Scripture	*1 Apol.* 35	*1 Apol.* 38	*Dial.* 97	Use in other literature
Exod 17:12			×	(*Barn.* 12.2)[1]
Isa 50:6–8		×		*Barn.* 5.1; 6.1–2; Matt 26:67; 27:30
Isa 53:9			×	1 Pet 2:22
Isa 57:1–2			×	
Isa 58:2	×			*Gos. Pet.* 3.6–7; John 19:13
Isa 65:2	×	×	×	*Barn.* 12.4
Ps 3:5–6		×	×	*1 Clem.* 26.2
Ps 21:8–9[2]		×		Matt 27:39
Ps 21:17, 19[3]	×	×	×	*Barn.* 6.6; 5.13; Matt 27:35; *Gos. Pet.* 4.12

These citations are drawn from traditional collections of prophecies,
and the accounts of the fulfillment of these scriptures reflect traditional narratives. In *1 Apol.* 35.6–8 Justin adds a brief narrative that
cites four details of a narrative about Jesus' passion and crucifixion,
and he adds that all of these are recorded in the "Acts of Pilate."[4] As
fulfillment of Isa 65:2 ("I have stretched out my hands . . ."), Justin
reports that "Jesus Christ stretched out his hands when he was
crucified by the Jews who contradicted him and said that he was not
the Christ." There is no such detail in the narratives about the
crucifixion in any known gospel.[5]

As fulfillment of Isa 58:2 ("They now request judgment from me"),
he gives a brief reference to the fulfillment which has parallels in the
Gospel of Peter[6] and perhaps in the Gospel of John.

---

[1] *Barnabas* does not quote the exact verse that appears in *Dial.* 97.1, but gives a
general abstract of Exod 17:8–11 with the report about Moses holding up his arms.

[2] According to the counting of the LXX, = Ps 22: 6–7 of the Hebrew Text.

[3] = Ps 22:16, 18 in the Hebrew text.

[4] On these references to the "Acts of Pilate" in Justin and elsewhere, see above,
1.7.

[5] On Isa 65:2 in the passion narrative, see Crossan, *The Cross that Spoke,* 229–231.

[6] See also above, # 3.2.3.2.

1 Apol. 35.6	*Gos. Pet.* 3.6, 8	John 19:13
... ridiculing (διασύροντες) him,	... they said, "Let us drag (σύρωμεν) the Son of God ..."	
they sat him on a judgment seat (ἐκάθισαν ἐπὶ βήματος)	... and sat him on the judgment seat (ἐκάθισαν αὐτὸν ἐπὶ καθέδραν κρίσεως) and	... and he sat down on the judgment seat (καὶ ἐκάθισεν ἐπὶ βήματος).
and said, "Judge us!"	said, "Judge righteously, O King of Israel!"	

The parallel in the *Gospel of Peter* requires a common source for this Gospel and Justin. The origin of the report about "dragging" (σύρειν) or "ridiculing" (διασύρειν) is obscure, but the parallel cannot be accidental. Nonetheless, the *Gospel of Peter* cannot have been Justin's source, because he uses the word βῆμα for "judgment seat," like John 19:13. Thus, all three parallels must derive from the same piece of information about Jesus' passion, whatever its character.

The fulfillment of Ps 21:17 [22:16] ("They pierced [ὤρυξαν] my hands and my feet") is said to point to the nails (ἥλοι) which were fixed through Jesus' hands and feet when he was crucified. There is no corresponding account in known gospel texts. Neither "nails" (ἥλοι) nor "fixing with nails" (καθηλοῦν) are mentioned in accounts of the crucifixion,[1] not is there a reference to "nails" in Ps 21:17 quoted by Justin. But *Barn.* 5.14 quotes Ps 118 [119]:120: "Nail my flesh" (Καθή-λωσόν μου τὰς σάρκας) in the context of prophecies referring to the crucifixion, and Ignatius, *Sm.* 1.1–2, addresses the Smyrneans as those who are established in faith "as if nailed (καθηλωμένοι) to the cross of the Lord Jesus Christ" and then refers to Christ as "being nailed for us in the flesh" (καθηλωμένος ὑπὲρ ἡμῶν τῇ σαρκί). It is, therefore, quite likely that Justin knew of an account of Jesus' crucifixion in which this detail was emphasized. That he did not develop this information independently is evident, for the passage from the Psalms quoted by him (Ps 21:17) does not contain a reference to piercing with nails.[2]

---

[1] However, *Gos. Pet.* 6.21 says that "they drew out the nails from the hands of the Lord" when they took him down from the cross for burial.

[2] See also the discussion in Crossan, *The Cross that Spoke*, 228–29. The mention of the marks of the nails in Jesus' hands at the appearance of his resurrection (John 20:25) would be a secondary reflection of this narrative detail. However, Crossan (ibid., 230) would rather connect this feature with Isa 65:2 (the stretching out of the hands).

The last of the details mentioned by Justin relates to the casting of lots and the dividing of the garments according to Ps 21:19. Only here does Justin reproduce a narrative detail that is also recorded in all the canonical Gospels: Mark 15:24 parr and John 19:23–24, in the latter instance with an explicit quotation of Ps 21:8, as well as in *Gos. Pet.* 4.12. However, dependence upon any of these canonical accounts is not very likely. Mark 15:24 (and, following Mark, also Matt 27:35 and Luke 23:34) first report the dividing of the garments (διαμερί-ζονται τὰ ἱμάτια αὐτοῦ) according to Ps 21:19a, then speak about distri-buting them by lot (βάλλοντες κλῆρον) according to Ps 21:19b. *Gos. Pet.* 4.12, though using different terminology, agrees with this Synoptic account. John 19:23–24 presents a more elaborate interpretation of Ps 21:19a/b: the garments (ἱμάτια) of Jesus are divided into four parts for the four soldiers, but then they decide not to divide the tunic (χιτών) but rather to cast lots about it. Justin first speaks about the casting of lots about the garment (ἱματισμός); this narrates the fulfillment of Ps 21:19b, that is, the part of this verse of the psalm that he had actually quoted. Then Justin adds that they divided it among them; this is the fulfillment of Ps 21:19a which Justin had not quoted before. Justin's narrative, thus, rests directly upon an interpretation of both halves of Ps 21:19, as does John 19:23–24, but without revealing any influence from the Johannine passage. However, Justin's account was not invented for this context on the basis of the scriptural passage, because the first half of the verse is not even quoted here. Therefore, Justin must have quoted selectively both a cluster of scriptural pro-phecies and a narrative account that was independent of the respec-tive passages in the canonical Gospels as well as of the *Gospel of Peter*.

In the cluster of prophecies quoted in *Dial.* 97, Ps 21:17, 19 is the last scripture that is quoted and the only one to which an account of the fulfillment is added. It begins with the piercing of Jesus' hands and feet with nails, in words very similar to those used in *1 Apol.* 35.7. Then follows the report about the dividing of the garments. But this time, both Ps 21:19a and 19b are quoted, and the dividing of the gar-ments is told before the mention of the casting of lots.[1] In the context of the systematic interpretation of all the verses of Psalm 21, Justin once more quotes Ps 21:17 and 19 (*Dial.* 104.1), but does not mention the piercing of the hands and feet; he only remarks that he had men-

---

[1] Justin expands the latter by saying "they cast lots (λαχμός), each leaving the selec-tion of what he wanted to the decision of the lot (κλῆρος)." This formulation does not necessarily require recourse to a different tradition; cf. *Gos. Pet.* 4.12: λαχμός, John 19:24: λάχωμεν αὐτῷ τίνος ἔσται.

tioned already that the soldiers divided the garments among themselves (*Dial.* 104.2).

In *1 Apology* 38, the last prophecy quoted is Ps 21:8–9, and Justin adds a few remarks which are drawn from the context of the mocking of the crucified Jesus. It is worth noting that the selection of sentences from the psalm quoted in *1 Apol.* 38.6 corresponds exactly to the sentences which describe the fulfillment (38.8):

Ps 21:8–9	Quote from the Psalm	Narrative of mocking
All who look at me mock at me,		When he was crucified,
they speak with lips, they shake the head.	they speak with lips, they shake the head saying,	they turned out the lips and shook the heads saying,
"He hoped for the Lord,		He who raised the dead,
he may rescue him, if he delights in him.	he may rescue him,	may he rescue himself.
πάντες οἱ θεωροῦντές με ἐξεμυκτέρισάν με, ἐλάλησαν ἐν χείλεσιν, ἐκίνησαν κεφαλήν·	Ἐλάλησαν ἐν χείλεσιν, ἐκίνησαν κεφαλήν λέγοντες·	σταυρωθέντος γὰρ αὐτοῦ ἐξέστρεφον τὰ χείλη καὶ ἐκίνουν τὰς κεφαλὰς λέγοντες·
Ἤλπισεν ἐπὶ κύριον, ῥυσάσθω αὐτόν, εἰ θέλει αὐτόν.	Ῥυσάσθω ἑαυτόν.	Ὁ νεκροὺς ἀνεγείρας ῥυσάσθω ἑαυτόν.

Whatever the relationship of this description of the mocking to the corresponding accounts of the Synoptic Gospels, it is clear that Justin quotes neither a full text of the Psalm 21 nor a full account of any written gospel. Rather, he copies a piece of scriptural proof that was developed in the school tradition of the early church.

All the citations of narrative materials about the passion and crucifixion of Jesus sofar discussed reveal Justin's indebtedness to the school tradition of scriptural proof. There is very little, if any, new contribution of Justin himself. However, Justin was not just a passive heir of this school tradition; he was an active participant. This becomes clear whenever Justin himself creatively constructs scriptural proof. The clearest evidence for this is his interpretation of

Psalm 21 [22] in *Dialogue* 99–107. In that context, Justin has once more presented the mocking of the crucified on the basis of Ps 21:8–9:

Ps 21:8–9[1]	1 Apol. 38.8	Dial. 101.3	Synoptic Gospels
			Luke 23:35a:
All those who look at me,		Those who looked at him	The people stood looking
			Matt 27:39
they	they	they	those who passed by
speak with lips,	turned out the lips	turned the lips.	blasphemed him,
they shake the head.	and shook the heads	each shook heads,	shaking their heads and saying . . .
			Luke 23:35b
They scoffed at me		and they scoffed together[2]	and the leaders scoffed at him
	saying, He who raised the dead,	and said sarcastically,	**Matt 27:40**
[may he save him]		"[He has called himself the Son of God;] may he come down and walk about.	"Save yourself, if you are the Son of God, come down from the cross."
[may he save him]	may he rescue himself.	Let God save him."	**Matt 27:43** "He trusts in God, (let God) rescue him now, if he delights in him; for he said, 'I am the Son of God.'"
He hoped upon the Lord; may he rescue him, may he save him, if he delights in him.		He has called himself the Son of God.	

Ps 21:8–9	1 Apol. 38.8	Dial. 101.3	Synoptic Gospels
			Luke 23:35a:
Πάντες οἱ θεωροῦντές με		οἱ θεωροῦντες αὐτὸν	εἱστήκει ὁ λαὸς θεωρῶν
			Matt 27:39[3]
καὶ ἐλάλησαν ἐν χείλεσιν, ἐκίνησαν κεφαλήν·	ἐξέστρεφον τὰ χείλη καὶ ἐκίνουν τὰς κεφαλὰς	καὶ τὰ χείλη διέστρεφον, τὰς κεφαλὰς ἕκαστος ἐκίνουν,	παραπορευόμενοι ἐβλασφήμουν αὐτὸν κινοῦντες τὰς κεφαλὰς αὐτῶν

---

[1] The text of Ps 21:8–9 is given here exactly as it is quoted in *Dial.* 103.3.
[2] Literally: "They crinkled their noses at each other."
[3] Cf. Mark 15:29.

			Luke 23:35b
ἐξεμυκτέρισάν με.		τὰς μυξωτῆρσιν ἐν ἀλλήλοις διαρρινοῦντες.	ἐξεμυκτήριζον δὲ καὶ ὁ ἄρχοντες.
	λέγοντες· Ὁ νεκροὺς ἀνεγείρας	ἔλεγον εἰρωνευόμενοι·	
[σωσάτω αὐτόν]			**Matt 27:40**[1] σῶσον σεαυτόν, εἰ
		[Υἱὸν θεοῦ ἑαυτὸν ἔλεγε] καταβὰς περιπατεῖτο·	υἱὸς εἶ τοῦ θεοῦ, καὶ κατάβηθι ἀπὸ τοῦ σταυροῦ.
[σωσάτω αὐτόν]		σωσάτω αὐτὸν ὁ θεός.	**Matt 27:43**[2]
Ἤλπισεν ἐπὶ κύριον,			πέποιθεν ἐπὶ τὸν θεόν,
ῥυσάσθω αὐτόν, σωσάτω αὐτόν,[3] ὅτι θέλει αὐτόν.	ῥυσάσθω ἑαυτόν.		ῥυσάσθω νῦν,
			εἰ θέλει αὐτόν· εἶπεν γὰρ ὅτι θεοῦ εἰμι υἱός.
		Yἱὸν θεοῦ ἑαυτὸν ἔλεγε.	

What becomes apparent here is typical of Justin's treatment of traditional materials about scripture and fulfillment. One could say that Justin is updating the traditional scriptural proof. First, he goes back to the entire and full text of the Greek Bible and quotes the complete text of Psalm 21, rather than only the excerpt that has been used in the traditional proof of scripture and fulfillment. Second, he makes recourse to the actual text of written gospels and uses relevant passages from Matthew and Luke that would demonstrate a more complete fulfillment of prophecy. In that process, sentences which do not fit the prophecy are omitted, for example, the narrative phrase "he who has raised the dead" (*1 Apol.* 38.8) is now left out, because it has no equivalent either in the prophecy of Psalm 21 or in the record of the written gospels. On the other hand, a phrase that is supported by the text of a gospel, like "let him come down from the cross," is preserved although there is no support for it in the text of the psalm. But Justin takes a third step: he updates the narrative itself. "They twist their lips" (καὶ τὰ χείλη διέστρεφον) is a sentence of Justin's narrative that has no equivalent in any written gospel; it is added by Justin, because there is a phrase in the psalm which requires a corresponding

---

[1] Cf. Mark 15:30; Luke 23:35b.

[2] There are no Synoptic parallels to this Matthean verse.

[3] This phrase is missing in Justin's quote of Ps 21:9 in *Dial* 101.3, but it appears in the quotation of the entire psalm in *Dial.* 98.3 as well as in the manuscripts of the LXX.

sentence in the story of the passion in order to make the fulfillment perfect.

In the narrative that tells the fulfillment of the prophecy of Ps 21:8–9, a convincingly complete account would not have been possible, unless Justin had drawn on all available evidence from written gospels. Thus, more than one Gospel, certainly Matthew and Luke, possibly also Mark, are required to serve. The result is a harmony of these Gospels. But it must have been a harmony that was not simply composed for the purpose of scriptural proof. In that case, only those sentences would have been quoted, which have a direct correspondence in the text of scripture. However, Justin's gospel quotations also contain sentences and phrases, which are not required for the demonstration, and to which there are no corresponding scriptural prophecies. One of these sentences without direct scriptural equivalent appears in the scene of the mocking of the crucified Jesus, in which he is challenged to descend from the cross.

Justin Martyr is the first Christian writer who is aware of the fact that the written gospels have become a "text." However, he may not have been the first to set down, side by side, texts from "scripture" and texts from written records of Jesus. That honor must be given to Marcion who, in his "Antitheses," juxtaposed gospel quotations with passages from scripture—albeit in order to emphasize the contrast. Justin is intent upon demonstrating the identity of scripture and fulfillment. The gospels become a historical record that proves this identity. However, many gospels would not do, either for Marcion or for Justin. While Marcion reduces the record to one single purified gospel, Justin includes as much of the tradition as is possible. A gospel harmony is the answer, and Justin reveals the process of its composition. Marcion rejects the traditions which he felt were falsified. Justin includes as much as was possible—and the criterion for inclusion is the scriptural prophecy. Had Justin prevailed, and not Irenaeus, a harmony of the available gospel literature would have been the answer. His student Tatian fulfilled that task, but, as will be seen in the next chapter, his work was accepted only in the Eastern church.

5.3 Tatian's Diatessaron

by William L. Peterson

5.3.1 THE DIATESSARON'S SIGNIFICANCE

The *Diatessaron* (Greek: διὰ τεσσάρων = "through [the] four [gospels]") is a gospel harmony, created about the year 172. Its putative composer, Tatian, combined the four canonical Gospels with one or more extra-canonical sources, and wove them into a single continuous account. Duplications were removed, contradictions were reconciled, and parallel passages were harmonized.

The importance of the *Diatessaron* rests upon four points. First, the *Diatessaron* is the most extensive, earliest collection of 2d-century gospel texts extant. Since it incorporated virtually the entire text of the four canonical Gospels, as well as some material from extra-canonical gospels, its comprehensiveness far outstrips the scattered parallels of other early sources. And as a creation of the mid-second century, its antiquity surpasses all other sources, save Justin, Marcion, Clement of Alexandria, the Jewish-Christian Gospel fragments, and, perhaps, some of the Nag Hammadi texts. "Pour retrouver les plus anciennes leçons évangeliques, la connaissance de l'oeuvre de Tatien est d'une importance primordiale."[1] Second, since the *Diatessaron* is the earliest specimen of a gospel harmony yet recovered *in extenso,* it affords us a unique opportunity to examine the techniques and concerns of a 2d-century harmonist. We know that numerous other 2d-century harmonies existed (Justin's harmony is one example); yet only the *Diatessaron* survives in blocks big enough to afford a panoramic view of the endeavor. Third, like any document created in a particular time and place, the *Diatessaron* reflects the theology and praxis of its locale. Consequently, the *Diatessaron* "offers extraordinary insights into the patterns of cultural transmission from the earliest Christian to the medieval world."[2] Fourth, it is not by chance that both Arthur Vööbus and Bruce Metzger begin their respective *Early Versions of the New Testament*[3] with chapters on the *Diatessaron*, for the *Diatessaron* is usually considered to be the most ancient of the versions. Furthermore, the *Diatessaron* is quite probably the form in which the gospels first appeared in Syriac, Latin, Armenian, and Georgian. As such, it

---

[1] Louis Leloir, "Le *Diatessaron* de Tatien," *OrSyr* 1 (1956), 209.

[2] Robert Murray, "The Gospel in the Medieval Netherlands," *HeyJ* 14 (1973) 309.

[3] Arthur Vööbus, *Early Versions of the New Testament* (PETSE 6; Stockholm: 1954); Bruce Metzger, *The Early Versions of the New Testament* (Oxford: Clarendon, 1977).

occupies a position unique in the history of the dissemination of the gospels, for it served as the foundation of four of the major New Testament versions, each of which bears the *Diatessaron*'s imprint.

5.3.2 AUTHORSHIP

Although we know that there were other early harmonies, and that a work called a Διὰ Τεσσάρων was composed by the otherwise obscure Ammonius of Alexandria,[1] tradition links only one name with the *Diatessaron*, that of Tatian. The citations upon which that statement rests are given below, in section 5.3.3; here we present the items in Tatian's biography to which we will refer (in section 5.3.7) when dating the *Diatessaron* and locating its place of composition.

Tatian's only other extant work, the *Oratio ad Graecos*,[2] provides some biographical details. He says he was born in the land of the Assyrians (*Or.* 42), which, technically, would mean east of the Euphrates, but which, taken colloquially, could mean Syria in general.[3] He appears to have had a disdain for power, wealth, adventure and sex (*Or.* 11). Leaving his home in the East, Tatian wandered westward, passing through various philosophic schools, until one day he read some "barbarian writings, older than the doctrines of the Greeks, more divine than their errors" (*Or.* 29). This was the Septuagint. Tatian converted to Christianity, and, in the one firm chronological fix we possess, became a student of Justin Martyr's in Rome. Irenaeus tells us that after Justin's death Tatian was expelled from the primitive Roman community for being an Encratite and a follower of the Gnostic Valentinus.[4] Epiphanius says that he left Rome and returned to the East, where his teachings had great influence.[5]

---

[1] *Ep. ad Carpianum* 1 (most readily available in Nestle-Aland, *NT Graece,* 73*).

[2] Molly Whittaker, ed., *Oratio ad Graecos and Fragments* (Oxford Early Christian Texts; Oxford: Clarendon, 1982); Whittaker's Introduction contains a good brief biography of Tatian.

[3] Lucian, whose home was Samosata, calls himself an "Assyrian," and calls Hierapolis an Assyrian city (*De Dea Syra* 1); cf. the treatment of Theodor Zahn, *Tatians Diatessaron* (FGNK 1/1; Erlangen: Deichert, 1881) 268–70. Also noteworthy is the fact that Tatian is called ὁ Σύρος by Clement of Alexandria (*Strom.* 3.12, 81.1) and Theodoret of Cyrrhus (*Haer. fab. comp.* 1.20; MPG 83, 372), while Epiphanius calls him τὸ γένος Σύρος (*Haer.* 46.1.6; eds. Holl and Dummer, 204).

[4] Irenaeus *Adv. haer.* 1.28.1 (eds. Rousseau and Doutreleau 354); on Encratism, see Henry Chadwick, "Enkrateia," *RAC* 5. 343–65, esp. 352–54.

[5] *Haer.* 46.1.8 (edd. Holl and Dummer 204).

5.3.3 ATTESTATION

Given the early and wide dissemination of the *Diatessaron* throughout the entire Christian world, it is convenient to divide our analysis into Western and Eastern attestation.

In the West, the first mention of the *Diatessaron* is in Eusebius *Hist. eccl.* 4.29.6:

> Tatian, their (the Encratites') first head, brought together a combination and collection—I do not know how—of the gospels. He called this the *Diatessaron*, which is still in circulation among some people.

Epiphanius, a later 4th-century writer, also speaks of the *Diatessaron* (*Haer.* 46.1.8–9[1]):

> It is said the gospel *Diatessaron* was created by him (Tatian), which some call according to the Hebrews.

In the 5th century, Theodoret, who from 423 to 457 was bishop of Cyrrhus, a small Syrian town two days' journey from Antioch, reports (*Haer. fab. comp.* 1. 20[2]):

> He (Tatian) composed the so-called *Diatessaron* by cutting out the genealogies and whatever goes to prove the Lord to have been born of the seed of David according to the flesh. And this work was in use not only among his own party but even among those who follow the tradition of the Apostles, who used it somewhat too innocently as a compendium of the Gospels, without recognizing the craftiness of its compositions. I myself found more than two hundred copies in reverential use in the churches of my diocese, all of which I removed, replacing them by the Gospels of the four Evangelists.

Finally, in the sixth century, Victor, bishop of Capua in Italy from 541 to 554, came across a manuscript of a harmonized gospel, but lacking a title or author's name. Victor directed that a copy of the manuscript be made and, in his preface to the new copy (which is our present Codex Fuldensis), he relates how, after much difficult research, he came to the conclusion that the work must be the harmony of Tatian. Inexplicably, however, Victor does not call Tatian's work a *Diatessaron* but a *Diapente* (= "Through five [gospels]").

Before leaving the West, two points bear mention. First, it is notable that Irenaeus never mentions that *Diatessaron*, although he knows Tatian. Similarly, the silence of Clement of Alexandria, who

---

[1] Epiphanius *Haer.* 34–64, eds. Holl and Dummer (GCS 66; 2d ed.; Berlin: Akademie-Verlag, 1980) 204–5.

[2] *MPG* 83. 372.

also mentions Tatian and may, in fact, have been one of Tatian's pupils,[1] remains puzzling—unless the *Diatessaron* was composed in the East, after Tatian left the West. Second, although the first mention of the *Diatessaron* is by Eusebius in the early 4th century, the *textual* imprint of the *Diatessaron* is found in many earlier western works, such as the writings of Novatian (d. 258),[2] the Roman Antiphonary,[3] and the Vetus Latina manuscripts.[4] We must conclude that the *Diatessaron* saw circulation in the West long before Eusebius's remark.

In the East, there is also abundant evidence of early circulation of the *Diatessaron*. Indeed, even the most casual reading of the Old Syriac Gospels (extant in two manuscripts: Codex Sinaiticus [sy^s, 4th century] and Codex Curetonianus [sy^c: 5th century]), shows that they have already been influenced by the textual variants and harmonistic readings of the *Diatessaron*.[5] And in the 4th century, many of the gospel quotations of the Syrian writers Aphrahat and Ephrem are in the form of the *Diatessaron*. Ephrem even wrote a commentary on "The Gospel of the Mixed," as the *Diatessaron* was known in Syria, but he fails to name Tatian or use the word *Diatessaron*.

The word *Diatessaron* first appears in Syriac in the 4th century, in the Syriac translation of Eusebius's *Church History,* where the Syriac translator not only translates Eusebius's words (4.29.6), but makes clear his firsthand knowledge of the harmony:

> Now this same Tatianus their former chief collected and mixed up and composed a gospel and called it *Diatessaron*; now this is (the Gospel) of the Mixed, the same that is in the hands of many unto this day.[6]

---

[1] Clement's remark about having studied Christianity with "an Assyrian" (*Strom.* 1.1, 11.2) is often interpreted as referencing Tatian.

[2] Anton Baumstark, "Die Evangelienzitate Novatians und das Diatessaron," *OrChr* 27 [3d series 5] (1930) 1–14.

[3] Idem, "Tatianismus im römischen Antiphonar," *OrChr* 27 [3d series 5] (1930) 165–74.

[4] Heinrich Joseph Vogels, *Beiträge zur Geschichte des Diatessaron im Abendland* (NTA 8/1; Münster: Aschendorff, 1919).

[5] See, e.g., the work of Friedrich Baethgen, *Evangelienfragmente: Der griechische Text des Cureton'schen Syrers* (Leipzig: Hinrichs, 1885), later supported by Vogels, Plooij, and Burkitt. This view holds the field today: cf. the *Early Versions of the New Testament* by either Bruce Metzger or by Arthur Vööbus; see also Matthew Black, "The Syriac Versional Tradition," in Aland, ed., *Die alten Übersetzungen,* 130–32.

[6] *The Ecclesiastical History of Eusebius in Syriac,* eds. William Wright and Norman McLean (Cambridge: Cambridge University Press, 1898) 243; the text is also given in F. C. Burkitt, ed., *Evangelion da-Mepharreshe: The Curetonian Version of the Four Gospels* (2 vols.; Cambridge: Cambridge University Press, 1904) 2. 175.

Notice how the translator deleted Eusebius's "I do not know how," and modified the last phrase, so that it emphasizes even more strongly the *Diatessaron*'s continuing use. Although the Greek διὰ τεσσάρων transliterated into Syriac, the name must not have meant anything to a Syriac reader, for the translator felt obliged to supply the *Diatessaron*'s common Syriac name, "of the Mixed."

In a 5th-century Syrian work, the *Doctrina Addai*, the *Diatessaron* is also named, but in an awkward way:

> Moreover, much people day by day assembled and came together for prayer and for the reading of the Old Testament and the New, the *Diatessaron*.[1]

The word "*Diatessaron*" in the *Doctrina Addai* is probably a later interpolation,[2] if for no other reason than that it is so anachronistic. After this, the word "*Diatessaron*" remains unused in Syriac literature until the 9th century, when the Syrian commentator Ishocdad of Merv names the work, tells us that Ephrem wrote a commentary on it, and then himself cites the *Diatessaron* as an authority.[3] Similarly, Tatian himself is not named in Syriac literature until the eighth century, when he is mentioned by Theodore bar Konai.[4] After this period, both Tatian and the *Diatessaron* are referenced in Syriac literature.

In order to have influenced the gospel citations of Aphrahat, Ephrem, and the oldest separated Syriac gospel manuscripts (sysc), the *Diatessaron* must have been in circulation in Syria from the beginnings of Syrian Christianity, where it appears to have been known as "the Gospel of the Mixed" (*da-Mehallete*). Only later—perhaps as late as the 8th or 9th century—did the name "*Diatessaron*" become the work's common designation in Syriac. This explains why the first use

---

[1] George Phillips, ed., *The Doctrine of Addai, the Apostle* (London: Truebner, 1876) 34 (folio 23a); a more recent edition is that of George Howard, ed., *The Teaching of Addai* (SBLTT 16; Chico, CA: Scholars Press, 1981) 73.

[2] The competition between the designations "New" and "*Diatessaron*" led Burkitt (*Evangelion da-Mepharreshe*, 2.174) to conclude that we have an interpolated text before us. However, Burkitt felt "New" was the intruder. This seems unlikely, once one realizes how anachronistic the use of the word "*Diatessaron*" is at this point in Syriac literature.

[3] Margret Dunlop Gibson, ed., *The Commentaries of Ishocdad of Merv* (HSem 5–7; 3 vols.; Cambridge. MA: Harvard University Press, 1911–16), e.g., 2. 45 (text); 1. 27 (translation). Ishocdad's report that Ephrem wrote a commentary on the *Diatessaron* appears in 2. 204 (text); 1. 123 (translation).

[4] Addai Scher, ed., *Theodorus bar Koni. Liber Scholiorum II* (CSCO 69; Louvain: Peeters, 1912) 305. Martin Elze (*Tatian und seine Theologie* [FKDG 9; Göttingen: Vandenhoeck & Ruprecht, 1960] 120–24) gives a review of the Syrian testimonies concerning Tatian.

of the word in Syriac, by the 4th-century translator of Eusebius's *Church History* appears to be a transliteration, which obliges the translator to append its standard Syriac name "of the Mixed." The use of *"Diatessaron"* in the *Doctrina Addai* is probably a later interpolation, if for no other reason than that it is so anachronistic: one must wait four centuries before the word will again be used in Syriac.

5.3.4 WITNESSES TO THE DIATESSARON

No direct copy of Tatian's *Diatessaron* exists. Instead, the scholar must be content with a wide array of sources, and attempt to reconstruct the *Diatessaron*'s text from them. These sources, called "witnesses" to the *Diatessaron*, range in genre from poems to commentaries, in language from Middle Dutch to Middle Persian, in extent from fragments to codices, in date from 3d to 19th century, in provenance from England to China. Mastering these sources is the key to Diatessaronic scholarship.

The most convenient way to classify the Diatessaronic witnesses is geographically, commencing with the most valuable (i.e., what scholarship views as the most reliable). Below is a partial list which begins with the Eastern witnesses

5.3.4.1 *Eastern Witnesses*

Ephrem's *Commentary*

The greatest Father of the Syrian church, Ephrem Syrus (obit 373), composed a *Commentary on the Gospel of the Mixed*. It survives in an Armenian recension[1] (two manuscripts: Venice: Bib. Mechitarist, nos. 312 and 452, both dating from 1195), as well as in the original Syriac[2] (Dublin: Chester Beatty Library, no. 709; late 5th or early 6th century). This lone Syriac manuscript was missing forty-one folios, which were recently discovered in 1987.[3] The editor of both recensions, Louis Leloir, suggests that neither is inherently superior, for sometimes one, then the other, seems to preserve the best text.[4] Ephrem's *Commentary* is the most important Eastern witness because of its early date,

---

[1] Louis Leloir, ed., *Saint Éphrem, Commentaire de l'Évangile concordant, version arménienne* (CSCO 137 [text] and 145; Louvain: Peeters, 1953 & 1954).

[2] Idem, ed., *Saint Éphrem, Commentaire de l'Évangile concordant, texte syriaque* (CBM 8; Dublin: Hoddaes Figgis, 1963).

[3] Idem, "Le Commentaire d'Éphrem sur le Diatessaron, Quarante et un folios retrouvés," *RB* 94 (1987) 481–518.

[4] See Louis Leloir's comments in his *Éphrem de Nisibe, Commentaire de l'Évangile concordant ou Diatessaron* (SC 121; Paris: Edition du Cerf, 1966) 28–29. This volume is a French translation of the Commentary, with a helpful introduction.

and the fact that Syriac is the language in which Tatian composed his harmony (see section 5.3.7). Consequently, the *Commentary* stands closest to Tatian not only in date, but also in diction.

The Arabic Harmony

This Arabic translation of the *Diatessaron* survives in six manuscripts, dating from the 12th to the 19th century.[1] Colophons in several of the manuscripts state that the text was translated from the Syriac by the Nestorian exegete Ibn at-Tayyib (obit 1043). Like most Diatessaronic witnesses, the Arabic Harmony has been "Vulgatized"; that is, the genuine Diatessaronic variants have often been removed and replaced with the "standard" gospel reading of a particular time and place. In the case of the Arabic Harmony, it appears that Peshitta readings were frequently substituted for the Diatessaronic reading. This suggests that the Harmony was translated from a Syriac exemplar which had already been Vulgatized. Although the text of the Arabic is not without value for recovering Diatessaronic readings, its chief importance is its witness to the *Diatessaron*'s sequence of the harmonization.

The Persian Harmony

This fascinating document survives in a single manuscripts (Florence: Bibl. Laurent., Cod. Orient. 81; dated to 1547).[2] Syriasms in the text show that it was translated from a Syriac *Vorlage*. First edited in 1951, the sequence of the Persian Harmony diverges from the other Diatessaronic witnesses. Because of this, Tjitze Baarda has questioned whether one can really speak of it as a witness to the *Diatessaron*, suggesting instead that it is a harmony which is independent of the *Diatessaron*.[3] Nevertheless, the text of the Persian Harmony contains numerous Diatessaronic readings—according to some stu-

---

[1] The standard edition is that of A.-S. Marmardji, *Diatessaron de Tatien* (Beyrouth: Imprimerie Catholique, 1935). The earlier edition of Agostino Ciasca, *Tatiani Evangeliorum Harmoniae Arabice* (Rome: Bibliographia Polyglotta, 1888), upon which the English translations of H. Hogg ("Tatian's *Diatessaron*," in *The Ante-Nicene Fathers*, Vol. 10 [additional volume], ed. A. Menzies [5th ed.; Grand Rapids, 1969], 63–129) and J. Hamlyn Hill (*The Earliest Life of Christ ever Compiled from the Four Gospels being the Diatessaron of Tatian . . . [Edinburgh: Clark, 1894]*) were based, is out-dated.

[2] *Edition: Diatessaron Persiano*, ed. Guiseppe Messina (BibOr 14; Rome: Pontificio Instituto Biblico, 1951).

[3] Tjitze Baarda, "In Search of the *Diatessaron* Text," *Vox Theologica* 17 (1963) 111; also in idem, *Early Transmission of the Words of Jesus: Thomas, Tatian and the Text of the New Testament* (Amsterdam: Uitgeverij, 1983) 69.

dies, far more, in fact, than the Arabic Harmony. Baarda suggests, probably correctly, that the gospel text used by the creator of the Persian Harmony contained Diatessaronic readings. In this manner, the Persian Harmony, composed in a sequence independent of Tatian's *Diatessaron*, acquired numerous Diatessaronic readings.

The Syriac Versions (sy[s] sy[c] sy[p] sy[pal])

The two manuscripts of the Old Syriac Gospels (Sinaiticus and Curetonianus) contain harmonizations and variant readings paralleled in the *Diatessaron*, as do the later Syriac versions, such as the Peshitta (sy[p])[1] and the Palestinian Syriac Lectionary (sy[pal]).[2] Harmonizations distinctive of the *Diatessaron* show that it preceded and influenced the oldest separated Syriac gospels known to us. This fact has led some scholars to argue that the *Diatessaron* was the form in which the gospels first appeared in Syriac.

The Gospel Quotations of Aphrahat, Ephrem, Rabbula of Edessa, Isho[c]dad of Merv, and the Liber Graduum

Given that a Syriac *Diatessaron* appears to antedate the oldest Syriac separated gospels, it is not surprising to find that virtually all of later Syriac literature is shot through with Diatessaronic readings. Among those works which have received scholarly scrutiny are the *Demonstrations* of Aphrahat (obit c. 367), one of the earliest Christian Syriac writers.[3] He frequently quotes the gospels in the form of the *Diatessaron*. Similarly, Ephrem Syrus (obit 373), who composed the *Commentary* on the *Diatessaron*, also cites the gospels in this form in his many hymns and sermons.[4] Coming from this same fourth-century period, the Syriac *Liber Graduum*, or "Book of Steps," fre-

---

[1] See the evidence in my *The Diatessaron and Ephrem Syrus as Sources of Romanos the Melodist* (CSCO 475; Leuven: Peeters 1985) 156–58.

[2] See my remarks ibid., as well as the study of Matthew Black, "The Palestinian Syriac Gospels and the Diatessaron," *OrChr* 36 [3d series 14] (1939) 101–11. The second part of Black's study never appeared.

[3] The presence of Diatessaronic readings was first noted by Theodor Zahn, in a review of George Phillips, *The Doctrine of Addai, the Apostle . . .*, in GGA 1877 (lacks vol. no.) 183–84. Aphrahat's citations from the Gospel of John have been studied by Tjitze Baarda, *The Gospel Quotations of Aphrahat, the Persian Sage*, vol. 1: *Aphraat's Text of the Fourth Gospel* (2 vols.; Amsterdam: Vrije Universiteit, 1975).

[4] These are available in an excellent edition, which spans more than eighteen volumes in CSCO, edited by Edmund Beck. Ephrem's gospel text has been studied by Louis Leloir, *Le Évangile d'Éphrem d'après les oeuvres éditées. Recueil des textes* (CSCO 180; Louvain: Peeters, 1958). Earlier, F. C. Burkitt (*Ephraim's Quotations from the Gospel* [TaS 7,2; Cambridge, 1901]) embarked upon a similar task.

quently offers quotations from the *Diatessaron*.[1] In the 5th century, the famous bishop of Edessa, Rabbula, who in his *Canons* insists on the use of the "separated gospels" in his churches (a canon undoubtedly directed against the *Diatessaron*, the gospel "of the mixed"), nevertheless sometimes cites the gospel in a form which contains Diatessaronic readings.[2] It is unclear whether this is a result of his gradual transition from use of a *Diatessaron* to the separated gospels, or of a lapse of memory, or of the above-mentioned imprint which the *Diatessaron* left upon the later separated gospels. Later, the 9th-century Syrian writer Isho^{c}dad of Merv quotes from the *Diatessaron* in his commentaries on the Four Gospels, and identifies it as the source of these quotations.[3]

The Old Armenian and Old Georgian Versions of the Gospels

Stanislaus Lyonnet scrutinized the gospel citations of the oldest extant Armenian liturgical and Patristic writers, and found that they often offer Diatessaronic readings.[4] Since Armenian Christianity was introduced from Syria, this discovery is not surprising. A parallel situation exists in the case of the oldest Georgian gospel citations, which also betray Diatessaronic influence.[5] Since Georgian Christianity was imported from Armenia, the route by which these texts arrived in Georgia is manifest. In both of these ancient churches, it appears that the gospels first circulated in the form of a *Diatessaron*.

Manichaean Documents

We know that the Manichaeans used the *Diatessaron*, for its readings have been found in the *Kephalaia,* the *Homilies* and the *Psalms,*

---

[1] Cf. A. Rücker, "Die Zitate aus dem Matthäusevangelium im syrischen 'Buche der Stufen'," *BZ* 20 (1932) 342–54; see also the unpublished dissertation of Fiona J. Parsons, *The Nature of the Gospel Quotations in the Syriac Liber Graduum* (Birmingham, 1969).

[2] Cf. Arthur Vööbus, "Investigations into the Text of the New Testament used by Rabbula," *Contributions of the Baltic University (Pinneburg)* 59 (1947). See also idem, *Studies in the History of the Gospel Text in Syriac* (CSCO 128; Louvain: Peeters 1951) 179–86; and the study of Tjitze Baarda, "The Gospel Text in the Biography of Rabbula," *VigChr* 14 (1960) 102–27; also idem, *Early Transmission,* 11–36.

[3] Edition: Gibson, ed., *The Commentaries of Isho^{c}dad.*

[4] *Les origines de la version arménienne et le Diatessaron* (BibOr 13; Rome, 1950).

[5] Cf. Anton Baumstark, "Zum georgischen Evangelientext," *OrChr* 26 [3d series 4] (1929) 117–21. See also the more recent remarks of Joseph Molitor, "Das Neue Testament in georgischer Sprache. Der gegenwärtige Stand seiner Erforschung und seine Bedeutung für die Gewinnung des griechischen Urtextes," in Aland, ed., *Die alten Übersetzungen,* 314–44.

as well as in such miscellaneous Manichaean works as the Turfan Fragments.[1] That Mani, who was raised in a Judaic-Christian community in the 3d century, should have known the *Diatessaron* is not surprising, for Tatian's creation seems to have incorporated Judaic-Christian elements.[2]

Romanos the Melodist

This 6th-century Syrian-born hymnographer quotes the *Diatessaron* in his Greek hymns, composed in Constantinople in the court of Justinian I. His use of the *Diatessaron*[3] in his *Kontakia* is significant, for not only are these hymns considered masterpieces of world literature, but they were also sung in the Imperial Court.

Arabic and Karsuni Gospel Manuscripts

Curt Peters logged thirteen Arabic and two Karsuni (a type of script used by Nestorian and Jacobite Christians when writing Arabic) gospel manuscripts which contain Diatessaronic readings.[4] Since they rest upon a Syriac *Vorlage,* the presence of Tatianisms is only to be expected.

The Dura Fragment

One of the earliest Christian parchments known to us is the so-called Dura Fragment, discovered at Dura-Europos in Syria in 1933. The *terminus ad quem* is set by the destruction of the town in the winter of 256–257 CE. The fragment (New Haven: Yale University,

---

[1] On the Manichaean Diatessaronic readings, see: Anton Baumstark, "Ein 'Evangelium'-Zitat der Manichäischen Kephalaia," *OrChr* 34 [3rd series 12] (1938) 169–91; idem, review of H. J. Polotsky, *Manichäische Homilien (Manichäische Handschriften der Sammlung A. Chester Beatty. Band I),* in *OrChr* 32 [3rd series 10] (1935) 257–68; Gilles Quispel, *Tatian and the Gospel of Thomas* (Leiden: Brill, 1975) 68; idem, "St. Augustin et l'Évangile selon Thomas," in *Mélanges d'histoire des religions offerts à Henri-Charles Puech* (Paris: Presses universitaires de France, 1974) 379–92; William L. Petersen, "An Important Unnoticed Diatessaronic Reading in Turfan Fragment M-18," in Tjitze Baarda, A. Hilhorst, G. P. Luttikhuizen, and A. S. van der Woude, eds., *Text and Testimony: Festschrift A. F. J. Klijn* (Kampen: Kok, 1988) 187–92.

[2] The Jewish-Christian *Gospel of the Hebrews* is the prime candidate for the extracanonical source employed by Tatian alongside the four canonical gospels.

[3] See my *The Diatessaron and Ephrem Syrus.*

[4] Curt Peters, *Das Diatessaron Tatians* (OrChrA 123; Roma: Pontificium institutum orientalium studiorum, 1939), 48–62; see also Anton Baumstark, "Das Problem eines vorislamischen christlich-kirchlichen Schrifttums in arabischer Sprache," *Islamica* 5 (1931) 562–75; idem, "Arabische Übersetzung eines altsyrischen Evangelientextes," in *OrChr* 31 [3rd series 9] (1934) 165–88.

Dura Parchment 24) contains fourteen legible lines of Greek text, from the passion narrative.[1] The text is harmonized. At first considered decisive evidence for a Greek original of the *Diatessaron*,[2] later studies were more cautious, and found signs of translation from Syriac.[3] Daniël Plooij also noted the existence of harmonized Syriac passion narrative collections, independent of the *Diatessaron*, and suggested that the fragment, whose sequence has some agreement with the *Diatessaron* but also some differences, might be from one of these unrelated passion narrative collections.[4] At present, our best evidence seems to indicate that the fragment is from a *Diatessaron* and translated from Syriac. It establishes an extremely early date for circulation of a Greek *Diatessaron*. Ironically enough, we have no other evidence of a Greek *Diatessaron* save this fragment, found deep in Syria.

5.3.4.2 Western Witnesses

Codex Fuldensis and the Latin Harmonies

Copied in 546 CE at the request of bishop Victor of Capua, this Latin codex (Fulda: Landesbib., Bonif. 1) is a harmonized life of Jesus, composed from the gospels.[5] Although its text is a very pure Vulgate, its sequence is distinctly Diatessaronic. That the document was Vulgatized at some point in its transmission is a demonstrable fact, for while the *text* of Fuldensis is Vulgate, the readings in the *capitularia* (the "table of contents," as it were) have *not* been revised accordingly; they preserve the original Diatessaronic readings.[6] This is irrefutable evi-

---

[1] Edition: Carl H. Kraeling, *A Greek Fragment of Tatian's Diatessaron from Dura* (StD 3; London: Christophers, 1935). A corrected edition is found in Charles B. Welles, et al., eds., *The Parchments and Papyri: The Excavations at Dura-Europos . . ., Final Report*, vol. 5, pt. 1 (New Haven: Yale University Press, 1959) 73–74.

[2] So the fragment's editor, Carl H. Kraeling, and F. C. Burkitt, "The Dura Fragment of Tatian," *JTS* 36 (1935) 255–59, who, while arguing for Latin, saw the Fragment as precluding a Syriac original.

[3] So Daniël Plooij, "A Fragment of Tatian's *Diatessaron* in Greek," *ET* 46 (1934–35) 471–76; and Anton Baumstark, "Das griechische 'Diatessaron'-Fragment von Dura-Europos," *OrChr* 32 [3rd series 10] (1935) 244–52.

[4] Plooij, ibid., 476.

[5] Edition: *Codex Fuldensis*, ed. Ernst Ranke (Marburgi/Lipsiae: Elwert, 1868).

[6] This phenomenon was first noted by Johann Christian Zahn, "Ist Ammon oder Tatian Verfasser der ins Lateinische, Altfränkische und Arabische übersetzten Evangelien-Harmonie? und was hat Tatian bei seinem bekannten Diatessaron oder Diapente vor sich gehabt und zum Grunde gelegt?" in C. A. G. Keil and H. G. Tzschirner, *Analekten für das Studium der exegetischen und systematischen Theologie*, vol. 2, pt. 1 (Leipzig, 1814) 183–88. It was later investigated in more detail by Theodor Zahn, *Tatian's Diatessaron* (FGNK 1; Erlangen: Deichert, 1881) 300–3; and Heinrich

dence that at some earlier date there existed in the West an unvulgatized (or "Old Latin," in the sense of the Vetus Latina, i.e., pre-Vulgate) Latin *Diatessaron*. While obviously impoverished as a source of Diatessaronic readings, Codex Fuldensis has the same sequence of harmonization as the Arabic Harmony, and as Ephrem's *Commentary*. Hence, it is an important witness for fixing the order of the *Diatessaron*'s text. It is also our oldest Western Diatessaronic witness.

In addition to Codex Fuldensis, no fewer than seventeen other Latin gospel harmonies, all related to the Diatessaronic tradition, have been noted by scholars. Only two have been edited: Codex Sangallensis (a Latin-Old High German bilingual: Stiftsbib. no. 56; dated ca. 830),[1] and Codex Cassellanus (Landesbib., Ms. theol. fol. 31; 9th century).[2] Some of these manuscripts descend from Codex Fuldensis and its Vulgatized Latin text. Others, however, have escaped much of the Vulgatization to which Fuldensis was subjected, and preserve many more Diatessaronic readings and sequential harmonizations. The fact that Codex Cassellanus, for example, interpolates the Diatessaronic reading *occurrit, ut tangeret eum* between John 20:16 and 17, a reading which is absent from Fuldensis, confirms the conclusion drawn on the basis of the disagreement between the *capitularia* and the text of Codex Fuldensis: at one time there existed an unvulgatized, "Old Latin" *Diatessaron*. This Old Latin *Diatessaron*, now lost, has not vanished without a trace, for its textual imprint is still to be found in many of these other Latin gospel harmonies.

The Old High German Harmonies

The oldest Old High German harmony is a bilingual manuscript, Codex Sangallensis (Stiftsbib. no. 56; dated ca. 830).[3] Each side of each folio contains two columns, with Latin on the left, and the Old High German (in the East Frankish dialect) on the right. The Latin is pure Vulgate, agreeing almost perfectly with Codex Fuldensis. Quite

---

Joseph Vogels, *Beiträge zur Geschichte des Diatessaron im Abendland* (NTA 8/1; Münster: Aschendorff, 1919).

[1] Edition: Eduard Sievers, *Tatian, lateinisch und altdeutsch* (Bibliothek der ältesten deutschen Literatur-Denkmäler 5; 2d ed.; Paderborn: Schöningh, 1892); studies: Anton Baumstark, *Die Vorlage des althochdeutschen Tatian, herausgegeben von Johannes Rathofer* (Niederdeutsche Studien 12; Köln: Böhlau, 1964); Gilles Quispel, *Tatian and the Gospel of Thomas: Studies in the History of the Western Diatessaron* (Leiden: Brill 1975).

[2] Edited and studied by: C. W. M. Grein, *Die Quellen des Heliand. Nebst einem Anhang: Tatians Evangelienharmonie herausgegeben nach dem Codex Cassellanus* (Cassel: Kay, 1869).

[3] Edition: Eduard Sievers, *Tatian, lateinisch und altdeutsch* (Bibliothek der ältesten deutschen Literatur-Denkmäler 5; 2d ed.; Paderborn: Schöningh, 1892).

naturally, scholars assumed that the Old High German column had been translated from its neighboring Latin column; and since the Latin was without significant variant readings, what variants there were in the Old High German column must be "geringfügig und fast bedeutungslos."[1] But in 1872 the Germanist O. Schade noticed agreements between the Old High German column and Vetus Latina (not Vulgate!) manuscripts—agreements which were lacking in the neighboring Latin column of Sangallensis.[2] The meaning of these agreements was clear: the Old High German column was *not* slavishly dependent upon its Vulgate neighbor, but had its own, independent textual tradition. Later investigations confirmed Schade's observation: Codex Sangallensis' Old High German column has suffered less Vulgatization than its Latin column.[3]

Today, in addition to Codex Sangallensis, two other manuscripts offer readings from the Old High German Tatian: Oxford, Bodleian, Junius 13 (17th century, but a copy of an older now lost manuscript),[4] and Paris, Bib. Nat., Ms. lat. 7641 (10th century).[5] Reports survive of three other Old High German Tatian manuscripts, but all of them have been lost.

The Vetus Latina, Novatian and the Roman Antiphonary[6]

The Vetus Latina group of manuscripts, which preserve a pre-Vulgate text, contain variants which find parallels in the *Diatessaron*. Since these reflect the oldest known separated gospel text in Latin, and since they too have been influenced by the *Diatessaron*, scholars conclude that the situation is analogous to the one in Syria, where the Vetus Syra manuscripts showed Diatessaronic influence. Therefore,

---

[1] So Sievers, ibid., p. xviii.

[2] Oskar Schade, *Altdeutsches Wörterbuch,* vol. 1 (Halle: Buchhandlung des Waisenhauses, 1872) pp. xviii–xix.

[3] See the extensive examples offered by Anton Baumstark, *Die Vorlage des althochdeutschen Tatian,* herausgegeben von Johannes Rathofer (Niederdeutsche Studien 12; Köln: Böhlau, 1964), and by Rathofer, "MS Junius 13 und die verschollene Tatian HS-B," *Beiträge zur Geschichte der deutschen Sprache und Literatur* (Ausgabe Tübingen) 95 (1973) 13–125. More recently, however, Rathofer has assumed a more skeptical position: "Die Einwirkung des Fuldischen Evangelientextes auf den althochdeutschen 'Tatian.' Abkehr von der Methode der Diatessaronforschung," in A. Oennerfors, *et al.,* eds., *Literatur und Sprache im europäischen Mittelalter: Festschrift Karl Langosch* (Darmstadt, 1973) 256–308.

[4] See P. Ganz, "Ms. Junius 13 und die althochdeutsche Tatianübersetzung," *Beiträge zur Geschichte der deutschen Sprache und Literatur* 91 (1969) 28–76.

[5] See D. Haacke, "Evangelienharmonie," in W. Kohlschmidt and W. Mohr, eds., *Reallexikon der Deutschen Literaturgeschichte* (2d ed.; Berlin: De Gruyter, 1958) 1. 410–413.

[6] See the references above $ 5.3.3.

in Latin, just as in Syriac, the *Diatessaron* must have seen circulation before the separated gospels were translated into the vernacular.

Parallel investigation into the text of the oldest Roman Father whose Latin writings are preserved, Novatian, and into the oldest Roman *Antiphonary,* show that the gospel citations of both reflect the readings of the *Diatessaron*. This led scholars to the conclusion that the gospels first saw circulation in Latin in the form of a Latin *Diatessaron*.

The Liège Harmony and its Middle Dutch and Middle High German Allies

The most important Western source of Diatessaronic readings is the Liège Harmony. Now in the Universiteitsbibliotheek in Liège (Manuscript no. 437), the work is composed in Limburgs (a dialect of Middle Dutch) and dates from about 1280 CE. First edited in 1835,[1] its connection with the Diatessaronic tradition was made public by J. A. Robinson in 1894.[2] The scholarly edition of Daniël Plooij set new standards for presenting the text of a Diatessaronic witness.[3] His edition contains an apparatus full of parallels from other Diatessaronic witnesses, and is an indispensable research tool. In the manuscript's Preface the Dutch scribe says he composed the harmony himself, working from Latin gospel texts; but the Liège Harmony's sequence is Diatessaronic, and its text is full of Vetus Latina and Diatessaronic readings—hardly the result if a 13th-century scribe were working from the by-then-standard Vulgate and creating a harmony *de novo*. Rather, in the Liège Harmony we possess a copy—albeit, several times removed and in Dutch—of the unvulgatized Latin *Diatessaron* which lies behind Codex Fuldensis. Consequently, the manuscript is a gold mine of Diatessaronic readings, some of which find their only parallel in Ephrem's *Commentary* or the Old Syriac Gospels. Together with a few Syriasms in the Dutch text, this fact led Plooij to conclude that the lost, unvulgatized Latin ancestor of the Liège Harmony had been translated directly from Syriac into Latin, without a Greek intermediary.[4] The presence of these Syriasms in a Western Harmony, and the manuscript's sometimes singular parallels with the Vetus Syra and

---

[1] G. J. Meijer, *Het Leven van Jezus, een Nederlandsch handschrift uit de dertiende eeuw* (Groningen: Oomkens, 1835).

[2] "Tatian's *Diatessaron* and a Dutch Harmony," *The Academy* 45 (1894) 249–50.

[3] Daniël Plooij, C. A. Phillips and A. H. A. Bakker, eds., *The Liège Diatessaron,* Parts 1–8 (VNAW 19/21; Amsterdam, 1929–1970).

[4] Cf. Plooij's two studies: *A Primitive Text of the Diatessaron* (Leiden: Sijthoff, 1923), and idem, *A Further Study of the Liège Diatessaron* (Leiden: Brill, 1925).

Ephrem support the conclusion that the original language of the *Diatessaron* was indeed Syriac and not Greek.

The Liège Harmony (or a similar manuscript) was the archetype for a series of harmonies in Middle Dutch. No fewer than seven manuscripts exist, the most famous of which are the Stuttgart Harmony (Landesbib., 140, 8°; dated 1332),[1] the Hague Harmony (Koninklijk Bib., M 421; dated 1473),[2] the Cambridge Harmony (Univ. Library, Dd. 12.25; dated to the 13th or 14th century),[3] and the Haaren Harmony (Groot-Seminarie; dated c. 1400).[4] Additionally, there are at least ten manuscripts or fragments of harmonies in Middle High German, which derive from the same Middle Dutch tradition transmitted in the Liège Harmony. Only one of the complete manuscripts has been edited, that of the Zürich Harmony (Zentralbib. G 170 App. 56; dated to the 13th or 14th century).[5] Generally speaking, these Middle High German harmonies, along with the Middle Dutch harmonies, are all secondary witnesses to the type of a text best preserved in the Liège Harmony, although there appear to be exceptions.[6]

The Medieval Italian Harmonies

Two recensions of the *Diatessaron* survive in Medieval Italian. The one, the Venetian recension, so-named because of its dialect, survives in a lone manuscript (Venice: Marciano, no. 4975; 13th or 14th century). The other recension, the Tuscan, survives in twenty-six manuscripts, dating from the 14th and 15th century.[7] Both recensions

---

[1] Edition: *De Levens van Jezus in het Middelnederlandsch*, ed. J. Bergsma (De Bibliotheek van Mittelnederlandsche Letterkunde 54, 55, 61; Leiden: Brill, 1895–98).

[2] The variant readings of the Hague (or Haagse) Harmony, as this MS is known, are found in the apparatus of J. Bergsma's edition of the Stuttgart Harmony (see previous note). Since the Hague Harmony is closely related to the Stuttgart Harmony, reconstructing the text of the former is an easy task.

[3] Edition: *Het Diatessaron van Cambridge*, ed. C. C. de Bruin (CSSN series minor, tome 1, vol. 3; Leiden: Brill, 1970).

[4] Edition: *Het Haarense Diatessaron*, ed. C. C. de Bruin (CSSN series minor, tome 1, vol. 2; Leiden: Brill, 1970).

[5] *Das Leben Jhesu*, ed. Christoph Gerhardt (CSSN series minor, tome 1, vol. 4; Leiden: Brill, 1970).

[6] For example, Anton Baumstark felt that two of the collections of fragments which have seen editions, the so-called "Himmelgarten" and "Schönbach" Fragments, reflected two different, older, less-Vulgatized Diatessaronic traditions than the rest of the Middle High German tradition: see Anton Baumstark, "Die Himmelgarten Bruchstücke eines niederdeutschen 'Diatessaron'-Textes des 13. Jahrhunderts," *OrChr* 33 [3rd series 11] (1936) 80–96; idem, "Die Schönbach'schen Bruchstücke einer Evangelienharmonie in bayrisch-österreichischer Mundart des 14. Jahrhunderts," *OrChr* 34 [3rd series 12] (1937) 103–26.

[7] Both are printed in the same volume: V. Todesco, A. Vaccari, and M. Vattasso, eds., *Il Diatessaron in Volgare Italiano* (Studi e Testi 81; Città del Vaticano, 1938),

come from a Latin *Diatessaron* other than Codex Fuldensis, for the number of Diatessaronic readings in them is quite high. This indicates that their archetype escaped much of the Vulgatization to which Fuldensis was subject. The lone manuscript of the Venetian Harmony offers a superior text, preserving more Diatessaronic readings than the twenty-six manuscripts of the Tuscan Harmony.

The Middle English Pepysian Harmony

The English diarist Samuel Pepys once owned this manuscript, hence its name. Dating from about 1400, the manuscript is now in the library of Magdalene College, Cambridge (Pepys 2498).[1] Although written in a charming Middle English, mistranslations show that its archetype was an Old French gospel harmony.[2] In this manner, the Pepysian Harmony serves a dual purpose: it is the lone example of a *Diatessaron* in English, and it is the sole evidence that an Old French *Diatessaron* once existed. Although its text has been abbreviated, resequenced, and Vulgatized, the Pepysian Harmony often surprises the researcher, for it is sometimes the only Western Diatessaronic witness to preserve a reading which finds parallels in the Eastern Diatessaronic witnesses.

Western Poetic Witnesses

The oldest monument of Old Saxon literature, the rhymed poem *The Heliand,* is a story of Jesus' life, in harmonized form.[3] The editor of the first modern edition, J. A. Schmeller, noted in 1840 that the *Diatessaron* had been one of the anonymous poet's sources.[4] Further studies confirmed this finding.[5]

---

with part 1 being "Il Diatessaron Veneto," ed. by V. Todesco, and part 2 being "Il Diatessaron Toscano," ed. by M. Vattasso and A. Vaccari. The user should be alerted to the fact that part 1 uses folio numbers for the running headers, while part 2 uses chapter numbers.

[1] Edition: *The Pepysian Harmony,* ed. Margory Goates (Early English Text Society, Old series 157; London: Oxford University Press, 1922).

[2] Ibid., p. xv.

[3] Old Saxon edition: *Heliand und Genesis,* ed. Otto Behaghel (Altdeutsche Textbibliothek 4; 9th ed.; Tübingen: Niemeyer, 1965). English translation: Marianne Scott, *The Heliand* (University of North Carolina Studies in the Germanic Languages and Literature 52; Chapel Hill, 1966).

[4] J. A. Schmeller, *Heliand oder die altsächsische Evangelien-Harmonie,* Erste Lieferung: *Text* (Monachii, Stutgartiae, Tubingae: Cotta, 1830); Zweite Lieferung: *Heliand: Wörterbuch und Grammatik nebst Einleitung und zwei Facsimilies* (Monachii, Stutgartiae, Tubingae: Cotta, 1840). The dependence of *The Heliand* upon the *Diatessaron* is noted in the 2d vol., p. xi.

[5] E.g., C. W. M. Grein, *Die Quellen des Heliand. Nebst einem Anhang: Tatians*

More recently, an early 13th-century Latin poem, the *Vita beate virginis Marie et salvatoris rhythmica*,[1] has been shown to have Diatessaronic readings. Although critics have contended that the allegedly "Diatessaronic" readings found in poetic sources such as these are probably not genuinely Diatessaronic, but the products of meter and "poetic licence,"[2] such charges are refuted by the agreement of these Western poetic sources with Eastern poetic sources (Ephrem's hymns and metrical sermons, Romanos's hymns) and with other, non-poetic Diatessaronic witnesses.

5.3.5 WORKING WITH THE DIATESSARON: RECONSTRUCTING READINGS

5.3.5.1 Rules for the Reconstruction

It is self-evident that working with such a vast and diverse array of sources makes *Diatessaron* research quite different—and much more difficult—than working with a single source, such as the *Gospel of Thomas*. However, over a century of experience has given *Diatessaron* scholars some benchmarks to use when reconstructing its text. The pitfalls have also been marked. In this section, guidelines as well as danger points for reconstructing Tatian's text will be given.

Heinrich Joseph Vogels suggested the first rule of Diatessaronic studies, namely, that where the Vetus Latina and the Vetus Syra agreed against the Greek, that was the reading of the *Diatessaron*.[3] Although such a simplistic rule must be rejected today, Vogels was on the right track, recognizing the primary position of the *Diatessaron* in both the Latin and Syriac textual traditions. What he failed to con-

---

Evangelienharmonie herausgegeben nach dem Codex Cassellanus (Cassel: Kay, 1869); Gilles Quispel, "Some Remarks on the Gospel of Thomas," *NTS* 5 (1958–59) 276–90, esp. 282–290; idem, "Der Heliand und das Thomasevangelium," *VigChr* 16 (1962) 121–53; idem, *Tatian and the Gospel of Thomas: Studies in the History of the Western Diatessaron* (Leiden: Brill 1975). See also J. fon Weringha (author's name also given as J. von Weringh), *Heliand and Diatessaron* (Studia Germanica 5; Assen, 1965).

[1] Ed. Adolf Vögtlin (Bibliothek des literarischen Vereins in Stuttgart 180; Tübingen, 1888). Study: R. van den Broek, "A Latin Diatessaron in the 'Vita Beate Virginis Marie et Salvatoris Rhythmica,'" *NTS* 21 (1974) 109–32.

[2] Cf. Willi Krogmann, "Heliand, Tatian und Thomasevangelium," *ZNW* 51 (1960) 255–68; idem, "Heliand und Thomasevangelium," *VigChr* 18 (1964) 65–73; Bonifatius Fischer, "Das Neue Testament in lateinischer Sprache," in: Aland, ed., Die alten Übersetzungen, 47–48, esp. in n. 158; and C. C. de Bruin, *Jezus: het verhaal van zijn leven* ('s-Gravenhage 1980) 48.

[3] Vogels, *Beiträge zur Geschichte des Diatessaron*, 27: "daß sämtliche Lesarten, die durch die Vetus Latina + Vetus Syra gegen die griechische Überlieferung bezeugt werden, Tatianlesarten darstellen . . ."

sider was the existence of the so-called Western Text, which also influenced the Latin and Syriac traditions at a very early stage in their development. And, indeed, the *Diatessaron* is thought either to have influenced the Western Text, or to have been created from gospels which were full of Western readings; but it is still unclear which scenario is correct.[1] Therefore, scholarship today sifts the individual Diatessaronic witnesses, searching for agreements among them, which, after screening for extraneous influences, may justly be called "Diatessaronic." One point of Vogels' rule, however, remains: by a quirk of logic, we can only be sure we have recovered the text of the *Diatessaron* in readings which *differ* from the standard canonical text. Since large portions of the Diatessaron's text agree with the current canonical text, there is no way to tell whether readings in Diatessaronic witnesses which *now* agree with the canonical text are the result of Vulgatization or part of the harmony's original text. Only in those passages where the harmony's text *diverges* from the canonical text, can a judgement be made. Consequently, all modern Diatessaronic research is a search for deviations from the canonical text.

Three rules aid in this search.[2] First, to be considered genuinely Diatessaronic, a reading should be found in both its Eastern and Western witnesses. The rationale is that while a "local" reading might have found its way into, say, the Vetus Syra and Ephrem, in the East, this same "local" reading could not have found its way into a Western witness, like the Liège Harmony, save via the medium of the *Diatessaron*. Second, the reading should be absent from all non-Diatessaronic sources whence our Diatessaronic witnesses might have acquired it. For example, if a reading found in the Liège Harmony also occurs in the Vulgate, then one must search for other Diatessaronic support, for the Liège reading may have come from no more exotic a source than the Vulgate. Similarly, even if a reading is widespread in Diatessaronic sources, both East and West, but is also found in numerous Patristic sources not connected with the *Diatessaron*, then

---

[1] The fundamental studies are by Frederick Henry Chase, *The Old Syriac Element in the Text of Codex Bezae* (London: Macmillan, 1893); idem, *The Syro-Latin Text of the Gospels* (London: Macmillan, 1895). The dissertation of A. F. J. Klijn, *A Survey of the Researches into the Western Text of the Gospels and Acts,* vol. 1 (Utrecht 1949), offers an excellent survey of researches since Chase and discussion of the problems involved. See also the more recent study of Walter Henss, *Das Verhältnis zwischen Diatessaron, christlicher Gnosis und "Western Text"* (BZNW 33; Berlin: De Gruyter, 1967).

[2] These were originally put forward in my article, "Romanos and the Diatessaron: Readings and Method," *NTS* 29 (1983) 484–507. A fuller discussion is found in my *The Diatessaron and Ephrem Syrus,* 55–57. This study also contains numerous readings derived using the three rules.

caution must be exercised, for these Patristic sources create "interference," and prevent one from drawing a direct line from the prospective witnesses back to Tatian's harmony. Third, the genre of all of the sources with the reading should be that of a gospel harmony, or, if different, the source should have come under the influence of the harmonized "Life of Jesus" genre. For example, the Liège Harmony and *The Heliand* are both harmonized lives of Jesus; they are clearly within the circle of harmonized texts. The Vetus Latina, Peshitta and the hymns of Romanos are not gospel harmonies. Yet, each has, in its history, been exposed to or been influenced by the harmonized "Life of Jesus" tradition. In the case of the Vetus Latina and the Peshitta, this contact appears to have been indirect, since the earliest gospel in these languages was almost certainly a *Diatessaron*; hence, Diatessaronic readings were in the eye, ear, and textual tradition of these languages when the separated gospels were translated. In the case of the hymns of Romanos, the influence appears to have been direct, for Romanos was, in fact, retelling Jesus' life in a harmonized form, drawing from all of the gospels and extra-canonical material. The fact that his gospel citations often agree with those of the *Diatessaron* mean that he must have been using the *Diatessaron* directly, as one of his literary sources.

Before considering some examples, the caveats must also be given. First, since we are dealing with texts which span more than a millennium, and whose languages are exceptionally diverse, we must be alert for apparent agreements which are nothing more than the result of the grammatical requirements or syntactic conventions of a language. For example, at Luke 7:42, five Western witnesses give a variant to the standard Greek text. While the Greek reads "Which of *them* will love him more?" the Liège Harmony (and its related allies, the Stuttgart, Hague and Zürich Harmonies) and the Venetian Harmony read, "Which of *these two* will love him more?" The identical variant occurs in the Arabic and Persian Harmonies. Although the variant appears Diatessaronic, it must be discounted, for the Eastern witnesses are suspect. The reason: although the Western languages do not have the dual, it is standard in such a construction in Arabic and Persian. Second, one must be alert to ambiguous translations in the many vernacular languages. For example, at John 20:17, Ephrem, Aphrahat, Romanos and the Venetian Harmony all have Jesus' words as "I *go* to my Father and your Father," against the canonical "I ascend to my Father and your Father." The reading of the Liège Harmony, "Ik *vare* te minen vader . . ." is ambiguous, for in Middle Dutch, *vare* may mean either "to fly" or "to go." The evidence of Liège is, therefore, a *non liquet,* despite the fact that it might well be in agreement with the *Diatessaron's* reading. Finally, one must always be on guard against variant readings from the parallel passages in the other gospels. Although von Soden attributed all cross-gospel harmonizations to the influence of the *Diatessaron*,[1] today we know that is not the case. Many such harmonizations are spontaneous, often scribal "errors." These may also arise, of course, in Diatessaronic witnesses. Therefore, one must constantly play the devil's advocate in the case of every reading, to be certain that it is genuinely the result of Diatessaronic influence, and not a chance.

With that in mind, let us examine a few Diatessaronic readings.

5.3.5.2 Reading 1

At 4.5 in his *Commentary,* Ephrem's text of the baptism of Jesus reads: "Et cum vidisset, *ex splendore lucis super aquas* et per vocem factam de caelis . . ."[2] Also in the East, Ishoᶜdad of Merv, in his *Commentary*, at Matt 3:15–16, states: "And straightway, as the Diatessaron testifies, *a great light shone,* and the Jordan was surrounded by white clouds . . ."[3] In the West, the Pepysian Harmony says: "And so John baptized Jesus. And when he was baptized, and was in prayer for them that received baptizing in his name, so came *the brightness of heaven* and the Holy Ghost, and alighted within him."[4] And the Latin poem, the *Vita Rhythmica* says: "Cum ergo Jesus a Johanne foret baptizatus / populusque plurimus cum ipso renovatus, / ecce celum est apertum, *lux magnaque refulsit* / in Jesum necnon universos presentes circumfulsit."[5] Finally, two Vetus Latina manuscripts, a (4th century) and g[1] (8th century), interpolate at Matt 3:16: ". . . *lumen ingens circumfulsit (lumen magnum fulgebat:* so g[1]) de aqua, ita ut timerent omnes.*"[6]

We have Eastern and Western support, and the reading deviates from the standard canonical text; might it be Diatessaronic? Looking further afield, we discover that Justin Martyr also knows the reading

---

[1] Hermann Freiherr von Soden, *Die Schriften des Neue Testaments* . . . (Berlin: Duncker, 1902–13) Teil 1, Abt. 2 (1907) p. 1633: "Tatian's Diatessaron ist im Grund die einzige Quelle für alle irgend bedeutsameren Abwandlungen des Evangelien-Textes."

[2] Armenian recension (Syriac *hiat*): Leloir, ed., *Saint Éphrem,* 36.

[3] Gibson, ed., *The Commentaries of Ishoᶜdad,* 1. 27.

[4] *The Pepysian Harmony,* ed. Marjory Goates (Early English Text Society, Old series 157; London: Oxford University Press, 1922) 10.

[5] *Vita Beate Virginis Marie et Salvatoris Rhythmica,* ed. Adolf Vögtlin, (Bibliothek des literarischen Vereins in Stuttgart 180; Tübingen 1888), 129.

[6] *Itala, I. Matthäusevangelium,* ed. Adolf Jülicher (2d ed.; Berlin: De Gruyter, 1972) 14.

(*Dial.* 88.3),[1] as does Epiphanius (*Haer.* 30.13),[2] who says that it stood in *Gospel of the Ebionites,* that is, one of the now-lost Jewish-Christian Gospels. This constellation of texts seems to indicate that the reading is genuinely Diatessaronic, for it is unlikely that all of the Diatessaronic witnesses should have independently drawn the reading from Justin or a Jewish-Christian Gospel. Rather, it would appear that Tatian acquired the reading from his teacher, Justin, and incorporated it into the *Diatessaron.* The reading may well have stood in the Jewish-Christian Gospel spoken of by Epiphanius, especially since that document appears to have been (1) a gospel harmony which (2) excluded John, and which (3) Epiphanius equated with the *Diatessaron.* Justin's Ἀπομνημονεύματα was a harmony, and it also excluded John.[3] Therefore, Justin's reading may come from the Jewish-Christian Gospel, which Tatian then used—either directly or indirectly—when he created his *Diatessaron,* or both Tatian and the *Gospel of the Ebionites* were dependent upon Justin's harmony.

5.3.5.3 *Reading 2*

At Luke 2:36, the standard canonical text reads, "Anna . . . was of a great age, having lived with her husband seven *years from* her virginity." This reading is supported by most Diatessaronic witnesses. But a few, namely, the Persian Harmony in the East ("[she] remained seven years *a virgin with* her husband"), and the Stuttgart and Zürich Harmonies in the West ("[she] remained with her husband seven years in her virginity"), offer variants which are, despite their small differences, essentially the same.[4] Is this the reading of the *Diatessaron*?

With Eastern and Western support, and no other known sources from which the reading might have come, one is forced to conclude that this reading stood in Tatian's *Diatessaron.* Only in this manner can one explain (1) its occurrence only in harmonized "Lives of Jesus," and (2) the unique agreement between a source in Persian and sources in Middle Dutch and Middle High German. Significantly, the reading is also congenial with Tatian's alleged Encratism. This also suggests that we have detected the hand of Tatian at work. The fact that all

---

[1] *Die ältesten Apologeten,* ed. J. Goodspeed (Göttingen: Vandenhoeck & Ruprecht, 1914) 202; see above # 5.2.2.3.

[2] *Epiphanius I, Anacorantus and Panarion (1–33) I,* ed. Karl Holl (GCS 25; Leipzig: Hinrichs, 1915) 350–51.

[3] See above # 5.2.

[4] The evidence is: Persian, 6 (ed. Messina 22): "era rimasta sette anni *vergine con* suo marito"; Stuttgart, 14 (Bergsma 20): "ende hadde gheleift met haren man VII jaar *in* haren magedomme"; Zürich, 15 (ed. Gerhardt 11): "vnd hat belebet irme manne siben iar *in* irme magtvme."

other Diatessaronic witnesses give the standard canonical reading is easily explicable: they have all been Vulgatized, that is, the deviant Diatessaronic reading—so obvious in this case—was removed and was replaced with the canonical reading.

5.3.5.4 Reading 3

Sometimes we stumble across readings which are arguably earlier than the present canonical text. One is in Matt 8:4 (and parallels), where the canonical text runs: "Go, show yourself to the priest and offer the gift *which Moses commanded,* in a testimony to them." No fewer than six Diatessaronic witnesses, four in the East (both recensions of Ephrem's *Commentary,* Isho{c}dad's *Commentary,* Romanos), and two in the West (the Liège and the Venetian Harmonies), give the following (with minor variants): "Go, show yourself to the priest(s) and fulfill the Law."[1] With Eastern and Western support, and no other known sources from which these Diatessaronic witnesses might have acquired the reading, we must conclude that it is the reading of Tatian. And in it, Jesus required that someone "fulfill the Law."

In the early church, the *Diatessaron* seems to have seen currency not in Gentile-Christian circles, but in Judaic-Christian communities. The reading of the *Diatessaron* is certainly more congenial to Judaic Christianity than to the group which later came to dominate the church, and which edited its canonical texts: Gentile Christians. We must hold open the possibility that the present canonical reading might be a later revision of an earlier, stricter, more explicit and more Judaic-Christian text, here preserved only in the *Diatessaron.*

5.3.5.5 Reading 4

A similar circumstance may be at work in the *Diatessaron* at Matt 27:52–53, where, the canonical text reads: "(52) And the graves were opened, and many bodies of the saints who had fallen asleep were raised. (53) And coming out of the tombs after his resurrection, they entered into the holy city and appeared to many." In the next verse, 54, the centurion offers his confession upon seeing the wonders sur-

---

[1] The evidence is: (1) Ephrem (Syriac): Leloir, ed., *Saint Éphrem*; (2) Ephrem (Armenian): *Commentaire,* ed. Louis Leloir (CSCO 145; Louvain: Peeters, 1954), 126; (3) Isho{c}dad: *Commentary,* ed. Gibson, 2. 70; (4) Romanos: *Romanos le Mélode. Hymnes II,* ed. J. Grosdidier de Matons (SC 110; Paris: Edition du Cerf, 1965) 376; (5) Liège: *The Liège Diatessaron,* eds. Daniël Plooij, C. A. Phillips and A. Bakker, parts 1–8 (VNAW 19/21; Amsterdam 1929–70) 104; (6) Venetian: *Il Diatessaron Veneto,* ed. V. Todesco, pt. 1 of *Il Diatessaron in Volgare Italiano,* StT 81 (Città del Vaticano 1938) 50.

rounding Jesus' death: "When the centurion and those who were with him, keeping watch over Jesus saw the earthquake and what took place, they were filled with awe, and said, 'Truly, this was the Son of God!'"

Source-critically, vss. 52 and 53 are from some special source of Matthew; they are missing from the other Synoptic Gospels. When we turn to the Diatessaronic witnesses, we discover an interesting fact: three of our Eastern sources (Ephrem, in his *Commentary* and in no fewer than three of his hymns, Ishoᶜdad, in his *Commentary,* and Romanos in two of his hymns), and three Western sources (twice in the Pepysian Harmony, the Venetian Harmony and *The Heliand*) speak only of "the dead" coming out of their tombs. The greater detail of the canonical account—all of which is theologically loaded: "bodies" (more specific and agreeing with Paul at 1 Cor 15:35–44), "of saints" (certainly superior to the mere "dead" of the *Diatessaron,* and therefore more developed, and also Pauline), "who had fallen asleep" (again a more elegant description, and again used by Paul in 1 Cor 15:20 and 1 Thess 4:14)—suggests that the *Diatessaron's* reading is earlier.

Supporting this conclusion is another apparent Diatessaronic reading in the same passage. It is an omission, and therefore one must be careful in arguing from it, for the argument is *e silentio.* But in this case, the omission is an active omission, that is, it changes the meaning of the text. Therefore, it elicits greater credence than a passive omission, that is, one which does not alter the meaning of the text. In numerous Diatessaronic witnesses, both East (Ephrem, twice in his *Commentary,* and in three of his hymns; twice in the *Commentary* of Ishoᶜdad; and twice in the hymns of Romanos) and West (twice in the Pepysian Harmony; *The Heliand*), the resurrection *and appearance of* the risen "dead" occur *simultaneously* with Jesus' death on the cross. In other words, the *Diatessaron* omitted the canonical "after his resurrection," which—most bizarrely—delays the appearance of those resurrected *for three days*! Rather, according to the *Diatessaron,* the "dead" were raised *and revealed there and then* as one more sign of the gravity of Jesus' death. The reading of the Pepysian Harmony gives some idea of the scene, according to Tatian:

> And with that, the veil that hung in the temple before the high alter burst in two pieces, the earth quaked, and the stones burst, and the dead men arose out of their graves. And entering the holy city, they appeared to many. And the centurion . . .[1]

---

[1] The evidence for this reading is too complex to give here; it is presented in my *The Diatessaron and Ephrem Syrus,* 95–112. The citation from the Pepysian Harmony is from Goates' edition, 100.

In the canonical account, the delay of the appearance of those resurrected for three days defeats the whole purpose of having them raised when Jesus dies on the cross; but the delay *does* bring the canonical account into line with Pauline theology, which proclaims Jesus the "first fruits" of the resurrection (1 Cor 15:20). According to Pauline theology, one cannot have the "saints" arising before Jesus himself has risen. It would appear that the *Diatessaron* preserves a more primitive version of the text at this point than does the canonical text, which has been revised to bring it into conformity with Pauline theology.

5.3.5.6 Reading 5

As an insight into Tatian's method of harmonization, consider the following canonical passages, and then compare them with the *Diatessaron*.

Matt 5:29
If your *right eye* causes you to sin, *pluck it out and throw it* away; it is better that you lose one of your members than that your whole body be thrown into hell.

Matt 18:9
And if your eye causes you to sin, pluck it out and throw it from you; it is better for you to enter life with *one eye* than with two eyes to be thrown into the hell of *fire*.

Mark 9:47–48
And if your eye causes you to sin, pluck it out; it is better for you to enter *the kingdom* of God with *one eye* than with two eyes to be thrown into hell, where their worm does not die, and the *fire* is not quenched.

Consistent features in the *Diatessaron's* harmonization of this passage are the italicized portions of text, drawn from all three passages. The conjunction of three Diatessaronic witnesses (the Persian Harmony;[1] the Syrian Father Aba;[2] and the Liège Harmony[3]) permits us to reconstruct the Diatessaronic text as follows:

---

[1] Messina, 63.

[2] Reading # 451 in *Biblia Polyglotta Matritensia, VI, Vetus Evangelium Syrorum, Diatessaron Tatiani*, ed. I. Ortiz de Urbina (Matriti 1967) 36, citing F. Nau, "Aba, comment. in Diatessaron," *Revue de l'Orient Chrétien* 17 (1912) 69–73. Aba is described as a student of Ephrem's: cf. Otto Bardenhewer, *Geschichte der altkirchlichen Literatur* (2d ed.; Freiburg: Herder, 1924) 4. 374; or Rubens Duval, *La littérature syriaque* (Paris, 1907; photomechanical reprint: Amsterdam: Philo Press, 1970) 313–314.

[3] Plooij et al., 70.

If your *right eye* (Matt 5:29) scandalizes you, *pluck it out and throw it* (Matt 5:29 or Matt 18:9) from you, for it is better to enter the kingdom (Mark 9:47) with one eye (Matt 18:9 or Mark 9:47) than to be cast with two eyes into *the fire* (Matt 18:9 or Mark 9:48).

To borrow a word from Arthur Vööbus, Tatian's creation is a fine "filigree" of texts crafted with bits from each of the three passages. In this case, however, we must be cautious in attributing this harmonization to Tatian, for the identical harmonization also occurs in Justin's *First Apology* (15.2).[1] While we can be certain that each of our Diatessaronic witnesses did not independently copy this reading from Justin, the fact that he also transmits the reading is one more indication that Tatian knew and used Justin's harmonized gospel.

5.3.5.7 Reading 6

Finally, as a reading of interest from a church-historical perspective, is the conjunction of at least four Diatessaronic witnesses (two hymns of Romanos in the East;[2] the Pepysian Harmony,[3] Vetus Latina MS *a*,[4] and perhaps the *Vita Rhythmica*[5] in the West) suggest that the *Diatessaron's* text at John 13:9 read "Simon Peter said to him: 'Lord, not only my feet, but also my hands and my head *and my whole body*.'" The passage is, of course, significant as an echo of baptism. Immersion ("wash my whole body"), not simply affusion ("wash my head"), was the practice of the Syrian church, and its form of baptism finds textual support in the *Diatessaron*. It is interesting to speculate whether (1) the *Diatessaron*, the first gospel in Syriac, dictated the practice of the Syrian church, or whether (2) the text of the *Diatessaron* was augmented to conform to preexisting Syrian rites, or whether (3) the omission of "and my whole body" in the Greek and Latin tradition was an adaptation of the sacred text to the practices of later Western regions.

5.3.6 SOURCES OF THE DIATESSARON

The Readings given above provide a sense of the *Diatessaron* and offer concrete evidence for some of its sources. First of all, it is evident

---

[1] Goodspeed, 35.

[2] *Romanos le Mélode. Hymnes IV*, ed. José Grosdidier de Matons (SC 128; Paris: Edition du Cerf, 1967) 82 and 392–94.

[3] Goates, 88.

[4] *Itala, IV. Johannesevangelium*, ed. Adolf Jülicher (Berlin: De Gruyter, 1963), 149.

[5] Vögtlin, 149, which betrays Diatessaronic influence by interpolating *totum*; nevertheless, it fails to interpolate the full Diatessaronic reading, for it does not read *corpus*. Its reading is: Et non solum pedes ad lavandum, / Dabo manus atque caput *totum* ad aquandum.

(Readings 1 and 5) that Tatian drew upon the harmonized gospel traditions used by his teacher, Justin.[1] Justin's harmony did not incorporate John; the *Diatessaron* does. This means that Tatian could not have simply "annotated" Justin's harmony; at the minimum, he had to do a rather thorough revision. Second, as seen in Reading 1, the *Diatessaron* has agreements with extra-canonical sources, most notably with the Jewish-Christian gospel tradition.[2] This suggests that Tatian used not just the four canonical Gospels, but at least one extra-canonical source. Third, Tatian appears to have used a redaction of the canonical Gospels which was very old—sometimes, perhaps, revealing a textual tradition that was *more* ancient than our present canonical text (Reading 3 and 4)—and which had a Jewish-Christian flavor. Into this mix, Tatian seems to have introduced his own distinctive Encratite views. The result was the *Diatessaron*.

There are readings in the *Diatessaron* which find parallel in the *Gospel of Thomas,* and the Diatessaron has an exceptional number of Western Text readings.[3] How this puzzle is to be resolved remains a mystery. It is the best working hypothesis to assume dependence by *Thomas* and the *Diatessaron* on a common tradition, which was "Western."

5.3.7 ORIGINAL LANGUAGE, DATE, AND PROVENANCE

Although Latin, Greek, and Syriac have been suggested as the language in which Tatian composed his harmony, experts today conclude that the deed was done in Syriac.[4] Only in this manner can one account for the Syriasms and Semitisms present in the Western witnesses. The hypothesis that the *Diatessaron* was composed in Greek or Latin, based on the Greek Gospels, makes it impossible to

---

[1] See my forthcoming article, "Textual Evidence of Tatian's Dependence Upon Justin's 'ΑΠΟΜΝΗΜΟΝΕΥΜΑΤΑ," *NTS* 36 (1990). See also above # 5.2.

[2] On this see especially C. A. Phillips, "Diatessaron—Diapente," *BBC* 9 (February 1931) 6–8; J. H. Charlesworth, "Tatian's Dependence upon Apocryphal Traditions," *HeyJ* 15 (1974) 5–17; and my *The Diatessaron and Ephrem Syrus,* 47–51.

[3] See Gilles Quispel, "L'Évangile selon Thomas et le Diatessaron," *VigChr* 13 (1959) 87–117; idem, "L'Évangile selon Thomas et le 'Texte Occidental' du nouveau Testament," *VigChr* 14 (1960) 204– 215; idem, *Tatian and the Gospel of Thomas: Studies in the History of the Western Diatessaron* (Leiden: Brill, 1975). See also the references above # 5.3.5.1.

[4] For a review of the arguments and the evidence for Syriac, see my "New Evidence for the Question of the Original Language of the Diatessaron," in: Wolfgang Schrage, ed., *Studien zum Text und zur Ethik des Neuen Testaments zum 80. Geburtstag Heinrich Greeven* (BZNW 47; Berlin: De Gruyter, 1986) 325–43.

account for the parataxis (where subordination is found in the Gospels) and variants which are paralleled only in the Old Syriac.

The date of the *Diatessaron's* composition can be fixed to between 163 (the earliest date of Justin's death) and the time of Tatian's own death (probably about 185). If Eusebius's report that Tatian was expelled from the Roman church in 172 is correct, and if, as is often surmised, the *Diatessaron* was composed after this date, then the range is narrowed to the time from 172 to ca. 185.

The matter of provenance is more difficult to determine, since there was a significant Syriac-speaking community in Rome about this time.[1] Therefore, although one might think that having determined the original language as Syriac would mean composition in the East, it is also possible that Tatian composed his harmony in Rome in Syriac. The early influence of the *Diatessaron* on the Latin gospel tradition, on Novatian, and on the Roman Antiphonary is more difficult to account for if composition is placed in the East. F. C. Burkitt, who suggested that Latin was the original language, opined that Tatian created his harmony in Rome, and then produced a second, revised edition once back in the East.[2] Burkitt's suggestion of Latin is unanimously rejected today, but the possibility of two *Diatessarons,* one Roman in origin, and one Syrian in origin, would go some way towards accounting for the early presence of Diatessaronic influence in both the East and the West, and also for some significant differences between the Eastern and Western witnesses in their sequence of harmonization. The matter remains *sub judice,* but composition in the East is difficult to reconcile with the empirical evidence of Diatessaronic readings in Rome in the second and third century.

A complicating factor in all this is the harmony of Justin, about which we know so little.[3] If it, and not Tatian's creation, accounted for what we "mistakenly" take for Diatessaronic influence in the early Latin texts, then a major obstacle to Eastern provenance is removed. Then the *Diatessaron* would almost certainly have been composed in the East. However, our meager knowledge of the influence of Justin's harmony makes this suggestion only informed speculation. Until further evidence can be assembled, Rome appears the most likely place of composition.

---

[1] The *Liber pontificalis* (ed. L. Duchesne [Paris 1886] 1. 134) states that Anicet, bishop of Rome from 154 to 165, was a Syrian; cf. the remarks of Arthur Vööbus, *Early Versions of the New Testament* (PETSE 6; Stockholm 1954) 4 and 6.

[2] F. C. Burkitt, "Tatian's Diatessaron and the Dutch Harmonies," *JTS* 25 (1924), 128–130.

[3] But see the discussion of Justin's harmony above # 5.2.

5.3.8 FEATURES AND CHARACTERISTICS OF THE DIATESSARON

Tatian's harmony appears to have lacked the genealogies and the ascension account.[1] Matthew, the most popular Gospel in the early church, appears to have been the skeleton upon which Tatian placed his harmony. At points the harmonization appears to be almost word by word; at other points, it appears that Tatian is working with larger blocks of text. The abbreviating nature of the *Diatessaron's* text has been noted by some scholars.[2] Whether this is due to editorial activity by Tatian, or due to the fact that the gospels he knew may not have been as developed as our current canonical Gospels (cf. Reading 4) is unknown. On the other hand, Tatian often appears to have added a clarifying word or phrase to the canonical text.[3]

Theologically, the most evident motif is Tatian's Encratism. One example has been discussed above: Anna's seven years of continence with her husband (Reading 2). It has also been suggested that the *Diatessaron* sought to distance Jesus from Judaism. Adolf von Harnack pointed to the omission in Ephrem's *Commentary* of passages where "Israel" was mentioned, or where Jesus was depicted as the Saviour of the Jews.[4] No comprehensive investigation of all the Diatessaronic witnesses has yet been undertaken to see if this is a genuine feature of Tatian's creation, or if it is only a feature of Ephrem's *Commentary*. Whatever its distancing of Jesus from Israel, it is clear (cp. Reading 3) that the *Diatessaron* was not anti-nomian or pro-Pauline.

As this brief survey has shown, the field of Diatessaronic studies is complex; but it is also hoped that this overview has revealed glimpses of the rich rewards which can be gained from study of the document which early Christians carried with them as far as the Gobi Desert in the East and to England in the West.

---

[1] This is stated by Theodoret (*Haer. fab. comp.* 1. 20; quoted above), and some witnesses do lack the genealogies. In other witnesses, where they are found, they fit awkwardly in the text.

[2] See the remarks of J. Neville Birdsall, "The Western Text in the Second Century," in: William L. Petersen, ed., *Gospel Traditions in the Second Century: Origins, Recensions, Text and Transmission* (Christianity and Judaism in Antiquity 3; Notre Dame: Notre Dame University Press, 1989) 8–9.

[3] See the remarks in my *The Diatessaron and Ephrem*, 162.

[4] Adolf Harnack, "Tatian's Diatessaron und Marcion's Commentar zum Evangelium bei Ephraem Syrus," *ZKG* 4 (1881) 492–494; cf. J. Rendal Harris, "Was the Diatessaron Anti-Judaic?" *HTR* 18 (1925) 103–9.

Index of Passages

New Testament

Apostolic
Tradition 21.11